THE GRAMMAR OF SOCIOLOGY

BOOKS BY DR. HARIDAS T. MUZUMDAR

The
Grammar of Sociology:

MAN IN SOCIETY

HARIDAS T. MUZUMDAR, M.A., Ph.D.

Chairman, Department of Sociology
Dean, Division of Arts and Sciences
Arkansas A. M. and N. College, U.S.A.

ASIA PUBLISHING HOUSE

BOMBAY • CALCUTTA • NEW DELHI • MADRAS
LUCKNOW • BANGALORE • LONDON • NEW YORK

THE GRAMMAR OF SOCIOLOGY: MAN IN SOCIETY

Copyright © 1966 by Haridas T. Muzumdar
U. S. Library of Congress Catalog Card No. 60-5378

PRINTED IN INDIA

BY PYARELAL SAH, AT THE TIMES OF INDIA PRESS,
BOMBAY, AND PUBLISHED BY P. S. JAYASINGHE,
ASIA PUBLISHING HOUSE, BOMBAY I

TO

THE YOUTH OF THE WORLD WHO
SHALL BE THE CITIZENS OF THE
WORLD ON THE MORROW

" The peoples of the world have two natural and two cultural traits in common. The natural traits they share in common are: their biological makeup and their being rooted to the earth—they all must eat food, derived from the earth. The two cultural traits they share in common, in the latter half of the twentieth century, are the nationalist culture-complex and the industrial-urban culture-complex."

PREFACE

THE number of introductory textbooks in sociology is legion. I therefore enter the field with trepidation. An attempt is made in this book to delimit the field of sociology and to set forth the categories and conceptual tools with which the sociologist must operate.

My main purpose has been to stimulate clear and precise thinking. The book may have many faults, but it has the virtue of consistency. The comparative approach in the study of society and culture, adopted in this book, should be an effective antidote to the inherent tendency of members of all societies to interpret society and cultural phenomena in ethnocentric terms.

I

My background has helped me to transcend the narrow, ethnocentric viewpoints of most authors of introductory sociology textbooks, oriental as well as occidental. Born and reared in India; recipient of higher education in some of the best American Midwestern Universities; participant observer of the American scene since 1920; interpreter of Gandhi and India to the American people; participant in the culture-streams of two great nations, India and America; naturalized citizen of the United States since July 7, 1947—this rich background has enabled me to view cultural phenomena from the intercultural standpoint and to look at national and societal problems from the international and intersocietal viewpoint.

As one who has experienced solidarity with the American people for forty years, as one who became an American citizen of his own volition, I have been driven to two conclusions in regard to cultural orientation: (1) that the fundamental values of a culture are taken for granted by the culture-bearing group, which is to say, by the members of that society; this "taking for granted" often leads to neglect of those fundamental values which, however, do tend to assert themselves in times of crisis ; (2) that the fundamental as well as auxiliary values of American culture are today better appreciated, more deeply cherished, and more stoutly defended and preserved by minority groups, by the New Americans, than by the descendants of old-stock Americans.

II

An attempt is made in this book to describe society and its functioning in general, and American society and its functioning in particular. Data from other societies have been drawn upon in order to throw light upon the functioning of American society and its adequacy or inadequacy. To give the student a clear picture of the American ethos is one of the aims of this book—a task not attempted by any other introductory sociology textbook.

Several considerations have guided me in selecting American society for intensive analysis : (1) I happen to be better acquainted with American society and its working than with any other society ; (2) the data on American society are not shielded from anybody's gaze either by a strongbox or by an iron curtain ; (3) as one of the youngest and most dynamic societies in the cultural landscape of the world, American society can be studied in terms of its roots and growth ; (4) a proper understanding of American society as well as Russian communist society is a MUST for every intelligent citizen in this One World of ours.

Even though data from American society have been extensively used, the book has been prepared to serve as a basic textbook for the study of society, regardless of the type of culture or society with which the student happens to be affiliated. In non-American societies where the textbook is used, the teacher may enrich the student's understanding of the working of his own society by supplementing the data on American institutional patterns and operations (Chapters 35-40) with data derived from his own society.

In this day and age, when the fate of our generation and of posterity depends upon the kinds of decisions mankind collectively makes, whatever insight in regard to policy-formulation and development we can gain from an interdisciplinary approach in social science is a positive gain. A study of this book should provide the student-citizen with data and conclusions for making decisions, calculated to benefit mankind. Professional practitioners, especially in the fields of applied sociology and social work, may, it is hoped, find useful the emphasis in the present work on social and cultural forces as a basis for the study of human behavior.

III

Some of the material appearing in the book has been used for papers read by me before learned societies, and has had the benefit of competent scholars' critical judgment. In addition, Dr. Conrad Taeuber, Assistant Director, U. S. Bureau of the Census, and Mr. Calvert L. Dedrick, associated with the U. S. Bureau of the Census, have read Chapter 20. Dr. Robert Schwenger, U. S. Department of Agriculture, now with the U. S. Department of Commerce, has supplied some comparative data on production. The Education Research Division of the Department of H.E.W. (Health, Education and Welfare) provided some of the latest data on education in the U. S. A.

Since 1945, I have been working on this book on and off for almost twenty years. During twenty years of teaching, I have read and used a great many introductory sociology textbooks. My debt to the authors of those textbooks is apparent throughout this book. Availing myself of the latest thinking in the field, I have attempted to make my own contributions to the conceptual framework of sociology in clear and precise language. In this task, I have not hesitated to redefine some of the basic terms of sociology, such as folkways, mores, institutions, etc.

The unique organization of the material in this textbook in three parts or Books—Groups, Processes, Culture—it is hoped, may commend itself to teaching sociologists as well as to students. Because the three parts are interrelated and interdependent, a significant point made in one part bears repetition in another part—certainly the teacher in the classroom is forced time and again to refer to a major point in half a dozen different contexts, with varying emphases.

The whole of Section II (Chapters 4-8) has been devoted to a discussion of original nature and human nature, nature and nurture, heredity and environment, individual and person, from several points of view. The same problem has been touched upon previously in Chapter 2 and later in appropriate contexts with varying emphases. Likewise, Hindu philosophical views of human nature have been expounded in more places than one. This arrangement lays the obligation for synthesis and integration where it belongs— upon the student himself.

Wherever possible, I have made every effort to utilize the latest publications and the latest data, but I have not hesitated to refer to older sources if they contained significant data, insights and theories. For people whose thinking is dominated by the cult of the new, this procedure requires an explanation. Let us put it this way: A valid theory or approach does not become invalid simply because it was formulated in 1907 or 1909, or 1924 or 1940—or, for that matter, in the fourth century B.C. or the sixth century B.C.—especially when no new theory of a fundamentally significant nature is contributed by a later publication.

Then, again, some of the masters of sociology, such as Max Weber (1864-1920) and Georg Simmel (1858-1918), Parsons and Merton, Ghurye and Lazarsfeld, are not mentioned in the book, not because the author is not impressed with their contributions to contemporary sociology but because their specific contributions are consistent with and do not detract from the conceptual framework of sociology developed in this book.

An introductory textbook in sociology, not a history of developments in sociological theory, the present work addresses itself to more basic sociological problems than most existing textbooks in the field. The contents of the book have been tried out in my classes as a basis of discussion, with very favorable results. It is hoped that the book in its present form may serve as a teachable tool to the teacher and may stimulate and help students in their study of human behavior within the context of groups and culture. Indeed, the present book is intended not only to give the student a proper grounding in the discipline of sociology but also to provide him a basic general education about the world in which he lives.

My indebtedness to my former teachers, Professors Thomas D. Eliot, Ernest W. Burgess, Kimball Young, the late Edward A. Ross (1866-1951), Robert E. Park (1864-1944) and John L. Gillin (1871-1958) can never be fully expressed. The stimulation I received from each one of them in class discussions, seminars and personal conferences will always remain with me as a cherished treasure. I would be remiss in my duty if I did not express special appreciation to Park and Burgess for the intellectual stimulation received by me from their trailblazing volume *Introduction to the Science of Sociology,* which has been rightly looked upon as the Bible of sociologists throughout the Midwest and promises not to be outdated. Footnotes and references acknowledge my debt to other respected authors in the field.

I am especially grateful to Professor John M. Howard for the artist's conception of the pecking order among hens and to R. V. Bowers and Luther Fry for the two charts on Rochester, New York, which appear on pages 48 and 49. These charts had appeared, originally, in *American Sociological Review,* April 1939.

Instead of summarizing the thoughts and viewpoints of scholars quoted in the textbook, I have deliberately inserted extended quotations, in some cases, in order to acquaint the student with the mode of thinking of some of the authorities in sociology, psychology, anthropology and economics as well as biology. It is with great pleasure that I acknowledge my thanks to the authors and publishers whose works have been drawn upon for extended quotations.

I wish to express my special thanks to Mildred F. Pettit of Cedar Rapids, Iowa, for typing the final copy for publication.

While thanking the many friends and associates for their help and cooperation and suggestions, I assume full responsibility for all the shortcomings and errors that may be found in the book.

HARIDAS T. MUZUMDAR

Ark. A. M. and N. College
Pine Bluff, Ark., U.S.A.
January 1966

CONTENTS

BOOK I

THE GROUP

SECTION I

SECTION II

Section III

BOOK II

PROCESSES

SECTION VI

BOOK III

CULTURE

SECTION VIII

CHARTS AND GRAPHS

TABLES

BOOK I

GROUPS

The sociological thesis does not maintain that human nature can be fashioned out of anything and everything by the sheer alchemy of group and culture. What it does maintain is that *original nature can develop into human nature only in a socio-cultural environment.* . . Given the potentialities of original human nature—the unlearned tendencies to react, to organize and systematize experiences of reactions, to represent and articulate experiences—the group environment and culture transform potentialities into actualities in consonance with the imperatives of a given culture. The human child at birth is endowed with the capacity to act, how to act is determined by culture. Says the *Vishnu Bhagavat* with great chivalry, " By birth everyone is a Shudra "—not an animal ! Participation in group-correlated culture transforms the individual into the person and original nature into human nature.

CHAPTER 1

THE TEACHING SOCIOLOGIST'S FRAME
OF REFERENCE *

1. The Quest for a Theoretical Framework

THE Introductory Sociology course is at once a source of comfort
and of headache to every teacher—comfort born of a desire to introduce students to a rewarding field of study; headache born of a
clash of opinions as to what should and should not be dealt with in
the introductory course. I do not know how our colleagues in other
disciplines feel about their specific introductory courses and textbooks, but I believe it would be revealing no secret to fellow sociologists to point out that each of us has on more occasions than one
expressed a desire to write our own introductory textbook in sociology containing what we believe to be just the right approach and
just the right data about society. In this understandable and com-
mendable desire to promote our discipline and serve our pupils
aright, many a sociologist lives under a delusion of grandeur, meets
with frustration, and perhaps nourishes a special neurosis or psychosis of his own. The present writer, too, has fallen victim to the
neurosis so prevalent among our tribe.

Before presenting the theoretical framework ideally suited to an
introductory sociology textbook (and course), we may briefly survey
the nature of treatment accorded to the subject by past and present
authors.

Prior to the days of Auguste Comte (1798-1857) there was no
textbook in sociology as such, for the simple reason that the word
itself did not exist in the language; but the subject matter allocated
to sociology by Comte used to be discussed by a variety of social
scientists—historians, economists, political scientists, psychologists,

* Paper read at the meeting of the Midwest Sociological Society held in Des
Moines, April 12-14, 1951; published in the *American Sociological Review*,
Vol. 16, No. 5, October 1951, pp. 713–18.

and by philosophers. Making an original contribution by creating sociology as the science of human behavior in society, Comte none the less imposed upon the new science a handicap which it had to struggle hard to overcome. For all practical purposes, Comte thought of his new science as the philosophy of history—as the evolution of the human mind from the mythological stage to the philosophical stage, and, later, to the scientific stage. Comte's English counterpart, Herbert Spencer (1820-1903), utilized a mass of anthropological data in describing what he called Social Statics and Social Dynamics. And Comte's American counterpart, Lester F. Ward (1841-1913), wrote *Dynamic Sociology* with a special eye on contemporary social processes and end-results. Early German writers on sociology were dominated by philosophical interests.

The best-known, earliest American textbooks in introductory sociology after Ward were those of Franklin H. Giddings (1855-1931), Albion W. Small (1854-1926) and Edward A. Ross (1866-1951). Two of them, Small and Ross, had German training and German orientation in social science, but all three were American enough and pragmatic enough to keep their eyes focused upon empirically observable social data. William Graham Sumner (1840-1910) and Charles Horton Cooley (1864-1929) likewise may be said to belong to the generation of American pioneers in sociology. All of them were concerned with the development of a conceptual framework within which social processes and human behavior might be studied and analyzed. The quintessence of the thinking of the pioneers in sociology, European as well as American, was set forth within a special theoretical framework of their own by Robert E. Park (1864-1944) and Ernest W. Burgess (1886-   ) in their monumental work: *Introduction to the Science of Sociology*, first published in 1922.

2. SOCIAL PROBLEMS AND OVER-ALL SOCIAL SCIENCE

This wholesome quest for a satisfactory theoretical framework for Introductory Sociology has recently suffered a setback by the rise of two schools of thought: (1) the social problems school, and (2) the over-all social science school. Some have conceived of Introductory

Sociology as a hodge-podge of social problems, while others have conceived of Introductory Sociology as a general survey of all sciences, natural as well as social.

Few Social Problems textbooks are concerned with a discussion of the theoretical framework within which social problems arise. And even those few textbooks in social problems that do undertake to present a theoretical framework make no appreciable contribution to the full understanding of social processes or human behavior within the socio-cultural setting. The Social Problems textbook is usually a compendium of conditions and situations viewed as "problems" by significant sections of a society at a given time. By the time it is printed, such a textbook is already out of date in regard to some of its data and conclusions. Hence there is the need for frequent revisions. The data learned by the student in the thirties or forties have no relevance to the citizen in the fifties and sixties—even if he should remember them! In spite of this glaring situation, we have respectable sociologists who maintain that the best introduction to the study of sociology is by way of a course in Social Problems. I am not questioning the validity of a course in Social Problems—I am only denying its validity or utility as an Introductory Sociology course.

Indeed, the Social Problems course in the role assigned to it as an Introductory Sociology course does more harm than good, because in many instances that is the one and only course in Sociology with which a student majoring in other fields has any acquaintance. The result is staggering: such a student develops a distorted conception of the discipline of Sociology on the one hand and becomes weighed down with the abnormalities of our society on the other. Under the circumstances, neither sociology nor society can be correctly appraised or fully appreciated by the student-citizen.

Now we come to the school of sociologists who would present Introductory Sociology as an over-all social science. There is nothing alien to this school—from soup to nuts, all is grist for their mill, if one may mix up metaphors. Indeed, this meaningless mixing up of metaphors is the only correct way to describe such textbooks palmed off as Introductory Sociology. I am not opposed to social science books as such, or even textbooks; they may conceivably serve a useful purpose. But I am opposed to such books being designated as Introductory Sociology. There is a dead give-away in most such pseudo-textbooks: All of them proudly point out that one of the virtues of the book is that, at the discretion of the teacher, certain sections may be omitted, the other virtue being that the book could be taught just as effectively backward as forward! To add injury to the insult, at the end of every chapter, they add a reading list and a list of topics and discussions covering other books.

Can we imagine an Introductory textbook in Geometry being taught backward as effectively as forward? Can we imagine a student getting the hang of things he is supposed to learn in Geometry if certain sections may be omitted at the discretion of teachers? The unpalatable conclusion is that a great deal of the matter included in such over-all social science textbooks palmed off as Introductory Sociology is irrelevant to the purposes of Sociology or is presented in a manner irrelevant to sociological analysis. Some Introductory textbooks frankly confess, among other things: (1) that many students enroll in the Introductory Sociology course because the hour just fits into their schedule and (2) because it is a "snap" course; (3) there is no guarantee that all introductory class students would go on with further studies in Sociology; (4) therefore, the textbook in question attempts to present all kinds of distilled information which may be helpful to the future citizen.

3. OBJECTIVES OF INTRODUCTORY SOCIOLOGY

What objectives should an Introductory Sociology course or textbook achieve? First, it must delimit the field of Sociology. Second, it must set forth the categories and conceptual tools with which the sociologist must operate. Third, it must provide a theoretical framework within which all problems of human behavior within the context of groups and culture can be fitted and analyzed. Fourth, the Introductory Sociology course or textbook should serve as basic orientation for further studies and researches in the field of sociology. Fifth and last, the course as well as the textbook ought to supply the student with a point of view, a perspective upon human living, a methodology for the understanding of social normalities and abnormalities.

A sound Introductory Sociology course ought to achieve three end-results. One of the end-results of the study of Introductory Sociology ought to be an appreciation of certain common-human collective traits in all cultures on the one hand and of the relativity of cultures in time and/or place on the other. Second, the student should be helped to a realization that social processes are conditioned by the value system of a given society and that the value system is itself part of the data to be studied by sociologists. Third and last, while so-called "laws" of social dynamics can be formulated only within the context of a given socio-cultural milieu, be it a national society or a cultural community, and are relevant only within the given milieu, the Introductory Sociology course has the obligation to point out the emergence of universal or global cultural categories transcending national, racial, and culture-area boundaries. A discussion of the emergence of the One World—of the small neighborhood world—should be left neither to political spell-binders nor to journalistic hacks, but should be undertaken by trained sociologists.

4. A PREFACE TO THE GRAMMAR OF SOCIOLOGY

In the grammars of Indo-European languages we speak of subject ←→ predicate ←→ complement as necessary elements in a sentence-structure. Does the grammar of sociology—within the limits of Indo-European modes of thinking—have an analogous structure in society? Yes, indeed! In sociology it will be entirely valid to speak of group as subject, process as predicate and culture as complement. Thus the group (subject) by operation creates and perpetuates (predicate) culture (object or complement):

$$Group \longleftrightarrow Process \longleftrightarrow Culture$$

The Grammar of Sociology is divided into three parts: (1) Groups (Subject), (2) Processes (Predicate), (3) Culture (Complement). Since the days of Comte and Le Play, Spencer and Ward, Gumplowicz and Ratzenhofer, Giddings and Small, Ross and Cooley, sociologists have gone a long way in delimiting our field of investigation and in defining the scope and methods of our discipline. Even so, it seems to the present writer that we are far behind our confreres in the natural sciences and in some of the social sciences. Any ten physicists would agree among themselves in regard to subject matter, conceptual tools, and laboratory procedures, to which the student should be introduced in the elementary course and in the first two or three courses. As for the economists, seven out of ten are apt to have similar agreement in regard to their discipline. It is only when we come to our own discipline of sociology that agreement becomes a rare phenomenon. To be sure, sociologists worth their salt are not disheartened by this state of affairs. Ours is a peculiarly dynamic field of investigation which lends itself to a multitude of approaches—mythological, philosophical, scientific. Furthermore, the scientific approach in the field of human behavior within the context of groups and cultures has necessitated a methodology all its own.

The group is the datum of Sociology. As sociologists we attempt to study human behavior in terms of groups and groupings. Groups and groupings operate (i.e. Processes) within the framework of culture. Hence the student must be introduced to the various types of groups and groupings in society. How different types of groups come into existence or how they are formed, how they are held together, how they operate—with this field the student must be acquainted at the very beginning of the study of sociology.

Next, the various processes characterizing individual and group behavior must be studied and known by the student at the introductory level. Sociologists have been using the word process both in the singular and in the plural quite frequently. But so far as the present writer knows, not one of them has taken the trouble to define the term. That deficiency must be made good. Then, again, the term socialization has been bandied about loosely, without a proper distinction between the processes of socialization and the processes of social participation. The other processes—cooperation, competition, conflict, accommodation, assimilation, social change, social control—have received fuller and more satisfactory treatment in some of the standard textbooks in Sociology and special monographs. In the field of Social Change, Satyagraha, both as process and as movement, is a new departure in the theory of social processes, and ought to find a place in our Introductory Sociology.

Finally, our students at the elementary level must develop a proper appreciation of the cultural framework, of the cultural environment, within which individuals and groups operate. Here, it seems to me, the sociologist must clearly define his field. As sociologists we are not called upon to trace the evolution of culture from the paleolithic to atomic artifacts and correlative social institutions. The study of preliterate cultures must properly be left to anthropologists. It is permissible to introduce the student at the introductory level to the stages of cultural growth—to the idea of cultural evolution. But the use of massive data from preliterate cultures in the formation of laws of social statics and dynamics, as was done by Herbert Spencer, is not within the province of the sociologist.

The discussion of culture, for purposes of introductory sociology, ought to start with the assumption of the earth-bound character of man. In a measure, man, collective man, is of the earth, earthy. Sociological study of culture begins with the rise of River Valley civilizations. The four institutional orders of society—the family order, the economic order, the dharmic (church-school) order, the socio-state order—are then studied in terms of their manifestations here and abroad and in terms of the five primary institutions and a host of secondary institutions. Finally, an attempt is made to study the interrelationships among institutions, and the emerging pattern of social organization.

In this section on Culture, many departures from traditional practices in standard textbooks in Sociology need to be undertaken. I have no patience with sociologists who say that their textbook needs periodic revision because statistics have become outmoded. A basic text in Astronomy or Physics needs to be revised not in terms of millions of new experiments, observations and facts, but only in terms of one or two fundamentally revolutionary discoveries. The Ptolemaic astronomy needed to be rewritten only after Copernicus's revolutionary discovery of the heliocentric nature of the universe began to be recognized as valid. The Newtonian physics textbook needed to be revised not in terms of millions of experiments and observations but only in terms of the revolutionary concept of matter being congealed energy and in terms of the time-space frame of Einsteinian relativity. The statistics gathered together in Census Volumes every ten years and in special surveys do not constitute analogous revolutionary discoveries.

Either Sociology is a science of society or it is not. If Sociology be a science, its basic principles cannot be affected by a temporary shortage of housing or by the dislocations born of man-made cataclysms like wars or by natural calamities like earthquakes and pestilences. As sociologists we are, ought to be, concerned with the discovery and exposition of abiding laws by which society maintains its integrity as an ongoing cooperative concern of mutual services.

When as sociologists we are reduced to saying it is difficult to define sociology, let us quit calling ourselves sociologists. When we are reduced to saying sociology is what sociologists are doing and talking about, let us be honest enough to confess that sociology is neither a science nor an art but a dodge. When we are reduced to saying that the whole book is an answer to what sociology is, let us not be arrogant enough to write a book on sociology. My English training in India leads me to believe that we have no right to use a term if we cannot define it. Let the definition be tentative; let it be wrong, to begin with, if need be, but let there be a definition of our discipline. The first two or three chapters of the Introductory Sociology textbook may well attempt to state exactly what Sociology is, what its methodological problems are, what its scope is conceived to be.

As a participant in two cultures, the author is deeply impressed with what he has called "cosmopolitan" or "global-universal" processes, i.e., the processes of interaction on a global scale leading to the emergence of One World. Fully mindful of the fact that human behavior is understandable primarily and solely within a given cultural setting, also recognizing the existence of a number of culture-areas, we must not be blind to the operation of forces leading to the emergence of certain fundamental cultural categories acceptable to mankind as a whole. If we cannot adequately deal with cosmopolitan or global-universal processes and global-universal cultural categories in the making, we may as well "shut up shop." The last chapter in each of the three sections of the book may well deal with the universal or global setup.

5. The Sociologist's Frame of Reference

The interrelationships between group (or groups), process (or processes) and culture are best understood by describing the group as a subject, process as a predicate and culture as the object or complement. The group (subject) by its operation and functioning creates and perpetuates (predicate) culture (object or complement). Once culture emerges and cultural categories are established, there comes into being the framework of ethos defining the possibilities and limitations in human behavior. Thus the group, the creator of culture, becomes a prisoner of its own creature; or, to put it in more flattering terms, the group as well as each constituent member thereof functions efficiently, effectively and satisfyingly, because of the definition of goals. The interrelationships between group, process and culture are reciprocal:

$$Group \longleftrightarrow Process \longleftrightarrow Culture$$

Group may be defined at its elementary level, for our purposes, as an aggregation of human beings. To be meaningful, however, group should imply that its members are *associated* with one another in a certain network of reciprocal relationships for a specific purpose or set of purposes. A group in this sense is the starting-point of sociological inquiry. It is the datum of sociology.

A distinction must be made between an aggregation or collection of individuals and a group. Professional social workers, working in the field of group work, are deeply concerned with the processes leading to the transformation of a collection of individuals into a group, into an operational group or an association. For purposes of social work as well as of sociology, a group means a group of associated members, reciprocally interacting on one another.

Process may be defined as the continuum of events whereby being is transformed into becoming. The process is thus always a dynamic affair. Change, it is said, is the one constant fact of nature. The process must always be thought of as a continuum. A river is a continuum. The particles of water observed at a certain point in the river at a certain time are replaced by similar particles of water at the same point in the river at the very next moment. Yet, such replacements take place so evenly and so uniformly that the river presents itself to the naked eye of the observer as a stable fact, not a fact as flux. Empirically man finds it possible to treat the river as a fact with a given structure, the waters flowing at a given speed. The structural concept enables man to utilize the river and to compare and contrast it with other rivers as well as with other phenomena that are not-rivers.

Functionally, process in sociology may be viewed in terms of interaction—interaction between the individual and person, inter-action between person and person, interaction between the person and the group, interaction between group and group, interaction between persons, groups, and culture. Interaction means more than a stimulus acting on the individual, person or group: true interaction implies stimulus leading to response, which in turn affects the stimulus. The process involves:

$$Stimulus \rightarrow Response \rightarrow Stimulus = Stimulus \longleftrightarrow Response$$

The stimulus-response formula of the psychologists needs to be interpreted sociologically. It is not the objective stimulus to which response is made; the response is always made to the subjective interpretation of the stimulus. The Hindus describe this pheno-menon as *Rajju-Sarpa-Nyaya,* "the logic of the rope-snake." A piece of rope, lying on the road, if it were subjectively thought to be a snake, would call forth the response as to a snake—either a fight or a flight.

Ideally, we should use the formula: stimulus-interpretation-response; but since the formula stimulus-response is widely used, we retain it with the specific understanding that a given stimulus in a given situation always implies either a subjective interpretation of the given stimulus or a culturally defined interpretation of the situation—or a subtle combination of both.

Process in sociology may also be viewed structurally for methodo-logical purposes, if the dynamic aspect is not forgotten. Structurally, process in sociology assumes the form of institution or institutional-ization. Institutions may be defined as collective modes of response by human beings (always assumed to be associated in groups) to given stimuli. That is the elementary definition of institution. Actu-

ally, institutions, to be sociologically valid, must be defined as collective modes of response formalized with ritual and carried out
through formal agencies. (See *infra* CHAPTER 13).

Culture may be defined as the sum-total of human achievements,
material as well as non-material. There is no consensus among sociologists and anthropologists and philosophers of history regarding the
definition of culture. Oswald Spengler would make a sharp distinction between culture and civilization. Anthropologists like A. A.
Goldenweiser would consider the two terms synonymous. (Ogburn
and Nimkoff, in the third edition of their textbook *Sociology*
(1958), define civilization as the latter phase of culture, characterized by *civil* social organization as in the cities, in contrast to
kinship organization in tribal societies).

Some would confine culture to immaterial phenomena only.
Thus, for instance, Sutherland and Woodward say: "If ... culture
exists only where there is communication, then the content of culture
can only be ideas or symbol-patterns. Culture is then an immaterial
phenomenon only, a matter of thoughts and meanings and habits
and not of visible and touchable material things or objects." For
"material elements that are made and used in accordance with socially inherited tradition," these two authors suggest the use of the
term "culture objects" (4, p. 21). In like manner, E. B. Tylor defines
culture as "that complex whole which includes knowledge, belief,
art, morals, law, custom and any other capabilities acquired by man
as a member of society" (2, p. 25, quoted). And Robert Redfield
speaks of culture as "an organized body of conventional understandings manifest in art and artifact, which, persisting through
tradition, characterizes a human group" (2, p. 25, quoted). Combining several of these ideas we may define culture as that complex
whole of the achievements of man, or the total social heritage of
man, which can be transmitted vertically as well as horizontally to
men through, and by, communication and tradition. The distinction
between the material aspects of culture and the non-material aspects
of culture is made only for methodological purposes. Material culture objects, such as typewriters and subway trains, are meaningless
except in terms of the "capability" of men to use them in terms of
the functions defined by the given cultural context.

We may then say that culture is the sum-total of human achievements capable of transmission by communication and tradition. There are two ways of looking at culture—material objects or artifacts and non-material phases of behavior, such as social organization and the specific uses of material culture-objects. The difference between material and non-material culture is more apparent than real, because the uses of artifacts are culturally conditioned. The discovery of an underground rectangular structure, built by the Indians of the Southwest, is interesting; but it becomes meaningful only when we discover to what use it had been placed. Not until the building is identified as the Kiva, as the secret place for worship and ceremonials, can we appreciate the role of the underground structure in the life and culture of the Indians who had built it.

To take an instance from contemporary experience, some of the G.I.'s in the South Pacific during World War II exchanged their alarm clocks for some highly prized native objects. But to the natives of the South Pacific the alarm clock served as an ornament to be worn around the neck. The artifact—the alarm clock—is the same; but in the culture of the native, it does not serve the purpose defined for it by our culture. Thus at the core of culture, either material or non-material, there is the element of cultural conditioning, the element of appropriate usage or the element of appreciation. Culture is a network of interrelationships, a configuration or a patterning.

The popular and literary usage of the term culture as refinement, as proper understanding, has a sound basis but its narrow connotation is unacceptable to the sociologist.

The cultural process, spoken of by Park and Burgess (3, pp. 52–54), would then involve acquisition and assimilation of the values of the culture of a given group.

Group → Operation, in terms of Interaction and Processes of Institutionalization → Culture: This nexus suggests the methods and techniques of investigation available to Sociology, indeed to all the social sciences.

A word of caution is in order. Groups, processes and culture are so integrally related that it is impossible to investigate any one of these elements of sociology without reference to the other two.

Man's behavior can only be understood in terms of what Professor Chang Tung-sun (1, *passim*) has called the immediate and remote forces, namely, groups and culture, respectively. It is only for the sake of convenience that we separately treat Groups, Processes, Culture.

6. DISCUSSION
By Joseph K. Johnson, Southern Illinois University

I must begin this discussion with a confession of agreement. Agreement with one's colleagues is not ordinarily cited as a cardinal academic virtue, and I must say, in my own defense, that it has never been a habit with me. In the course of my career as a teaching sociologist, I have clashed with many sociological opinions, and, far from finding these clashes a source of headaches, I have found in them both keen enjoyment and righteous satisfaction. For one so conditioned, discussion of a paper with which one is in enthusiastic and almost complete agreement presents problems. I think my task would be easier if I had the assistance of an organ and a choir, so that I could simply chant a sevenfold AMEN, but lacking these liturgical reinforcements, I shall have to do the best I can. I shall underline a passage here and there, I shall add a few footnotes, I shall ask a question or two, and make a few comments.

First, a couple of footnotes on the Problem Approach:

1. In the *problem* textbooks, the theoretical framework most often used, until recently, has been that of *social disorganization*. Not only has this approach failed to contribute significantly to the understanding of the problems studied, but it has led to serious misunderstandings and has directed successive generations of research workers down scientific blind alleys. For example, in connection with the problems of delinquency and crime, this approach has led to the expenditure of much time and money in seeking for "causes" of crime in the criminal man as an individual, and in his physical environment, while the study of the total socio-cultural context within which criminal behavior patterns develop has been sadly neglected. Only a few have followed the brilliant lead of the late E. L. Sutherland, adopting his assumption that criminal behavior patterns are developed, in the same way that any other behavior patterns are developed and turning their attention, accordingly, to the criminal community and its culture—matters which, up to now, have been better known to the fiction writer than to the sociologist.

2. It is a mark of the logical immaturity of sociology as a science, and of the opportunistic, *ad hoc* character of many of its curricular developments that the *problem approach,* as such, should ever have developed or gained acceptance. Certainly, the suggestion of a "problem" approach, as distinguished from, or as an alternative for, a "principles" approach in physics or chemisty would be greeted with consternation, if not derision, by the exponents of these sciences. Most modern textbooks in these fields strive for an integration of principles and problems; that is, of theory and application. The pedagogical soundness of this procedure is rather well established and it would seem that sociologists might well follow the practices of the physical sciences in this respect. But one difficulty has been that departments of sociology, anxious to expand their enrollments, have catered to that numerous group of students which has a mildly altruistic (or morbidly curious) interest in certain social problems, but has no desire to acquire the conceptual tools with which to deal with such problems scientifically. Hence we give them brightly written journalistic descriptions, a few statistics to make it look "scientific," a list of proposed solutions, and a passing grade if they can remember one of the solutions.

Next, a footnote on the dated character of introductory textbooks:
3. Those of us who have not yet written our introductory textbooks may view with some apprehension the suggestion that the day may come when sociology textbooks will not become obsolete in from three to five years. Nevertheless, we may hope that when the day arrives, sociologists, relieved of the onerous task of revising footnotes in terms of later surveys, and substituting 1950 census data for 1940 data, will find more time for reflective thinking and for the construction of long-range research designs which will extend the frontiers of understanding in our field.

And now a bit of underlining of Professor Muzumdar's statement of the proper objectives and end-results of the introductory course:
4. The list of objectives is admirable for its conceptual adequacy as well as its brevity. In line with his rejection of the omnibus or "soup-to-nuts" course, he has made no provision for the discussion of organic evolution, Mendelian law, or the latest research on mutations; nor has he left room for a "quickie" course in paleontology or an evaluation of the controversy between the advocates of diffusionism and the exponents of the theory of parallel invention. Neither does he propose to steal the thunder of the economists by a discussion of the origins and consequences of the Industrial Revolution, nor that of the political scientists by a brief survey of the

current political "—isms." Surely, he is to be commended for his modesty and restraint, though it is just possible that he is motivated, in part, by a basely selfish desire to hold back something for his advanced courses.

At this point, lest the author feel that I have buttered him too freely, I feel obliged to raise a question:

Is it true, as certain statements in the preface to his *Grammar of Sociology* suggest, that the author is committed to the position of *social realism,* that is, the view that the ultimate social datum is the group?

Notwithstanding the advantages of such a position from the standpoint of delimiting the field of sociology, it must be noted that it is an extraordinarily difficult position for American students, brought up on the traditions of religious, political and economic individualism, to assume. My personal view, which I am sure is not unshared, is that the issue of *nominalism* vs. *realism* is a relic of pre-scientific thinking : that the individual-in-the-group and the group-of-individuals are both perfectly objective realities, and that one cannot possibly study the group analytically without giving some attention to the individuals who compose it, or *vice versa.*

Moreover, it is impossible for the sociologist to correct some of the fallacies of the individualistic approach if he does not bring the individual into focus under his lens. The individual must be brought into the picture so that the student can see to what degree and in what manner his own habits, tastes, attitudes and values are the products of cultural pressures brought to bear upon him through the various groups in which he participates. Also, the individual must be brought into the picture so the student can see clearly how he, by his own decisions and acts, can influence the course of group processes and contribute to the growth and evolution of culture.

Having written the above statements, I hasten to invoke a curse upon the head of any one who shall twist them into a defense of the practice, so common in introductory textbooks, of presenting a 'short' summary of individual and social psychology before taking up the subject of groups. This summary is seldom accomplished in fewer than two chapters, and in one widely used textbook, four chapters are devoted to the task ; and since the discussion of groups comes later, and the discussion of processes follows that, the class which follows the textbook order of topics seldom learns much about processes. I speak with feeling and there is no use in my trying to conceal the fact that I have aided and abetted the textbook writers in the sin which I have just denounced. I might plead in justification the fact that Professor Muzumdar's textbook has not yet been published, nor my own either, for that matter. But I shall not stoop to alibis. I take comfort in the fact that to commit sin is less culpable than to advocate sin. What I wish to be understood as advocating is simply that the group be represented as composed of individual people or *socii,* and that the individual person or *socius* be represented, not merely as a group member, but as a group product.

From question to suggestion is an easy and natural progression:
Accordingly, I presume to offer a suggestion that the linear representation of the relationship between Group←—→Process←—→Culture be replaced by a closed figure (ideally a circle) composed of the four words, Individual, Group, Process, Culture, connected by double-headed arrows to signify reciprocal relationships. Reasons for including the individual in the schema have been stated. Representation of the relationship in the form of a circle helps to express the principle of organic unity and continuity. Of course, this arrangement fails to indicate a starting point—the point at which the instructor and the freshmen committed to his care should break into the circle of concepts. But I think this question can be answered in terms of a well established canon of science which holds that scientific inquiry should proceed from the simple and immediate to the complex and abstract. To the naive observer, the simple, immediate datum of experience is neither *individual* nor *group* (both are abstractions), but *group-of-individuals.* This is the logical starting point.

Comments on the treatment of social processes:
Nowhere is the conceptual equipment of sociology less adequate than in the representation of social process or processes. Though we clearly recognize today the extent to which conceptual thinking is framed and limited by language, a third generation of sociologists continues to worry along with a make-shift set of terms borrowed from the language of common-sense to differentiate and designate the many forms and aspects of social process. All of us recognize the inadequacy of terms such as *conflict, competition, accommodation, cooperation,* with their fuzzy and shifting denotations and their moral and emotional connotations, to represent the complex play of action and change to be observed in the simplest human group. Yet we continue to employ these terms, defining and redefining them to

the point where there are almost as many definitions as textbooks. It seems high time to strike out afresh and undertake the development of a new set of terms, soundly based upon observation and analysis of group behavior and uncluttered by popular meanings and connotations. This is clearly the task of sociology as a generalizing science, yet it is a task in which we have failed for want of a start.

Professor Muzumdar's proposal that we begin with groups (not with words people have used in the past to indicate what happens in groups) is a sound and constructive one. His conception of social process as a dynamic continuum provides a logical and empirically sound starting point for analysis. His proposal that process be viewed functionally in terms of the varied patterns of interaction—*person with person, person with group, group with group,* etc.—suggests a promising approach, as does his proposal for a structural approach in terms of what we now call *institutionalization.* I submit, however, that the term *institution* is too cluttered a term for scientific use. A term which can be employed to designate such diverse objects as (a) the Papacy, (b) a mental hospital, and (c) the rights of primogeniture is hardly precise enough for scientific discourse. The task is not an easy one. It is not a task for a single sociologist. It is a task in which all should join with grim determination to *observe* and *think* our way out of the present confusion.

7. RESPONSE TO DR. JOHNSON'S DISCUSSION
By Haridas T. Muzumdar

When a new approach to a theoretical framework is suggested, one is never sure how one's colleagues will react to it. To be sure, there is nothing new about the ingredients of the theoretical framework suggested by me, but the configuration is certainly a bit unorthodox—and new. I have been particularly fortunate in having as the discussant of my paper Professor J. K. Johnson, Chairman of the Department of Sociology, Southern Illinois University, whose generous and kind words will serve as a most welcome encouragement to me. I am gratified that my theoretical framework is acceptable; I cannot guarantee that the execution will meet with the same enthusiastic response. I can only say that I have been striving and will continue to strive to finish this project in a way not to belie the high hopes raised.

Now, concerning a couple of points raised by Dr. Johnson. As for social realism, I have completely bypassed the problem of so-called group ascendancy versus so-called individual ascendancy. The problem of the so-called group mind is severely let alone. Starting with the group as the smallest unit of sociological analysis, I have attempted in three chapters to deal with the nature of "Centers of Internal Dynamics in the Group." (CHAPTERS 4, 5, 6.) In other words, I do possess some acquaintance with the individual—but I have deliberately refrained from analyzing *in extenso* the physiology and the anatomy of the individual human organism. In that field I accept the findings of scholars more competent than sociologists can ever expect to be. Those elements of the biophysical nature of man that are relevant to an understanding of man's behavior within a socio-cultural framework are dealt with; and the elements of the psycho-social nature of the human organism are exploited for all they are worth. In the discussion of Socialization and Social Participation, as indeed in the discussion of the whole range of social processes, the social fact accepted is, in Professor Johnson's happy phrase, the group-of-individuals or individuals-in-the-group, a dynamic concept of interrelationship and interaction. The discussion of Group Dynamics, in spite of its phrasing, is based on the role of the individual in the social context and the effect of the group situation upon the individuals involved.

Dr. Johnson's suggestion for the substitution of the circular schema for the linear one with the addition of an extra term is welcome; but I hesitate to accept it for two reasons: (1) There is the danger of our getting bogged down in a comprehensive analysis of the individual; (2) in my scheme the group always implies an aggregation of individuals associated for a specific purpose or set of purposes.

I am happy to have Professor Johnson raise the perennial problem of social science, namely, Shall we redefine terms of ordinary usage or shall we coin new terms to designate processes and culture traits? For good or for ill, as it appears at the present moment, we are doomed to the use of words of ordinary and literary speech; the utmost we can do is to give a precise content or connotation to the words and terms we use as conceptual tools in our discipline. That, of course, as Professor Johnson rightly observes, "is not a task for a single sociologist; it is a task in which all should join, with grim determination to *observe* and *think* our way out of the present confusion."

REFERENCES

1. CHANG TUNG-SUN: "A Chinese Philosopher's Theory of Knowledge." *The Yenching Journal of Social Studies,* Vol. I, No. 2, January, 1939.
2. WILLIAM F. OGBURN and MEYER F. NIMKOFF: *Sociology,* p. 25. Boston: Houghton Mifflin Co., 1940.
3. ROBERT E. PARK and ERNEST W. BURGESS: *Introduction to the Science of Sociology,* 2nd ed., pp. 52–54. Chicago: The University of Chicago Press, 1924; eighth impression, 1933.
4. ROBERT L. SUTHERLAND and JULIAN L. WOODWARD: *Introductory Sociology,* 2nd ed., p. 21. Philadelphia: J. B. Lippincott Co., 1940.

CHAPTER 2

THE STUDENT'S FRAME OF REFERENCE

1. VARIOUS WAYS TO DESCRIBE MAN

EVER since he achieved cognition and the ability to communicate, man has been engaged in describing himself and his activities, in an effort to understand himself. Since the attainment of sophistication, that is to say, since the dawn of high cultures, systematic attempts have been made to describe man and his activities. These attempts have led to the rise of various disciplines, well-organized bodies of knowledge.

Biology studies man as an organism: the physical structure, the properties of the different limbs or organs of the body; the functioning of the human body; the nerves, the tissues, the bones, the muscles, the ductless glands, the reflexes; the circulation of the blood; the digestive system; the processes of birth, growth, maturation, senescence, death; the mechanism of reproduction and the transmission of unit traits through the germ plasm.

Psychology studies man in terms of his behavior, both latent and manifest. Some psychologists have attempted to understand man in terms of his physiology; they view man merely as a structural unit, as a mechanism. This school of psychology, known as the Behaviorist School, founded by John B. Watson, looks upon human behavior as predetermined or preconditioned and therefore made up of predictable responses of man to the outer world.

The Dynamic School of Psychology, ranging from *Gestalt* to Psycho-analysis, studies man as a thinking and feeling subject, an animal that responds to the outer world by deliberate effort and will. *Economics* studies man in terms of his wealth-producing and wealth-consuming activities. *Political Science* studies man in terms of his activities within the framework of an organized state structure. *History* studies and describes unique events and personages that have affected the flow of collective human life. It may be pointed out that philosophers and historians like Oswald Spengler and Arnold Toynbee, when they indulge in deducing certain laws or generalizations from the unique events of history, are using not the tools of history but the refined techniques of sociology and anthropology.

Anthropology studies man, first, in terms of his physical characteristics (Physical Anthropology); second and more significantly, it studies man in terms of his cultural characteristics (Cultural Anthropology). In the past, anthropologists devoted themselves to studying tribal and primitive cultures; but now they are applying themselves to an investigation of man's behavior in high cultures. Thus the line of demarcation between anthropology and sociology is becoming somewhat blurred.

Social Psychology, analyzing human behavior within the context of groups, provides a bridge between psychology and sociology. *Sociology,* alone among the social sciences, undertakes to study man as a member of the group and as a participant in culture—as a group-living as well as a culture-building and culture-bearing animal. According to sociology, man is never an individual in isolation; he is always related to other human beings, to a group or groups; he always lives and moves and has his being in a cultural setting. Man is never an individual; he is ever the collective man.

High *religion* views man in terms of his destiny: salvation or damnation; release from the cycle of births and deaths or involvement in indefinite transmigrations. The concern with man's destiny has led religious teachers to expound the "nature" of man. Practically all religions ascribe to man a dual nature, the noble and the ignoble. Practically all religions ascribe to man freedom of will to work out his salvation if he so chooses. High religion posits a soul. While it rarely attempts to describe the nature or anatomy of the soul, high religion affirms a certain bond or kinship between the human soul and the Supreme Soul or God. Finally, all religions tend to set man off from the subhuman creation in terms of three distinctive human traits or attributes: (1) reason, (2) conscience, (3) will.

Hindu philosophy views man as an emanation from the Supreme Soul, from the Godhead. The formula, *Tat-Twam-Asi* (That thou art), suggests that man is part of That (God), and has within him some of the divine attributes. In Quaker phraseology, every man has *that* of God in him. In the language of the *Bhagavad Gita*, man is a complex of animal-human-divine attributes. In some the animal traits predominate, in others the human and in still others the divine. To the extent that man, by deliberate effort, achieves a way of living in which animal traits are subordinated to the distinctively human, to that extent does he realize his *Dharma* (see *Infra* for definition) and his true self. According to this view, the realization of man's soul, of his self, becomes tantamount to realization of the Supreme Soul, the Supreme Self, or God.

These are some of the ways in which man has attempted to understand himself and his fellows.

2. MAN AND CULTURE

Sociology has thrown considerable light upon the processes of human behavior. The results of sociological inquiry at once exalt the individual human being and deflate his ego. The individual human being is puny compared to the elephant or the tiger. Even the tiny ant surpasses the human creature in its capacity to attend to its chores in a methodical manner. "Go to the ant, thou sluggard," admonished the wise man, "consider her ways and be wise!" These facts are hardly calculated to enhance man's ego. And yet, in a real sense, man, collective man, is the supreme creature on this planet, exercising dominion over birds and beasts. How do we account for this seeming contradiction?

In the lower forms of life, behavior is conditioned mainly by heredity, by instincts, and only slightly by learning. Thus the ant and the beaver could do little else but respond to the outer world in terms of their instincts. These instincts serve the lower forms of life well by securing their survival and propagation. The higher we ascend in the scale of life, the less important becomes the role of instincts and the more significant the role of learning. Living by instinct is good so far as it goes, but it tends to develop a lack of adaptability to changed conditions. The dinosaurs perished because they were not capable of adapting themselves to the changed conditions on this planet. Living by learning, in contrast to living by instinct, has the merit of flexibility and adaptability. Adaptability makes for growth, rigidity makes for death.

Man has achieved pre-eminence on this planet by his ability to learn, by his ability to condition his behavior in the light of experience and learning. And how does learning take place? Human learning takes place within the context of the group (or groups) and within a cultural framework. Thus the human individual's supremacy in nature rests upon his group-relatedness and upon his participation in culture. Indeed, an individual, abstracted from the group and from culture, is less than human: he is what we call a feral man. The physical characteristics of the feral man are human in every respect—limbs and organs of the body—but he lacks the distinguishing traits of human behavior which separate man from the subhuman creation. (See *infra,* CHAPTER 6). The indisputable conclusion of sociology is that the human individual, to be truly human, must move, live and have his being within the group and thereby participate in the cultural stream.

Man's behavior is not transmitted biologically; it is conditioned by the accumulated culture of the past and by the voice of his contemporaries. *Communication* is the key word in human behavior. Language, the tool of communication, sets man off from the non-human creation. And language is a product of the group. The role of language in the accumulation of culture and in the communication of culture cannot be overestimated. Man is the only creature that builds culture. In the process of evolving culture, man climbs to ever higher planes of living. Man's cultural environment has been referred to as the superorganic environment. We may say that just as it is natural and inevitable that fish must live in water, so it is natural and inevitable that man must live in the superorganic environment, that is to say, within a cultural framework. The existence of the superorganic presupposes the existence of the group in the past as well as in the present.

The group is the "carrier" of the culture. An individual may be said to be a "bearer" of a culture insofar as he is related to the particular culture-group and embodies its values and ways. The contemporary American population group (1960) composed of one hundred and eighty million men, women and children, is the carrier of American culture. An individual American citizen traveling abroad or working abroad is a culture-bearer from America, precisely because he is related to the American group as a member of the American nation, and carries with him specific American values and ways of doing things.

It would be helpful if at this stage we were to define some of the key terms used in this discussion.

Group may be defined at its elementary level, for our purposes, as an aggregation of human beings. To be meaningful, however, group should imply that its members are associated with one another in a certain network of relationships for a specific purpose or set of purposes. A group in this sense is the starting-point of sociological inquiry. It is the datum of sociology.

Culture is the sum-total of human achievements, material as well as non-material, capable of transmission by communication and tradition. Culture is a network of interrelationships, a configuration or a patterning; it is acquired, and leads to learned behavior.

3. CULTURE AND PERSONALITY

For purposes of analysis, culture may be thought of as patterned behavior or a set of behavior patterns, learned and shared by the members of a group. *Certain ideas, attitudes, values and norms are expected and accepted in each society.* In complex societies, with a heterogeneous population, we find groups or categories of people who share subcultures, i.e., distinctive sets of learned and shared behavior patterns peculiar to these groups. Such groups are referred to as ethnic groups. The Muslims of India or the Adivasis (indigenous tribes of India) each have a subculture of their own within the larger framework of Hindese culture. The American Negroes and American Indians as well as the Spanish-speaking groups and other minority groups in the United States of America, each, have, likewise, a subculture of their own.

While all the members of a national society are characterized by what is called the national ethos, i.e., "the soul of the people," members of ethnic groups within the nation also participate in their distinctive subculture with its norms and values. Thus it would be correct to say that the American personality is the resultant of the American's participation in the national culture plus his participation in the subculture of the ethnic group to which he belongs. The same reasoning would apply to the Hindese personality pattern. The culture of the dominant ethnic group—Anglo-Saxon, White, Protestant, Urban in the U.S.A.; Hindu in India—may well be, but need not be, coterminous with the ethos of the given society; even so, the personality pattern of the dominant ethnic group is regarded as a criterion by ethnic minorities.

To summarize: The general behavior patterns shared by the members of a group constitute the culture of that group. The specific behavior patterns shared by the members of a subgroup within the larger group constitute the subculture of that subgroup. Personality is a function of the total (generic) culture of a society as modified by the subculture.

We may now turn to a discussion of the emergence of human nature and personality.

4. The Emergence of Human Nature and Personality

The term individual, strictly speaking, refers to the biological organism, or to the human being in general without specific reference to his relation to the group. The individual with a status in the group is called a person.

The term "human nature" needs to be properly analyzed as consisting of (1) the original nature of man, and (2) the acquired or truly human nature of man. The original nature is the same the world over, it is the same today as it was a hundred thousand years ago in its potentiality. But the acquired nature of man, which is what human nature is, changes and develops in response to the superorganic or cultural environment.

The child is born with certain prepotent tendencies to act. All children, regardless of race or clime, are born with a certain innate structure of the individual organism—i.e., with a complex of organic interrelationships which determine reactions to stimuli, such as cold, heat, light, darkness, etc. This capacity for response, for experiencing sensations, is common to all children at birth, barring the exceptional. Hence it may be called the original nature of man, or the common-human nature of man. (A fuller discussion of the original nature of man will be found in CHAPTERS 4, 5, and 6.)

Endowed with an innate structure of the individual organism, the child is born, so to say, into the stream of the social process, into a cultural milieu. Hence the original nature of man from the very outset begins to be acted and reacted upon and modified by the structure of the social organization. As the late Professor Robert E. Park aptly suggested, "Man is not born human," but to be made human (1, pp. 79–84). Human nature as we know it in action, i.e., in its manifestations in the social context, should be regarded on the whole "as a superstructure founded on instincts, dispositions, and tendencies, inherited from a long line of human and animal ancestors" (1, p. 80).

Endowed with "instincts, dispositions and tendencies," human nature is compounded of physical, mental, and emotional elements. Body, mind and heart are intertwined and interrelated parts of the original endowment of the child.

The child, however, is born not in a vacuum but in a social context. Therefore, the full description of the constituent elements of human nature would encompass the bio-physical and the psycho-social traits. The biological trait of human nature is correlated to the institution of the family, and the physical to the economic order. The psychological trait is correlated to the *dharmic* (church-school) order. (For want of a better term the present writer has applied the Sanskrit word *Dharma* to the church-school order. Both church and school are used symbolically as instruments that "hold together" or "uphold" the unity of the individual as well as of society. *Dharma* literally means "that which holds together;" derivatively, it is used synonymously with religion and duty whose function it is to hold together or uphold the unity of the individual, of society, of the cosmos.) The social trait of human nature is correlated to the organized social order with its many institutions, culminating in the state.

Such a view of human nature has obvious merits. It enables us to correlate the individual to groups and institutions. How do social institutions affect the individual? How does the individual, either as leader or as follower, affect social institutions? We need definitive answers to both these questions before we can have a complete "psychograph" or "sociograph" of the individual—i.e., before we can have a definite understanding of human personality.

5. THREE APPROACHES TO THE STUDY OF PERSONALITY

There are three approaches to the study of human personality: (1) the biological, (2) the psychological, (3) the sociological.

The biological definition of personality comprehends the biophysical characteristics of the individual organism. Valuable as this approach is, its inadequacy is immediately obvious to all discerning persons. How many of us, when we think of Shakespeare or Goethe, are prone to meditate on their biophysical characteristics? Are you satisfied to be looked upon by your friends merely as an interesting piece of anatomy? Hardly. Thus we are forced to the conclusion that the organism as personality is merely a substructure upon which is built the psychological and sociological personality.

The psychological definition of personality is based upon the unity of mental life, upon the integration of the intellectual and emotional elements in the life of the individual. In this sense, personality includes "not only the memories of the individual and his stream of consciousness but also the characteristic organization of mental complexes and trends which may be thought of as a supercomplex" (1, pp. 69–70). Personality thus conceived means a certain *style* peculiar to the individual. The style of the person is determined by the characteristic organization of mental trends, complexes, emotions and sentiments. The trends, complexes, emotions and sentiments are apt to be reorganized from time to time but *except in the case of conversion* the reorganization would always conform to the original pattern, to the style, to the dominant trend which has been referred to as a sort of supercomplex. This unity of mental life gives us a clue to the probable behavior of a person in differing situations. As William James so aptly said, "The philosopher and the lady-killer could not very well keep house in the same tenement of clay." If the psychological style of a person is philosophic, the chances are a hundred to one that he will not be a lady-murderer.

The psychological approach to the study of personality has led to a proper understanding of personality malaise, such as schizophrenia, paranoia, the divided self, multiple personality, etc. The psycho-analytic techniques have given us further insight into the role of wishes, of mental conflict, and of repression and sublimation in the growth of personality.

The sociological definition of personality is in terms of the status of the individual in the group, in terms of his own conception of his role in the group of which he is a member. Let us remember that personality is derived from the Latin *persona* which means a mask. A number of factors determine the individual's conception of his role in the group: physical traits; temperament; character; social expression, as by facial expression, gesture, manner, speech, writing, etc.; prestige, as by birth or by past success; the past experiences of the individual. (1, p. 70) Indeed, what others think of us, rather what we imagine others think of us, plays a large part in the deter-mination of our social self, or personality as viewed sociologically.

A comprehensive definition of personality, combining both the psychological and sociological definitions, may be best set forth in the words of Dr. Kimball Young: "Personality is a . . . .patterned body (characteristic organization, in our terminology—H.T.M.) of habits, traits, attitudes, and ideas of an individual, as these are organized externally into roles and statuses, and as they relate inter-nally to motivation, goals, and various aspects of selfhood" (2, p. 58).

6. THE CRUCIAL ROLE OF THE FAMILY IN THE FORMATION OF PERSONALITY

The child's growth, biological, psychological and sociological, takes place within the home at the start of its career. The family presents itself to the child as a concrete manifestation of the cultural process, indeed, of the cultural milieu as a whole. In the home is fashioned the style of personality that will by and large characterize the individual throughout his life. Adjustments to the biological and physiological demands of the organism are here mastered. Social rituals, ranging from table manners to getting along with others, are consciously inculcated in the child by the parents. Language, the tool of communication, is acquired by the child through the processes of imitation, inculcation and suggestion. Problems of psychological and emotional adjustments arise and are solved appropriately by each child in terms of the cultural values and the standards of the family. Finally, through familial relationships the child is constantly involved in and experiencing the processes of socialization and social control as well as accommodation to fellow-man.

The family setup tends to bring the child into contact with children and adults of other families as well as with his kinsfolk near and distant. From the home the child, in modern times, is translated to the school to the end that his latent powers may be "drawn out" and his rough edges polished. Here he becomes enmeshed in an intricate network of new group relationships, perhaps as leader in one, as follower in another. And all the time he is being subjected to cultural forces—that is to say, he is learning from culture, a veritable storehouse of stimuli for correct behavior. He is thus constantly developing a sense of solidarity with his culture-group.

While the process of physical maturation plays its part in creating in the growing child new wishes, new interests and new tensions, the sociological process at work relates him to a multiplicity of new groups, large and small, as a teen-ager, as an adolescent and, later, as an adult. As an adult he marries and begets children, the culture-bearers of the morrow. An endless chain of this sort has made possible the evolving and maintenance of culture, the environmental framework within which human nature develops and man attains his true stature as man.

7. THE UNIVERSALITY OF THE SOCIO-CULTURAL PROCESS

This socio-cultural process is universal; that is to say, it is present wherever human beings are to be found. Generalized human behavior is the same the world over—i.e., eating, drinking, sleeping, mating, procreating, recreating, working, cooperating, competing, fighting, loving, etc. But the specific forms of human behavior, i.e., how to eat or what to eat or when to eat; how, when, with whom, to cooperate or compete, etc.—such specific forms of behavior are conditioned by the cultural framework within which a given person or group operates. Hence a study of the cultural environment is essential to the understanding of human behavior.

The cultural framework sets man off from other forms of animal life. A given cultural environment sets its participant members off from other human beings operating under differing cultural environments. We must be careful not to confuse specific American or Euro-American forms of behavior with generalized human behavior patterns.

In the first two books, The Group and The Processes, an attempt is made to study certain aspects of human behavior from the generalized standpoint, though I must confess that the American cultural environment is very much in the background implicitly if not explicitly. In the third book, namely, Culture, the specifically American scene is taken as the subject for analysis.

REFERENCES

1. ROBERT E. PARK and ERNEST W. BURGESS: *Introduction to the Science of Sociology,* 2nd ed. Chicago: University of Chicago Press, 1924; eighth impression, 1933.

2. KIMBALL YOUNG: *Social Psychology,* 3rd ed. New York: Appleton-Century-Crofts, 1956.

NOTE: Studies of the divided self and of multiple personality have been made, among others, by William James (1842-1910), Morton Prince (1854-1929), Theodule A. Ribot (1839-1916), Pierre Janet (1859-1947), and others. *Dr. Jekyll and Mr. Hyde* by Robert Louis Stevenson (1850-94) is a classic portrayal of the divided self. Contemporaneously, the problem of multiple personality has been vividly illustrated in *Three Faces of Eve* by Corbett H. Thigpen and Hervey M. Clecky (New York: McGraw-Hill, 1957) and *The Final Face of Eve* by Evelyn Lancaster (with James Poling) (New York: McGraw-Hill, 1958). For two cases of inner conflict within the personality, see the stories of Irene and the Country Squire (CHAPTER 25).

CHAPTER 3

INTRODUCTION TO SOCIOLOGY

SOCIOLOGY is the science of society. Here we have two terms that need to be defined: science and society.

1. A DEFINITION OF SCIENCE

Science is defined by competent scholars as organized knowledge. The science of society in this sense would mean organized knowledge about society.

Science is also viewed by competent scholars as a technique of arriving at knowledge, as a technique of organizing knowledge. The distinctive characteristic of science, from this standpoint, is method. The end and means of science are alike directed toward reducing a mass of observable facts into a self-consistent system of general principles and laws.

1. The Nature of "Thinking" and of the "Mind"

In their efforts to respond to the objective conditions of life, men in the very earliest history of humankind developed "thinking." Thinking soon became a most useful aid in responding to the objective conditions of life. Thinking is localized neither in certain neurons nor in any particular organs of the human organism: it *emerges* from the particular functional arrangement and interaction of all the parts of the organism. A cave in a rock made by the forces of nature was a part of nature. Before it could be utilized by men as a place of refuge, as a shelter, some sort of thinking—or beginning of thinking —would be involved. When by usage the cave proved competent to serve men's purposes, thinking in terms of the establishing of correspondence was matured: cave←→shelter ←→security. The idea of shelter, the idea of security—non-material events—would become

2   33

fixed as stereotypes. Now the cave would cease to be an object of nature; it would become part of man's "culture." Similarly, the branch of a tree lying on the ground was but a part of nature. If through idle curiosity on man's part, or through necessity, the picking up of the branch and its use as an instrumentality could serve as an extension of the human organism in its struggle to respond to the objective conditions of life, the former object of nature would become part of man's "culture." Again the idea of the handle, the idea of the club, the idea of the crowbar or the lever, would develop through the processes of establishing correspondences. The branch, now a stick, an artifact <—->handle, club, crowbar, lever.

Again, to take another illustration, nature has provided fire in volcanoes and in forest fires. If a terrific gale of wind created friction between two branches of a tree, there might be fire. If there were human beings to observe fire springing up "from nowhere" and burning the tree that was standing a little while ago, the idea of fire being generated or made to order would dawn in the "mind" of our savage ancestors. A new correspondence would be established: branches of trees rubbing furiously<—->fire. Once this correspondence was established, through the trial-and-error method men would devise means to make fire.

Observation and the establishing of correspondences have been essentials in the process of thinking from the very beginning of man's history on this planet. *Ur-correspondences,* that is to say, objective realities, exist in nature. Man's discovery of these ur-correspondences entails or involves thinking. Once the correspondences are established, they become part of man's culture, part of his conceptual world. The process of establishing and accumulating correspondences is identical with the process of the emergence of the "mind." The mind may best be defined as the capacity for organizing and systematizing experiences. The larger the number of experiences and the better (i.e., the more serviceable) the organization of experiences, the richer the mind. Mind, like thinking, is a generalized characteristic of the organism, human as well as non-human; neither can be located in any special sense-organ. Even so, the dominant role of the brain in the development of the mind and of thinking must be conceded.

2. Mind, Thinking and Language

Mind and thinking cannot progress very far until they become articulated through gestures and symbols, through "collective representations" and words. The human organism is very nimble and flexible. It can walk on all fours or on two legs. It can grasp objects with the aid of the prehensile thumb. It can emit sounds. The pointing with a finger or fingers or with outstretched hands or with uttered sounds would be easy of accomplishment for the human organism. Whenever men in groups stumbled upon the notion that articulating such-like symbols and sounds could, by correspondence and integration, mean specific things uniformly and collectively to all members of the group, language had its start.

The first type of language evolved by collective man was the same type that had been evolved by birds and beasts, namely, emotive language. Certain sounds signified danger, certain other sounds signified joy ; some sound suggested, "Let us move on," while some other sound suggested, "Let us stay here awhile," and so on and so forth.

Spoken language is of two types : emotive and referential. Emotive language is to be found among birds and beasts as well as among men—among our distant ancestors, among contemporary infants and babies, and even among adolescents and adults. The development of referential language, that is to say, of spoken words referring to objects, events and ideas, marked a milestone in man's upward march and in his cultural evolution.

At what stage in man's psychological and cultural growth, emotive language was supplemented—and/or supplanted—by referential language we do not know. But whenever that crucial event happened, sounds become words and words became collective representations.

Soon the reciprocal relationship between thinking, mind and language became so intimate that none of these three non-material traits of man could function without the aid of the other two. Today we say that we think with our mind and that we think in language, i.e., with the aid of words, symbols, collective representations. These three traits of collective man—thinking, mind, and language—have given rise to culture, non-material as well as material.

Science, a species of theoretical knowledge, is part of the non-material culture of man. For thousands and thousands of years, a relatively small body of empirically tested and reliable knowledge was built up, as a result of trial and error, primarily through the instrumentality of the spoken language. When man began to devise written or painted symbols to correspond to sounds which stood for objects or ideas, the prehistoric period of culture came to an end and history, in the modern sense, began. But let us remember that written language, the language in which you are reading this book, is itself a product of cultural growth and evolution. Written language has appeared in the following forms: (1) the earliest, picture-writing, i.e., the picture of a bird to designate a bird; (2) pictograph, i.e., a bird on wings to denote flying; (3) ideograph, i.e., written symbols standing for certain ideas ; (4) syllabic symbols, i.e., symbols standing for certain syllable sounds ; (5) alphabetic writing, as in Sanskrit, Greek and Latin as well as in English and most modern languages.

Just as the development of referential language had in the past enhanced thinking and enlarged the mind, so now written language began to facilitate thinking, to promote the accumulation of culture, and to enrich the mind.

3. The Mind, an Open System

Nature and mind are alike integral parts of the cosmic system. Self-consistency is the essential attribute of any system. Nature, however, is what I would call a built-in system, while mind is an open and creative system. By saying nature is a built-in or closed system I mean that changes in nature must take place in terms of its inner consistency. The open or creative system of the mind implies that the human mind, in terms of *its* inner consistency, can impose upon the universe any one of a dozen self-consistent systems—that is to say, the human mind can view the universe as compounded of matter or of energy (spirit or mind) or of both mind and matter ; the human mind can view the universe in terms of freedom of will or predetermination, in terms of life after death or in terms of no life after death. The human mind at one time imposed upon the universe the geocentric system of Ptolemy and no one was the worse off for it.

Today we impose upon the universe the helio-centric system of Arya Bhatta (5th century A.D.) and of Copernicus (1473-1543 A.D.). The medieval scholastic imposed upon the universe a system in which thousands of angels could dance on the point of a needle; modern physicists foist upon us a system in which thousands of electrons dance in an atom which cannot be seen by the naked eye.

Even so, inasmuch as it is a system, albeit an open system, the human mind must conform to the laws of its own self-consistency.

4. The Four Axioms Underlying Natural Science

The integrity—integrality, unity—of the universe is maintained (1) by the law of the uniformity of nature and (2) by the law of causation. If, in terms of everyday ordinary experiences, water chose to boil at one hundred degrees centigrade one day and to freeze at the same temperature the next day, the universe *as we know it* would cease to exist. Nor could the universe *as we know it* exist without the operation of the law of causation. For every event in the universe there must be a cause; indeed, the effect lies in the cause, said the Hindu philosopher Kapila, author of the *Sankhya Upanishad*. A given event may be the effect of a particular cause and may in turn be the cause of another event. Under any and every condition, the cause-effect relationships subsist within phenomena. To discover this relationship in a given situation is to discover the Truth in the situation. The best definition of scientific law is in terms of Buddha's statement formulated about 2,500 years ago: namely, that Truth consists in the discovery of cause-effect relationships subsisting between phenomena.

These objective realities of the universe—namely, the law of the uniformity of nature and the law of causation—must be accepted as axioms by the human mind if it is to maintain its integrity. In addition, the human mind, by the very nature of its makeup, has to accept two more laws as axiomatic: namely, the law of identity and the law of contradiction. If A equals B and B equals C, then A equals C—the Law of Identity. The mass production of our industrial-technological civilization is made possible by the utilization of the Law of Identity—standardized, replaceable parts. A cannot be not-A—the Law of Contradiction: that is to say, A and not-A are mutually exclusive terms and categories. Fire and water behave differently—that is the judgment of our sensory perceptions. Fire burns, water cools. Such judgments of the sensory perceptions compel the human mind to assume the Law of Contradiction.

To summarize: In order to maintain its self-consistency and integrity the human mind must accept the four fundamental axioms of logic:

1. The Law of the Uniformity of Nature
2. The Law of Causation
3. The Law of Identity
4. The Law of Contradiction

Science must assume these four laws as axiomatic. Without the acceptance of these laws the human mind is unable to organize and systematize its experiences. Science which claims to take nothing on faith is forced to accept these four laws of nature and mind on faith. Within the limitations imposed by the four laws of logic the human mind attempts to investigate phenomena and to establish the relations of identity or contradiction, or of causation or correlation.

5. *The Fifth Axiom of Social Science: The Law of Surplus Power*

The natural sciences have evolved vast systems consistent with these four laws of logic. The student of human behavior, the social scientist, likewise, is forced to accept the four fundamental propositions of logic. Social science differs from natural science in that the social scientist observes phenomena in which he himself is an active participant. Furthermore, as attested by empirical observation, the power of a group, i.e., its capability to achieve a desired end, is greater than the sum-total of the power of each member of the group. This fact leads to the enunciation of a fifth axiom, peculiar to social science: namely, that *a group, an association, has more power than the sum-total of the power of each associated member.* The Friends (Quakers) have a saying: God and one man make a majority. Sociologically we may say that a dynamic, small group plus a cause, i.e., a group wedded to a cause, would generate more power than all other groups in society. The handful of followers of Buddha and Jesus and Mohammed, of Lenin and Mussolini and Hitler, each constituted a more powerful group than all the other apathetic groups of their day within the social context in which they operated. Much of social-science thinking has been vitiated by the neglect of this fundamental aspect of social behavior. A handful of the citizens of a nation plus their national flag constitute a greater strength than the sum-total of the strength of each national. For that matter, the piece of cloth with interesting designs becomes more powerful than all the members of the nation when that piece of cloth is collectively accepted by the group as its collective emblem, as its national flag. The compulsions of collective representations in human behavior have been only recently analyzed by eminent sociologists, such as Emile Durkheim (1858-1917). The sociologist has been driven to the conclusion that in human affairs power resides in the collective representation more than in the group of persons espousing the particular collective representation.

From these observable and demonstrable facts the social scientist is led to add to the four laws of logic the fifth law specially applicable to social science. In a variant form, we may rephrase the fifth axiom as follows: A group of persons bound together by a collective representation generates greater power than the sum-total of the strength of each member of the group; such a group also generates greater power than apathetic groups, however large or small, in society. Such is the Law of Surplus Power.

6. Comte: The Three Stages of the Human Mind

The human mind has gone through three stages: (1) Mythological, (2) Philosophical, (3) Scientific. For the term Theological, suggested by Auguste Comte (1798-1857), the Father of Sociology, I substitute the term Mythological as being more appropriate. Compelled to account for the universe and the cosmic process, the human mind in the early stages of its evolution created myths and legends. Descent from the sun or the moon was and is popularly ascribed to royal families in most of the "civilized" countries of our day. The

Emperor of Japan was believed to have been born of the Sun-Goddess. The Hindus thought of the successive incarnations of God from the lowest form of life, conceivable to them, to the highest—from the fish and the turtle, through the lion, to the human form. The Hebrews thought of the universe as having been created by the fiat of the Supreme Being in the course of six days.

6A. Myth-making Stage

Myth-making was one of the outstanding achievements of the emergent human mind. It is still present with us—in adults as well as in children. The purpose of myth-making has always been to give a consistent and ordered view of the universe. And that is precisely the purpose of philosophy and of science. It is difficult to draw sharp lines of demarcation between myth-making on the one hand and philosophy and science on the other. Modern science, natural no less than social, has forged ahead with the aid of myths and fictions. Modern astronomy is built on the myth of gravitational pulls. Modern physics accepted the myth of ether and the myth of the atom and later proved these myths to be true. (A question : May we not be going in a circle? Each culture poses its problems and tries to find answers to those problems. This is especially true in the social sciences.) Modern mathematics is built on the myth of numbers. In the realm of social science, the myth of a corporation as a fictitious person, capable of suing and being sued at law, was the basis of the legal system long before the sociological concept of the corporation, or of any association, for that matter, as a Mahajana was ever evolved and proved to be valid. (See CHAPTERS 9 and 18.)

6B. Philosophical Stage

In the process of myth-making the human mind attained a certain measure of sophistication. With sophistication came the philosophical approach to an understanding of the universe. Philosophy was developed and cultivated in order to answer the self-same questions as myth-making undertook to answer—with this difference that myth-making answered isolated questions and gave *ad hoc*

answers to problems as they arose. Philosophy systematically formulated all the questions regarding the universe and sought to
answer them in terms of a self-consistent system of thought. The
Hindu philosophers, for instance, raised, among others, the following questions: What is this universe? How did it arise? What is
the nature of the universe? What is its end? What is man's relation
to the universe? How does man know? What is the nature of
man? Does man have a soul? How did man come into being?
What is the end of human life? Is there a life after death? What
are the highest purposes of human life? What is the role of the
Creator if there be One?

In the Western world, in the historic period, philosophy has been
cultivated in terms of ontology, metaphysics, logic, psychology,
epistemology, ethics, esthetics. The realm of values was discovered
and systematically investigated by the early philosophers of all
modern "civilized" nations—the Chinese, the Hindus, the Greeks,
the Romans, the Europeans. Plato was concerned with the investigation of justice and with discovering how this value could be realized
by collective man. A modern American philosopher, Will Durant,
wrote his doctoral dissertation on *Philosophy and the Social Problem*. The Chinese have at all times conceived of philosophy in
terms of problems of interpersonal relationships.

6C. Scientific Stage

With the discovery of the experimental method as a tool of insight
into the processes of nature, the universe and the cosmic process, the
human mind entered the scientific age. Science helped man unlock
many a secret of nature. In terms of the four axioms of logic and
with the aid of rules of logic science helped man to *deduce* particular
truths from general truths empirically known to be valid, and to
induce or *arrive at* general truths or principles or laws from isolated
facts. The trial-and-error method whereby primitive man solved his
problems and arrived at new knowledge partook of both the *deductive* and *inductive* methods of science. With the attainment of
sophistication, man set forth elaborate rules and procedures for
deductive and inductive methods of research and investigation.

The Hindu system of logic, formulated some three centuries before Aristotle, combines both deductive and inductive methods of reasoning. It contains five parts:

1. Wherever there is smoke, there is fire
2. It is the nature of fire to create smoke
3. This mountain is smoky
4. Because smoke is always associated with fire
5. Therefore, this mountain has fire or is a volcano

Omit two parts of this Hindu syllogism, and you have the Aristotelian syllogism whose classic example is:

All men are mortal
Socrates is a man
Therefore, Socrates is mortal

The first proposition, alike in the Hindu and in the Aristotelian syllogism, embodies a general truth which had not been, and has not been, disproved in the experience of man. But the potential handicap of deductive logic has been that it is easy to affirm a plausible valid proposition, which in reality may not be true to objective facts. Given a false or a half-true major premise, no amount of rigorous and logical reasoning can give us a valid conclusion. False or half-true major premises can be easily shown up by accurate observation of the facts and by pointing out exceptions. The doubting of the validity of a major premise gave rise to the elaboration of the methods of inductive logic: observation of facts, classification of facts, the framing of a hypothesis, verification of the hypothesis by experiment under the most rigid controls, generalization or enunciation of a law which may serve as a major premise in deductive reasoning.

It may be pointed out that the mythological, philosophical and scientific "stages" in the development of the human mind are really not stages—they are co-eval. The so-called stage is merely characterized by the predominance of a particular approach and the subordination of the other two.

7. Bertrand Russell: Three Approaches to the Universe

Bertrand Russell suggests three approaches of man to the universe:

1. The Common Sense Approach
2. The Mystic Approach
3. The Scientific Approach

These three approaches have validity in the experience of man—they were present when human life began, they are present with us today. What a particular person does is simply to have one of the three approaches as dominant and the other two as subordinate. Life is a continuum. Experience is a continuum. Experience begets knowledge and knowledge is validated only by reference to experience.

In the post-Renaissance Age science has been accepted by man both as an outlook and as a technique. Scientific methods of observation and analysis of facts are being more and more applied to the social scene. Sociology has made significant contributions to an understanding of man's behavior in society. Unfortunately, however, sociologists have been too preoccupied with the massing of data to set forth a consistent set of valid sociological laws. We shall attempt to set forth some of these laws making use of the mass of isolated social data gathered by scholars in the field.

Two special handicaps of social science may be noted in passing. (1) In addition to the fact that the social scientist is involved in the social phenomena he is observing and studying, our cultural imperative does not permit us to experiment with or upon human beings. Hence we are compelled to set up an experimental design from existing situations or conditions—a highly unsatisfactory state of affairs, since many variables, known and unknown, cannot be controlled. In social science we are, therefore, not able to establish foolproof cause-effect relationships except in a few cases. But we can establish co-relationships: Given A 100 times, B is found 80 times or 60 times. (2) Social science terminology suffers from the fact that most of our conceptual tools are expressed in words of ordinary usage: culture, human nature, accommodation, institution, individual, person, etc.

Sociology as the science of society may now be defined as that body of knowledge about society which has been empirically tested and found to be valid.

2. A DEFINITION OF SOCIETY

Now we come to the other part of the definition of sociology, namely, society.

8. The Functional Definition of Society

Society may be defined as a complex of groups in reciprocal relationships, interacting upon one another, enabling human organisms to carry on their life-activities and helping each person to fulfill his special wishes and accomplish his special interests in association with his fellows. This is the functional definition of society. "From this standpoint society is an immense cooperative concern of mutual services," as is rightly observed by Park and Burgess. (5, p. 162).

Here we have five terms that need to be defined: (1) "interaction," (2) "life-activities of human organisms," (3) "person," (4) "wishes," (5) "interests." Interaction is dealt with in BOOK II. Wishes and interests are defined elsewhere subsequently. Here we may briefly allude to the life-activities of human organisms and the concept of the person.

A human organism, an individual, may be viewed, from the standpoint of sociology, as a biological entity. The child at birth is at best an individual. The individual with a status in the group—or in a set of groups—is to be viewed as a person. The life-activities of human organisms comprise birth, nutrition, growth, maturity, reproduction, senescence, death. This life-cycle of human organisms is lived out within the context of groups—in society. The human individual is not only born in a group but is also surrounded by culture from the very moment of his birth. This means that the strictly biological functions of the human organism, of the individual, must be carried out within the cultural context by the person in accordance with formalized and conventionalized procedures. A child born in America usually satisfies his biological function of nutrition with the aid of the milk-bottle, the spoon, and later the knife and fork.

9. The Functional-Structural Definition of Society

The functioning of the individual as well as the person, of the group as well as society, can be understood and analyzed only within the cultural context. In a sense, society and culture are co-eval. Collective man could no more live apart from culture than could fish live outside water. The cultural environment is as necessary for the person as air and sunshine are for the individual. Neither collective man nor society can be thought of apart from culture.

Therefore, the second definition of society is from the structural standpoint.

Structurally, society may be defined as the total social heritage of folkways, mores and institutions; of habits, sentiments, and ideals; in short, of all the non-material elements of culture in all their intricate interrelationships within a given context.

Now we are ready to set forth a combined functional-structural definition of society:

Society is a complex of groups in reciprocal relationships, interacting upon one another within the cultural context, enabling human organisms to carry on their life-activities and helping each person to fulfill his special wishes and accomplish his special interests in association with his fellows.

10. The Dynamic Definition of Society

Anticipating our discussion of society as process in BOOK II, we may here include our dynamic definition of society as well:

Dynamically, society is the process of stimulus-response relationships culminating in interaction, communication, and consensus .... *Society is the network of reciprocal relationships and interactions among persons and groups within a cultural context.* (CHAPTER 21)

Sociology is the science of society, thus defined.

3. SOCIOLOGICAL ANALYSIS

As a science, sociology should help us analyze the nature of groups, processes, social organizations, societal organization, cultural patterns, and human behavior within the context of groups and culture. Analysis presupposes a valid body of knowledge—in this case, about society.

11. Two Sources of Knowledge: Percepts and Concepts

Knowledge is gained from two sources: through perceptions and through conceptions. Percepts are private and individual, and may be experienced differentially by different individuals. Concepts are public and collective, and are shared in common by different members of the group. For instance, the intensity of heat or cold endured —or enjoyed—by different individuals differs with each individual —an experience in the realm of perception. But the image of the horse, recalled by the utterance or appearance in print of the word "horse," is common to all members of the group, i.e., to all moving in a common universe of discourse—an experience in the realm of conception. The word "horse" would not conjure up an image of a tiger or a tiger-lily to any member of the group.

All knowledge, including even the perceptual variety, exists in the world of concepts—in the conceptual order. Sociological knowledge, therefore, is the body of concepts about the behavior of man in the socio-cultural milieu. Hence special conceptual tools must be devised for sociology if we are to succeed in analyzing society.

12. Natural Science and Social Science Methods

The inductive analytical method of natural science is available to sociology, but cannot be used successfully by sociologists because of the order of phenomena we investigate. The phenomena of the socio-cultural order do lend themselves to (1) observation and collection of data, (2) classification of data, and (3) the postulation of a hypothesis; but they do not easily lend themselves to (4) experimentation under controlled conditions for the purpose of (5) verification.

For one thing, our cultural imperative does not permit us to experiment with or upon human beings (except with the voluntary consent of human guineapigs); second, the bias of the social scientist, in his role as participant observer, is an ever-present danger. Third, human behavior is compounded not just of neurons and chemical processes but of wishes, attitudes and interests, will-power and motivation, group pressures and cultural compulsives as well.

13. Tools of Sociological Analysis

Hence, for sociological analysis, special conceptual tools must be devised and natural science methods must be adapted to the socio-cultural order of phenomena. While as sociologists we would be happy to establish cause-effect relationships between social phenomena whenever possible, we would approach our task of sociological analysis through specific methodological tools, such as (1) the establishing of co-relationship if not causal relationship, (2) the statistical distribution of certain socio-cultural traits in the time-space framework, (3) sharply defined conceptual tools for the definition of our problems, (4) the setting up of an experimental design.

Since we cannot affirm that slum conditions are responsible for juvenile delinquency (because there are many slum-dwelling youngsters who do not become delinquents), we attempt to correlate slum-dwelling and juvenile delinquency. If out of 100 juvenile delinquents, 60 or 70 were to come from slums, the correlation would be meaningful; and this fact, *if fact it were,* would then be useful to policy-makers as well as to citizens.

14. Causation or Correlation?

The following two charts (pp. 48-49), one a composite of ten social indices in the City of Rochester and the other, showing families on public relief in that city, tell an interesting story. Chart number 1 indicates that the indices of social disorganization are most prevalent in the center of the city and decrease toward the periphery. The next chart points out that the highest percentage of families on relief is concentrated precisely in the area which bristles with indices of social disorganization.

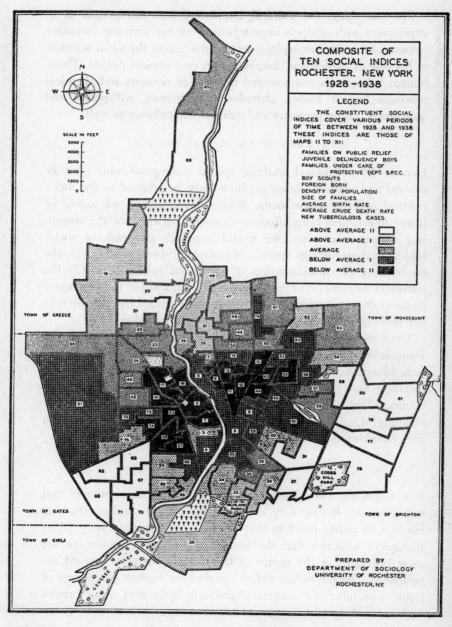

COMPOSITE OF
TEN SOCIAL INDICES
ROCHESTER. NEW YORK
1928–1938

LEGEND

THE CONSTITUENT SOCIAL
INDICES COVER VARIOUS PERIODS
OF TIME BETWEEN 1928 AND 1938
THESE INDICES ARE THOSE OF
MAPS II TO XI:

FAMILIES ON PUBLIC RELIEF
JUVENILE DELINQUENCY BOYS
FAMILIES UNDER CARE OF
  PROTECTIVE DEPT. S.P.C.C.
BOY SCOUTS
FOREIGN BORN
DENSITY OF POPULATION
SIZE OF FAMILIES
AVERAGE BIRTH RATE
AVERAGE CRUDE DEATH RATE
NEW TUBERCULOSIS CASES

ABOVE AVERAGE II
ABOVE AVERAGE I
AVERAGE
BELOW AVERAGE I
BELOW AVERAGE II

PREPARED BY
DEPARTMENT OF SOCIOLOGY
UNIVERSITY OF ROCHESTER
ROCHESTER, N.Y.

The indices of social disorganization and of other social phenomena correlated with it are found to be highest in the center of the city and to decrease toward the periphery. From R. V. BOWERS, "ECOLOGICAL PATTERNING OF ROCHESTER, NEW YORK," AMERICAN SOCIOLOGICAL REVIEW, 4:181, April, 1939. Data for map collected by LUTHER FRY.

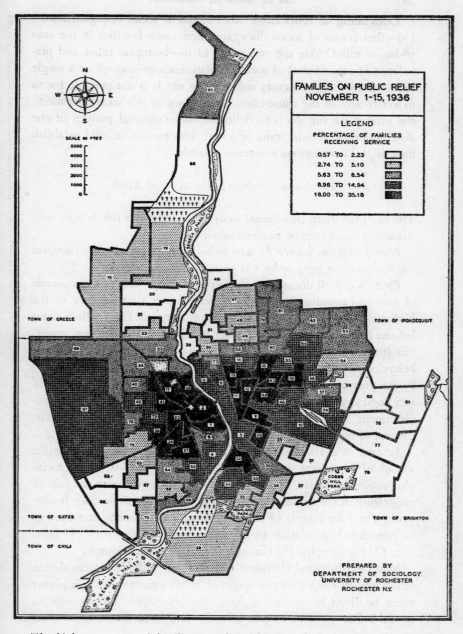

CHART 2
THE DISTRIBUTION OF FAMILIES ON RELIEF
IN ROCHESTER, NEW YORK (1936)

FAMILIES ON PUBLIC RELIEF
NOVEMBER 1-15, 1936

LEGEND
PERCENTAGE OF FAMILIES
RECEIVING SERVICE

0.57 TO 2.23	
2.74 TO 5.10	
5.63 TO 8.54	
8.96 TO 14.94	
16.00 TO 35.18	

SCALE IN FEET
5000
4000
3000
2000
1000
0

TOWN OF GREECE

TOWN OF IRONDEQUOIT

TOWN OF GATES

TOWN OF BRIGHTON

TOWN OF CHILI

COBBS
HILL
PARK

PREPARED BY
DEPARTMENT OF SOCIOLOGY.
UNIVERSITY OF ROCHESTER
ROCHESTER N.Y.

*The highest per cent of families on relief, like the indices of social disorganization,
is found near the center of the city. From R. V. BOWERS, "ECOLOGICAL PATTERNING
OF ROCHESTER, NEW YORK," AMERICAN SOCIOLOGICAL REVIEW, 4:188, April, 1939.
Data for map collected by LUTHER FRY.*

Does being on relief *cause* other forms of social disorganization? Do other forms of social disorganization *cause* families in the area to be on relief? Are the two social facts—being on relief and prevalence of other forms of social disorganization—*caused* by a single factor or by a set of factors unknown to us? It is not possible for us to verify any of the cause-effect hypotheses in this social situation; the utmost we can do is to delineate the ecological pattern of the distribution of certain traits of social disorganization, and establish meaningful correlations wherever possible.

15. Need for Sharp Conceptual Tools

The need for sharp conceptual tools of sociology for the definition of situations can never be overestimated.

Four factors influence human behavior: (1) *heredity,* (2) *natural environment or geography,* (3) *groups, and* (4) *culture.*

First. We shall discuss heredity in connection with our discussions of race and socialization. Suffice it here to note that heredity, or the biological factor in man, provides the substratum from which arises human behavior. Heredity, in other words, provides the raw materials from which is fashioned the human personality with its specific behavior patterns, some unique to the individual, others generalized by the pressures of groups and cultural compulsives. For purposes of sociological analysis, we discard the dichotomy heredity versus environment (natural as well as cultural) and substitute for it the concept of heredity-and-environment.

Second. We also discard the emphasis of the environmentalist school of historians, such as H. T. Buckle (1821-62), and social philosophers. Instead, as sociologists we attempt to assess the role of geography in the fashioning of culture within the time-space framework. The four aspects of the geographic environment that need to be considered in relation to man's evolving culture are: (1) location, (2) topography, (3) climate, and (4) natural resources.

Man's earth-bound character has changed with the accumulation of culture. In the very early stages of man's existence on this planet when he lived by gathering food, the geographic factors exerted crucial influence upon human behavior and upon the human horde.

Rivers and mountains, abundance or scarcity of rainfall, warm or cold climate, availability or unavailability of fruit, nuts and berries and game, would determine collective man's response to his "world" and would set limits to the growth of his culture.

Even so, it must not be assumed that the presence of certain geographic factors would automatically elicit a predetermined type of response. For instance, the Eskimos, living in the frigid Arctic zone, have evolved a high type of cultural adjustment to their environment by inventing the igloo, the harpoon, fur and skin clothing for the body; whereas the Onas, living in the identical type of frigid zone in the Antarctic, have failed to develop any kind of habitation (made of ice bricks) or any kind of clothing!

On empirical grounds, three conclusions are drawn by sociologists: (1) That even in prehistoric times, geography acted merely as a limiting factor in the growth of culture; the Eskimos could not build a steel structure or a log cabin, because these resources, timber and iron, were not present. (2) That geography does not act as a creative or causative factor in the growth of culture; the Onas failed to utilize the self-same resources that were utilized successfully by the Eskimos (4, p. 59). (3) That with cultural accumulation and with man's increasing mastery over the forces of nature, the geographic factor is, or may be rendered, comparatively insignificant in the growth of culture and in the moulding of human behavior: Today we can build air-conditioned houses and offices in the tropics and steel structures in the Arctic, thanks to modern technology.

Third. Sociological analysis requires a sharp delineation of types and categories of groups in society, and a proper understanding of how groups arise, are held together, and function. This task is undertaken in the rest of BOOK I.

Fourth. The culture concept as well as the concept of the culture area, developed by anthropologists, is a most useful tool of sociological analysis. Culture may be thought of as a conceptual house built in a geographic setting for human beings to live in. Or, culture may be likened to the atmosphere which surrounds us but of which we are serenely oblivious except when with sharp tools of analysis fashioned by competent scholars we try to analyze its nature.

We shall analyze the elements of culture in BOOK III, though it must be stressed that the cultural framework is implicit in our discussions of groups (BOOK I) and processes (BOOK II).

16. Experimental Designs in Sociological Research

Finally, the sociologist may be able to set up a control situation by getting full data on a given factor present in population A and absent in population B (1, *passim*). For instance, the Salk polio vaccine was administered to thousands of children in a given State; perhaps several thousands of children in the same State failed to receive the vaccine either because of the shortage of vaccine or medical personnel or because of the parents' refusal to permit vaccination. Here is a ready-made control social situation, made to order for the sociologist to analyze. The more refined the two samples, that is to say, the more alike the two samples are in every respect excepting vaccination, the more reliable would be the correlation between Salk-vaccination and the absence of subsequent polio attack.

Again, suppose there is disagreement over the desirability of large farms or small farms, how can we objectively verify a given judgment? Well, we simply look about ourselves in the nation and conceptually create an experimental design for our sociological research.

First, we must set forth an inventory of traits comprehended by the term "desirability"—traits that make for vital community living. Next, we would select two analogous communities sharing most of the basic traits in common, such as similar location, comparable size of population, same ethnic composition, etc., but differing in the fact that one community is inhabited by people with large farms and the other inhabited by people with small farms. Then we check off and compare the traits of "desirability" prevalent in each community.

This is precisely what was done by Walter R. Goldschmidt in his paper, "Large Farms or Small: The Social Side" (1944). He selected two California communities, one representing the large-farm economy and the other the small-farm economy (3, pp. 274–

75). In Public Affairs pamphlet No. 100, *Small Farm and Big Farm,* Carey McWilliams utilized Dr. Goldschmidt's findings and arranged them in a comparative chart for ready references (2, p. 3). (CHART 3.)

CHART 3

A COMPARISON OF THE SOCIAL AND ECONOMIC DIFFERENCES
BETWEEN A COMMUNITY OF LARGE FARMS AND
ONE OF SMALL FARMS [1]

Traits	ARVIN (*Large Farms*)	DINUBA (*Small Farms*)
Population	6,300	7,800
Tributary Trade Area	70,000 Acres	77,000 Acres
Banks	NONE	TWO
Newspapers	ONE	TWO (one vigorous, a real force in the community)
All Business Establishments	60	156
Schools	One Grammar School (no high school)	Four grammar schools (one high school)
Local Government	COUNTY ONLY	Incorporated, elects own local officials
Service and Commercial Clubs	TWO	FIVE
Fraternal and Women's Clubs	NONE	SEVEN
Veterans' Associations	NONE	TWO
Churches	six (only three are adequately housed)	Fourteen (mostly substantial and in good condition)
Housing	Very poor ; houses badly crowded on small lots ; very few brick or other permanent buildings	Modest but generally adequate ; most houses on lots of 50x120 ft.; lawns, trees, etc.
Youth and Juvenile Delinquency	Fairly serious, few recreational opportunities	Almost nonexistent ; numerous recreational facilities

[1] Carey McWilliams: *Op. Cit.,* p. 3.

The sociologist has to be ingenious in "creating" or "setting up" such experimental designs in research from existing socio-cultural realities.

REFERENCES

1. F. STUART CHAPIN: *Experimental Designs in Sociological Research.* New York: Harper & Brothers, 1947.
2. CAREY MCWILLIAMS: *Small Farm and Big Farm.* Public Affairs Pamphlet No. 100. New York: Public Affairs Committee, Inc., 1945.
3. LOWRY NELSON: *Rural Sociology.* New York: American Book Company, 1948.
4. WILLIAM F. OGBURN: & MEYER F. NIMKOFF: *Sociology,* 2nd ed. Boston: Houghton Mifflin Co., 1950.
5. ROBERT E. PARK and E. W. BURGESS: *Introduction to the Science of Sociology,* 2nd ed. Chicago: University of Chicago Press, 1924: eighth impression, 1933.

CHAPTER 4

THE NATURE OF THE GROUP-RELATED INDIVIDUAL

1. THE GROUP-RELATEDNESS OF THE INDIVIDUAL

INDIVIDUALS composing a group constitute so many force-centers or centers of power. They impart internal dynamics to the group, but they generate power only within a group setting. It may truly be affirmed that the individual lives, moves, and has his being in the group. It is the purpose of the present section (CHAPTERS 4–8) to elucidate and reinforce the meaning of these statements.

Grouping is a reality in the social process, but the group need not be thought of as a mystical reality. The postulation of the group mind is likewise out of the question. What is called the ethos of a group, of the ancient Greeks for instance, has a sociological validity. The ethos of a group is the characteristic way in which *members* of that group collectively react to hypothetical situations in terms of the logic of their culture. The ethos is the characteristic organization of the value systems and behavior patterns of a group—it is the "soul" of the group or of a people.

The group is the datum of sociology, not the individual human organism. To begin with, the very existence of the human organism postulates for its birth the association of male and female parents, of father and mother. The child is never born in a vacuum—he is born to a group within a cultural context. He grows up in groups—the immediate family group, the large family group, the friendly group, the play group, the neighborhood group, (the school group as well, in modern culture, Western or Westernized).

The prolongation of human infancy, first discussed by John Fiske (1842-1901), is the mechanism whereby the individual is socialized and becomes a person and a participant in the social heritage of his forebears.

The genetic group is the one to which the human individual at birth belongs. The diagram on the next page depicts the inter-relationship of the person to some of the groups.

The person's membership in a group is determined by the presence and awareness of a common interest or set of interests. Thus, for instance, his membership in the family is conditioned by biological and affectional interests, to cite but two of the many functions performed by the family. The membership in the neighborhood group is dependent upon a common locale, a geographically common habitat, wherein he dwells in association with others. The membership in the community group is derived from the *common* perquisites of life, material as well as non-material, shared by all the persons living in a common habitat, psychological or physical. The community is predicated upon a common sharing of modes of living, spatial, temporal, material and ideational, even ideological. The membership in the state or province is dependent upon a common political, administrative unit with territorial boundaries. The membership in the region or the section—the New England States region or the Mountain States region—is derived from the common fea-

CHART 4

THE INDIVIDUAL AND HIS RELATIONS TO EXPANDING GROUP
LIFE [1]

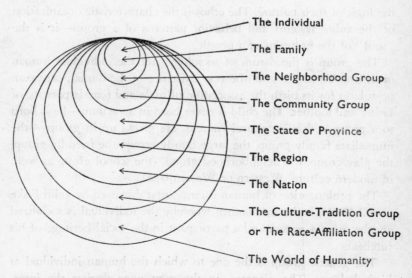

The Individual

The Family

The Neighborhood Group

The Community Group

The State or Province

The Region

The Nation

The Culture-Tradition Group
or The Race-Affiliation Group

The World of Humanity

[1] Adapted from John L. Gillin & Others: *Social Problems*, 3rd ed., p. 11. New York: D. Appleton-Century Co., 1943.

tures and culture complexes peculiar to the region. Membership in the nation is based upon a common loyalty to the great group, a civic and political unit, living within a geographically delimited area with a strong sense of in-group solidarity and with reverence to its cultural traditions and values.

The culture-tradition group as well as the race-affiliation group in which the person holds "membership," may transcend the limits of national boundaries—the Western democracies, or the Caucasian group, for instance—or it may be an island of likeminded or like-blooded people within the nation—the Ainus of Japan, the "colored" people of America, etc. Not only the presence but also the awareness of the common bonds is essential to this membership.

Membership in what has been called the Great Society, in the World of Humanity, is predicated upon common characteristics setting apart the world of *homo sapiens* from all others and upon an awareness of these common characteristics: "God hath made of one blood all the nations of the world to dwell on the face of the earth."

The feature common to all "members" of humanity is the original nature of man. This original nature of man is transformed into human nature by the categories of culture obtaining within a given nation or a given culture area.

The group represents a twofold dynamic set of relationships: internal and external. The intragroup and intergroup relationships constitute the core of sociological analysis.

A given group is constantly in interaction with other groups—in terms of cooperation or opposition, the spectrum of cooperation-opposition ranging all the way from corporate action based on friendliness to active hostility, with correlative accommodation and equilibrium. This, in fact, is the central theme of sociology. The diagram on the next page depicts a continuum of interpersonal and intergroup relationships.

Therefore, for a proper understanding of groups and groupings, we are obliged to study, on the one hand, the nature of the "members" of the group and, on the other hand, the processes of group-formation and group-interaction. In this and the two succeeding chapters we may address ourselves to an analysis of the nature of the members of the group.

CHART 5

A CONTINUUM OF INTERPERSONAL AND INTERGROUP RELATIONSHIPS[1]

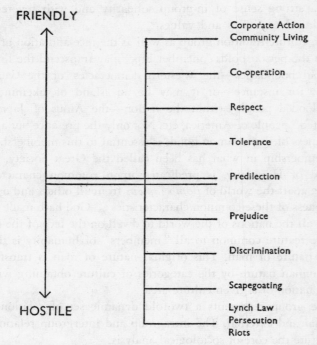

FRIENDLY

Corporate Action
Community Living

Co-operation

Respect

Tolerance

Predilection

Prejudice

Discrimination

Scapegoating

HOSTILE

Lynch Law
Persecution
Riots

[1]Adapted from *ABC's of Scapegoating,* with a Foreword by Gordon W. Allport, p. 10. Chicago: Central Y.M.C.A. College, n.d.

2. A DEFINITION OF THE ORIGINAL NATURE OF MAN

The human being at birth represents but a bundle of prepotent tendencies to act—to react to the environment. In this respect, the human individual is not different from other forms of organic life. The original nature of man, what has also been called the common-human nature of man, at birth consists of unlearned tendencies to respond to the objective conditions of life—reflex actions, instinctive actions, emotive actions. In this respect, man shares his original nature with all forms of organic life above the vegetable kingdom.

There is another ingredient in the common-human nature of man, namely, the capacity to organize and systematize the experiences of responses; this trait of the original nature of man seems to be shared by the more advanced forms of mammalian life, certainly by the higher apes, so far as modern research can be relied upon. Original human nature has still another trait, namely, the capacity to " represent" and "articulate" experiences symbolically. Whether the higher anthropoid apes have this capacity we do not know.

We may then define the original nature of man as consisting of:
(1) unlearned tendencies to react or to respond to the environment, as manifested in reflex, instinctive and emotive actions;
(2) the capacity to organize and systematize the experiences of reactions or responses;
(3) the capacity to represent and articulate experiences symbolically.

Of these three ingredients of the original nature of man, the first two are studied by psychology and the third by social psychology. Sociologists are content to accept the findings of psychology and social psychology insofar as they are scientifically valid, and build on these findings a sociological theory for the behavior of man—of collective man. It may be noted in passing that while individualist psychology studies the structures and mechanisms of human behavior mostly in terms of the physical organism, social psychology studies the responses of organic structures and mechanisms to the social situation. The sociologist goes a step farther and addresses himself to an investigation of the individual organism's responses to the social and cultural milieu as well as the natural environment. While we are primarily concerned with the sociological approach in the analysis of human behavior within the group and within a given cultural context, it may not be amiss to summarize briefly the standpoints of individualist psychology and social psychology.

In their attempt to account for human behavior, psychologists of the individualist school start off with the organism's unlearned tendencies to react to stimuli. These tendencies are analyzed in terms of physiological structures—reflex actions, instinctive actions and emotive actions. The word "instinct" is taboo to some psychologists. Sensations are studied in terms of the five organs—sight, touch smell, hearing, taste. Laboratory equipments are set up to measure the intensity of these sensations. Then they branch off into a study of learning in terms of attention, retention, memory, association, organization of experience—all without ever mentioning the other tabooed word "mind." The magic of the laboratory experiment is invoked by these individualist psychologists, blissfully ignorant of the fact that the cult of the laboratory is a part of our modern culture.

3. A SOCIAL-PSYCHOLOGICAL VIEW OF THE INDIVIDUAL

The role of language and ideas, of collective representations and thinking; of imitation and valuation; of fads and fashions; of groups and collective action, neglected by the individualist psychologist, are studied by the social psychologist. The social psychologist, like the individualist psychologist, takes the individual organism as his datum and, on the basis of the original nature of man, tries to formulate the mechanisms and procedures of man's social behavior. Unwilling to use the word "instinct," the American social psychologist, F. H. Allport, postulates the following six "prepotent tendencies to react" on the part of the human organism (1, p. 50):

1. starting and withdrawing
2. rejecting
3. struggling
4. hunger reactions
5. sensitive zone reactions
6. sex reactions

The social consequences of these six prepotent tendencies to react, on the part of the human organism, will be dealt with in the next chapter.

The Hindese authors, Mukerjee and Sen-Gupta, in their book, *Introduction to Social Psychology: Mind in Society,* place a major emphasis on the role of the group in the social behavior of man. Thus (3, pp. 37–38):

The foundation or basis of the group is a series of responses evoked from a number of individuals by a stimulus, and modified by another set of responses mutually evoked by the individuals in action. This analysis holds good throughout the scale of group life, from the simplest to the most complex. At a certain level of organic life, which we have no way of determining, there arise conscious processes: impression, ideation, emotion, and conative attitudes. These are superadded to the unconscious responses. A series of psychic factors, therefore, is superadded to the primary fact of stimulus-response. The psychic factors are: (1) representations of the stimulus; (2) representations of the responses to the stimulus; (3) the affective processes connected with these; (4) representations of the moving fellow-beings; (5) representations of the responses to the moving fellow-beings; (6) the emotive processes connected with these. Usually all of these are not experiences. Some stimuli and responses may remain mere physical facts. For example, a person may be aware of the stimulus but totally unconscious of his responses; he may be vividly conscious of his fellow-beings and may react emotionally to their presence, but the primary stimulus may recede from the field of attention. If the first three preponderate in consciousness, the stimulus becomes the primary fact in the mind of the individual; if the latter three claim exclusive attention, the awareness of the group displaces that of the physical environment. Both these mental conditions arise in course of the same process of adjustment of a number of individual beings to the environment.

One important corollary follows from the foregoing discussion. Group formation is but an episode in the adaptation of the individual to the environmental stimulus. The group is called into being because individuals are so constituted that they respond to the same stimulus in a specific manner. The influence of the group upon the individual arises through the exigencies of the sameness of the stimulus and the similarity of responses. If the individual were perfectly adapted to the environment, or if there were no call upon the individual to respond, obviously there would be no group life. In the state of lunacy, similarity with fellow-beings with respect to responses is, to a large extent, absent. This leads to the withdrawal of the individual from the group; thus there is little group life in a lunatic asylum. Likewise in the final stage of dementia praecox, there is a disinclination to all forms of action, save probably to a few mechanical and repetitive ones. Here, also, the individual cannot participate in group life, but fights shy of company. Group life, then, is an adjunct to the normal give and take between the organism and the environment. There is no group life *per se,* apart from the main function of adaptation to the environment. Consequently, a group mind or a group soul, transcending the normal course of the mind of an individual and influencing the latter *ab extra,* does not exist.

Affirming that the contents of the mental stream are determined by the environment, natural as well as social, these authors describe how a human being "primarily appeals to the motor-side of our nature." First, the human being is a moving object, with dynamic qualities. Second, "the moving object carries a greater potential attention-value." Third, "attention in a certain sense is but a preparatory stage to action. Thus all living and moving objects are calculated to set the motor mechanism of the human body on the very edge of action." Fourth, "every individual feels himself capable of a large variety of responses. The organisms which are structurally similar thus appear to one another as possessing a large potentiality of reactions. Each person represents to another a moving environment and calls forth a rapid adjustment in terms of actual or incipient movements." Fifth, "a rapid motor adjustment . . . . always involves compensatory internal changes, of respiration, of circulation, and of glandular secretions. These, however, are correlates of emotion, be they causes or effects. Therefore, a human environment would always give rise to particular emotional qualities." (3, pp. 40–45).

The human group, as an environment, [continue the authors] thus acts upon the individual organism in a definite way, primarily by influencing the motor-mechanism, voluntary and involuntary. It also develops the mental pattern of a special kind; for the mental contents begin from the nucleus of kinaesthetic impressions, and the associated ideas called up are determined by the character of the nucleus. We know also that special types of emotion arise in the course of the motor response and these must inevitably blend with the impressions and ideas. A psychic pattern, accordingly, is formed with emotions, kinaesthetic impressions, and ideas, and with a determinate motor attitude. This, in its ultimate analysis, represents the primary type of behavior of man in society. (3, pp. 45–46)

Individual habit and social behavior are correlated, maintain these authors (3, pp. 46–47):

The motor responses, like the psychic contents, have their own patterns. Such patterns, when they are common to all the members of a species, and determined by hereditary factors, are called *instincts*. But the peculiar environment in which each individual is placed elicits from him certain typical courses of action to meet the adaptive needs of daily life. These, like instincts, are invariable within limits; but, unlike the former, are peculiar to the individual. These are what we call *habits*. Such, for instance, are the modes of showing courtesy, the types of behavior demanded at parties and ceremonials, obedience to customs, modes of worship, food-getting, marriage, etc. These show a large amount of variability, though they are common to a large number of people—people belonging to the same group or class or region. They supervene upon habits and serve to modify them. Lastly, there are modes of behavior following upon and determined by the psychic patterns. These are the voluntary or purposive actions.

These types of action, reflex, instinctive, habitual, customary, and voluntary, are not mutually exclusive. The classification is not horizontal but vertical. Each is modified by the next in the hierarchical order, and each is more variable than the preceding one. Moreover, in every concrete instance of human behavior, there is a coalescence of all the orders of action. In a panic, the instinctive dominates over the voluntary, habitual, and customary modes of action, though the traces of all may be seen. The action patterns blend just as do the psychic patterns.

And, like the psychic patterns, the action patterns are determined socially. This determination is principally of a negative character. It is through the inhibition of particular modes of responses that the surviving type of action is selected. From the primitive taboo to the present day penal law, all inhibitions serve the same purpose, that of limiting the range of conduct.

Finally, these two Hindese authors sum up the central theme of social psychology in terms of the subservience of man to two masters, nature and the group (3, pp. 52–53):

Man has two masters to serve. Physical nature holds him fast; her commands must be obeyed. The human group in which the individual lives is equally insistent in its demands. The individual normally strikes a middle course, placating both nature and society. All individuals in the group have to accept the terms offered by the physical world; hence, in ordinary cases, there is hardly any conflict between the two courses of action. A group of agricultural laborers has its pastimes and recreations, its jokes and arguments consonant with the hard physical exertion that nature calls for in exchange for the wherewithal to live. The individuals agree remarkably in their psycho-physical make-up, inasmuch as the amount of physical labor, fatigue, and vicissitudes of work leave little opportunity for the mind to develop divergent varieties. Accordingly, likes and dislikes, ideas and impulses of different individuals have the same pattern. The responses to nature and to the group converge and blend.

Occasions, however, arise when there is conflict between the demands of nature, or between the habits formed in the daily occupation of life and the responses to the group. Nature and habit alike demand that in rain and hailstorm the individual seek a covered shelter. Yet the festive merry-making of the group drags the individual from his shelter and gives predominance to the psycho-physical pattern prepared by the group. Between the complete union and the complete divergence, there are shades and gradations that elude notice.

But group behavior rarely bars the way of man's adaptation to the physical environment. It is true that holiday rejoicing goes on in the open air regardless of the inclemencies of the weather. Loyalty to the trade union demands starvation of the family. Patriotism calls for the supreme sacrifice. Yet the biting cold breaks up the holiday gathering. The agony of hungry children produces the blackleg (scab). The love of life and fear of death snap the bonds of loyalty. In the normal routine of life, the group patterns offer easy guidance to man's adaptation to the physical environment. For, biologically speaking, this adaptation is primary, and social adjustment is only an aid to it.

4. A HINDU PHILOSOPHICAL VIEW OF THE INDIVIDUAL

Hindu philosophy conceives the universe as compounded of five classes of stimuli, generically called Air, Fire, Water, Earth, and Ether (Akasa); and original human nature as compounded of the capacities for responding to these stimuli in terms of Temperature, Color, Flavor, Odor, and Sound. The human being represents a reciprocal network of the physical or material and the vital elements of being. In Western terminology, the human being is compounded of physico-chemical elements and processes and of biological elements and processes. This biophysical organism, partaking of the nature of *Tat* or *Brahman*, is capable of experiencing five sensations-in-general (*Bhuta Matras*):

1. Sound-in-general (sound undifferentiated)
2. Temperature-in-general
3. Color-in-general
4. Flavor-in-general
5. Odor-in-general

Color-in-general, for instance, is the standard to which we refer when we perceive and experience particular colors, such as yellow, blue, red, etc. It is maintained by Hindu metaphysicians that if we had no capacity for experiencing sensations-in-general, we could not experience any of the millions of particular sensations.

Furthermore, Hindu psychology treats the human self in terms of the three aspects of consciousness, the subconscious, the conscious, the superconscious. Western psychologists have attempted to study the conscious self of man. The psychoanalytical school has attempted to probe into the subconscious self of man. But the Hindu psychologists believe that in addition to the experiences of this incarnation, the subconscious serves as a storehouse for the memories of the experiences of past incarnations as well—what Carl Jung would call "racial memory." The superconscious self of man, manifested in mystical experiences, culminating in the attainment of Buddhahood by Gautama or in the experience of Jesus—"I and My Father are One"—is not yet considered a fit subject for scientific investigation by the psychologists of the Western world, with the notable exception of William James, Hugo Münsterberg, J. B. Rhine, and a few others.

5. INDIVIDUALS AS CENTERS OF ENERGY AND POWER

Whatever be our view of the nature of the individual—Western, Chinese or Hindu—the fact remains that the individual organism is endowed with capacities for neuromuscular activities and for cognition and representation as well as with capacities for growth and decay. The human individual may be likened to a dynamo generating energy and power. Individuals are both alike and unlike—alike in their possession of common-human nature, unlike in the amount of energy and power they generate. The power of hearing is shared in common by all individuals but some may have a keen power of hearing, others a dull power of hearing; and some others yet may be completely or almost completely devoid of the power of hearing. These individuals with unlike powers function as persons, as members of the group in which they are born and the groups with which they. become associated.

The internal dynamic of the group is derived from the relationships of "members," who are alike in being human and unlike in their individual human traits and capacities: some are males, some are females, some are children; some are very old, some are very young; some are healthy, some are sick; some are tall, some are short; some can read, some cannot read; some are auditory-minded, some are visual-minded; some can sing, some cannot sing; some are characterized by emotionalism, some by intellectualism; some are extroverts, some are introverts, and so on and so forth. It is needless to elaborate the point that every group is composed of individuals with differences in background and experience and knowledge; every group, therefore, represents the resultant of the reciprocal interaction of differing degrees of energy and power generated by different autonomous individuals—centers of energy and power.

REFERENCES

1. FLOYD H. ALLPORT: *Social Psychology.* Boston: Houghton Mifflin Co., 1924.
2. J. C. CHATTERJI: *India's Outlook on Life.* New York: Kailas Press, 1931.
3. JOHN L. GILLIN, et al: *Social Problems,* 3rd ed. New York: D. Appleton-Century Co., 1943.
4. RADHAKAMAL MUKERJEE and N. N. SEN-GUPTA: *Introduction to Social Psychology: Mind in Society.* Boston: D. C. Heath and Co., 1928.

NOTE: For the Hindu philosophical view of the individual, see Swami Akhilananda: *Hindu Psychology* (New York: Harper & Brothers, 1946) and J. C. Chatterji: *India's Outlook on Life* (New York: Kailas Press, 1931).

CHAPTER 5

THE INTERNAL DYNAMICS OF THE GROUP I

THE group receives internal dynamics from its members, who are at once alike in some respects and unlike in others, who at once strive for the same things and for different things. Having set forth varying interpretations of the human self in the last chapter, we are now ready to embark upon a sociological analysis of human nature characterizing individual human organisms, the centers of energy and power within the group. This analysis of human nature and human behavior is undertaken in terms of concrete situations including man's beliefs and activities.

"War is a biological necessity," we were told on the eve of World War I by von Treitschke, von Bernhardi and Nietzsche. "War is a necessary instrument for the rectification of wrongs suffered by the 'have-not' nations," said the spiritual descendants of Treitschke, Bernhardi and Nietzsche on the eve of World War II. The difference between the two statements, between the two outlooks, is the measure of the change in the temper of our generation. It also neatly disposes of the whole question of violence as being rooted in human nature.

1. HUMAN NATURE AND RELIGION

Perhaps more contradictory statements have been made about human nature than about anything else one can think of. For instance, it is vehemently contended, on the one hand, that human nature cannot be changed; and it is contended, on the other hand, with equal vehemence that human nature can be changed.

The phrase (human nature) is sometimes employed with cynical deprecation as, 'Oh, that's human nature,' or as often, perhaps, as an expression of approbation, 'He's so human!' (8, p. 65)

Philosophers and religious leaders have been using the term "human nature" in a generic sense, without specifying whether they are referring to original nature or to acquired nature. Thus Buddha,

Laotze, Jesus, Locke, Rousseau, Kropotkin, Gandhi, and a considerable school of religious thinkers accept the altruistic traits of human nature as their point of departure and build their *Weltanschauung* upon that belief. Hobbes, Darwin, Hitler, Reinhold Niebuhr, and a considerable school of religious and pseudo-religious thinkers, on the other hand, accept the egotistical traits of human nature as their point of departure and build their *Weltanschauung* upon that belief.

Every historic religion has had these two contradictory schools of thought: one affirming the divinity of man, the other affirming the devilishness, the original sin, of man. The evils of our society are traced by the former school to the corruptions of human nature brought about by man-made institutions; in the judgment of the latter school, the evils of our society stem directly from the original sin of man, from the limitations of human nature.

In between, there is a school of thought in religion which affirms the duality of human nature. Zarathustra (Zoroaster) is the outstanding exponent of this point of view. It may be pointed out, however, that most religious leaders, including Mahatma Gandhi in India and the Friends in Christendom, while affirming the divine nature of man, do not preclude the existence of wicked propensities in human nature.

In his commentary upon the Bhagavad Gita, for instance, Mahatma Gandhi says: "Man's self is a perpetual battleground between the forces of evil and the forces of good." (4, INTRODUCTION)

Logic and science are incapable of throwing much light on certain basic problems of human existence. Immanuel Kant postulated four possible antinomies wherein from the same set of premises two contradictory conclusions could be drawn. Whether one is to believe in the essential and inherent goodness of man, or in the essential and inherent wickedness of man, falls within the purview neither of logic nor of science. The belief in this realm is the result of interaction between one's own temperament and one's cultural heritage. There are perfectly good Christians who believe in the wickedness of human nature and there are equally good Christians who believe in the divinity of human nature. The matter being extralogical, the judgment of right and wrong does not apply here.

Both schools of thought believe in progress and in human perfectibility, but advocate different paths in order to arrive at these common goals.

The problem for the "wickedness" school is: Human nature is compounded of evil propensities; therefore, we have evils, injustices, wrongs, in society. But it is possible for man to redeem himself by confession of his sins, by repentance, by divine grace. Thus redeemed, he can overcome the wickedness of the world; aye, he may become a partner in the building of the Kingdom of God.

The problem for the "goodness" school is: Human nature is compounded of divine potentialities as well as of evil propensities. The evils, the injustices and the wrongs in society are produced by the inevitable necessity for man to function in a cultural milieu with the aid of institutions as instrumentalities. In this process of interaction man's divine potential becomes obscured and his less lovely traits find expression. Therefore, man must by supreme effort transcend the limitations of his institutional mode of operation and by inner communion become aware of his higher and truer self. Thus redeemed, he must set about the task of transforming and redeeming the institutions of his generation; aye, he may thus become a partner in the building of the Kingdom of God.

Two absolutely opposed points of view, as far apart as the North Pole is from the South, in regard to human nature are propounded by opposite schools of thought in every religious tradition. Here are two statements—one representing an extreme of the "wickedness" school in Christendom, the other an extreme of the "goodness" school in Hinduism (the Upanishads):

Human nature is a rogue and a scoundrel, or why would it perpetually stand in need of laws and religion?

—An English clergyman (8, p. 65, quoted)

Tat-Twam-Asi, i.e. *That* thou art! That is to say, the human self is the Supreme Self in miniature; or, human nature partakes of Divine Nature. Thou hast *that* of God in thee.

—A Hindu saying (9)

2. HUMAN NATURE: A SOCIOLOGICAL ANALYSIS

Human nature, sociologically viewed, is capable of two definitions: (1) Human nature is the sum-total of the organism's unlearned tendencies to react to stimuli, inner as well as outer; (2) Human nature is the organization of learned responses to stimuli. In the first sense, human nature is referred to as *the original nature of man* or the common-human nature of man, that is to say, the nature common to all mankind; in the second sense, it is looked upon as the acquired nature of man.

On the first (primitive) level, for instance, it is human nature for the organism to feel heat and cold. On the second (acquired) level, it is human nature for man to ward off the effects of heat and cold by providing himself with shelter and clothing. Again, on the primitive level, it is human nature to feel hunger. On the second level, it is human nature not only to experience the biological stimulus of hunger but also to work out the techniques for satisfying hunger.

The techniques for the satisfaction of biologic urges become part of man's culture. The techniques differ in different climes, in different cultures. In India hunger is satisfied without the aid of knife and fork or chop-sticks; in China it is satisfied with the aid of chopsticks, whereas in the Western World, during the last three hundred years or so, knife and fork are ritualistically essential for the satisfaction of hunger.

The child—a bundle of prepotent tendencies to act—is confronted at birth with the task of learning the techniques of his forefathers' culture. Armed with a mastery of the techniques, man becomes part of the cultural milieu. But culture is never static. From time to time an increment is added to culture; and even when nothing critically new has been added to it, culture is experienced *differentially* by different participants. A change in the physical environment or the invention of a new technique, such as fire-making or bow-and-arrow or the automobile, may call for a new type of adjustment, a new mode of operation.

The task of human nature is a dynamic one: to translate *prepotent tendencies to react* into *concrete behavior patterns*. This it does in two ways: (1) by acquiring knowledge of and mastery over

known techniques; (2) by creating new techniques for the solution
of problems created by a change, or a new element, in culture.

Human nature in this sense is culturally conditioned. Well may
Professor Park say: "Man is not born human but to be made
human" (8, pp. 79–84). In contradistinction to original nature,
human nature is the result of social interaction in a cultural milieu;
abstracted from contact with his fellows at birth, the child will
grow up into a "feral man"—without knowledge of human speech,
without any concept of "right" and "wrong," without awareness of,
or the ability to use, cultural techniques. (For case studies, consult
CHAPTER 6)

The constituent elements of common-human nature are:

(1) Biological
(2) Physical
(3) Psychic
(4) Social

The biological element of our common-human nature gives rise
to the family order with its institutions of marriage, divorce, christening, etc. The physical element gives rise to the economic order,
with its institutions of the market-place. The psychic element
leads to the *dharmic* or church-school order with its institutions of
education and religious ministration. Finally, the social trait of our
common-human nature gives rise to the social order with its
normative institutions culminating in the State.

A great deal of confusion in the discussion of human nature and
its role in human behavior springs from a lack of precise statement
about the two levels of human nature and the two levels of institutions. The family order, for instance, does spring from the biological
trait of original nature. But the primary institution of the family and
its derivative or secondary institutions, such as marriage, divorce,
engagement ring, christening, baptism, etc., are culturally conditioned. It is permissible to say that original nature requires or
postulates the existence of the family order the world over; but it is
not permissible to say that original nature requires the celebration of
the marriage ceremony only by a Christian priest or only by a Hindu

priest the world over. Man must eat food to satisfy the pangs of hunger the world over—that is part of common-human nature; but whether he shall eat meat or vegetables, whether he shall use his fingers or implements to eat with—these are matters dictated by the environment and the institutions of man's society and culture, by human nature.

3. HUMAN NATURE: A PSYCHOLOGICAL VIEW (BEHAVIORISTIC)

The psychological view of human nature is as varied as the number of schools of psychology. The "instinct" school would interpret all human behavior in terms of "instinct," whereas the "behaviorist" school would account for human behavior in terms of conditioned and reconditioned reflexes and habit patterns. The "vitalists" are concerned with "consciousness" and "mind," while the "structuralists" deal with physical structures as clues to human behavior. In spite of these different accents, most psychologists accept "drives" and primitive reflexes, or what Allport calls "prepotent reflexes," as conditioning factors in human behavior.

Allport, as already pointed out in the last chapter, postulates six important classes of human prepotent reflexes (2, p. 50):

(1) starting and withdrawing
(2) rejecting
(3) struggling
(4) hunger reactions
(5) sensitive zone reactions
(6) sex reactions

Starting and Withdrawing

The response of starting may be produced in the newborn infant by removal of support, loud sounds, a sudden tug or push when drowsy, and immersion in water. Turning the head so that the nostrils will not be buried in the pillow, and blinking at objects threatening the face (at about one hundred days of age) are examples of special *withdrawing* responses. The latter is connected in older children with retreating movements of the head and body. (2, pp. 50–51)

Rejecting

By the third day of life the use of hands and feet in pushing away noxious stimuli from the body is clearly seen. There has been observed in the infant, four days of age, a response of pushing at the hand of the experimenter who was pinching the nose of the infant. When the newborn baby is lying on its back with legs extended, a slight pinch on the inner surface of one knee will cause the opposite foot to be drawn up, somewhat awkwardly at first, until the sole finds and presses against the hand that is pinching. This reflex, although slow and crude at the start, has a deep evolutionary foundation. Well before the age of a year the infant pushes out toward the approaching nursing bottle, when in no mood for its contents. A little later the same response is shown toward bitter medicine and toward toys which are proffered in an attempt to beguile his stormy moods. These are reactions of 'rejection in advance,' just as . . . concealment (is) a 'withdrawal in advance.' . . . The use of the hands in self-defense or attack is attributable rather to an efferent development of protective reflexes than to a 'fighting instinct.' (2, pp. 56–57)

Struggling

If the limbs or the head of a newborn child are held so that the usual random motions are impossible a struggle ensues which grows more violent as the restraint continues, involving more and more of bodily musculature, and accentuated by crying and, later, screaming. The restraint of movement is no doubt to be considered biologically as a nocuous stimulus. The struggle response is a compound of the two more elementary reflexes of rejection and withdrawal. Attempts are made both to push away the restraining agent, and to escape its force by withdrawal. The accompanying emotion is, therefore, often a mixture of anger and fear. The two reactions are readily seen in certain wild animals when captured and held in the hands. Many creatures, pursued and brought to bay, quickly substitute for the withdrawing response of flight the rejecting or repelling response of fighting. It is probable that the habit of *pugnacity* arises genetically from the rejection employed in self-defense. When the efferent development is complete—that is, when one has learned how to fight—the use of the ability for offensive purposes is likely to follow . . . (. . . There is an innate reflex basis for self-defense; but there is none for fighting itself. . . .)

At the beginning of life the human infant struggles indiscriminately against any restraining force, whether it be another human being or a blanket which confines his movements. There is no inherited susceptibility to *social* stimuli, as distinct from other stimulations, in anger. At a later date the child *learns* that certain actions, such as striking, scolding and screaming, are effective toward persons, but not toward things. In adults, although the infantile response is still sometimes seen, the fighting reaction becomes fairly well limited to stimuli whose hurting or restraining influence can be thrown off by physical violence.

The various prepotent reflexes are prominent among the movements whose blocking leads to an angry struggle. Interference with the nursing activity (hunger reflexes) is an invariable stimulus for this response. There is an extension of an ever-widening circle of stimuli as the child develops, so that the restriction, not only of the innate mechanisms, but of all kinds of acquired habits based upon them (for example, blocking of the habits of manipulation through withholding a desired plaything) is certain to evoke the struggle. At a later stage, an insult, which thwarts one's habitual bearing of self-esteem, has often a more potent effect than direct bodily attack. Finally, our readiness to struggle against the thwarting or restraint of others, under conditions which we term 'injustice,' is the final development in the transfer of the fighting response to situations of a social character.

The activities of sexual and family love are particularly liable, when opposed, to lead to struggle. The ferocity of sexual jealousy and the blood feuds of the mountaineers are well known instances. The hunger reactions are equally potent in the fierceness of the struggle to which they lead when blocked. Aggression, unsatisfied hunger, crowded conditions, and limitations which hamper both the economic and the sex life are, when they evoke struggle responses on a large scale, the cause both of industrial conflict and war. (2, pp. 58–60)

Hunger, Sensitive Zone and Sex Reactions

The first three classes of responses—*starting and withdrawing, rejecting, struggling*—have been aptly described as *avoiding responses.* "The biological function of these activities is protection ; and their stimuli arise from contacts which the organism makes with external objects" (2, p. 61). Could we perchance denominate the other three classes of reactions—hunger, sensitive zone, sex—as *grasping reactions?* The biological function of these activities is not so much protection as thriving, not so much survival as prospering, not so much life as the good life.

Endowed with the prepotent tendencies, with unlearned capacities for response, with 'drives,' the child is born in a cultural milieu, surrounded by nature as well as by the parents and by other human beings. The attempt on the part of the child to come to terms with nature as well as with culture results in struggle, and struggle calls for adjustments—biological adaptations and social accommodations.

4. HUMAN NATURE AND THE STRUGGLE FOR EXISTENCE

Struggling, as used by Allport, is neither moral nor immoral; it is a reflex action calculated to foster the growth of the organism. In the social context, this struggling mechanism is translated into the "struggle for existence." This "struggle for existence," this striving for the satisfaction of the whole man, is neither moral nor immoral in itself; it tends to be moral or immoral in accordance with the means and instrumentalities utilized by man in the process of struggle, living and growth.

Using the term "struggle for existence" in a large sense, the late Professor Franklin H. Giddings (1855-1931) broke it down into the following "four distinct and specific struggles," namely:

1. The struggle to react, to endure heat and cold and storm, to draw the next breath, to crawl the next yard, to hold out against fatigue and despair, to explore and analyze the situation;

2. The struggle for subsistence to repair the waste of reaction;

3. The struggle for adaptation by every organism to the objective conditions of its life;

4. The struggle for adjustment by group-living individuals to one another. (6, p. 14)

Be it noted that the struggle for adaptation is part of the biological process, while the struggle for adjustment (accommodation) is part of the sociological process.

With the fourfold struggle for existence as a tool of analysis, Giddings traced the source, rise and growth of (a) religious, esthetic, and scientific activities; (b) economic activities; (c) ethical norms; (d) group cohesion and solidarity, "the precedent condition" of human society and culture (6, pp. 15-16):

The struggle to endure and, notwithstanding fatigue, to go on, to keep up courage and to maintain faith, develops into religion. It avails, however, only if sensitiveness to the situation warns of danger, and reaction to peril achieves safety. Sensitiveness to electrical and chemical conditions, to temperature, pressure and sound, to light and shade, to color and form (in all their objective degrees and proportions, dissonances and harmonies) and alert reaction to them, are the beginnings of esthetic interest and discrimination, which therefore, it seems, are vital concerns . . . They are the unwearying guardians of immediate safety. For assurance of safety or continuing security, yet other reactions are necessary. There must be an exploration of each situation and an analysis of it. This is an intellectual business, an affair of ideas and of thought processes, for which only man is competent. His attempt to develop it is his scientific life.

Religion, then, the esthetic life, and the scientific life, are initial products of the struggle to react, to hold out, to go on.

The struggle for subsistence initiates and broadens into the economic life. The struggle for adaptation becomes the ethical life. For adaptation, in its beginnings a mere taking on or perfecting of useful characters, develops, in time, into self-control, self-direction and self-shaping.

Adaptation—which, as it goes on, widens into and includes the ethical life—at first is a mere conforming of the organism, through variation, selection and inheritance, to the physical conditions under which it happens to live; that is to say, to altitude, temperature, light or darkness, dryness or moisture, enemies, food supply, and so on. Through adaptation, and because non-adaptation means extinction, the individuals of any given species, congregated and dwelling in any given region where food supplies are found, become increasingly alike ; and the first two conditions of social life, . . . namely, grouping and substantial resemblance, are provided. But since they are alike, individuals of the same variety or race, so brought together in one habitat, necessarily want the same things, and, as often as not, try in like ways to get them, reacting in one manner to any stimulus that incites all of them, or to a common situation. They compete in obtaining things which each is able to get by his own efforts, or (unconsciously or consciously) they combine their efforts to obtain things that no one could get unaided. In either case their interests and activities are not altogether harmonious and easily become antagonistic.

Competition tends to engender conflicts inimical to group cohesion; but in aggregations of animals or of human beings, in which individuals generally are substantially similar in behavior and approximately equal in strength, conflicts are self-limiting in a degree. An equilibrium of 'live and let live' is arrived at, which makes gregarious life possible for animals and conscious association possible for human beings. In human communities the let live habit of non-interference becomes a conscious toleration, in which adaptation passes into adjustment, a reciprocal adaptation. It is a precarious adjustment at first because rivalries continue and conflicts recur. When, however, these provoke collective (i.e. group) reactions in defense of the let live status, the struggle then begun is a struggle to maintain adjustment and to improve it. On its success group cohesion depends, and on group cohesion social evolution depends.

Professor Giddings' analysis and conclusions may be summed up in his own words (6, pp. 16–17):

(1) The struggle to react with ongoing will and discriminating intelligence becomes differentiated into religious, esthetic and scientific activities;

(2) The struggle for subsistence becomes the economic life;

(3) The struggle for adaptation broadens into the ethical life;

(4) The sruggle of resembling creatures to adjust themselves (together with their competitions and their adaptations) to one another is the beginning and the continuing process of group cohesion, the precedent condition of human society and all that it signifies.

Through success in all of these struggles, and not in one or another of them only, there results a survival of the fit, namely, [of those] organisms that are so equipped with proper parts and habits that on the whole they fit into and conform to the essential conditions of life incident to the environment in which they are forced or elect to dwell.

The stimulus-response relationships of the organism and the objective conditions of life constitute an essay at transforming tension into equilibrium. This tension is inherent in the very nature of being. But the interpretation of tension has created doubts about its validity in some quarters. "The struggle for existence" in the large sense in which Giddings used it cannot be and need not be disputed. But when "the struggle for existence" is identified with tooth and claw, with so-called jungle law, we have a right to enter a demurrer regarding its universality. Struggle, in the Giddings and Allport sense, is neither moral nor immoral; far from being brutal and destructive, it provides the only type of soil on which growth can take place.

We do not consider the resistance of air immoral nor do we consider it a destructive phenomenon ; without the resistance of air, so far as our knowledge of physics goes, there could be no motion. Air-resistance, friction, motion—the three are related. Similarly, struggle, adaptations and adjustments, growth—these three, too, are related.

5. HUMAN NATURE AND THE INFERIORITY COMPLEX

In the whole animal kingdom there is no offspring less weak and less self-reliant at birth than the human offspring. The young of no species require so long a time as does the human infant to acquire strength and to be self-reliant. This very weakness of the human organism, implanted by nature, is the source of man's strength and his superior achievements. The prolongation of human infancy, as John Fiske (1842-1901) pointed out, renders it possible for the child, by imitation and suggestion and inculcation, to gather up and acquire the experience of the race, including moral judgments and esthetic values, desirable goals and institutional means. (5, pp. 100–21).

There is yet another weakness the human child must constantly strive to transform into a source of strength. The objective conditions of life on the one hand and the child on the other constitute a stimulus-response relationship of superiority-inferiority. The inferiority complex is present in every child (1, *Passim*). But this very inferiority of the child *vis-a-vis* the world is a challenge to him and sets before him desired goals which must be achieved if the inner integrity of the growing child is to be upheld. One set of goals realized, another set of a yet higher type challenges the child. Progress, in other words, becomes possible precisely because of the presence of the inferiority complex. To be sure, if the inferiority complex leads to frustration through inability to attain the goals demanded by the objective conditions of life, then it becomes a source of disintegration of the human self—a case of personality malaise. But the fact that the majority of mankind have survived the ordeal and thrived on it would suggest that the inferiority complex, like the helplessness of the human infant at birth, is a mechanism provided by nature for man's growth.

6. HUMAN NATURE AND CULTURE

On the basis of the preceding discussion, we are now ready to set forth in brief compass the problem of human nature.

One. We must distinguish between the "original nature" of man and the "acquired nature" of man. Human nature in the sense of "original nature" is a constant. But the "original nature" of man, of the infant at birth, *isolated from society,* does not develop into what we call "human nature"; it is, therefore, logical to deduce that "human nature" as we know it is fashioned from the raw materials provided by nature, i.e., by the "original nature" of man. Human nature, in the sense in which it is ordinarily used, is the product of social interaction, of cultural conditioning. We are thus in a position to accept Professor Park's definition (8, p. 80):

Human nature may therefore be regarded on the whole as a superstructure founded on instincts, dispositions, and tendencies, inherited from a long line of human and animal ancestors. It consists mainly in a higher organization of forces, a more subtle distillation of potencies latent in what (E.L.) Thorndike calls 'the original nature of man.'

Two. The facile attempt made by certain psychologists and by the man in the street to account for any and every phase of human behavior in terms of so-called 'human nature,' in terms of inborn 'instincts,' is unscientific, in the judgment of most competent scholars. Among respectable social scientists, those who still espouse the instinct theory are best represented by William McDougall, who could produce or adapt an instinct *ad hoc* to account for any type of human behavior. In *Instinct: A Study in Social Psychology,* Professor L. L. Bernard (1881-1951) once and for all exploded the all-too-convenient instinct-myth. He found no less than 5,759 so-called instincts used by 412 authors in 495 books, referred to 14,046 times! (3, *passim*)

Three. The situational approach, the stimulus-response relationship between the organism and the environment, is the most satisfactory and the most scientific method for the study of human behavior.

Starting with certain 'prepotent reflexes,' with certain prepotent tendencies to react, human organisms in the infancy of man's existence grew through (1) the struggle to react, (2) the struggle for subsistence, (3) the struggle for adaptation, (4) the struggle for social adjustment or accommodation, and evolved culture.

Four. By the trial and error method, in the process of living, human organisms developed patterns of behavior that had a growth value as well as a survival value. In this fashion there arose in each tribal group folkways and mores, customs and laws (taboos), techniques and institutions. These became part of their culture, of their social heritage, the transmission of which to posterity soon became a dominant concern of each generation. Language, education, imitation, inculcation and a host of other devices, including social control, conscious as well as unconscious, began to be perfected by each group for transmitting the social heritage.

Five. Each society, each tribe, discouraged variation from type. As a "type-conforming group of associates," (6, p. 18) with the "consciousness of kind" as a motive force in their behavior, each tribe lived its life more or less satisfactorily—until a "non-conformist" in its midst, or a "stranger" from beyond, brought into being a new invention, a new mode of operation, a new outlook. If the new invention had pre-eminent growth and survival values for the group, it would be adopted—not, however, before the intransigent conservatives, that is to say, those who wished to conserve the old order of things, had been successfully overcome.

The new invention might be either made by the group or introduced within it through the processes of culture-contact, peaceful or warlike. Some inventions, such as fire-making, tool-making, bow-and-arrow, and the wheel, profoundly transformed the mode of living of the group. Discovery of metal and application of metal to tools, such as spits for roasting and spears and swords for fighting, constituted a milestone in man's upward march from savagery toward civilization. Growth in material culture was accompanied by growth in non-material culture—in ideas, institutions, social techniques and philosophies of life.

We need not enter into the futile discussion which preceded which—whether the idea was responsible for the material invention or *vice versa*. Suffice it to note that either may be father to the other : in some cases, no doubt, in the past as in the present, the idea might have led to exploration and experimentation and to the creation of the invention; in other cases, the invention might have happened through the sheer weight of the accumulated traits of culture, without any design or forethought, and then might have given rise to a train of new thought.

The interaction between material and non-material culture is reciprocal. The idea of the automobile could be born only after—and not before—the invention of the wheel and its use in transportation had been social realities. Seeing horse-drawn carriages may give rise to the idea of the horseless carriage, but the automobile could not be born until technical inventions in the field of harnessing energy, self-propulsion, had been made.

Six. Man was never born in a vacuum. He was always born within a group, surrounded by fellow human beings and by culture as well as by nature. The primitive man's world was circumscribed geographically as well as culturally. Within his cultural milieu he was called upon to solve problems in order to survive and to prosper. With inter-tribal contacts, peaceful or warlike, his mental horizon extended and his problems multiplied. With the rise of empires and with the consolidation of tribes into nations, man entered the so-called modern period of history. Modern methods of transportation and communication having well-nigh annihilated distances in time and space, man has today become a member of the Great Society.

(10, *passim*). His problems have multiplied a thousandfold, but so has his cultural legacy multiplied a thousandfold. For his guidance, for his spiritual resources, he is no longer compelled to look merely to his in-group ancestral wisdom and cultural legacy; today he can avail himself of the wisdom and cultural legacies of all peoples, of all nations, of all races, of all religions.

Seven. To understand man's behavior today, in our generation, we must take into account not only the "original nature" of man, not only "human nature," but also the accumulated cultural legacy of man through the centuries of his existence upon this planet. The world of today, such as it is, is the product pre-eminently of man's nurture rather than of his original nature. Human behavior may be understood better through the cultural approach than through the biological approach.

Eight. Culture is the outgrowth of man's living on this planet. Culture is the product of interaction between man's original nature, man's acquired nature and man's environment. Man's environment includes nature, fellow human beings and the cultural milieu with its folkways and mores, customs and institutions, laws and philosophies of life.

The relation between human behavior and culture is so integral that it is permissible to affirm two complementary propositions at the same time, namely, that (1) culture is a function of human nature, and (2) human nature is a function of culture.

Culture is the outgrowth of the process of man's living; and the process of living, from one standpoint, may be said to be the process of solving problems—problems caused by man's need for food, for protection against the inclemency of weather; problems caused by deviation from the norms of the group. Problems of this nature are the common lot of all mankind, of primitive tribes as well as of civilized nations, of Oriental society as well as of Occidental society.

Nine. To obviate misunderstanding we may sharply distinguish between original nature and human nature from the sociological standpoint.

Original nature is the sum-total of the organism's unlearned tendencies to react to stimuli, inner as well as outer. Human nature is the organization of learned responses to stimuli. The component parts of original nature are natural traits: biological, physical, psychological, social. The component parts of human nature are the experiences of responses to stimuli as conditioned by original nature. Functionally, original nature consists of (1) unlearned tendencies to react to the environment, as manifested in reflex, instinctive and emotive actions; (2) the capacity to organize and systematize the experiences of reactions; (3) the capacity to represent and articulate experiences symbolically. These potential capacities of original nature are translated into actual realities as original nature becomes transformed into human nature through the organism's participation in the socio-cultural process. Human nature is truly a product of social interaction.

Ten. The sociological approach to the study of human behavior does not imply that man must deliberately involve himself into group relationships every moment of his waking hours. It simply implies that man becomes what he is as a result of his experiences gathered from his relation to groups and participation in culture. On empirical grounds, however, it is known that deliberate isolation from the group, or solitude, from time to time, affords man an opportunity for meditation, for developing a detached perspective on the "world" around him, for deepening his insights, for establishing right relations with collective man and with God. The desire cherished by some individuals, such as hermits and recluses and philosophers, to be "above the battle," to be far from the "madding crowd," does not contradict the sociological analysis that man acquires or develops his true self in the socio-cultural milieu and in no other milieu.

Indeed, some would argue, and argue cogently and validly, that once selfhood is developed, man must deliberately strive from time to time to retire from group activities and stimulations in order to "create" his personal and unique "universe." Religious experience is of this nature. Gandhi lived his life, alternating between group-involvement and solitude. Sociological analysis does not militate against such a prescription for the living of the abundant and full life.

And yet, how intimately man's life is entwined with the lives of other men may be illustrated from Mahatma Gandhi's experiment with his search for solitude (7, pp. 59–60):

Gandhi's private utopia would be an idyllic existence on the Himalayan heights, perhaps by himself, perhaps with a few others of like mind; an existence in which he could live in harmony with nature, labor for himself a few hours, and commune with his inner self and with God. There would be no need to minister to others since none would need ministration.

In a grand gesture of living his phantasy as a reality, the Mahatma did actually establish a solitary abode in the open country-side near Wardha, with the hope of "living and working there in solitude" (1936)—the famous Sevagram Ashram. In the beginning a single mud hut was built. The late Dr. John R. Mott (1865-1955), the famous Y.M.C.A. leader, interviewed Gandhi there in 1937. Village reconstruction workers would visit Gandhi there from time to time. Soon the sick and the infirm began to come in. Other cottages had to be built. A dispensary was established. A barn had to be built to accommodate cows. Dairy workers were needed, and new cottages went up. Thus, ruefully commented Gandhi, "In spite of myself, the place has developed into an Ashram without any rules and regulations. It is growing and new huts are springing up. Today it has become a hospital. In jest I have called it a 'Home for the Invalids. . . . I have likened it to a Lunatic Asylum. . . ."

The Sevagram Ashram illustrates the story of the Hindu recluse all over again. He lived in solitude the better to perform his *sadhana* or meditation. A mouse began to distract his attention. He decided to get a cat in order to chase the mouse away. The cat needed milk, and he bought a cow. It soon appeared that if he was to devote himself to meditation, he had to have someone to take care of the cow. And so on and so forth.

REFERENCES

1. ALFRED ADLER: *Social Interest: A Challenge to Mankind*. New York: Putnam, 1939. See especially Chapters VI and VII.
2. FLOYD H. ALLPORT: *Social Psychology*. Boston: Houghton Mifflin Company, 1924.
3. L. L. BERNARD: *Instinct: A Study in Social Psychology*. New York: Henry Holt & Co., 1924.
4. *Bhagavad Gita*: Gujarati Translation, with an Introduction by Mohandas K. Gandhi. Ahmedabad: Navajivan Press, 1929.
5. JOHN FISKE: *A Century of Science*. Boston: Houghton Mifflin Company, 1899.

6. FRANKLIN H. GIDDINGS: *Studies in the Theory of Human Society*. New York: Macmillan, 1922.
7. HARIDAS T. MUZUMDAR: *Mahatma Gandhi: Peaceful Revolutionary*. New York: Charles Scribner's Sons, 1952.
8. ROBERT E. PARK and ERNEST W. BURGESS: *Introduction to the Science of Sociology*, 2nd ed. Chicago: University of Chicago Press, 1924; eighth impression, 1933.
9. *Upanishads*: Hindu Religio-Philosophical Treatises.
10. GRAHAM WALLAS: *The Great Society*. New York: Macmillan, 1914.

THE INTERNAL DYNAMICS OF THE GROUP II

OUR quest for an understanding of the individual, a veritable dynamo generating power, a center of force in the group, has led us thus far to a definition of the original nature of man (CHAPTERS 4 and 5). In this chapter we shall attempt, by a process analogous to experimentation, to validate our hypothesis that human nature is a product of group-relatedness, of participation in culture; in short, of social interaction.

1. AN EXPERIMENTAL DESIGN

In order to study the role of the group in the fashioning of the child from an individual into a person, we may adopt one of two methods: positively, to observe the behavior of the growing child within the context of the group; negatively, to observe the behavior of the growing child abstracted or isolated from the human group. The positive approach is permissible to us but it requires refined scientific techniques of observation and generalization. The negative approach is not available to us because of the compulsions of our cultural categories.

Even so, the sociologist has been unwittingly aided by the discoveries of human individuals who grew up in isolation from society. These individuals, under careful study, have been found to be organically "human," but in what we call "human nature," they have been deficient. Maurice H. Small describes some of these individuals as "feral men" (10, pp. 240–43, quoted):

2. CASES OF FERAL MEN

According to a letter which he (Kaspar or Caspar Hauser) bore when found at Nürnberg one afternoon in 1828, he was born in 1812, left on the doorstep of a Hungarian peasant's hut, adopted by him, and reared in strict seclusion.

At the time of his appearance in Nürnberg, he could walk only with difficulty. He knew no German, understood but little that was said to him, paid no heed to what went on about him, and was ignorant of social customs. When taken to a stable, he at once fell asleep on a heap of straw. In time it was learned that he had been kept in a low dark cell on the ground; that he had never seen the face of the man who brought him food, that sometimes he went to sleep after the man gave him a drink; that on awakening he found his nails cut and clean clothing on his body; and that his only plaything had been two wooden horses with red ribbons.

When first found, he suffered much pain from the light, but he could see well at night. He could distinguish fruit from leaves on a tree, and read (see—H.T.M.) the name on a doorplate where others could see nothing in the darkness. He had no visual idea of distance and would grasp at remote objects as though they were near. He called both men and women *Bua* and all animals *Rosz*. His memory span for names was marvelous. Drawing upon the pages of Von Kolb and Stanhope, a writer in *The Living Age* says that he burned his hand in the first flame that he saw and that he had no fear of being struck with swords, but that the noise of a drum threw him into convulsions. He thought that pictures and statuary were alive, as were plants and trees, bits of papers, and anything that chanced to be in motion. He delighted in whistles and glittering objects, but disliked the odor of paint, fabrics and most flowers. His hearing was acute and his touch sensitive at first, but after interest in him had lessened, all his senses showed evidence of rapid deterioration. He seemed to be wanting in sex instinct and to be unable to understand the meaning of religious ceremonies. Merker, who observed him secretly during the early days which he spent in jail, declared that he was "in all respects like a child." Meyer, of the school at Ansbach, found him "idle, stupid, and vain." Dr. Osterhausen found a deviation from the normal in the shape of his legs, which made walking difficult, but Kaspar never wearied of riding on horseback.

His autopsy revealed a small brain without abnormalities. It simply gave evidence of a lack of development.

To speak of children who have made the struggle for life with only animals for nurses and instructors is to recall the rearing of Cyrus in a kennel and the fabulous story of the foundling of Rome. Yet Rauber has collected many cases of wild men and some of them, taken as they are from municipal chronicles and guaranteed by trustworthy writers, must be accepted as authentic.

(a) *The Hessian Boy.* Was discovered by hunters in 1341, running on all fours with wolves; was captured and turned over to the landgrave. Was always restless, could not adapt himself to civilized life, and died untamed. The case is recorded in the Hessian chronicles by Wilhelm Dilich. Rousseau refers to it in his *Discours sur l'origine et les fondements de l'inégalité parmi les hommes.*

(b) *The Irish Boy.* Studied and described by Dr. Tulp, curator of the gymnasium at Amsterdam; features animal, body covered with hair; lived with sheep and bleated like them; stolid, unconscious of self; did not notice people; fierce, untamable, and indocible; skin thick, sense of touch blunted so that thorns and stones were unnoticed. Age about sixteen. (Rauber)

(c) *The Lithuanian Boys.* Three are described. The first was found with bears in 1657; face not repulsive nor beastlike; hair thick and white; skin dry and insensitive; voice a growl; great physical strength. He was carefully instructed and learned to obey his trainer to some degree but always kept the bear habit; ate vegetable food, raw flesh, and anything not containing oils; had a habit of rolling up in secluded places and taking long naps. The second, said to have been captured in 1669, is not so well described as the third, which Dr. Connor, in the *History of Poland,* says was found in 1694. This one learned to walk erect with difficulty, but was always leaping restlessly about; he learned to eat from a table, but mastered only a few words, which he spoke in a voice harsh and inhuman. He showed great sagacity in wood life.

(d) *The Girl of Cranenburg.* Born in 1700; lost when sixteen months old; skin dark, rough, hard; understood but little that was said to her; spoke little and stammeringly; food—roots, leaves, and milk. (Rauber)

(e) *Clemens of Overdyke.* This boy brought to Count von der Ricke's Asylum after the German struggle with Napoleon. He knew little and said little. After careful training it was gathered that his parents were dead and that a peasant had adopted him and set him to herd pigs. Little food was given him, and he learned to suck a cow and eat grass with the pigs. At Overdyke he would get down on his hands and knees and pull up vegetables with his teeth. He was of low intelligence, subject to fits of passion, and fonder of pigs than of men.

(f) *Jean de Liege.* Lost at five; lived in the woods for sixteen years; food—roots, plants, and wild fruit; sense of smell extraordinarily keen; could distinguish people by odor as a dog would recognize his master; restless in manner and always trying to escape. (Rauber)

(g) *The Savage of Aveyron.* After capture, was given into the care of Dr. Itard by Abbé Sicard. Dermal sense duller than in animals; gaze wandering; language wanting and ideas few; food—raw potatoes, acorns, and fruit; would eagerly tear open a bird and eat it raw; indolent, secretive; would hide in the garden until hunger drove him to the kitchen; rolled in new snow like an animal; paid no heed to the firing of a gun, became alert at the cracking of a nut; sometimes grew wildly angry; all his powers were then enlarged; was delighted with hills and woods, and always tried to escape after being taken to them; when angry would gnaw clothing and hurl furniture about; feared to look from a height; and Itard cured him of spasms of rage by holding his head out of a window; met all efforts to teach him with apathy, and learned but little of language.

(h) *The Wolf Children of India.* The two cases described by a writer in *Chambers' Journal* and by Rauber were boys of about ten years. Both ate raw food but refused cooked food; one never spoke, smiled, or laughed; both shunned human beings of both sexes, but would permit a dog to eat with them; they pined in captivity, and lived but a short time.

(i) *Peter of Hanover.* Found in the woods of Hanover; food—buds, barks, roots, frogs, eggs of birds, and anything else that he could get out of doors; had a habit of wandering away in the spring; always went to bed as soon as he had his supper; was unable to walk in shoes at first, and it was long before he would tolerate a covering for his head. Although Queen Caroline furnished him a teacher, he could never learn to speak; he became docile, but remained stoical in manner; he learned to do farm work willingly unless he was compelled to do it; his sense of hearing and of smell was acute, and before changes in the weather he was sullen and irritable; he lived to be nearly seventy years old.

(j) *The Savage of Kronstadt.* Of middle size, wild-eyed, deep-jawed, and thick-throated; elbows and knees thick; cuticle insensitive; unable to understand words or gestures perfectly; generally indifferent; found 1784.

(k) *The Girl of Songi.* According to Rauber, this is one of the most frequently quoted of feral cases. The girl came out of the forest near Chalons in 1731. She was thought to be nine years old. She carried a club in her hand, with which she killed a dog that attacked her. She climbed trees easily, and made niches on walls and roofs, over which she ran like a squirrel. She caught fish and ate them raw; a cry served for speech. She showed an instinct (sic!) for decorating herself with leaves and flowers. She found it difficult to adapt herself to the customs of civilized life and suffered many fits of sickness. In 1747 she was put into a convent at Chalons. She learned something of the French language, of domestic science, and embroidery. She readily understood what was pointed out to her but always had certain sounds which were not understood. She claimed to have first begun to reflect after the beginning of her education. In her wild life she thought only of her own needs. She believed that the earth and the trees had produced her, and her earliest memory of shelter was of holes in the ground.

3. The Wolf-Children of India: Amala and Kamala

Some social scientists have cast doubts upon the authenticity of some of the cases of feral men, enumerated by Maurice H. Small. It is not to be assumed that any of the eminent men connected with the history of some of these "feral men" intended to commit a fraud; at the worst, we can only say that perhaps they were gullible or that their tools of observation and analysis were not sharp enough. No such doubts can be cast upon the recent story of the two wolf-children of India, Amala and Kamala, whose history has been authenticated by the most rigorous canons of scientific observation and analysis. (11, *passim*)

It is a story oft told: (1) Arnold Gesell: *Wolf Child and Human Child* (1941); Arnold Gesell: "The Biography of a Wolf-Child," *The Harper's Magazine,* January, 1941; Robert M. Zingg: "India's Wolf-Children: Two Human Infants Reared by Wolves," *Scientific American,* Vol. 164; March 1941; J. A. L. Singh and R. M. Zingg: *Wolf Children and Feral Men* (1942).

The facts about Kamala (1912-1929) and Amala (1919-21), as reconstructed by Dr. Arnold Gesell (6, pp. 183–93), from Rev. J. A. L. Singh's diary, are these:

Spring, 1912: A baby girl, later to be called Kamala, is born in a mud-hut to a mother (probably belonging to the primitive tribe of Kora), in Godamuri.

Fall, 1912: At the age of six months, this baby girl, left in a field by the mother for a while, was picked up by a she-wolf, who took her to her den containing four cubs. The human child, here, began to grow up as a fifth cub, nourished and breast-fed by the mother wolf.

1919: For seven years, the human child had been learning the ways of the wolf family, when, all of a sudden, the mother wolf brought into the den another human child, about six months of age. This latter human child was later to be called Amala. Amala began to be breast-fed and raised as a wolf-cub by the mother wolf exactly as Kamala had been seven years earlier. What the introduction of the new human cub must have meant for Kamala, in terms of her experiences, we have no way of knowing.

October 9, 1920: The two wolf-children in the company of wolves were sighted about 5 : 00 p.m. by Rev. J. A. L. Singh and his party perched on a machan (i.e. a hunter's perch built on a tree). With the aid of field glasses, the two mysterious creatures were identified as "human" children.

October 10, 1920: The two wolf-children were again seen under the same circumstances.

October 17, 1920: The two wolf-children were rescued from their wolf family by a party, organized and headed by Rev. J. A. L. Singh. In the attempt the mother wolf was killed.

October 23, 1920: For a week, the two children, barricaded in a courtyard, were almost starved by the frightened village attendant, during Rev. J. A. L. Singh's journey on a pastoral visitation. Upon return, Mr. Singh gave them water and milk.

October 28, 1920: In a bullock-cart they journeyed to Midnapore.

November 4, 1920: The two children arrived at the Midnapore Orphanage, managed by Mr. and Mrs. Singh.

September 21, 1921: Cared for with love and sympathy, the two wolf-children began to grow up in a socio-cultural environment. Wolf ways persisted for the most part in spite of the human environment. One special aspect of the human environment must have meant a specially tingling sensation to the children—the early morning massage by Mrs. Singh. Amala, the younger, not fully wolfized, would take the lead and give the cue to Kamala in all matters of contacts with animals and human beings. With the socializing process at work—that is, with the gradual transformation of original nature into human nature—Amala, the younger of the two, the monitor in the process, died, on September 21, 1921, of an illness—Nephritis—contracted on September 4, 1921.

This was the third and, perhaps, most serious crisis in Kamala's young life. Her first crisis had been experienced when at the age of six months she was abstracted from society and taken into a den of wolves. Her second crisis came when somebody in Rev. J. A. L. Singh's party inadvertently shot the mother wolf with an arrow. And now, within a year, this third crisis befell Kamala. Says Dr. Gesell: "There are no more pathetic lines in the diary than those which describe the grief and confusion of Kamala after the death of her human companion of the den." (6, p. 190) Upon this bereavement, so far as we know, she shed her first tears (two) of grief and sorrow. But in accordance with the ways of the wolf, she "clung with doglike tenacity to the spot where Amala lay dead. For two days she would neither eat nor drink. . . . For six days she sat in a corner by herself. Water had to be forced upon her. Ten days later (October 8th) she was found smelling all the places where Amala had been." (6, p. 190)

October 16, 1921: Kamala began to howl and prowl by night, reverting to her wolf ways. Whereupon Mrs. Singh intensified and prolonged her early morning massage of Kamala. With care and patience, with sympathy and love, Kamala began to be gradually weaned from wolf ways and inducted into human ways. For instance:

November 1, 1921: Kamala made the first attempt to adopt a goat as a pet.

November 18, 1921: She did finally adopt one of the goats as her pet. This act symbolized her consciousness of self, of her separation from the world of animals. The "psychological gradations" in Kamala's development of human nature may be listed, after Gesell, as follows: "(a) consorting with Amala; (b) taking the cue from Amala in social contacts; (c) watching with some vague identification dogs and puppies; (d) playing with the pet goats; (e) seeking out Mrs. Singh; (f) associating with fellow orphans." (6, p. 191)

1922: Kamala said Ma for Mrs. Singh and later *bhoo bhoo* when she was hungry or thirsty. She learned to pull the pankha (fan) and would pull it for hours. She would voluntarily go out for strolls with the Singhs and the babies, though "she was animal enough to run on all fours." In truly human child-like fashion, she began to be afraid of the dark.

1924: By February, she had six words in her spoken vocabulary, and understood questions addressed to her. Later she would combine two words. By the end of the year, her vocabulary increased "by leaps and bounds, with small sentences." (6, p. 191) She could name one color.

1925: Change from animal to human ways continued. Her motor coordination improved. She could stand alone on her feet and drink from a glass. Her use of words increased steadily.

1926: "In 1926 Kamala was a different person altogether," wrote Mr. Singh in his diary.

1927: She could use complicated though short sentences; used conversational jargon, comprehended verbal instructions, and went on simple errands. She took to singing, was *en rapport* with her associates, and delighted in communicating with them. She now wanted to be dressed like the other children, and would blush with bashfulness if reminded of her previous lack of clothing. She displayed initiative and responsibility. At the age of 15, she behaved like a child two and a half years of age. But then eight years of her life had been spent in association with wolves, away from human contacts and devoid of participation in culture. "In contrast to her earlier solitary behavior, she now spent about twelve hours a day in sociable contact with others and not more than three waking hours alone." (6, p. 193) Her human nature now taken for granted, Mr. Singh's diary has henceforth "meager entries."

November 14, 1929: At 4.00 A.M., as the result of an illness, Kamala, at the age of seventeen, died of uraemia, having attained the mental age level of a three-and-a-half-year-old child.

With these facts before us, we may draw attention to certain psychological and sociological situations involved in the transition from wolf society to human society, from wolfized nature to human nature.

(1) Separation from their human mother and from human society at a tender age must have been a serious crisis for both Amala and

Kamala, but since they had not yet developed a sense of their own selfhood, the crisis was perhaps not of major importance in their young lives.

(2) Separation from the wolf "mother" and from wolf "siblings" was the second major crisis for the two wolf-children.

(3) The death of Amala at the orphanage was the third major crisis for Kamala, now well on the way to socialization.

From raw meat to cooked food, from grunts and howls to language, from naked innocence to bashfulness, from going on all fours to walking erect on two legs, from hostility to "strangers" to dependence upon other members of the orphanage, from inability to discriminate between animals and human beings to the dawning of selfhood and the adoption of a goat as a pet, from absence of fear of darkness to fear of the dark, from the biotic level of catch-as-catch-can of wolf society to human society with a complex culture of regular time schedules, verbal communication, collective representations, and all sorts of material and non-material culture traits—this transition from original nature, wolfized, to human nature was accomplished thanks to the loving tender care and sympathy of Mrs. Singh.

It may be mentioned in passing that several American sociologists of note have doubted the authenticity of Rev. J. A. L. Singh's diary and his story of the two wolf-children, Amala and Kamala. I do not share their skepticism. Professor R. M. Zingg has gone to great lengths in order to check the authenticity of Mr. Singh's diary, and his findings and conclusions should be acceptable to sociologists.

From the story of Amala and Kamala and from the stories of other feral men recounted by M. H. Small, certain inescapable conclusions may be drawn. Abstracted from the group, the child does not grow up speaking Sanskrit or Hebrew—the only sound it learns to emit is a grunt, a groan, a bleat, a roar, or something like that in imitation of the animals it was associated with. It learns to walk on all fours. The nervous system and the brain of the "feral" child or man are more or less similar to those of "normal" human beings; but he (or she) has no idea of "right" and "wrong," no referential language, no intellectual tools, no esthetic feelings, as understood by human beings. Problems of the self and the not-self do not plague the feral men. They operate with the aid of reflexes and instincts, their one concern being the preservation of their biophysical self.

It is a moot question: which is the more remarkable—the growing up of these human children in the company of wolves? Or the subsequent learning of human ways by Kamala after the forces of group and culture were brought to bear upon her?

4. ANNA AND ISABELLE

Perhaps India is a bit too far away for Americans. Amala and Kamala present interesting case histories. But have we any instance in America proving or disproving our hypothesis regarding human nature? Well, it just happens that we have two interesting cases—Anna and Isabelle.

The facts in these two cases of "extreme isolation," as Kingsley Davis has called them, are these (1 and 2):

Anna (March 1 *or* 6, 1932-*August* 6, 1942) : (1) born out of wedlock in a nurse's home; two weeks later, brought to her grandfather's home, seventeen miles from a small Pennsylvania city; because of grandfather's ire, was soon removed to the house of one of her mother's friends. A minister took her with a view to adoption but decided against it because of vaginitis. At the age of three weeks, taken to a children's home in the nearest large city, where she spent eight weeks. Turned over by the mother to a couple, pronounced unfit by the social worker. Soon removed from them, at the age of a little over four months, taken to another children's home in a nearby town, where she remained for nearly three weeks. Transferred to a private foster home. Because of lack of funds, was brought to irate grandfather's home at the age of five and a half months.

(2) From approximately six months of age to six years of age, lived in grandfather's house, in an attic-like upstairs room, neither loved nor cared for by mother; having had only physical contact with her mother who brought her milk, the only food she lived on. Seldom moved by mother from one position to another, her clothing and bedding being filthy. No caresses, no little talks, no visiting with mother or elder illegitimate brother or with grandfather. Occasional physical contact with mother and brother—yes; communicative contact, never. As a result, at the age of six, she could neither talk

nor walk, neither control elimination nor do any of the things learned as part of the process of socialization. Was extremely emaciated and under-nourished, with skeleton-like legs and a bloated abdomen.

(3) At the age of six years less one month, discovered by officers of the humane society, "wedged into the chair, which was tilted backwards to rest on a coal bucket, her spindly hands tied above her head," unable to talk or move. "The child was dressed in a dirty shirt and napkin," the officer said. "Her hands, arms and legs were just bones, with skin drawn over them, so frail she couldn't use them. She never had enough nourishment. She never grew normally, and the chair on which she lay, half reclining and half sitting, was so small the child had to double her legs partly under her."—*The New York Times*, February 6, 1938. (1, p. 554, quoted)

(4) Went through a marathon of changing scenes, only surpassed by her changes of address during the first five and a half months: (a) put into the old folks' county home, which had but one lone nurse to look after her as well as three hundred and twenty-four other inmates. Here spent nine months (Feb.-Nov. 11, 1938) in a socio-cultural environment, learning and developing some rudimentary motor coordinations. In the first fifteen days, her listlessness and apathy were partly gone; she was now more alert and looked healthier. She "found" her tongue and could discriminate between tastes. Could distinguish colors to some extent. Could sit up better, and smiled. By the time she was removed from the county home, her legs had calves in them; she would laugh heartily emoting a "Tsha-tsha-tsha." But she could barely stand while holding onto something. "She visibly liked people, as manifested by smiling, rough-housing, and hair-pulling." (b) November 11, 1938, moved to a foster home, where she remained until August 30, 1939. Here, at the foster home Anna underwent "a remarkable transformation"—she began to "learn." (We shall later recount her learning accomplishments at the foster home.) (c) For the next three years (August 30, 1939-August 6, 1942), Anna lived in a small school for retarded children. Here she began to develop speech. While she talked mainly in phrases, "she would repeat words and try to carry on a conversation." Died of hemorrhagic jaundice on August 6, 1942.

Isabelle (*April 1932-*   ): (*1*) born out of wedlock, like Anna; her mother, who had become a deaf-mute at the age of two, raised her "in a dark room shut off from the rest of the mother's family." Her mother, however, gave her love and affection, taught her sign-language. Thus mother and daughter could "converse" with each other by means of the sign-language of deaf-mutes. But the girl had little contact with the outside world; besides, her food was inadequate. Says Dr. Davis: "Lack of sunshine and inadequacy of diet had caused Isabelle to become rachitic. Her legs in particular were affected . . . bowed . . . "

(*2*) Discovered in November, 1938, nine months after Anna had been, Isabelle was promptly brought to the attention of clinical psychologists and speech pathologists at Ohio State University. She manifested much fear and hostility toward strangers, especially men whom she had never seen before. "In lieu of speech she made only a strange croaking sound. In many ways she acted like an infant . . . Many of her actions resembled those of deaf children."

(*3*) The psychological tests were most disappointing—on the Stanford-Binet she was 19 months, and on the Vineland social maturity scale she scored 39 months. Obviously "feeble-minded," said the specialists. Failure seemed to be the foregone conclusion.

(*4*) But those in charge of her persisted against seemingly impossible odds, and succeeded in reconditioning her to vocalize. This opened to her the world of representations, of *Vorstellungen.* Overcoming her early handicap of "extreme isolation," Isabelle, like other normal American children, went to school and made good.

How shall we interpret Anna and Isabelle within our frame of reference?

Our problem is not to assess the relative role of biogenic versus sociogenic factors. Our task is much simpler—and more significant. One of the fundamental theses of sociology is that an individual, abstracted from group and culture, grows up, if at all, not as a human being with human nature but as a feral being with feral nature. The best biological equipment would avail naught if contact with group and participation in culture were missing. To be able to participate in culture one needs the ability to manipulate concepts, and the ability to manipulate concepts is acquired, *solely and*

4

exclusively, through social interaction. Concepts, we know, are integrally related to language. And language is not only a social product in a historical setting but it can be learned and acquired only by and through the individual's relationships to contemporary groups.

Whether Anna was feeble-minded is not so important for our purposes as it is to know what kind of socializing influences played upon her. Isabelle, too, was pronounced "feeble-minded" by specialists. Isabelle developed the ways of normal human beings, but Anna did not. Can we account for these differences on a non-biological or non-hereditary level?

First, Isabelle was accepted by her mother while Anna was rejected by her mother.

Second, Isabelle's mother loved and cared for her and taught her, through sign language, certain concepts and a rudimentary control over the limited cultural environment to be experienced in the seclusion of an isolated dark room. Anna's mother neither loved nor cared for her, and failed to teach her the implications of the world of *Vorstellungen,* of representations, of concepts.

Third, Isabelle knew security in her mother's bosom; Anna had been tossed around like a football from one agency to another, from one foster home to another, before she was five and a half months old. And after that for full five years she knew neither security nor love from her mother.

Fourth, Isabelle was fortunate in having kindly, concerned specialists who persisted in "drawing out" her powers even when all outward signs spelled the impossibility of the task. Anna, on the other hand, was thrust into an old folks' county home with a lone nurse having to look after three hundred and twenty-four other inmates—hardly an ideal situation for developing the retarded girl's powers.

Even at that, Anna's amazing progress during nine months (February-November 11, 1938) at the old folks' county home brings into sharp relief the dynamic role of relation to group and participation in culture. For another nine months (November 11, 1938-August 30, 1939), Anna was placed in a foster home, presumably by the Pennsylvania State Welfare Department. Here, under the benign care of the foster-parent, Anna, still unable to speak, learned several things. She began to develop bodily coordination, with the vaguest sort of conceptual manipulation. For instance, "she could descend the stairs (by sitting successively on each one), could hold a doughnut in her hand and eat it (munching like a child), could grasp a glass of tomato juice and drink it by herself, could take a step or two while holding to something, and could feed herself with a spoon." Some of the later accomplishments of Anna at the foster-home have been listed by Kingsley Davis as follows (1, pp. 561–62):

She was able to walk alone for a few steps without falling; she was responsive to the verbal commands of her foster-mother, seeming to understand in a vague sort of way what the latter wanted her to do; she definitely recognized the social worker who took her weekly to the doctor and who therefore symbolized to her the pleasure of an automobile ride; she expressed by anxious bodily movements her desire to go out for a ride; she seemed unmistakably to seek and to like attention, though she did not sulk when left alone; she was able to push a doll carriage in front of her and to show some skill in manipulating it. She was, furthermore, much improved physically, being almost fat, with chubby arms and legs and having more energy and alertness. On the visit prior to this one she had shown that she could quickly find and eat candy which she saw placed behind a pillow, could perform a knee-bending exercise, could use ordinary utensils in eating (e.g. could convey liquid to her mouth in a spoon), could manifest a sense of neatness (by putting bread back on a plate after taking a bite from it). Limitations still remaining, however, were as follows: she said nothing—could not even be taught to say "bye-bye"; she had to be watched to tell when elimination was imminent; she hardly played when alone; she had little curiosity, little initiative; it seemed still impossible to establish any communicative contact with her.

This means that within two years after her discovery, as a result of group-relationship and cultural participation, Anna "could walk, understand simple commands, feed herself, and achieve some neatness, remember people, etc. But she still did not speak . . . " (2, p. 433)

From August 30, 1939, until her death (August 6, 1942), that is to say, for a period of three years Anna lived in a small school for retarded children. In 1941 Anna reached 46 inches in height and weighed 60 pounds.

She could bounce and catch a ball and was said to conform to group socialization, though as a follower rather than a leader. Toilet habits were firmly established. Food habits were normal, except that she still used a spoon as her sole implement. She could dress herself except for fastening her clothes. Most remarkable of all, she had finally begun to develop speech. She was characterized as being at about the two-year level in this regard. She could call attendants by name and bring in one when she was asked to. She had a few complete sentences to express her wants. (2, p. 434)

In the middle of 1942, the school report said:

Anna could follow directions, string beads, identify a few colors, build with blocks, and differentiate between attractive and unattractive pictures. She had a good sense of rhythm and loved a doll. She talked mainly in phrases but would repeat words and try to carry on a conversation. She was clean about clothing. She habitually washed her hands and brushed her teeth. She would try to help other children. She walked well and could run fairly well, though clumsily. Although easily excited, she had a pleasant disposition. (2, p. 434)

Compare these *ad hoc* arrangements made for Anna with "the prolonged and expert attention that Isabelle received." Once Isabelle came to the attention of experts associated with Ohio State University, Dr. Marie K. Mason and Dr. Francis N. Maxfield, no stone was left unturned in the task of helping her to experience the world of Vorstellungen. The results of psychological tests, as already pointed out, were most discouraging: on the Stanford-Binet test her score was 19 months, and on the Vineland social maturity scale "her first score was 39, representing an age level of two and a half years." Said Dr. Marie Mason: "The general impression was that she was wholly uneducable and that any attempt to teach her to speak, after so long a period of silence, would meet with failure."

In spite of this interpretation [says Davis], the individuals in charge of Isabelle launched a systematic and skilful program of training. It seemed hopeless at first. The approach had to be through pantomime and dramatization, suitable to an infant. It required one week of intensive effort before she even made her first attempt at vocalization. Gradually she began to respond, however, and, after the first hurdles had at last been overcome, a curious thing happened. She went through the usual stages of learning characteristic of the years from one to six not only in proper succession but far more rapidly than normal. In a little over two months after her first vocalization she was putting sentences together. Nine months after that she could identify words and sentences on the printed page, could write well, could add to ten, and could retell a story after hearing it. Seven months beyond this point she had a vocabulary of 1,500–2,000 words and was asking complicated questions. Starting from an educational level of between one and three years (depending on what aspect one considers), she had reached a normal level by the time she was eight and a half years old. In short, she covered in two years the stages of learning that ordinarily require six. Or, to put it another way, her I.Q. trebled in a year and a half. The speed with which she reached the normal level of mental development seems analogous to the recovery of body weight in a growing child after an illness, the recovery being achieved by an extra fast rate of growth for a period after the illness until normal weight for the given age is again attained. (2, p. 436)

In her fifteenth year (1947) Isabelle passed the sixth grade in the public school, participating in all school activities like other normal children. She was then speaking well, walking and running without trouble, and singing with gusto and accuracy.

The rest of Isabelle's story will be very much like the story of any other American youngster. But Anna did not live long enough for us to judge whether she was really feeble-minded. That problem, however, is peripheral to our purposes; because we accept the proposition that given lack of mentality—amentia—no amount of group-relatedness or participation in culture would fashion a normally functioning human being. On the other hand, we have proved that, abstracted from group and culture, the very best biological endowment is impotent to transform original nature into human nature. Had it not been for her extreme isolation during the first six years of her life, Isabelle might well have developed her latent powers—her biogenic potentialities—normally like other children.

5. THE OBJECTIONS OF A PSYCHOLOGIST

May not "feral" children be really idiots? Their behavior patterns, points out Dr. Wayne Dennis (3, pp. 425–32) very cogently, do correspond to those of idiots as described by Tredgold (12, *passim*). The question is raised, and quite pertinently, Would a human infant survive if uncared for by human beings?

As to self-selection of the right food by infants in C. M. Davis's experiment, Dennis says: "Her subjects had before them every element which they needed and none which would harm them, whereas the wild child would have before him but little food and a multitude of harmful objects." Let us say, "little food," as we in our cultural environment know it. The jungle is full of nutritious elements capable of supporting beasts, birds and men, both encultured and feral.

A further point needs to be noted. The feral child, according to our hypothesis, would grow up in a non-human, non-cultural environment; which means, his psyche would have less stimulation to develop as in the pattern of human association. But the psyche would develop—on a biogenic plane—on the first two levels in our definition of original nature: (1) capacity to respond to the environment, (2) capacity to organize and systematize the experiences of responses—leaving the third part undeveloped, namely, the capacity to articulate and represent symbolically the experiences of responses.

Now it is a well-known fact, attested by animal lovers, that on the animal level any non-human creature—say, a monkey—develops an uncanny sense for distinguishing harmful from harmless food. The case of a GI in World War II illustrates this point. He had adopted a monkey as his pet. In the course of a march he and his monkey pal came across a mud hole with water. Being thirsty, he was about to drink the water when the monkey let out a big screeching howl. Every time he made the attempt to drink the water, the monkey would howl. Finally, the GI gave up the idea of drinking water from that mud hole. Later he was informed that the water in that mud hole had been polluted and poisoned. On the basis of this undisputed fact, and hundreds like it, namely, that animals instinctively differentiate between harmful and harmless food and drink, it is permissible to entertain the hypothesis that the feral child too develops the same capacity. The keener development of the olfactory sense, a part of the psyche, is merely a compensation for the non-development of some other parts of the psyche.

Disbelieving the stories of wolf-children, Dr. Dennis makes a strong point when he argues that the folklore of India contains the wolf-child myth and that the myth may well have provided the perspective for judging subnormal, idiotic children. The point is well taken and deserves to be studied seriously. Most of the previous stories of wolf-children in India may well be explained on this basis. But the Midnapore Orphanage children are in a peculiar class: (1) photographs do not lie; (2) it has not been proved that any entry in Rev. J. A. L. Singh's diary was invented. Dennis is quite right in asserting that most wolf-children stories are based on hear-say, that nobody ever saw any of them actually live in the company of wolves; but Amala and Kamala were actually rescued not only from the wolf-den but also from their wolf companions—from their wolf family.

As to mental retardation caused by extreme isolation, a socio-logical thesis, Dr. Dennis (4, p. 750) counters with an experiment he conducted, and "refutes" the thesis to his satisfaction. As re-ported in The Psychological Bulletin, 1936, 33: 750, two infants were isolated from the group, with minimum social contacts and minimum bodily manipulations. For the first nine months they were kept mostly in a horizontal position. Here is a summary of the experiment, as given by Dr. A. H. Hobbs (7, p. 31):

Attendants were carefully instructed not to smile or show any other response to the infants' behavior. Despite these conditions, little retardation was noticed. The infants raised their heads, smiled, noted objects, and babbled at about the same time and to the same degree as other infants of similar age. After nine months the re-strained and isolated infants began to lag, but when conditions were modified to permit behavior normal for their age they soon caught up.

Instead of refuting it, this account bears out the sociological thesis. In this experiment there is abstraction of the infants neither from the group nor from culture. A clean bed, clean diapers, bodily cleanliness, wholesome food, the being "kept" in a horizontal position by someone from time to time or when the infants might get into trouble—the only thing missing was the fuss of the parents. No, this experiment cannot be counted as an instance of isolation from group and culture. At best it can be construed as an experiment in which the warm love of the mother is missing. Even so, the warm love of the mother expresses itself precisely in doing the sort of things that were done by the attendants. The experiment proves nothing to invalidate the sociological thesis; it only proves the obtuseness and inhumanity of the experimenter.

Let us, once and for all, remove the misunderstandings of our psychologist and geneticist friends. The sociological thesis does not maintain that human nature can be fashioned out of anything and everything by the sheer alchemy of group and culture. What it does maintain is that *original nature can develop into human nature only in a socio-cultural environment.* Let us take an analogy. An acorn, a tiny seed, is necessary for the mighty oak to grow. But given the best acorn in the world, if the soil were not right, if the temperature were not proper, if sun and water were not to be had in right amount, there would be no oak, mighty or puny. Now it is legitimate for some specialists intensively to study the acorn and to communicate their conclusions regarding good and bad varieties. But it is equally legitimate, indeed more necessary, that some other specialists study and tell us about the type of soil, temperature, water, needed for the acorn to grow. Our psychologist and geneticist friends are concerned with the acorn—certainly, we want to avail ourselves of their discoveries and conclusions. At the same time it may well be profitable for them to take to heart the discoveries and conclusions of sociologists.

Let us recapituate the sociological point of view in regard to human nature:

The absence of the environment of human group and culture results in feral nature in consonance with the imperatives of biophysical existence of the human organism. Contrariwise, the presence of human group and culture and participation in culture and group life do transform original nature into human nature, as attested universally. Even so, it is worth noting that the presence of human group and culture is impotent to "create" human nature if the original nature of man is missing, to begin with. Given the potentialities of human nature—the unlearned tendencies to react, to organize and systematize experiences of reactions, to represent and articulate experiences—the group environment and culture transform potentialities into actualities in consonance with the imperatives of a given culture. The human child at birth is endowed with the capacity to act, how to act is determined by culture. Says the *Vishnu Bhagavat* with great chivalry, "By birth everyone is a Shudra"—not an animal! Participation in group-correlated culture transforms the individual into the person and original nature into human nature.

6. DONALD AND GUA

What happens when the full endowment of original human nature is not present is best illustrated by the experiment conducted by Mr. and Mrs. W. N. Kellogg who raised a female chimpanzee, "Gua," as a sort of sibling to their son Donald (9, pp. 3–4):

At the time of adoption, "Gua," the chimpanzee, was seven and a half months old; their son, Donald, was ten months old. Both were treated with the same kindly care. They ate, slept, and played together. Gua, being stronger and physically more mature than Donald, was naturally more adept at motor activities, such as climbing and acrobatics. She showed greater speed of movement. More interesting, Gua very readily learned some of the so-called humanizing and acrobatics. She showed greater speed of movement. More adroitly with a spoon, to drink liquids out of a glass, to skip rope, and to open doors. Indeed she learned to do these things better than did Donald, and in general was more cooperative and obedient. But in respect to the crucial matter of speech, Gua lagged behind. The ape came to 'comprehend' a large number of words and phrases, but she never learned to speak. Donald, of course, learned in the customary manner of children.

This experiment points to the twofold conclusion: (1) that the chimpanzee, not endowed with the original nature of man, could not develop human nature; and (2) that Donald, endowed with the original nature of man, did develop human nature through association with human groups and through participation in culture.

We may set forth four interrelated generalizations: (1) Human nature is the product of social interaction; (2) Abstracted from group and culture, the very best biological endowment, by itself, is impotent to transform original nature into human nature; (3) Given amentia, a lack of mentality, culture and group are impotent to transform original nature into full functioning human nature; (4) No amount of group-relatedness and participation in culture could transform a non-human original nature into human nature.

REFERENCES

1. KINGSLEY DAVIS: "Extreme Social Isolation of a Child." *The American Journal of Sociology*, Vol. XLV, No. 4, January, 1940, pp. 554–65.
2. KINGSLEY DAVIS: "Final Note on a Case of Extreme Isolation." *The American Journal of Sociology*, Vol. LII, No. 5, March, 1947, pp. 432–37.
3. WAYNE DENNIS: "The Significance of Feral Man." *American Journal of Psychology*, Vol. 54, No. 3, July, 1941, pp. 425–32.
4. WAYNE DENNIS: "Infant Development under Minimum Social Stimulation." *Psychological Bulletin*, Vol. 33, No. 9, November, 1936, p. 750.
5. ARNOLD GESELL: *Wolf Child and Human Child.* New York: Harper & Brothers, 1941.
6. ARNOLD GESELL: "The Biography of a Wolf-Child." *The Harper's Magazine*, No. 1088, January, 1941, pp. 183–93.
7. A. H. HOBBS: *The Claims of Sociology: A Critique of Textbooks.* Harrisburg: The Stackpole Co., 1951.
8. W. N. & L. A. KELLOGG: *The Ape and the Child.* New York: McGraw-Hill Book Co., 1933.
9. WILLIAM F. OGBURN and MEYER F. NIMKOFF: *Sociology.* Boston: Houghton Mifflin Co., 1940.
10. ROBERT E. PARK and ERNEST W. BURGESS: *Introduction to the Science of Sociology*, 2nd ed. Chicago: University of Chicago Press, 1924; eighth impression, 1933.
11. J. A. L. SINGH & R. M. ZINGG: *Wolf Children and Feral Men.* New York: Harper & Brothers, 1942.
12. ALFRED F. TREDGOLD: *Mental Deficiency*, 3rd ed., Revised. New York: W. Wood & Co., 1920.
13. R. M. ZINGG: "India's Wolf Children: Two Human Infants Reared by Wolves." *Scientific American*, Vol. 164, No. 3, March, 1941, pp. 135–37.

CHAPTER 7

THE GROUP AS THE SCHOOL OF SOCIAL EXPERIENCE

THE trouble with the feral men is that they grew up unrelated to human groups and culture. The logical inference is valid, namely, that for the development of human nature and human personality the environment of the group and culture is essential. Phrases, such as the school of hard knocks, the school of experience, the school of social experience, are bandied about by laymen and scientists alike, without a proper appreciation of the meaning of those terms. In this chapter, and the next, an attempt will be made, in terms of concrete situations, to set forth the meaning of the term " the school of social experience."

1. On Definitions

Definition is the beginning and the end of study, of education, indeed of living as such.

Definitions of events, situations, processes, are culturally conditioned. In order to avail myself of the use of the typewriter, I need not know how to make it or to repair it, nor need I go into a philosophical disquisition on the meaning of the typewriter. My culture has defined the use of the typewriter and I so use it. I have not the vaguest notion of electricity, but I, like millions of Americans, use it by the switching on of a button.

In the conceptual realm there does arise the acute problem of apprehending in its totality the meaning of the culturally conditioned definition of events, situations, processes.

The initial definition is a sort of dim outline, a delimitation of the field of inquiry. The final definition is a precise statement of the subject under investigation, containing the full connotation thereof, neither a detail superfluous included nor a detail necessary omitted.

Let us investigate how an unsophisticated child would proceed in his study of man.

To begin with, he will impose upon himself a delimitation of the field of inquiry. In order to know what man is like—what man is— he will not gaze at the stars, nor will he permit his toys or books to confound the issue. He has seen in action his father and mother and other friends and relatives and strangers. By a subtle process of ratiocination whose nature we do not as yet know, he "abstracts" the peculiar qualities pertaining to father, to mother and to each of the rest of the people whom he has "experienced." This process of abstracting creates the generic concept man. The abstracting and generalizing qualities go hand-in-hand with, if indeed they do not precede, the capacity for specific experiencing.

The frame of reference which furnishes the yardstick for measuring, abstracting and generalizing is not the child's self but a more fundamental thing than the child's self, namely, the *élan vital*, to use Bergson's term. (Note the Hindu metaphysicians' insistence that the human self can be known and understood only in relation to the Supreme Self.) It is the *élan vital* that furnishes the groundwork for the child's capacity for experiencing in individual situations and in generic (abstract) terms.

Given the capacity for experiencing in specific and generic terms, given the capacity for abstracting and generalizing, the child will, after demarcating man from not-man, proceed to a study of his *Weltanschauung*. The final definition of man will, in other words contain a precise statement of man's *Weltanschauung*. No other definition of man would complete the study of man. And in the attempt to comprehend man's *Weltanschauung*, the growing child will be going through the experiences of his own evolving *Weltanschauung*. Such a study should span the life-time of each one of us.

It is in this sphere that education could tremendously help the growing child.

2. EDUCATION AND THE SOCIAL PROCESS

Education takes in its broad sweep not merely the school but the whole complex of society. Therefore, we must adopt the sociological approach if we want to comprehend the full meaning of education.

A study of educational sociology, in fact, is being promoted at several of our largest universities. Educational Sociology views society from the standpoint of the educative process and education from the standpoint of the social process. To put it differently, Educational Sociology concerns itself with the educative aspect of the social process and with the social aspect of the educative process.

The child, both as a biological organism, that is to say, as an individual, and as a sociological entity, that is to say, as a person or an individual with a status in the group, is confronted ever since birth with the stimulus-response relationship. The stimuli, either bio-physical or psycho-social, may be internal or external. Whatever be their nature, the stimuli unfailingly call forth in each instance a specific response, even if it be the response of passivity and indifference. Like stimuli evoking like responses build up in the individual, functionally if not constitutionally, certain modes of behavior. These modes, in terms of self-consistency, build up trends, physical, psychic, emotional. Interacting with one another, these trends—mental sets, habits, attitudes, sentiments, complexes—determine the personality of the individual.

Thanks to the essential sanity of the *élan vital*—thanks to the goodness of God as the theologian would say—in a majority of cases the trends organize themselves harmoniously and give us a workably integrated personality. Should the trends, for one reason or another which can be objectively ascertained in each specific case, be at odds and inharmonious, the result would be a personality malaise—a split personality, a divided self, a multiple self, a fragmented personality, in short, a disorganized personality.

Cases of constitutional defects, giving rise to functional mishaps and thereby leading to personality malaise, ought to be sharply distinguished from cases of personality malaise brought about by pressure from without and consequent repression from within. Society owes a responsibility for both types of malaise, more for the latter than for the former.

The individual derives his full meaning, both as a biological organism and as a person, from the group—it is the group, father-mother, that brings him into being and sustains him physically and otherwise during his dependent stage; again, it is the group that gives him a social meaning in terms of status. Such being the fundamental aspect of the relationship between the individual and the group, in the social process the survival of the group is rated more important than the survival of the individual.

During social crises, all sorts of mechanisms are at work imbuing the individual with a sense of exaltation to the end that he may volunteer his services—nay, sacrifice his very life—for the good of the group: the group exalts him, the individual feels elated; the group is superordinate, the individual is subordinate. This essential subordination of the individual to the group, whether or not it flatters our vanity, is a characteristic part of the normal social process as well.

Society and the social process have been variously defined. The uninstructed layman is apt to speak of society as a collection of persons. The well-read layman is apt to conceive society as the sumtotal of social institutions, such as the family, the church, the school, the economic order, the state. Neither of these two concepts is adequate, though each of them may have some truth. The following definition of society by the late Professor C. H. Cooley (1864-1929), in terms of the social process of interaction is fundamentally sound (1, p. 28):

"Society is a complex of forms or processes each of which is living and growing by interaction with the others, the whole being so unified that what takes place in one part affects all the rest. It is a vast tissue of reciprocal activity, differentiated into innumerable systems, some of them quite distinct, others not readily traceable, and all interwoven to such a degree that you see different systems according to the point of view you take."

We have already given our own definitions of society from the structural, functional, and dynamic standpoints. The functional definition of society, given by Park and Burgess, has special relevance in the present context. Hence we may reproduce it here (2, p. 162):

From the functional standpoint, "society, either as a sum of institutions or as a collection of persons, may be conceived of as a sum-total of instrumentalities, extensions of the functions of the human organism which enable individuals to carry on life-activities.

From this standpoint society is an immense cooperative concern of mutual services."

Society "an immense cooperative concern of mutual services!" Yes, a complex of interrelated parts each serving the others and thereby maintaining the whole concern. But whether we emphasize instrumentalism or mutualism in the definition, the central core of society is the "immense cooperative concern." In other words, the parts derive their meaning from the whole: without the whole they would cease to be—without society there could be no socii. Such, indeed, is the meaning of Aristotle's dictum: "The *polis* (the Socio-State) is prior to the individual."

From the plowman in the field and the policeman on the beat to all imaginable persons at all imaginable types of activity, every person is rendering a twofold service to his fellow man: directly, by producing something that is useful to others; indirectly, by not being a burden to others—and thereby helping maintain the integrity of society. The law of this social process is: The more you give of yourself the more are you rewarded by your fellows. The fundamental truth of Jesus's saying, "He who loses his life shall gain it," becomes dynamically obvious to every one during social crises, such as wars and revolutions.

The mechanism of praise and blame, of approbation and disapprobation, by one's fellows, is an excellent device for social control under whose impulsion man feels himself highly exalted at one extreme and deeply mortified at the other.

From the cradle to the grave, man is swimming along in the stream of the social process within a cultural context, either actively and in a definite direction or just passively and with no end in view. Participation in the socio-cultural process, with its subtle mechanisms of social control and its superordination of society over the individual, is as natural for man as is swimming in the water for fish. In other words, the socio-cultural frame, a veritable storehouse of stimuli, constantly acts and reacts upon the individual, and the individual must needs respond to these stimuli. *In these stimulus-response relationships the individual learns. And that, precisely, is the educative aspect of the social process.* Long before formal schooling was invented, society the world over was carrying on its educative work with the new-born as well as with the adult through myriads of rituals and institutions. Even today, the greater part of our education is derived from the social process rather than from formal schooling. Hence the importance of a sociological orientation for our educators.

3. SOCIETY AND THE EDUCATIVE PROCESS

That education has to do with learning may be readily granted. Each stimulus-response situation provides the individual with an occasion for new experience. These experiences, properly organized and integrated, even without intellectualized systematization, constitute the elementary form of learning. The larger the number of experiences the vaster the fund of learning. Inasmuch as the socio-cultural framework is a veritable storehouse of stimuli, participation in the socio-cultural process automatically becomes the fundamental and most important technique of learning—that is to say, outside the generalized technique of stimulus-response relationship.

There are two other techniques of learning: through manipulation and through formal training.

The capacity for manipulation—to manipulate objects, to "monkey with things"—is part of the original endowment of human nature, a prepotent tendency to act or react. By the trial and error method, manipulation helps us to add to our fund of learning. Manipulation may be entirely individual and erratic or it may be highly socialized, formal, elaborate and purposive, as is attested by modern research foundations.

Manipulation is thus seen to be part and parcel of the educative process.

Formal training is a highly significant social ritual. It has the twofold purpose of: (1) transmitting to the learner the experience of the human race so far as it lies within the ken of the group and can be objectified, and (2) enabling the individual to develop his personality, to find his place in the milieu, to contribute to the ongoing stream of the social process. One's contribution to the social process may be made by fulfilling certain essential functions according to the accepted standard, such as engaging in matrimony and bringing into the world new individuals as well as by becoming an active partner in the "immense cooperative concern of mutual services."

Precisely because it is a social ritual, formal training has been part and parcel of the social existence of man from the very beginning. No, formal training is not an invention of modern times nor of the historic ancient world: it may be said to have been part of the experience of prehistoric, even preliterate, man—a social heritage transmitted somewhat enriched from generation to generation.

What is new today is not the concept nor the institution of formal training but the changed method of formal training and the changed nature of the institution. Rituals connected with initiation, marriage, hunting, etc., served as formal training—as schooling—to primitive man.

Among historic peoples of the ancient world, schooling was carried on by the monarchy and the feudal hierarchy through their laws and dictates; by the organized priesthood through religious and secular ministrations; by the itinerant teacher, the yogi, the sannyasi (recluse), the mendicant, the monk, through occasional ministrations to persons and groups; by the bard and the wandering minstrel through their ballads and songs; by the definitive rituals of each group and tribe. Indeed, long before the rise of Christianity, temples (Hindu, Buddhist, etc.) and synagogues (Jewish) had a system of imparting instruction through formal training. These temple and synagogue schools and the subsequent church schools, the monasteries, and the still later mosque schools were the precursors of the modern school as we know it today.

From Socrates's "school" in the market-place of Athens, from Plato's academy in the garden near Athens, from Aristotle's peripatetic school in Hellas, we have traveled far—to the post-colonial red school building of a century ago, to the magnificent public school no. xyz in the metropolitan area of today and to the equally magnificent structure of the consolidated school in rural areas. These beautiful buildings, intended to be veritable temples of learning, suffer from the industrial complex of our day, but that they are complete in their equipment to the nth degree there is no denying.

To what extent progress in outer structure in architecture has carried with it progress in inner function is an interesting question to pursue. Indeed, it is precisely in this phase of the question that the social aspect of the educative process comes to the fore concretely and continuously.

The public school system is but a unit in the larger "school" system evolved in America and elsewhere, embracing the college and the university and the research laboratory of foundations, corporations and government bureaus. (May I be permitted to coin the word *researchtory* for the research laboratory?)

The problem of learning through formal training ought to be viewed in its totality, that is to say, in terms of the larger school system—the school-college-university-researchtory. The question ought to be formulated somewhat as follows: What is the posture of learning at each successive level of formal training, the school, the college, the university, the researchtory? What, in other words, is the *Weltanschauung* of the learner at each of the successive stages of formal training?

To sum up: Stimulus-response relationship, social participation, manipulation and formal training, the four techniques of learning, have been with mankind from the very beginning of our social existence. The nature of each of the techniques changes in response to the changing patterns of a cultural milieu. The range of participation of the growing American child is today widened by his experience of the India chudder-shawl, Persian rug, Japanese print, Chinese painting as well as distinctively American objects. Unlike his prototype in the ancient world, he plays not with simple toys but with mechanical toys, with automobiles, with engines, with trains, with airplanes, etc. The changes in the nature of formal training are too obvious to be missed.

Participation and manipulation arise from the "primitive" biologic stratum of the organism and ascend to the social level as the child grows. Formal training, on the other hand, arises from the social level and ascends to the intellectual plane. Indeed, formal training is the product of a highly intellectualized systematization. The objective of formal training, thus conceived, is threefold: (1) to impart the tools of learning, (2) to impart the content of learning, (3) to prepare the learner for membership in the "immense cooperative concern of mutual services."

THE SCHOOL OF SOCIAL EXPERIENCE 115

REFERENCES

1. CHARLES H. COOLEY: *Social Process*. New York: Charles S. Scribners, 1918.
2. ROBERT E. PARK and ERNEST W. BURGESS: *Introduction to the Science of Sociology*, 2nd edition. Chicago: The University of Chicago Press, 1924; eighth impression, 1933.

CHAPTER 8

THE CHILD AND HIS WORLD

1. BIOLOGIC AND CULTURAL RECAPITULATION

IN the prenatal state of being, the child "recapitulates" the evolutionary scheme of nature—i.e., he roughly passes through the whole history of his animal ancestors. Long before this theory of organic recapitulation was advanced by biologists as a result of careful investigations, Johann Friedrich Herbart (1776-1841) had put forth in 1804 the so-called "culture epoch" theory. The number of Herbartians and neo-Herbartians is legion. According to a modern representative of the school, the late Dr. Maximilian P. E. Groszmann, founder of the Educational Clinic of the National Association for the Study and Education of Exceptional Children at Plainfield, N.J., the culture epoch theory implies that "each individual born into this world passes from infancy to childhood and maturity through a series of developmental stages which broadly represent the consecutive stages of civilization through which the human race has passed." (3, p. 40)

Inasmuch as it is a moot problem whether we could neatly divide the stages of civilization into savagery, barbarism, "civilization," I am not sure that we could properly attribute the savage's mode of thinking to the child or of the barbarian's to the growing boy. That the mature person must adopt the mode of thinking and behavior acceptable to his milieu, to his civilization, on pain of disability or annihilation, goes without saying.

In a broad sense, however, we might agree with Dr. Groszmann when he says that the growing child's "methods of thinking, feeling and symbolizing, his instinctive activity, the sequence of his modes of conduct, will reincarnate the development of the race." (3, p. 41) But when someone suggests, as did Jack London, that the boy, "in his brief years of boyhood, rehearses the history of primitive man in acts of cruelty and sagavery, from wantonness of inflicting pain on

116

lesser creatures to tribal consciousness expressed by the desire to run in gangs" (4, p. 296), when some one expresses such an opinion, we must admit there is too much "reading" into the behavior of the child. Wanton cruelty on the part of boys and their tendency to run in gangs are induced not so much by a psycho-social throwback to so-called primitivity as by the contemporary culture patterns and the social process.

The "culture epoch" theory, however, is at once intriguing and sobering: the child is born with potentials that could make of him a subhuman "feral man," a savage, a barbarian, or a civilized person. Remove him from human contact and he will grow up, if at all, into a "feral man." (*Supra*, CHAPTER 6). Let his growth take place undirected by purposive social forces and he will turn out to be a "savage" or a "barbarian."

2. THE NATURAL HISTORY OF THE NEWBORN

What is the child at birth? A bio-physical bundle of "instincts, dispositions, and tendencies, inherited from a long line of human and animal ancestors." (5, p. 80). A rough inventory of the special instinctive tendencies with which human beings are equipped at birth would have to be divided into three parts: first, the simpler reflexes; second, the more complex tendencies; third, the unidentifiable power of systematization, organization, articulation, and representation of experiences.

Among the simpler reflexes may be mentioned: "'crying, sneezing, snoring, coughing, sighing, sobbing, gagging, vomiting, hiccuping, starting; moving the limb in response to its being touched, tickled, or stroked on the sole of the foot; extending and raising the arms at any sudden sensory stimulus, or the quick pulsation of the eyelid.'" (5, pp. 80–81).

Among the more complex original tendencies may be mentioned: "sucking, chewing, sitting up, and gurgling. Among the more general unlearned (*sic*! learned?—H.T.M.) responses of children are fear, anger, pugnacity, envy, jealousy, curiosity, constructiveness, love of festivities, ceremonials and ordeals, sociability and shyness, secretiveness, etc." (5, p. 81).

The third part of the inventory, namely, the unidentifiable power of systematization, organization, articulation, and representation of experience is overlooked by psychologists, first, because it cannot be statistically measured; second, because the modern psychologist is anxious not to lay himself open to the charge of being a "vitalist," a believer in "mind."

Be that as it may, it is with these three types of endowment that the child is born. Into what sort of a world is it born? Into a world that to the child is what William James called a "big booming, buzzing confusion"—an inchoate mass of stimuli. Light and darkness, the touch of the mother as well as of clothes and wrappings, movement and rest, form and distance—these are perhaps among the elemental experiences of the newborn child.

3. THE BIOGRAPHY OF A BABY

In an interesting pioneer work entitled *The Biography of a Baby,* Milicent W. Shinn gives us a significant picture of the evolving baby :

She (my little niece) evidently felt a difference between light and darkness from the first hour, for she stopped crying when her face was exposed to gentle light . . . The baby showed no sign of hearing anything until the third day, when she started violently at the sound of tearing paper, some eight feet from her. Taste and smell were senses that the baby gave no sign of owning till much later. The satisfaction of hunger was quite enough to account for the contentment she showed in nursing ; and when she was not hungry she would suck the most tasteless object as cheerfully as any other . . . Our baby showed from the first that she was aware when she was touched. She stopped crying when she was cuddled or patted. She showed comfort in the bath. . . . She responded with sucking motions to the first touch of the nipple on her lips. (6, pp. 41, 43, 45, 46, 47).

Our baby showed temperament—luckily of the easygoing and cheerful kind—from her first day, though we could hardly see this except by looking backward . . . On the twenty-fifth day, toward evening, when the baby was lying on her grandmother's knee by the fire, in a condition of high well-being and content, gazing at her grandmother's face with an expression of attention, I came and sat down close by, leaning over the baby, so that my face must have come within the indirect range of her vision. At that she turned her eyes to my face and gazed at it with the same appearance of attention, and even of some effort shown by the slight tension of brows and lips, then turned her eyes back to her grandmother's face, and again to mine, and so several times. The last time, she seemed to catch sight of my shoulder, on which a high light struck from the lamp, and not only moved her eyes but threw her head far back to see it better, and gazed for some time with a new expression on her face—"a sort of dim and rudimentary eagerness," says my note. She no longer stared, but really looked. (6, pp. 53, 54, 65, 66, adapted).

Here in this significant statement we have a description of the surface behavior of the child which definitely points to the child's possession of the unidentifiable power of systematizing and organizing experience. This interpretation is reinformed by Miss Shinn's subsequent statements of the baby's behavior:

The baby's increased interest in seeing centered especially on the faces about her, at which she gazed with rapt interest. Even during the period of mere staring, faces had oftenest held her eyes, probably because they were oftener brought within the range of her clearest seeing than other light surfaces. The large, light, moving patch of the human face . . . is calculated to excite the highest degree of attention a baby is capable of at a month old. So from the very first—before the baby has yet really seen his mother—her face and that of his other nearest friends become the most active agents in his development and the most interesting things in his experience. (6, pp. 70–1).

The observation is entirely accurate and the statement valid except in one respect. It is not necessarily the *light* surface of the face (as contrasted with the *dark*) that engages the month-old baby's interest with rapt attention. Millions of non-white month-old babies are equally entranced by the non-white—coal-black, swarthy, brown, yellow—faces of their mothers and relatives. The magnet is in reality the "moving patch of the human face," whose text is a miracle in that it can express varied feelings and emotions. If "light" means "lighted," there is no quarrel with Miss Shinn's description.

To continue Miss Shinn's account:

Our baby was at this time in a way aware of the difference between companionship and solitude. In the latter days of the first month she would lie contentedly in the room with people near by, but would fret if left alone. But by the end of the month she was apt to fret when she was laid down on a chair or lounge, and to become content only when taken into the lap. This was not yet distinct memory and desire, but it showed that associations of pleasure had been formed with the lap, and that she felt a vague discomfort in the absence of these.

Nature has provided an educational appliance, almost ideally adapted to the child's sense condition, in the mother's face, hovering close above him, smiling, laughing, nodding, with all manner of delightful changes in the high light; in the thousand little meaningless caressing sounds, the singing, talking, calling, that proceed from it; the patting, cuddling, lifting, and all the ministrations that the baby feels while gazing at it, and associates with it, till finally they group together and round out into the idea of his mother as a whole. (6, pp. 71, 72, 76).

In Miss Shinn's *Biography of a Baby* there is an attempt made to give a description of the natural history of a baby's emerging "mind"—of the unidentifiable power of systematizing and organizing experience. Whether the "mind" is pre-existent or whether it emerges from the interaction of sensory organs as a result of the stimulus-response relationship is a question that may be safely set aside so far as this discussion is concerned. Suffice it to note that the emergence of the "mind" is part and parcel of the natural history of the child, the senses being the media of experience and the gateway to knowledge.

Subsequent clinical analyses of the growing infant's behavior by psychologists emphasize the significant point that the natural history of the baby and of his growth is integrally tied up with the emergence of "the mind."

At first, the mother is experienced by the newborn as a collection of detached phenomena: the moving patch of the human face, breasts, hands, eyes, etc., in terms of their function and utility to itself; as it grows the baby mentally correlates the detached phenomena into the functioning organic whole, namely, the mother.

No natural history of the baby is complete without a mention of "touch relationships" between child and parents (5, p. 56). Because of this affinity and attraction, the growing child is peculiarly susceptible to the actions and behavior patterns of its nearest group—father-mother. Susceptibility to the behavior of others having been induced in the first instance, the child "carries over" that experience to its stimulus-response relationships with the larger group, embracing relatives, friends, acquaintances, visitors, household help, sweet-heart, et al.

4. Nursery—the Birthplace of Intelligence

Call it "mind," call it the capacity to organize and systematize experiences, call it what you will, the fact remains that the emergence of intelligence in the baby is indissolubly bound up with the nursery, which may be viewed both as a set of relationships between child and parents and as a place. The human offspring is more helpless at birth than the offspring of any other species. In prolonged human infancy nature has provided an excellent medium for the transforming of the biologic baby into the cultural man through the multitudinous interplay of social forces which, by presenting problems, call forth the child's intelligence.

Under the circumstances it would be unmitigated cruelty to the newborn as well as a gross injustice to society, to humanity, if parents were to overlook the importance of the nursery as the basic school of the child. Here is Dr. Groszmann's exhortation to parents and parents-to-be (3, pp. 425–26):

The nursery should be a sacred place in every home. Here past and present join hands in the growing and maturing of the child. In the child of today we may observe the gradual unfolding of civilizing powers and factors which have been at work from the dawn of civilization to the most modern phases of human life. The evolution of the individual repeats the experiences of the race. As the savage man was surrounded by a world of wonders and mysteries which he only vaguely divined and which filled him with terror and strange longings, so the infant finds himself confronted with a world of forces which he realizes but indistinctly, and whose indefinite and infinite content and extent he learns gradually to reduce to symbolic terms, in his own consciousness, through language, measurement, organization, coordination. He learns to grasp the mysteries of his life by grasping with his feeble hand the objects which are nearest to him—through them he will learn to understand and interpret the possibilities of the infinite.

The nursery is a temple in which the divine manifests itself in its eternal creativeness; it is a laboratory in which a new soul is formed by the thousand and one experiments which the child undertakes instinctively to build up a conceptual world through the medium of his senses, from the messages which the outside world sends him incessantly along the wires of his nervous system.

In the nursery the foundation is laid for all future education. During the first seven years of his life a child assimilates more, " learns " more, than in all his subsequent life. Instinctively the child is constantly studying, experimenting, storing up experiences, concepts and ideas. There is divine wisdom in his activity. . . .

In the nursery much can be done for the training of the observing powers; there should be plenty of objects for manual and visual inspection. Children will and must touch all things. Their muscular activity must not be checked; it means health and knowledge to them. Rather let us dispense with costly and superfluous bric-a-brac if we are afraid it will be broken. Let us rather sacrifice a cherished piece of breakable material than the valuable information your child will receive from handling it. Bric-a-brac costs only money. Checking the child's instinctive tendency (impulse—H.T.M.) for inspection may cost a soul.

Denying that educational treatment of the child in the home could be easily reduced to a patent formula, Dr. Groszmann urges upon parents the closest attention to and interest in their children (3, pp. 424–25):

"If parents would give some of the time they devote to the fluctuations of the stock-market or of the fashions to a loving observation of the fluctuations of the soul activities in their children, they would render a greater service to them and to the race at large than by attempting to control the price of wheat or by conducting a charity ball. Froebel's words, 'Lasst uns unsern Kindern leben!' mean that we must live not only *for* our children, but *with* them and *among* them, so that we may enter into their very souls and understand the subtle workings of their budding minds. Only then can we do justice to them."

More important than "objects for manual and visual inspection," lying about and inviting manipulation by the child, is the behavior of the parents toward the child and toward each other in the presence of the child.

5. PLAYGROUND—THE BIRTHPLACE OF IDEALS

Even as the nursery is the birthplace of intelligence, even so the playground is the birthplace of ideals. The nursery itself often partakes of the nature of the playground for the growing child in the initial stages—especially during the first year or two. In course of time, the entire house or apartment, or a corner in the house or the apartment, or yet a courtyard or a garden, or the children's recreation center, may become the growing child's playground.

When the play is the thing, father and mother lose for the moment their role of father and mother: to the child they become just co-players. This tingling sensation, this thrilling experience, on the part of the child visualizing the parents in a new role, constitutes a tremendous extension of the thinking process.

Indeed, the implications of the play activity of the child go deeper yet. (1) All games have a set of rules of their own. (2) Some can win a game more easily than others. (3) While one is playing the others have to watch. (4) If you break the rules you lose. (5) Each player tries to win within the framework of the rules of the game. (6) To play the game you must cooperate with others. Points one and four give rise to respect for the rules of the game, for certain accepted and approved ways of doing things, for the folkways and mores of the group, for societal patterns of behavior. Point number two gives rise to the sentiment of admiration for achievement as well as for the winner. Point number three gives rise to a regard for the rights of others, to the sentiment of patience awaiting one's turn, to a consideration for one's fellow man. Point number five vividly brings home to the child the role of goals, of purposiveness, in human behavior and in the social process. Finally, (6) the playing of the game with members of the group gives the growing child an experience and an appreciation of cooperation.

No, the child of two or three does not neatly analyze the implications of the play activity as suggested above; nor, for that matter, are many adults capable of consciously realizing all the implications of the play activity. Even so, the six factors, the six values, set forth in our analysis, are subsumed in the game-play situation; without understanding them fully and intelligently, the child still adopts them all as a frame of reference in his future dealings with and researches into the "world" round about him.

The primary ideals of purposiveness in life, of fairness, of regard for others, of achievement and of admiration for achievement, of respect for the rules of the game, of the ego-expanding value of social approbation—these primary ideals, so vital for the integrity of personality as well as of society, are nurtured in the young breast as a result of the stimulus-response relationships on the playground.

"Pluralistically responding (i.e. in plural numbers reacting) to common stimulation, communicating and associating, acting upon one another by suggestion and example, and imitating one another in a thousand ways, individuals generate similar feelings and develop closely resembling ideas." (2, p. 17) The playground, in other words, gives rise to a "consciousness of kind," to likemindedness; nay, more. In terms of its patterns of competitions and accommodations, surcharged as they are partly with feeling, partly with emotion, partly with sentiment, partly with reason, the playground provides a miniature framework for the social process of the adult world.

The value of the playground as the birthplace of idealism and of harmonious personality must be fully appreciated by us all.

6. The World of Representations

Besides exercising the intelligence or the intellect and giving rise to the primary ideals, the playground extends the capacity of the child in yet another significant respect. The transformation of father or mother from the usual role to that of co-player, as already pointed out, opens to the child the beautiful vista of the infinite world of *Vorstellung* (representation).

The world of make-believe, of fantasy, of dereistic or unrealistic thinking, plays a large part in the life of the growing child. Under proper guidance, the child's world of make-believe can become an educational agency of unsurpassed merit giving information as well as fostering imaginativeness and learning.

Far from being a source of danger to the child or his personality, this world of make-believe is the very spring of the highest values of life, namely, spiritual values. Have we not seen the little girl endow the doll with all the essential qualities of humanity? And when boys are playing a game of make-believe using a match for a knife (let us say)—have we not seen how in such circumstances they would rigidly treat the match as though it were an actual knife? In the world of make-believe, in other words, children develop notions and values approximating totem and taboo.

The flag standing for one's country, salutation to the flag as being equivalent to patriotism—these putative values belong to the world of representation through make-believe, through idealization. The concept of the flag as standing for one's country—indeed, as one's country—becomes transformed and reified, through the mechanism of totem and taboo, into a spiritual value.

Dereistic thinking and idealization, it is evident, lie in dangerous proximity even as do insanity and genius.

The failure to utilize consciously and purposively the world of *Vorstellung,* the children's world of make-believe, as a pedagogical technique has been responsible for many an instance of personality malaise, of anti-sociableness, of incipient and full-fledged criminality.

The pedagogy of Ancient India was based upon a proper appreciation of the manner in which the child grows physically, mentally, morally, spiritually. The *Pancha-tantra* and the *Hitopadesha,* teaching moral counsel through stories about animals, are best suited for the inquiring growing "mind" of the child. The Aesop's Fables, derived from Hindu sources, have served a similar purpose in the Occident.

Modern pedagogy has been utilizing the visual and auditory factors as useful aids in the fostering of learning. Following in the footsteps of Ancient India, we may profitably utilize the mechanism of *Vorstellungen,* of representations, as the most important technique in the teaching of little children.

And without resorting to the rod or the drill we may yet excite the child's interest in developing his retentive powers, in exercising his "memory," through rhythmic recitation, as does India to this day. Be it a recitation of numbers or a retelling or redramatization of a story once told or dramatized, rhythm will hold the attention of the children and teach them many things.

7. FROM CHAOS TO COSMOS

At birth the child finds himself surrounded and confronted by a "world" which is an inchoate mass of stimuli—a "big booming buzzing confusion." The "world" may have a logic and a harmony and a unity of its own; to the newborn, however, it is nothing more than confusion. The inborn "capacity to organize and systematize experience"—to wit, "mind"—begins to function under the impact of the mass of stimuli. Regardless of whether order and unity inhere in the "world" or not, the mind, which by definition is the capacity to organize and systematize experience, must needs postulate order and unity in the phenomenal world. Order and unity, in other words, must be *imposed* at the very outset by the child "mind." This imposition or superscription (superstition) of order and unity upon the universe may or may not be in accord with the objective reality—that, however, is a problem for philosophers. Suffice it for the child to endeavor to create—yes, *create for himself*—a workable world by differentiating himself from his environment, by differentiating a number of component elements of the environment from one another. A subtle process of reasoning and ratiocination within the framework of law, order and unity comes into play, unbeknown to the child, from the very start of the career of the newborn. In spite of its all-pervasiveness, few even among adults are aware of the constant functioning of this process of reasoning and ratiocination as part of their experience of living from moment to moment!

Indeed, the child is constantly, perhaps unbeknown to himself, engaged in creating cosmos out of chaos. Let us analyze the implications of the proposition: A burned child avoids the fire.

To begin with, the child has his finger (let us say) burned by contact with a chunk of fire lying outside the wire fence of the fireplace. The child cries, lets go the fire, and is attended to by his mother. But that is not all. This stimulus-response relationship of fire and burned finger constitutes for the uninstructed child the very epitome of the fundamentals of epistemology:

(1) Fire burned the finger, fire *caused* the burned finger. The Law of Causation. (2) The fire burned his finger when the finger and the fire came into contact, the fire would burn his finger once again if that very finger or another were to come into contact with that same chunk of fire or another; yes, on the morrow, too, fire would burn his finger; hence the avoidance. The Law of the Uniformity of Nature. (3) The fire from the fireplace of his own house burned his finger, the fire from the fireplace of his playmate's house, too, would burn it. The Law of Identity. (4) Table, chair, sofa, fireplace when no fire is burning it—these and a host of other things do not burn the finger; the concept of fire and not-fire. The Law of Contradiction.

In other words, all the laws of logic are utilized by the uninstructed child in arriving at the judgment: "Fire burns the finger and therefore contact with fire must be avoided." Not all children need to undergo the tingling sensation of a burning finger in order to be enabled to put into operation the laws of logic. The intellectual type of child, as contrasted with the visual and the auditory, would form an equally valid judgment by means of *Vorstellung* (representation)—through the advice given by parents: "Don't go too near the fire, it will burn you."

The child's explorations into and analyses of situations are indeed very complex and subtle—and highly rational.

8. INFERIORITY LEADS TO ACHIEVEMENT

The child vis-a-vis the "world"—i.e., his environment including father and mother—realizes his inferiority. This sense or feeling of inferiority must be overcome: subconsciously argues the uninstructed child. In other words, inferiority, the liability of childhood, becomes at once an asset inasmuch as it immediately brings into play its antidote, namely, goal-seeking.

The child imposes order upon the universe; the universe in its turn imposes unity of personality upon the child through his goal-seeking activity. And the child's development, be it noted, "is determined by his personal, individual interpretation of things"; his points of view decide the directions he will take, not the objective facts themselves. (1, p. 29)

Such a view of the child mind has a profound bearing upon education. From the very start, parents and teachers and the community as a whole may well take for granted the child's capacity to impose "order" upon the chaotic "world" in terms of the fundamental laws of logic, unless the original endowments of a particular child be subnormal. Such an attitude, especially on the part of parents and teachers, would tend to accelerate the child's mental development and emotional maturity.

REFERENCES

1. ALFRED ADLER: *The Education of Children.* New York: Greenburg, 1930.
2. FRANKLIN H. GIDDINGS: *Studies in the Theory of Human Society.* New York: Macmillan, 1922.
3. MAXIMILIAN P. E. GROSZMANN: *The Exceptional Child.* New York: Scribners, 1917.
4. JACK LONDON: *The Star Rover.* New York: Macmillan, 1920. Sonoma Edition.
5. ROBERT E. PARK and ERNEST W. BURGESS: *Introduction to the Science of Sociology,* 2nd ed. Chicago: The University of Chicago Press, 1924; eighth impression, 1933.
6. MILICENT W. SHINN: *The Biography of a Baby.* Boston: Houghton Mifflin Company, 1900.

SPECIAL NOTE NO. 1: The student is urged to familiarize himself with the stimulating little book, *The Making of Modern Mind,* (Houston: The Elsevier Press, 1956) by Leonard Carmichael, Secretary of the Smithsonian Institution. The book contains the Rockwell Lectures, delivered by Dr. Carmichael at The Rice Institute, Houston, Texas, in 1956.

SPECIAL NOTE NO. 2: The student will find interesting case histories of some noted persons, who by will power overcame their respective inferiorities, in *The Importance of Feeling Inferior* (New York: Harper & Bros., 1957) by Marie Benyon Ray.

CHAPTER 9

TYPES OF GROUPS AND GROUPINGS

THUS far we have attempted to describe how the group-related child, participating in culture, creates a cosmos out of chaos. Now we are ready to embark upon a classification of groups and upon a consideration of the dynamics of the group. Eminent sociologists have wrestled with this problem and laid us under a heavy debt by their prior investigations. No one scheme of classification is, however, entirely satisfactory. Hence, reserving for later consideration the categories of group, we may here address ourselves to a classification of *types* or kinds of groups and groupings from as many angles as possible:

1. TEN DICHOTOMOUS GROUPINGS

CHART 6

TEN DICHOTOMOUS GROUPINGS

1. Primary Group	...	Secondary Group (Cooley)
2. In-Group	...	Out-Group (Sumner)
3. Permanent Group	...	Transitory Group
4. Vertical Group	...	Horizontal Group (Miller)
5. Institutional Group	...	Non-Institutional Group
6. Formal Group	...	Informal Group
7. Contractual Group	...	Non-Contractual Group
8. Voluntary Group	...	Involuntary Group
9. Homogeneous Group	...	Heterogeneous Group
10. Community	...	Society

While each pair of classification implies more or less mutually exclusive categories, the ten bases of classification are not necessarily mutually exclusive. Indeed, the family, a primary group, may also be viewed as an in-group, as a permanent group, as a vertical group, as an institutional group, as a formal group and as a contractual group in the Occident, as a non-contractual, organic group in the Orient; as an involuntary group from the standpoint of the child's membership, or as a voluntary group from the standpoint of the romantic couple entering into matrimony. But this tenfold classification does yield us valuable tools for the analysis of group behavior and the social process.

2. PRIMARY AND SECONDARY GROUPS

The primary group is characterized by intimate, face-to-face relations and relationships. Examples: the family, the kinship group, the playgroup, the gang, the congeniality group, the friendship group, the neighborhood group, the community group. It may be noted that spatial proximity is an aid to the functioning of the primary group—but not essential in every case. The kinship, congeniality and friendship groups can manage to function on the level of primary-group relationships even when their members are separated from one another by vast distances. As already pointed out, the primary group is the birthplace of human nature and of the primary ideals of cooperation, mutual aid, regard for others, sympathy, love. The judgments of the primary group are matters of crucial moment to its members. The judgment, adverse or favorable, of one or more members of the primary group acts as a norm for one's behavior. Through the mechanism of praise and blame, the primary group exercises control over its members. The primary group acts as a normative and regulatory group.

When intimacy and face-to-face contacts are not present in the relation of members, we have the secondary group. With the onset of industrialism and the rise of urbanism, society tends to become a network of multitudinous secondary groups, with a core of a few primary groups still extant. Many of the problems of our day— social, economic, political, cultural—arise from the host of secondary groups that have emerged in the wake of industrialization and urbanization. In the anonymity of the city one's behavior is controlled by institutional mechanisms and by the fundamental categories of the given culture, not by sentiment, not by the judgment of " strangers," not by approbation and disapprobation as such. Examples of the secondary group: political parties, trade unions, the United States Chamber of Commerce, the business corporation, national fraternities, the public, etc. The secondary group should not be viewed as being antagonistic to the primary group.

3. IN-GROUP OUT-GROUP PROBLEMS

The in-group is antagonistic to the out-group. The in-group comes into being when one identifies oneself with the group in contrast to others, who are conceived to be members of other groups, of out-groups. The Catholic Church, for instance, is an in-group with reference to the Protestant Churches; the Baptist Church is an in-group with reference to the Methodist Church, and so on. The in-group may be primary or secondary, permanent or transitory, institutional or non-institutional. The in-group is a sympathetic group so far as its members are concerned; to the in-group, the out-group is an antagonistic group. It is possible to have within a large in-group or we-group a number of out-groups more or less at odds with one another. The nation today is the largest in-group unit, commanding the loyalty of all its citizens who may be variously grouped, each group striving to realize its interest which, however, must not conflict with the putative or real interest of the nation. The history of mankind is in a sense the story of the extension of in-group loyalty from small units to large units—from the family and the clan to the tribe, to the city, to the nation. Today mankind is struggling to expand the national in-group loyalty to embrace the inter-nation or world in-group loyalty.

As for permanent and transitory groups, the meaning of these terms is obvious. Some groups, such as nations and races, classes and castes, are permanent, that is to say, more or less permanent; while such groups as crowds and mobs and lynching parties are transitory.

4. VERTICAL AND HORIZONTAL GROUPS

The vertical group embraces persons of different strata or statuses while the horizontal group holds together persons of the same status. A nation or a religious denomination constitutes a vertical grouping, while a class or a caste represents horizontal grouping. In the trade union movement of our day, craft unionism—i.e., unionism by crafts,

such as carpenters or plumbers—represents horizontal grouping
(A.F.L.), while industrial unionism—i.e., unionism by industry or an
industrial plant embracing workers of all categories from the janitor
to the skilled mechanic—represents vertical grouping (C.I.O.).

5. INSTITUTIONAL, FORMAL AND CONTRACTUAL GROUPS

The institutional group functions through rituals, symbols, officers, codes of conduct, regulatory power (*Danda*) including the
power to punish. The nation is an institutional group in contrast to
the public which is a non-institutional group. The state, as an association of citizens for power, is an institutional group in contrast
to a picnic party which is a non-institutional group. Certain classificatory groups, such as those enumerated ("created"?) by the
Census—Age groups, Sex groups, National Origins groups, Colored
and White groups, Gainfully Employed groups, Unemployed
groups, etc.—fall within the category of non-institutional groups.

Formal groups may be either permanent or transitory. They rest
upon agreement short of contract. When formal groups become
institutionalized, contract for admission or continued membership
and *Danda* (regulatory power) become the efficient mode of operation. Informal groups rest upon consensus with a leeway for "take it
or leave it." Informal groups in some cases tend to become formal
groups.

The contractual group is born of a contract with a definition of
powers and responsibilities of the members as well as of the group
as an entity. The contractual group is a formal group with a definite tendency toward institutionalization. The Mayflower Compact
group, the signers of the Declaration of Independence including
their constituencies, the framers of the United States Constitution
and their constituencies, are all examples of contractual groups. The
carving out of Pakistan out of India has had ultimately to rest upon
a contract between Hindus and Muslims who were developing in-
group out-group attitudes of hostility within the tenuously held
together entity called the Hindese group. The corporation in the
legal sense is essentially a contractual group when it is started, even
though the State "certifies" its birth. A labor union, likewise, is

essentially a contractual group and an entity in its own right, just like the corporation, even if it may not take out papers of incorporation. Sentiment and sympathy apart, a union and a corporation are sociologically birds of the same feather and must be treated as such. If a corporation must keep its books open to inspection, so must the union. If the corporation is called upon to pay income tax, so must the union be called upon to pay tax on its income. Both are using the device of becoming a Mahajana, engaged in corporate activity, not just cooperative activity.

6. The Concept of the Mahajana

The Mahajana, a Sanskrit word, literally means the great man, but it is applied to the collective entity, the body, of many men who constitute it. We may call it the Corpus Magnum or the Homo Magnus. Aristotle's description of the association fits the Mahajana concept neatly : "When they (the individuals) meet together, they become in a manner one man who has many feet, and hands, and senses." (*Politics,* BK. III, CH. 11). The caste Mahajana is greater than all the members of the caste, taken simply or all together in a simple additive fashion. The Mahajana is greater than all its members precisely because it is á functional group. In the Mahajana there is an emergent plus value, exactly as there is an emergent plus value in a bundle of sticks tied together contrasted with the sticks lying together or away from one another. The Mahajana's plus value emerges from loyalty—from the loyalty of its members. The business corporation functions as a Mahajana because of the loyalty of its "members"—stockholders—to profit through production and/or service; the union functions as a Mahajana because of the loyalty of its members to higher wages and shorter hours, to elimination of industrial hazards and to security of tenure, even to industrial democracy in some cases.

7. Groups in Democratic and Totalitarian Societies

The social malaise of our twentieth century civilization in non-totalitarian countries may partly be traced to the fact that the

genetic primary group is receding more and more into the background and the contractual group with its special axe to grind is
mushrooming forth in every direction. Each contractual group comes
into being to promote its interest. Now the interests are varied and
conflicting, hence the interplay of different contractual groups
creates social harmonies and disharmonies—social pathologies.

The classification of groups into voluntary and involuntary is
useful in defining cultural limits within which human beings may
or must group themselves. Membership in the family is inevitable
for the newborn; there is no choice. Indeed, the newborn was not
consulted whether he (or she) ever wanted to be born or whether he
(or she) wanted to be born to the particular parents. Ecological
groupings are more or less involuntary. One may choose one's
friends outside the neighborhood, but one cannot deny one's
physical relation to the neighborhood in which one dwells. One's
membership in the race-group is likewise predetermined by birth.
Membership in the religious group is predetermined for 99 per cent
of the population by the religious affiliation of the parents. Membership in the State, in modern society, is determined by the place
of birth. One has the right, later in life, to move away from a given
neighborhood, from a given community, from a given religious
grouping, from a given Nation-State and choose one's group affiliations in terms of a new neighborhood, a new community, a new
religious grouping, a new Nation-State. This particular classification
drives home the point that certain group relationships are imposed
upon us all at birth; that, later in life, we are at liberty to enter into
new group relationships with existing groups or with newly formed
groups.

The classification of groups into voluntary and involuntary gives
us an insight into the workings of a democracy and a totalitarian
setup. A democratic society permits, even encourages, the rise and
growth of all types of voluntary groups for the attainment of their
objectives, for the enrichment of man's enjoyment, in conformity
with the categories of its culture, while a totalitarian society, dominated by an authoritarian government, bans and suppresses voluntary groups. In totalitarian States the so-called voluntary groups are
in fact adjuncts of the government. To discover whether a State is

democratic or not we need only to know whether voluntary groupings are permitted or not.

8. HOMOGENEOUS AND HETEROGENEOUS GROUPS

The classification of groups into homogeneous and heterogeneous gives us a clue to the nature of the internal and external dynamics of the group. In formal education, educators are constrained to keep in mind the heterogeneity of the school population they deal with: heterogeneity in regard to age, sex, grade, physical maturation, intellectual attainments, family and community backgrounds from which the students come. The American nation is a medley of heterogeneous groups, when viewed from the standpoint of national or racial origins or religious persuasions. And yet, culturally, while not monolithic, America is a homogeneous entity: an American, regardless of his subcultural background, can be easily identified and set apart from a European or an Asian. America's historic task has been to forge a homogeneous entity and loyalty out of a multiplicity of subcultural groups and loyalties. The formula is: *E pluribus unum*—the emergence of American culture out of subcultural pluralism. This task has succeeded, and it is a marvel for the world to behold. Imperialists have striven to forge cultural homogeneity by crushing the cultures of their heterogeneous subject peoples— and have failed. It remains to be seen if the ruthless effort of the Soviet Union to forge homogeneity out of heterogeneous peoples and cultures will ever succeed.

9. GEMEINSCHAFT (COMMUNITY) AND GESELLSCHAFT (SOCIETY)

Ferdinand Toennies has pioneered in distinguishing between the community and society, between *Gemeinschaft* and *Gesellschaft*.

We have already defined society as "a complex of groups in reciprocal relationships, interacting upon one another within the cultural context, enabling human organisms to carry on their life-activities and helping each person to fulfill his special wishes and accomplish his special interests in association with his fellows." By juxtaposition, we may define the community as follows: *Community comprises the entire group sympathetically entering into a common life within a given area, regardless of the extent of area or state boundaries.* In society the dominant motif is interaction between groups, in community it is the integral quality, the wholeness, of the group.

Zimmerman and Frampton describe the distinctions between community (*Gemeinschaft*) and society (*Gesellschaft*) as follows (5, p. 280):

> In the *Gemeinschaft* the group has a life of its own, superior to that of its temporary members. The group is an end in itself. In the *Gesellschaft* the group is merely a means to an end. In the *Gemeinschaft* we have faith, customs, natural solidarity, common ownership of property, and a common will. In the *Gesellschaft* we have doctrine, public opinion, fashion, contractual solidarity, private property, and individual will.

Community and community spirit are, in other words, distinguished from society and its contractual solidarity by the fact that members of the community emphasize their common will and commonweal—parks, for instance, in the domain of material culture and mores in the domain of non-material culture—whereas members of society emphasize their rights, rely on laws, and operate on the basis of contract and formal legalism.

Community, thus defined, is the focus of social life. The community, local, national or worldwide, provides the background for the interplay of social forces—including persons, groups, the social heritage—and for the manifestation of the social processes.

The community is a natural entity, while society is an intangible artifact. The community is a network of reciprocal relationships and interdependences derived from the sharing in common not only of the preconditions of collective living but also of certain perquisites of living by all its members. Society, on the other hand, is a network of reciprocal relationships and interdependences derived from the sharing in common of the two preconditions of collective life, namely, grouping and substantial resemblance, leading to the emergence of laws and contracts, of formal rules and procedures. Ideally, community is characterized by crescive institutions, while society is characterized by enacted institutions. In a complex culture, community and society overlap, with the emergence of enacted institutions in a community as well as in a society. But the constituent elements and behavior patterns of the two groupings—society and community—are distinctive and must be borne in mind.

We need to have a conscious sense both of relating ourselves to society and of participating in community, the former to ensure our privacy and to maintain our ego, the latter to enrich our inner being.

Having briefly discussed types of groups and groupings, we may next turn to a discussion of group categories. This will be followed by an investigation of how groups are formed, how they are held together, and how they function or operate in general situations (within the institutional order) and in specific situations (classes, castes, races, nations).

REFERENCES

1. ARISTOTLE: *Politics.* Jowett's translation.
2. CHARLES H. COOLEY: *Human Nature and the Social Order.* New York: Scribners, 1902.
3. HERBERT A. MILLER: *Races, Nations and Classes.* Philadelphia: Lippincott, 1924.
4. WILLIAM G. SUMNER: *Folkways.* Boston: Ginn & Co., 1906.
5. C. C. ZIMMERMAN and M. E. FRAMPTON: *Family and Society—A Study of the Sociology of Reconstruction.* New York (now Princeton) : D. Van Nostrand Co., 1935.

CHAPTER 10

GROUP CATEGORIES

1. FROM THE CROWD TO THE CORPORATION

THE functioning of the sociogenic group—sociogenic in contrast to biogenic or genetic—may be viewed as ranging all the way from the mass and the crowd as its most elemental level to the corporation at its highest level. The rainbow of group behavior, or the, categories of the group, may be seen as: the mass, the crowd, the audience, the public, the assembly, the association, the corporation. These group functionings shade off into one another as imperceptibly as do the colors in the rainbow. Every corporation is an association but not every association is a corporation. Every association is an assembly but not every assembly is an association. Every assembly is a public but not every public is an assembly. Every public is an audience but not every audience is a public. Every audience is a crowd or a mass but not every crowd or mass is an audience.

The mass is an anonymous group of individuals, physically separated from one another, exhibiting little direct interaction or exchange of experience, unable to act collectively, but capable of generating symbols and stereotypes which, in turn, can galvanize localized groups into crowds or audiences. (1, pp. 241–45).

The crowd is an aggregation of individuals drawn together by an interest without premeditation on the part of any of them and without even tentative prevision of what to expect.

The audience is an aggregation of persons drawn together by an interest with premeditation on the part of some or all of them and with tentative prevision of what to expect, on the part of some or all of them.

The public is an aggregation of persons, moving in a common universe of discourse, confronted by an issue or a value, divided in their opinions regarding ways to meet the issue or to appraise the value, and engaging in discussion.

138

The assembly is a temporary association of persons, drawn together by an interest, moving in a common universe of discourse, with definite collective awareness of the value to be realized.

The association is a functional group that comes into existence for a well-defined purpose and that strives for the accomplishment of the purpose by culturally defined processes of collective action and functioning.

The corporation is an association, whose corporate entity is an accepted part of the social process—i.e., an association that has usually outlived a generation. This sociological concept of corporation is not widely used, though the distinction between association and corporation, conceived sociologically, is helpful in analysis.

Only the corporation and the association achieve the status of Mahajana and act as a Mahajana whose behavior can be predicted in advance. The other forms of grouping and group functioning, visible as amorphous Mahajana, fail to achieve continuity except when they become transformed into an association or a corporation.

In common usage we have several terms which stand for the sociological concept of association (or corporation): club, society, party, group, etc. The Shakespeare Club, the Browning Society, the Republican Party, the A.F.L., the C.I.O., the Carpenters Union: Local No. X, the Delta Social Group, the ABC Fraternity, the XYZ Sorority, etc.—these descriptive terms and similar ones are used to denote associations or corporations.

The American Sociological Society is at present (1959) in the throes of wrestling with the problem whether to call this national organization Society or Association. Sociologically, it would be fitting and more accurate to call this professional organization the American Sociological Association.

2. HERD, MASS AND CROWD

What the herd is in the subhuman world, the mass is in human society. The mass, a spontaneous collective grouping like the crowd, resembles the crowd in many respects but is "fundamentally different from it in other ways. The mass is represented by people who participate in mass behavior, such as those who are excited by some national event, those who are interested in a murder trial which is

CHART 7
THE RAINBOW OF GROUP CATEGORIES

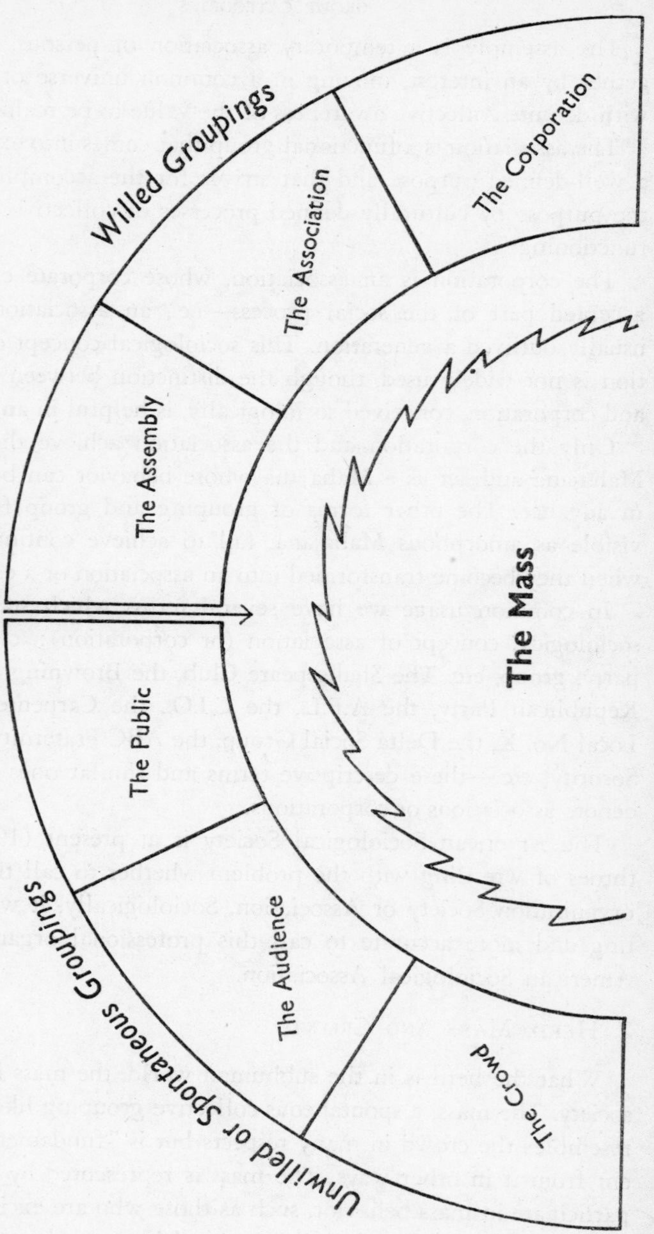

The Population

Willed Groupings
- The Corporation
- The Association
- The Assembly

Unwilled or Spontaneous Groupings
- The Crowd
- The Audience
- The Public

The Mass

reported in the press, or those who participate in some large migration." (1, p. 241)

In recent times we have witnessed the emergence of the Massen-Mensch, the mass-man, or the mass-mind, in totalitarian countries—Nazi Germany, Fascist Italy, Militarist Japan, Soviet Russia. Mass advertising in the United States results in mass-mindedness, even though it is not regimented to the purposes of a police state. Furthermore, our technological civilization with its increasing urbanization has given rise to a host of secondary groups, uprooted from their primary group relationships and from the primary ideals; the members of these secondary groups think and act anonymously as a mass. Finally, the price for our industrial development is the creation of a vast proletarian mass in highly industrialized countries.

While the mass and the crowd are distinctly different phenomena, mass-mindedness and crowd-mindedness are closely akin in that they are equally dangerous to the smooth operation of cultural categories in certain situations.

The crowd, another spontaneous collective group operating on an elemental level, has been intensively studied here and abroad, among others, by Gustave Le Bon (1841-1931), Gabriel Tarde (1843-1904), S. Sighele (1868-1913), and Everett Dean Martin (1880-1941).

Using the psychoanalytical technique of Freud and his disciples, viewing the crowd as a collective compulsion neurosis, Martin interpreted the crowd situation as an occasion and an instrumentality for release of the repressed wishes of its members (2, *passim*). This interpretation is helpful in accounting for certain types of crowd behavior; but it is wrong to imply that the crowd as such is a pathological social situation. The crowd is as natural as the family so far as sociogenic factors are concerned. The matter of crucial moment for any culture is to discover the gap between sanctioned behavior for willed groups and for unwilled, spontaneous groups such as crowds. If the gap between sanctioned behavior for the crowd and sanctioned behavior for the citizen or an association be very wide, cultural restraints may lead to frequent crowd behavior. There is nothing wrong or abnormal about the crowd so long as it operates in harmony with the cultural categories.

Le Bon divided crowds into two categories: Homogeneous and Heterogeneous (3, pp. 202–03, quoted).

Le Bon's Division of Crowds

I. Heterogeneous Crowds:
  1. Anonymous (street crowds, for example)
  2. Not anonymous (parliamentary assemblies, for example)

II. Homogeneous Crowds:
  1. Sects (political, religious, etc.)
  2. Castes (military, sacerdotal, etc.)
  3. Classes (bourgeois, working-men, etc.)

This classification of Le Bon's is interesting and suggestive, but it is open to criticism and unacceptable to us. First, in our scheme of ascending classification any and every conceivable group in society can be fitted, while in Le Bon's scheme there is a mixing up of categories. Second, it is an open question whether we should view a parliamentary assembly as behaving primarily on the crowd level. That an assembly is capable of degenerating into a crowd there is no denying; but, ordinarily, a parliamentary assembly functions on a higher level than the crowd. Third, it is not clear why Le Bon should classify parliamentary assemblies among heterogeneous *crowds* and sects among homogeneous *crowds*. Fourth, it is debatable whether a sect should be classified as a crowd in operation. That a sect may well have had its origin in a crowd situation we can believe; but if it can persist in society as a combat group in conflict with the status quo or with certain elements in the status quo, it must have attained the status of an association, if indeed not that of a corporation.

3. BLUMER'S CLASSIFICATION OF CROWDS

Dr. Blumer (1, pp. 233–34) divides crowds into four categories.

Blumer's Classification of Crowds

1. The casual crowd (a street crowd)
2. The conventionalized crowd (a football crowd)

3. The expressive crowd (a dancing crowd)

4. The active crowd (a lynching mob or a revolutionary crowd)

The casual crowd and the conventionalized crowd are easy to understand. The expressive crowd, geared to rhythmic repetitive act, generates ecstasy and exaltation, whether of a religious nature or of a sensual nature. The origin of the religious ritual of dance has been sought by some social scientists in this expressive type of crowd behavior.

4. How an Active Crowd is Formed

The formation of the active crowd is attended by the following stages and processes: 1. An exciting event catches the attention and arouses the interest of the people. 2. A disturbance in the routine activity of life takes place, creating some sort of unrest. 3. If the exciting event be more than casual or conventional, unrest will lead to "milling." 4. Milling will tend to collective excitement. 5. Social contagion and a high degree of suggestibility will set up interstimulation, highly charged with emotionalism, and intensify collective excitement by circular reaction. 6. The crowd is now *en rapport,* and its anonymous members are in process of throwing off their cultural conditionings while enjoying a sense of power, of bigness, through identification with the amorphous group. The person is now steadily regressing into the individual, moved by elemental passions. 7. The apt word uttered anonymously, the apt slogan cried anonymously, or the apt gesture or suggestion made by a self-constituted leader will create in the crowd a frenzy—and a readiness for action. The crowd is now transformed into a mob. By definition, the mob is a crowd in action.

The crowd can not only be converted into a mob, it can also be turned into an audience under proper circumstances. When primary interest is focused on the human actor and his doings, a casual crowd that gathered together on a street corner at his sight may stay on to listen to him or to watch his tricks. The crowd in this new situation has become an audience. And, of course, the audience can be drawn together from persons with a common interest, some or all of whom have more or less thought out beforehand what the nature of the interest is and what to expect. Thus arise our audiences in theatres, at operas, at political rallies, at revival meetings, etc.

At the Chicago fire, caused by Mrs. O'Leary's cow, as is popularly supposed, the panicky crowd of citizens was saved from mutually trampling upon one another by an anonymous person's cry: "Keep to the right!" Momentarily, the crowd was turned into an audience, listened to the injunction, and abided by it because the injunction was in perfect harmony with the cultural categories of America.

5. OVERLAPPING GROUP CATEGORIES

Physical propinquity is essential to the formation of a crowd. The mass may become a special type of audience for a particular football player through the newspapers or the radio, or TV, even as the crowd may become a localized audience under certain circumstances. When the audience, moving in a common universe of discourse, confronted by an issue or a value, begins to discuss the problem pro and con, we witness the emergence of the public. When members of the public form a temporary association to meet together for the realization of a predetermined value, the assembly comes into being. Should the assembly decide to implement the value already realized, to promote the interest that brought them together in the first instance, there would emerge an association, a functional group. The association, functioning over a generation, would become structuralized into a corporation.

Of these categories of group behavior, the mass and the crowd are unwilled. The audience, and the public *can* come into being spontaneously without collective premeditation on the part of members to form the particular type of group. But the mechanisms of these types of behavior easily lend themselves to scrupulous or unscrupulous manipulation by capable persons well-versed in the study of human behavior. Thus, in the evening, a speaker in Columbus Circle, New York City, could in the twenties and the thirties attract a crowd, if he had a soapbox or a raised platform to stand on; in Hyde Park, London, a speaker can still draw a crowd. Passers-by would stop to see what was going on. Gathered together by curiosity, those members of the crowd that stay on to listen to the speaker, become transformed into an audience.

6. A Case History of the Spectrum of Group Behavior

Let me describe a typical example of the way progression in group functioning takes place. In 1920, I decided to "educate" the American people about India's struggle for freedom. Having seen some speakers and crowds surrounding them on street corners, I decided to select Columbus Circle, New York City, as my corner. I borrowed a stepladder from one of the corner stores, and took my time placing it in the right position. By this time a small group of people gathered together, out of curiosity, to see what was going to happen. Slowly I began to tie a turban on my head. The crowd increased in size. While still tying the turban, I told the crowd that soon I would talk to them on India. Then I started to speak to the crowd. Those who had pressing business to attend to moved on and vanished into the anonymous street crowd. Those who stayed on to listen to me became my audience. I spoke for half an hour or so; asked the members of my audience to ask me questions, but none of them did. Then, half jokingly half seriously, I gave them a sales talk on a "great" pamphlet on India—"great," because it had been written by me—which they could get for 25 cents only. That first evening the sale of the pamphlets brought in a little over $15.00. Those who still stayed on were informed that next week, the same evening, at the same place, I would speak to them again.

From week to week, people began to gather at the specified spot well in advance of the scheduled meeting. (After the first two meetings, the turban as "an attraction" was discarded by me.) On an off evening, while strolling by Columbus Circle, I heard an Irish-American speaker denounce British imperialism. I joined the crowd. One of the members of "the crowd" recognized me, and suggested to one of the two Irish-American speakers that they invite me to address the crowd. Evidently, this "member of the crowd" must have been an influential person. As soon as the speaker was through, the other speaker ascended the platform and introduced me to the " crowd." Amidst applause I shared the Irish-American platform and spoke on India and British imperialism. That was the beginning of my making common cause with the Irish-Americans. Now I had a definite following—and the public against British imperialism had now to think through the problem in terms of India as well as Ireland.

Soon I was invited by the two Irish-American speakers to attend a weekly gathering of all their speakers, where the leaders of the movement for Ireland's freedom would give the speakers pointers as to what aspects to emphasize and how to put over their argument in favor of Ireland's freedom.

At a "mass meeting" held in a big theatre in New York City I was invited to be one of the speakers when Mr. Emmon De Valera was the guest of the evening and main speaker. This assembly, of course, had been carefully planned by the leaders of the movement for Ireland's freedom and those who attended it had a definite notion of the value to be realized—seeing Mr. De Valera, hearing him, encouraging him in his fight for Ireland's freedom, contributing funds for the movement, boosting the morale of the people associated with the movement both in Ireland and in the United States.

At this time, in cooperation with two Hindese friends, I organized the Young India Association whose general purposes were, upon consultation, approved by one of the Irish-American leaders. Young India Association functioned until 1922 when I left New York City for the Middle West. This association did not function long enough to become a corporation.

This description shows the gradual merging of one group functioning into another on a higher level. It also demonstrates that spontaneous groupings—the mass, the crowd, the audience, the public—can be purposively brought into being by a "leader" or "leaders."

7. The Spectrum of Group Behavior Under Totalitarianism

Human susceptibility to these spontaneous groupings has been in recent times exploited by "spell-binders," by "ideologists," by unscrupulous persons who rely more on emotion than on intellect, more on violence and brute force than on non-violence and soul force. Leaders of totalitarianism prefer a mass to the crowd, a crowd to the audience, an audience to the public, a public to the assembly. Under totalitarianism the police set rigid limits to the possible number of values around which the public can be created.

The assembly and the association can function in a totalitarian setup only as adjuncts of the State, never autonomously. And, of course, no corporation could possibly function which did not serve the needs of the police State.

8. WILLED AND UNWILLED GROUPINGS

The assembly, the association and the corporation are collectively willed groupings in contrast to the public, the audience, the crowd, the mass, which are collectively unwilled groupings. None of the willed groups can come into being without action on the part of some or all of the members of the particular group. The willed group is usually brought into being by a far-seeing person—a seer, a leader—or a set of far-seeing persons. The leader is keenly aware of the fact that the interest, which has become his "concern," is shared by a significant number of persons in the population. He puts his whole self—all his energies—into the task of accomplishing the interest. Others, to whom the interest has not become a dominant concern, give him only part of their self—part of their time and energy—in the common task. The leader may be viewed as the nucleus, as the nucleated person, around whom revolve others with fractional interest; the organization of the interest gives rise to the association. The persistency and the activity of the association are determined by the nucleated person.

In the early stages, the association exhibits more color than power, more motion than result, more dynamic than achievement. In the mature stage, the association in the form of a corporation exhibits more power than color, more achievement than dynamic, more structure than function.

The business corporation, the trade union, the research founda-tion, the educational foundation, the humanitarian foundation—these are all instances of corporation sociologically conceived. The legal concept of the corporation is different from the sociological concept of the corporation. By legal fiat, the State "creates" a corporation by issuing papers of incorporation to a duly organized association; by legal fiat, the corporation becomes a legal person, immutable and immortal. If all the members of the association that had taken out papers of incorporation stepped aside or died or were replaced, the legal existence of the corporation would not be affected.

A corporation, sociologically speaking, is not a creature of the State, is not dependent upon the State for its birth, is neither immutable nor immortal; to the sociologist, any association whose corporate entity is an accepted part of the social process over a long period of time, usually a generation or longer, is a corporation. The corporate entity of the association is to be determined by function, not by legalism.

This discussion of group functioning, especially of the association, is valuable for a proper understanding of the functioning of institutions. A great deal of misunderstanding has arisen from failure to correlate institutions and associations. No institution can function without the active functioning of its correlative, the association. The State, for instance, may be viewed either as an institution or as an association. As an institution the State embodies collective modes of behavior; as an association the citizens operate the State machinery from generation to generation. As the institution of the State embodies rules of procedure, the association of citizens is provided with ready-made, workable rules. The State as citizens, therefore, does not question the validity of the State as an institution—except in a crisis. And in a crisis the State as institution usually triumphs over the State as citizens.

That the institution and the association are correlates is a point which needs to be driven home as sharply and as clearly as possible. (See CHAPTER 13).

REFERENCES

1. H. BLUMER: "Collective Behavior" in *An Outline of the Principles of Sociology*, edited by R. E. Park. New York: Barnes and Noble, 1939.
2. E. D. MARTIN: *The Behavior of Crowds.* New York: Harper and Brothers, 1920.
3. R. E. PARK and E. W. BURGESS: *Introduction to the Science of Sociology*, 2nd Edition. Chicago: University of Chicago Press, 1924; eighth impression, 1933.

CHAPTER 11

PROCESSES OF GROUP FORMATION

HAVING described the types and categories of grouping in human society, we may legitimately raise the question: How do human groups arise?—From what sources do groups spring?

A river may have its source in a subterranean spring, in a waterfall, or in the melting snows on a mountain. The mighty Mississippi has its source in a trickle from an underground spring in northern Minnesota and rushes down to the Gulf of Mexico. The three great rivers of India, the Indus, the Ganges and the Brahmaputra have their origin in the melting snows of the Himalayas, "the eternal abode of snow." Is it possible, in like manner, to discover the sources from which human groups spring? The answer is an emphatic Yes.

Human groups arise from three possible sources: (1) genetic, (2) ecological, (3) sociological.

1. GENETIC GROUPS

The family and kinship groups may be cited as instances of genetic groups; they are held together by genetic, biological interrelationships. Bonds of blood characterize the genetic group.

In America, the family—a genetic group—is composed of husband-wife-children. Adopted children legally enjoy the same status as children begotten by parents. Kinship groups are thought of in terms of blood relationships both on the husband's side and on the wife's side. Uncles, aunts, cousins—paternal or maternal—are among the child's kinship group in addition to father, mother and siblings.

In India and China, the family—a genetic group—embraces a larger number of people. With Grandfather and Grandmother at the head, all sons and their wives and grandchildren and all unmarried daughters—these constitute the joint family (or the extended family or the large family), whose members share a common hearth and a common shelter.

Clans and tribes arose from the interrelationships of several families through marriages. In primitive tribes, several interest and professional groups did arise, but these subgroups were controlled by common genetic ties.

2. ECOLOGICAL GROUPS

Ecological groups are characterized by the interrelationships and interdependences between human organisms and their habitat. Neighborhoods and communities, large or small, may be studied as groups that arise ecologically and are held together sociologically.

The study of human ecology resolves itself into a study of demography within a territorial context: how a population acts upon the environment, how the environment acts upon the population, how members of the population compete and cooperate with one another in the struggle for existence and the struggle for thriving. Human ecology, therefore, may be studied under the three heads: (1) the biology of the population, (2) the territorial distribution of the population, (3) the economic struggle of the population in its efforts to perpetuate itself, to survive, and to thrive.

The biology of the population is studied by sociologists in a special field of investigation, called Population Problems. A course entitled "Population Problems" is offered by most Departments of Sociology in American colleges and universities. Here we study such classificatory groups as the population group as a whole and its subdivisions, age groups, sex groups, racial groups, national origins groups, etc. The quantitative aspects of the population are supplemented with a study of the quality of the population—with eugenics and euthenics.

Under the heading, the territorial distribution of the population, the sociologist studies human groups in terms of their earth-bound character: the population of the world spread over the world, the density of the population in different regions of the world, the population of different nations, the man-land ratio, the population of rural areas, the population of urban areas. The concept of the community, i.e., a population sharing a *common habitat* and *common perquisites of group life,* emerges in this area of sociological study. *A community is characterized by four elements: (1) people,*

(2) geographic locale or setting, (3) common services, institutions and value systems, and (4) commonly cherished sense of integral loyalty.

Rural society and urban society, the rural community and the urban community, the hamlet community containing a group of less than 250 persons inhabiting a functionally well defined area and the metropolitan community containing a group of over 50,000 persons, likewise, inhabiting a functionally well defined area—all these groupings and patterns, processes and relationships come under the purview of the sociologist when he is studying the territorial distribution of the human population. The study of man-land ratio is supplemented by a study of man-technology ratio, and the transition is effected for the study of the third aspect of human ecology in the modern setting.

The economic struggle of the population for perpetuation, survival and thriving is studied by a special class of social scientists, called economists. The sociologist is interested in the economic struggle of the population in terms of social groupings brought about in processes of competition and cooperation, of superordination and subordination. The occupational hierarchy of unskilled workers, skilled mechanics, professional workers, employers, constitutes as significant a social fact as an economic fact. The standard of living and the plane or level of living of different groups in society are of vital concern to the sociologist (2, *passim*). The incidence of poverty and dependency, i.e., of poor groups and of dependent groups, in society has great social significance. Substandard living and public relief, juvenile delinquency and crime are likewise socially significant. These and many other facts and processes, involved in the economic struggle of the population, are studied by sociologists to discover possible causes and correlations and prescriptions.

Three points, emerging from the discussion thus far, may now be stressed:

1. That genetic groups may without violence be subsumed under ecological groups;
2. That groups which arise from the ecological background, such as the family and occupational hierarchy groups, are

constantly subject to the sociological processes, inasmuch as they needs must operate within the cultural framework.

3. That the community is the focus of social life; that the community, whether local, national or worldwide, provides the background for the interplay of social forces and for the manifestation of the social processes.

3. A Footnote to the Definition of Community

The definition of community in a democratic setting, as given by us, fits neither the concept nor the operation of a community in a non-democratic society, especially in a feudal or feudalistic society resting upon ascribed rights of precedence and deference. In hierarchy-conscious India, valiantly striving to be a democracy, the societal organization rests upon tight-knit groups, each acting as a "community." The British Raj had coined the terms, "the Hindu community," "the Muslim community," "the Sikh community," "the Anglo-Indian community," etc., and had referred to the separate representation of these groups as "communal" representation. Thus in India, the territorial ingredient in community is regarded as insignificant compared to the common sharing of blood or ideology as a criterion for community-consciousness.

This, also, means that a Hindese village is not a community in the strict sense of the term. The responsibility of Community Development workers in the rural areas of India is, first and foremost, to create a community consciousness among the villagefolk and then to promote community development.

4. Ecological and Sociological Groupings

Groups may be said to have had a sociological origin when they arise from the psycho-social needs and interests of persons and are held together by psycho-social interrelationships within a cultural context. Ecological groupings and sociological groupings in a number of cases arise from the perspective and point of view of the investigator. The family and the community may, for instance, be studied either from the standpoint of the interrelationships between the vital and spatial elements or from the standpoint of consciously cherished aims and objectives of members either of the family or of the community. In the former case, we are trying to discover the configuration of the network of relationships between human organisms and the human habitation; in the latter case, we are trying to study the configuration of socio-cultural relationships of persons engaged in the struggle for the achievement of status and for the realization of interests that brought them together in the first instance or that hold them together once they are thrown together. The labor union movement (the A.F.L. and the C.I.O.) arose from the economic struggle for higher wages and shorter hours, for security of job and steady employment; but the labor movement, including unionism, must be viewed as part of the sociological process. The same is true of the National Association of Manufacturers and the United States Chamber of Commerce. Sociological groups arise from the association of persons to realize certain cherished interests: (1) family and kinship groups; (2) employers' organizations, corporations, employees' organizations; (3) church groups; (4) educational organizations; (5) friendship groups, playgroups, civic clubs, women's clubs, the Townsend clubs; (6) political parties, the nation, the state, to mention but a few illustrative groupings in our society.

These six illustrations of sociological groupings are studied by sociologists as well as by other social scientists. The family and kinship groups are studied by anthropologists as well as by sociologists. Unions and corporations are studied by economists as well as by sociologists. Church groups are studied by theologians, church historians, census enumerators, as well as by sociologists. Educational organizations are studied by educators, historians of education, as well as by sociologists. The composition and functioning of friendship groups, playgroups, civic clubs, women's clubs and similar groups are most advantageously analyzed by sociologists in terms of primary and secondary group relationships or in terms of in-group and out-group relationships, or in terms of social movements. Political parties, the nation and the State are studied by political scientists as well as by sociologists. The study of social movements, regardless of whether they are correlated to economics or politics, falls within the purview of sociology—be it socialism or woman suffrage, prohibition or anti-prohibition, the Grange or the international cartel movement.

5. THE NATURAL HISTORY OF A SOCIAL MOVEMENT

Let us now briefly set forth the natural history of a social movement and its grouping from the sociological background:

First, there is a felt need for something which the existing order, the status quo, does not have. But the need, even when felt, is not enough to bring people together. The need must be transformed into an interest, into a consciously cherished aim. One or more persons should share the interest in common, and at least a few of them should be "concerned" enough to deem the accomplishment of the interest as vital to their very being. Need, interest, "concern" in the Quaker sense—this progressive psychological motivation accounts for the birth of any and every social movement.

Second, the concern is communicated to others with the aid of all possible techniques of communication present in the culture. The spoken word and the printed word, private conversations and public addresses, the radio and the TV, the telephone and the telegraph, postal service and personal travel—all these and many other devices are utilized by concerned persons to share their interest with the public, to "put across" their point of view, and to win new friends and advocates for the interest. Some concerned persons rely only on moral suasion and intellectual persuasion, on truthful facts and interpretations, fully confident that their "cause" is worthy enough in its own right to commend itself to all intelligent persons. Some others resort to intimidation and bribery, to fraud and distortion, to special pleading and theatricality. Whatever be the device utilized and the means employed, there is created a stir in society, an agitation. This stage is characterized by some groups in society as "educational," by others as "propaganda," depending upon whether they are in agreement or disagreement with the purpose of the agitation. In this context, there is a very thin line dividing "propaganda" and "education." The listener is apt to say that the speaker is engaged in "educational" work if he happens to agree with the speaker's point of view; and he is apt to refer to the speaker's work as "propaganda" if he happens to disagree with the speaker. (For a fuller treatment of propaganda and prejudice, see CHAPTER 23.)

Third, the agitation creates a growing consciousness of the particular need in cross-sections of society, in variegated groups large or small. The interest now is shared by a larger circle of persons, each of them related to scores of different groups.

Fourth, these persons, with varying backgrounds and drawn from different groups, organize themselves into a group, a functional group, an association, to promote the achievement of the interest. Ordinarily, the original set of concerned persons becomes the nucleus of the organization and provides leadership; sometimes new leadership is provided from among the newly won converts. A significant instance of the latter type is to be found in the role of Paul in the establishment of the Christian Church.

Fifth, the organized group plans concerted actions and "drives" in order to win more adherents for the "cause." The interest is now definitely converted into a cause. New converts continue to support the cause. Norms and rituals begin to develop and the cause and its psycho-social complex become fairly well known to the public at large. The "ideology" of the new group is on the way to a sharp definition.

Sixth, if by now the cause has not been won and if the original impulse for change continues to be shared dynamically by the adherents of the cause, the stage is set for the launching of a well defined movement with a statement of its goals and methods, in short, its ideology. The movement, if it touches significant aspects of life, will divide the reflecting public into two groups—those for and those against. Woman suffrage and socialism, prohibition and anti-prohibition, pacifism and militarism are instances of movements that affect the public vitally and therefore are either praised or denounced by significant groups in society. As soon as the cause attains the status of a movement, formal membership rules are worked out and enforced, and in-group controls set in. Should it outlast a "generation" without achieving its objective, the movement would be transformed into an institution, a collective mode of response within the total social process. The trade union movement, for instance, has become a definite institution in capitalist society.

Seventh, within the institutionalized movement there arises a bureaucracy which glorifies the original interest and remains impervious to social changes which might have rendered the founding fathers' interest invalid in the present context or which might have realized that interest in an oblique fashion. The best instances of rigid bureaucracy are to be found in the labor union movement—Caesar Petrillo and John L. Lewis. Sometimes, the bureaucracy of the institutionalized movement merely pays lip-service to the "cause" of the founding fathers and actually becomes an obstacle in the path of those who would carry on the work of the founding fathers. For apt illustrations of this process, one may study the history of reform movements within established religious traditions. Paying lip service to the reformer, members of the institutionalized reform movement often forget the reformer's original purposes. The Daughters of the American Revolution (D.A.R.) are today frightened by the very word "revolution," even though their ostensible purpose is to revere the memory of the revolutionary founders of the nation.

Eighth, when rigidity, inflexibility or reaction permeates an institution and is upheld by its bureaucracy, some persons either affiliated with the movement or outside of it feel a new need for change in the status quo and the whole cycle is repeated. The rise of various Protestant denominations within Christendom attests to this cyclic nature of social movements.

It may be noted, first, that if the original interest did not rest on a genuine need of the people, or a segment of the people, propaganda might succeed in floating the movement; but it would not become vital in the socio-cultural context—unless, of course, the propaganda were high-powered. Second, if the interest were not of a significant nature, i.e., if the interest did not call into question the fundamental categories of culture, the movement would merely enlist the loyalty of faddists and of the lunatic fringe in the population. Calendar reformers, foes of superstition concerning Friday the 13th, believers in spirit seances, etc., continue to operate as groups without much disturbance to the cultural process. Third, if the interest is realized in the stage of agitation, no social movement will be born. Fourth, if the interest is accomplished after it is organized, the movement will liquidate itself: the woman suffrage movement, for instance. And again, after the accomplishment of the interest, the movement may espouse a related cause—the League of Women Voters, for instance, or the Women's International League for Peace and Freedom. Or, sometimes, the movement may just continue in existence as a social grouping without any compelling interest or binding loyalty—just to perpetuate the memory of past achievements.

The number of interests human beings can develop is legion and the possible number of sociogenic groupings in society is also legion.

Thus arise sociological or sociogenic groups in society in contradistinction to ecological groups and groupings.

It may be pointed out that biogenic and ecological groups develop psycho-social interests and operate as sociological groups in society. Here we have been concerned with the sources from which groups arise.

6. A SUPPLEMENTARY NOTE ON IDEOLOGY

The ideology of a movement is more than its platform. The platform of a political party, for instance, sets forth on the intellectual plane principles and programs for action; while the ideology of a movement, in addition to principles and programs, contains an appeal to the sentiments and beliefs, to the aspirations and ideals, cherished by the group, i.e., by a section of the total population. The platform demonstrates the stand taken by the group on grand issues as well as on petty problems of the day; it may consist of a compilation of issues and problems. The ideology, on the other hand, is an integrated whole revolving around the core issue; petty problems of the day, it is understood, would be dealt with in the light of the general goals and methods enunciated by the founders and promoters of the movement. The various social isms—socialism, communism, capitalism—have ideologies, not platforms. Vital religion, too, has an ideology, not a platform; indeed, the ideology of religion is so thoroughly accepted by the people that it becomes part of the value system.

It must be emphasized that a "well defined movement with a statement of its goals and methods" may be viewed as an ideology only when it characterizes a section or segment of the total population. When the whole population becomes involved in it, the ideology is translated into the value system and becomes related to the ethos. Today Communist and Democratic ideologies are characteristic of significant sections of the total population of the world as well as of different nations. To the American people, democracy is more than an ideology—it is a value, a part of their ethos.

REFERENCES

1. JEROME DAVIS, so far as the present writer is aware, is the first sociologist who dealt with the origin, rise and career of social movements, both theoretically and concretely. See his *Contemporary Social Movements* (New York: The Century Co., 1930). For later discussions of social movements, see Harry W. Laidler's *Social-Economic Movements* (New York: Thomas Y. Crowell Co., 1947, 4th printing) and Rudolf Heberle's *Social Movements: An Introduction to Political Sociology* (New York: Appleton-Century-Crofts, 1951).

2. THOMAS D. ELIOT: *American Standards and Planes of Living.* Boston: Ginn and Co., 1931.

CHAPTER 12

PROCESSES OF GROUP COHESION

How do the members of the group cohere? How does group cohesion or solidarity develop? The members of the group cohere and group cohesion or solidarity is maintained by certain well-known sociological mechanisms. The entity of the group is preserved and its members are bound or held together: (1) by folkways, mores and institutions; (2) by esprit de corps and morale; (3) by collective representations.

1. How Folkways and Mores Arise

These sociological mechanisms are part of the non-material culture of man. The question before us now is: How do these traits of culture arise? Giddings's analysis of the struggle for existence gives us a partial clue in answering this question. (*Supra,* CHAPTER 5).

First, organisms, human or subhuman, must "struggle to react" to the objective conditions of the physical universe; second, organisms must "struggle for subsistence to repair the waste of reaction"; third, organisms must struggle for adaptation to the objective conditions of life; fourth, group-living organisms must struggle for adjustment or accommodation to one another.

The struggle to react is predicted upon the élan vital and upon faith, giving rise, in the case of man, to religion, to the esthetic life and to the scientific life.

The struggle for subsistence initiates and broadens into the economic life.

The struggle for adaptation widens into the ethical life of man. This struggle, at first, involves merely a conforming of human organisms—through variation, selection and inheritance—to the physical conditions under which they happen to live, i.e., to altitude, temperature, light or darkness, dryness or moisture, enemies, food

159

supply, and so on. Non-adaptation means extinction of the members of the species; hence adaptation is good inherently and the processes of adaptation are right. Whatever helps in the preservation, survival and thriving of the species is good and right; whatever thwarts these goals is bad and wrong. Subhuman species may not realize this fact in terms of thought-processes, but they all act on this premise. Man—collective man—not only realizes the validity of this thought but he also articulates it and thereby initiates the formulation of ethics.

Through the processes of adaptation, members of the human species, congregated and dwelling in any given region where food supplies were found, became increasingly alike. This biological struggle for adaptation, thus, provided the first two conditions of social life, namely, grouping and substantial resemblance.

Grouping and substantial resemblance gave rise, in the case of man, to a "consciousness of kind." This group of resembling creatures—human beings—wanted the same things, and, as often as not, tried to get them in like ways. Successful responses would be repeated over and over again, unconsciously, in order to ensure survival and growth values. In course of time these unconscious successful responses blossomed forth into "folkways."

Originally folkways came into being as unconscious collective modes of response or behavior that ensured the survival and growth of the group—of the folk. Today, we must define folkways as those unconscious collective modes of response or behavior that are *believed* to ensure the survival and/or growth of the group. No member of the group ever questions a folkway nor is anyone needed to enforce the practice of the folkway. The folkway is there and one just abides by it without giving any thought to it. The questioning of the folkway is as likely as the questioning of man walking on two legs. Loosely, custom is quite often referred to as a folkway, even though not necessarily related to the survival and growth of the group.

The emergence of folkways marks the beginning of culture. Folkways in a sense become the first instalment of capital in the accumulation and growth of culture. In their own right folkways begin to bind the members of the group together, and the emergence of the cultural imperative in the realm of the superorganic reinforces the process of group solidarity.

The folkway, let us say, dictated the use of bodily covering for protection against the inclemency of weather; there would inevitably be a wide variety of material to choose from for the making of the bodily covering: the bark of trees, the skin of animals, etc. If it is the bark of trees that is to be used, the question would arise concerning the type of tree or trees to be chosen. The same would apply to the skin of animals: which category of animals? Further, the animal that is killed or the animal that has died a natural death? Group solidarity would suffer if each member were permitted leeway to make his own choice. To remedy this situation, there would arise mores embodying value-judgments: the bark of such and such trees alone may be used, or the skin of such and such animals alone may be used. When a particular folkway becomes associated with value-judgments of right and wrong, the mores come into being. Mores may arise from the practice sanctioned by one of the groups in the population and rated by that group as being right, observed by other groups, later held as an ideal by other groups as well as by the original group and transformed into compulsive modes of behavior by society at large. In other words, mores come into being when value-judgment are imported into, or attached to, certain folkways.

The mores of the group provide a criterion for right and wrong and add another significant installment to the cultural capital. As Sumner has pointed out, the mores can make anything right for the time and place and the group concerned. Here we witness the emergence of collective subjective evaluation. "*O tempora, O mores!*" said the Latin poet. It must be emphasized, however, that while the mores of two cultures may and usually do differ from each other, the mores of each culture constitute a self-consistent system.

2. ANALYSIS BY BAGEHOT AND SUMNER

Walter Bagehot (1826-77) in his book *Physics and Politics* (1867-68) discussed the group-binding role of folkways and mores, without using those terms, under the term custom or the cake of

6

custom. Cooperation and likemindedness ("likeness"), requisite for group formation and cohesiveness, were "produced by one of the strongest yokes . . . and the most terrible tyrannies ever known among men—the authority of customary law!" (1, p. 213). Furthermore, "the fixed custom which public opinion alone tolerates is imposed on all minds, whether it suits them or not. . . . Only one check, one sole shield for life and good, is then possible—usage." (1, pp. 54–55.) Usage, i.e., collective repetitive action, is made still more sacrosanct by "the propensity of man to imitate what is before him" (1, p. 92). The "persecuting tendency" of the group ensures the survival and enforcement of the cake of custom. "National character is but a name for a collection of habits more or less universal. . . . In time an ingrained type is sure to be formed, and sure to be passed on," by sociological processes (1, p. 106).

William Graham Sumner (1840-1910), in his book *Folkways* (1906), analyzed the cake of custom into folkways and mores, pointing out that folkways ensured societal welfare and mores embodied value-judgments.

3. FOLKWAYS, MORES AND INSTITUTIONS COMPARED

Folkways and mores, alike, exert a constraining influence upon members of the group. But while the folkways are never susceptible to questioning, the mores or part of the mores may conceivably be questioned by those members of the group who find the constraint intolerable or who think a new procedure is more serviceable in holding the group together. To obviate the confusion, sure to be created by non-conformists, there arise institutions.

An institution may be defined as that collective mode of response or behavior which has outlasted a generation, which prescribes a well-defined way of doing things, and which binds the members of the group together into an association by means of rituals, symbols, procedures and officers possessed of regulatory power or *Danda*.

A clear-cut distinction must be made between folkways, mores and institutions. They all have certain features in common—for instance, folkways, mores and institutions are alike "collective modes of response or behavior," have all "outlasted a generation," all "prescribe a well-defined way of doing things," all "bind the members of the group together." But the practice of folkways and conformity to mores do not require the formation of an association, nor are they dependent upon the exercise of regulatory powers by designated officers; institutional modes of behavior are practised by an association and *enforced* by officers possessed of *Danda.*

The folkways outline the general frame of reference of a culture; the mores embody value-judgments within the framework of the folkways; the institutions create elaborate structural patterns for the promotion of the functions of the culture. The non-acceptance of folkways marks out one as an outlandish person, as a marginal man. The non-acceptance of mores marks out one as a stranger, as a rebel, as a fit object for ostracism, for persecution, for extermination, by the group. The institutions provide techniques including *Danda* for imposing comformity to the folkways and mores upon all members of the group.

Are not folkways and mores compulsive enough, and rational enough for a given time, to secure conformity? Why does human society need institutions? Folkways and mores are, to be sure, compulsive and rational enough for a given time, but without the emergence of institutional procedures every member of the group would have to be a policeman, ever on the alert for spotting non-conformists and for dealing with them appropriately in order that group solidarity might not be endangered. Far from securing group stability, each member of the group acting as a policeman over all others may easily lead to the disruption of the group. The elaborated, institutionalized procedures render it unnecessary for every member of the group to assume the responsibility of acting as a policeman over all others every moment of his life; and at the same time these procedures secure conformity to group standards through the instrumentality of *Danda,* wielded by designated officers.

4. DIFFERING FOLKWAYS, DIFFERING MORES

Let us take three different folkways of greeting among Euro-Americans, Chinese and Hindus. When two Chinese gentlemen meet, each greets the other by pressing his own two hands. The more elaborately ritualized the pressure the warmer the greeting. (Under the impact of the cult of modernism this folkway is on the way out, I am assured by Chinese students.) When two Hindu gentlemen meet, each folds his two hands and greets the other with the words *Namas-Té*—a bow to thee, i.e., to the divine in thee. When two Euro-Americans meet, they shake each other's right hand. The firmer the grip the warmer the greeting. I do not know the origin of these three different modes of greeting, but the practice of handshaking may be speculatively accounted for. The rude barbarians of Europe were in the habit of carrying weapons. The shaking of right hands implied that the weapon could not be used by either party against the other. This practice thus ensured and assured each other survival. Today we have travelled far from the rude days of European barbarism, but the practice of handshake has survived as part of our folkways, as a cultural lag. Among us today, in America, the handshake has been transformed into a measure of warm greeting.

Like the folkways, the mores, too, inject (import) into a given culture specific categories. The women of Bali are properly dressed when their breasts are entirely uncovered and their genital organ is properly covered from the waist to the thigh. An American woman, so dressed, and appearing at a formal dance, will not be permitted to become a member of the dancing group—our mores so dictate. Furthermore, our mores dictate that the swimming suit, however abbreviated or elongated, is fit for wear at a bathing beach; it is not fit for wear in a class room or at a public meeting held in Madison Square Garden in New York City.

5. THE INSTITUTION OF PROPERTY

Institutions make the most significant increment to cultural categories. Let us take the institution of property. The institution of property, whether common or private, rests upon a highly subtle concept. Actually, the property of a thing is its dharma—"what holds it together"—its highest possibility; in Greek terminology, the property of a thing is its entelechy, its implicit destiny. The property of the sun is to give out heat and light; of the moon to receive light and reflect it ; of the earth to give rise to organic forms of life ; of man to build the superorganic or the cultural world.

The institution of property is, however, very different from this philosophic concept of property. When we say we have property in the canoe, we mean we have the right to use the canoe in terms of its dharma or entelechy. Now the property—i.e., the inherent characteristic—of the canoe as such is to float in water ; man's property in the canoe means man's right to the use of the canoe as a floating conveyance. The property in a canoe may belong to a whole tribe— to the entire group as among the Trobriand Islanders—or to the builder, as among some other primitive tribes ; or to the one who by superior strength gets it from the original builder, or to the one who acquires it by due process of exchange or, as we say, by due process of law. In any of these situations, property in the canoe implies the right to use and to dispose of it in accordance with the folkways and mores of the group, i.e., in accordance with the cultural categories. And in every case, this right is enforced by officers, self-constituted or appointed or elected. The institution of private property, brought about by sophistication and high intellectual attainments, is a relatively late development in culture.

The cultural categories in America are tied up with the institution of private property both in production goods and in consumption goods. The cultural categories of a socialized society would deny private property in production goods while granting private property in consumption goods.

6. CULTURAL CATEGORIES AND CONSENSUS

Folkways, mores and institutions determine the categories of a culture ; once the cultural categories have emerged, folkways, mores and institutions cannot markedly deviate from the categories of culture. Culture and its categories, society and its culture must be studied simultaneously if we are to arrive at significant insights into the social process.

The momentous role of folkways, mores and institutions in promoting group cohesion or solidarity can never be overestimated. The members of the group, characterized though they be by a consciousness of kind, are at once competing and cooperating with one another for the good things of this life and for status ; they are held in line, so to say, by the constraints and prescribed procedures of folkways, mores and institutions. On the foundation of these cultural categories rests group solidarity.

Once group solidarity has been achieved in this fashion, there arise other sociological devices to make group solidarity more dynamic and to secure more effective group action. These devices are esprit de corps, morale, and collective representations.

7. Esprit de Corps, Morale, Collective Representations

Esprit de corps may be defined as group feeling; it is the intensification of in-group solidarity in a given situation. "The enthusiasm of the two sides in a football contest, the ecstasy of religious ceremonial, the fellowship of members of a fraternity, the brotherhood of a monastic band are all manifestations of group spirit" (2, p. 166). General Charles George ("Chinese") Gordon of the Royal Engineers exemplified esprit de corps in a marked fashion. Captured by the fanatical Mahdi at Khartum, Gordon was given the choice to renounce Christianity and embrace Islam, thereby saving his life, or be slain. Gordon, who had never identified himself with Christianity in any of its religious manifestations, was compelled by the crisis to realize that renunciation of Christianity would mean renunciation of his identification with the British people. The esprit de corps surged in his soldier-breast and he gave up his life in preference to giving up his identification with his group, his people.

Morale may be defined as group will (2, p. 166). Group will or collective will is always present in the social process, but in a crisis it comes to the fore. Morale-building activities are undertaken by all governments engaged in war. Speakers stress what *we* must do, even if it should involve minor discomforts to *us* as citizens for the time being. Victory gardens, victory war bonds, help win the war by driving 35 miles an hour, the Atlantic Charter—these and other slogans and activities were devised in America as morale-boosters. Mobilizing the community for winning the war was in the air everywhere in the land. The citizen felt he was part of the group will— on what he did depended the success of the war effort. Propaganda and education are valuable aids in morale-building, and no person or group can be wholly free from either propaganda or education, for the simple reason that they are both integral parts of the primary social process (see CHAPTER 23).

Collective representations may be defined, after Park and Burgess, as "the concepts which embody the objectives of group activity" (2, p. 166). But inasmuch as objectives are reciprocally related to available or possible procedures and instrumentalities, collective representations may be said to arise simultaneously with the existence of group life. The very constitution of the human mind rests upon the capacity for experiencing the world both in terms of precepts and concepts. While perceptions are private and individual, conceptions are always public and collective. Language, the repository of collective representations, is itself a social product. No one human mind gives rise to a collective representation; what each human mind does is to integrate collective representations as parts of its experience. The concept of the tribe or the nation, the concept of patriotism, the concept of the flag as a symbol of one's nation— these are all instances of collective representation, and they all call forth loyalty. *The cement of loyalty binds the members of the group together as no other cement does.*

Thus, the processes of group cohesion involve the binding or holding together of its members (1) by folkways, mores and institutions, (2) by esprit de corps and morale, (3) by collective representations. Furthermore, we have pointed out the interdependence between human behavior and cultural categories. Human behavior can be understood in terms of group affiliations, and group affiliations are a function of culture. Therefore, the study of group and culture involves an acceptance of the anthropologist's concept of culture-area. Within a given culture-area, such and such cultural categories prevail, such and such group affiliations are possible, such and such human behavior is to be found conditioned.

Society, the great group, or "a complex of groups" as defined by us, is held together by the same six mechanisms which make for group solidarity. Indeed, these mechanisms, especially four of them, namely, folkways, mores, institutions, and collective representations (including values), constitute the framework of society. It is not people as such that make society; it is *people functioning within the socio-cultural framework,* making for cohesiveness or solidarity, that constitutes society.

REFERENCES

1. WALTER BAGEHOT: *Physics and Politics.* New York: D. Appleton and Company, 1873. The articles originally appeared in *The London Economist* (1867-68).
2. ROBERT E. PARK and ERNEST W. BURGESS: *Introduction to the Science of Sociology,* 2nd ed. Chicago: University of Chicago Press, 1924; 8th impression, 1933.
3. WILLIAM G. SUMNER: *Folkways.* Boston: Ginn and Company, 1906.

CHAPTER 13

PROCESSES OF GROUP FUNCTIONING: ASSOCIATIONS AND INSTITUTIONS *

"THE number of interests human beings can develop is legion and the possible number of sociogenic (i.e., in contrast to genetic and ecological) groupings in society is also legion." (*Supra*, CHAPTER 11).

1. GROUP COTERMINOUS WITH INTEREST

We may now go a step farther and say that the term interest is coterminous, if not synonymous, with the term group. It would not be far-fetched to say that group equals interest or interest equals group, in terms of activity in the social context. Indeed, this very point was made as early as 1908 by one of Small's pupils, Arthur F. Bentley (2, pp. 211–12):

There is no group without its interest. An interest . . . is the equivalent of a group. We may also speak of an interest group or of a group interest, again merely for the sake of clearness in expression. The group and the interest are not separate. There exists only the one thing, that is, so many men bound together in or along the path of a certain activity. Sometimes we may be emphasizing the interest phase, sometimes the group phase, but if ever we push them too far apart we soon land in the barren wilderness. There may be a beyond-scientific question as to whether the interest is responsible for the existence of the group, or the group responsible for the existence of the interest. . . . What we actually find in this world, what we can observe and study, is interested men, nothing more and nothing less. This is our raw material. . . .

The term "interest group" is in a sense tautologous, since there can be no group without an interest, and no genuine interest without

* The material in this Chapter was presented as a Paper, entitled "A Redefinition of Institution as a Conceptual Tool," at the 48th Annual Meeting of the American Sociological Association, held in Berkeley, Calif., August 30-31, September 1, 1953.

a group. What is meant by the term "interest group" is simply that a given interest—say, the concerns and viewpoints, needs and aspirations of farmers as a class over against the industrial laborers as a class, or of laborers over against employers, etc.—serves as a focus for organizing a working team, an association, in order to achieve the specific objectives represented by the interest. The "interest group," in other words, or simply the group, is a functional association of its members for the accomplishment of a commonly shared interest (9, pp. 425–36). This statement is applicable to all groups —from the crowd to the corporation.

2. GROUP, ASSOCIATION, OPERATION

Association may be viewed either as a process or as a structure. The organization of an interest—let us say, providing a summer camp experience to children of underprivileged families living in urban slum areas—simply means the organization of the concerned individuals into a functional group, or into an association, for the realization of that interest. The progression is: 1. *Interest*←→ *Group,* 2. *Organization*←→*Association,* 3. *Operation of the Functional Group.*

A functional group may be defined as a group which functions (i.e., operates) as a unit and which has a function (i.e., a purpose) in the social order and which, therefore, by the fact of its operation and purposiveness enables its members to realize their interests. Such is the functional group—the association.

The processes of association will be dealt with in the SECOND BOOK. Here it may be pointed out, as it had been implied in our discussion of the natural history of a social movement, that in the rise of every association there is to be found either a nucleated person with consuming interest or a core group of nucleated persons. How does an association operate?

There are four essential elements involved in the operation of an association. To begin with, (*a*) a collective mode of response to the objective situation is developed, (*b*) this collective mode of behavior binds the members of the group together, (*c*) by means of rituals, symbols and procedures. Finally, (*d*) there emerge elected, appointed or self-constituted officers possessed of regulatory power or *Danda*. (*Danda*, a Sanskrit word, means the symbol of power as well as the power to regulate and to punish.) Now any outsider who shares this interest can become a member of the association—of this voluntary functional grouping—by subscribing to all four operational parts of the association, upon being accepted into membership.

3. Association, Corporation, Institution

Some associations achieve their objective and fold up; others continue to function from generation to generation and become an integral part of the social process. Such associations that have outlasted a generation may be called corporations, viewed structurally. But (1) *the collective modes of behavior* of associations or corporations, (2) outlasting a generation, (3) prescribing a well-defined way of doing things, (4) binding the members together, (5) by means of rituals, symbols and procedures, and (6) with officers wielding *Danda* are appropriately to be called institutions. *The addition of the second requirement, namely, "outlasting a generation," transforms the functional operation of an association into an institution.* The term generation is relative. For instance, the grade school generation covers eight years, while the high school or college generation spans only four years. The biological generation encompasses twenty-eight to thirty years. The generation for a professional association, such as The American Sociological Association or The American Economic Association or The Bar Association, may be conservatively placed at about six to ten years.

By this definition, then, a group of incorporators possessed of a "birth certificate" for a non-profit organization or "corporation" called a college, do not launch an institution from the blue skies in the midst of a community. Nor does the college, on the first day or in the first year of its operation, become a full-blown institution. Until a generation passes, that is to say, until sufficient time elapses for relationship to be established and structuralized both within the college community and with the outside world, the college functions merely as an association. After the passing of a generation, the college, that is to say, its operational part, becomes an institution;

and the college in terms of its operator part—i.e., contemporary students, faculty, administration, alumni—remains as an association. In course of time some parts of this association—the Board of Trustees, for example—are bound to become corporations, sociologically viewed. After a generation the college association itself may be viewed as a sociological corporation.

4. Folkways, Mores, and Institutions

In the wide range of sociological literature, no term has been more abused and ill-used than the term institution. The layman's conception of an institution embraces a building where certain activities are carried on. Some eminent sociologists and anthropologists confuse an institution with the group of people associated with the operation of it. Furthermore, the confusion is made worse confounded by the mixing up of primary and secondary institutions. Hence an endeavor was made in the preceding chapter to present a consistent theoretical framework within which the institutional setup of any society could be studied. There we distinguished clearly between folkways, mores, and institutions, belonging as they do to the same category in that they are all collective modes of response. Furthermore, we pointed out that their structural and operational differences set them off one from another.

Among the pioneers who have analyzed and described institutions, we must mention the noted anthropologists of Europe and of America. While their descriptive material is valid, the conceptual tool devised by them is inadequate. In America, the problem has been explored by Sumner, Park and Burgess, Chapin, Malinowski, and MacIver. All of these pioneers have valuable suggestions to offer in the interpretation and analysis of institutions. But none of them has emphasized the point that institutions are, fundamentally, of the nature of folkways and mores, in that they are collective modes of response.

5. Sumner's Definition of Istitution

Many anthropologists and students of cultures have described institutions without attempting a formal definition. We are indebted to Sumner not only for the concepts, folkways and mores, but also for his pioneer approach at a formal definition of institution. An institution, according to Sumner, embodies a concept and a structure —i.e., the objective to be achieved and the method of achieving the objective. Institutions, said Sumner, may be either crescive or enacted —that is to say, they may either grow up by the same processes of natural evolution as do the folkways and mores, monogamy, for instance; or they may be developed by deliberate choice and action, state sanction for marriage in our day, for instance.

Park and Burgess, in their trail-blazing volume, not only gathered up all previous valid sociological theories but also made their own rich contributions to the evolving framework of sociological orientation. Here is their discussion of Sumner's definition of an institution as consisting of a concept and a structure (8, pp. 796–97):

The concept defines the purpose, interest, or function of the institution. The structure embodies the idea of the institution and furnishes the instrumentalities through which the idea is put into action. The process by which purposes, whether they are individual or collective, are embodied in structures is a continuous one. But the structures thus formed are not physical, at least not entirely so. Structure, in the sense that Sumner uses the term, belongs, as he says, to a category of its own. "It is a category in which custom produces continuity, coherence, and consistency, so that the word 'structure' may properly be applied to the fabric of relations and prescribed positions with which functions are permanently connected." Just as every individual member of a community participates in the process by which custom and public opinion are made, so also he participates in the creation of the structure, that "cake of custom" which, when it embodies a definite social function, we call an institution.

Institutions may be created just as laws are enacted; but only when a social situation exists to which they correspond, will they become operative and effective. Institutions, like laws, rest upon the mores and are supported by public opinion. Otherwise they remain mere paper projects . . . that perform no real function.

The pioneer analyses of folkways, mores and institutions by Bagehot (CHAPTER 12), Sumner, and Park and Burgess serve as a stepping-stone for our own approach to institution.

6. DERIVATION OF INSTITUTIONS FROM ORIGINAL HUMAN NATURE

Sociogenic groups arise, as already pointed out, from a commonly shared interest. Interest itself is based on a need—biological, psychological, sociological—a need that has been consciously thought about and transformed into a cherished aim. We may then affirm: No interest no group; given an interest there is bound to be a group; given complementary interests, there will be cooperative, accommodative groups in society; given conflicting interests, there will be in society opposing groups, each striving for the realization of its interest—which is the same thing as to say, each striving for mastery. (1, *passim*)

Interest as the atom in social science was first developed by Gumplowicz (1838-1909) and Ratzenhoper (1842-1904) in Central Europe, and imported into American sociology by Albion W. Small (1854-1926). Small's definition of interest, though worded abstractly, agrees with our definition: namely, that *interest is a need transformed into a consciously cherished aim.* Here is Small's definition: "In general an interest is an unsatisfied capacity, corresponding to an unrealized condition, and it is predisposition to such rearrangements as would tend to realize the indicated condition . . . . The whole life-process . . . is at last the process of developing, adjusting, and satisfying interests" (9, p. 433).

From this standpoint, then, the functioning of groups in society may be best understood in terms of the fundamental interests of man, of collective man. Inasmuch as human interests are derived from human needs, an investigation of the basic needs—and expressions—of common-human nature may answer our problem. Here is a serviceable schema (p. 176) originally worked out by the present writer in 1926, in his Master's thesis, *Group Concepts, Oriental and Occidental,* at Northwestern University, under Professor Thomas D. Eliot (7, pp. 203–05).

The basic pattern of this schema was worked out by me in 1926, but the present schema represents the refinements I have been able to make over a period of years. No discussion of institutions has been quite satisfactory. Sumner's and Chapin's discussions come closest to being satisfactory. The present schema has the virtue of consistency and is competent to answer any and all questions regarding a given collective mode of behavior or response and positively to identify whether or not it is an institution.

Let us illustrate the point by a few examples. The gait of the Americans is largely uniform when compared to the gait of the Chinese. Even though the two gaits are collective modes of response, have been formalized and ritualized and have outlasted a generation, they are not institutions because officers to enforce them are not to be found. On the whole, Americans get intoxicated quicker and on less liquor than do Europeans—collective modes of response, etc., etc., but not institutions. On the other hand, the American system of working one's way through college is definitely an institution of the economic order, of the business world. Here are to be found all the elements of an institution according to our definition : (a) a collective mode of response or behavior, (b) which has outlasted a generation, (c) which prescribes a well-defined way of doing things, (d) and which binds the members of the group—employer-employee—together into an association (e) by means of rituals, symbols, procedures, i.e., hours of work, etc., (f) and officers possessed of regulatory power or *Danda*—the employer usually, but the State as well when a contract is broken, or the rituals, symbols and/or procedures are violated. Likewise, the potlatch is an institution among the Kwakiutl. In devious ways it serves as a mechanism for exchange and trade, while directly it acts as a mechanism for the preservation of rank and status in the social hierarchy.

For a social phenomenon to be called an instituiton all six requirements of the definition must be satisfied, not just one or two, or even any four or five. The misuse of the term institution even in *The Encyclopedia of Social Sciences* stems from lack of rigorous insistence upon all six parts of the definition. There is something soothing about the word which leads the layman to dignify an old janitor on the college campus as an institution. Even if it be conceded that the janitor, having outlived several college generations, in a sense satisfied most of the requirements of our definition, he cannot be called an institution simply because *he* is *not* a collective

CHART 8

THE DERIVATION OF INSTITUTIONS FROM ORIGINAL HUMAN NATURE

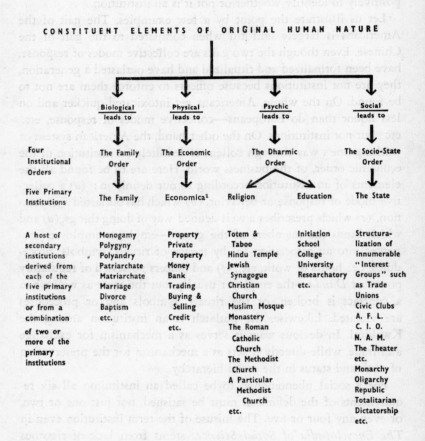

CONSTITUENT ELEMENTS OF ORIGINAL HUMAN NATURE				
Biological leads to	Physical leads to	Psychic leads to		Social leads to
Four Institutional Orders The Family Order	The Economic Order	The Dharmic Order		The Socio-State Order
Five Primary Institutions The Family	Economica[1]	Religion	Education	The State
A host of secondary institutions derived from each of the five primary institutions or from a combination of two or more of the primary institutions	Monogamy Polygyny Polyandry Patriarchate Matriarchate Marriage Divorce Baptism etc.	Property Private Property Money Bank Trading Buying & Selling Credit etc.	Totem & Taboo Hindu Temple Jewish Synagogue Christian Church Muslim Mosque Monastery The Roman Catholic Church The Methodist Church A Particular Methodist Church etc.	Initiation School College University Researchatory etc.	Structuralization of innumerable "Interest Groups" such as Trade Unions Civic Clubs A. F. L. C. I. O. N. A. M. The Theater etc. Monarchy Oligarchy Republic Totalitarian Dictatorship etc.

[1] Professor F. Stuart Chapin designated this primary institution as "business", meaning by that term not business in contradistinction to agriculture or labor or manufacture but essentially what we mean to convey by the term "economica", viz., the structured pattern of securing a livelihood. Chapin's term business, as interpreted by him, may be used synonymously with our term economica, and we have used the two terms interchangeably in the text.

mode of response. He is a responder, not a response. Janitoring in American culture is an institution and the janitor's union is an association or a corporation. Similarly, Emerson was on the right track when he spoke of an institution as being the lengthened shadow of an individual—but not precise enough. Let us say Hull House in Chicago is the lengthened shadow of Jane Addams. Even so, the core of Hull House as an institution is to be found in its being a collective mode of response, etc., not in the fact that Jane Addams founded it and guided its destiny for over a generation. An understanding of Jane Addams will help us understand Hull House better, and a knowledge of Hull House will throw light upon Jane Addams. But the institution of Hull House is much more than merely the lengthened shadow of Jane Addams.

We can avoid all confusion and misunderstanding in the use of the term institution by the simple device of separating the particular species of collective mode of response (institution) from its correlate, the group of people who engage in that mode of response, namely, the association or the corporation as the case may be:

$$Institution \longleftrightarrow Association \; or \; Corporation$$

Without the association to operate it there can be no institution.

7. THE FOUR INSTITUTIONAL ORDERS

Let us see how the four institutional orders—the family order, the economic order, the dharmic order, the socio-state order—stand up under rigorous scrutiny. The point of departure for this discussion is man's past of long ago when there was little cultural accumulation.

To begin with, the family order involves (a) a collective mode of response, namely, getting together of male and female, mating, begetting of children, rearing of children, etc.; (b) this collective mode of response or behavior has certainly outlasted a generation; (c) it binds the members of the group together, father-mother-and-children-and-kinsfolk, (d) by means of rituals, symbols and procedures. Finally, (e) the officers possessed of regulatory power or *Danda* are present; but they are not human, they are natural forces —hence the term institutional order rather than institution. If male and female did not get together and did not indulge in the collective mode of behavior comprising, mating, begetting progeny, rearing children, there would be no human beings left after a while, either as individuals or as groups, to perpetuate the family order. Thus all the requirements of our definition are met except that the officers wielding *Danda* are natural forces, not human beings; hence *there is validity in referring to the family order as one of the four institutional orders.* An institutional order is simply an order (comprising modes of behavior) instituted or foreordained by nature.

Now let us take the economic order. This institutional order involves (*a*) the collective mode of response—securing of food, clothing and shelter; (*b*) this collective behavior has certainly outlasted a generation; (*c*) it binds together the members of the group—the horde, the clan, the tribe—(*d*) by means of rituals, symbols and procedures. Again, (*e*) the officers wielding *Danda* are natural forces. If the group did not indulge in this collective behavior, namely, the securing of food, clothing and shelter, nature would make short shrift of them.

Third, the Dharmic Order involves (*a*) the collective behavior of participation and communication, of learning and teaching, of preserving the lore of the past and adding to it; (*b*) this collective behavior, outlasting a generation, (*c*) binds the members of the group together (*d*) by rituals, symbols and procedures. Again (*e*) the officers wielding *Danda* are natural forces. If the group did not indulge in this collective behavior, namely, participation and communication, learning and teaching, conserving and creating, man's dominance over birds and beasts would be at an end.

Fourth, the socio-state order involves (*a*) the collective behavior of leadership and followership, of freedom under rules and authority, of cooperative and corporative activity, (*b*) outlasting a generation, (*c*) binding the members of the group together (*d*) by rituals, symbols and procedures. Again, (*e*) the officers wielding *Danda* are natural forces. If the group did not indulge in this collective behavior, namely, cooperative and corporative action under authority and rules, internal tensions and conflicts would render the group an easy prey to another group or to the onslaughts of birds and beasts.

It is safe to assume that our savage ancestors in the dim, dim past had by the trial-and-error method developed certain folkways and mores and were in possession of the fundamental framework of culture comprising the family order, the economic order, the dharmic order, the socio-state order.

8. THE FIVE PRIMARY INSTITUTIONS

With the accumulation of culture, five basic or primary institutions emerged: family, economica, religion, education, state. The process of the emergence of the five primary institutions carried with it a peculiar and far-reaching change, namely, an extension of the gradual sway of *Danda* or regulatory power by the State over the other four primary institutions as well as over "citizens." While folkways, mores and institutional patterns still carried weight, the State would now exert its authority by laws and regulations. Sometimes folkways and mores might be incorporated into laws; sometimes new dictates might be enacted into law in harmony with the cultural categories of the group. In course of time, "officers possessed of regulatory power or Danda" might as well be empowered by the State as by the self-governing association itself. Today the primary institution of the family is being circumscribed and regulated by the State in a score of ways. Secondary institutions, such as marriage, divorce, adoption, share the same fate. The sway of state authority has, similarly, been extended to economica or "business," to education, and to religion. Notice: it is the State that guarantees freedom of religion; and it is the State that exempts the property of a religious body from taxation.

It is evident that the five primary institutions fully satisfy all the requirements of our definition of institution. That secondary institutions would fulfill all the requirements of our definition goes without saying.

9. MACIVER'S CORRELATION BETWEEN ASSOCIATION AND INSTITUTION

So far as the present writer's knowledge goes, among the English-speaking writers R. M. MacIver was the first one to distinguish between association and institution and to correlate the two. If only we could somehow eliminate the concept *association as process* by substituting for it some such word as groupation or groupalization, or simply sociation, most of our difficulties would vanish instantaneously. It is to MacIver's credit that he steadfastly held on to the functional concept of association and was thus able to correlate it to institution in his masterly work, *Community: A Sociological Study* (1917). Here are three significant passages from MacIver's discussion of the relation between an association and an institution (5, pp. 23–27):

An association is an organization of social beings (or a body of social beings *as organized*) for the pursuit of some common interest or interests. It is a determinate social unity built upon common purposes. Every end which men seek is more easily attained for all when all whom it concerns unite to seek it, when all cooperate in seeking it. Thus you may have an association corresponding to every possible interest of social beings. Community bubbles into associations permanent and transient . . . the enormous number of associations of every kind, political, economic, religious, educational, scientific, artistic, literary, recreative, philanthropic, professional. . . .

A community is a focus of social life, the common living of social beings; an association is an organization of social life, definitely established for the pursuit of one or more common interests. An association is partial, a community is integral. The members of one association may be members of many other and distinct associations. Within a community there may exist not only numerous associations, but also antagonistic associations. . . . Community is something wider and freer than even the greatest associations; it is the greater common life out of which associations rise, into which associations bring order, but which associations never completely fulfill. If we reflect, we perceive at once that there is a vast difference between the living together of men which makes a village or city or country on the one hand, and the association of men in a church or trade union—or even . . . in a state—on the other. . . .

To a permanent purpose there always answers, in the nature of things, a permanent association. . . . (Indeed) Church and State . . . rest on purposes more lasting than any individuals, and are thus maintained through periods of time infinitely larger than the life-periods of individuals. Insofar as they are purposes necessary to the fulfillment of life, they create associations as immortal as life (i.e., corporations sociologically conceived—H.T.M.).

10. CHAPIN'S FOUR-TYPE PARTS OF THE STRUCTURE OF PRIMARY INSTITUTIONS

Sumner had supplemented his definition of an institution as embodying a concept and a structure with the further elaboration that an institution had four parts:

(1) Personnel
(2) Equipment
(3) Organization
(4) Ritual

Professor Chapin's analysis of an institution into four-type parts is the most original and serviceable contribution to sociology since Sumner's pioneering contributions in this field. Carrying forward Sumner's analysis of the structure of an institution as consisting of (*a*) personnel, (*b*) equipment, (*c*) organization, and (*d*) ritual, Professor Chapin suggests the following four-type parts as being integral to the structure of a given institution (3, p. 16):

(1) Attitudes and Behavior Patterns
(2) Symbolic Culture Traits or "Symbols"
(3) Utilitarian Culture Traits (Real Property)
(4) Code of Oral or Written Specifications

Professor Chapin illustrates these type parts with reference to four primary institutions. In conformity with our frame of reference, we shall rearrange the order in Chapin's chart and also include education (omitted by him)—see page 182.

This analysis by Chapin has the merit of consistency and objectivity. While the description of type parts is in terms of contemporary American culture, the analysis would hold good for any and every culture—with modifications in detail dictated by the specific categories of a given culture. Chapin's conceptual scheme is likewise useful in that it identifies five *major* social institutions, which match

CHART 9

TYPE PARTS OF THE STRUCTURE OF PRIMARY INSTITUTIONS[1]

Four-Type Parts	Family	Business	Religion (Church)	Education (School)	State
I. Attitudes and behavior patterns	Affection Love Loyalty Respect	Workmanship Thrift Cooperation Loyalty	Reverence Loyalty Fear Devotion	Learning Teaching Communication Participation Loyalty	Subordination Cooperativeness Fear Obedience
II. Symbolic culture traits, "symbols"	Marriage Ring, Crest Coat of Arms Heirloom	Trade-mark, Patent sign Emblem	Cross Ikon Shrine Altar	Certificate Pennants School Colors School Songs	Flag Seal Emblem Anthem
III. Utilitarian Culture traits (real property)	Home Dwelling Furniture	Shop Store Factory Office	Church Edifice Cathedral Temple	School building Class-room equipment Gymnasium Playground	Public buildings Public works
IV. Code of oral or written specifications	Marriage license Will Genealogy Mores	Contracts Licenses Franchises Articles of Incorporation	Creed Doctrine Bible Hymn	State law Charter Local Autonomy of School District	Charter Constitution Treaties Laws Ordinances

182

[1] F. Stuart Chapin: *Contemporary Social Institutions*, p. 16. New York: Harper and Brothers, 1935. Chapin's term is "Major Social Institutions," and he left out Education from the table; likewise his order was: Family, Church, Government, Business.

our five Primary Institutions. Inferentially, Chapin's anlaysis implies the existence of secondary institutions. But it is difficult to see how this four-type-part analysis of the structure of primary institutions could apply to secondary institutions, such as the institution of property, for example.

11. A CRITIQUE OF MALINOWSKI'S DEFINITION OF INSTITUTION

Malinowski, the famous cultural anthropologist, likewise, analyzed the institution into four constituent elements, though of a different nature (6, pp. 162–67):

(1) Activities
(2) Personnel
(3) "Charter" and Norms
(4) Material Apparatus

An institution, according to Malinowski, will have to comprise: (1) a system of concerted and specialized activities, (2) carried on by an organized, specially designated group of people, (3) who operate under a system of values, (4) which are put into effect through material apparatus. Like Chapin's, this definition by Malinowski is admirable and serviceable. If in the above description by Malinowski, the word material were to be interpreted as or replaced by "enforcing" or "regulatory," Malinowski's definition would almost wholly coincide with the one we have given. The word material is, however, used in a gross sense.

Malinowski classified institutions into the following categories: the family, the neighborhood, the state (i.e., the political organization), the nation (i.e., the culturally integrated unit), occupational and professional groups, free (i.e., voluntary) associations, and the groups based on status, race, and age. Concerning the last category, it is pointed out that in certain societies age, race, rank, caste, and class severally form bases for organization that becomes institutionalized. Such a classification of institutions is unsatisfactory, first, because it mixes up the dimensions of categories; and, second, because it does violence to Malinowski's own definition, if I understand him aright, that the institution is basically, as we have stressed time and again, a mode of collective behavior, not a group of people. To speak of an occupational group, for instance, as an institution is to commit lese-majeste against the conceptual framework of sociology.

How defective the conceptual framework has been thus far may be gathered from the fact that the eminent anthropologist Robert H. Lowie, in his book *Social Organization* (1948), mixes up primary with secondary institutions and lumps them together. To quote Lowie: "The most important institutions sociologically are probably kinship, marriage, law, property, religion, and education." (4, p. 4.)

12. ANALYSIS OF CHURCH AND PROPERTY AS INSTITUTIONS

In terms of our frame of reference, the correlation between an association and an institution may be picturesquely brought out by an analogy. If we were to compare the institution to railroad tracks, then the swiftly running train would be analogous to the association. The institution provides procedures, it requires an association to utilize the procedures. The four institutional orders come into being by the fact of human aggregation and association. The five primary institutions and a host of secondary institutions, either crescive or enacted, emerge as part of the continuing process of human aggregation and association within a cultural framework, continuously expanding and enriching as a result of cultural accumulations.

In terms of our thesis, namely, the correlation between an institution and an association, let us analyze two institutions of our society, church and property, from the standpoint of their emergence, growth and functioning in our day.

The Christian Church as an institution exists not because Jesus preached the gospel of the Kingdom of God on earth to be realized by love, but because his disciples, the Apostles, decided to band themselves together into an association to propagate the message of Jesus. This tiny association got reinforcement from the dynamic Saul turned into Paul. New members joined the association through the preachings of the Apostles, especially Paul. Members of the association began to be despised as "Christians" and persecuted as rebels against the Roman State. Thriving on persecution, the association won new converts in Asia Minor, in Egypt, in Greece, and in Rome. By the time all the original members of the association passed away, the converts under new leaders carried on the work of propagating the gospel of Christ. And this went on from generation to generation in spite of persecution by the Roman State until the year 323 A.D., when Constantine, the Emperor of Rome, became a convert to Christianity, i.e., a new member of the association dedicated to propagating the teachings of Christ. Under Imperial patronage, the symbol of the cross was brought up from the catacombs into the open air; church buildings began to rise; a standard form of liturgy began to emerge; new rituals and new officers evolved—all cherishing the memory of Jesus, glorifying the activities of past associations, creating a sense of continuity from Jesus, through the Apostles, the various associations, down to the establishment of the headship of the Church at Rome. Today the institution of the Christian Church persists only because there are associations of interested persons in the contemporary world to promote the gospel of Christ in their own lives and in the lives of others. Once the institution of the Christian Church arose in the Occident, it became one of the categories of Occidental culture, as binding upon the Occidental group as that group's folkways and mores.

The correlation between institution and association is evident in the case of the Christian Church. What sort of association is correlated, say, to the institution of property?

Property is the intangible right to the use and disposal of a good, material or non-material, in which ownership rights are affirmed for the group, or a member or a set of members of the group, by the folkways and mores. This intangible right is enforced by collectively devised procedures and rituals. The institution of property emerges when the group acts, so to say, as a committee of the whole, as an association, accepting the dictates of the tribal chief, the medicineman, the warrior group, the autocratic monarch, or the parliamentary assembly. The State as an association of citizens, in other words, guarantees the institution of property. Once the institution of property arises, it becomes one of the categories of culture, as binding upon the group as are the folkways and mores.

In conclusion, then, no institution can function without an association.

13. SUMMARY

Our frame of reference obviates unnecessary confusion. Let us, then, summarize our point of view. Ultimately, all the institutions in society may be traced to original human nature, the descending series being: secondary institution, usually referred to merely as institution; primary institution, institutional order, human nature, original nature.

CHART 10

THE ASCENDING-DESCENDING SERIES CONNECTING ORIGINAL NATURE WITH INSTITUTIONS

↓	Secondary Institutions	↑
↓	Primary Institutions	↑
↓	Institutional Orders	↑
↓	Human Nature	↑
↓	Original Nature	↑

Every institution consists of six parts: (1) a collective mode of response, (2) that has outlasted a generation, (3) prescribing a well-defined way of doing things, (4) binding the members of the group together into an association, (5) by means of rituals, symbols, procedures, and (6) with officers wielding *Danda*. In the case of the four institutional orders, the officers wielding *Danda* are natural forces;

in the case of the five primary institutions and the host of derivative institutions, the officers wielding *Danda* are human.

Finally, anticipating discussion in BOOK III, we may point out that while an institution, either created by deliberate choice or evolved crescively, aims to fulfill the dominant purpose, interest and need, it nevertheless may and does subserve auxiliary purposes, needs and interests. The primary purpose of the family, for instance, is the perpetuation of the species through procreation; but precisely because it is operated by human beings, the family as an institution also subserves other purposes, interests, and needs: educational, religious, recreational, economic, emotional, etc. Even so, the most serviceable way to study an institution is to discover its dominant purpose or purposes as defined by the cultural context and then to analyze it into its component parts.

REFERENCES

1. HARRY ELMER BARNES : *Sociology and Political Theory*. New York: Alfred A. Knopf, 1924.
2. ARTHUR F. BENTLEY: *The Process of Government*: *A Study of Social Pressures*. Chicago: University of Chicago Press, 1908.
3. F. STUART CHAPIN: *Contemporary American Institutions*. New York: Harper and Brothers, 1935.
4. ROBERT H. LOWIE: *Social Organization*. New York: Rinehart & Co., 1948.
5. R. M. MACIVER: *Community*: *A Sociological Study*. New York: Macmillan, 1931. (London edition, Macmillan, 1917).
6. BRONISLAW MALINOWSKI: *A Scientific Study of Culture and Other Essays*. Chapel Hill: University of North Carolina Press, 1944. *Cf.* "Culture," *Encyclopedia of Social Sciences*.
7. HARIDAS T. MUZUMDAR: *Group Concepts, Oriental and Occidental*. Unpublished Master's Thesis, Evanston, Illinois: Northwestern University, 1926.
8. ROBERT E. PARK and ERNEST W. BURGESS: *Introduction to the Science of Sociology*, 2nd ed. Chicago: The University of Chicago Press, 1924; 8th impression, 1933.
9. ALBION W. SMALL: *General Sociology*. Chicago: University of Chicago Press, 1905.
10. WILLIAM GRAHAM SUMNER: *Folkways*. Boston: Ginn & Co., 1906.

CHAPTER 14

CLASS GROUPINGS

HAVING discussed how groups originate, cohere and function, we may now address ourselves to an analysis of four significant groupings in the modern world—(1) the class group, (2) the caste group, (3) the race group, and (4) the nation or the national group. In this chapter and the succeeding one we shall discuss classes and castes, and in the next two chapters races and nations.

1. DEFINITIONS OF CASTE AND CLASS

In terms of our system of classification, how do we locate classes and castes? Both these groups, the class and the caste, have their origin in the sociological setting and function dynamically in the social process. The class functions as one of the publics in society, unless deliberately organized into an association, such as the Workingmen's Association, while the caste functions as one of the many corporations in the social order. Both class and caste are horizontal groups, and both define the rank and position of the person in the social hierarchy. Both involve stratification, i.e., the concept of the higher and lower, or upper and lower.

When classes cease to be open and become rigid, we have the emergence of caste groupings in society. Caste groupings may be said to exist in society when there is a prohibition among groups in regard to the sharing of *roti* (bread) and *betty* (daughter). When breaking of bread together and intermarriage between groups are not permissible, there we have the caste structure in society. India is the classic example of a caste organization of society, even though traces of caste are to be found in almost every country and society. The Japanese and the Ainus, the Chinese Mandarin and the rikshawman, the English classes and masses, the American whites and colored, the "Aryan" German and the Jew, the Slavic Pole and the Jew, the Greek and the barbarian, the Roman and the barbarian, the Jew and the Gentile, the Christian and the pagan, the believing Muslim and the "infidel"—these dichotomous categories savor of the nature of caste.

With social relationships having been structuralized over a long period of time and with status determined by birth in a hereditary hierarchy, caste groupings function in society on the basis of live and let live. Thus castes are accommodation groups. But when a hereditary status is brought into question, when a person or a group of persons becomes unreconciled to the assigned status, the caste structure of society becomes split wide open and we witness the emergence of classes which function as conflict groups. Thus the unwillingness of the Negro in American society to accept the status assigned by traditional patterns, especially in the South, is transforming Southern caste society into a class society. Whites and colored in the South today are facing each other, with the old frame of reference challenged by the underprivileged Negro.

The Negroes are no longer content with their classification and status as a horizontal group. They are aspiring to be, and to be considered, a vertical group with a hierarchy of their own. The professional Negro has more in common with the professional white than with the Negro domestic servant. The Negro scientist, Dr. George Washington Carver (1864-1943), had more in common with his white colleagues than with the Negro share-cropper.

A new realignment is appearing before our eyes, calling into question old values and bringing into being new values. This period of transvaluation of values is inevitably fraught with tensions and conflicts. Be that as it may, the end in sight is clear: the substitution of class patterns of behavior for caste patterns of behavior.

A vital democracy abhors the caste structure of society. Witness the attempt of the Republic of India not to enumerate castes for its 1951 census but to enumerate occupational groups. Within the democratic framework, classes arrive at a nice balance—the balance of the rope in a tug of war, so to say. Such a tug of war between classes is preferable to caste society on the one hand and to a so-called classless society on the other. The quest for a classless society is a mirage. Both on theoretical and practical grounds, the existence of a classless society is an impossibility. Every attempt to submerge classes leads to the emergence of a mass society dominated by totalitarian dictatorship. In Soviet Russia striving to achieve a classless society, we witness on the one hand rule by the elite class at the top and mass-mindedness at the bottom layer on the other. Democracy, to be meaningful, must permit the emergence, organization and functioning of voluntary and semi-voluntary groups and associations; it must set forth rules for the minimization of conflict between classes.

What, then, are classes? A class in logic is an aggregation of units with common characteristics. In sociology, classes are sections of the population with differential access to the rights and privileges as well as to the goods and services available in a community. Thus violin-players of this country—or of the whole world, for that matter—constitute a class, markedly different from the class of professors, or from the subclass, professors of sociology. I cannot and do not choose to belong to the class of violin-players, because by background, training and temperament I am incapable of inducing the violin to do its tricks. I admire the class of violin-players but am satisfied with my affiliation to the class of professors.

Between the class of violin-players and the class of professors there may emerge a wholesome rivalry as to who may render better service to the community. Or, there may emerge a jealousy that in the matter of prestige, remuneration and utility of services rendered, the class of violin-players is overrated and the class of professors underrated. But there need be no class warfare between the two.

It is necessary to formulate such a broad conception of class, especially because most discussions of class are based upon economic considerations alone. Classifications of groups on the basis of income are important, but they do not exhaust the field.

Membership in a class means location of the member's rank and position both within the class and with reference to other classes. This location of rank and position is technically called status, as pointed out by Ralph Linton. "Behavior associated with a particular status is called by the sociologist a role. A person's role in the group is the dynamic aspect of his status. Since status is position in a group, a person has as many statuses as he has group affiliations. . . . (But) when we speak about a man's social status, we ordinarily make not a generalization but a selection. We have in mind one status in particular: his social class status. . . . Class status seems to overshadow all other kinds of status. . . . A social class is the aggregate of persons having essentially the same social status in a given society. . . . The fundamental attribute of a social class is thus its social position of superiority or inferiority to other social classes. The arrangement is much like that of the college with its freshman, sophomore, junior and senior classes." (16, pp. 307–09)

All societies, primitive or civilized, with the exception of the most underdeveloped, such as food-gathering tribes (see *infra*, p. 210), we know anything about have had classes; not all of them, however, assign to a class "its social position of superiority or inferiority to other classes" on the basis of material wealth and power. Hindu society, for instance, assigns the topmost rank to the Brahmins, the class—rather caste—of teachers-priests. The functions of teaching and religious ministration were considered most valuable in society and their performers as a class were assigned the highest position. The Kshattriyas, soldiers-administrators, were assigned the second highest position, because the function of maintaining law, order and good government was deemed the next most important function in society. The Vaishyas, agriculturists-craftsmen-merchants-manufacturers, were third in the hierarchy even though they might have more wealth. Last came the Shudras, servants. Such a functional class hierarchy conforms neither to the premises nor to the conclusions of the class sociology of Marxism.

2. PLANES AND STANDARDS OF LIVING

In the Western world, dominated by a money economy, class affiliation is determined by the income of the person and his family. On this basis, there are roughly three classes in our society: the upper class, the middle class, the lower class. W. Lloyd Warner (21, *passim*) has refined these categories into: upper-upper, lower-upper; upper-middle, lower-middle; upper-lower, lower-lower. Affiliation to any one of these class groupings is determined, sociologically if not psychologically, by the plane of living; and such affiliation determines one's standard of living.

The standard of living is a relative concept—relative to time and place. What may be considered minimum requirements for decent living in our Southland with its warm climate may be rated substandard in the North with its cold climate. The relativity of the standard of living becomes more vivid when two societies or cultures are compared. The amount of goods and services commanded by the "lower class" in America would entitle its possessor to be ranked as a member of the middle class throughout the Orient and in most of Europe.

Then, too, a distinction must be made between the standard of living and the plane of living or the level of living. Technically, the standard of living implies cultural or subcultural criteria as to what is necessary for decent living; the plane of living denotes the actual amount of goods and services at the disposal of an individual, family, class or nation. There is bound to be a gap between the standard of living and the plane of living for the majority of us; the wealthiest class at the top experience no gap between the two. Social policy in a democracy attempts so far as possible to bridge the gulf between the standard of living and the plane of living of its citizens.

The problem is, however, a little more intricate than appears on the surface. *In a general sense* the cultural framework suggests and embodies the standard of living; for instance, the wearing of shoes is deemed essential to decency and efficient functioning in American culture, not so in many Oriental countries. *Specifically,* however, our standard of living is determined by the group—the class—to which we belong. The professional person at work must wear a "white collar," while the unskilled or even skilled laborer at work must wear an overall. The white-collar worker's standards and actual expenditures are determined by his desire to keep up with the Joneses in the white-collar class, not in the unskilled worker class. The Rockefeller family's standard of living is determined by that of the Ford family and the Morgan family, not by your family or mine.

The lower class—approximately one-third of the population of the United States, according to the Roosevelt New Dealers—consists of dependent unemployables, the unemployed, and those employed at wages not sufficient to maintain themselves and their families on a "decent standard of living." The concept of the standard of living constantly changes with dynamic changes in society. The automobile was considered a luxury in the early twenties; in the early thirties families on relief in metropolitan areas in the U.S.A. drove out to the relief center in their cars and secured the wherewithal for food, shelter and clothing for themselves—and fuel for their cars!

Whether viewed from the standpoint of the standard of living or the plane of living, the American lower class is less destitute, indeed more prosperous, than the middle classes in most of the rest of the world.

Less than 10 per cent of the American population may be bracketed in the upper class. This means that the majority of the American population, somewhere in the neighbourhood of 60 per cent, belong to the middle class. The self-appraisal of the American people, as revealed in the following chart, is interesting:

CHART 11

THE SELF-APPRAISAL OF THE AMERICAN POPULATION[1]

Upper Class   7.3%

Middle Class   70.4%

Lower Class   22.3%

[1] *Fortune Magazine*, February, 1940, p. 14.

3. IMPLICATIONS OF PLANES OF LIVING

That a vast number of families in the United States received in the thirties income under $1,000 per year and only a tiny fraction received over $10,000 per year (16, p. 331) is not so significant as the fact that the income level is tied up with the plane of living and with attitudes. The income and the plane of living determine whether necessary medical services must be availed of or denied by the family; whether the children are to go to a public school or to a private school, to a second-rate college near at hand or to a first-class college far away; whether the head of the family should belong to the National Association of Manufacturers or to the Trade Union. In England, for instance, children of working class families could not aspire to go to the "public" school at Eton or Harrow; the limited income of the family and the status of the family would not permit that. The "school tie" happens to be important in the public life of England. This means that facilities for entering public life are accorded to children of wealthy families and denied to those of poor families. World War II and the strength of the Labor Party have recently tended to blur old class lines and weaken "school ties" in England.

The birth rate as well as the infant mortality rate is inversely related to income: the lower the income the higher the birth rate and, also, the higher the infant mortality rate; the higher the income the lower the birth rate and, also, the lower the infant mortality rate. A study of seven cities made in the thirties by the Children's Bureau, Washington, D.C., revealed that the infant mortality rate was 167 for families with an annual income under $450 and only 59 for families with an annual income of $1,250 and over (16, p. 311, quoted). During the last two decades, the relation of income and birth rate has been changing in the United States, with an increase in the number of children in upper and middle class families. (See CHAPTER 36)

While the inverse relation between infant mortality and income is still operative in the U.S.A. as well as abroad, we may cite the latest available figures for the average income in the U.S.A. in 1957, in order to keep the record straight and up to date.

According to an official release by the Department of Commerce, U.S. Government (April 20, 1958), the average family income in 1957 in the U.S. was $6,130—about 50 per cent higher than in 1947, an actual increase of 20 per cent when adjustment is made for increased living costs between 1947 and 1957. The total income (including wages, dividends, interests and rents) of all Americans —44,000,000 families and 9,500,000 single households—was $328,000,000,000 before taxes, while the average income of full time workers was $4,190.

The percentage of families in certain income brackets in 1957 was as follows:

$10,000 and over   11 per cent
$6,000 to $9,999   27 per cent
$4,000 to $5,999   25 per cent
$2,000 to $3,999   23 per cent
Below $2,000   14 per cent

The following table from Bertillon's study of trends in birth-rate bears out the inverse correlation between income, as reflected in living quarters, and the birth rate:

TABLE 1

ANNUAL BIRTHS PER 1,000 WOMEN OF FERTILE AGE IN DIFFERENT ECONOMIC STRATA OF CERTAIN EUROPEAN CITIES[1]

Classification	Paris	Berlin	Vienna	London
Very poor quarters	108	157	200	147
Poor quarters	95	129	164	140
Comfortable quarters	72	114	155	107
Very comfortable quarters	65	96	153	107
Rich quarters	53	63	107	87
Very rich quarters	34	47	71	63

[1] Quoted from E. B. Reuter: *Population Problems*, 2nd ed., p. 346, Philadelphia: J. B. Lippincott Co., 1937.

The same trend is found to obtain in the United States. "The number of children born varies inversely with the income or prestige of the occupation," according to an analysis of the data published by the Census Bureau. "Of the mothers from 35 to 44 years of age who bore children in 1929, the average number of children they had borne was 6.2. The average of the wives of coal mine operatives was 8.0; the average of the wives of physicians and surgeons was 3.4. Between these extremes, the number of children were: farmers' wives, 7.1; carpenters' wives, 6.0; wives of locomotive engineers, 5.1; wives of men in clerical occupations, 4.1; wives of men in professional service, 3.9." (17, pp. 347–49)

These and other significant demographic facts determine the composition of a population. And the composition of the population has a direct bearing on the constitution of society—on the types of groupings and interactions in the social process. A comprehension of class structure in society is, therefore, very important to the sociologist.

4. CONCEPTS OF SOCIAL STRATIFICATION AND SOCIAL MOBILITY

Sociologists have borrowed from geologists the notion of stratification and have developed the concept of social stratification. By careful investigation and analysis geologists have been able to establish several strata or layers of sedimentary rock, each stratum being identified with a specific geological period. The precise classification of the earth's strata has enabled paleontologists to identify fossil remains as belonging to specific periods in the history of the earth. The date of the Java man, or *Pithecanthropus erectus,* was thus established; he flourished in the Pleistocene Epoch, that is to say, between the First and the Fourth Glacial Period in geology, roughly between 1,000,000 B.C. and 20,000 B.C. By identifying the exact sequences in the glacial period, we can narrow down the precise date of the Java man still further. Most authorities incline to the view that the Java man lived in the early Pleistocene, that is, nearly a million years ago.

In like manner, sociologists have been investigating whether the location (and identification) of a person in a certain social stratum may help us understand his behavior. Is there a constellation of specific traits and behavior patterns associated with certain classes— the upper class, the middle class, the lower class? A number of studies of the American scene have been made by American sociologists to determine an answer to this question. The classic analysis of the class structure in American society is to be found in the study of "Yankee City," Newburyport, Massachusetts (1941), by W. Lloyd Warner and Paul S. Lunt (21, *passim*).

Both objective criteria, such as income, membership in certain clubs, etc., and subjective criteria, such as self-evaluation and evaluation of oneself by other members of the community, were used in classifying the citizens of "Yankee City" into upper-upper, lower-upper; upper-middle, lower-middle; upper-lower, lower-lower.

James West has studied a Missouri agricultural community with a small-town center in *Plainville, U.S.A.* (1945); and John Dollard has described the differential advantages and disadvantages associated with various class statuses in his book, *Caste and Class in a Southern Town* (1937).

In *Elmtown's Youth* (1949), A. B. Hollingshead analyzes the influence of the class structure of a Mid-Western Corn Belt community upon the social behavior of teen-agers. The Lynds' classic studies of Muncie, Indiana, in *Middletown* (1929) and *Middletown in Transition* (1937) are sociological classics. And Gunnar Myrdal's famous study of Negro-White relations in the context of the democratic tradition, in his two-volume work, *An American Dilemma* (1944), postulates a caste structure of social relationships as between whites and Negroes.

We are not concerned, in the present context, with the relative merits of the conclusions arrived at nor with the validity of the techniques of investigation used by these and other authors in the field; suffice it to note that the concept of class structure of society, i.e., of stratification, is a useful tool of analysis of certain facets or phases of human behavior. These analyses do raise the question whether we are headed toward a stratification, or class rigidity, in American society. To this question we shall address ourselves later in this chapter.

The counterpoint of social stratification is the process of social mobility. Social mobility implies movement up and down class lines, or a translation from one status to another. Such movement is possible only in an open class society.

In spite of the lingering effects here and there of European society's premium upon pedigree, American society, from its very inception, started out as an open class society, which ascribed a higher or a lower status to a person in terms of his achievements rather than in terms of his pedigree or heredity. The former we call achieved status, while the latter is called the ascribed status. Nobody quarrels with the thesis that the logic of American culture is to put a premium on achieved status, not on ascribed status. The question is: Is this logic of the American heritage still valid in the latter half of the twentieth century, or is it merely a romantic illusion?

This question we shall attempt to answer in connection with our discussion of trends toward class rigidity. Here it may be pointed out that outside of the class of slaves, there were no closed classes in pioneer America; even the indentured laborers were permitted to become free citizens after they had served their period of indenture. As for the rest of the citizens, the expansive frontier, beckoning to all resourceful pioneers, made mince-meat of any possible tendency toward structuralization of classes on the Eastern seaboard. One of the earliest exponents of the American spirit, of the emerging American ethos, was Hector St. John de Crevecoeur (1735-1813) (18, *passim*).

It is worthy of note that some of the Founding Fathers were afraid that the "wild" frontiersmen, who disdained class distinctions, might make the orderly processes of government impossible. And when Andrew Jackson was elected President, he was hailed as a representative of the frontier which respected guts and guns, not birth nor name nor class affiliation.

Two questions seem to be pertinent: (1) Is it possible that such a heritage of over two hundred years can be radically changed overnight? Or (2) is it possible that the change in the direction of structuralized classes has been going on imperceptibly for several decades, and we are just waking up to it?

5. TRENDS TOWARD CLASS RIGIDITY

Relying upon four research studies—*Middletown in Transition* by the Lynds (1937), *American Business Leaders* by Taussig and Joslyn (1932), *Social Mobility* by Sorokin (1927), and *Occupational Mobility in an American Community* by Davidson and Anderson (1937), two noted American sociologists, Ogburn and Nimkoff, are impelled to remark: "Gone are many of the social conditions that gave us open classes. . . . American business leaders are being increasingly recruited from the upper classes . . . (We are now witnessing) an increase in the hereditary transmission of economic status (in America)." (16, p. 333)

These statements were first made by them in the first edition of their textbook *Sociology* (1940), and have been repeated in their second edition (1950). We shall examine whether the conclusions drawn by Ogburn and Nimkoff are valid.*

We have a saying in this country: "From shirt sleeves to shirt sleeves in three generations." The first generation, the pioneer, working in his shirt sleeves, would build up a fortune. His children would mismanage it. His grandchildren would be reduced to working in shirt sleeves. The question is: Is it possible today for anyone to build up a vast fortune and become a millionnaire, now that the frontier has disappeared?

Sorokin's study of two generations, 1860-90 and 1891-1921, revealed that the doors to fabulous riches were closed fifty per cent against "the poor" and opened fifty per cent in favor of "the rich."

* For 18 years, from 1940 to 1958, the Ogburn-Nimkoff Sociology textbook had been used as a staple by Sociology Departments all over this country. The student generations, brought up on the Ogburn-Nimkoff generalization that American society was heading toward class rigidity, will continue to go through life with that image of America in their minds. I doubt very much whether any of them will re-orient their outlook toward the changed point of view of Ogburn and Nimkoff (1958) in regard to "inconclusive" trends toward class rigidity in America.

This *volte face*, on the part of Ogburn and Nimkoff, from dogmatic assertion to cautious skepticism in regard to *impending* class rigidity in American society, was discovered by me in May, 1959, when I examined their third edition for possible adoption in my Principles of Sociology course (1959-1960). Since many sociologists have taken their cue from the first two editions of Ogburn and Nimkoff, I have decided to leave intact my arguments designed to demolish the early incorrect conclusion of my good friends, Professors Ogburn and Nimkoff.

It is a pleasure for me to note that my criticism of the original Ogburn-Nimkoff thesis finds strong reinforcement in their own rebuttal of their previous stand. Here is what they say in their third edition of *Sociology* (1958 ; p. 192) :

"This discussion has been concerned with whether social-class lines have been getting tighter or looser in the United States. A review of inferences drawn from historical trends, as well as the direct study of the mobility of various groups, shows that the evidence is inconclusive and that there is no clear answer to the question of whether there is any significant change in vertical mobility in American society. There have, however, been great changes in the size of occupational groups and in income levels, representing a general upgrading of the population. If the per capita income in the United States rises during the years 1950 to 2000 as it did from 1900 to 1950, the wage-earners of the second half of the century will have the purchasing power of the middle class of the first half of the century. . . ."

This is how Sorokin arrived at his conclusion. Of "the present generation" of millionnaires (1891-1921), 19.6 per cent started life as "poor" and 52.7 per cent started life as "rich," while in "the deceased generation" of millionnaires (1860-90), 38.8 per cent started life as "poor" and 29.7 per cent started life as "rich." (19, pp. 464-65).

Next, in the sample study of San Jose, California, in 1930, Davidson and Anderson, (3, CHAPTER 2) found that in spite of the phenomenal mobility of the American population, both occupationally and territorially, 41.7 per cent of the sons of unskilled workers became unskilled workers and only 4.1 per cent of their children became professionals, others becoming semi-skilled (16.5 per cent), skilled workers (13.7 per cent), proprietors (10.3 per cent). How shall we interpret these figures: "upgrading" or freezing the status quo by heredity? Are we really approaching the conditions of frontierless Europe with its closed class system?

6. ARE WE REALLY HEADING TOWARD CLASS RIGIDITY?

The studies referred to by Ogburn and Nimkoff lead me to a diametrically opposite conclusion. No, the open class system of America is not in process of becoming a closed class system.

First, Professor Sorokin's study, published in 1927, took for his two generations the years 1891-1921 as the present and 1860-90 as the deceased. The deceased generation (1860-90) witnessed the rise of the empire of the machine. The industrial revolution really began to operate full blast in this country after the end of the Civil War. Thus there were opportunities in this new, unexplored field alike for rich and poor, for everybody with initiative and the daredevil spirit. It is not at all surprising, therefore, to discover that 40 out of the 100 millionnaires of the deceased generation (1860-90) started life as "poor" and made their way up. Nor is it surprising that in the next generation (1891-1921), 53 out of 100 millionnaires started life as "rich." What is really surprising is that as many as 20 out of 100 millionnaires started life as "poor" in the 1891-1921 generation! With combines, trusts, monopolies and holding companies pre-empting the field of industrial and business enterprises during 1891-1921, in no other cultural milieu except the American would a hundred millionnaires in that generation have 20 stemming from "poor" origins.

The study of 25,000 executives of "big business" by Taussig and Joslyn (1932) throws interesting light upon the possibility of success by the not-rich in the contemporary generation. A sample of 7,371 executives revealed (20, CHAPTER 10) that:

44 per cent came from homes with father who was a major executive, or a large owner, or a professional;

44 per cent came from homes of farmers, clerks, salesmen, minor business executives, or small proprietors;

11 per cent came from homes of manual laborers.

It was revealed, furthermore, that 31 per cent of the fathers of the business leaders examined had been big-business executives in their generation. This means one-third inbreeding and two-thirds outbreeding, so far as executives of " big business " were concerned.

Second, regarding the figures about social mobility, it is pertinent to point out that the data are derived from a study of San Jose, California, in 1930, by Davidson and Anderson. Two questions may be raised: (1) Is San Jose, California, typical of America? (2) Is the year 1930 typical? We need more extensive studies and data before categorical assertions concerning the dawn of the closed class system in America can be made.

Interestingly enough, Davidson and Anderson themselves reported that their statistics showed "substantial upgrading," and they reaffirmed their position in a later work.

TABLE 2

UPGRADING IN STATUS AS REVEALED BY
THE SAN JOSE STUDY [1]

Professional Men:	20% came from homes with fathers, skilled, semi-skilled, unskilled laborers
Proprietors:	ditto
White-collar Clerks:	18% came from homes with fathers, semi-skilled or unskilled laborers
Skilled Artisans:	10% came from homes with fathers, unskilled laborers

[1] H. D. Anderson and P. E. Davidson: *Ballots and the Democratic Class Struggle,* pp. 232 ff. Stanford University Press, 1943.

Again, we cannot make precise statements concerning the percentage of upgrading in America without more extensive studies, but upgrading as a part of the American contemporary cultural scene cannot be denied.

Third, it is true that our frontier did disappear in 1890. But ever since the disappearance of the physical frontier, the American people have been engaged in the still more challenging and pioneering task of exploring the technological frontier. Hence the open class concept of a pioneer society still persists with us, even if some amount of rigidity seems to have crept into our class system because of the inability of the average citizen to command costly capital goods.

Fourth, there is yet another consideration relevant to the issue. The rise of the corporation, especially of the "modern quasi-public corporation," is tending to depersonalize ownership. "The American Telephone and Telegraph Company (is) perhaps the most advanced development of the corporate system. With assets of almost five billions of dollars (early 1930's) with 454,000 employees, and stockholders to the number of 567,694, this company may indeed be called an economic empire—an empire bounded by no geographical limits, but held together by centralized control. One hundred companies of this size would control the whole of American wealth; would employ all of the gainfully employed; *and if there were no duplication of stockholders, would be owned by practically every family in the country.*" (2, p. 3; *italics ours.*) At the end of 1935, it may be noted, the American Telephone and Telegraph Company had on its books 659,000 stockholders, "a number almost equal to the number of potential voters living in the five smallest states," according to the National Resources Committee report, 1939-40.

The very concept of property has been revolutionized by the modern corporation, which "has divided ownership into (a) nominal ownership and (b) the power formerly joined to it" (2, p. 7). Ownership is diffused, scattered, among thousands of stockholders; while the power of ownership, namely, management of the resources and assets, is vested in the hands of a new elite class, namely, the management. Possessing, if at all, an insignificant share in corporate property, the class of managers specialize in the task of efficient and abundant production, regardless of the nature of the ownership of property—whether by one-man, by one-family, by a plutocracy, by the middle class, by the working class, by a cross-section of society, or by the state.

Under the circumstances, millionnaires and non-millionnaires are irrelevant terms—interesting relics of an era on the way out. The modern corporation, the managerial class and the technocrat class are making mince-meat of old notions of upper, middle and lower class. The impact of these three newly emerged forces in our society —the rise of the corporation, divorce between ownership and power, rise of the managerial class—has brought about three startling results: (1) wide diffusion of property, (2) abundant production, (3) equitable distribution. (*Cf.* 4, pp. 156–75, for an excellent abstract of Berle and Means' central thesis, in their own words, as made by Kingsley Davis and associates.)

Fifth, the long-term or "secular" trend in America has been in the direction of a steady and spectacular rise in the income from labor, i.e., wages and salaries, compared to the income from property, i.e., royalties, interests, dividends, etc. The comparative incomes from labor and capital show an unmistakable trend. "Official data indicate that hourly earnings of industrial workers rose almost 800 per cent between 1840 and 1940, while the proportion of the national income which goes to 'wealth' in the form of profits, rent and interest has remained virtually constant. Per capita income almost trebled between 1932 and 1945 alone." (9, p. 81).

In the four years, 1929, the peak year before the depression; 1933, at the bottom of the depression; 1940, when the U.S.A. began to shift gears to become an arsenal of democracy; 1945, the year which witnessed the end of shooting hostilities of World War II, we find income from labor and capital as in Table 3 (p. 204).

After an intensive analysis of the distribution of the national income in the U.S.A., Professors Benham and Boddy conclude that "in peacetime the portion going to property averages about 25 per cent of the total . . . . The share of wages and salaries is about 65 per cent . . . . In fact, labor seems to have improved its position relatively to property, as well as absolutely, during the last fifty years or more." (1, pp. 228–30).

TABLE 3

PERSONAL INCOMES FROM LABOR AND CAPITAL IN SPECIFIED YEARS IN THE U.S.A.[1]

Class of Income	Personal Incomes (billions of dollars)			
	1929	1933	1940	1945
From Capital, i.e., net rents and royalties, interest, and dividends	17.25	9.7	13.2	16.3
From Labor, i.e., Salaries and Wages	52.2	28.5	48.9	111.4

[1] Adapted from Frederic Benham & Francis M. Boddy: *Principles of Economics*, p. 228. New York: Pitman Publishing Corporation, 1947.

Finally, instead of becoming more rigid, the open class system of America is becoming ever more open under the impact of the impersonal logic of technology. Urbanization, an outgrowth of industrialization, with its anonymity and secondary group relationships, has actually reversed the trend toward class rigidity in America. Clarence Day's *Life With Father* in the horse-and-buggy era vividly depicts American urban society, at the turn of the century, sharply divided into upper, middle and lower classes, each class with its appropriate code of etiquette. The observance of social distance was part of the amenities of life—one of the graces inculcated in high and low. The power of "Society"—of the upper class—was taken for granted. The upper classes had more wealth, higher income, better education, more power and authority, greater prestige, than either or both of the other two classes. Family name and status, a sure sign of class rigidity, meant much.

Today, under the impact of urbanization, the family name and status mean so little that the concerned families get out a bluebook or a directory of the so-called upper four hundred. Wealth and income are today more widely diffused than at the turn of the century. Indeed, some of the middle class professional technicians and some of the skilled and semi-skilled laborers of the so-called lower class receive higher incomes than name families. In which category shall we place the plumber or the carpenter who receives a higher income than the teacher or the minister? And where shall we place the members of trade unions, with their concentration of power partly derived from organization and partly from benevolent grant by the state?

The open class system of America is today more open than it was at the turn of the century. The structuralization of classes has not markedly taken place. This proposition may be affirmed in the face of the observed fact that in middle-sized towns the class configuration is very evident. Let us remember that over fifty per cent of the American population lives in metropolitan areas, where classes are in flux.

7. CLASSES IN EUROPE AND AMERICA

Even so, we must recognize that compared to the completely open class system of America's frontier days, we have today a less open class system. Not everyone today can become a railroad tycoon: the cost of capital goods is beyond the reach of the average citizen. And if 42 per cent of the sons of unskilled workers tended to become unskilled workers even in one community in an abnormal year, there is an ever-present threat to the promise of American life, to the values of American democracy based upon the open class system. One of the implications of this threat is: Are we on the way to developing class-consciousness, especially for the working class?

To find an answer to that question we must understand the contrasting backgrounds of European and American societies. Even though it had its roots in European culture and society, American society started as an association of pioneers, who had cut loose from their old-world moorings, in an expansive land with a seemingly limitless frontier.

In early Middle Ages European society was made up of two main classes: Lords and Serfs, with a sprinkling of Burghers or townspeople. In late Middle Ages there were: Peasants, Burghers, and Aristocracy. The burghers were either tradesmen or craftsmen. The aristocracy was made up of nobility, clergy and knights. The commercial revolution endowed towns with power. With the rise of the industrial revolution, some members of the aristocracy joined the ranks of the burghers, and among the burghers themselves a new class, the proletariat, began to emerge—the class of workers who possessed no tools, who had only their labor power to sell, and who were dependent upon employment for their livelihood. As the industrial revolution progressed, the ranks of the proletariat swelled by additions from peasants, traders, craftsmen, and even the aristocracy. Looking at the class structure of his day (1848), Karl Marx described two broad classes, the employer and the employee, the capitalist and the proletariat, the exploiter and the exploited, and spoke of the burghers who fell in neither category as bourgeoisie. The term bourgeois or bourgeoisie simply means "town dwellers," but Marx gave it a peculiar connotation by suggesting that the bourgeoisie were on the side of the exploiter and against the exploited.

Neither in the period of Colonization nor in the period of industrialization did American society know such sharp distinctions between groups. Here the pioneer was a worker, mostly self-employed, a farmer, a craftsman, even a tradesman of a sort, all rolled into one. American society had neither serfs nor peasants on the one hand nor an hereditary aristocracy on the other, even though it did have slaves and indentured laborers. From its very inception American society began to prize achieved status more than ascribed status or status assigned by heredity. Furthermore, American society from its inception began to exalt and glorify the common man as no previous society had ever done. The well-being of the common man became, and is to this day, the dominant concern of American society.

Because of these differing backgrounds between Europe and America, we should be careful in the use of European terms and conceptual tools, some of which are definitely irrelevant to the American scene. With this caution we may proceed to a study of the class analysis of society.

8. THE MARXIAN ANALYSIS OF THE SOCIAL PROCESS

The class analysis of the social process was first set forth systematically by Karl Marx (1818-83) and Friedrich Engels (1820-95).

"The history of all hitherto existing society," states the Communist Manifesto, "is the history of class struggles. Freeman and slave, patrician and plebeian, lord and serf, guild-master and journeyman, in a word, oppressor and oppressed, stood in constant opposition to one another, carried on uninterrupted, now hidden, now open fight, a fight that each time ended, either in a revolutionary reconstitution of society at large or in the common ruin of the contending classes" (13, p. 321). In the present epoch of capitalist ascendancy, "society as a whole is more and more splitting up into two great hostile camps, into two great classes directly facing each other: Bourgeoisie and Proletariat" (13, p. 322).

With the aid of this conceptual tool of investigation, namely, the theory of the class struggle, Marx reared an elaborate structure of class sociology, professing to interpret history past and present and to predict the future.

The essential elements of Marxism are:

1. The existence of the class struggle;
2. The labor theory of value, i.e., labor is the creator of value;
3. The theory of the exploitation of labor by capital—the laborer is paid less than the full reward for his labor;
4. The theory of surplus value—that part of the value created by the laborer which is withheld from him becomes the surplus value, pocketed by the capitalist;
5. The economic interpretation of history—i.e., "The mode of production in material life determines the general character of the social, political, and spiritual processes of life." (11, p. 162 quoted);
6. The revolutionary role of the proletariat in abolishing capitalism and bringing into being a classless society; capitalism has created the weapons of its own destruction, namely, the increasing misery of the workers in the midst of plenty and recurring industrial crises; "it has also called into existence the men who are to wield those weapons—the modern working-class—the proletarians." (13, pp. 327–28);
7. The proletariat as a mass, however, cannot bring about the classless society. The proletariat, organized as a class—as a class-conscious association—can become the revolutionary force in society. Combinations of workers, i.e., trade unions,

and labor parties, and other labor activities should create among workers a sense of their class-belonging, an awareness of their revolutionary role in society, a readiness to follow the leadership of the vanguard of the labor movement, namely, the Communist Party;

8. The purpose of the working-class movement, according to Marx, is not to remedy defects in the *status quo* but to pull down the *status quo* and erect in its place a revolutionary new social order affecting every phase of human activity including legal foundations and ideology. This is the long-range view in contrast to the short-range opportunistic tactic;

9. The social revolution can be brought about by the capture of power, by the capture of the State machinery, by the militant minority, the Communists, who should immediately impose upon the country a dictatorship of the proletariat. The State, which had been used as a class tool of exploitation by the capitalists, must now be used by the workers as a class tool of expropriation and liquidation of the propertied class. When the transitional period is over, said Marx, the bourgeois class will have been liquidated, the classless society will emerge, and the State will "wither away," the workers, i.e., the producers, being the only citizens in society;

10. Patriotism, fatherland, loyalty to the State, religion are myths created by the bourgeoisie for the exploitation of the masses. "The working men have no country" (13, p. 340). The workers of the world are united as a class, as producers; their common interest is to end exploitation and to usher in distributive justice the world over. Hence the revolutionary call of the Communist Manifesto: "Workers of the world, unite! You have nothing to lose but your chains, and a whole world to gain!"

Such, in brief outline, is the Marxist analysis of the social process. On the foundation of this analysis there have arisen ideologies of a world-shaking nature. Sociology becomes a parlor science if it ignores Karl Marx and his *Communist Manifesto* and *Das Kapital* or Henry George and his *Progress and Poverty*.

9. A Critique of Marxian Analysis

Marxism gave rise, directly, to the Communist movement and the Communist police State in Russia as well as to Communist movements the world over; it gave rise to Fabianism, to Guild Socialism, and to the Labor Party in Great Britain which believes in ballots instead of bullets in bringing about the social revolution; it gave rise to the I.W.W. in America with its revolutionary watchword: "Not a fair day's wages for a fair day's work, but abolition of the wage system," and to Syndicalism in France which believes in economic weapons of "direct action," such as the label, boycott, sabotage, the local strike, the sympathetic strike, the general strike. By reflex action Marxism gave rise to Italian Fascism and to National Socialism in Germany. Marxism is today dividing national societies and the world into hostile camps.

Some of the points made by Marx are correct and some are incorrect. For instance, there is a great deal of truth in the existence of the class struggle in society, in the labor theory of value and in the theory of surplus value. The economic interpretation of history, likewise, has an important element of truth; but as an all-sufficient explanation of human behavior it is misleading, false and mischievous. The Marxian thesis that the mode of production does have some causative correlation to the social process is well brought out (see p. 210) by Dr. Richard T. Ely (1854-1943).

Marx underrated the dynamic of national loyalty. His prediction that the social revolution would first take place in highly industrialized countries has been proved to be wrong: it took place in Russia, an industrially underdeveloped country. He was equally wrong in his categorical assumption that with advance in technology and increase in production, the worker's share of the national income would steadily diminish: as a matter of fact, the worker in the United States of America today enjoys luxuries such as were unavailable to royalty in Marx' day. Again, the business corporation in America with millions of its stockholders is actually tending to establish partnership between capital and labor. Finally, granted there is some amount of distributive injustice under capitalism, the answer is to be sought, in a democratic society, not in bullets but in ballots.

Being a German and a European, Marx inevitably thought in terms of the European scene. It is true that workers in his day did not enjoy universal suffrage on the continent of Europe. In England

TABLE 4

A CORRELATION BETWEEN THE MODE OF PRODUCTION AND CERTAIN OTHER FACTORS IN THE ECONOMIC ORGANIZATION OF SOCIETY [1]

From the Standpoint of Production	From the Standpoint of Exchange	From the Standpoint of Labor	From the Standpoint of the General Economic Organization
1. Direct appropriation	Conquest and Seizure	Laboring class not differentiated; Beginning of slavery and serfdom	Tribal and independent economy
2. Pastoral	Barter	Slavery and Serfdom	Household and neighborhood economy
3. Agricultural	Barter and money	Serfdom and free labor	Village economy
4. Handicraft	Money	Free labor governed by custom	Custom work (Domestic or putting-out economy-HTM)
5. Industrial	Credit	Individual contract and group contract	National or capitalistic and world economy

[1] Reproduced, with adaptation, from Richard T. Ely: *Outlines of Economics*, 6th ed., p. 26. New York: Macmillan, 1937.

the Reform Bill of 1832 strove to extend the right of vote to several categories of male workers. It was promptly utilized by the British workers to initiate changes and reforms in favor of the working-class, so much so that after the 1946 election Great Britain formed a Labor Government to run the affairs of Great Britain and the vast British Empire and Commonwealth without a single shot having been fired. The rights of workers to organize themselves into voluntary associations are more scrupulously recognized and upheld in capitalist America under a democracy than in "Communist" Russia under a dictatorship.

The Soviet government of Russia, which had come into power on the premise of the solidarity of the workers of the world, is today more nationalistic and chauvinistic than capitalist America. The tables seem to have been turned. The Soviet government is more capitalistically motivated than the bourgeois democracy of America. And the American government is more socialistically oriented than the so-called "Workers' Government" of Russia. It is not America that demanded heavy reparations from defeated Germany; it is the workers' government of the Soviet Union that demanded and exacted heavy reparations from the workers of Germany! Stalin gave the lie direct to Marx' assertion that "the working men have no country." The East German working men have Germany as their country, to be exploited by the Russian working men who have Russia as their country! The same relation of exploiter and exploited exists between communist Russia and other satellite countries!

10. LIBERTY VERSUS SECURITY

Even so, one fundamental point raised by Marxism remains unanswered. When the citizens of a country are confronted with a choice between political liberty and economic security, *as a mass* they have elected to sacrifice liberty in favor of security. The Communists in Russia rode to power on the crest of slogans, such as: Bread to the people, factories to the workers, land to the peasants, peace to all the world. Hitler, on his part, promised a job to every unemployed German citizen, and took over the reins of government in Germany. The question is: Can political democracy, granting the utmost liberty to the citizen, guarantee economic security to the citizen? If it can, there is no need to be afraid of the future of democracy in America or elsewhere in the world.

Tied up with security is the question of the definition of democracy itself. Democracy, to be valid, implies the right of the citizen to participate in the making of national policy. The citizen spends eight hours a day at his work. The question is: Does he have a right to participate in the making of the policy of the establishment where he works and which functions as an on-going concern because of his work? What are the limits and possibilities of partnership between labor and capital?

Are we ready to implement political democracy with industrial democracy? Is the present situation ideal? Do we need any changes in the *status quo*? Is the Golden Age of America to be found in the past, in the present, or in the future? These questions every American is called upon to answer, in the light of his conscience, in the light of his best judgment.

On the basis of the answers given, American society, indeed any society, will be found divided into four groupings: from left to right, radical, progressive or liberal, conservative, reactionary.

Radical→ Progressive → Conservative → Reactionary
or
Liberal

The reactionary posits his utopia in the past, the conservative in the *status quo*, the progressive or liberal in the evolutionary future, the radical in the revolutionary future (23, *passim*). Whether one is to be a reactionary or a radical, a conservative or a liberal, will be determined by the background of one's experiences and in large measure, though not solely, by one's group or class affiliation.

This brings us back to the problem of classes in society and the significant role played by class affiliations in the social process.

With "increasing" rigidity of class structure in American society, are we headed toward a class-conscious workers' movement patterned after Marxism? The answer is a tentative No. First, the

American heritage of liberty and equality militates against the development of such a movement. Second, the very mobility of the American population, occupationally and territorially, acts as a deterrent to the development of a strong working-class consciousness. Third, the American worker believes in the workability of capitalism as earnestly as does the capitalist; indeed, not only is every worker in America a capitalist at heart but he is also striving to be a capitalist in his own right. Fourth, even though the physical frontier has vanished, we are today engaged in exploring the technological frontier; and the pioneer traits of self-confidence, self-reliance, personal initiative, and private enterprise are still in the ascendant among Americans. Fifth, coming out on top through competition is a value still highly regarded in America. Sixth, the American believes in a precise definition of the rules of competition: today he is witnessing the interplay and competition between Big Business, Big Labor, Big Agriculture, and Big Government. Finally, there is no danger of the emergence of a revolutionary class-conscious workers' movement in America so long as the American can translate the American Declaration of Independence into the spicy American lingo (after Mencken): "You and me is as good as anybody else, and maybe a damn sight better!" (14, pp. 583–84; also may be found in *The American Language,* 2nd ed., p. 389, by the same author.)

REFERENCES

1. FREDERIC BENHAM and FRANCIS M. BODDY: *Principles of Economics.* New York: Pitman Publishing Corp., 1947.
2. A. A. BERLE and G. C. MEANS: *The Modern Corporation and Private Property.* New York: Macmillan, 1935.
3. P. E. DAVIDSON and H. D. ANDERSON: *Occupational Mobility in an American Community.* Stanford, Calif: Stanford University Press, 1937.
3a. H. D. ANDERSON and P. E. DAVIDSON: *Ballots and the Democratic Class Struggle.* Stanford: Stanford University Press, 1943.
4. KINGSLEY DAVIS *et al*: *Modern American Society.* New York: Rinehart and Company, 1949.
5. CLARENCE DAY: *Life with Father.* New York: Alfred A. Knopf, 1935.
6. JOHN DOLLARD: *Caste and Class in a Southern Town.* New Haven: Yale University Press, 1937.

7. RICHARD T. ELY: *Outlines of Economics*, 6th ed. New York: Macmillan, 1937.

8. HENRY GEORGE: *Progress and Poverty*. Available in several editions.

9. A. H. HOBBS: *The Claims of Sociology: A Critique of Textbooks*. Harrisburg, Pa: The Stackpole Publishing Company, 1951.

10. A. B. HOLLIGSHEAD: *Elmtown's Youth*. New York: John Wiley and Sons, 1949.

11. H. W. LAIDLER: *Social-Economic Movements*. New York: Thomas Y. Crowell, 1944.

12. ROBERT and HELEN LYND: *Middletown* (1929) and *Middletown in Transition* (1937) New York: Harcourt, Brace & Co.

13. KARL MARX: *Capital and Other Writings*, ed. by Max Eastman. New York: The Modern Library, 1932.

14. H. L. MENCKEN: *The Mencken Chrestomathy*. New York: Knopf, 1949.

15. GUNNAR MYRDAL *et al*: *An American Dilemma* (2 vols.). New York: Harper and Brothers, 1944.

16. WILLIAM F. OGBURN and MEYER F. NIMKOFF: *Sociology*. Boston: Houghton Mifflin Co., 1940.

17. E. B. REUTER: *Population Problems*, 2nd ed. Philadelphia: J. B. Lippincott Co., 1937.

18. HECTOR ST. JOHN DE CREVECOEUR: *Letters from an American Farmer*. New York: A & C Boni, 1925.

19. PITRIM SOROKIN: *Social Mobility*. New York: Harper & Brothers, 1927.

20. F. W. TAUSSIG and C. S. JOSLYN: *American Business Leaders*. New York: Macmillan, 1932.

21. W. LLOYD WARNER and PAUL S. LUNT: *The Social Life of a Modern Community* (Yankee City Series, Vol. 1). New Haven: Yale University Press, 1941.

22. JAMES WEST: *Plainville, U.S.A.* New York: Columbia University Press, 1945.

23. A. B. WOLFE: *Conservatism, Radicalism and Scientific Method*. New York: Macmillan, 1923.

CHAPTER 15

CASTE GROUPINGS

In the last chapter, it was suggested that when classes cease to be open and become rigid, we have the emergence of caste groupings in society, characterized especially by a prohibition in regard to the sharing of *roti* (bread) and *betty* (daughter). We also pointed out the existence of dichotomous categories savoring of caste in practically every culture. Finally, the point was made that while classes tend to become conflict groups, castes are always accommodation groups.

Inasmuch as the caste structure of Hindu society is in process of disruption, a brief statement of the sociology of caste may be in order.

1. THE ARYAS

The migrations of the Aryas from the Caucasus region to Europe and to India have profoundly shaped the course of human history. That branch of the Aryas or Caucasians which went to Europe became the progenitor of modern Europeans and Americans, while the other branch that went to India became the progenitor of modern Hindus.

The Arya invaders, who came to India from the Caucasus region in successive waves between 4000 B.C. and 2000 B.C., had, as befitted a pioneer group, a classless and a casteless society. Every male had to participate in the common task of conquering the Dashyu, the dark-skinned enemy, and of colonizing, first, the fertile land of the Five Rivers (Punjab) and the Indus Valley and, later, the Gangetic Plains. Not only did this pioneer group know nothing of caste or class, but their womenfolk stood on a par with men, if not an inch higher. That absence of classes and equality of the sexes are characteristic of pioneer societies was several millennia later

215

demonstrated once again in the case of American pioneers in the New World.

Having driven the Dravidians to the South of the Vindhya Mountains, the Aryas settled in the fertile Indo-Gangetic regions in the North, which they began to call Aryavarta, the land of the Aryas, in contrast to Dakshinadesha, the Southland, which became the abode of the Dravidians. Having secured plenty of elbow-room—lebensraum—in a land flowing with milk and honey, the Aryas, true to their proud name, settled down to elaborate a code of conduct befitting an Arya, a nobleman, a gentleman.

These rambunctious people had proudly called themselves Aryas, *agriculturists*, in contradistinction to the "lower breeds"—hunters, fishers, nomads and shepherds. Arya is derived from the Sanskrit root Rü or Ar (to cultivate the soil), from which we have our English word *ar*able. By derivation the term Arya came to mean a superior person, a nobleman, a gentleman, in contrast to the Un-Arya, the uncivilized barbarian.

Parenthetically, it may be noted that when the late Orientalist, F. Max Müller (1823-1900), imported the word Arya or Aryan into the European languages, he took pains to point out that he was using the word to describe a family of closely related languages. By Aryan, Max Müller meant the family of Indo-European languages. He had not the faintest idea that the word would be misused by later generations of racialists. "I have declared again and again," wrote Max Müller, "that when I say Aryas (Aryans) I mean neither blood nor bones, neither hair nor skull; I mean simply those who speak an Aryan language. When I speak of them I commit myself to no anatomical characteristics. To me an ethnologist who speaks of Aryan race, Aryan blood, Aryan eyes and hair, is as great a sinner as a linguist who speaks of a dolichocephalic dictionary or a brachycephalic grammar." (3, p. 12, quoted.) If we must refer to any people as Aryan, the only people to whom the term fits are the Hindus of India. But by consensus, philologists and social scientists have agreed to restrict the usage of the term Aryan to the Indo-European family of languages including Sanskrit, Old Persian, Greek, Latin, German, English, Armenian and Slavic. (3, p. 11.)

2. THE FUNCTIONAL ORGANIZATION OF SOCIETY

The code of conduct evolved by the Aryas of India through the centuries came generically to be called Arya-Dharma, the Dharma or Religion (duties and obligations) of an Arya, of a gentleman. The starting-point of this code of conduct was duty, not right; collective well-being, not individual aggrandizement; the sacredness and primacy of function, not of functionaries. The Arya-Dharma also came to be known as Sanatana Dharma, the Eternal Religion.

Hindu lawgivers reasoned: No well-regulated society could possibly exist if it did not have the functions of teaching and religious ministration properly performed; no society could endure peacefully for long if it did not have the functions of administration and defense properly performed; no society could subsist for long if economic functions, such as agricultural, industrial, commercial, were not fully provided for.

No more efficient method for the upholding of Dharma and culture could be devised than to call upon fit persons to specialize in these functions, each according to his ability and temperament. Thus was formulated the principle of Varnashrama-Dharma, the fourfold functional organization of society:

1. Brahmins (Teachers-Priests)⎫⠀⠀The
2. Kshattriyas (Warriors-Administrators)⎬⠀Twice-
3. Vaishyas (Merchants-Agriculturists)⎭⠀Born
4. Shudras, also spelled as Sudras (Servants)

Those members of society who could not perform any of the first three functions of culture were called upon to minister to the needs of others. This service function was not so exalted as the first three, but it was sacred none the less. Those who performed the first three functions could be invested with the sacred thread—an emblem of the twice-born. They could study the Vedas and other sacred Scriptures. To reconcile the Shudras to their lot, the Hindu lawgivers endowed the act of ministration with great merit.

3. THE PRIMACY OF THE FUNCTION OVER THE FUNCTIONARY

In order to establish the primacy of function over the functionary, Hindu lawgivers, viewing caste merely as a mechanism for the functional organization of society, explicitly stated (9, pp. 160–61):

Of Brahmins or Teachers-Priests, Kshattriyas or Warriors-Administrators, Vaishyas or Merchants-Agriculturists and Shudras (Sudras) or Servants, the obligations have been distributed according to the qualities born of their nature. (We should say nurture instead of nature.—H.T.M.)

Serenity, self-restraint, austerity, purity, forgiveness, and also uprightness, wisdom, knowldege, belief in God—these are the obligations of the Brahmin, implicit in his nature (nurture—H.T.M.) and vocation.

Prowess, splendor, firmness, dexterity, and also not fleeing in battle, generosity, rulership—these are incumbent upon the Kshattriya.

Agriculture, protection of cows, and commerce are the obligations of the Vaishya, while action of the nature of service is to be rendered by the Shudra.

—*Bhagavad Gita.*

The Shudra becomes a Brahmin and a Brahmin becomes a Shudra by conduct. Know this same rule to apply to him who is born of the Kshattriya or of the Vaishya.

—*Manu Smriti.*

Truth, gift, forgiveness, good conduct, gentleness, austerity, and mercy—where these are seen, there we have a Brahmin.

If these marks exist in a Shudra and not in a Brahmin, the Shudra is not a Shudra nor is the Brahmin a Brahmin.

Only when his conduct conforms to this standard do we have a right to call him a Brahmin; otherwise he must be regarded as a Shudra.

—*Mahabharata.*

What is said as to the marks of conduct indicative of a man's caste, if those marks are found in another, designate him by the caste of his marks, not by the caste of his birth.

By birth every one is a Shudra. By Samskara (performance of obligatory duties) he becomes a twice-born.

—*Vishnu Bhagavat.*

Neither birth nor Samskara, neither study of the Vedas nor ancestry is the cause of Brahminhood. Conduct alone is the cause thereof.

—*Mahabharata.*

Beyond the pale of the caste system, outside the four caste groupings in society, was the Panchama, literally the *fifth* group, the so-called "untouchables." The defeated, dark-skinned Dravidians constituted the fifth group, so far as the conquering, fair-complexioned Aryas were concerned. Whether prompted by eugenic considerations or by arrogance, the Aryas devised methods to keep their "race" pure by forbidding inter-marriage and interdining. In course of time, the Dravidian nucleus of the Panchama group was reinforced by the castaways of Hindu society. Those Aryas who failed properly to perform their dharmas, duties, by their inner self, by their neighbor, by society, by God, were "out-casted," excommunicated, and were driven into the Panchama group. The majority of those who suffered excommunication came from the Kshattriya caste; the soldiers who ran away from battle had no place in the ordered relations of society. And since suicide was religiously frowned upon, harakiri could not solve the problem as it did with the Japanese. Hence the only alternative for the excommunicated was to swell the ranks of the Panchama.

Here it may be noted that in course of time each of the four— rather five—castes developed a host of subcastes, an intricate hierarchy with each subcaste having its own sanctions and strictures, structure and status.

4. Four Stages in the Individual's Career

Before setting forth the sociological implications of the functional organization of society on the basis of caste among the Hindus, it may be pointed out that the Varnashrama system not only postulated a fourfold division of society according to functions but it also divided the life of the twice-born persons into four "ashramas" or stages:

1. Brahmacharya or the Stage of Student-Celibate, 6–24 years;
2. Grihasthya or the Stage of Householder, 25–50 years;
3. Vanaprasthya or the Stage of Semi-Detachment from the World, 51–60 years;
4. Sannyastya or the Stage of Renunciation, 61-onward.

The Brahmachari or student-celibate lived with his preceptor, Guru, in the Ashram—the forest hermitage university. He went to the surrounding communities with the beggar's bowl and brought food and other necessities for the upkeep of the University including himself, his fellow students and the Guru. In other words, society maintained the student. The Grihastha or householder undertook his duties as a member of the polity of Arya-Dharma, maintaining Brahmacharis, students-celibate, and Sannyasis, recluses. As a Vanaprastha, the householder began the process of detaching himself from the work of the world and was supported by his son, the new head of the house. Finally, he betook himself to the forest and lived at a forest hermitage in company with others like himself, meditating on God, or at a forest hermitage university imparting instruction to worthy pupils; or he moved about from place to place, doing good to others, ministering to the needs of others, imparting wisdom to the people as an itinerant teacher or troubadour. Because of his vow of poverty and chastity and his dedication to the pursuit of Truth, he would be maintained by society in old age as he had been maintained by the same society during his student days when he had embraced poverty and chastity and undertaken to pursue Truth.

5. TEN CHARACTERISTICS OF CASTE IN INDIA

In the functional organization of Hindu society the operation of ten sociological mechanisms is worth noting:

1. the caste as a primary group,
2. the ever-present tendency for functions to become structuralized,

3. the emergence of rationalization for the defense of the *status quo,*

4. the mechanism for transcending caste barriers,

5. the mechanism for incorporation of out-groups within the polity of Arya-Dharma, or Hindu society,

6. acculturation rather than imposition,

7. the safeguarding of security and status, of recognition and response, to all members of society, and of new experiences only to the elite,

8. social solidarity through division of labor,

9. a significant scale of values for appraising the functions of culture,

10. caste organization of society in process of disruption through social change, thanks to the impact of Occidental technology and ideology.

6. THE CASTE PANCHAYAT

Dominated by the concept of social division of labor, the Aryas lived in small compact communities, never in isolated farmsteads as was done by the early Saxons in Germany and by later American pioneers. In the small community, different castes performed specified functions. One was born into the caste, into the function, as well as into the community. The caste and the community were alike primary groups, exerting social control on the individual members. Inasmuch as the different castes were in reciprocal relationship with one another, procedures had to be developed on the basis of folkways and mores. Thus arose in each caste its Panchayat or Council of Five, and the caste itself became a Mahajana (a functional corporation).

The caste Panchayat, especially the village Panchayat, according to Sir M. Monier-Williams, was "the original type, the first germ of all the divisions of rural and civic society in medieval and modern Europe" (7, p. 455). The word of the Panch (five), or of the Panchayat, was said to be the word of God. Compare the Latin : *Vox populi, vox dei.* (The English word punch, meaning either a drink containing five ingredients or a boxing with five fingers held tightly into a fist, is derived from the Sanskrit word spelled in English either as Panch or Punch and pronounced exactly like Punch, meaning five.)

7. TRAITS OF THE CASTE SYSTEM IN INDIA

In addition to prohibition in regard to *roti* and *betty,* the caste system of India has been characterized by a number of other traits.

The primary group relationships of the caste made it possible for all members to satisfy three wishes—the wish for security, the wish for recognition, and the wish for response. The wish for new experience could be attained only by those who were willing to renounce "the world, the flesh and the devil," and thus to transcend the restrictions of caste barriers.

The joint-family system and the caste Mahajana cared for the dependents and the unemployables, thus obviating the need for social work agencies. In modern urban centers, where caste bonds are loose, social work agencies have become necessary and are springing up.

The caste guaranteed a job to the youngster in consonance with his station in life, and it inculcated the virtue of craftsmanship. While the choice of jobs was non-existent, there were no "blind alley jobs" either.

Through the ages, the untouchables have been victims of rationalization on the part of the high caste Hindus. Denied opportunities for economic and educational advancement, the untouchables developed unclean habits of living including the eating of carrion. These unclean habits of living were then used as a "justification" by the high caste to avoid "touching" them. Today, reasoning is gradually replacing rationalization in the treatment of the untouchables by the high caste Hindus. The late Mahatma Gandhi (1869-1948) gave them the endearing title of Harijans, which means "children of God."

The cardinal tenet of Hindu society and of Arya Dharma is the doctrine of *Adhikara* or fitness. One may not interfere with the spiritual evolution of the other person or group. This meant that there was no standard formula for salvation applicable to all. Promises of heaven contingent upon the acceptance of one religion or another had little force; this meant, too, an absence of missionary zeal and a readiness to accept outgroups not bent upon disturbing the *status quo*.

Indeed, hospitality to outgroups is a characteristic of Hindu society. The Jews were welcomed by Hindu society in the second century B.C., perhaps earlier, and have never been persecuted. The Apostle St. Thomas established a Christian community in India in the first century A.D., and these *peaceful* Christians have never been persecuted by Hindu society. The first group of Pilgrim Fathers who left their land in search of freedom of conscience, the Zoroastrians of Iran, went to India in the seventh century A.D., and have never been persecuted. If anything, these progressive Parsees are highly esteemed and looked upon as a group with a high status in the polity of Arya Dharma.

In addition to Hindu castes, there are some professional or craft castes composed exclusively of Muslims, and some others composed of Hindus and Muslims. The Roman Catholic Church in India, and some Protestant Churches, too, have accommodated themselves to the caste rituals of Hindu society—in the matter of the communion cup, for instance. The tenacity of caste may be appreciated from the fact that reformist groups invariably have ended up by having a caste status assigned to them. A group of reformers advocating inter-marriage and interdining have usually ended up in the past as a caste-that-is-opposed-to-the-caste-system!

The best instance of the incorporation of out-groups within the polity of Arya Dharma is afforded by the Dravidians. Those Dravidians who stayed up North were treated as the Panchama, the fifth group. Those who elected to make their home South of the Vindhya Mountains began to be wooed by itinerant Teachers from the North. These Aryan Teachers studied the customs and mode of living of the Dravidians, familiarized themselves with the many gods and goddesses of the Dravidians, and then began to present the polity of Arya Dharma in terms intelligible to the Dravidians. In the process of imparting their religio-philosophical teachings to the Dravidians, the Aryas took over a great many ideas and ceremonials from the Dravidians. Through this process of acculturation arose the pantheon of Hinduism. Probably by 1,000 B.C., this process may have attained its climax.

The Dravidians accepted the fourfold functional organization of society with their own Brahmins, Kshattriyas, Vaishyas and Shudras —and their own untouchables! Another sociological law has been demonstrated in the behavior of the Hinduized, or culturally Aryanized, Dravidians, namely, that the convert is more zealous than the one born to the faith. While in the North only the touch of the Panchama would constitute pollution, in the South the very shadow of the Panchama would spell pollution for the high castes! Now the Brahmins of the South could share *roti* (bread) and *betty* (daughter) with the Brahmins of the North, and so on. But the South became the stronghold of Hindu orthodoxy. Some of the greatest systematizers and revivalists of Hinduism, such as Shankara or Sankara (eighth century A.D.) arose in the South. This emphasis on acculturation to the neglect of imposition has given Hindu society a stability unknown to other societies. In the same way, the Rajputs, originally an out-group, have become the staunchest defenders of Arya Dharma in the North.

Finally, Hindu society with its caste structure has never persecuted or crucified a single Truth-Seeker, however wide of the mark his thinking may have been. (The tragic martyrdom of Mahatma Gandhi on January 30, 1948, was motivated by political considerations, not religious.) With full and unfettered freedom of thought, these Seers elaborated all kinds of systems of thought and founded such variant schools as atheistic, agnostic, nihilistic, materialistic, idealistic, spiritualistic, pluralistic, dualistic, transcendentalistic, monotheistic, monistic, etc. They had thus anticipated the conclusions of Plato, Spinoza, Berkeley, Hume, Hegel, Kant, Schopenhauer, Herbert Spencer, Haeckel, Emerson, and other Occidental thinkers. (1, p. 14). " Indeed, if I may be allowed the anachronism," remarked Sir M. Monier-Williams, "the Hindus were Spinozaites more than 2,000 years before the existence of Spinoza; and Darwinians many centuries before Darwin, and evolutionists many centuries before the doctrine of evolution had been accepted by the scientists of our time, and before any word like 'evolution' existed in any language of the world [other than Sanskrit]." (7, p. xiii). " The mind of man can penetrate where the rays of the sun cannot," says an ancient Hindu proverb. These new experiences of the thinkers would in course of time become the common legacy of the masses. And, of course, new experiences beyond the caste structure are always available to those who dedicate themselves to the pursuit of Truth and who embrace poverty and chastity.

8. CASTE AND "ORGANIC SOLIDARITY"

Durkheim spoke of two kinds of solidarity, mechanical and organic. Mechanical solidarity is derived from resemblance and likeness, while organic solidarity springs from the division of labor (4, *passim*). In Durkheim's terminology, castes may be spoken of as "corporations professionelles" or as "groupes professionelles." The Brahmin priest-teacher at the top, the Kshattriya warrior-administrator in the middle and the Vaishya banker at the bottom, each of these twice-born performing his allotted task, made for organic solidarity. The Shudras and the Panchamas, who were not among the twice-born, had specific tasks allotted to them.

Organic solidarity rests upon division of labor, not necessarily upon hereditary castes. The open class society in America is characterized by division of labor and by organic solidarity.

9. ROLE OF GOVERNMENT IN CASTE REGULATIONS

Innovations in caste status and function, including reinstatement of excommunicated persons, can be ordered only by government decree—not even by the say-so of the Brahmin. Of course, it was assumed that the Brahmin would give his counsel to the State authorities. Thus we had the peculiar spectacle of Muslim rulers being called in to adjudicate in matters of Hindu caste functioning. The British Raj inherited this prerogative of Hindu Kings by way of the Muslim Raj it had supplanted. (6, pp. 82–84).

A Hindu Raj would have introduced changes in the caste system progressively to conform to the requirements of social change; as it was, the British Raj developed the policy of neutrality in social and religious matters. Thus, while it guaranteed security of person and property and a measure of civil freedom, according to Hindese nationalists the British Raj failed to keep Hindu society abreast of the times because of its differing conception of its social role in

India. This accounts for the persistence of early marriage and caste rigidity well into the first quarter of the twentieth century. (It may be noted that the ban against early marriage was enacted legislatively by the Legislative Assembly of India in the twenties, and that the Constituent Assembly of India legislatively forbade the practice of untouchability in 1947.)

10. The Disrupting Impact of Occidental Culture

With English education came mobility territorially, occupationally and intellectually. Equality began to be posed against caste stratification, national freedom against caste well-being, democracy against hierarchy. Movements for the purification of Hindu society arose: in Bengal, the Brahmo Samaj, led by Raja Ram Mohan Roy (1772-1833); in Punjab and North India, the Arya Samaj, led by Swami Dayananda Saraswati (1824-83); in Bombay and the South, the Prarthana Samaj, led by M. G. Ranade (1842-1901), and others.

British aggressions and exploitation in the land created discontent among the people. The emancipation of the mind through acquaintance with the English language and with Euro-American culture led to the rise of nationalism in India. National loyalty cut across the caste hierarchy. The discovery of Sanskrit literature by European scholars gave Hindus just the needed sense of pride in their Motherland. This pride became grist for the mill of the nationalist. (8, pp. 11 ff.)

Added to English education and the newly emerging nationalism as factors tending to break down the caste structure of society, there came into operation an entirely strange factor, namely, technology, respecting neither high nor low, neither rich nor poor. The impersonal logic of technology tended to affect Hindu society to its very roots. The newly created emporia of the seaborne invader— Bombay, Calcutta, Madras—became magnets attracting the ambitious and energetic elements of all caste groups. In these metropolises secondary group relations tended to loosen the bonds of caste. And when urbanism became reinforced by industrialism, the very foundations of Hindu society began to shake. The untouchable could buy his railroad ticket and sit anywhere he liked; the high caste man had the option not to travel by train or to sit side by side with the untouchable. The rituals and taboos connected with eating began to be modified under the impact of urbanism and industrialism. In a factory, the high caste man had the option not to work or to work in company of all kinds of people.

Besides English education and the impersonal logic of technology, there was yet another disintegrating factor. By a peculiar system of beliefs of the Hindus for which I can find no rational explanation, an untouchable would be treated as a person unfit for "touch" by the high caste Hindus so long as he remained a Hindu; but the moment he became a Muslim or a Christian, the high caste Hindu would not object to "touching" him or treating him civilly. Thus the Christian missionary movement brought hope of "social uplift" as well as "salvation" to many an untouchable. Motivated by the desire to prevent desertion of the untouchables from the Hindu fold to the Christian, Hindu reform movements, such as the Arya Samaj, decided in the twenties and thirties to woo the untouchables. They evolved the *Shuddhi* or "purification" ceremonies which would entitle the untouchable to become a "twice-born," on a par with all the Aryas or noble people of India. By contrast, Gandhi's crusade to abolish untouchability was motivated purely by the desire to serve the underprivileged and to rectify a monstrous injustice. Whichever way we look at it, be it in terms of Christian missionary endeavors or Hindu revivalist efforts or Mahatma Gandhi's crusade on behalf of the untouchables (renamed by him Harijans or children of God), this underprivileged Panchama or Fifth Group became the beneficiary of new social forces. Today the Constitution of the Republic of India forbids the practice of untouchability, and Prime Minister Nehru's cabinet had had at least two Harijans holding important portfolios.

Thus, culture-contacts and emergence of new ideas, the rise of nationalism and the impersonal logic of technology—all these factors have been acting as catalytic agents in Hindu society.

Early marriage was banned by legislation in the twenties. Caste rigidity is conspicuous by its absence in large cities, and is slowly melting away in rural areas. The crusade against untouchability, launched by Mahatma Gandhi in 1931, has been further disturbing the stability of the caste structure of India ever since. And, as already pointed out, the Constituent Assembly of India in 1947 legislatively forbade untouchability; and the new constitution of the Republic of India (January 26, 1950) specifically forbids the practice of untouchability (*Vide* Section on Fundamental Rights).

As for the future, it is my judgment that, so far as possible, the leaders of India will still think in terms of the functions of culture that must be performed. Setting their face deadset against rigid barriers of caste, they will strive to organize their society on a functional basis. The new practice of enumerating occupational groups rather than castes for purposes of the census promises to strengthen democracy. In spite of a Marxist slant here and there, I do not foresee the possibility of India giving less respect to the teacher than to the merchant prince or the labor tsar.

11. THE IMPACT OF CASTE UPON OCCIDENTAL CULTURE

The mechanism of caste has been discussed by us in great detail, first, because outsiders have failed fully to appraise its role in Hindu society; second, because it has played a pervasive role in the history of Europe since Plato wrote his *Republic*. It is not necessary for us here to prove the point that from Pythagoras down Greek thinkers were deeply influenced by the philosophy and polity of ancient India. The Pythagorean theorem, so-called, was known in India a couple of centuries before Pythagoras was born. And Pythagoras' beliefs and teachings—the pre-existence and transmigration of the soul, accent on asceticism, prohibition of meat-eating, advocacy of vegetarianism, the conception of the virtue and mystic quality of numbers, and belief in ether as the fifth element in addition to the recognized four, fire, air, water, earth—these beliefs and teachings of Pythagoras are alien to the Greek temper and Hellenic culture; they are more Hindu than Hellenic. Indeed, "Before the sixth century B.C. all the religious-philosophical ideas of Pythagoras are current in India" (5, p. 559). And Eusebius records that "Certain learned Indians actually visited Athens and conversed with Socrates" (10, p. 8).

Students of Hindu and Greek cultures have drawn our attention to "the resemblance between the Hindu Varnas or Castes, Brahmins,

Kshattriyas or warriors, Vaishyas or townsfolk, and Shudras, and the division of the ideal polity in Plato's *Republic* into Guardians, Auxiliaries, and Craftsmen. The story that Socrates proposes to tell about their divine origin, in order that the system may be perpetuated, 'otherwise the State will certainly perish,' is curiously like the Vedic myth about the origin of the four castes from the mouth, arms, thighs, and feet of Purusha, the Primeval Man." (10, p. 8). Compare Plato's *Republic*, BOOK III, and the *Rig Veda*, X, 90.

The Platonic threefold division of society became an actuality in Mediaeval Europe: (1) oratores or the clergy, (2) bellatores or the soldiers, and (3) laboratores or the workers. The clergy, like Plato's guardians, were placed in authority not by the suffrage of the people but by their talent. (2, pp. 110–12). That is precisely how the Brahmins acquired their authority in Hindu society—by *Adhikara* or fitness.

Plato's ideal Republic was without checks and balances, hence it would tend to degenerate into a totalitarianism as the experiences of the Middle Ages and of our own times suggest. When Church and State did not act as a check upon each other in Mediaeval Europe, we had one-party domination and totalitarianism. In our day those of us who saw no virtue in "kicking out of office one set of scoundrels and putting another set in" have been thoroughly chastened by the havoc wrought by Platonism in action even today in Soviet Russia—and in Fascist Italy, Nazi Germany, and Militarist Japan not so long ago.

The Nazi Germans in their day and the Soviet Russians today have succeeded in realizing the Platonic ideal in practice: (1) the Elite at the top, (2) the Nazi or the Communist Party along with the army, in the middle, (3) the non-Nazi or the non-Communist mass at the bottom. Thus the underlying philosophy of the caste system of India by way of Plato is today vigorously operating in Europe!

In our analysis of the caste system in India, we pointed out the inherent tendency toward structuralization of functions. In the Soviet Union this tendency toward structuralization of functions has been in operation ever since Lenin's death (1924) with a violence unknown to India and unimaginable to a democracy. Would-be poachers, disturbers and dissenters have been "liquidated," so that the elite may continue to reign for the glory of the Soviet Union! This is a significant fact in the contemporary world scene, and we may ignore its implications at our own peril.

The open class system of America permitted the structuralization of caste relations as between white and colored during the period of slavery. Since the War between the States, this structuralized relationship between white and colored has been gradually undergoing modifications. The Park Avenue set, the bluebook set with their subdebs and debutantes, have not yet become definitely structuralized; nor has the Hollywood set. But the proletarian mass is in process of becoming structuralized. The sociologist has an obligation to investigate and analyze the implications of these "caste" situations in Russia as well as in America.

REFERENCES

1. SWAMI ABBEDANANDA: *India and Her People*. New York: Vedanta Society, 1906.

2. ERNEST BARKER: "Unity in the Middle Ages," Chapter in *Unity of Western Civilization*, 2nd ed., ed. by F. S. Marvin. London: Humphrey Milford, 1922.

3. RUTH BENEDICT: *Race: Science and Politics*. New York: The Viking Press, 1945.

4. G. E. GHELKE: *Emile Durkheim's Contributions to Sociological Theory*. New York: Columbia University Studies in History, Economics and Public Law, Vol. LXIII, No. 1, 1915.

5. E. W. HOPKINS: *Religions of India*. Boston: Ginn and Company, 1895.

6. J. H. HUTTON: *Caste in India*. Cambridge: University Press, 1946.

7. SIR M. MONIER-WILLIAMS: *Brahmanism and Hinduism*, 4th ed., New York: Macmillan, 1891.

8. HARIDAS T. MUZUMDAR: *Gandhi the Apostle*. Chicago: Universal Publishing Co., 1923.

9. HARIDAS T. MUZUMDAR: *The United Nations of the World*. New York: Universal Publishing Company, 1942 (2nd ed., 1944).

10. H. G. RAWLINSON: "India in European Literature and Thought," Chapter I in *The Legacy of India*, ed. by G. T. Garratt. Oxford: Clarendon Press, 1945.

CHAPTER 16

RACE-GROUPS

RACE is strictly a classificatory term in the field of biology and genetics, embracing a group of people, while nation is a sociological grouping.

1. RACE, ORIGINAL NATURE, GENETICS

A group of individuals is said to belong to a race when all its members share in common certain significant physical traits that are transmitted biologically through the mechanism of heredity. Among the physical traits that can be inherited from generation to generation are: the color of the skin, eye color and eye form, hair color and hair form, shape of the nose, bodily stature, shape of the head, blood type.

We must also assume that the original nature of man—the capacity to respond and to systematize and articulate the experiences of responses—is also biologically inherited from generation to generation. But inasmuch as original nature is simply a potential and becomes a serviceable tool of human behavior only after its transformation into human nature through the processes of socialization, all attempts to classify the inheritable original nature of man into good or bad, superior or inferior, become meaningless. Geneticists and psychologists incline to the view that certain mental traits and abilities may be inherited, the musical ability for instance. Even if we grant this, we are compelled to accept the fact that the inherited musical ability of a Hottentot musical genius will have to express itself in terms of the musical lore of the Hottentot people. The musical ability of a Bach or a Beethoven, whether inborn or acquired, has to express itself in terms of the musical lore of Occidental culture. All children, Hottentot or Icelandic or Germanic, are born with the ability to manipulate things ; but whether they will manipulate a toy engine, a toy typewriter or a stone or a reed, is conditioned by the given culture. Hence scientists are baffled to classify inherited mental traits into good and bad, efficient and inefficient, superior and inferior.

A study of samples of new-born babies among different peoples would reveal the fact that some are quick of reaction, others slow of reaction. But the quickness or intensity of response is found to be the monopoly of no particular people. Some new-born babies in every group are quick and others slow of reaction; each group is apt to conform to the curve of normal distribution, the so-called bell-shaped curve, in regard to biological characteristics:

CHART 12

BIOLOGICAL CHARACTERISTICS

The curve of Normal Distribution

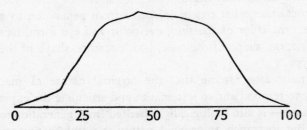

Among a large sample of new-born babies of any race, measured for quickness of response, a few will fall within the 0-25 range, practically the same number within the 75-100 range, and the vast majority within the 25-75 range.

This yields little of significance in classifying race-groups on the basis of their inherited mental traits and abilities. The only phenomenon in this field we can scientifically observe and analyze and classify is human behavior as conditioned by culture. But then this differentiation in human behavior, susceptible of scientific observation, is a function of culture, not of heredity.

Geneticists and psychologists are still wrestling with this problem in the hope of discovering reliable tools for the investigation and classification of inherited mental traits and abilities of different peoples. The quest, however, is entirely fruitless unless the very basis of sociology and cultural anthropology is proved to be invalid.

With the aid of psychological measurements, it is possible to identify two extreme cases in any group—the genius and the idiot. Let us, however, remember that even this identification can at times be wrong—Isabelle had been pronounced "feeble-minded" by clinical psychologists. Even so, mental testing has its validity; but the attempt to locate whole culture-groups or race-groups on a scale from superior to average to inferior, in terms of native ability or biologically inherited mental traits, is foredoomed to failure. To begin with, the criteria of "superior" are vague, flexible, and relative. Whatever physical traits or mental capacities make for optimum adjustment of the group to its environment are "good," even "superior." In terms of adjustment to the tropics, the Negro's dark skin is a value; in the same environment, the European's white skin would be a liability. Contrariwise, in temperate and cold climates, the Negro's dark skin would be a liability.

Inherited *physical* traits are capable of measurement and analysis and classification. The problem for the physical anthropologist, in cooperation with geneticists, is to discover which physical traits are transmitted by heredity from generation to generation, and not affected by nurture. A little English girl aboard a steamer once remarked to a Hindu, "My, but you must not be washing your hands and face with soap; that is why they are so dark!" Well, of course, no amount of soap will turn the dark-brown skin of the modern Hindu into colorless white, despite the naiveté of the little girl!

2. MECHANISMS OF INHERITANCE

The quest for the classification of the human species into races, ultimately, reduces itself to a study of the mechanisms of heredity, the genes and the chromosomes, and the identification of those unit-traits or genes in the chromosomes which translate themselves into the physical traits of the new-born. This quest has been greatly aided by biologists and geneticists.

Students who specialize in studying the mechanism of inheritance are agreed upon four fundamental principles: (1) the principle of independent unit-traits or genes, (2) the principle of "determiners" in the germ cells, (3) the continuity of the germ plasm, (4) the principle of "dominant" and "recessive" traits.

First, the male sperm and the female egg fuse together to produce a "zygote." This zygote is the individual-in-the-making (in the mother's womb), made up of chromosomes containing genes. The chromosome, literally a colored body, is like a string of beads; it is made up of a string of genes. Each human being has 48 chromosomes, 24 received from the father and 24 from the mother.

The following illustration (p. 235) prepared by Amram Scheinfeld, vividly describes the heredity process (11, p. 102).

The germ plasm contains unit-traits or genes for the different characteristics that will be manifested in the newborn—color of skin, color and shape of the eyes, the shape of the nose, the color and texture of the hair, the shape of the head, blood type, etc. Each of these unit-traits is independent, though some of them may be associated with one another in a cluster, such as fair skin, blue eyes and blond hair.

Second, it is obvious that the son does not "inherit" his father's nose; rather the germ plasm which matured into the son carried within it a "determiner" for the shape of the nose the son would have.

Third, there is really no inheritance from parent to child; rather, parent and child resemble each other because they are both derived from the same germ plasm—because they are both chips off the same old block. The son is in a real sense half-brother to his father, by another mother. The continuity—and immortality—of the germ plasm is one of the miracles of life.

Fourth, Mendel established the principle that certain unit-traits are dominant and certain other unit-traits are recessive. The unit-trait for blue eyes is, for instance, recessive as compared to the unit-trait for brown eyes which is dominant. This means that if one parent has blue eyes and the other has brown eyes, the offspring will have brown eyes.

The problem of inheritance is, however, more complicated than the simple statement that the offspring will have brown eyes. Here we must pause for a moment to explain the Mendelian law of inheritance.

CHART 13

THE HEREDITY PROCESS [1]

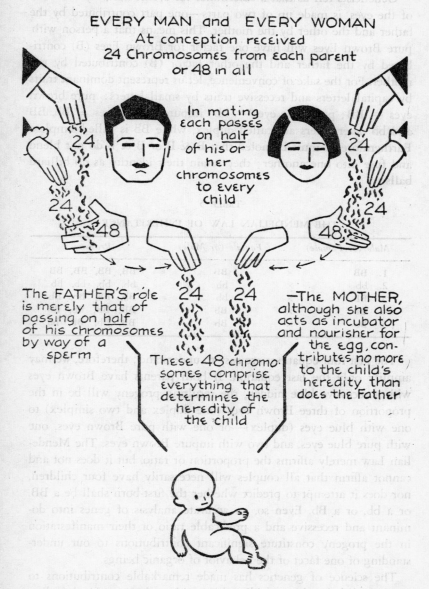

EVERY MAN and EVERY WOMAN
At conception received
24 Chromosomes from each parent
or 48 in all

In mating
each passes
on half
of his or
her
chromosomes
to every
child

24

24

24

24

48

48

24

24

The FATHER'S role
is merely that of
passing on half
of his chromosomes
by way of a
sperm

—The MOTHER,
although she also
acts as incubator
and nourisher for
the egg, con-
tributes no more
to the child's
heredity than
does the Father

These 48 chromo-
somes comprise
everything that
determines the
heredity of
the child

[1] Reproduced from Amram Scheinfeld: *The New You and Heredity* (1950), p. 102, with the permission of the author and the publisher, J. B. Lippincott, Co.

Geneticists tell us that a determiner for a unit-trait, say the color of the eyes, is made up of two parts—one part contributed by the father and the other by the mother. This means that a person with pure Brown Eyes will have one factor for Brown Eyes (B) contributed by the father and the other factor (B) contributed by the mother. For the sake of convenience, let us represent dominant traits by capital letters and recessive traits by small letters: pure brown eyes = BB; pure blue eyes = bb; impure brown eyes = Bb. BB and bb determiners are called duplex, while Bb is called simplex. Furthermore, it must be noted that B & B or B & b do not blend and fuse into one another; they retain their identity as do billiard balls.

TABLE 5

THE MENDELIAN LAW OF INHERITANCE

Male (or Female)		Female (or Male)		Progeny
1. BB	×	BB	=	BB, BB, BB, BB
2. bb	×	bb	=	bb, bb, bb, bb
3. BB	×	bb	=	Bb, Bb, Bb, Bb
4. BB	×	Bb	=	BB, BB, Bb, Bb
5. Bb	×	Bb	=	BB, Bb, Bb, bb

The first four equations are easy to understand; therefore, we may amplify only the last equation. If both parents have Brown eyes with a recessive blue hidden, the resulting progeny will be in the proportion of three Brown eyes (one duplex and two simplex) to one with blue eyes (duplex)—or one with pure Brown eyes, one with pure blue eyes, and two with impure Brown eyes. The Mendelian Law merely affirms the proportion or ratio, but it does not and cannot affirm that all couples will necessarily have four children, nor does it attempt to predict whether the first-born shall be a BB, or a bb, or a Bb. Even so, an accurate analysis of genes into dominant and recessive and a predicable ratio of their manifestation in the progeny constitute significant contributions to our understanding of one facet of the behavior of organic beings.

The science of genetics has made remarkable contributions to man's well-being by providing him with techniques for breeding better cattle and horses, for improving the quality of the grain, for cross-breeding existing fruits and vegetables and flowers to evolve new ones—e.g., grapefruit, tangerine, etc.

3. EUGENICS AND EUTHENICS

So far as the human species is concerned, programs for betterment are geared both to eugenics, or improvement of man through an improvement of his hereditary qualities, and to euthenics, improvement of man through an improvement of his environment.

The eugenic approach is twofold: positive and negative. The negative aspect of the eugenic program attempts to discourage matings between dysgenic persons and to breed out undesirable hereditary traits. The positive eugenic program, on the other hand, attempts to encourage the propagation of wholesome hereditary strains.

Later we shall discuss the classic cases of the Jukes, the Kallikaks, and the Edwardses (*infra,* CHAPTER 26).

4. FOUR BIOLOGICALLY DETERMINED DIFFERENCES

The study of genetics clearly points out that certain differences may be biologically determined or inherited. Both the psychologist and the sociologist are interested in studying the possible implications of biological differences for human behavior, social organization, and culture.

The biologically determined differences are four: (1) individual differences, (2) sex differences, (3) age differences, and (4) race differences.

The problem of individual differences is of crucial importance to educators. Should we penalize the superior student by compelling him to advance in his school work at the pace set by the average student? Should we overtax the dull student by compelling him to try to achieve beyond his capacity? Is democracy inherently opposed to special treatment for the gifted?

Does the basic sex difference between men and women imply differences in intellectual and emotional capacities? Are sex roles, such as active "pursuer" or passive "pursued," determined by biology or by culture? Answers to these and other questions may throw light on some of the problems of human behavior and social relationships.

At what age does a child grow into maturity? Are the behavior patterns of teenagers in a given society determined by biology or by culture? Do different people mature at different ages? Does the I.Q.

$\left(\dfrac{\text{Mental Age}}{\text{Chronological Age}} \times 100\right)$ test inherited mental ability or acquired ability and actual accomplishment? What is the role of different age-groups in our culture? Answers to these and similar questions would throw light on some of the problems of social organization and relationships.

In this chapter, we are primarily concerned with a study of race, race differences, and the impact of race on modern civilization.

5. CRITERIA FOR CLASSIFICATION OF MANKIND INTO RACES

The problem of classification of mankind into races on the basis of similarity of certain significant physical traits is much more complicated than the layman realizes. There is the fundamental problem of the determination of basic, relevant traits whose possession may entitle their possessors to a common grouping. This problem is neatly set forth by Ruth Benedict (1887-1948) in *Race: Science and Politics* (1, p. 23):

In zoology a classification is considered artificial, if, for instance, it classes a whale with fishes simply because whales swim; the classification is basic when it classes a whale with mammals, whose processes of reproduction and need for breathing air into their lungs the whale shares. For the study of mammals, it is necessary to subordinate many obvious physical differences that appear among mammals and to consider together not only whales, which swim like fishes, but also bats, which fly like birds. Whales and bats moreover must be studied alongside hoofed animals and men, for they are all mammals.

Students of human races, therefore, hoped to establish classifications of man which were more than superficially descriptive and which might have a validity such as the classification of mammals has.

The questions we must answer are : (1) What inheritable stable physical traits are basic for purposes of sound classification? (2) How did these traits become stabilized in a given group and differentiated from similar stable traits in other groups—skin color, eye color and form, stature, shape of the nose, shape of the head, etc.? (3) What significance do these differentiations have in the behavior of people?

In view of popular misconceptions regarding the validity of certain bases of classification, we may reproduce the authoritative statement of Ruth Benedict on (1) skin color, (2) eye color and form, (3) hair color and hair form, (4) shape of the nose, (5) stature, (6) cephalic index, (7) blood types (1, 25-30, 174-75, 31) :

Skin Color

The racial difference that at once arrests attention is skin color. The wall paintings of ancient Egyptians used four pigments for the complexions of the four peoples they knew ; red for themselves, yellow for their enemies in Asia, white for people from the north, and black for Negroes. This classification has been reduced by one and given a Greek terminology. Its value consists in that it is the most generalized category into which human beings are zoologically divided :

Leucodermi—white-skinned
Xanthodermi—yellow-skinned
Melanodermi—black-skinned

In general usage this classification corresponds to the division into Caucasoid (white), Mongoloid (yellow), and Negroid (black); these are the obvious and striking human varieties. Further physical characteristics, as we shall see, can be associated with these three groups. They have each a large geographical range, and represent real differentiations.

Skin color, of itself, however, has very limited scientific use as a criterion of these primary races. The range in each group is very large, and some groups of Whites are darker than some Negroes. Broca, the French physical anthropologist, used thirty-four shades of skin color and Deniker nine. Differentiation into shades is a help in one direction but it makes the overlapping even more serious.

The superficial character of skin color as a criterion of race becomes a serious difficulty when the question is one of assigning problematic groups to the primary races. Are the "Australians"

Negroid because their skin color is nearest the range for Negroes; are light-colored Armenian types Caucasoid because theirs is nearest the range for Whites? All students agree that such arguments are superficial.

Skin color, therefore, as a means of differentiating the ethnic groups of man with the widest geographical range has some advantage if it is loosely applied. As a scientific criterion it has a gross rather than a specific usefulness.

Eye Color and Eye Form

Eye pigmentation is commonly recorded in physical measurements of populations but it does not identify an individual as a member of a particular race. Dark eyes are common to all human races and cannot therefore be used to differentiate them. Even more special types of eye color, such as blueness, have never been found coextensive with a whole ethnic group.

Eye form appears in racial descriptions primarily in reference to the "slanting" eyes typical of yellow-skinned Asiatics. It is called the Mongoloid eye, and the slant-eye appearance is caused by a fold of skin, the epicanthic fold, which covers the inner angle of the eye. It occurs in infancy among many Whites but does not usually persist into adulthood; it occurs among some Negroes and is characteristic of some American Indians (also Mongoloids) though most of these latter do not have it.

Hair Color and Hair Form

Dark hair color, like dark eyes, is so widely distributed among mankind that it does not serve to define race, and, as with blue eyes, even the special trait of blond hair does not run uniformly through any ethnic group.

Hair form can also be classified. There are three major types:
Leiotrichy—straight lank hair (e.g., Chinese, Eskimo)
Cymotrichy—wavy hair (e.g., inhabitants of Europe, India, Australia)
Ulotrichy—woolly or frizzy hair (e.g., Negroes, Melanesians)

These differences in hair appearance are due to the form of the individual hair as seen in cross section under a microscope; straight hair is round, woolly hair extremely oval, and wavy hair falls in between.

Again like skin color, these different hair forms are found in ethnic groups of wide geographical distribution, and when used as characteristics of these major groups they have descriptive value.

The trouble with them as racial traits is that they cross-cut races as described in other terms. Because Australian black-fellows have smooth wavy hair, like that of Europeans, they are not therefore Europeans, nor are the Eskimos Chinese because they have straight lank hair. Smooth wavy hair is typical of Europe, Egypt, and the Asiatic peoples who live from the eastern Mediterranean down to and including India, and is therefore characteristic of peoples who are unlike in other physical traits. Hair form nevertheless has a certain value in the study of the distribution of races, and no one doubts, on other grounds as well as hair form, that the dark Melanesians of Western Oceania—for instance, the natives of the Solomon Islands—are genetically related to African Negroes.

Shape of the Nose

Physical anthropologists have paid considerable attention to measuring the types of human nose. There are two chief categories:

Leptorrhine—narrow nostrils (e.g., European, Eskimo)
Platyrrhine—flat broad nostrils (e.g., Negroes, Tasmanians)

Besides these, various descriptions of the nose bridge are in use: concave, convex, aquiline, or straight.

Here again, though certain extreme nose shapes are found only in certain groups in the world—certain broad flat forms among certain Negroes and certain narrow aquiline ones among certain Caucasians —even these do not identify a man who on other counts is a Negro or a Caucasian, both races having a great range of nose shapes.

Stature

Bodily height is the extreme case of a physical trait, which, though it is also hereditary, is easily modified by environment. Many studies have demonstrated that stature as well as body weight is influenced by diet, sickness, and other conditions of life. It is therefore in most cases not a reliable index of genetic relationship. A good exception to this rule is the case of the pygmies, among whom stature is clearly hereditary and can be used for zoological classification. In other cases, however, even when stature is hereditary, tall groups jostle short groups within each race as it is defined in other terms. The tallest and the shortest group measured are both Negro, and even on the remote island of Tierra del Fuego, an extremely tall American Indian tribe is the neighbor of an extremely short tribe. Stature is a very fallible racial criterion.

$$Cephalic\ Index: \frac{Breadth\ of\ Head}{Length\ of\ Head} \times 100$$

The cephalic index is the ratio of the maximum breadth to the maximum length of the head seen from on top, and is expressed in a percentage. This aspect of the head has been arbitrarily divided into three types:

Dolichocephalic—narrow-headed, with cephalic index under 75
Mesocephalic—medium-headed, with cephalic index 75–80
Brachycephalic—broad-headed, with cephalic index over 80

Of all human measurements, the cephalic index is the commonest in physical anthropology and the data on it in a given population are the most often available. This is because it is definite and easy to measure, and because, with certain allowances for the thickness of the skin, it can be used in measurements of skulls of dead people as well as of heads of living people.

The cephalic index does not serve to distinguish the White race from the Mongoloid nor from the Negro, nor has it any constant value for any primary race. For instance, some American Indian groups have the narrowest skulls ever measured and some the broadest skulls, and these are groups which, judged by other characteristics, fall together into one race. Similarly, the cephalic index distinguishes between certain sub-groups of the White race rather than having a constant value for all Caucasians. In other words, a graph of the cephalic index shows peaks and valleys *within* large groups otherwise similar and is chiefly used to describe small local variations.

Blood Types

There are four types of blood, O, A, B, and AB, and although blood type O can be mixed successfully with the other three, none of these can be mixed with one another without clumping.

These four types of blood are inherited by each child from its forebears. But Whites, Negroes, Mongols,—all races of man have all these blood types. The color of their skin does not tell which blood type they have. You and an Australian bushman may have the same blood type. Because you inherit your bodily traits from your many different ancestors, you may have a different blood type from your mother or your father or your brothers and sisters. You may have eyes like your mother's, teeth and hair like your father's, feet like your grandfather's, and a blood type like your great-grandmother's.

Blood types are strictly hereditary and very stable; any individual having blood type A, for example, must have had an ancestor whose blood type was A. Therefore when different blood types are present in any population, it is one of the surest signs of mixed ancestry. But even such isolated races as the aboriginal Australians have a high percentage of blood group A, which is that most characteristic of Western Europe. And in Europe 10 to 30 per cent of the population everywhere have blood type B, which is that most characteristic of India and Eastern Asia. The evidence from the study of blood groups emphasizes in the strongest possible manner the great amount of biological mixture that must have taken place from the earliest times.

6. DIFFICULTIES IN CLASSIFICATION

In spicy language Professor E. A. Hooton (1887-1954) points out the difficulties and confusions present in the field of classification of human races (3, pp. 446-47):

Zoologists, in classifying animals, fling about families, genera, and species like drunken sailors scattering their wages. These terms connote little more than relationship based upon morphological features. Families are groups of animals of common descent, the members of which bear to each other fundamental structural resemblances. Genera are smaller groups within the families, and the members of a genus are more like and more closely related to each other than they are to animals belonging to any different genus. The species is merely another splitting up of the genus into still smaller, more similar, and more nearly related groups. Varieties or races constitute a still further subdivision. Linnaeus gave to the term "species" a definite conception of fixity when he formulated the aphorism *species tot sunt diversae, quot diversae formae ab initio sunt creatae*—"just so many species are to be reckoned as there were forms created at the beginning." According to him a species was a sort of eternal biological verity—immutable, objective, requiring only to be discovered and named. Darwin in *The Origin of Species* rejected the objective concept of species, not only because he could not satisfy himself as to the existence of any dependable criteria whereby a group of animals could be ranked as a genus, the less important classification of a species, or degraded into a variety. An attempt to distinguish as a physiological criterion of species the ability to inter-breed without loss of fertility is futile, since many forms universally recognized as species produce hybrids with other species. So the term "species" is little more than an artificial rank in classification, a label for a pigeonhole of a certain size into which may be thrust conveniently subjects closely related to each other in form and by origin. Hence, the modern systematist has no qualms about the recognition of a new species, providing it is sufficiently distinct from those already known; he does not feel as if he were interfering with the works of the Creator in so doing.

In dealing with man, however, anthropologists have usually been very chary in their use of zoological terms of classification. Usually all human types, extinct and recent, except, perhaps, Pithecanthropus erectus, have been included in the family Hominidae. In the matter of species subdivision, such archaic and apelike forms as Neanderthal man, Heidelberg man, Sinanthropus, and Eoanthropus have usually been assigned separate specific rank and have sometimes been elevated to the grade of a genus. Everything seems to depend upon the systematist's idea as to the distinctness of the form he describes and its nearness or remoteness of relationship to other human types. Obviously, this is a very subjective and arbitrary procedure. All existing forms of man are usually included in one species, *Homo sapiens,* although the differences between the several races are quite as marked as usually serve to distinguish species in other animals. The purely academic nature of any discussion as to the unity or diversity of species in modern groups of men makes it a sheer waste of time. We avoid difficulties by talking about "races."

Even the term "race" as applied to man is commonly employed with no accurate and well defined meaning. One often sees references to the "White race," the "Jewish race," the "Latin race," the "Irish race." Such indiscriminate use of the word "race" implies a linguistic criterion, and finally any reference to an "Irish race" must mean a race characterized either by geographical position or, failing that, by temperament. Such confusions of usage are usually confined to the non-anthropological writing public. All anthropologists agree that the criteria of race are physical characters.

7. KROEBER'S CLASSIFICATION OF RACES

The most widely accepted scheme of race classification is the one originally given us by Dr. A. L. Kroeber (5, p. 140)—(see next page):

The late Professor Franz Boas (1858-1942) was of the opinion that the three main stocks—Caucasoid, Mongoloid, Negroid—could be more appropriately reduced to two, the Mongoloid and the Negroid, and that the Caucasoid might be conveniently conceived to be a specialized differentiation of the Mongoloid. This way the existence of Ainus in Japan, with white skin and hairiness, may be accounted for without resort to the theory of migration. (1, p. 35).

CHART 14

THE RACES OF MANKIND *

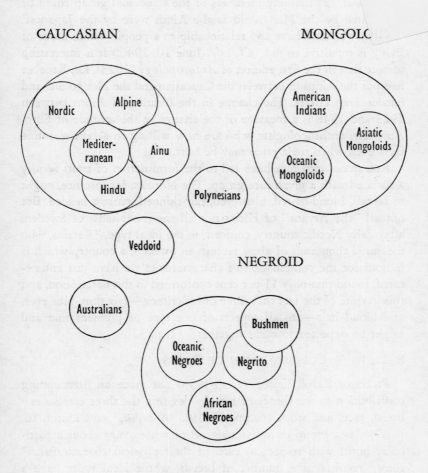

CAUCASIAN   MONGOLO

Nordic

Alpine

Mediter-
ranean

Ainu

Hindu

Polynesians

Veddoid

American
Indians

Asiatic
Mongoloids

Oceanic
Mongoloids

NEGROID

Australians

Bushmen

Oceanic
Negroes

Negrito

African
Negroes

* Relationship of human races. Distances between the centers of circles are indicative of the degree of similarity. Reproduced from A. L. Kroeber: *Anthropology,* 2nd. ed., p. 140. (New York: Harcourt Brace & Co. 1948).

But books on race are written by members of the Caucasoid group and it hurts our pride to believe (1) that we are descended from the Mongoloid, (2) that any members of the Caucasoid group could be subjugated by the Mongoloid as the Ainus were by the Japanese, (3) that we could have any relationship to a people whose mode of living is repulsive to us! (*Cf. Life,* June 10, 1946.) It is interesting to note that in the first edition of *Anthropology* (1923), Dr. Kroeber had put the Ainus in between the Caucasian and the Mongoloid, and outside both circles. The change in the location of Ainus between 1923 and 1948 is a measure of the change in the attitude of Euro-American anthropologists, who are now willing to accept scientific facts even when their pride may be hurt.

Researches into race have led to the formulation of traits *ideally* associated with a given race group. The Nordics, for instance, ought to be tall, blond-haired, blue-eyed, fair-skinned, narrow-headed. But not all "the Aryans" of Hitler nor all the inhabitants of Sweden, a typically Nordic country, conform to the ideal type. "Retzius, who measured thousands of army recruits in Sweden, a country which is famous for the combination of characteristics we have just enume-rated, found that only 11 per cent conformed to this description, and this in spite of the fact that three of his criteria—fair skin, blue eyes, and blond hair—are all aspects of one type of pigmentation and might be expected to occur together." (1, p. 32).

8. LINTON'S CLASSIFICATION OF RACES

Professor Ralph Linton (1893-1953) has made an illuminating contribution to the theory of race by devising the three categories: breed, race, and stock (6, pp. 22–59). "A *breed*," says Linton (6, p. 37), "is a group of individuals, all of whom vary about a parti-cular norm with respect to each of their physical characteristics." *Race* "consists of a number of breeds, whose ideal types have a series of characteristics in common" (6, p. 39). Finally, "*Stocks* are groups of races, the content of any stock being established by the same techniques as those used for establishing racial classifications" (6, p. 40).

Linton's special contribution to a proper understanding of race is well brought out by Schermerhorn (10, pp. 21–24):

The anthropologist approaches the problem from both above and below; the view from above may be called a general conception, while the view from below may be termed specific. In the general conception, the anthropologist begins with the biologist's method of classification (sometimes called taxonomy). Thus, just like the biologist classifying animals, he takes the first step:

Genus: Homo
        Species: Sapiens
                Subspecies: 1, 2, 3, etc.

These subspecies then receive the name of stocks. The human species, Homo sapiens, has three main subspecies or stocks known as the Caucasian, Negroid, and Mongolian stocks. Then each of these subspecies has several sub-subspecies.

SUBSPECIES: Caucasian
            Sub-subspecies: Nordic, Alpine, Mediterranean, Armenoid, Hindese
SUBSPECIES: Negroid
            Sub-subspecies: Nilotic, Forest, Pygmy, Negrito, Oceanic
SUBSPECIES: Mongolian
            Sub-subspecies: I. Old World
                            North Chinese, Malay, Siberian
            Sub-subspecies: II. New World
                            American Indians

In the specific conception, the anthropologist begins with groups that have a homogeneous heritage; i.e., groups that are small and isolated from other groups chiefly by geographical boundaries and that have practiced inbreeding until there is a kind of family resemblance. This genetic group is called the *breed*. There are few examples of this kind left in the world today, but Linton illustrates the type by citing the Cape York Eskimo with something under five hundred persons who have interbred for three hundred years. According to the present hypothesis, many of these breeds who lived close together and began to marry members of other breeds in nearby territory gradually came to resemble each other as well. This gave rise to the type that is now called a race. Thus a race, according to the specific conception, is a group of breeds having physical characteristics sufficiently alike so that they can be grouped together into a single type. Race, as defined by this hypothesis, is for all practical purposes identical with the sub-subspecies mentioned above. And finally, a group of races that resemble each other sufficiently would be called a *stock,* the three main ones being, as before, the Caucasian, the Negroid, and the Mongolian. The diagram for the specific conception would differ only in its point of reference but in other details would resemble the one presented by the general conception above. Hence it would be:

Breeds (genuine biological entities): 1, 2, 3, 4, etc.
Races (groups of similar breeds): Nordic, Alpine, Mediterranean, Armenoid, Hindese
Stock (a group of similar races): Caucasian

It will now be easy for the reader to follow through the classificatory process with the other stocks. There is, however, one important distinction which belongs to the *specific* conception, and that is that the positing of breeds is at present hypothetical, for none of the pure breeds that make up the races any longer exist. They are inferred entities, and we have good reason for inferring them because of the laws of genetics developed since Mendel.

The question immediately arises: what about the white race, the yellow race, and the black race? The answer is that anthropologists and social scientists in general who are careful of their terminology, never use the terms "black race" or "yellow race" or "white race" because those terms refer more specifically to stocks than to races. Furthermore, it is not entirely accurate to say that the Caucasian stock is composed of white races, because many anthropologists include the Hindese race with the other Caucasian groups, and the Hindese people live in India and have a brown skin. This means that color of skin is less important for the anthropologist, who finds in the Hindese other measurable characteristics very similar to those of the Mediterranean groups. Thus, even though there may be a variant skin color, the other characteristics compel him to call the Hindese a Caucasian race (though it should be explained that this classification does not include all the Indian [i.e., Hindese] groups). . . . Anthropology knows nothing whatever of "the white race" or "the black race."

9. ORIGIN OF RACE DIFFERENCES

How did race differences arise? Through isolation, inbreeding, interbreeding, selection, and mutation.

A given group of people, let us call it a tribe, lived in a given area. All the human organisms in that area would have had to make appropriate responses to the objective conditions of life, to heat, humidity, temperature, altitude, etc. Those who failed to make successful responses to these conditions would perish; those who survived would be selected organisms capable of flourishing in that habitat. Let us say our tribe was endogamous. The successful would mate from generation to generation. All the successful organisms would have had to develop somatic characters capable of adjustment to the environment. "Tropics and polar regions, deserts and swamps, valleys and mountain tops, would seem to be variations sufficiently wide to produce differences in man. The narrow slit-like opening of the nose of the Eskimo is perhaps the result of a geographical influence, for such nasal openings serve the purpose of warming a little the air taken into the nostrils. The dark skin of the African native protects the blood from too much penetration of the ultra-violet rays of light. The polar bear and the rhinoceros are adapted to their particular geographical environments and neither could live in the habitation of the other. . . . Blue eyes and fair hair survive more readily around the Baltic than at the Sahara." (9, p. 86).

Furthermore, if our tribe were endogamous, inbreeding would tend to stabilize the tribe. "Inbreeding is likely to occur in regions where there are barriers such as rivers, mountains, deserts, or stretches of land without much food, and among peoples who do not have many inventions for transportation, and whose technology is so crude as to support only a small population." (9, p. 87). And, of course, the tribe might be hostile to out-groups.

In this isolation there arises what anthropologists call the "area of characterization." (1, p. 42). In this area of characterization not only would the stabilized physical type be unique but its culture too would be unique and specialized. Thus in primitive societies we often find certain race characteristics and certain culture traits, including the morphology of language, associated together. But it must be remembered that culture is not a function of race; the co-existence of a given culture and a given race can be easily accounted for in terms of simple sociological processes.

Suppose our tribe were exogamous, then interbreeding would selectively stabilize the type most capable of adjustment to the environment. The two tribes would now form the area of characterization, giving rise to a specialized racial type and an emergent culture. Nor must we overlook the role of mutation in the fixing of physical type. A mutant within a group may intermarry with the "normal" type and establish a new hereditary line. Or, two mutants may intermarry and establish a new hereditary line. The process of selection will determine the fixation and ascendancy of the mutant type if it has greater survival value.

Interbreeding need not be restricted to two contiguous tribes. Migration of human beings from place to place has taken place on this planet from almost the very beginning of the origin of the species, homo sapiens. Migration would thus account for the distribution of certain physical traits and culture traits over areas separated by vast distances.

To summarize: In our discussion of race thus far, we have affirmed that it is a classificatory term; that the term race has to do with physical traits, with anatomy, not with culture; that different racial types arise in different areas of characterization; that the processes consummating stabilization of race types are isolation, inbreeding, interbreeding, selection, and mutation; that in a given area of characterization a race type and a culture type may grow up intimately associated with each other, but that race, as such, does not determine the type of culture evolved. The role of human migrations and of diffusion of culture traits is most significant in the evolution of culture. Culture is learned behavior acquired with the aid of sociological mechanisms, while race is anatomy inherited through the mechanisms of biological inheritance.

10. RACE AND CULTURE

Certain race groups and certain types or patterns of culture are found associated together—for example, the Caucasoid groups in Europe and European culture patterns. This fortuitous circumstance has given rise to the racialist theory that certain types of culture, high culture, can be originated, maintained, or enriched only by certain race groups. Anthropology and sociology disprove this racialist notion of the biological determinism of types of culture.

For instance, the Finns, the Hungarians and the Turks are Mongoloid racially, yet they have accepted the European culture pattern and enriched it. The Negroes in America are racially akin to some of the Negro tribes in Africa, and yet they effectively participate in the American cultural stream. Indeed, the two distinctively American contributions to the world of art, jazz in its musical form and in its dance form, are Negro contributions to American culture.

The ability to speak a certain language does not rest upon the color of the skin. American Negroes speak English, rather American; Alexandre Dumas, *pere et fils,* with Negro blood in their veins, enriched the French language and French literature; and Aleksander Pushkin, likewise with Negro blood in his veins, enriched the Russian language and Russian literature.

In the photograph of what he calls "cultural turnabouts" (facing p. 252) Mr. Scheinfeld has dramatized the pre-eminent role of culture rather than of biology in the formation of personality. Mr. Paul Fung, Jr., a Chinese-American, is as American as the corn we grow in Iowa, even though racially he belongs with the Chinese of China. Mr. Joseph Rhinehart, on the other hand, a member of the Caucasian stock, was reared in China by a Chinese family practically from infancy under the name of Fung Kwok-Keung, and was as Chinese in his speech, outlook and temperament as any son of the Celestial Kingdom when he returned to America, the land of his birth as well as of his biological parents. (11, pp. 505–06).

11. RACE AND RACISM

The fortuitous association of race and culture has had profound effects on human behavior throughout history. Ethnocentrism—i.e., exalting one's group and judging out-groups by the norms of one's own group—is an inevitable byproduct of group cohesion. My forebears in India divided the world into Aryas, the noblemen, and the Un-Aryas (the ignoble), usually referred to as the Mlechchhas, the unclean. To the Chinese the world consisted of civilized Chinese and rude barbarians. The Greeks, on the one hand, and the Romans, on the other, each looked upon themselves as "civilized" and the rest of the world as "barbarians." For the Israelite the world consisted of Jews and Gentiles. The Christians looked upon the rest of the world as heathens. The Muslims divided the world into "believers" and "non-believers." It is not necessary for us to sit in judgment upon these varied ethnocentric value-judgments. Whether they were good or bad, right or wrong, justifiable or unjustifiable, is irrelevant. A group that has no ethnocentric pride is headed toward extinction. The point to note is that these judgments of superiority and inferiority were premised on cultural criteria. The "inferior" were deemed to be inferior because of their backward culture, not because of the color of their skin nor because of their cephalic index. If the culturally inferior happened to have a different color of skin, that was purely accidental—interesting but not relevant.

With the rise of modernism, in the wake of the Renaissance and the Reformation in Europe, and with the rise of the scientific concept of race, there came into being the vogue of imputing cultural superiority and inferiority to anatomical traits—the doctrine of racism or racialism. Racialism may be defined as the doctrine that correlates mental abilities to physical traits and attributes superiority or inferiority to certain physical traits, such as fair complexion *versus* dark complexion, thin lips *versus* thick lips, etc. The logic was simple: Certain physical traits are associated with certain mental traits; certain mental traits alone can create certain culture traits; the cultural inferiority of some people is due to their mental inferiority which finds manifestation in their physical traits. This fantastic mode of thinking, which completely eliminated the role of human migrations and culture contacts, is called racism or racialism. While ethnocentrism has been with mankind from the beginning, racialism is a recent phenomenon.

12. RACISM REFUTED: BENEDICT AND LINTON

The assumptions of racialists are refuted by biology and psychology as well as by historical facts. In three remarkable passages, Ruth Benedict explodes the racialist myth (1, pp. 14–16):

CHART 15

CULTURAL TURNABOUTS *

"Paul Fung, Jr. left, racially Chinese but completely American in culture, is shown here with Joseph Rhinehart (Fung Kwok-Keung), White-American by birth, but 'Chinese' in rearing and basic culture. Photographed on the evening when they met at the author's (Scheinfeld's) studio (February, 1950), Paul, a professional cartoonist, has just completed a sketch of Joseph, and the latter has written below it his name in Chinese." (For further description of the two men, see *infra,* Chapter 26).

* Reproduced from Amram Scheinfeld: *The New You and Heredity* (1950), opposite p. 506, with the permission of the author and the publisher, J. B. Lippincott, Co.

The more we know about the fortunes and the vicissitudes of any civilization, the less it proves to be the peculiar offspring of an unmixed race. This is true even far back in prehistory, and an eminent archeologist has said that the great social truth made clear by archeology is that culture lives on and maintains itself though the race perish; either as conquerors or as peaceable settlers a new racial type carries on the old ways of life of the conquered or earlier occupants of the land. The archeologist looking back over the long centuries sees, not the destruction of that civilization when one racial carrier was superseded, but the continuity of its history in the hands of one racial type after another. The growth of human civilization in the European Paleolithic (Old Stone) Age has cultural, but not racial, continuity. The culture which Neanderthal Man possessed was after his disappearance carried forward by Cro-Magnon man, given new embellishments by men of the later Old Stone Age, and elaborated by the races of the New Stone Age. Only the last two types are racially ancestral to modern man. This lack of racial continuity in one small corner of Europe during prehistory is better established for Europe than for other parts of the world because the archeology of Europe is better known, but all that research into prehistory is uncovering in Africa, in Asia, and in Central America tells the same story.

This story has been repeated in Western civilization since the dawn of history and the evidence of it constantly accumulates. A century ago the historian of Western civilization was content to begin with Greece, but today this is inadequate. Historical study has unrolled a longer history under our eyes. Greece was the inheritor of earlier Oriental civilizations and its early culture owed much to Egyptian influences. Essential cornerstones of our civilization are the inventions of other races. Perhaps we prefer to identify our Western culture by its printing presses and literateness. But paper and printing were both borrowed from China. Our economic life with its great concentration of population is based on the cultivation of grains and of animals which are Neolithic inventions from Asia; corn and tobacco were first domesticated by the American Indian. Our control of Nature is overwhelmingly dependent on mathematical calculations. But the so-called Arabic system of notation which is essential to all complicated mathematics was unknown in Europe in the Roman era; it was invented in Asia and introduced to our civilization by the Moors. Algebra was a method of calculation also borrowed by Europeans from Asiatic peoples.

Wherever we look, the truth is forced upon us that many different races have contributed to the growth of our culture, and that when we hold culture as the constant, race is a variable. The "white race" was once the borrower, as today Japan is. The "white race" spent long centuries at the process and Japan a few decades, but by that token some literalists could argue the racial superiority of the Japanese over the "white race."

In four passages, Professor Linton deflates the ego of the American prone to suffer from the superiority complex (6, pp. 346–47): [1]

Our solid American citizen awakens in a bed built on a pattern which originated in the Near East but which was modified in Northern Europe before it was transmitted to America. He throws back covers made from cotton, domesticated in India, or linen domesticated in the Near East, or wool from sheep, also domesticated in the Near East, or silk, the use of which was discovered in China. All of these materials have been spun and woven by processes invented in the Near East. He slips into his moccasins, invented by the Indians of the Eastern woodlands, and goes to the bathroom, whose fixtures are a mixture of European and American inventions, both of recent date. He takes off his pajamas, a garment invented in India, and washes with soap invented by the ancient Gauls. He then shaves, a masochistic rite which seems to have been derived from either Sumer or ancient Egypt.

Returning to the bedroom, he removes his clothes from a chair of southern European type and proceeds to dress. He puts on garments whose form originally derived from the skin clothing of the nomads of the Asiatic steppes, puts on shoes made from skins tanned by a process invented in ancient Eygpt and cut to a pattern derived from the classical civilizations of the Mediterranean, and ties around his neck a strip of bright-colored cloth which is a vestigial survival of the shoulder shawls worn by the seventeenth-century Croatians. Before going out for breakfast he glances through the window, made of glass invented in Egypt, and if it is raining he puts on overshoes made of rubber discovered by the Central American Indians and takes an umbrella, invented in southeastern Asia. Upon his head he puts a hat made of felt, a material invented in the Asiatic steppes.

On his way to breakfast he stops to buy a paper, paying for it with coins, an ancient Lydian invention. At the restaurant a whole

[1] In the following quotation, place names imply places where the invention was first made, not necessarily the places from which we today get the particular article referred to. For instance, "a cantaloupe from Persia" means that the cantaloupe was first grown in Persia or Iran, and not that we get it today from that country.

new series of borrowed elements confronts him. His plate is made of a form of pottery invented in China. His knife is of steel, an alloy first made in southern India, his fork a medieval Italian invention, and his spoon a derivative of a Roman original. He begins breakfast with an orange from the eastern Mediterranean, a cantaloupe from Persia, or perhaps a piece of African watermelon. With this he has coffee, an Abyssinian plant, with cream and sugar. Both the domestication of cows and the idea of milking them originated in the Near East, while sugar was first made in India. After his fruit and first coffee he goes to waffles, cakes made by a Scandinavian technique from wheat domesticated in Asia Minor. Over these he pours maple syrup, invented by the Indians of the Eastern woodlands. As a side dish he may have the egg of a species of bird domesticated in Indo-China, or thin strips of the flesh of an animal domesticated in Eastern Asia which have been salted and smoked by a process developed in northern Europe.

When our friend has finished eating he settles back to smoke, an American Indian habit, consuming a plant domesticated in Brazil in either a pipe, derived from the Indians of Virginia, or a cigarette derived from Mexico. If he is hardy enough he may even attempt a cigar, transmitted to us from the Antilles by way of Spain. While smoking he reads the news of the day, imprinted in characters invented by the ancient Semites upon a material invented in China by a process invented in Germany. As he absorbs the accounts of foreign troubles he will, if he is a good conservative citizen, thank a Hebrew deity in an Indo-European language that he is 100 per cent American.

13. A Pseudo-Scientific Myth Exploded

There is a spicy saying to the effect that there are three types of lies: plain lies, damn lies, and statistical lies. That statistics may be used, or misused, to prove one's preconceived notions is a matter of everyday observation. But it is not realized that social scientists, too, may fall victim to wishful thinking and manipulate statistical data to suit themselves.

The classic example of the social scientists victimizing themselves by statistical data is to be found in the use made of the results of the intelligence tests given to the American Expeditionary Forces in World War I. The gross result showed that, on the average, Negroes made a lower score on these intelligence tests than the whites. And since the samples of Negro and white recruits were larger in number than the size required for statistical generalization, the validity of the results could not be questioned.

When the results of the U.S. Army tests were made available to the public, eminent psychologists and sociologists, secretly suffering from a superiority complex, rushed forth into print in the twenties and early thirties in order to "prove" scientifically that the Negro was innately inferior to the white! And this in spite of the fact that refutations were appearing at the same time in some responsible journals and writings!

Memoirs of the National Academy of Sciences, 15 : 1921, carried "Psychological Examining in the U.S. Army," edited by R. M. Yerkes, in which sectional differences as between Negroes and Negroes and between Negroes and whites were pointed out (12, *passim*).

Only after the appearance, in 1935, of *Race Differences* by Dr. Otto Klineberg, Professor of Psychology at Columbia University, did social scientists begin to retract their wish-fulfilling generalization. Now it began to be allowed that Negro recruits from the North were far superior to the Negro recruits from the South, and that Negro recruits from certain Northern States had a higher median score than white recruits from certain Southern States (4, p. 182).

TABLE 6

MEDIAN SCORES ON A.E.F. (AMERICAN EXPEDITIONARY FORCE) INTELLIGENCE TESTS FOR WHITES FROM CERTAIN SOUTHERN STATES AND FOR NEGROES FROM CERTAIN NORTHERN STATES [1]

Whites		Negroes	
State	*Median Score*	*State*	*Median Score*
Mississippi	41.25	Pennsylvania	42.00
Kentucky	41.50	New York	45.02
Arkansas	41.55	Illinois	47.35
Georgia	42.12	Ohio	49.50

[1] Otto Klineberg: *Race Differences*, p. 182. New York: Harper and Brothers, 1935.

. The comment upon this table by Ruth Benedict and Gene Weltfish in their Public Affairs Pamphlet No. 85 (1943), "The Races of
Mankind," is illuminating (2, p. 18):

Negroes with better luck after they were born got higher scores
than whites with less luck. The white race (sic!) did badly where
economic conditions were bad and schooling was not provided, and
Negroes living under better conditions surpassed them. *The differences did not arise because people were from the North or the
South, or because they were white or black, but because of differences in income, education, cultural advantages, and other
opportunities.*

For reproducing the above table and for these remarks, the
pamphlet was not permitted to be distributed among American
armed forces during World War II, at the behest of a few sensitive
Southern Congressmen and Senators.

14. RACIALISM, A PRODUCT OF MODERN CIVILIZATION

The rise of racialism is intimately tied up with the rise of modern
civilization and forms an integral part of the intellectual history of
our recent past. (1, *passim.*) I can best set forth the natural history
of racialism in our times by reproducing my own discussion of this
problem in another context (8, pp. 113–19):

The Free Spirit of the Renaissance

The Renaissance in Europe freed men's minds from narrow moulds
of thinking. Seafaring adventure, national loyalty, industry and commerce, invention and technology, education and freedom—these
traits made their appearance in human culture, some of them for
the first time, and began to flourish. In the Age of Discovery—a
concomitant of the New Learning—the farthest corners of the world
were discovered and "contacted" by the seafaring Europeans.

National Armies

Over these accomplishments the Europeans were naturally flushed
with pride, with a sense of superiority. The newly emerged Levia-
thans, the National States of Europe, maintained and enriched themselves with the aid of disciplined troops. The French Revolution
created the " national " army brought about by universal conscription

9

of the population. All Europe save Great Britain adopted conscription as a national policy.

Britain's Naval Forces

Seagirt Britain contented herself with fighting on the continent of Europe and on other continents, whenever the need arose, with mercenaries, with professional soldiers, who were willing to hire themselves out for a price, for gold. These mercenaries used to be reinforced with the cream of the British volunteer fighting forces derived from royalty, aristocracy, and commonalty. Protected by the seas on all sides, Great Britain did not need a national conscripted army as badly as did the other nations of Europe. Defended by the sea and depending on the sea for protection, Great Britain invested in her navy more money per capita than did any other country of Europe.

Engines of Brute Force

Be that as it may, the National States of Europe emerged in the post-renaissance period with mighty engines of brute force as their most characteristic feature. These States could be best described as embodiments of brute force, one poised against another, one bloc poised against another, each State changing sides in response to the need for a balance of power.

The Original Sin of the Nation-State

Political Nationalism—the Nation-State—was born of the original sin of competition and conflict. The Nation-State arose against the background of Mercantilism. Now, what did Mercantilism stand for? Well, Mercantilism postulated that your country was richer than your neighbor country if you as a nation had more gold. Gold, a very much scarcer commodity in those days than now, could be secured by means fair or foul. Fair means embraced commercial transactions—export of merchandise to be paid for in gold. Foul means embraced buccaneering expeditions, piracy on the high seas, laying claim to the gold of the New World "discovered" and "conquered" by freebooting adventurers, looting the gold of the Old World—of India—by mercantile-imperialist ventures and exploits.

"Consciousness of Kind"

Competition and conflict made each person, bound to a country, conscious of his kinship with others bound to the same country, in juxtaposition to those who "belonged to other countries." This is how the consciousness of a common culture and of a common allegiance under the Holy Roman Empire—the wag has said, "It was neither Holy nor Roman nor yet Empire"—gave way to nationalist "consciousness of kind," to adapt a phrase of the late Professor Franklin H. Giddings. National or particularistic languages, literatures and folklores grew up as part of the experience of the new in-group solidarity, of national "consciousness of kind." Some of the new traits of nationalism were invented and some were rescued from oblivion to the end that the mighty god of the Nation-State might be enthroned.

15. Racialism and Nationalism

Malthus and Darwin

A while ago we said that the Europeans became flushed, and had a right to become flushed, with pride and a sense of superiority over their remarkable accomplishments in the wake of the Renaissance. The intellectual climate of Europe had to conform to the new conditions, vibrant, dynamic, changing, shot through with conflict. Rev. Thomas R. Malthus (1766-1834), in his *Essay on Population* (first edition, 1798) developed the theory of population pressure upon food supplies and the consequent "struggle for existence." The phrase "struggle for existence" caught the imagination of Charles R. Darwin (1809-1882), whose studies of nature led him to propound in his book *The Origin of Species* (1859) the thesis that the whole case of evolution rested upon the struggle for existence and upon the survival of the fittest.

Evolutionism, Ethnocentricism, Racialism

The application of the theory of evolution to mankind was flattering to the conquering Europeans. And why not? They had discovered and colonized the New World. They had come in contact with the red-skinned in America, the black-skinned in Africa, and overpowered them. Nor did they have a very difficult time imposing themselves and their will upon the brown-skinned and the yellow-skinned of Asia. One cannot blame the European for thinking that white skin represented the acme of creation, that the white man's culture and its institutions were the highest toward which the rest of the world was slowly, mayhap falteringly, marching. The mighty god of the Nation-State began to look at the world from ethnocentric norms. And if the brown-skinned and the yellow-skinned of Asia refused to accept the white man at his self-proclaimed worth—well, it was just a case of the cussedness and backwardness of the "natives"!

At any rate, the doctrine of evolution, tied to the racialist dogma, provided the rambunctious Europeans a rationalization, if not justification, for their depredation and exploitation of peoples all over the world.

Nordic Superiority

Ironically enough, it was a Frenchman, Count Gobineau (1816-82), who propounded the doctrine of Nordic superiority in his four-volume work, *Essai, sur l'inégalité des races humaines* (1853, 1855). The Germans were not averse to accepting the thesis; the school of racialism flourished all over Europe, with reverberations in America (Madison Grant, Lothrop Stoddard). But it was reserved for the British to carry out in actual practice the thesis of the "white man's burden" upon the "natives," the so-called "lesser breed," all over their far-flung Empire.

Racialism was the besetting sin of my forefathers, the Aryas, in the days when they had white skin. Racialism is today the besetting sin of the white-skinned European—and, to some extent, of the white-skinned American. And this racialism is tied to the god of the Nation-State and has manifested itself as imperialism.

16. RACE-CONSCIOUSNESS, ETHNOCENTRISM, BRUTE FORCE

Race is neither good nor bad; racialism is positively bad and mischievous because it is based on superstition. In the eighties of the last century Vacher de Lapouge wrote: " I am convinced that in the next century millions will cut each other's throat because of 1 or 2 degrees more or less of cephalic index" (1, p. 3, quoted). This portentous warning was realized almost fully by the Nazi ethnomaniacs. But we are not at the end of the road.

More and more the peoples of the world acting as masses are tending, quite unscientifically, to identify mental traits and culture with race characteristics. Many Americans are speaking of the "Jewish race" and the "Irish race." The melting-pot of America is boiling. The attempt to create a single unified type of American character by the elimination of differences has not quite succeeded. It is gratifying that for a generation or so we have been taking a new tack: to create a new American character synthesizing the positive contributions of the many races and nations that are in our midst.

A course in "Race Relations" or "Ethnic Minorities" is offered by every well-organized Department of Sociology in the U.S.A.

On the world scene, the creation of race-consciousness and the emergence of race-conscious groups threaten to fulfill Vacher de Lapouge's dire forebodings.

What is the answer of social science to this new threat to world peace? The answer of sociology, to be meaningful, must be in harmony with the mechanisms of human behavior. To begin with, it is not possible to legislate out of existence, either nationally or internationally, ethnocentrism. Ethnocentric judgments, whether valid or invalid, are inherent in the relationships between in-groups and out-groups. Racialism, foolish and ill-conceived as it is, is a specialized and dogmatic form of ethnocentrism. Neither ethnocentrism nor racialism is a particular source of danger so long as each group is content with its own group-megalomania. But when ethnocentrism or racialism is implemented with the weapons of brute force and attempts to force its conception of superiority upon other people at the point of the bayonet, then indeed do ethnocentric and racialist groups become a menace to themselves and a source of danger to others. In a contest of pseudo-intellectual and emotional belief as to which is superior, each group is bound to hold its own. There is no danger in this situation ; the danger arises when an attempt is made to impose ethnocentric norms or racialist dogmas of one group upon other groups by violence. The "white man's burden" imposed upon the "natives" of Asia and Africa by European imperialists, the "master race" concept of Hitler's followers, the East Asia Co-Prosperity Bloc with the Japanese at the top of the hierarchy—these events of the very recent past illustrate how dangerous ethnocentrism and racialism can become when backed up by brute force.

The discountenancing of racialist dogmas by the Soviet Union is a positive gain to our generation. But the ruthless persecution of dissident minorities in the Soviet Union, and ruthless imposition of rule upon satellite nations, in the name of an economic gospel, have all the earmarks of racialism run amok—and have the odor of the "master race" concept.

To summarize : One, we have pointed out that race is simply a classificatory term applicable to a group of individuals possessing certain well defined physical traits. Two, we have discussed how race differences arose, in the first instance, through isolation, inbreeding, interbreeding, selection, and mutation; this process is still going on in our day—witness the Eurasians of India, not to mention the polyglot called American. Three, while race differentiations afford an interesting subject for scientific investigation, in our time race is being conceived en masse as a badge either of superiority or of inferiority. The so-called race problem, within a nation or in the world at large, resolves itself into the problem of power relations between the dominant group and subject or minority groups.

To the sociologist, race is a vertical group embracing all classes and categories of people possessing certain physical traits in common. In the social process, however, that is, in the actual behavior of *race-conscious* persons, race functions as a horizontal group. "The Negro is all right in his place"—this, regardless of whether the Negro be George Washington Carver, the noted scientist; or a noted banker like Richard R. Wright, President of Philadelphia's Citizens and Southern Bank and Trust Co.; or a noted sociologist like Professor E. Franklin Frazier, at one time President of the American Sociological Society; or Professor Ralph Bunche who negotiated the Israeli-Arab truce in 1948.

Race relations in the United States, thus, become caste relations as between "white" and "colored," and class relations when the term race is misused, as is popularly done, to embrace minorities, racial, religious, cultural or national. Each "race" group is expected to behave according to certain preconceived patterns of social relationships—it may do this and not that, it may go so far and no farther. Thus, virtually "race" becomes a caste grouping, at most a class grouping, with a specialization of functions. The Hawaiians must be entertainers, the Negroes must be domestic servants and in the movies they cannot be heroes unless the movie happens to be all-Negro. In recent times these patterns have been rapidly changing.

On a world scale, the same sort of caste grouping had taken place as between the "white" man and the "native." The recent attempt of Asians and Africans to overthrow the "white man's burden" is, in effect, an uprising of a vertical group, treated as a horizontal group, against the privileged, intrenched hierarchy; as such, in the words of Professor H. A. Miller it constitutes a revolution (7, pp. 35–36).

The degradation of race into caste and class is a fruitful field of investigation.

India might well have been the first country to degrade race (*Varna*) into caste—a challenging hypothesis which needs to be investigated.

REFERENCES

1. RUTH BENEDICT: *Race : Science and Politics,* rev. ed. New York ; The Viking Press, 1945.

2. RUTH BENEDICT and GENE WELTFISH: *The Races of Mankind.* New York : Public Affairs Committee, 1943.

3. E. A. HOOTON: *Up From the Ape,* rev. ed. New York : Macmillan, 1946.

4. OTTO KLINEBERG: *Race Differences.* New York : Harper and Brothers, 1935.

5. A. L. KROEBER: *Anthropology,* 2nd ed. New York : Harcourt, Brace and Company, 1948.

6. RALPH LINTON: *The Study of Man.* New York : D. Appleton-Century Company, 1936.

7. H. A. MILLER: *The Beginnings of Tomorrow.* Boston : D. C. Heath and Company, 1933.

8. H. T. MUZUMDAR: *The United Nations of the World.* New York : Universal Publishing Company, 1st ed. 1942 ; 2nd ed. 1944.

9. WILLIAM F. OGBURN and MEYER F. NIMKOFF: *Sociology,* 2nd ed. Boston : Houghton Mifflin Company, 1950.

10. R. A. SCHERMERHORN: *These Our People.* Boston : D. C. Heath and Company, 1949.

11. AMRAM SCHEINFELD: *The New You and Heredity.* Philadelphia : J. B. Lippincott Company, 1950.

12. R. M. YERKES: "Psychological Examining in the U.S. Army." *Memoirs of the National Academy of Sciences,* 15 : 1921.

CHAPTER 17

NATION-GROUPS

To think a person as a member of a "race" is relatively a new social phenomenon—only about a hundred years old. To think of a person as a member of a "nation" has been part of our intellectual tradition and emotional beliefs for at least four hundred years— ever since the Age of Discovery (1492). From the ashes of feudalism in Europe arose the modern political nation; indeed, feudalism itself had been dealt a death-blow by the rising consciousness of nationalism buttressed by the rise of particularistic or "national" languages, literatures and folklores, and by the onset of the commercial and industrial revolutions.

1. CONFLICT, THE ORIGINAL SIN OF THE NATION

We pointed out, in the preceding chapter, that the political nation was born of the original sin of competition and conflict. Here is the record of history (2, pp. 115–17):

The Hundred Years' War (1337-1453) gave rise to two rival groups across the English Channel, each feeling a "consciousness of kind"—the English and the French. The Wars of the Roses (1453-1485) gave rise to a United English nation under the Tudor Dictatorship. Rivalry in discovery and piracy on the high seas cemented national solidarity among the participants—the English, the French, the Portuguese, the Spaniards. The American Nation was born of conflict (1776-83). Napoleon of the French Revolution of Liberty, Equality, Fraternity, overran most of Europe (1798-1815) and thereby sowed the seeds of national consciousness among defeated countries. The Kingdom of Prussia, whose Bluecher helped defeat Napoleon, was one of the notable products of the Napoleonic wars. The German Nation was born of conflict—of war with France (1870-71). The Italian Nation, under Mazzini and Garibaldi, came into being as a resurgent movement in protest against Austrian domination (1859-70). The Hindese Nation came into being in 1885 with the establishment of the All-India National Congress, as

a protest against British exploitation and against Occidental en-
croachments upon her ancient cultural legacy (and achieved the
status of a sovereign nation in 1947).

The list can be indefinitely expanded, embracing the hundred
odd nations of the world, covering especially—if one were so
minded—the cases of China, Japan, Korea, Turkey, and Russia.
The thesis is irrefutable. Either competition or conflict, or possibly
a combination of both, has given rise to political nationalism.

Indeed, not only did the Nation-State arise from competition and
conflict; it also thrived on competition and conflict, and it has been
armed to the teeth for ever-present competitions and conflicts.

The national consciousness of kind has become thoroughly patterned during the last four hundred years. When we meet a person,
we immediately tend to identify him as an Englishman, a Frenchman, a German, a Chinese, a Japanese, etc., and then establish the
basis of our contact with him. National belonging has become an
inextricable part of our intellectual tradition. Anybody not belonging to a nation is viewed either as a "native" or as a member of
a primitive tribe. All civilized persons are expected to be nationals,
i.e., members of one or another national in-group. As a "national"
you are studied by the sociologist; as a "native," you are investigated
by the anthropologist.

The racialist, by his very motivation, tends to overlook the unique
life experiences of a person belonging to an out-group; to him all
out-group members are cast in one mould, or stereotyped. The
nationalist, likewise, tends to define the unique life experiences of
an out-group national in terms of preconceived notions about the
particular out-group—in terms of stereotypes. The nationalist is not
concerned with the man in the Englishman, the man in the German, the man in the Japanese, or the man in the Russian; he is primarily concerned with the Englishman or the German or the
Japanese or the Russian as he is moulded by the system of nation-
belonging or nationalism. *Nationalism,* in other words, *has become
a dominant culture-complex in the modern world.* Indeed, it is safe
to assert that nationalism has become a cult, a religion, demanding
total loyalty from the members of the nation.

2. MILLER: THE NATION AS A VERTICAL GROUP

"The nation," says Professor Herbert A. Miller (1875-1951), "may be defined as a vertical group, including within its membership people of every class or horizontal level. It is an enlarged family or community which, whatever the disparity of its members in social position, has a sense of solidarity from top to bottom. The recent emphasis on race and the possibility of interracial conflict have begun to make a corresponding vertical racial grouping. Both may use geographical boundaries to set their limits." (1, p. 33).

The vertical organization is more irrational than the horizontal, because, within the vertical group, there are individuals and classes that are more closely related to those in other vertical groups than to classes within their own vertical group. Paderewski the artist belongs to the musical world and has only a sentimental and historical relation to the Polish peasant. (1, p. 36).

There is no concrete and permanent definition of a nation. It usually has some geographical relations, but may exist without them; it may inhere in a consciousness of blood relationship, but aliens may be adopted into it; it may turn about tradition and history, but myth may be just as effective; it may claim high moral justification and purpose, but an analysis of its history may show that it came into existence by ruthless injustice.

The artificial rationalization about each nation drives one to the conclusion that the real reason for it is the psychological yearning of the individual to belong to a group that will give him social dignity; the nation was created in part to satisfy this yearning. In others words, the intrinsic qualities of the nation are identifiable, but the subjective satisfactions that it gives have made it seem paramount to the minds of those who can see no alternative equal to it . . . the nation is a vertical grouping in which the practical value of class interests is ignored, because the individual thinks he can find his greatest self-realization in his nation. Formerly he found it in religion; now he is transferring much of his religious emotion to nationalism. (1, p. 46).

3. DEFINITION OF A NATION

What, then, is a nation: Is it composed of people of one blood? Hardly; in every national group we have different types of blood—

O, A, B, AB—widely distributed. Is the nation a matter of race? America is a nation even though we have many "race" groups in our midst. Is the nation, perchance, a matter of language? Switzerland has three different languages and is yet a nation. Is the nation then a matter of religion? Not at all; because every nation contains adherents of different religions and different communions. Is the nation synonymous with culture? Well, America, Britain and Germany are more united than disunited culturally, and yet each functions as a well defined national entity. As Professor Miller rightly observes, "There is always a metaphysical element in the consciousness of each national" (1, p. 49). The metaphysical element spoken of by Professor Miller is nothing more nor less than the loyalty given by the members of a group to an imagined national entity.

At the beginning of this century nobody in the world knew of an entity called Pakistan. In the early twenties of this century, Iqbal coined the world Pakistan—P for Punjab, A for Afghan, i.e., North-West Frontier Province, K for Kashmir, S for Sind—as a cultural concept, suggesting the area where Islam and Islamic influences were dominant. In the late twenties four Muslim Hindese students in London gave Pakistan a political coloring. At first the political concept of Pakistan seemed to be still-born; but within less than a generation, under the dynamic leadership of Mr. M. A. Jinnah (1876-1948), the Muslims of India switched their loyalty to an imagined national entity called Pakistan. On August 14, 1947, the Muslim nation of Pakistan was born with its own geographical territories and political machinery.

The Zionist movement of the last seventy-five years culminating in the emergence and rise of Jewish nationalism and the State of Israel affords another interesting illustration of the psychological mechanisms involved in the creation of a national entity.

Since loyalty to the cultural framework is the core of national functioning, we may define the nation as a community delimited by the State. Community involves, as pointed out in Chapters 9 and 11, a commonly shared sense of integral loyalty. And the State, in its structural aspect, is a militant organization, an embodiment of *Danda*.

4. EVOLUTION OF THE NATION

Under what conditions does a group called the nation come into being, and how does it function?

The area of characterization, on the one hand, tends to stabilize the race type of a group or tribe, as pointed out in the preceding chapter, and, on the other hand, provides a background for the emergence of a unique and specialized culture. The processes of group formation, group cohesion and group functioning give rise, in the first instance, to elements of culture and are later moulded by the given culture.

A tribe may be viewed as a group of people living together in an area of characterization, bound together by a common culture and by loyalty to the tribe and its culture. More often than not, the tribe must have developed common physical traits. So long as loyalty to the tribe is given by its members predominantly on the basis of folkways and mores, so long is the consciousness of tribalism incipient and automatic. But when loyalty is enforced by the tribe in accordance with institutional procedures, we are on the threshold of the cult of tribalism. Tribes and tribalisms flourished in the preliterate era all over the world and continued to flourish until the rise of empires. The emergence of unique cultures in the different areas of characterization, human migrations and conquests, culture contacts and borrowings—these traits of tribalism constitute the stuff of human history in the periods of savagery and barbarism.

After graduating from hunting, fishing, sheep-herding and nomadism to agriculture, man, collective man, in his civilized state, was once again on the march looking for the best place to settle in, carrying with him his implements of war and his implements of agriculture. Some of the implements of agriculture he carried with him were material, i.e., domestic animals and tools; others were nonmaterial, i.e., skills concerning the making and use of agricultural implements.

Thus did the Arya (agricultural) tribe split off into two branches, one going from the Caucasus region southeastward to India and Iran, the other westward to Europe. This Aryan migration, in successive waves, eastward and westward, roughly from 4000 B.C. to

2000 B.C., has had profound effects upon human history in the period of civilization. They fashioned the face of Mother India; in Iran they created a great civilization; in Europe, as in Asia, borrowing from others significant traits of culture, the Aryas laid the foundation of modern culture. The culture of the Aryas, in Europe as in Asia, rested on the broad base of agriculture. As handicrafts began to supplement agricultural activity and as division of social labor began to emerge, the essential conditions for the development of organic solidarity came into being. Soon, portions of the non-agricultural population tended to congregate in small areas. This small compact area with specialization of functions, with division of labor, and with interdependence, became the Pooree or Nagar of the Hindus, the polis of the Greeks and the civitas of the Romans.

Tribalism was now transformed into the City-State as a "power center." The City-State embarked upon a career of conquest, transforming the original tribalism into imperialism.

The Roman Empire (roughly, 325 B.C.–475 A.D.) functioned with Rome as its power center—secular until the end of the 3rd century A.D., both secular and religious from the 4th century A.D. until its downfall. The Holy Roman Empire (roughly from 476 or from 800 A.D. to 1500 A.D.) functioned with Rome as its religious power center and with the seat of authority of the Emperor as its political power center. (Technically, the Holy Roman Empire, which was neither holy nor Roman nor yet empire, came to an end in 1806 when Francis II resigned the elective imperial crown for the hereditary crown of Austria.)

The very people who broke up the Roman Empire, the Germanic tribes, carried on the imperial tradition until the onset of the Renaissance and the Reformation. And we have already discussed how the political nation arose in the wake of the Renaissance and the Reformation.

These historical data deserve to be interpreted in sociological terms. Our discussion points to the following stages of political development: 1. Tribalism, 2. City-State, 3. City-State as a power center for Empire, 4. The Empire Structure, 5. The Nation-State, 6. Imperialism, 7. The Inter-Nation State. In other words, the trend has been from tribalism to civitas-imperialism, from civitas-imperialism to nationalism, from nationalism to imperialism—and from nationalism to internationalism.

5. NATIONALISM, GREAT POWER, POWER POLITICS, EMPIRE

Clark Wissler rightly suggests that modern nationalism is of the same species as tribalism (3, *passim*). Let us now enumerate the elements making up a nation: (1) population, (2) territory, (3) common cultural framework, including historical experiences, and sentiments and values, (4) in-group loyalty, and (5) sovereignty. The role of loyalty in nation-building and nation-functioning must be fully appreciated.

Since the well-nigh complete annihilation of time and space distances by modern inventions, the world has been experiencing the slow but sure emergence of several cultural categories binding upon all the peoples of the world. Nationalism or nation-belonging is one of these cultural categories or cultural compulsives.

A population, living in a given territory, sharing a common social heritage, bound together by in-group loyalty, strives to impose its will (rule) upon another people living in a specified territory, and succeeds because: (1) the out-group is bound together by a weaker cement of loyalty, or (2) the population of the out-group is smaller in number, or (3) the territory of the out-group is strategically vulnerable, or (4) the technology of war of the out-group is inferior to that of the in-group.

Unless democratic traditions and values impose compulsive restraints upon an in-group, each nation strives to attain the status of a Great Power and to play Power Politics. This sociological point needs to be emphasized. From another context I may reproduce my discussion of the sociological implications of power politics and the empire system (2, pp. 88–92):

Power Politics

What does constitute a Great Power in international affairs today, and what are its terms of peace? What is meant by Power Politics? Well, a nation's status as a Great Power is determined by its striking power, actual and potential, offensive as well as defensive. The

striking power of a nation is dependent upon a suitable combination
of :

(1) man-power
(2) national resources
(3) industrial equipments
(4) armaments of destruction
(5) morale

Given these ingredients of power, derived either from domestic
sources or from empire, a nation is ready to play the game of Power
Politics; which simply means that that nation now assumes the role
of the arbiter of the destiny of mankind, at least of that portion of
mankind whose misfortune it is to dwell within its orbit.

Without the consent of a Great Power or Great Powers, no
changes may be made in the internal or external relations of the
rest of the world. Anybody, any country, venturing to suggest
changes, without the consent of the Power Politics "boys," is dubbed
a disturber of world peace, a menace to the stability of society, a
danger to the orderly processes of civilization !

Simply stated, Europe's perennial problem has been the problem
of Power Politics. Germany has felt for over a century that she was
as good and as great as England and France combined but that she
had been at a disadvantage in Power Politics because England and
France owned far-flung empires.

The only way Germany could tip the scale in her favor in the
game of Power Politics was by changing the map of the world. And
hell has been let loose upon this earth by every such effort on the
part of Germany.

(Since the end of World War II, the Soviet Union, Red China
and the United States, with their allies, have been striving for
ascendancy in world affairs through Power Politics, by resorting to
persuasion whenever possible, to economic and military aid to other
nations wherever practical, to intimidation and use of force where
necessary.)

The truth is, aggression in our times is rooted in Power Politics
and Power Politics is rooted in the empire system, which may be
defined as congealed aggression.

Empire, Foster Parent of Totalitarianism

The empire system rests upon domination, upon denial of self-
government to citizens, upon imposition of rule from above, upon
denial of civil liberties, upon denial of the four freedoms. The kinship between imperialism on the one hand and fascism and

communism on the other is more than skin-deep. All the patterns of fascism and communism were first worked out by the empire system which is totalitarian in form and function.

TABLE 7

PATTERNS OF TOTALITARIANISM

Empire System	Fascist and Communist Systems
1. Rule imposed	1. Rule imposed
2. Ruling Party—Alien	2. Ruling Party—Native
3. Denial of Self-Government	3. Denial of Self-Government
4. Denial of Civil Rights	4. Denial of Civil Rights
5. Denial of some or all of the Four Freedoms	5. Denial of some or all of the Four Freedoms
6. Secret Service—the most vital arm of government	6. Secret Service—the most vital arm of government
7. "Detention Camps" for "non-conformists"	7. "Concentration Camps" for "non-conformists"
8. Superiority Complex	8. Superiority Complex
Totalitarianism	Totalitarianism

So far as the problem of power relations is concerned, there is no difference between the totalitarian dictatorship of communism and that of fascism. Communists as well as fascists rule their own country with an iron hand and extend their tentacles to neighboring countries whom they would fain convert into satellites by peaceful methods of infiltration if possible, by intimidation and brute force if necessary. Since the end of the shooting hostilities of World War II, the Soviet Russian and Communist Chinese totalitarian dictatorships have been engaged in carving out an ideological empire, which appears less galling to subject peoples in satellite countries because of "native" leadership, but which is more mischievous than old-style political empires ever were.

The empire system, new-style as well as old-style, creates fear and necessitates armaments. Therefore, the abolition of the empire system, colonial-political as well as communist-totalitarian, would seem to be a precondition to freedom from fear, to disarmament, and to the outlawry of war. (For an extended discussion, see 2, pp. 88–92.)

6. THE EMERGENCE OF THE TWO SOVEREIGNTIES

By the beginning of the twentieth century nearly all the countries of Europe had been patterned and were functioning as nations—some of them as imperiums or empire nations, i.e., nations with empire, such as Great Britain, France, Spain, Portugal, Italy, Turkey, Austria-Hungary, Germany, Belgium, Netherlands, Denmark, Russia. All of Africa was under the domination of one imperium or another directly or indirectly; even China, nominally free, was subject to the play of Power Politics by the Great Powers. The New World had 20 Latin American nations, free from foreign control, but effectively led by the United States of America. Canada, a member of the British Commonwealth, was actually a free nation, though technically subject to Great Britain. A few islands in the Atlantic and small territories in Central and South America were subject to British, French, Dutch and Danish imperiums. In the Pacific, Australia and New Zealand were, like Canada, free nations, though technically dominions of Great Britain.

At the beginning of the present century, seven imperiums acted as Great Powers—Great Britain, France, Germany, Italy, Russia, Japan, the United States of America, the last not quite conscious, then or even now, of its historic role in world affairs.

Every imperium is in a sense a Great Power in that it effectively interferes with the internal and external affairs of nations subject to it. But in terms of Power Politics, i.e., the capability to interfere in the internal and external affairs of nations not politically subjected, " the title to greatness as a Power is derived by a nation from its striking power, offensive as well as defensive." (2, p. 111.)

Thus at the beginning of the twentieth century we had the following categories of political group-entities operating:

1. GREAT POWERS: Great Britain, France, Germany, Italy, Russia, Japan, the U.S.A.;
2. IMPERIUMS: In addition to the above seven: Spain, Portugal, Denmark, Belgium, Netherlands, Austria-Hungary, Turkey;
3. NATIONS: All free and self-governing political entities, such as Scandinavia and Switzerland in Europe, the 21 nations of the Western Hemisphere (including 20 Latin American countries and Canada), Australia and New Zealand;

4. NATIONALITIES: Populations, living in well-defined areas, shar-ing a common social heritage and outlook bound together by common in-group loyalty, denied self-government: all the countries of Asia excluding Japan, Thailand and Tur-key; all the countries of Africa; some of the countries of Europe subject to Austria-Hungary, Turkey and Russia. These nationalities were striving for nationhood. Spurred on by the oppression psychosis, nationalities developed the con-sciousness of political nationalism as a defence mechanism and operated within the imperium as conflict groups.

With these categories as our conceptual tool, we are enabled to make a distinction between international relations and power politics. The relations between the Soviet Union and one of its satellites are, for instance, in the domain of power politics, not in the field of international relations.

The first half of the twentieth century saw the rise and fall of some Great Powers. At the end of the First World War (1914-18), two Powers dropped from the list—Germany and Russia. By the time the Second World War came around those two nations once again took their place alongside of the other five Great Powers that had survived the First World War. At the end of the Second World War (1939-45) only three Powers survived—the U.S.A., Great Britain and the Soviet Union.

Thanks to the democratic compulsions lately experienced by her people, Great Britain as an imperium is counting its last days—and must play second fiddle to one of the two remaining Great Powers, the U.S.A. or the U.S.S.R. The U.S.A. does not believe in establish-ing an imperium but is forced by the logic of events to play the role of a Great Power. The Soviet Union, uninhibited by democratic compulsions, has been embarking upon a new career of expan-sionism and imperialism. In the fifties and the sixties, Communist China flung the challenge to the U.S.S.R. and the U.S.A. to be counted as a member of the exclusive club of Great Powers.

Before breathing its last, before being destroyed by the weapons of its own making, or before being ended by new creative social forces on a world scale, the civilization of nation-states is already in process of creating a new set of relationships. No longer are nations self-competent and "independent"—they must choose between rival blocs, the democratic bloc led by the United States of America and the communist bloc led by the Soviet Union and/or Communist China.

The leaders of the Soviet Union realize this new trend in "international" relations; the leaders of democratic America and Britain have not yet fully awakened to the reality of the new situation. Be that as it may, in terms of our sociological analysis, it is permissible to assert that the significant aspect of the history of the next few years will not be the history of the rise of new nations and their accomplishments, important as Swaraj (or self-government) is; rather, it will be the history of interaction between the democratic bloc led by the U.S.A. and the communist bloc led by the Soviet Union, climaxing either in a world imperium of a totalitarian nature under the aegis of the Soviet Union or in the emergence of the democratic United Nations of the World under the aegis of the United States of America.

Unhappy as the problem of alignment may be, sociologically speaking, neutralism and the desire to create a "third force" advocated by some eminent statesmen seem like the will-o-the-wisp— a snare and a delusion. When a house is on fire, no neighbor has the right to enjoy the luxury of being a neutral spectator. The do-nothing action of the bystander serves as an encouragement to the fire to run its destructive course.

According to exponents of Western democracies, communist trickery and deceit have set the world community on fire: One has to be either for it or against it—not neutral toward it. According to Communist Russian spokesmen, Western democracies, based on capitalism, are intent upon overthrowing the communist structure of society built up in Russia during the last forty years or so.

The central core of the problem in the relations between the USSR and the USA is the non-existence of mutual trust and confidence.

If the "third force," to the creation of which Prime Minister Jawaharlal Nehru and India's foreign policy are committed, could create conditions for the establishing of mutual trust and confidence between the USA and the USSR, the philosophy of neutralism and the "third force" would be abundantly justified.

The leaders of the newly freed nations of Asia and Africa are thinking in terms of creating a "third force" as a buffer or intermediary between the USSR and the USA. A "third force" resting upon moral power rather than armaments has a great deal of merit, but whether it can be strong enough and dynamic enough in time to exert itself in the contest between the two power blocs is an open question.

Co-existence of communism and democracy is possible under one of two conditions: (1) that the democratic countries give up their cherished values and accept Russian dictation, or (2) that Russian communists and their co-workers abroad give up their cherished notion of winning the world for communism and sincerely abide by the norms of civilized society, without deceit and trickery.

7. THE NATION AS A MAHAJANA

Race and nation often become confused in the thinking of people because both function as Mahajanas. We have discovered that race represents a classificatory group, that a racial group functions either as a caste or as a class, and that a race-conscious group functions as an association, as a Mahajana. The nation, too, functions as a Mahajana. We may define the nation as "a militant organization—militant potentially or actually—of a community delimited by the State." Therefore, it is legitimate, from one standpoint, to define the State as an embodiment of *Danda*—of regulatory power, including brute force. Thus it is in the nature of a nation-group to be, and to act as, an association, as a corporation, as a Mahajana, armed with weapons of war.

In the Mahajana the "members" engage not only in cooperative activity but also, and more pointedly, in corporate action. This galvanizing of different horizontal and vertical groups into the supreme vertical group, this cementing together of a vast array of secondary groups by a common loyalty, is no mean achievement of nationalism.

When we view the nation functioning as an association or as a corporation, the structural correlate is to be found in the State as an institution. When we view the State as an association of citizens, the structural correlate is to be found in the social heritage of the nation.

The reciprocal co-relationship between the nation, the State and the community must be particularly noted. The community provides the background for the rise of associations and for the interplay of social forces. The community may be larger than the nation, the English-speaking countries forming a community so to say; but no nation can exist without its correlative community. Nor can the nation function without the instrumentality of the State.

8. THE DYNAMICS OF RACE AND NATION

Race is hard to define, race affiliation is difficult to locate, by strictly scientific criteria. But race affiliation, as a mystic consciousness of kind, is invoked in the modern world, even if the invocation should involve misuse of the term race. The national and cultural minorities in the American population are vaguely referred to as racial minorities, though conceptual precision requires us to refer to them as ethnic minorities. Thus race as a stereotype has attained in American society a dynamic entirely unrelated to race as a scientific concept.

The nation as a sociological grouping, with a common cultural heritage, is easy to define and easier still to locate. The consciousness of kind binding the members of a nation together is born of a common cultural framework. Whether it arose purely as an area of characterization in utter isolation, an untenable proposition, or as a result of culture contacts and diffusion, each national cultural framework has certain unique traits to distinguish it from all others. This cultural framework is called the ethos. The loyalty given by each citizen to his national in-group, to the ethos of his people, makes for solidarity within and divisiveness without. The idealist says: "Love of my country does not demand that I shall hate and slay those noble and faithful souls who also love theirs, but rather that I should honor them and seek to unite with them for our common good" (Romain Rolland). But in actual practice, love of one's country, loyalty to one's country, has spelled hate and depredations against the out-group nation.

When we develop an in-group loyalty to embrace all the nations of the world, war will vanish (even if rumors of war should persist). This consummation may be hastened if not brought about by the impersonal logic of technology—by the frightening prospect of extinction of man and all his works by nuclear and thermonuclear warfare. The collective wisdom of man, too, will have to play its part if a warless world is ever to be realized.

REFERENCES

1. HERBERT A. MILLER: *The Beginnings of Tomorrow.* Boston: D. C. Heath and Company, 1933.
2. HARIDAS T. MUZUMDAR: *The United Nations of the World.* New York: Universal Publishing Company, 1st ed., 1942 ; 2nd ed., 1944.
3. CLARK WISSLER: *Man and Culture.* New York: Thomas Y. Crowell Company, 1923.

CHAPTER 18

THEORIES ABOUT THE GROUP

1. THEORIES ABOUT THE RISE OF GROUPS

WE have pointed out three possible sources from which groups may spring: (1) the biogenic source (family and kinship groups), (2) the ecological source (neighborhood and community groups), (3) the sociogenic source (interest-inspired groups of all kinds, voluntary as well as involuntary). (See *supra*, CHAPTER 11).

We have also pointed out that groups are held together by: (1) folkways, mores and institutions; (2) by esprit de corps and morale, and (3) by collective representations. Likewise we brought out how mechanical solidarity, based upon resemblance, differs from organic solidarity based upon division of labor. (CHAPTER 15).

Finally, we have suggested how the group may function, on a sort of rainbow spectrum, from the mass and the crowd at the bottom to the audience, the public, the assembly, and the association and the corporation at the top. (CHAPTER 10).

Ever since man began to think and reflect, he has been curious to know about himself and his kind. In the process, he has developed all kinds of theories about himself and his group—theological, metaphysical, and scientific or positive.

We may distinguish at least five different theories about the rise of groups: (1) the theological or supernatural theory, (2) the natural or organic theory, (3) the contractual or the social contract theory, (4) the theory of war and violence, (5) the theory of mutual aid.

2. THEOLOGICAL OR SUPERNATURAL THEORIES

The earliest theological theory about the rise of groups is to be found in the Hindu scriptures. The Rig Veda, the oldest scriptural writing of the world, describes the *Brahman,* or the Creative Spirit, as the source of the four castes—the Brahmins issuing from His

279

mouth, the Kshattriyas issuing from His arms, the Vaishyas issuing from His thighs, and the Shudras issuing from His feet (X, 90). This is one of the earliest theological theories concerning the rise of groups.

When the four castes are viewed as issuing from the body of the *Brahman,* we have the *organismic* theory of society—society itself an organism springing from the Super-Organism, the *Brahman.* When the four castes are viewed as constituting a vast Mahajana of humanity, we have an organic theory of society, implying the inter-dependence of the four castes upon one another.

Echoes of the organismic and organic theories of society are to be found in Plato. "God has framed you differently. Some of you have the power of command, and in the composition of these he has mingled gold, wherefore also they have the greatest honor; others he has made of silver, to be auxiliaries; others again who are to be husbandmen and craftsmen he has composed of brass and iron; and the species will generally be preserved in the children. But . . . all are of the same original stock. . . ." (*The Republic,* BOOK III, SECTION 415). "In a well-ordered State," said Plato, "when any one of the citizens experiences any good or evil, the whole State will make his case their own and will either rejoice or sorrow with him," even as "the whole frame . . . feels the hurt and sympathizes all together with the part affected, say a hurt finger" (*The Republic,* BOOK V, SECTION 462). This is one of the earliest attempts in European thought to institute an analogy between the group (the polis in this case) and the human organism.

3. The Natural or Organic Theory

According to Aristotle, society has its origin and growth, not in the perception of utility and the search for justice as with Socrates and Plato, but in the very scheme of nature, in the instinctive being of man and woman. The successive organic stages of social develop-ment, according to him, are the family, the village, and the city-state.

Aristotle maintained that the union of male and female, of master and slave, culminating in the development of a household, was natural. Likewise it was natural for several households to band themselves, thus giving rise to the village. The polis, the city-state, was but the inevitable product of such natural aggregations.

Aristotle's contribution to our study may be summed up as follows: (1) *The polis* is a natural product, being an organic development of the social nature of man. (2) The most elemental fact in the social process is not the individual but the family. (3) Families getting together for purposes of satisfying their daily needs constitute a village, villages in union constitute a state; hence the state is a complex of groups, territorial and functional. (4) The purpose of the state is to provide not life as such but good life. (5) The group is a real unit and greater in power than the individuals composing it: "When they (the individuals) meet together they become in a manner one man, who has many feet, and hands and senses" (*Politics*, BK. III, 11: 1–4).

Aristotle's theory of the organic development of society and state led, on the one hand, to the concept of the functional unity of society and, on the other, to the organismic theories of later times.

The New Testament, for instance, abounds in references to the organismic nature of society. The Christian Church, i.e., the Christian fellowship group, is described as the mystical body of Jesus Christ.

Auguste Comte (1798-1857) spoke of the Humanity-Organism. And Herbert Spencer (1820-1903) instituted elaborate analogies between society and the human organism, comparing the system of alimentary organs of the human body to the industrial system of society (the "sustaining system"), the vascular circulatory system to the commercial system of society (the "distributing system"), etc.

4. SOCIAL CONTRACT THEORY

Plato accounted for the origin of society and state in terms of "perceived utility" and contractual relationship. The polis arises "out of the needs of mankind; no one is self-sufficing, but all have many wants. Can any other origin of a State be imagined?" (*The Republic*, BOOK II, SECTION 369).

Social contract theorists assumed the existence of a "state of nature" in which man lived in idyllic bliss, according to one school, and in constant danger of life and limb, according to another school. Thomas Hobbes (1588-1679) espoused the latter point of view and characterized the "state of nature" as "a war of each against all." The former point of view was advocated by John Locke (1632-1704) and Jean Jacques Rousseau (1712–78) who glorified the "state of nature" as the state of freedom and bliss.

Among Hindu social contract theorists, likewise, we find these two schools of thought. The Hobbesian position is well stated in the following verse: "Whenever there is drought, the stronger seizes the weaker, for the waters dictate the law." This is technically known as Matsya-Nyaya, i.e., the logic of the fish, the stronger ones devouring the weaker.

To avert chaos, according to Hindu social contract theorists, was created the King possessed of the attributes of the Creator, according to some versions, or of the principal gods, according to others. The King derives his authority from divine ordination. Here we have an anticipation of Hobbes's "war of each against all" and his theory of absolute monarchy as well as the theory of the divine right of kings.

The Buddhist view of the state of nature and the origin of kingship is more like that of Locke and Rousseau. "At first," Buddha is reported to have said, "the people were altogether perfect—having no corporeal body, living in satisfaction, resplendent, capable of traversing the air, and long-living. As they declined more and more from their original state of purity, there gradually appeared among them the differences of color and sex, while the institutions of family and property, punishment and the division of the four classes, were introduced into their midst by a series of mutual agreements. . . .

"When it was found that theft had appeared in society, the people assembled together and agreed to choose as king one who would punish those deserving punishment, blame those deserving blame, banish those deserving banishment, and in return would get a share of paddy from the people. Then they selected the most beautiful, gracious and powerful individual from among themselves and made a contract with him on the above terms. He was called the Great Elect (*Mahasammaté*) . . . and King (Rajan)." (6, pp. 118-19). Such is the Buddhist theory of social contract.

Not only the social contract theory but also the organic and organismic theories of society had been developed by Hindu philosophers.

5. MUTUAL AID AND VIOLENCE AS MECHANISMS FOR INTEGRATING THE GROUP

In contrast to the "perceived utility" of Plato and the social contract theorists, and Aristotle's natural inevitability of the sociopolitical order among men as the basis for group formation and functioning, there are two other theories, diametrically opposed to each other, which profess to account for the integration of groups and groupings, namely, (1) the theory of mutual aid and (2) the theory of violence and war.

Adam Smith (1723-90), who in his *Wealth of Nations* (1776) propounded the beneficent role of competition as "the unseen hand" promoting individual well-being as well as the general good, had previously taught, in his *Theory of Moral Sentiments* (1759) that sympathy was the cohesive bond in society. Jesus and Gandhi claimed love as the integrating force in society.

Why love force, so pervasive in society, is overlooked by historians is picturesquely brought out by Mahatma Gandhi (1869-1948):

Thousands, indeed tens of thousands, depend for their existence on a very active working of this force (namely, the force of love or truth). Little quarrels of millions of families in their daily lives disappear before the exercise of this force. Hundreds of nations live in peace. History does not, and cannot, take note of this fact. History is really a record of every interruption in the even working of the force of love or of the soul. Two brothers quarrel ; one of them repents and re-awakens the love that was lying dormant in him ; the two again begin to live in peace ; nobody takes note of this. But if the two brothers, through the intervention of solicitors or for some other reason, take up arms or go to law—which is another form of the exhibition of brute force—their doings would be immediately noticed in the press, they would be the talk of their neighbors, and would probably go down in history. And what is true of families and communities is true of nations. There is no reason to believe that there is one law for families and another for nations.

History, then, is a record of interruptions in the course of nature. Soul-force, being natural, is not noted in history. (5, pp. 92–93).

Mutual aid and spontaneous cooperation have been stressed by Kropotkin, Benjamin Kidd, J. Novicow and Graham Wallas (1858-1932) as mechanisms integrating the group. Peter Kropotkin (1842-1921) maintained that mutual aid was a significant factor in evolution (10, *passim*). And Benjamin Kidd (1858-1916) held that in order to survive and prosper a species must practise cooperation and mutual aid (9, *passim*).

Jacques Novicow (1849-1912) shares Gandhi's view that love binds individuals together in social relationships. "The active adaptation of the social environment can be designated by the general term love. Indeed to love any one is to desire to make that person like oneself. Charity (love) has for its goal to procure for others the material well-being which we ourselves enjoy." (2, p. 270, quoted). While he viewed the universe as an arena of endless combats and alliances, Novicow maintained that organic conflict has ascended from the physiological level to the economic and the political and, finally, to the intellectual level.

William McDougall (1871-1938), W. Trotter (1872-1939), and Herbert A. Miller (1875-1951) arrived at the notion of group solidarity and functioning through the positing of an instinct. Mc-Dougall spoke of a "gregarious instinct," Trotter of a "herd instinct," and Miller of a "group instinct." Giddings's notion of the "consciousness of kind," the theory of imitation propounded by Bagehot, Tarde, Ross and others, and the theory of prolonged human infancy by John Fiske (1842-1901) may all be subsumed under the heading of mutual aid in one form or another.

In contrast to the mutual aid theorists, the school of "social Darwinists" maintains that dynamic groups come into being and flourish as a result either of intragroup conflict or intergroup conflict. Interests, domination, conflict, competition, rivalry—these, according to the violence school, are the basic mechanisms of group dynamics.

Charles R. Darwin (1809-82) had postulated (1) natural selection through (2) the struggle for existence and (3) the survival of the fittest. This was the tooth and claw theory of evolution, a struggle of each against all, in contrast to the love and mutual aid theory of Kropotkin and Kidd.

Ludwig Gumplowicz (1839-1909), Gustav Ratzenhofer (1842-1904) and Albion W. Small (1854-1926) viewed interest as the mechanism for fusing the group together. Interest can and does serve either as a cohesive force or as a divisive force in the group. Resembling creatures that they are, sharing the same or similar interests, men may as often strive against one another as join forces with one another for the fulfilment of commonly cherished interests. Thus interest may lead to war as easily as to mutual aid.

Gumplowicz, for instance, believed in (1) polygenesis, (2) race conflict, (3) conflict of syngenetic groups, (4) group ascendancy over the individual, (5) coercion of the majority by the minority—all derived from his basic theory of interests. (8, *passim*).

According to Ratzenhofer the "innate interest" in every fertilized germ cell develops into (1) the racial interest or sexual, (2) the physiological interest or nutritive, the second leading to (3) the individual interest and the first to (4) the social interest; finally (5) the transcendental interest. (2, p. 172, quoted). Expounding Ratzenhofer's principles, Small says: "*The latest word of sociology is that human experience yields the most and the deepest meaning when read from first to last in terms of the evolution, expression, and accommodation of interest*" (12, p. 282). "Speaking somewhat roughly and symbolically, we may say again that all the acts which human beings have ever been known to perform have been for the sake of (six interests): (a) *health*, or (b) *wealth*, or (c) *sociability*, or (d) *knowledge*, or (e) *beauty*, or (f) *rightness*, or for the sake of some combination of ends which may be distributed among these six" (12, p. 444).

Ratzenhofer's main thesis is "that conflict is primarily universal but that it tends to resolve itself into cooperation. Socialization (shall we say civilization?—H.T.M.) indeed is the transformation of conflict into cooperation" (12, p. 499). In his system of thought group ascendancy is not emphasized. The following brief citation from Small's adaptation of Ratzenhofer's doctrines clearly sets forth their point of view:

The modern state is both a political organization and an economic system, but it is much more. The state is a microcosm of the whole human process . . . . The state is not a rigid entity but a process— " a becoming"—which changes with the variation of interests of the component individuals and groups. . . . The various institutions, political, ecclesiastical, professional, industrial, etc., including the government, are devices, means, gradually brought into existence to serve interests that develop within the state. . . . The constant and fundamental role of the state is to bring to bear upon the individuals composing it a certain power of constraint to secure from them, in all their struggles with each other, the observance of minimum established limits of struggle. . . . Civil society organized as the state is composed of individual and group factors, each of which has in itself certain elements of political independence. That is, each has interests seemingly distinct from the interests of the others. Each has some degree of impulse to assert these interests in spite of the others. Thus the state is an arrangement of combinations by which mutually repellent forces are brought into some measure of concurrent action. . . . We thus make out the main tendency of civic struggle to be the ultimate harmonization of all interests. This result we call civilization. (12, pp. 226–53, adapted.)

The doctrine of interest, so essential in Gumplowicz's system, formed the cornerstone of Ratzenhofer's sociology. Ratzenhofer's pupil, the late Professor Albion W. Small, popularized the concept in America. One of Small's pupils, A. F. Bentley, utilized the sociology of interest in his investigation of political behavior (*supra,* CHAPTER 13). Mary P. Follett (*infra*) has adroitly manipulated the concepts of the group and interest to arrive at social realism.

Marx and Marxists have emphasized class struggle as a mechanism for developing in-group solidarity and cohesiveness among contending classes. (11, *passim*). Two of the basic goals of Marxism, namely, a classless society and the withering away of the State, are theoretically a chimera and practically a mirage.

Anthropologists have described primitive tribes and tribal societies and their growth and expansion in terms of intergroup as well as intragroup conflict. Indeed, the origin of the State, according to reputable anthropologists, must be sought in either intergroup or intragroup conflict. Whether sociologists are under obligation to accept this theory is a different matter.

6. SOCIOLOGICAL ANALYSIS OF SOCIETY

For the sociological analysis of the group and its role in society as well as in the eye of the individual (the socius), we are indebted to Jean Bodin (1530-96), Johannes Althusius (1557-1638), Otto von Gierke (1844-1921), F. W. Maitland (1850-1906), and Miss Mary P. Follett (1868-1933).

Bodin viewed society as made up of "a series of associations, from the family at the bottom to the state at the top." (3, p. 92, quoted). Building upon Bodin's thesis that society was a complex of groups arranged in an ordered hierarchy, Althusius enunciated his own doctrine of the reality of group as a juristic person. (1, p. 30).

In legal terminology, a corporation is a person at law that can sue and be sued. To call a corporation a person at law, say the lawyers, is to indulge in a fiction, but a very useful fiction. And the "fiction theory" leads straightway to the "concession theory." For instance, a corporation comes into being when the state issues a birth certificate: the state makes a *concession* to a group of individuals, gives them a franchise, to operate as an entity in society. (7, Introduction by Maitland, pp. xxxi–xxxii).

Gierke and Maitland elaborated the concept of real personality of the group by throwing overboard the concession theory as well as the fiction theory. A group is real because it operates as such within society. Sociologically, a trade union is a corporation regardless of whether it ever took out its birth certificate of incorporation. (7, pp. xxxiii–xxxviii).

Finally, Miss Follett in her two books, *The New State* (1918) and *Creative Experience* (1924), re-emphasizes the importance of group for the development of human personality.

7. SMALL GROUPS AND GROUP DYNAMICS

Within the context of a given era or period of time, social events and felt needs give rise to new types of sociological investigation. After World War I (1914-18), the Inquiry into the Christian Way of Life—The Inquiry Group or The Inquiry, for short—explored the techniques of cooperative thinking as a device to reconcile opposing points of view (1923-32). Another group, operating as The Institute for Propaganda Analysis (1937-41), opened up for investigation and study the area of propagating ideas and attitudes on a mass scale.

During and since World War II (1939-45), the studies of (*a*) types of leadership, (*b*) the nature of small groups, and (*c*) the functioning of small groups have been carried on under the general heading of "group dynamics." This is a promising field of investigation, first, because empirical data can be secured by careful observation and, second, because the results of the analysis of these data throw significant light on the motivation and functioning of human beings in reciprocal interaction one with another. (Cf. the works of Kurt Lewin, Robert F. Bales, D. Cartwright and A. Zander, and others.)

REFERENCES

1. H. E. BARNES: *Sociology and Political Theory*. New York: Knopf, 1924.

2. L. M. BRISTOL: *Social Adaptation*. Cambridge, Mass.: Harvard University Press, 1915.

3. W. A. DUNNING: *From Luther to Montesquieu*. New York: Macmillan, 1905.

4. M. P. FOLLETT: *The New State*. New York: Longmans, Green & Co., 1918.
   : *Creative Experience*. New York: Longman's, Green & Co., 1924.

5. M. K. GANDHI: *Sermon on the Sea,* ed. by H. T. Muzumdar. Chicago: Universal Publishing Co., 1924.

6. U. GHOSHAL: *History of Hindu Political Theories*. Calcutta: Humphrey Milford, 1923.

7. OTTO VON GIERKE: *Political Theories in the Middle Ages,* tr. with an Introduction by F. W. Maitland. Cambridge, England: University Press, 1900.

8. L. GUMPLOWICZ: *The Outlines of Sociology,* tr. by F. W. Moore. Philadelphia: The Academy of Political and Social Science, 1899.

9. BENJAMIN KIDD: *Social Evolution*. New York: Macmillan, 1894. (Several later reprints also available.)

10. PETER KROPOTKIN: *Mutual Aid: A Factor in Evolution*. New York: Knopf, 1922.

11. K. MARX & F. ENGELS: *The Communist Manifesto*. Available in several editions and in the collected works of Karl Marx.

12. A. W. SMALL: *General Sociology*. Chicago: University of Chicago Press, 1905.

NOTE: I have contented myself with listing the minimum number of sources for reference. To give a full bibliography on the subject would smack of pedantry—and would also mean waste of energy and time and space. There are excellent histories of political thought (W. A. Dunning; F. W. Coker) as well as excellent histories of social thought (J. P. Lichtenberger; Emory S. Bogardus; Pitrim Sorokin; Howard Becker and Harry Elmer Barnes), which would introduce the student to differing conceptions of the group.

CHAPTER 19
THE GROUP CALLED AMERICA

1. THE AMERICAN PEOPLE HAVE GROWN BY FOUR METHODS OF INCREASE

THE United States of America is today (1960) inhabited by approximately 180,000,000 people, called Americans. How from humble beginnings (in terms of numbers), this group has multiplied itself into 180,000,000 strong is one of the most remarkable stories in the annals of demography. The American population has increased by all of the four methods by which the population of any country may grow: (1) natural increase, i.e., excess of births over deaths, (2) immigration, (3) incorporation, such as the Louisiana Purchase, the acceptance of the Republic of Texas into the Union, the acquisition of the Oregon Territory by agreement with Great Britain, the Purchase of Alaska; (4) conquest—acquisition of the Southwest Territories and California from Mexico after the American-Mexican War.

2. THE INDIANS AND THE SPANIARDS

At the time of the discovery of the New World by Columbus (1492), the inhabitants of what is today called the United States of America—America, for short—were various Indian (Amerind) tribes. Soon the Spaniards made incursions into the mainland of Central and South America. From Mexico in Central America, they began to make their way up toward the Southwest.

Thus the country had two main groups: the Indian tribes and the Spaniards. It is difficult to estimate the exact number of Spaniards in America during the next hundred years, nor is it possible to estimate the population of the Indian tribes living between the Atlantic and the Pacific coast, within the boundaries of the present day United States. Suffice it to say that the Spaniards introduced the Roman Catholic religion in the New World. They treated the Indians as inferior people, fit to be enslaved and drafted into work, because they were "pagans" and not Christians.

3. EARLY ENGLISH ATTEMPTS AT SETTLEMENT

Two English explorers, dispatched by Sir Walter Raleigh, brought back to England in 1584 glowing accounts of Roanoke Island, off Virginia. Immediately he dispatched a colonizing expedition under Sir Richard Greenville and Sir Ralph Lane. These colonists landed on Roanoke in August, 1585, and built the "Citie of Raleigh," but were compelled by adverse circumstances to return to England in 1586. In 1587 Raleigh sent out another colonizing expedition under John White. Forced to return to England for supplies, White was unable to come back to Roanoke until 1591; by that time the colonists had all disappeared.

Rather an inauspicious beginning for the colonization of America by a people destined to leave a permanent stamp of their culture upon the country! According to an estimate, there were but 210 Britishers in America in 1610. But the next decade was to see a rise in population by 1,090 per cent, though in absolute numbers the population was meagre indeed—2,499.

This increase was made possible by the founding of Jamestown, Virginia, in 1607, and by the landing of the Pilgrim Fathers from the Mayflower at Plymouth Rock, Massachusetts, in December, 1620.

It may also be noted that the first shipload of Negro slaves was brought to Virginia by a Dutch privateer in 1619.

These beginnings give us a glimpse into the composition of the emerging American people: Indians with their tribal organization all over the country, the Spaniards with Spanish law, language and customs in the Southwest and California, and in Florida, the English on the Atlantic seaboard, and the Negro slaves also on the Atlantic seaboard.

4. THE THIRTEEN COLONIES

Let us briefly look at the growth of the thirteen colonies settled or controlled by the British on the eve of the Revolution (1776-83):

1. Virginia, founded by *settlement* at Jamestown in 1607, made under the London Company, chartered by King James I in 1606.

2. Massachusetts, founded in 1630 by *Puritans* under the Massachusetts Bay Company. With it became associated the Colony of Plymouth, which had been established by the *Pilgrims* in 1620 on land belonging to the Plymouth Company, chartered by James I in 1606.

3. New York, founded as New Netherland under the Dutch West India Company in 1624; seized by the English in 1664 and renamed New York.

4. Pennsylvania, granted to William Penn as proprietary by Charles II in 1681; first settlement in Philadelphia in 1682. Here William Penn initiated his holy experiment of a commonwealth in which politics would conform to the highest tenets of religion.

5. Delaware, first settled by the Dutch under the Dutch West India Company and by the Swedes under the Swedish South Company, taken by the English in 1664 and placed under the proprietorship of William Penn in 1682. With the Governor of Pennsylvania as its governor, Delaware acquired an Assembly in 1702.

6. New Jersey, founded under Dutch auspices, seized by England in 1664, and given its present name.

7. Maryland, granted to Lord Baltimore as proprietary in 1632 and started by settlements, mostly of *Roman Catholics*, on Chesapeake Bay in 1634.

8. Connecticut, made up of offshoots from Massachusetts (1635) and settlements on the shore, united under a royal charter in 1662.

9. Rhode Island, made up of two offshoots from Massachusetts, Rhode Island and Providence Plantations, united under a royal charter in 1663.

10. New Hampshire, an offshoot of Massachusetts, given a separate status in 1679.

11. North Carolina, settled by pioneers from other colonies, passed under the jurisdiction of an association of proprietors in 1665 by royal grant; given a separate status as North Carolina in 1729.

12. South Carolina, part of the Carolina region (1665), given independent status in 1729.

13. Georgia, founded as an experiment in *philanthropy*, under a board of trustees, or company, in 1732. (1, pp. 8–9, 22–23).

5. THE EMERGENCE OF THE AMERICAN ETHOS

By the middle of the eighteenth century, America had become an outpost of English culture. The Colonies, subject to the British Crown, had immense resources of raw materials and had a growing population which meant good customers for Britain's manufactured products. Indeed, the mercantile policy of England of those days deliberately discouraged any kind of manufacturing enterprises in America.

But a new spirit was abroad. Either through the connivance of English governors or through laxity in administration, the American had been developing certain types of industry and manufacture: (a) at home, spinning and weaving, smoking and salting meat, soap and candle, etc.; (b) in the household shop, products for the market, such as nails and shingles, barrels and casks, and liquor ; (c) village industry, such as sawmill, gristmill, fulling mill ; (d) openly, ship-building on a limited scale, and naval supplies for England, such as lumber, tar, pitch, rosin and turpentine, and deep-sea fishing and whaling (3, pp. 84–90).

The colonists had brought with them their own English and European arts of agriculture, but they had to learn a great deal from the Indians regarding agriculture in the New World. Corn and tobacco, potato and squash and beans were borrowed from the Indians and the art of growing them, too, was borrowed from them. Thus the Colonists prospered. At the first harvest in 1621, the Pilgrims on bended knees thanked God for His kindness. This is the origin of Thanksgiving Day, which is now celebrated by Americans with a turkey dinner and all the trimmings.

At the middle of the eighteenth century when the stamp of English culture was noticeable everywhere in this land, a curious thing was happening underneath—the emergence of a specific American ethos and outlook. A keen observer of the American scene whom we should know better, a Norman-French gentleman, Hector St. John de Crevecoeur, also known as Michel Guillaume Jean de Crevecoeur (1735-1813), arriving here from France via Canada in 1759, began ten years later (1769-80) to write *Letters from an American Farmer* (6, pp. 142–44, quoted):

The rich stay in Europe, it is only the middling and the poor that emigrate. . . . Everything (here) tends to regenerate them: new laws, a new mode of living, a new social system. Here they have become men. In Europe they were so many useless plants, wanting vegetable mould and refreshing showers; they withered and were mowed down by want, hunger, and war; but now by the power of transplantation, like all other plants, they have taken root and flourished! Formerly they were not numbered in any civil lists of their country, except in those of the poor; here they rank as citizens.

A European, when he first arrives, seems limited in his intentions as well as in his views; but he very suddenly alters his scale. . . . He no sooner breathes our air than he forms new schemes, and embarks on designs he never would have thought of in his own country. There the plenitude of society confines many useful ideas, and often extinguishes the most laudable schemes which here ripen into maturity. . . .

He begins to feel the effects of a sort of resurrection; hitherto he had not lived, but simply vegetated; he now feels himself a man, because he is treated as such; the laws of his own country had overlooked him in his insignificancy; the laws of this cover him with their mantle. Judge what an alteration there must arise in the mind and thoughts of this man! He begins to forget his former servitude and dependence, his heart involuntarily swells and glows; this first swell inspires him with those new thoughts which constitute an American. From nothing (to begin with), . . . to become a free man, invested with land to which every municipal blessing is added! What a change indeed! It is in consequence of this change that he becomes an American.

He is an American who, leaving behind him all his ancient prejudices and manners, receives new ones from the mode of life he has embraced, the new government he obeys, and the new rank (of citizen) he holds. He becomes an American by being received in the broad lap of our great *Alma Mater*. Here individuals of all nations are melted into a new race of men, whose labors and posterity will one day cause great changes in the world.

This analysis of the emerging American ethos and this prognostication of the role of America in world affairs, made on the eve of the American Revolution, certainly stamp Hector St. John de Crevecoeur as a keen observer and reliable interpreter of the American scene.

6. GROWTH OF THE AMERICAN POPULATION: 1610-1790

Let the figures now tell the story of the increase of the American people, then known as colonists, from 1610 to 1790, when the first census was taken by the newly (*contractually*) established United States of America.

TABLE 8

THE COLONIAL POPULATION, WITH DECENNIAL
INCREASE: 1610-1790[1]

Year	Population Number	Per Cent Increase
1610	210	...
1620	2,499	1,090.0
1630	5,700	128.1
1640	27,947	390.3
1650	51,700	85.0
1660	84,800	64.0
1670	114.500	35.0
1680	155,600	35.9
1690	213,500	37.2
1700	275,000	28.8
1710	357,500	30.0
1720	474,388	32.7
1730	654,950	38.1
1740	889,000	35.7
1750	1,207,000	35.8
1760	1,610,000	33.4
1770	2,205,000	37.0
1780	2,781,000	26.1
1790	3,929,214	41.3

[1] E. B. Reuter: *Population Problems*, 2nd ed., p. 52. Philadelphia: Lippincott, 1937.

During the first half century of their existence, 1610 to 1660, the colonies were dependent mainly upon immigration (referred to as colonization, practically up to 1790) for their population growth. After 1660 when the population had reached 85,000, the growth of population was made possible by two factors: (1) natural increase, i.e., excess of births over deaths, and (2) immigration. From 1670 to 1790, the decennial increase has been in the neighborhood of 35 per cent. This means that the American population doubled every twenty-five years.

Even at that America started its national existence with a population slightly less than 4,000,000 which would be just about half the population of New York City (1960).

7. NATIONAL CONSOLIDATION: 1790-1865

Between 1790 and 1860, prior to the Civil War, the American population, again, registered a decennial increase of about 35 per cent, doubling itself every twenty-five years, as may be observed from the following table:

TABLE 9

DECENNIAL INCREASE OF THE POPULATION OF
THE UNITED STATES: 1790-1860[1]

Census Year	Population Number	Per Cent Increase
1790	3,929,214	41.3
1800	5,308,483	35.1
1810	7,239,881	36.4
1820	9,638,453	33.1
1830	12,866,020	33.5
1840	17,069,453	32.7
1850	23,191,876	35.9
1860	31,443,321	35.6

[1] Reuter: *Op. cit.*, p. 53.

The period between 1790 and the Civil War (1861-65) is the period of national consolidation. The geographical shape of the United States was fully defined before the War Between the States ended. In 1783 the writ of the United States ran as far west as the eastern bank of the Mississippi though frontiersmen reserved their right to be a law unto themselves. The Louisiana Purchase of 1803 from France carried the U.S. writ westward as far as the Rockies.

The purchase of Florida from Spain in 1819 made the entire Atlantic seaboard American and national. Of course, each of these and later accessions of territory also meant addition to the American population.

The annexation of the Republic of Texas in 1845 and the cession of the territory by Mexico in 1848, after the Mexican-American War, brought the U.S. clear across the Rockies to the Pacific. And with the recognition of the U.S. claim to the Oregon Territory by Great Britain in 1846, the shape of the United States was firmly fixed. With the purchase of Alaska in 1867 from Russia, the boundaries of the Continental United States were definitely set. The annexation of Hawaii in the Pacific and of Puerto Rico in the Atlantic in 1898 completed American territorial boundaries. Puerto Rico has enjoyed the American Territorial form of self-government, as also did Alaska and Hawaii until their entrance into the Union as self-governing States in 1959-60.

The student may, at this stage, advantageously familiarize himself with two appropriate maps of the United States of America—one showing the territorial growth of the United States from the original 13 states, through the Louisiana Purchase, to the purchase of Alaska; and the other showing the existing states and territories with the dates of their entrance into the Union as states.

8. REPERCUSSIONS OF THE WAR BETWEEN THE STATES

The War Between the States (1861-65) involved some of the bloodiest battles and caused wholesale, wanton destruction in the South, especially in Georgia. One wishes that Sherman's March to the Sea through Georgia could have been as non-violent and peaceful as Gandhi's March to the Sea was in March-April, 1930!

The Civil War as an episode in the history of the American people deserves more than passing reference. First, it brought to the fore one of the seven greatest men of history: (1) Buddha, (2) Asoka, (3) Aristotle, (4) Jesus, (5) Bacon, (6) Lincoln, (7) Gandhi. (The first six were named by Mr. H. G. Wells in the early 1920's as the six greatest men of history.) From rail-splitting to legal practice, from the log cabin to the White House—this saga of Abraham

Lincoln is the patrimony not only of America but also of the whole world.

Second, the New England abolitionists, in spite of their impatience, demonstrated the true idealism of America which would brook no slavery, no injustice, no inequality among the children of God, regardless of the color of their skin or their former status of servitude. That brother was willing to fight against brother in a cause that he believed to be right is a sight the gods do not witness very often on this earth.

Third, while the Civil War broke out over the issue of *extension* of slavery to new states, in the course of the war the issue became *existence* or *extinction* of slavery itself. President Lincoln and his fellow citizens were prepared to make any and every sacrifice for the " unrequited toil" of the bondsman for two hundred and fifty years, if need be, "until every drop of blood drawn with the lash shall be paid by another drawn with the sword" (Lincoln).

Thus, even before the conflict was over, Lincoln's Proclamation of Emancipation (January 1, 1863) became the Negro's Charter of human liberty and civil rights. And Lincoln's inspired words of wisdom in the Second Inaugural Address (March 4, 1865) shall ever remain enshrined in the heart of the American people :

With malice toward none, with charity for all; with firmness in the right, as God gives us to see the right, let us strive on to finish the work we are in : to bind up the nation's wounds, to care for him who shall have borne the battle, and for his widow and his orphan —to do all, which may achieve and cherish a just and lasting peace among ourselves and with all nations.

Fourth, the sharp edge of ill feeling and hatred, resulting from the havoc wrought by the Northern Armies, notably by Sherman's march to the sea, was blunted by the chivalry exhibited by Lincoln and his military commanders. In all history there is no parallel to the return of the sword to the surrendering General Robert E. Lee by the conquering General U. S. Grant! Once the surrender was accepted and the war terminated, the military commanders on the winning side treated the battered and exhausted men on the other side with consideration, with fellow feeling, so much so that the "rebels" of yesterday were permitted to take along with them their horses for the plowing and for the harvesting.

Neither Lincoln nor his military commanders did anything to pour salt over the wounds of war; rather did they honestly strive "to bind up the nation's wounds." But the unconscionable carpet-baggers, who rode to power on the crest of the wave of anti-slavery, marred the smooth work of reconstruction along the pathway of charity and goodwill prescribed by Lincoln. This sad episode in the post-Civil War era of America holds a lesson for us—and we hope for the rest of the world as well. (How Lincoln's strategy could have been applied to world reconstruction after World War II has been dealt with by the author elsewhere: 4, CHAPTER 5.)

Fifth, it is evident, at least from hindsight, that the war between the states was entirely unnecessary, because the economics of slavery and the economics of free labor, when juxtaposed one against the other, made the choice for the slaveholders crystal-clear.

Indeed, on the eve of the war between the states, the economic realities were forcing slave-owners to appraise the situation anew. "The incomplete figures of the Census of 1860 put the number of slaves manumitted in that year at 3,018, a ratio of one to every 1,309 slaves. In that year there were about 262,000 free Negroes in the slave states." (3, p. 329).

Prior to the Civil War, slave labor was becoming economically more expensive than free labor. "The yearly expense for an able-bodied slave was not far from $ 135.00 . . . but afterward, under a system of free labor, Negroes could be obtained for $120.00 a year with board" (3, p. 332). Add to this the constant pangs of conscience the Southern Whites were experiencing by being a party to the maintenance of an essentially un-American system of enslavement, and you come to the conclusion that slavery would have died a natural death without benefit of blood-letting, without the horror of brother fighting against brother! This point needs to be emphasized today because many Northern whites and many Negroes seem to be suffering from the delusion that without the Civil War the Negroes would not have been freed.

Finally, the reconstruction era, marked by a surplus of scalawags and carpetbaggers from the North—a surplus more injurious to our nation than the surplus of corn today—deeply wounded the pride of Southern white citizens. Economic realities and political forces brought "reconstruction" to a halt, and the Negro by and large became a sharecropper for the same master for whom he had worked as a slave—without benefit of "social security" from the master! This unhappy state of affairs could have been avoided had the North not forced the issue of anti-slavery on the South. *Within less than a generation, under the impact of the impersonal logic of technology, slavery would have passed away from the American scene, without bitterness between North and South and without tension between white and colored in the South.* While this reading of history is tantamount to being wise after the event, it holds a moral lesson for us today.

To relieve the seriousness of this discussion, I may end this section with a true-life anecdote which depicts the lighter side of the American people (*The Reader's Digest*, December, 1956, p. 71):

When Albert Woolson, last surviving Union veteran of the Civil War, died in Minnesota at 109 years of age, I needed information on the funeral arrangements for *Army Times*, which was about to go to press. I telephoned Colonel Bud Larecy in Chicago, who would know about this matter.

In a Southern drawl soft as spoon bread Colonel Larecy allowed, " Suh, we are offering every assistance : marching band with muffled drums, firing squad, flag for the casket, and officers and men to act as pallbearers."

"Are you a pallbearer, Colonel?" I asked.

" No, suh," he said firmly. "Ah bugged out before mah name got on orders. Mah Confederate ancestors' graves have been disturbed enough! Mah car license reads ' Land of Lincoln.' Ah live on Scott Loop at Fort Sheridan, and drive down General Wood Street to work. And Ah thought it was going too far for me to help carry the last Yankee to his Eternal Camping Ground!"

—Col. John M. Virden (Washington, D.C.)

A footnote may be added to this genial encounter between the Northern Colonel and the Southern Colonel. The Civil War episode in American history has been described by someone as "feudin', fission, fusion." The outside world will continue blithely to refer to

Col. Bud Larecy and other stalwart descendants of Confederate ancestors as "Yankees"!

9. GROWTH OF THE AMERICAN POPULATION: 1860-90

Let us resume our story of the growth of the American people since 1860. "The rate of growth, roughly a doubling in each 25-year period, which had prevailed for approximately two centuries, was violently disturbed in the decade of the Civil War" (7, p. 54). The increase in the decade 1860-70 was 26.6 per cent, 8 to 9 per cent less than in previous decennial counts.

This decrease was caused by many factors. For one thing, immigration was checked. Second, increase in the death rate, especially of males in the prime of youth, as a result of the war, curtailed the number of marriages and depressed the birth rate. Third, for some curious reason unknown to population experts, the large-scale industrial development which in its initial stages is usually accompanied by a phenomenal exuberance in population growth failed to materialize in the aftermath of the Civil War. Perhaps the psychological dislocation caused by the Civil War might account for the relative decline in the rate of growth of the American population during 1860-70. But the next two decades, too, registered the low rate of population growth which had characterized the Civil War decade—just about 25 to 26 per cent.

TABLE 10

DECENNIAL INCREASE OF THE POPULATION OF
THE UNITED STATES: 1870-90[1]

Census Year	Population Number	Percentage Increase
1870	39,818,449	26.6
1880	50,155,783	26.0
1890	62,947,714	25.5

[1] E. B. Reuter: *Op. cit.,* p. 54.

10. SIGNIFICANCE OF 1890: THE NEW IMMIGRATION

The year 1890 is important in American history for a variety of reasons. First, that year marked the end of the frontier; according to the Census authorities, a frontier is an area with less than six inhabitants per square mile. The West which had beckoned resourceful men and women had no more land for free appropriation by frontiersmen, by the right of settlement.

Second, from 1890 on, America was to see the rise of great moguls of finance, industrial tycoons, railroad builders, and the era of monopolies, trusts, and holding companies—all working in the direction of more abundant production of goods and services.

Third, an era in immigration came to an end in 1880-90 and a new one set in. Population students usually speak of the years 1790-1882 (some say 1830-82) as the era of the Old Immigration. These Old Immigrants came mostly from Northern and Western Europe. These people were either Anglo-Saxons and Nordics or not too markedly different in language and outlook from the Americans whose culture-patterns were preponderantly British. Between 1830 and 1882, the Irish and the Germans constituted the largest portion of this Old Immigration.

The Irish and the Germans had already come to this country in the Colonial Period and taken an active part in the Revolutionary War. But during the period we are considering, they began to come in ever-increasing numbers every year.

The flow of Irish immigration was caused by the potato famine of 1840, by general poverty at home, and by a keen desire not to be ruled by England. Because of their Roman Catholic affiliation, the Irish were at first frowned upon and distrusted, but they soon made themselves an integral part of the American people. The cities of New York and Boston have had more often than not Irish-American Mayors. In the councils of the Democratic Party, especially in the North, the Irish-Americans play a significant part. The Irish-American priest is noticeable in many an American Catholic Church. The police forces and fire department forces of our great metropolises are in large or small measure manned by these competent and genial Irish-Americans. And today it would be difficult for an outside visitor to realize that St. Patrick's Day celebrations, including the colorful parades in all metropolises, are Irish importations into American culture. Indeed, it would be nearer the mark to say that St. Patrick's Day is as much an American holiday as it is Irish.

During the period under review, the Germans came in large numbers to this country for a variety of reasons. Some of them had taken part in the abortive reform movements of their country in the 1840's and sought political refuge here. These were idealists, chief among whom was Carl Schurz, a great statesman. Some others came here seeking wider scope for their talents and industriousness. Skilled farmers and skilled craftsmen, talented educationists and great music lovers, these German-Americans have contributed in large measure to the making of America what it is today. Just as Minnesota is a shining example of the efficiency of the Scandinavian-Americans, so is Wisconsin a bright example of the efficiency of our German-Americans.

Beginning with the decade 1880-90, roughly from 1882 through 1917, is the era of the New Immigration. This new immigration was made up of peoples from Southern Europe and from Eastern Europe—Latins and Slavs. The culture-patterns and languages of these new immigrants were very different from the dominant and evolving culture-patterns of the American people. Thus arose the problem of Americanizing, of assimilating, these peoples with variant culture-patterns.

"Between 1820 and 1930, over 4,628,000 Italians came to the United States, of which number over 3,500,000 arrived in the present century" (2, p. 44). After overcoming the barrier of language and other cultural disadvantages, the Italian-Americans have been able to make use of the opportunities afforded by this country for advancement both educationally and economically.

Besides the Italians, the South European tide of immigration brought in Greeks, Spanish, Portuguese, and Albanians. The Slavic immigrants included Russians, Ukrainians, Poles, Czechoslovaks, Yugoslavs, and Bulgarians. These people are to be found in all kinds of occupation—on the farm, in the factories, and in the professions.

11. EMERGENCE OF ETHNIC SUBCULTURAL ISLANDS

All these ethnic groups from Europe as well as others from Asia and Africa (to be mentioned) have enriched the American social heritage. I shall never forget the wonderment and respect I felt for America when, for the first time, I saw in the reading room, on the

open shelves of the New York Public Library, great works of literature from the different countries of the world placed side by side
with American classics. In no other country, I mused to myself,
would people be able to transcend their narrow cultural provincial-
ism and ethnocentrism to the extent of considering their own works
as being no better than those of other peoples.

Some of these ethnic groups have enriched America by importing
some of their specific culture-traits. The Irish gave us St. Patrick's
Day. The Germans gave us the Christmas tree. The Jews, who were
part of the German and Slavic immigration tide, have brought to
America their distinctive skills and talents in business and in the
professions.

Withal, it must be noted that all ethnic groups tend to congregate
together, especially the newly arrived immigrants. Thus we have our
"Little Italy," "Little Sicily," "Chinatown," "Maxwell Street,"
"Little Poland," "Deutschland," and similar communities in our
metropolises. By the third generation, the children of immigrants
tend to become thoroughly Americanized.

The following table reveals the shift in the sources of immigration between 1860 and 1910:

TABLE 11

THE SHIFT IN THE SOURCES OF IMMIGRATION, 1860-1910[1]

Country of Origin	Immigrant Arrivals in Each Decade					
	1861-70		1881-90		1901-10	
	Number	Per Cent	Number	Per Cent	Number	Per Cent
All countries	2,314,824	100	5,245,613	100	8,795,386	100
United Kingdom	1,042,674	45	1,462,839	28	865,015	10
Germany	787,468	34	1,452,970	28	341,498	4
Italy	11,725	0.5	307,309	6	2,045,877	23
Austria-Hungary	7,800	0.3	353,719	7	2,145,266	24
Russia	2,512	0.1	213,282	4	1,597,306	18
All others	462,645	20	1,456,494	27	1,800,424	21

[1] J. L. Gillin et al: *Social Problems,* 3rd ed., p. 181. New York: D. Appleton-Century Co., 1943.

12. GROWTH OF THE AMERICAN POPULATION: 1900-60

We may now look at the rate of growth of the American people as a whole between 1890 and 1960. The following table suggests (1) that the doubling of the American population every twenty-five years is strictly a matter of the past, (2) that the decennial rate of growth of the population may stabilize itself somewhere between 10 and 20 per cent.

TABLE 12

DECENNIAL INCREASE OF THE POPULATION OF
THE UNITED STATES: 1900-60[1]

Census Year	Population Number	Percentage Increase
1900	75,994,575	20.7
1910	91,972,266	21.0
1920	105,710,620	14.9
1930	122,775,046	16.1
1940	131,669,275	7.2
1950	150,697,361	14.5
1960	180,000,000[2]	20.0

[1] Data gathered from *Statistical Abstract of the U.S.*, 1956, p. 5.
[2] Estimate in round numbers.

A quick glance at Table 12, giving the decennial increase of the population of the U.S. between 1900 and 1960, reveals that whereas the percentage increase in the last two decades has been only 14.5 and 20.0 respectively, the increase of the population in absolute numbers has been practically 20,000,000 and 30,000,000 respectively, during 1940-50 and 1950-60.

While the depression years of the thirties were marked by an increase of only 9 million (1930-40), the period of World War II (1941-45) and the Korean War (1950-53) has been marked by what may be called a bumper crop of babies. These babies of the 1940's made necessary expanded school facilities and an increased number of teachers in the grade schools and in high schools. Toward the end of the 1950's, some of the babies of the 40's began to knock at the gates of our institutions of higher learning, entailing increased enrollments in our colleges and universities and expanded classroom facilities and teaching personnel. Educators have been keenly alive to this "battle of the bulge," and have been valiantly meeting the challenge of increased enrollment.

One psychological problem remains unanswered: Why did the American people experience a let-down in their population growth after the Civil War and a spurt in population growth during and after World War II? One possible psychological explanation may be that while the Civil War youths were suddenly thrust into a disruptive situation, World War II youths, having been inured to disruption as a normal part of their experience, decided to make the most of marriage before going off to war and during the war. This hypothesis deserves to be studied and analyzed on the basis of empirical data.

13. THE NEGRO MINORITY IN THE U.S.A.

The largest ethnic group in the American population is, of course, the Negro. This group has been part of America from the time of the Pilgrim Fathers' landing at Plymouth Rock. Having constituted almost 20 per cent of the total population in the early decades of this nation's history, since 1880 the Negro has been just about 10 per cent of the total population. But in absolute numbers, 15,042,286 (1950), the Negro population must be reckoned as a powerful force socially, politically and economically. (Cf. TABLE 13.)

That both under slavery and after Emancipation the Negro has had a differential and disadvantageous access to the goods and services of this country is an open secret. That the dominant white group has attempted, by means fair and foul, to keep the Negro in his place is also too true. It is also true that both in the South and in the North upstanding white men and women have championed the Negro's cause for equal treatment.

The two significant Negro organizations devoted to the betterment of the lot of the Negroes were founded at white initiative and have had white members on their boards. The National Association for the Advancement of Colored People (NAACP), founded in 1909, and the National Urban League, founded in 1911, have done

TABLE 13

A COMPARISON OF NEGROES AND WHITES AT
EACH DECENNIAL CENSUS: 1790-1960 [1]

Year	Total	White	Negro	All Others
1790	3,929,214	3,172,006	757,208	
1800	5,308,483	4,306,446	1,002,037	
1810	7,239,881	5,862,073	1,337,808	
1820	9,638,453	7,886,797	1,771,656	
1830	12,866,020	10,537,378	2,328,642	
1840	17,069,453	14,195,805	2,873,648	
1850	23,191,876	19,553,068	3,638,808	
1860	31,443,321	26,922,537	4,441,830	78,954
1870	39,818,449	33,589,377	4,880,009	88,985
1880	50,155,783	43,402,970	6,580,793	172,020
1890	62,947,744	55,101,258	7,488,676	357,780
1900	75,994,575	66,809,196	8,833,994	351,385
1910	91,972,266	81,731,957	9,827,763	412,546
1920	105,710,620	94,820,915	10,463,131	426,574
1930	122,775,046	110,286,740	11,891,143	597,163
1940	131,669,275	118,214,870	12,865,518	588,887
1950	150,697,361	134,942,028	15,042,286	713,047
1960[2]	179,323,175	158,831,732	18,871,831	1,619,612

[1] Data gathered from *Statistical Abstract of the U.S.*, 1956, p. 21.
[2] *U. S. Census of Population 1960 : Final Report PC(1)—1B ;* p. 1-164.
Washington, D.C.: U. S. Dept. of Commerce, Bureau of the Census, 1961.

creditable work in integrating Negroes into American society as equal citizens. While the Urban League has been mainly concerned with helping Negroes secure jobs and adjust themselves to the urban-industrial complex of the North, the NAACP has devoted its major efforts to securing and safeguarding the civil rights of the Negroes and equal rights for them to participate in American democracy as full citizens.

The Negro's rapid advance, economically and educationally, within less than a hundred years after Emancipation, is worthy of note. This underprivileged group of yesteryear has made notable contributions to arts and literature, to athletics and science, to education and nation-building. And since the integration of the Negroes into the armed forces of this nation during the Korean

War (1950-53), especially since the historic decision of the U.S. Supreme Court on May 17, 1954, outlawing segregation in the public schools, the Negro is gradually losing his status as a second class citizen and attaining the status of first class citizenship.

The so-called race problem in America is at bottom the problem of Negro-White relations. The Southern White's opposition to the Negro's first class citizenship is rooted in psycho-social reasons. To begin with, he has directly or vicariously known of the Negro as a slave. Second, he has met hundreds of Negroes who are inefficient and uneducated. Third, he feels, rightly or wrongly, that acceptance of race equality would lead to mixed unions and marriages.

Withal, as an American the Southern white man believes in the American Declaration of Independence and in the Constitution; both by religious persuasion and by American upbringing he believes in the equality of all God's children. And there is the crux of the American Dilemma. The American dilemma consists in the gap between our profession (of equality) and our practice (of inequality, segregation).

Under the prodding of the U.S. Supreme Court, most of the disabilities imposed upon the Negroes are on the way out. But goodwill cannot be legislated; goodwill can arise only in the day-to-day relations of living as neighbors at the local community level. It is a psychological problem, not a juridical nor a legislative problem.

Is there a psychological common-ground between Negroes and Whites in the South? Gunnar Myrdal (5, *passim*), in his epoch-making study, *An American Dilemma* (1944), answers the question in the affirmative.

When asked to rank, in order of importance, the types of discrimination they consider most important, Southern whites and Negroes exhibited differing scales of values. The ban the white man considered most important—intermarriage and sex relations between white women and colored men—was considered least important by the Negroes. Inequality in jobs and relief, considered least important by the whites, was rated most important by the Negroes. Here is the white Southerner's ranking of the nine types of discrimination.

CHART 16

A RANKING OF NINE TYPES OF DISCRIMINATION
BY SOUTHERN WHITES[1]

1. The ban on intermarriage and sex relations involving white women and colored men ;
2. The established etiquette governing personal relations between individuals of two races ;
3. Segregation in the schools and churches ;
4. Segregation in hotels, restaurants, and theaters ;
5. Segregation in trains, street cars, and buses;
6. Discrimination in public service ;
7. Inequality in political rights ;
8. Inequality before the law ;
9. Inequality in jobs and relief.

[1] Maxwell S. Stewart: *The Negro in America,* p. 30. New York: Public Affairs Committee, Inc., 1944.

It is worthy of note that since Mr. Myrdal wrote his book (1944), discriminations 3 to 9 have been on the way out, sometimes by mutual agreement, sometimes by the intervention of the Federal Government. Discrimination items one and two are not susceptible to judicial interpretations. However, since about 1960, the practice of addressing Negroes as Mr. or Mrs. or Miss in our media of mass communication is growing even in our Southland.

Competent British observers of the English social scene assure us that one of the wholesome byproducts of World War II was the impact it had on the class structure of English society: Lord Tweedmuir and Mr. Hornbeck and Johnny the frequenter of the pub all had to take shelter in a common bomb shelter and rub shoulders one with another. Similarly, in America, having fought for the freedom and civil rights of other peoples in two World Wars, American Negro youths naturally thought in terms of their own freedom from segregation and other legal restrictions. Resort to the Gandhi technique of non-violent resistance to the intrenched system of segregation by the Negro citizens of Montgomery, Alabama, under the leadership of Rev. Martin Luther King, Jr., and his associates in 1955-57 has had profound effects on the interracial situation in America. Its logical end-result is bound to be the attainment of first-class citizenship by our fellow citizens belonging to the Negro minority.

The CENTENNIAL of Lincoln's Emancipation Proclamation (1963) saw an upsurge of activities both by Whites and Negroes for the removal of the last vestiges of differential treatment accorded to American citizens belonging to the Negro ethnic group. On the FIRST of January, 1863, President Lincoln had proclaimed: "I do order and declare that all persons held as slaves within (the Confederate States) are, and henceforth shall be, free." The American people, both white and colored, celebrated the CENTENNIAL of this epoch-making Proclamation by insisting upon the attainment of first-class citizenship by Negroes. This insistence manifested itself in non-violent agitations as well as in court actions.

The Gandhi technique of non-violent resistance assumed various forms, such as: sit-ins, kneel-ins, voter-registrations, parades, pickettings, and mass demonstrations, leading to arrests and temporary imprisonments of a few white and colored demonstrators. Foremost among those espousing the Gandhi technique of non-violence were the Southern Christian Leadership Conference, established and headed by Rev. Martin Luther King, Jr., and CORE (Congress of Racial Equality), headed by American citizens who had received inspiration from the pacifist organization, the Fellowship of Reconciliation. The "Black Muslims," who are theologically poles apart from the teachings of the Prophet Mohammed of Arabia (570–632), reasserted, during the CENTENNIAL, their militant and violent philosophy more vigorously than ever before. And the powerful NAACP, at its 54th annual convention in Chicago, during the first week of July, 1963, set up machinery for the creation of "task forces of NAACP commandos," made up of young Negroes who would be available for participation in any form of non-violent activity whenever and wherever needed. A. Phillip Randolph, the redoubtable Negro Head of the Brotherhood of Sleeping Car Porters for over a generation, exerted his influence in favor of non-violent demonstration. The Student Non-Violent Coordinating Committee (SNCC) has also been active in the field.

The U.S. Judiciary stepped up its demands for integrating the remaining few public schools, colleges and universities that had been denying admission to eligible Negro students; it also stepped up its demands for integrating other public facilities, such as parks, as well as quasi-public facilities, such as hotels, restaurants, business establishments, etc. The Executive Branch of the Government exerted its full power and authority to the end that the Negro might enjoy all the rights and privileges of American citizenship. Leading Congressmen and Senators, likewise, became intent upon transferring the upsurge of Negro demands for equality from the streets to the courts. Churches, Chambers of Commerce, and professional and civic groups and businessmen all over the country went on record as being in favor of removing discrimination and segregation.

We may pause for a moment to discuss the usage of the word discrimination. Discrimination, literally, means acute discernment, keen judgment, ability to distinguish between objects of differing values or between objects of greater or lesser values. For instance, we may be said to exercise discrimination when we make nice distinctions between two works of art. A man of discriminating judgment is a man of fastidious judgment and tastes. Thus, discrimination, in a literal sense, means making nice distinctions, separating the grain from the chaff, so to say. But within the context of social situations, especially in the field of intergroup relations, discrimination connotes denying a certain individual or group some of the rights and privileges available in the community. Thus discrimination may involve denial of political rights or of economic or educational opportunities for advancement, or even segregation. Discrimination passes over from subjective judgment to overt action. While segregation in the sociological sense, not in the ecological sense, is the end-result of discrimination, prejudice is a subjective feeling, often crystallized into an attitude. The progression is: prejudice, attitude, discrimination, segregation.

14. THE AMERICAN INDIAN MINORITY IN THE U.S.A.

The other significant ethnic minority in America is the American Indian. We have reliable statistics concerning Indian (American) population since 1890.

TABLE 14

AMERICAN INDIANS IN AMERICA

1890-1950[1]

Year	Number	Increase (+) or Decrease (−)
1890	248,253	
1900	237,196	−
1910	265,683	+
1920	244,437	−
1930	332,397	+
1940	333,969	+
1950	343,410	+

[1] *Statistical Abstract of the U.S.* 1956, p. 33.

It is obvious that the Indian is not dying out, nor is he multiplying profusely. The vast majority of these Indians live on reservations as wards of the United States Government. These reservations and their residents are under the direct jurisdiction of the Indian Affairs Bureau in the Department of the Interior.

There are two schools of thought regarding the Indian's status as a ward: one maintains that the U.S. Government should encourage the Indians to perpetuate their tribal organization and rituals as wards of the government; the other maintains that we should educate them out of their reservations and into the full stream of American life.

During World War II, many Indian youths went to various battle fronts in Uncle Sam's uniform. Having seen how the other Americans live, most of these young men would rather give up the reservation with its social security and brave the world of competition and make a place for themselves by their own abilities.

In 1492, according to some estimates, there were about 900,000 Indians north of Mexico, but by 1870, thanks to wars, starvation and epidemics of measles, small-pox and cholera, their number dwindled to about 300,000. In most South and Central American countries, Indians outnumber citizens of the European stock; but north of Mexico they constitute a small minority in the U.S.A. and Canada.

15. THE SPANISH-SPEAKING MINORITY

In our Southwest, we discover three contemporary layers of culture : at the bottom the Indian, above it the Spanish, and above both the "Anglo." Also in the Southwest and in California we have another distinctive ethnic minority, recent immigrants from Mexico.

The Spanish-speaking ethnic minority in the U.S.A., about three million in number, reside mostly in California, Texas, Arizona and New Mexico; but migratory Mexican laborers are to be found in many parts of the country during the harvesting season. Then, too, a number of the "Mexican-Americans" have found jobs as industrial workers in Chicago, Detroit and New York, the last abounding in Spanish-speaking Puerto Ricans as well.

According to estimates based on the 1940 Census returns, approximately two million residents of the U.S. claimed Spanish as their mother tongue. Though all of them are referred to as "Mexicans," only about four hundred thousand of them were born in Mexico, and perhaps twice that number had one or both of the parents of Mexican birth.

In some communities these "Mexicans" have fared worse than Negroes or Indians. But the inferiority complex of the Spanish-speaking minority is fast disappearing, and in their ranks are emerging trained and professional men and women whose leadership will in the not distant future secure this "forgotten" minority their rightful place in the sun.

16. ORIENTAL MINORITIES IN THE U.S.A.

Finally, we come to a heterogeneous grouping called Orientals, consisting of those who came from various countries of the Orient and chose to make their home in America. From the Near East, over 100,000 Armenians, Syrians, Arabs and Turks had migrated to the United States by 1920.

The Gold Rush of California (1848-49) lured a number of Chinese as well as Europeans and Americans to the Pacific Coast "Paradise." By 1852, there were about 52,000 Chinese in this country, most of them in California. The transcontinental railroad builders needed laborers, and the Chinese were invited to get their share of the jobs and their share in the building of the great railroad empire. Between 1850 and 1880, almost 100,000 Chinese came to America, and in the single year 1882, nearly 40,000 arrived. It was in the same year, 1882, that the first Chinese Exclusion Act was passed by Congress.

With Chinese immigration effectively cut off, the Japanese began to take their place. In 1890, there were 2,039 Japanese; between 1890 and 1900, some 22,000 Japanese came here, and in the decade 1901-10, the number of Japanese immigrants exceeded 45,000. By the "gentleman's agreement" of 1907, the Japanese Government undertook to restrict Japanese immigration to the United States.

The following table gives the exact figures for the Chinese and Japanese by decades.

TABLE 15

DECENNIAL FIGURES FOR CHINESE, JAPANESE, AND
OTHER ORIENTALS: 1880-1950[1]

Year	Chinese	Japanese	All Other[2]
1880	105,465	148	
1890	107,488	2,039	
1900	89,863	24,326	
1910	71,531	72,157	3,175
1920	61,639	111,010	9,488
1930	74,954	138,834	50,978
1940	77,504	126,947	50,467
1950	117,629	141,628	110,240

[1] *Statistical Abstract of the U.S.*, 1947, p. 19, and *Ibid*, 1956, p. 33.
[2] "All Other" includes Filipinos, Hindus, Koreans. Hawaiians, Malays, Siamese, Samoans, and Maoris.

It is to the "All Other" group category that the present writer belongs—one of some 2,000 Hindus, rather Hindese, in this country, most of them on the Pacific Coast, engaged in farming. There are a few Hindese working in the factories of Detroit and the New York metropolitan region; and a handful of professional persons are to be found scattered over the country.

The Chinese, Japanese and Hindese made a success of rice culture in California. Being frugal and hard-working, they became formidable competitors of American farmers.

The Chinese Exclusion Act having been finalized in 1904, Congress enacted in 1917 a longitude and latitude act creating a barred zone in most of Asia—barred to immigration in the U.S.A.—and in 1924, the policy of Oriental Exclusion was enacted by Congress into law.

In 1943, during World War II, the Chinese Exclusion Act was repealed as a gesture of friendliness to our ally China. And in 1946, after a series of hearings before Congressional Committees, initiated by the present writer and his co-workers in the 1930's, India was put on a quota basis. The Walter-McCarran Act of 1952 put all countries, including Japan, on a quota basis. In 1965 the U.S. Congress abolished the National Quota System.

17. IMMIGRANTS ALL, AMERICANS ALL

East and West, Orient and Occident—America considers all peoples as equals and welcomes all those who knock at her gates within the limits set by law.

Even the limits set by law are sometimes overriden by this country to welcome political refugees, as was done in 1956-57 when some 25,000 Hungarian political refugees sought asylum here.

These are the people who make up the group called America: immigrants all, Americans all!

It is interesting to note that California which had agitated against Oriental immigration during the first four decades of the present century should send India-born Dr. Dalip Singh Saund to Congress in the biennial elections of 1956-58-60. That I should have been able in 1956 to enter the Republican Party primary as Candidate for U.S. Representative from the Second District of Iowa and get as many as 5,600 votes at an expenditure of $253.15, without any ethnic group to back me, is an authentic expression of American democracy.

18. WHO AND WHAT IS AN AMERICAN?

Now who is an American? And what is an American? It is easy to answer the first question: An American is one who is either born in this country or who has become a naturalized citizen of this country. The second question is more difficult to answer. It was an American—the copper-colored "original American," the American Indian, Corporal Ira Hamilton Hayes from the Southwest (Arizona) —who was among the immortal six that raised the U.S. Flag on Iwo Jima. "The six men—five Marines and a sailor—who took part in the historic flag-raising, were representative Americans. They came from the Allegheny Mountains in Pennsylvania (Sergeant Michael Strank, son of Czechoslovak immigrants), the dairy lands of Wisconsin (John Henry Bradley, Pharmacist's Mate, Second Class, USN), an Indian reservation in Arizona (Corporal Ira Hamilton Hayes, Pima Indian), the hills of New Hampshire (Corporal Rene Arthur Gagnon, son of French-Canadian immigrants), the oil fields of southernmost Texas (Corporal Harlan Henry Block), and the tobacco fields of Kentucky (Private First Class Franklin Runyon Sousley, the youngest of the six, 19 years and 5 months old)." It may be noted that Corporal Gagnon was one month shy of 20 years. (Joel D. Thacker: "History of the Iwo Jima Flag Raising," a multi-lith release by the Historical Division Headquarters, U.S. Marine Corps, August 15, 1951.) These young Americans, derived from different racial, national and religious backgrounds, working as a team, covered themselves with glory and made history. And the most decorated battalion in World War II was composed of true and loyal Americans—the Niseis, second-generation Americans, some of whom had been ousted, with their families, from their homes on the Pacific Coast soon after Pearl Harbor!

America is its people—180,000,000 strong. America is its social heritage of the Declaration of Independence and the Constitution with its Bill of Rights. America is Washington and Franklin, Jefferson and Lincoln, Edison and Ford, Steinmetz and Pupin; it is Smiths and Schmidts, Johnsons and Johansons, Murphys and Wolinskys, and Fujiwaras and Changs and Singhs, and a host of other sovereign citizens whose names can be found in the telephone directories of the leading cities of the world.

What, then is an American? Well, you can spot an American by the way he walks, head erect, eager to look the world in the eye; by the way he works, industriously and with many units of horse power harnessed in his labor-saving devices and tools; by the way he talks, freely, easily, open-heartedly; by the way he dresses, comfortably and luxuriously; by the way he eats—the European finds it difficult to juggle the knife and fork as does the American.

The collective representation of this America is "Old Glory"— "The Stars and Stripes For Ever!" The spiritual emblem of this group called America is the Cross of Christ. The ethical and political doctrines of this group, of this nation, are enshrined in the Declaration of Independence and the Constitution, exalting the dignity of man. The watchword of the American is industriousness, efficiency, power-driven machinery, maximum productivity. The expression of the American spirit is in generosity, hospitality, and sharing with the world the good things of this life produced by the sweat of the brow of the American people.

America is the Open Road and the Libertad, glorified by Walt Whitman, the poet of democracy.

This is the group called America.

REFERENCES

1. CHARLES, A. and MARY R. BEARD: *The Beards' Basic History of the United States.* New York: The New Home Library, 1944.
2. LUKE EBERSOLE: *American Society.* New York: McGraw-Hill Book Co., 1955.
3. H. U. FAULKNER: *American Economic History,* 5th ed. New York: Harper and Brothers, 1943.
4. H. T. MUZUMDAR: *The United Nations of the World.* New York: Universal Publishing Co., 1942 (2nd ed. 1944).
5. GUNNAR MYRDAL, et al: *An American Dilemma* (2 vols.). New York: Harper and Brothers, 1944.
6. V. L. PARRINGTON: *The Colonial Mind* 1620-1800. New York: Harcourt, Brace and Co., 1927.
7. E. B. REUTER: *Population Problems,* 2nd ed. Philadelphia: J. B. Lippincott Co., 1937.
8. *Statistical Abstract of the U.S.,* 1947; 1956. Washington: U.S. Government Printing Office.
9. MAXWELL S. STEWART: *The Negro in America.* New York: Public Affairs Committee, Inc., 1944.

CHAPTER 20

THE GREAT GROUP CALLED MANKIND

1. MAN'S ANTIQUITY

MAN, who belongs to the species *homo sapiens*, has been on this planet for perhaps as long as a million years and perhaps for as short a time as half a million years. The Java Man and the Peking Man are considered by competent authorities to have flourished in the early Pleistocene.

How and why man and the anthropoid ape—the chimpanzee, the orangutan, the gorilla—branched off, and when, are among the mysteries of nature. Suffice it to note that the skeleton forms of the anthropoid apes and of the hominidae (human beings) have not only many resemblances but also many affinities.

CHART 17
APES AND MEN

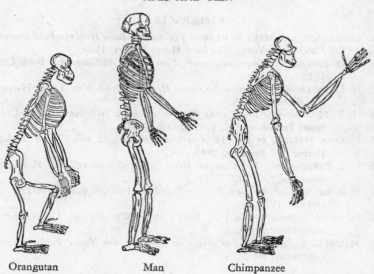

Orangutan   Man   Chimpanzee

It is conceivable that at an early age man delighted in swinging from one branch of the tree to another like his simian cousins. Then some non-conformist or a set of non-conformists decided to walk erect on two legs. Man's bodily frame was suitable for erect posture, even though it was easier to walk on all fours and to dwell in trees.

Once the advantages of walking erect on *terra firma* became evident—such advantages as a sense of power and dominion over those who were doomed to dwell in trees—collective man's upward march to progress began. With his prehensible or opposable thumb, he could grasp the branch of a tree or a stone and use those as implements in his dominion over birds and beasts.

2. THE OLD AND THE NEW STONE AGE

In time he began to fashion crude tools of stone for use, or just to while away the time. Anthropologists refer to this period as the Paleolithic or Old Stone Age. Having achieved mastery in the fashioning of stone implements, elaborate, ornamental and utilitarian, man entered the Neolithic or the New Stone Age.

Competent authorities estimate that the Paleolithic Age may have started as far back as 500000 B.C. and continued till 13000 B.C., when Cro-Magnon man held sway; that the Mesolithic (Middle Stone Age) may be dated around 10000 B.C. simultaneously with the emergence of modern man; that the Neolithic Age lasted almost up to 5000 B.C., when the metallic age dawned, even though some groups did discover the use of metal much earlier—as early as 7000 B.C. or even earlier.

Stone, flint, bone, and, later, bronze, copper and iron and steel implements—such is the rough road over which man ascended to his present position. During the Neolithic Age, man had domesticated the dog, sheep, goats and swine; he had made pottery, and had developed hoe culture, a rudimentary form of agriculture in which he cooperated with nature in raising barley, millet, peas and flax (8, p. 43).

3. FROM PREHISTORY TO HISTORY

Broadly speaking, man has passed from the food-gathering to the food-producing stage. (*Cf.* TABLE 4, CHAPTER 14, *supra.*) When he was dependent solely upon direct appropriation of the gifts of nature—fruits and berries and nuts—his numbers must have been very small indeed. Roughly, man has passed through the food-gathering, hunting-and-fishing, and nomadic existence—moving with the seasons to pasture his cattle and sheep—to the agricultural form of economy.

Man shared in common with other animals the capacity to vocalize, to emit sounds. In course of time, the rudimentary grunts and groans—a form of emotive language—gave way to referential language. For many, many centuries, this referential language was spoken, not written; even so, it gave man a tool possessed neither by birds nor beasts. Now he could pass on the accumulated wisdom of the ages by word of mouth. Later when pictographs, ideographs, and alphabetic writing were invented, man began to pass from the haze of prehistory into the clear light of history and his superorganic began to increase by leaps and bounds, by means of diffusion as well as by means of new inventions.

4. HUMAN MIGRATIONS

Once he mastered the art of locomotion, collective man kept on walking from place to place. Men crossed the oceans by land-bridges, or by island-hopping in their tiny rafts. In the long perspective of history, the history of man on this planet is the history of human migrations. This has meant the admixtures of race groups and the diffusion of culture traits the world over. We do not know who invented the wheel or where, or when, but it is to be found all over the world except in pre-Columbian America. The bow-and-arrow, having been once invented, travelled around the world. In our modern day, the so-called Arabic numeral system, invented by the Hindus of India, borrowed by the Arabs, and introduced by them to the Europeans, has been brought back to the Hindus and the Arabs by the Europeans as it girdled the whole world.

5. CORRELATION BETWEEN ECONOMY AND POPULATION

We have no exact, reliable data to show how large a population would be supported by a given form of economy, but the following table, prepared by K. Weichel and cited by Mark Jefferson, is highly suggestive:

TABLE 16

SUGGESTED CORRELATION BETWEEN DENSITY OF POPULATION
AND THE TYPE OF ECONOMY OF A GIVEN REGION[1]

Density Per Square Mile	Type of Economy
0 to 8	Hunting and fishing
8 to 26	Grazing and forestry
26 to 64	Beginnings of agriculture
64 to 192	Agriculture
192 to 256	Beginnings of industry
256 to 381	Agriculture and industry
381 to 512	Industry predominates
512 to 2,560	Industrial towns or suburbs
2,560 to 5,120	Centers of small cities
5,120 to 12,800	Centers of moderate cities
12,800 to 25,600	Centers of large cities

[1] Reproduced from N. P. Gist and L. A. Halbert: *Urban Society*, 2nd ed., p. 5. New York: Thomas Y. Crowell Co., 1941.

6. THE INVENTION OF AGRICULTURE

The invention of agriculture was the most momentous event in the life of early man. With oxen to plough the land, with pottery for storing the harvested grain, with the wheel to accelerate transportation and to make it less arduous, collective man had to settle down in a given place if he was to reap the full rewards of his agricultural pursuits. Thus arose the first continuous settled community, the agricultural village.

My forefathers and the forefathers of the Europeans, at one time living in the Caucasus region (*Cf.* the term Caucasian), called themselves Aryas, agriculturists. By derivation, the word Arya came to mean "nobleman," in contrast to the lower breeds, culturally, the hunters, the fishers, the nomads.

In the United States, agriculture is carried on typically by farmers living in isolated farm-houses in the open country, in contrast to the rest of the world where agriculture is carried on by farmers living in

11

villages. A community of less than 250—usually farmers and their families—is referred to as a hamlet in the United States, while a center of population containing more than 250 but less than 2,500 is called a village—a part of the rural population whose livelihood is dependent, directly or indirectly, upon agriculture.

7. THE ARYAN AND OTHER MIGRATIONS

Why these Caucasians decided to leave their homeland is not known. Whether spurred on by adventure and the pioneering impulse, or goaded by starvation incident to a possible change in climate, these Aryas began to move around 4000 B.C. northwestward, toward Greece and Italy and Germany, and southeastward toward India and Iran.

The momentous role of this twofold Aryan migration in the evolution of modern culture is not fully appreciated by historians, anthropologists or sociologists. These Aryas fashioned the culture of Hellas, Rome and Germany on the one hand and of India and Iran on the other. Two of the world's great religions, Hinduism and Buddhism, were evolved by them in India; and Hellenic, Roman and Germanic culture-traits are interwoven into the very fabric of present-day Euro-American culture.

The second most significant migration in human history is not so much permanent migration on a large scale as culture clash and contact between the Cross and the Crescent—the Crusades.

The third momentous migration took place after the dawn of the Age of Discovery (1492), from Europe to the Americas and to Australasia or Oceania. Associated with this migration for permanent transplantation, there occurred an equally significant event in human history, the military conquest of the world by Europeans and extension of their sway over practically all corners of the earth (1600-1950). This extension of European influence throughout the world laid the foundation for the emergence of modern civilization on a global scale.

Three minor migrations may be mentioned, all into Southeast Asia: Hindu-Buddhist, Chinese, and Muslim. There is no reliable estimate of the number of Hindus in Southeast Asia but their cultural stamp all over the region is unmistakable. In 1948, there were possibly as many as nine million Chinese in Southeast Asia (11, pp. 69–70). While the migration of Muslims from Arabia has been negligible, practically non-existent, the diffusion of the Muslim's religion and of Islamic culture traits in Southeast Asia is a potent factor in the evolving cultural framework of these people. The Japanese have not migrated to any Southeast Asian country in any significant numbers.

The story of the rise of the five River Valley civilizations and their spread throughout the world has been recounted by us in CHAPTER 34.

8. MAN'S EARLY ATTEMPTS TO COUNT HIS NUMBERS

In historic times we meet with several attempts made by man to find out how many of his kind lived in a given region. "In Babylon and China, population censuses go back as far as the third millennium B.C. Censuses have never been popular. They have foreshadowed some unpleasant event. Conscription, confiscation, or higher taxes were in the offing when a king or conqueror counted the men in a province or the sheep or the serfs. The Bible tells of violent opposition to a census in Judea at the time of King David." (11, p. 32). In the New Testament, we are told that Mary and Joseph went to Bethlehem to be counted by the census-takers of the Roman Empire.

The Domesday Book of England, compiled at the Order of William the Conqueror in 1086, was a kind of inventory of the country intended to help the king in levying taxes; it also contained a partial enumeration of the population of England at the time. China began to compile data on population, revenue and other matters as early as 1651; but the interpretation of items recorded has been difficult: for instance, did these records enumerate all males and females, only males, or males between the ages of 16 and 60?

9. JAPAN'S CENSUS RELIABLE SINCE 1721

The population figures for Japan, on the other hand, are fairly satisfactory beginning with 1721, when the population of Japan was

28.1 million. In 1792, it was 26.9 million; in 1828, 29.2 million, and in 1846 it was 28.9. Thus with minor fluctuations, the population of Japan was stationary for a hundred and twenty-five years, 1721-1846 (1, p. 28). According to Carr-Saunders, there had been "a rapid growh of the population of Japan between 1650 and 1720, ... (attributable) to a decline in the death-rate consequent upon the restoration and maintenance of internal order. Between 1720 and 1848 population was stable, and this stability was apparently attained by the extensive practice of abortion and infanticide. There is a gap in our knowledge of Japanese population history between 1848 and 1873. From the latter date onwards we begin to get figures again ... population began to increase before 1870, (and) ... the growth has been continuous." (1, p. 261).

TABLE 17

THE POPULATION OF JAPAN IN CERTAIN YEARS[1]

Year	Population Number
1721	28,100,000
1792	26,900,000
1828	29,200,000
1846	28,900,000
1873	31,100,000
1898	43,800,000
1930	64,500,000
1940	71,540,000[2]
1945	72,410,000[2]
1952	85,500,000[3]

[1] Data gathered from A. M. Carr-Saunders: *World Population*, pp. 28, 261. Oxford: Clarendon Press, 1936.

[2] Warren S. Thompson: *Population Problems*, 4th ed., pp. 351–352. New York: McGraw-Hill Book Co., 1953.

[3] U. N. estimate for 1952 (*The World Almanac*, 1954).

Between 1873 and 1898, the average annual rate of increase was 1.1 per cent, or an eleven (11) per cent decennial increase; this is less than half of the decennial increase for the United States (1870, 26.6 per cent; 1880, 26.0 per cent; 1890, 25.5 per cent). And between 1898 and 1930, the Japanese population grew annually at the rate of 1.2 per cent, or at a decennial increase of 12 per cent; this rate of increase is also lower than that for the United States in the comparable period (1900, 20.7 per cent; 1910, 21.0 per cent; 1920, 14.9 per cent; 1930, 16.1 per cent).

It would appear that the "yellow peril" of the early part of this century was a figment of the imagination of the propagandist, at least so far as Japan was concerned in terms of its population growth.

Japan is a small country, 147,690 square miles, smaller than the state of California (158,693 square miles); not more than one-fifth of the area of Japan can ever be cultivated, and most of it is already under cultivation. Judged by the number of persons per square mile, the density of Japan is quite high (575), compared to the density of the United States (50.7)—the figure for the density of Japan being for 1952, and the figure for the density of the U.S. being for 1950. But when we compare the number of persons per square mile of arable land, Japan leads the world in this specific type of density.

TABLE 18

PERSONS PER SQUARE MILE OF ARABLE LAND IN
CERTAIN SELECTED COUNTRIES: 1950[1]

Country	Persons per Square Mile of Arable Land	
Canada	98	
Australia	149	
United States	293	
Spain	459	
Sweden	489	
New Zealand	634	
France	511	(711?)
Union of India	786	
Italy	936	
Belgium	2,155	
Switzerland	2,406	
Netherlands	2,395	(2,495?)
United Kingdom	2,551	
Japan	3,575	

[1] Warren S. Thompson: *Op. cit.*, p. 353.

Had not Japan become the workshop of Asia in the wake of the Meiji Restoration (1868), it would have been impossible for the population to exert so much pressure on the land and yet survive.

10. Organization of Modern Censuses

The honor for having organized the first reliable census in Europe goes to Sweden—1750. "In 1749 the Swedish clergy, who had long been compiling lists of parishioners, were compelled (by law) to render (to the government) returns from which a total for the population was obtained; this was repeated at five-yearly intervals, and the population of Sweden is still enumerated in this unusual but very efficient manner. Until 1809, when Finland fell under the supremacy of Russia, it was united with Sweden, and the same system of enumerating the population obtained as in that country." (1, p. 6).

The next modern census in Occidental culture was organized by the United States of America in 1790. This census became necessary because of the constitutional provision that while each state would be entitled to two seats in the Senate, the number of seats in the House of Representatives would be allocated to each state in proportion to its population.

The U.S. Census, conducted at the end of each decade since 1790, is a huge undertaking. The Director of the Bureau of the Census is under the jurisdiction of the U.S. Department of Commerce. The U.S. Census volumes, like the census volumes of other nations, are veritable mines of information. Professor E. A. Ross (1866-1951) used to tell his students that whenever he was travelling abroad, he would enlighten and amuse himself by reading the census volumes or the statistical abstracts of the countries he was visiting. The average student is not likely to be thrilled by the type of figures one meets in census volumes; but he would find it profitable to leaf through the pages of Census Reports and Statistical Abstracts and to discover the variety of subjects on which data are available.

The next important census was organized by Great Britain (United Kingdom) in 1801. And England conducted the first census in India in 1872 ; every decennial census since 1881 until 1941 was conducted in India under British guidance and direction. In 1951, the new government of the Republic of India invited a Swedish expert to help with the census for that year. With an area of 1,221,880 square miles, India had a population of 356,829,485 in 1951 and 438,000,000 in 1961.

Carved out of the subcontinent of India and created in 1947 as a separate State, Pakistan conducted its first census in 1951. With an area of 365,907 square miles, Pakistan had a population of 75,687,000 (1951) and 93,812,000 in 1961.

All European nations, excepting those in the Balkans and Russia, have had reliable censuses for several decades. China's population has never been counted according to the scientific procedures worked out by census-takers. We have had to rely on estimates and guesses concerning the number of Chinese on the mainland of China. And at the present time, the situation has become vitiated by the communist Chinese regime's flair for inflating figures. Dr. Hu Shih told the present writer in a personal conversation in 1956 that the then population of China could not be very much above the 400,000,000 mark, but that the communist rulers of China were inflating the figure to 650,000,000 (1955) for political-psychological reasons.

The specialized agencies of the United Nations Organization, especially UNESCO and the Social and Economic Council, have been engaged in gathering uniform and reliable data on the population of the different countries of the world, and on their health conditions, on employment, on the plane of living, etc.

11. WORLD POPULATION BY CONTINENTS

The question may be raised: Which continent of the world is multiplying slowest? Availing themselves of the researches of other scholars, Woytinsky and Woytinsky give the following estimates of population in different parts of the world between 1650 and 1950 (11, p. 34)—TABLE 19, next page.

It is evident from TABLE 20 of percentage distribution of the world's population that North America has gained most, percentage-wise, in the last three hundred years; the second highest gain has been registered by Central and South America, and the third highest gain has been made by Europe. It is also evident that Africa has

TABLE 19

ESTIMATED POPULATION IN EACH CONTINENT, 1650-1950[1]
(MILLIONS)

Continent	1650	1700	1750	1800	1850	1900	1950
World Total	545	623	728	906	1,171	1,608	2,400
North America	1	1	1	6	26	81	166
Middle America	6	6	5	10	13	25	55
South America	6	6	6	9	20	38	111
Europe	100	110	140	187	266	401	559
Asia	330	400	479	602	749	937	1,302
Africa	100	98	95	90	95	120	198
Oceania	2	2	2	2	2	6	13

[1] W. S. Woytinsky and E. S. Woytinsky: *World Population and Production*, p. 34. New York: The Twentieth Century Fund, 1953.

TABLE 20

PERCENTAGE DISTRIBUTION OF THE WORLD'S POPULATION,
1650-1950[1]

Continent	1650	1700	1750	1800	1850	1900	1950
North America	0.2	0.2	0.1	0.7	2.3	5.1	6.9
Central and South America	2.2	2.0	1.5	2.1	2.8	3.9	6.9
Oceania	0.4	0.3	0.3	0.2	0.2	0.4	0.5
Africa	18.3	15.7	13.1	9.9	8.1	7.4	8.2
Asia	60.6	64.2	65.8	66.4	63.9	58.3	54.2
Europe	18.3	17.6	19.2	20.7	22.7	24.9	23.3
World Total	100.00	100.00	100.00	100.00	100.00	100.00	100.00

[1] Data worked from the preceding table.

lost most, percentagewise, during this period, while Asia has registered a significant loss.

12. RACIAL, LINGUISTIC AND RELIGIOUS CENSUS OF THE WORLD

Here is a breakdown of mankind in terms of race distribution: Caucasians in a majority with 57 per cent of the total population; Mongoloid second in rank with 34 per cent, and the Negroid less than 10 per cent. People of the European stock, spread over Europe, the Americas, and elsewhere, constitute but one-third of mankind. (11, p. 49).

Of the main languages spoken in the world, we may mention: Sino-Tibetan (Chinese) spoken by 500 million people in Asia; Korean-Japanese by 100 million; Indo-Aryan (Sanskritic) and Dravidian languages by 460 million, one among which, namely, Urdu or Hindustani, is spoken by almost 200 million people in India and Pakistan. English is spoken by some 240 million people in the British Isles, in the United States, Canada, Australia, New Zealand, the Philippine Islands, and elsewhere. It is today the most important medium of international communication. Russian is spoken by 120 to 150 million in the U.S.S.R., German is spoken by 100 million, French by 75 million, Spanish by 108 million. A knowledge of one or more of these languages is essential for the scholar, the elite and the diplomat. (11, pp. 52–54).

We may now set forth the religions professed by mankind.

TABLE 21

THE NUMBER OF ADHERENTS OF DIFFERENT RELIGIONS
OF MANKIND (1950) [1]

Name of Religion		Number of Followers in millions
All		2,400
Christianity		780
1) Roman Catholic	380	
2) Protestant	300	
3) Eastern Churches	100	
Judaism		12
Islam		322
Buddhism		645
Hinduism		400
Others		241

[1] Woytinsky and Woytinsky: *Op. cit.*, p. 55.

13. NATIONS WITH POPULATION EXCEEDING TEN MILLION

Race, religion, and language tend to cut across geographic and national boundaries, but inasmuch as the world of the twentieth century is dominated by the "nation" culture-complex, we may here give a rank order of the nations of the world with a population exceeding ten million.

TABLE 22

A RANK ORDER OF NATIONS WITH A
POPULATION EXCEEDING TEN MILLION (1950)[1]

Name of the Nation	Number in Millions
1. China	463.5[2]
2. India	358.0
3. USSR	193.0
4. United States	151.7
5. Japan	82.9[3]
6. Pakistan	75.0[4]
7. Indonesia	73.5[4]
8. Germany	69.0
9. Brazil	52.1
10. United Kingdom	50.6
11. Italy	46.3
12. France	41.9
13. Korea	29.5
14. Spain	28.3
15. Indochina	27.6
16. Mexico	25.4
17. Poland	25.0
18. Nigeria	24.0
19. Turkey	20.9
20. Egypt	20.4
21. Philippines	19.6
22. Iran	18.8
23. Burma	18.5
24. Thailand	18.3
25. Argentina	17.2
26. French West Africa	16.9
27. Yugoslavia	16.3
28. Romania	16.1
29. Ethiopia	15.0
30. Canada	13.8
31. Czechoslovakia	12.6
32. Union of South Africa	12.3
33. Afghanistan	12.0
34. Colombia	11.3
35. Belgian Congo	11.3
36. Netherlands	10.1

[1] Woytinsky and Woytinsky: *Op. cit.*, p. 46.

14. Four Universal Traits of Modern Man

These are the people of the world—the great group called man-kind, 2,400 million of them. They have two natural and two cultural traits in common. The natural traits they share in common are: their biological makeup and their being rooted to the earth—they all must eat food, derived from the earth. The two cultural traits they share in common are the nationalist culture-complex and the industrial-urban culture-complex.

Weichel's table, reproduced earlier in this chapter, reveals the significant fact that a given form of economy is capable of sustain-ing a certain number of people. It is pointed out that while the hunting and fishing type of economy could sustain no more than eight inhabitants per square mile, the agricultural economy could easily sustain almost 200 inhabitants per square mile. And when agriculture is reinforced by industry, as many as 400 inhabitants per square mile may be able to live and make a living. And in a highly developed industrial economy, the metropolitan city may be able to sustain as many as 25,000 per square mile. These figures are rough approximations, but the proportions are apt to be correct.

15. Industrialism Increases Output

It needs to be pointed out that industrialism not only produces manufactured goods on an unheard-of scale but it also helps to multiply agricultural production by supplying labor-saving devices,

---

[2] 1948 figures for China. In *The U.N. Statistical Yearbook* 1956, p. 29 (New York: United Nations, 1956), the 1953 figure given for mainland China is: 582,603,417. And in *The U.N. Statistical Yearbook* 1957, the population for mainland China, as of July 1956, is given as: 621,225,000. We must bear in mind that all population figures for mainland China, including the U.N. figures, depend upon educated guesses.—H.T.M.

[3] Japan's population for 1955 was 89,275,529 (*The U.N. Statistical Yearbook* 1956, p. 29).—H.T.M.

[4] During the last few years, Indonesia and Pakistan have been playing a seesaw game in their annual population figures. Sometimes, Indonesia shows a slight gain in population over Pakistan, and vice versa. It must be borne in mind, how-ever, that while Pakistan census figures are scientifically computed and thoroughly reliable, Indonesia's figures are based on estimates.—H.T.M.

mechanical implements, scientifically tested and improved seeds, chemical and natural fertilizers, etc.

This is the seedbed of revolutionary changes throughout the world—industrialism uprooting families from the farms and yet producing more than before; industrialism spawning large manufacturing cities, satellite manufacturing villages and towns; industrialism giving rise to the anonymity and loneliness of the city with its impersonal secondary group relations, a break with the primary group relationships of an agrarian society.

16. INDUSTRIALIZATION AND URBANIZATION

The experience of the United States is typical of what is gradually happening the world over: in 1787, nine (9) farm families were required to produce enough food for themselves and for one extra family in the city, town or village; in 1957, *by contrast, please note*, one farm family produced enough food to feed itself and about twenty (20) urban families.

TABLE 23

URBAN POPULATION IN THE U.S. IN SELECTED YEARS[1]

Year	Total Pop. (in millions)	Urban Pop. (in millions)	Percentage of People Living in Urban Areas
1800	5.3	0.3	6.1
1850	23.2	3.5	15.3
1900	76.0	30.2	39.7
1950[2]	150.7	88.9	59.1

[1] Data gathered from Woytinsky and Woytinsky: *Op. cit.*, p. 124.

[2] Data for 1950 secured from *U.S. Census of Population*: 1950, Vol. I, p. xviii; Washington: U.S. Government Printing Office, 1952.

The industrial revolution has brought into being centers of large population, serving as service centers for the suburbs and the hinterland, as commercial marts, as transportation centers, as manufacturing cities, as workshops for people encompassed within easy transportation radius. The industrial revolution first started in England around 1750, and therefore urbanization was experienced by England earlier than by any other country.

In the economy of the United States, agriculture has always played a significant part; therefore, the predominance of the rural population over the urban population during the greater part of the American nation's existence is understandable. Beginning in 1920, however, the urban population began to show an increase over the rural population: 51.4 (1920), 56.2 (1930), 56.5 (1940), 59.1 (1950), 69.9 (1960).

Most of the industrialized countries of Europe, likewise, have larger urban population than rural. In Australia, with its wide open spaces, and with its sheep-herding and cattle-breeding and wheat-growing industries requiring large tracts of uninhabited land, we find most of the population concentrated in towns and cities.

It took Japan between 50 and 60 years to double her agricultural production (9, p. 324) and about the same time to double her population (1898: 43,800,000; 1952: 85,500,000 pop.). During the same period, the average real income per capita has also doubled (1, p. 265).

Between 1900 and 1950, Japan's rural population increased in numbers only by 10 per cent while her total population doubled. Since the end of World War II, Tokyo has grown so rapidly and so far out that it has joined with the seaport city of Yokohama to the south. These twin cities have a total population of 8,315,000, which would be larger than that of New York City (7,891,000) and almost up to London's 8,346,000. (Associated Press news story, July 7, 1953). More recently Tokyo's population has outstripped that of London.

Japan's population, like that of the United States and like the populations of industrialized European countries, is preponderantly urban; municipalities of 30,000 or more inhabitants contain 50.9 per cent of the total population.

17. The Degree of Urbanization in Certain Nations

Since there is no uniform definition of "urban" agreed upon internationally, it is difficult to compare the degree of urbanization in different countries. Indeed, until the 1920 census, the U.S. Census itself used to take 8,000 or more population as a basis for an urban center; but since the 1920 Census, the basis has been changed to

2,500 or more inhabitants for a center of population to be called urban.

Even so, the self-evaluation of "urban" by each nation has its own psychological and sociological justification. On the basis of self-estimated criteria of urban, here is a rank ordering of certain nations in the contemporary world.

TABLE 24

A RANK ORDERING OF THE DEGREE OF URBANIZATION
IN CERTAIN NATIONS (1945)[1]

Country	Basis of Urbanism	Percentage of Pop. in Urban Areas
1. United Kingdom (1931)	Urban areas	79.2
2. Germany (1939)[2]		70.0
3. Australia (1947)	Urban communities	68.9
4. Argentina (1947)	Towns with 2000 or more	61.4
5. Belgium (1930)	Communities with 5000 or more	60.5
6. New Zealand (1945)	Towns with 1000 or more	60.5
7. United States (1940)	2,500 or more inhabitants	56.5
8. Cuba (1943)	Populated centers of all sizes	54.6
9. Canada (1941)	Incorporated places all sizes	54.3
10. Netherlands (1946)	Municipalities of 20,000 or more inhabitants	54.1
11. France (1946)	Towns with 2,000 or more inhabitants	53.2
12. Japan (1948)	Municipalities with 30,000 or more inhabitants	50.9
13. Italy (1936)	Communities with less than 50 per cent of the active population engaged in agriculture	44.6
14. Sweden (1945)	Urban Areas	42.3
15. Republic of India (1951)[3]	Cities and towns	17.3

[1] Data gathered from Woytinsky and Woytinsky: *Op. cit.,* p. 116.
[2] From Warren S. Thompson: *Op. cit.,* p. 106.
[3] From *India,* 1954, p. 15.

18. SIGNIFICANCE OF THE RURAL-URBAN RATIO

The rural-urban ratio helps us in our understanding of a nation as well as the world as a whole. The rural-agricultural communities are by experience and temperament, as well as by the slow tempo of change, predominantly conservative and traditional in outlook, while the urban communities tend to experiment with the new and are hospitable to change.

Women's fashions for France and for the whole of the Occidental world are set in Paris, Hollywood, New York and London. New experiments in art forms—cubism, futurism, etc.—are undertaken in Paris and radiate out to the French provinces as well as to the cities of other nations. The revolutionary upsurge of France was centered in Paris, and the rest of the French nation caught it by social contagion from Paris. And, of course, the best French is spoken in Paris. And so on and so forth.

The role of the country-city or rural-urban ways of living has been well delineated by Gardner Murphy in regard to India, one of the least highly industrialized among the great nations of the world.

19. Impact of Rural and Urban Ways of Life on India

"The term 'village' is used in the Census of India," rightly observes Murphy, "to describe a settlement of less than 5,000 people and is often loosely used to include also small 'towns,' as we should call them, of several thousand or even up to 20,000 population" (7, p. 59). Here is his description of "the divided village" (7, pp. 59–62):

Using the term as the Census does, there are about 600,000 villages in India. This staggering figure can be kept in mind with the aid of this device: Imagine India as ruled off with vertical lines a mile apart, and with horizontal lines a mile apart. On the average there is one village in each of the little cells, or each of the little square miles, which you will create in this way. Often villages are in only limited communication with one another. Even today it is common to find only a footpath connecting adjacent villages; if economic or other motives warrant it, it is possible to broaden this so that a bullock cart can pass. Dirt roads lead from small village to larger village, and horse-drawn or bullock-drawn vehicles deliver goods to market, and even at times for the world market.

The typical mentality of the mass of people, however, is the rural mentality which we well know from the pre-motorcar era of

American and European life, a mentality still found in those parts of the Western world where communication is poor. Into this relatively isolated village life there has emerged recently the kind of communication which goes with the spread of newspaper-reading habits. Excitement greets the return of a villager who has gone to a neighboring town and picked up some news, or the word of some literate person who has read the newspaper and can pass around among his eager listeners reports and gossip regarding national or world events. The death of Gandhi apparently reached most of the people of India within a few hours, by a network of communication based partly in the first instance upon radio and press, but very largely upon the fact that each person who received the news managed to radiate it out through many channels with incredible rapidity.

This fact is of very great importance with regard to social cohesion and social hostility. The channels of communication are inevitably established to a large degree along the lines of language and along the lines of community (religion) and caste. Since the Muslim press is independent of the Hindu press, it is not surprising that stories related to Hindu-Muslim strife take on two essentially different forms, one of which is circulated through Hindu sources and the other through Muslim sources. Supposedly authentic and factually well-documented news therefore becomes "a matter of course" to all members of one religious group but not to the other. The basic facts and interpretations are unknown to the other group which through its own system of communication provides a different approach.

We see something of this sort in our own country. But after all, Roman Catholics and Jews do see something of what is in a press that is read primarily by Protestants, and even the newspapers and magazines aimed at one religious group are likely to be restrained somewhat by the fact that any sectarian view will be subject to some criticism in a nonsectarian press. People do mingle and move about in exposure to a common language and ideology filtered through the radio. Often one can hear political discussion for a considerable period before knowing the sources through which the speaker has drawn his information. All of this is very hard indeed to duplicate in India.

While we may use the word "village" as noted above, for collections of habitations comprising a few hundred or even some thousands of people, huge importance attaches in India to the few great cities, mostly the courts of the great potentates, which have always been the centers of culture and progress. These cities were developed by the British regime, were emphasized by the British a hundred years ago, and became fundamental nerve centers in the military, economic, and political unification of India. These cities today are of enormous importance in regard to problems of social integration or disintegration. In countless instances the cities have been the focal points within which movements toward either unification or dissension were carried forward. The great riots in Calcutta in 1946 had a typical effect in crystallizing Hindu-Muslim hostility. Large-scale group hostilities are often quickly aroused in cities, as in the race riots (Detroit) and outrages (Miami) of recent history in the United States.

Another very obvious reason for emphasis on Indian cities is the fact that the *new* in almost every type of institutional practice makes its appearance first in the cities. Scientific and engineering enterprises, new ideas in the arts, religion, and philosophy are typically city products. In the city is the money which makes possible the development of productive enterprises such as the mills of recent decades. The village is inevitably conservative, inevitably the bastion of traditional stability, poise, reverence for the past. It follows that the movements of the village population into the cities, in response to industrial opportunities or by economic forces which have driven them off their land, are among the factors making for the most rapid social change and at the same time making for bitterness, hostility, and inter-group tension.

Thus, what has been happening in the ratio of rural-urban population in highly industrialized countries, such as Great Britain, Germany, the United States, Japan, will sooner or later happen in the newly freed nations of the world, at present feverishly engaged in industrializing themselves. We are justified in concluding that with technological and industrial advances, sociological implications of urbanism will manifest themselves in the Orient.

20. "URBANIZED AREA" AND "STANDARD METROPOLITAN AREA"

Two concepts are being developed by the U.S. Census authorities to classify "urban" populations in conformity with the social realities—the "urbanized area" concept, and the "standard metropolitan area" concept. A large city of 50,000 or more inhabitants may be surrounded, within easy radius of transportation and communication, by several outlying satellite communities, incorporated or unincorporated, each with a population under 2,500. Are these people in the urban fringe to be counted, and considered, as rural or urban? The U.S. Census wisely decided to include these urban-fringe population, regardless of the size of their communities, into the urban category, first, because of the economic, social and cultural interdependence of these fringe-area people upon the central city and, second, because of the genuine urban outlook of these people. "As a result of the urban-area concept, 6,203,596 persons were counted as urban who under earlier definitions would have been regarded as rural" (2, p. 204).

The *standard metropolitan area* concept is another useful tool of analysis. "In 1940 metropolitan districts were delimited for every city of 50,000 population or more, some districts having two or more such cities. Metropolitan districts included, 'in addition to the central city or cities, all adjacent and contiguous minor civil divisions or incorporated places having a population density of 150 or more per square mile.' On the basis of this definition, 140 metropolitan districts were identified in 1940." (2, p. 242).

In 1950, *metropolitan districts* were replaced by *standard metropolitan areas*. "The criteria of metropolitan character relate primarily to the character of the county as a place of work or as a home for concentrations of non-agricultural workers and dependents . . . (In New England) towns and cities were the units used in defining standard metropolitan areas."

On this basis of calculation, there were in the United States in 1950 "168 standard metropolitan areas. Their total population was 84,500,680. This was 56.1 per cent of the total population, whereas they covered only 7 per cent of the total area of the United States." (2, p. 244).

Of the 157 urbanized areas in the United States in 1950, the New York-northeastern New Jersey urbanized area had a population of over twelve million (12,296,117). The New York City standard metropolitan area would be perhaps as large as 13 to 14 million. This would compare with the London standard metropolitan area population of 10 to 11 million, and with the Tokyo (-Yokohama) standard metropolitan area population of almost 11 million people.

CHART 18

A COMPARISON OF THE AREA AND POPULATION OF 168 STANDARD METROPOLITAN AREAS AND THE REST OF THE U.S.A. (1950)

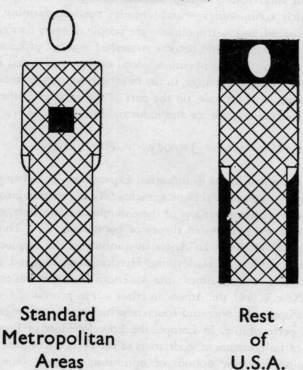

Standard Metropolitan Areas   **Rest of U.S.A.**

■ Land Areas

21. RURAL-URBAN TRENDS

These figures tell an interesting story: (1) that the vast majority of the population of industrialized nations is becoming urbanized; (2) that a large proportion of the urban population is tending to concentrate in standard metropolitan areas; (3) that, so far as the United States is concerned, the difference in outlook between the ruralite and the urbanite is fast disappearing under the impact of direct mail order catalogs of Sears, Roebuck and Co. and of

Montgomery, Ward and Co., as well as under the impact of radio, TV, telephone, rural free delivery (RFD: mail service), metropolitan newspapers, national periodicals, and ever-increasing enrollments of rural youths in high schools, colleges and universities.

In such communities—rural-farming, rural-nonfarming, urban and urbanized, and metropolitan—the people of every nation and of the whole world live and become enmeshed in social processes, such as co-operation and competition, social control and social change. The most significant change, in the twentieth century, is to be found in the hospitable attitude, on the part of the peoples of the world, toward technology, science and industrialism.

22. THE MALTHUSIAN THEORY OF POPULATION

Are there any limits to industrial expansion? To urban concentrations? To agricultural improvements? To population growth?

Before we can answer any of these questions adequately, we must understand the Malthusian theory of population. Rev. Thomas R. Malthus (1766-1834), an Anglican minister in the employ of the East India College at Haileyburg, Hertfordshire, England, lived in intellectually exciting times: the American character was emerging in the New World, the American ethos was in process of formation with its optimistic note and concrete achievements in progress and human perfectibility. In Europe, the Encyclopedists of France, the School of Enlightenment, godfathers of the French Revolution, were developing romantic notions of optimism, progress, human perfectibility, and social justice involving the abolition of want, poverty, misery, war, etc.

The Encyclopedists maintained that social welfare would accompany human perfectibility and dismissed the fear of overpopulation, as did Condorcet, with the thesis that in that far-off day, when abundant food supply would make possible an ever-increasing population, men would know that "the duties they may be under, relative to propagation, will consist not in the question of *existence* to a greater number of beings, but *happiness* . . . and not the puerile idea of encumbering the earth with useless and wretched mortals." (6, p. 273, quoted).

These ideas travelled over to England and won several converts. One of the outstanding advocates of the ideas of the French Encyclopedists was William Godwin (1756-1836). In his book, *Political Justice* (1793), Godwin explained poverty as the result of the exploitation of labor for profit under private property arrangements; political justice he equated with communism under which reason would hold sway, production would be increased, profit curtailed, labor adequately rewarded, and the general prosperity enhanced. The publication of another book, called *The Enquirer*, by Godwin in 1797, prompted Malthus to write a book refuting the Encyclopedists' thesis that we could achieve perfection here on earth both in terms of individual well-being and social well-being.

Malthus set forth his classic argument in his book, *An Essay on the Principle of Population as it affects the future improvement of society, with remarks on the speculations of Mr. Godwin, M. Condorcet and other writers.* The first edition of *The Essay on Population*, as it is usually called, was published in 1798 anonymously, and the much enlarged and revised second edition appeared in 1803 over the author's own name.

Malthus's argument in substance maintained that Godwin, Condorcet and others were barking up the wrong tree, because the more food you supplied and the better conditions you provided above the level of existence, the more would human beings multiply; the greater food supply which was to provide a higher plane of living would now be needed to feed more mouths—thus setting at naught the Encyclopedists' vision of a perfect and happy world.

Indeed, Malthus maintained that the human propensity to multiply always tended to outstrip the food supply. He stated this proposition picturesquely in terms of the two ratios, namely, that whereas population increased at a geometric ratio, the food supply increased only at an arithmetic ratio:

Population: 1, 2, 4, 8, 16, 32
Food Supply: 1, 2, 3, 4, 5, 6

That population could double itself every twenty-five years was being demonstrated by the United States at the time Malthus was writing.

Some critics have attempted to refute Malthus by criticizing the validity of the two ratios in exact proportion. The essence of the Malthusian theory, however, consists not in the ratio but in the hypothesis that *population tends to outstrip the food supply*.

Unchecked, population would tend to press upon the food supply : in the two ratios at stage three, 4 : 3, either some would have less than necessary for subsistence or all would have less than they had in stage two, 2 : 2. In stage four, 8 : 4, some of the population must either not come into being or quickly die off, making it possible for the 4 : 4 or 5 : 4 ratio to be operative.

How is population growth checked ? Two types of checks tend to limit population growth beyond the capacity of space and food to maintain : (1) preventive or prudential checks and (2) positive checks. These checks are "all resolvable into moral restraint, vice and misery," to quote Malthus's own words. The moral restraint or prudential checks (preventive) would involve late marriages and celibacy or continence for Malthus (and Gandhi), and birth control for the Neo-Malthusians. The positive checks to population growth, which are beyond the control of man, such as floods, earthquakes, epidemics, diseases, droughts, etc., are called by Malthus "misery," while man-made positive checks, such as wars, are called by him "vice."

The tendency of the population to "increase beyond the means of subsistence," argued Malthus, "tends to subject the lower classes of society to distress and to prevent any great permanent melioration of their condition." Thus, concluded Malthus, the quest of the Encyclopedists for perfection and happiness for all was a mirage.

We may sum up Malthus's theory of population in his own words, in the following three propositions :

1. Population is necessarily limited by the means of subsistence.
2. Population invariably increases where the means of subsistence increase, unless prevented by some very powerful and obvious checks.
3. These checks, and the checks which repress the superior power of population and keep its effects on a level with the means of subsistence, are all resolvable into moral restraint, vice and misery.

Population on a global scale can grow only by natural increase, though the different countries of the world, among themselves, may register an increment of population by immigration, incorporation and conquest as well. Limits to natural increase of population on a global scale are set by the amount of space and food available. But within each nation, two other factors play a part in increasing or decreasing the population: social organization and the state of the arts and technology. Thus we have four variables: (1) population, (2) food supply, (3) social organization, (4) state of the arts and technology. If society, for instance, were to sanction infanticide or to encourage a large number of sons, these facts would have a definite impact on the population. And, of course, the state of technology would influence production and therefore population growth.

23. INDUSTRIAL-URBAN EXPANSION

Now we are ready to take up a consideration of the questions whether there are any limits (*a*) to industrial expansion, (*b*) to urban concentration, (*c*) to agricultural improvements, (*d*) to population growth.

Theoretically, there are no limits to industrial expansion. With automation and the assembly line, three or four shifts of workers during 24 hours could keep power-driven machinery humming and producing day in and day out, week in and week out, month in and month out, year in and year out. But after a certain limit has been reached, a diminishing return sets in so far as the size of the industrial plant is concerned. Then again, while it may be possible to replace worn-out machinery, some of the raw materials going into manufacture may begin to dwindle, thus discouraging full production. Even so, man can depend upon his machine to multiply manufactured goods in such abundance as to supply everyone with an automobile or a bathtub or a house. But manufactured goods will be produced in proportion to the effective demand, that is to say, in proportion to the purchasing power of potential and actual buyers.

Limits to urban concentrations, to agricultural improvements, and to population growth can be stated in simpler terms.

Urban concentrations are made possible by and in turn make possible: a large number of jobs, a large number of customers, a large number of cultural opportunities and facilities, such as the theater, the opera, etc., and an efficient system of transportation and communication. The Greeks believed that the size of the city should be limited to a certain number of citizens by decree and regulation— 5,000 (Plato), and 10,000 (Hippodamas), while Aristotle would limit the size of the city to the point beyond which a citizen might not be able to know all others by sight. (5, pp. 65–66).

Modern nations do not believe in such regulations for the size of the city. With us, the state of the arts and technology and the logic of the socio-cultural world determine the size of the city. Manhattan, New York, for instance, being an island, could not expand horizontally; so it has expanded vertically, with skyscrapers housing offices, office-workers and apartment-dwellers.

In a metropolis, vibrant and dynamic, the demand for space being greater than the supply, value of real estate and rental prices go up ; in these circumstances, some people find it more economical to reside in the suburbs or to establish their factory or office in outlying regions. Thus arise satellite cities, urbanized areas, and metropolitan districts. As for the transportation system, the bumper-to-bumper travel by automobiles on the boulevards of our great cities and the over-crowded conditions of our transit systems are limiting factors in the size of urban concentration.

Thus we may look forward to well-knit metropolitan areas or districts but not to the rise of many more megapolises like London, New York and Tokyo.

24. Agricultural Improvements and Scarcity of Arable Land

The increase in agricultural yield is one of the wonders of our scientific age. An average dairy cow in the United States produces as much milk as do three to four average cows in India. The yield of corn per acre in the United States was two to three times that of the USSR until 1955-56, when the Russian "farmers" bought hybrid corn seed from the U.S.A. (These figures are tentative, but fairly reliable, even though actual research data are unavailable.) And there is a whole new world of synthetic foods and vitamins opened up by modern research. Collective man need not go hungry for a long time if he has ingenuity and know-how, science and soil.

But soil is limited. The surface of the globe comprises 197 million square miles. At a rough approximation, land, including rivers and inland lakes, constitutes slightly over 29 per cent of the total surface of the earth (or about 57.4 million square miles) and the water area, made up of oceans and the enclosed and fringing seas, is about 71 per cent (or 139.6 million square miles). (11, p. 3).

There is no way for man to increase the size of land surface of the earth, as he may increase the size of his manufacturing establishment. And not all the surface land is cultivable. As already pointed out, in Japan only one-fifth of the area can be cultivated. While some other countries are more fortunate in the ratio of cultivable land to the area of the country, the limited size of arable land throughout the world is visible to all investigators. According to the Food and Agriculture Organization (FAO) of the United Nations, only 9 per cent of the land in the world is cultivated, and some of this land is mediocre or marginal. The U.S. Department of Agriculture estimates are still lower: only 7.5 per cent.

Of the total surface land area in the world, 33,381,000,000 acres, 3,039,000,000 acres are arable, 5,405,000,000 acres are given over to permanent meadows and pastures, and 9,943,000,000 acres to forests and woodlands, while 14,994,000,000 acres cover built-on area, wasteland and some potentially productive land not in use at present (11, pp. 470–71).

Thus, the question whether there are any limits to population growth is tied in with the question of improvements in agricultural yield—with the question of the food supply. Weichel's chart (*supra*) and Ely's table (Chapter 14) throw interesting light on this question. A society which has developed the arts of agriculture supports a larger population than a society living in the hunting, fishing and/or nomadic form of economy. And it may be pointed out that agriculture reinforced by technology, at least in the United States, today produces fifty times as much as it did in 1787, and that with one-tenth the agricultural man-power.

Thus it would appear that population growth is a function of (*a*) food supply, (*b*) the state of the arts and technology, and (*c*) social organization with its totems and taboos. For instance, the Hindus of India need never starve if they but decide to eat meat, especially beef. There are scrawny, unyielding milch-cows by the thousands that, if not supported as a social ritual, could yield hundreds of tons of beef.

25. Two Determinants of Man's Future History

Collective man—2,400,000,000 of his kind (1950)—on this globe must be reconciled to living on 57.4 million square miles of the land surface, or 33 billion acres (excluding the areas occupied by rivers and inland lakes), of which only 3 billion acres are arable. The future story of man will be the story of the kind of optimum relationship he establishes with these resources, bestowed by nature.

There is yet another factor which will determine man's future history, and that is the way he establishes, or fails to establish, a *modus vivendi* between democracy and communist dictatorship. Whether the communist dictatorship will ever change its totalitarian nature and permit voluntary associations to function in its midst is a moot point. On no other terms, however, is coexistence between the two possible, inspiring confidence, trust and mutual goodwill. To coexist or not to coexist, on what terms to coexist or to go to war— these questions and answers to them will determine the shape of the world during the rest of the twentieth century.

26. A Footnote to the Malthusian Theory

The propensity to multiply is universal. No species could survive if it did not reproduce itself; indeed, a species would tend to disappear from the earth if it did not reproduce itself beyond replacement of the preceding generation, the hazards of life being what they are at every level of existence. Man, a rational creature, can safeguard himself and his species against certain hazards to life and limb by developing the superorganic, the cultural environment with its material and non-material traits. But even man cannot regulate drought, excessive rainfall, epidemics, landslides, volcanic eruptions, earthquakes, etc.

Religious orders, such as the Shakers who forbid marriage and reproduction, die out because of lack of replacement unless new bachelor members are recruited from society in every generation. The Roman Catholic orders of monks and nuns and priests have continued to flourish because of their ability to recruit new members into their ranks continuously from generation to generation. But so far as mankind as a whole is concerned, the species *homo sapiens* would perish if it did not reproduce itself biologically.

The injunction, "Go thou and multiply!" seems to be unnecessary because every species tends to multiply itself. This point is well brought out by the late Professor E. B. Reuter (1886-1946; 7a, pp. 111–17):

The Reproductive Tendency

The active force in the increase of population is the biological phenomenon of reproduction. This is the step in the cycle of the individual life which, like germination, growth, development, and decay, is essential to the evolution and continuance of a species.

This urge to reproduce is characteristic of all living matter. It finds expression in a wide variety of ways. In complexity of expression, the method varies from the simple budding and analogous methods of the simpler forms to the highly specialized types of bi-sexual reproduction of the vertebrate animals. In intensity it varies between species and, within the same species, from individual to individual. It may be a purely mechanical and non-conscious matter of cell division or it may take the intensely conscious form of sex instincts and maternal tendencies of certain higher animal forms. But in every group that is to maintain itself the urge is, on an average, of an intensity sufficient to more than counteract the destructive action of the environmental conditions to which the species is adjusted.

The Increase of Microscopic Forms

Uncontrolled and unmodified, the sex urge leads to reproduction at the physiological rate characteristic of the particular form. The rate of reproduction varies greatly from species to species. It may be slow or rapid, but this rate alone does not control the size of the group. The growth and ultimate size of the population are dependent also upon factors outside the biological equipment of the form itself. The inherent tendency of every species is to increase without limit.

The highest rates of reproduction and the greatest possibilities of increase would seem to lie with the simpler forms of life.

Certain minute organisms, of which the bacteria and certain disease bacilli are typical, reproduce themselves at a rate so rapid that no conception can be formed in terms of number. By a simple process of growth and division the numbers increase in a geometric ratio. Assuming an hourly rate, and many forms exceed this, the descendants of a single individual would exceed ten million in number before the end of the first day. It has been estimated of one microscopic organism that, given a culture medium in which growth and reproduction could proceed unhindered, in the period of one calendar month the descendants of a single individual would be sufficiently numerous to form a mass a million times larger than the sun.

Increase in the Plant World

The potential increase in the plant world is a fairly obvious phenomenon. Here, as in the animal kingdom, the rate is much less rapid in the higher than in the lower orders. Yet even the higher flowering plants tend to reproduce their kind at an astonishing rate. The marguerite daisy, common to so many sections of the country, is fairly typical in this respect. The blooming season of this plant covers a period of about sixty days. During this time a single plant produces approximately one hundred twenty-five heads of bloom of five hundred seeds to the head; a total of over sixty thousand seeds produced each season by a single plant.

The Oyster

The oyster is an excellent example of a fairly prolific animal form. An average size female oyster of the Maryland variety lays about sixteen million eggs per season. If one-half of these develop into female oysters there would be eight million female descendants from a single oyster in one year. The second season there would be 64,000,000,000,000 children of the single mother. The great-grandchildren would number 512,000,000,000,000,000. The fifth generation would total 66,000,000,000,000,000,000,000,000,000,000,000. And this goes on the assumption that each female laid but a single brood of eggs. But the oyster lives many years and produces a new brood each season. So the actual number would greatly exceed the figures given. Allowing eight cubic inches as the amount of space occupied by a single oyster, the fifth generation descendants from a single female would make a mass eight times as large as the earth.

Increase of the Higher Animal Forms

In the higher animal forms the reproductive power may seem slight as compared with the bacteria or the oyster, yet it is by no means negligible. The difference lies in the need for a few additional generations. The friendly robin raises one to three broods annually. To be well below the mark, set the yearly offspring of each pair at four young. The second season the parent pair would produce four more and the two pairs produced the first year, mating, would produce eight, making a total of eighteen at the end of the second season. If this increase continued for a period of ten years the descendants of the original pair would exceed one hundred thousand. By the end of twenty years the number would exceed twenty billion.

The same facts hold true of any form. The elephant, one of the slowest breeding of animals, has the physiological capacity to produce a progeny so numerous that in a very few centuries the earth would not furnish them standing room. Any species, allowed an opportunity freely to reproduce and for each individual to complete its normal span of life, would soon completely fill the world with members of its kind.

Limitations on Natural Increase

It is evident that the earth could not support the numbers of even a single species that would result, were the natural increase of the species not held in check. The result of the two factors, that the amount of space and food on the earth is limited and that, unhindered by adverse circumstances, the process of reproduction results in a geometrical ratio of increase, is the endless and stressful struggle for life.

In spite of the enormous reproductive rate and possibilities of increase of plants and animals, there is relatively slight variation in the number of a given species. Under ordinary circumstances the numbers do not increase; the fluctuations from year to year are not great. Obviously the death rate is always high; in most species more die each year than survive. If each pair of mated robins produce four young each season and the number of robins remains constant, the yearly death rate must be twice as great as the total permanent population. Four die for each two that survive. In other forms with a higher reproductive rate there is a correspondingly higher death rate. If the number of these plants remains constant then of the thousands of seeds produced each year by the flowering daisy all but one are destined to perish, even if the mother plant should die, which is by no means always the case. In the prolific oyster, millions must die for each one that survives else the bay would not hold the increase of a single season.

The Elimination of Excess Life

Nature is fertile in expedients for the destruction of excess life. Starvation is the fate of the largest number. There is a constant shifting and balancing in the ratio of living forms and their food supply, but the maximum number is set by the available food. Eggs in a great number are destroyed by enemies and the chances of climate. The oyster throws her eggs into the water to be fertilized by accidental contact with the male cells similarly thrown out; millions fail of fertilization. In all low forms the production of eggs is enormously in excess of the hatch, and the less the protection provided for the eggs or the offspring the greater must be the number produced if the species is to survive. Heat, cold, floods, drought, storms, take a share. Disease kills many. Multitudes perish that other species may have food. Life is a continual struggle, and in spite of the great energy put forth, the usual result is failure and death. Success is the exception, but not the rule.

The Reproductive Capacity of Man

What is true of the other animals is true of man; the reproductive tendency is the same. In spite of the long period of incubation, of childhood and immaturity, and of the relatively short fertile period of the female's life, the human species nevertheless has the physiological capacity to double its numbers in about seventeen-year periods. This is slow as compared to the lower forms, but it is all-sufficient to people the earth with unnumbered millions within an historic epoch. Assuming a doubling in twenty-five-year periods, to be well within the historic as well as the physiological limit, the descendants of a single pair living at the time of Christ would today be sufficiently numerous so that the entire surface of the earth would furnish standing room for about one-eleventh of their number. Assuming that they doubled in numbers in fifty-year periods, the numbers of the descendants of the single pair would today approximate one thousand times the present population of the globe.

Variable Reproductive Rates of Men and Societies

But men have quite variable reproductive tendencies. Within every society there are numerous women who produce offspring in uninterrupted series throughout the fertile period of life. Single families of twelve or even twenty or more were common in America a generation or so ago, and while less usual than formerly, are by no means a great rarity today. Some women still produce children with all the rapidity of unobstructed nature. With other women the reproductive capacity is less or is allowed less opportunity to function. Aside from those women who never have opportunity of sex experience and whose consequent sterility is beyond their control, there are others who produce few or no children. The individual variation in fecundity runs the whole gamut from complete sterility to reproduction at the physiological maximum.

Societies as well as individuals differ in their reproductive tendencies. As between races there appears to be some native difference in this respect. The culturally backward peoples in nearly all cases show a higher birth rate than those more advanced. Among groups of similar race and culture there are marked differences in this respect. There are periods and places where even among advanced peoples the reproductive capacity has apparently been exercised without let or hindrance. In a physical environment that placed a minimum of restriction on growth in numbers and with a public sentiment strongly favoring early marriage and an unrestricted birth rate, the American population in the early decades showed a birth rate approaching the capacity of the species. On the other hand, the birth rate of the French people during the recent decades has been little more than sufficient to maintain a stationary population.

In spite of the variable reproductive tendencies in different individuals and societies, the biological impulse which urges the human as well as other animals to reproduce their kind is itself fairly constant and everywhere sufficient to give a birth rate in excess of social needs. But neither this sex impulse nor the birth rate to which its uncontrolled expression would lead controls the actual increase of population. They set the upper limit to the possible rate of increase. Other factors and conditions control the actual expression allowed the native impulse as well as the average span of life, and so determine the growth in numbers. Neither the actual birth nor the growth of population is in proportion either to the sex impulse or to the natural fecundity of the group.

Theoretically, the same forces which serve to keep the animal population within bounds operate with no less force in the human realm. The human group cannot increase beyond its food and space limitations. But in the human group there are other and additional factors which operate to restrict and control human increase. . . .

27. DEFINITIONS OF DEMOGRAPHIC TERMS

It may be relevant here to define some of the demographic terms used by students of population. Fecundity, for instance, is the potential capacity for reproduction by the female, while fertility stands for the actual number of children borne by the female. The American woman's fecundity has not been lowered since 1790, but her fertility has definitely decreased as a result of social pressures, new values, and contraceptives.

Birth rate is measured by the number of children born in a year per 1,000 population. This is sometimes referred to as the crude birth rate. The refined birth rate is measured in terms of children per 1,000 females in the reproductive age group, usually 14 to 44 or 15 to 45. Death rate is computed as the number of deaths per 1,000 population in a year. Thus we can measure the natural increase of a population by deducting the total number of deaths in the population per year from the total number of births for the year; and the rate of natural increase would be computed by deducting the death rate from the birth rate per thousand. Infant mortality rate is computed on the basis of the number of deaths of infants below one year of age per 1,000 live births in a twelve-month period.

The student of population would find useful tools of analysis in morbidity rates, net reproduction rates, differential fertility rates, and their consequences for society.

REFERENCES

1. A. M. CARR-SAUNDERS: *World Population.* Oxford: Clarendon Press, 1936.
2. LUKE EBERSOLE: *American Society.* New York: McGraw-Hill Book Co., 1955.
3. N. P. GIST and L. A. HALBERT: *Urban Society,* 2nd ed. New York: Thomas Y. Crowell Co., 1941.
4. *India 1954.* Delhi: Publications Division. Government of India, 1954.
5. H. D. F. KITTO: *The Greeks.* Baltimore: Penguin Books, Inc., 1951.
6. J. P. LICHTENBERGER: *Development of Social Theory.* New York: D. Appleton-Century Co., 1936 reprint (originally published in 1923).
7. GARDNER MURPHY: *In the Minds of Men.* New York: Basic Books, Inc., 1953.
7a. E. B. REUTER: *Population Problems,* 1st ed. Philadelphia: J. B. Lippincott Co., 1923.
8. R. L. SUTHERLAND, J. L. WOODWARD and M. A. MAXWELL: *Introductory Sociology,* 5th ed. Philadelphia: J. B. Lippincott Co., 1956.
9. WARREN S. THOMPSON: *Population Problems,* 4th ed., New York: McGraw-Hill Book Co., 1953.
10. *The World Almanac 1954.* New York: N. Y. World-Telegram and the Sun, 1954.
11. W. S. WOYTINSKY and E. S. WOYTINSKY: *World Population and Production.* New York : The Twentieth Century Fund, 1953.

BOOK II

PROCESSES

Social interaction involves compounded stimulus-response relationships and is predicated upon communication. Communication may be either horizontal, from group to group of the same generation status, or vertical, from father to son, from teacher to pupil, from the older generation to the younger. On the stimulus side, communication involves suggestion, inculcation, indoctrination, education, propaganda; on the response side, it involves imitation, reconditioned response or changed behavior. Communication, the significant form of social interaction, defines the limits of society which may be said to exist not only by communication but also, and more significantly, in communication. In sociology, tradition may be viewed as a structuralized form of vertical communication—somewhat analogous to heredity in biology. Finally, consensus, which gives us the most satisfactory dynamic definition of society, is possible only through communication.

CHAPTER 21

PROCESS: AN INTRODUCTORY STATEMENT

1. PROCESS AS STIMULUS-RESPONSE RELATIONSHIP

EVERY manifestation of the vital principle, every form of organic life, that is known to us and that can be objectivley studied, arises within the context of Mother Earth. Earth, in the sense used here, includes land, water and the ocean of atmosphere surrounding our planet.

Organic life, whether plant, reptilian, bird, animal, or human, must successfully respond to the objective conditions of life if it is to survive and prosper. The stimulus-response relationship is at the core of organic living. The stimulus may be internal: hunger, maturation or sex; or it may be external: hardness or softness of the earth's surface, atmospheric pressure and altitude, sunlight and darkness, heat and cold, night and day, rain and snow and sunshine, seasonal change, in short, cosmic forces. An appropriate response must be made to all kinds of stimuli impinging on the organism.

2. THE BUDDHIST VIEW OF PROCESS

Tension, in Buddhist terminology suffering, gives rise to life and maintains it. The Buddha set forth "four noble truths." The *first* "noble truth about suffering," he expounded in the following words: "Birth is painful, disease is painful, death is painful; contact with the unpleasant is painful, and painful is separation from the pleasant." Tension is, indeed, at the core of life.

The cause of the tension or suffering, said Buddha, is the thirst or craving for life, for the gratification of passions, for success in this life, and for a future life. This is the *second* noble truth expounded by Buddha.

The *third* noble truth deals with the minimization or elimination of tension, with the cessation of suffering, which can be achieved by "the quenching of this very thirst, by the laying aside of the thirst."

355

The *fourth* noble truth suggests how the cessation of suffering can be consummated by treading the path of right responses to the universe, the path of right relations with the cosmic process—"the noble eightfold path" (1, pp. 60–61):

1. RIGHT VIEWS: free from superstition or delusion.
2. RIGHT AIMS: high and worthy of an intelligent, earnest man.
3. RIGHT SPEECH: kindly, open, truthful.
4. RIGHT CONDUCT: peaceful, honest, pure.
5. RIGHT LIVELIHOOD: bringing hurt or danger to no living thing.
6. RIGHT EFFORT: in self-training or self-control.
7. RIGHT MINDFULNESS: the active, watchful mind.
8. RIGHT CONTEMPLATION: earnest thought on the deep mysteries of life.

The four noble truths of Buddha remarkably anticipate the methodology of psychoanalysis and psychiatry. The first noble truth, in psychoanalysis, is the recognition of inner conflict. The second is the tracing of the roots of conflict. The third is the creation of confidence in the patient that the conflict can be minimized and eventually completely eliminated. The fourth noble truth or stage is prophylaxis, the prescription of the way conflict can be overcome and harmony established. (See *infra*, CHAPTERS 24 and 25).

3. THE HINDU CONCEPT OF PROCESS

The Hindu concept of process, from which the Buddhist concept **is** derived, is even more comprehensive and philosophical. In the Hindu view, life is conceived as an eternal drama, a divine play, in which Being constantly strives to Become. The becoming of being, the translation of will into action, the transformation of spirit into matter and of matter into spirit, the creation of institutions for functions, the relating of man's self to the Supreme Self—this constant process of what the Hindus call *samsara*, of ceaseless activity, or ongoing movement, constitutes the glory of man's existence. This drama of ceaseless activity is marked by cataclysms as well as by peaceful, rhythmic undulations of quiet processes. The end of the process, cosmic as well as social, according to the Hindus, is the attainment of *Satt-Chit-Ananda*: *Satt*, Supreme Being or Truth; *Chit*, Supreme Mind or Intelligence; *Ananda*, Supreme Bliss, "the peace that passeth human understanding."

Inorganic forms of existence set up mechanical tensions—pulls and pressures. Organic forms of life set up not only mechanical pulls and pressures but also vital tensions in the form of stimulations, responses and adjustments.

4. INTERACTION

The existence of organic life, therefore, involves a continuous resolution of tensions by proper responses. Organic life flourishes by achieving a nice balance between constantly changing, unstable elements. Life involves continuous equilibration of forces posed either in opposition or cooperation.

In order to survive and prosper, man must make successful responses to "earth, air, water, fire, ether," and to altitude, seasons, etc.; in addition, he must make successful responses to fellow man, and to the culture of his group, a veritable storehouse of stimuli.

Social processes arise from man's attempts to respond to nature, to the group, and to culture, especially the latter two.

The stimulus-response relationship is predicated upon the existence of forces, social forces, and interaction.

The social force may be represented by a geographical fact—the frontier in American history, the Niagara Falls in the age of electricity—or by a leader, or potentially by any and all of the thousands of groups making up society, or by any and all of the millions of traits of culture or social heritage.

Interaction among organic beings, human beings whom we are studying, is predicated upon contact, social contact, and involves interstimulation or circular reaction.

Contact between inanimate objects under appropriate conditions, such as high pressure, heat, or porosity, may lead to fusion or blending and the loss of individuality on the part of the entities concerned: two pieces of metal, similar or dissimilar, rain and dirt, etc., illustrate fusion or blending.

Contact between human beings involves no loss of individualities; the fusion it involves is on the psychological plane, in terms of wishes, interests, attitudes. The best way to picture interaction and interstimulation among human beings in contact is to think of the cue ball hitting one or more balls on the billiard table. No ball merges into the other but the cue ball imparts motion to the ball it hits and suffers a retardation of its own momentum.

CHART 19

SOCIAL CONTACT INVOLVES CIRCULAR REACTION

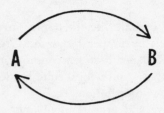

To summarize: All life, including human, is a constant essay at resolving tensions. The stimulus-response relationship is the beginning of the social process among human beings. The social process subsumes social forces and social contacts. The most elementary social process is that of interaction and interstimulation.

5. HISTORY OF THE CONCEPT OF SOCIAL FORCES

The concept of "social forces" is today well recognized among sociologists. The term "social forces" was coined and the concept developed first by social reformers in America—in the era of the "muck-rakers," especially in the last decade of the nineteenth century. Prompted by a highly sensitized conscience, aghast at the abuses of the newly emerging industrial-urban complex, social reformers began to analyze the problems of city life, municipal corruption and need for reform, relations between labor and capital, slums and housing, problems of social economy and local, state and national politics.

In the rural community, with its primary group relationships, the individual had counted for much; in the newly rising or newly expanding city with its secondary group relationships and impersonal, categorical contacts, since the Civil War, the individual tended to be lost. "It was the declining weight of the individual in the life of great cities, as compared with that of impersonal social organizations, the parties, the unions, and the clubs, that first suggested, perhaps, the propriety of the term social forces. In 1897, Washington Gladden published a volume entitled *Social Facts and Forces: the Labor Union, the Corporation, the Railway, the City, the Church.* The term soon gained wide currency and general acceptance." (2, p. 491).

In 1901, at the twenty-eighth annual National Conference of Charities and Correction, held in Washington, D.C., Mary E. Richmond, one of the pioneer social workers, read a paper on "Charitable Cooperation" in which she presented a diagram of (social) forces with which the charity worker (social worker, in modern terminology) might cooperate. (Chart 20, next page).

Then, beginning in October, 1906, E. T. Devine, author of *When Social Work Was Young* (New York: Macmillan, 1939), began to conduct a column called Social Forces in the pages of *Charities and Commons*, which later changed its name to *The Survey*. In the first article (1906), Mr. Devine stated: "In this column the editor intends to have his say from month to month about the persons, books, and events which have significance as social forces. . . . Not all the social forces are obviously forces of good, although they are all under the ultimate control of a power which makes for righteousness."

In 1916 the National Conference of Social Work formed a section, called "The Organization of the Social Forces of the Community"—obviously the parent of the present day term "Community Welfare Organization." This concern with the social forces operating in a community, on the part of social workers, gave rise to a valuable sociological concept, namely, that every community may be viewed as "a definite constellation of social forces." This sociological concept has made possible modern community surveys, such as the monumental Pittsburgh Survey of 1904-14 and subsequent surveys in this country and abroad (3, *passim*, especially CHAPTERS 1–2). The survey is predicated on the theory that every community is "a complex of social forces embodied in (its) institutions and organizations." (2, pp. 491–93).

CHART 20

SOCIAL FORCES WITH WHICH THE SOCIAL
WORKER MAY COOPERATE *

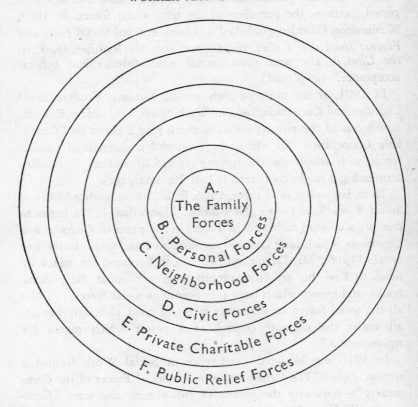

A.
The Family
Forces

B. Personal Forces

C. Neighborhood Forces

D. Civic Forces

E. Private Charitable Forces

F. Public Relief Forces

* Reproduced from Park and Burgess: *Op. cit.,* p. 492.

The concept of social forces has thrown significant light upon social processes—and upon various elements in man's culture and society.

6. PROCESS AND STRUCTURE

The term process is derived, etymologically, from the word "proceed," which means to go on or to go forward. Process is thus a going-on or a going forward. Going-on involves a continuous series of change from one point either in space or time to another indefinitely, that is, until the going-on is halted. We may, therefore, say that process is a continuum of change. In philosophical language, process involves a continuum of transformations from being into becoming.

A process may be viewed as a happening in flux. For methodological purposes, a happening in flux may be viewed as a structuralized event imprisoned in a point or a series of points within the time-space framework. The river is a happening in constant flux, but we can view it as a stabilized event in the time-space dimension. Similarly, society may be viewed either as a complex of groups in reciprocal interaction, or as the process of reciprocal interaction within the complex of groups. In the study of society thus far, we have emphasized the entity (event) aspect of society; in this section we shall study the process aspect of society.

7. SOCIETY AS PROCESS

Society may be viewed from one of three points of view: (1) structurally, (2) functionally, (3) dynamically, i.e., in terms of process.

Structurally, society is the cultural framework, or "the total social heritage of folkways, mores and institutions; of habits, sentiments and ideals; in short, of all the non-material elements of culture." (*Supra*, CHAPTER 3).

Functionally, "society is a complex of groups in reciprocal relationships, interacting upon one another within the cultural context, enabling human organisms to carry on their life-activities and helping each person to fulfill his special wishes and accomplish his special interests in association with his fellows." (*Supra*, CHAPTER 3). From this standpoint, society is an "immense cooperative concern of mutual services." (2, p. 162).

Dynamically, society is the process of stimulus-response relationships culminating in interaction, communication, and consensus.

If we must have but one comprehensive definition of society, we might formulate it in some such terms as the following:

Society is the network of reciprocal relationships and interactions among persons and groups within a cultural context.

Regardless of whether attention be focussed upon (a) persons and groups, or (b) upon institutions and other traits of culture, society becomes a sort of "extension of human organisms" for the fulfillment of life-activities, as suggested by Park and Burgess (2, pp. 161–62), because of the presence of the dynamic factor of process.

The fundamental sociological processes to be studied are social interaction and socialization, association and cooperation, opposition and accommodation, acculturation and assimilation, social control, social change, and social progress. In the following chapters of BOOK II, we shall delineate the operation of the basic social processes.

REFERENCES

1. ALFRED W. MARTIN: *Great Religious Teachers of the East.* New York: Macmillan, 1911.
2. ROBERT E. PARK & ERNEST W. BURGESS: *Introduction to the Science of Sociology,* 2nd ed., Chicago: University of Chicago Press, 1924 (eighth impression, 1933).
3. PAULINE V. YOUNG: *Scientific Social Surveys and Research,* 3rd ed., New York: Prentice-Hall, 1956.

CHAPTER 22

SOCIAL INTERACTION: COMMUNICATION AND CONSENSUS

SOCIAL interaction may be divided into two categories: (1) the personal and (2) the impersonal.

1. THE IMPERSONAL LOGIC OF TECHNOLOGY

Several years ago I invented the phrase, "the impersonal logic of technology." Let us analyze the impersonal interactions involved in that statement. Who invented the wheel and when, we do not know definitively. All kinds of claims have been put forth regarding the inventor of the wheel. Once the wheel was invented, once the facility for motion inherent in its circular form was realized by man, by collective man, the impersonal logic of technology began to work itself out. Two wheels joined together by an axis or axle made for greater stability and greater motion. Pushing the axle or pulling it would be the next step. Attaching a yoke to the axle and pulling it at the front end of the yoke would involve less energy, and greater speed and faster motion. Hitching one or more of the domesticated animals to the yoke would do away with the need for human labor in pulling the vehicle. The idea of the chassis to be mounted on the axle would logically follow; and we have the full-fledged ox-cart or the horse-and-buggy. A carriage drawn by horses would give rise to the idea of a horseless carriage, and we would enter the modern era of automobiles.

Necessity, they say, is the mother of invention; but a necessity is defined by the culture of the time and place. The necessity for a horseless carriage would not be experienced by people unacquainted with the horse-drawn or ox-drawn carriage; even the imagination of a horseless carriage would be impossible to a people unacquainted with the wheel.

This is not to deny the active role of an inventor or of an association of people in adding new increments to the basic invention. We are here concerned with affirming the existence of the internal, impersonal logic of an invention to carry itself forward to what the Greeks called its entelechy or implicit destiny, or to what the Hindus would call its dharma.

2. THE LOGIC OF THE CULTURAL COMPULSIVE

An interesting illustration of cultural compulsive is afforded by a group of head-hunting South Sea islanders. After occupying the island, the British authorities forbade head-hunting.

Not a single [other] native custom, art, law, or organization was modified, yet within a few years the inhabitants of the island passed from an industrious life to one of languor and indifference. The fields remained uncultivated, the huts fell into decay, and even the birth rate declined. At first the British were at a complete loss to explain the sudden and disastrous change. Only when a group of anthropologists were sent to the island to study the situation was the real cause discovered. All activity among the tribes on that island had been organized around head-hunting. The social status of each individual depended upon what he had done to increase the number of enemy heads taken by his group. Grain was grown, huts were built and repaired, boats constructed, implements produced, and children born only for one supreme purpose—to increase the head-hunting ability of the group. With this gone, life had no purpose or meaning. (3, pp. 8–9).

Interactions among the five primary institutions together with their multifarious secondary institutions afford further illustrations of cultural compulsives. In the determination of human behavior, the "cultural compulsive" (1, pp. 1–37) is of greater moment than the impersonal logic of technology. The cherished value or scale of values of a group, when endangered either internally or externally, galvanizes the whole group into action in defense of the cultural categories. Such impersonal interactions lead to conflict and even open hostility—wars between the cross and the crescent, the "cold war" between the democratic ideology and the communist ideology. This field of interaction has not yet been adequately explored because the concept of the interrelationships among the constituent elements of culture has been formulated only recently by sociologists. The anthropologists have much to teach us in this particular area of investigation.

3. Personal Interaction and Social Forces

The mechanisms of social interaction involving the person and the group have been more adequately analyzed by sociologists. In this field as in many others of a theoretical nature Park and Burgess have blazed the trail for us.

The social forces in personal interaction are human beings, one or many, on the one hand, and other human beings arrayed in groups, "the immediate forces" of Professor Chang, and culture laden with "the remote forces," on the other (2, *passim ; see* APPENDIX). It is questionable whether culture with its compulsives is a remote force. Ever since collective man began to live by folkways, mores and institutions, culture has provided man's specific and true environment, the superorganic environment spoken of by Herbert Spencer (1820-1903) and by A. L. Kroeber (1876-   ). Man can no more live apart from culture than can fish live apart from water. Perhaps, Professor Chang's thought may be more happily expressed by the terms "tangible" and "intangible." Be that as it may, man is constantly in interaction with other men and with culture.

Society as process may as well be viewed in terms of interaction. "A person is a member of society so long as he responds to social forces ; when interaction ends, he is isolated and detached ; he ceases to be a person and becomes a 'lost soul.' This is the reason that the limits of society are coterminous with the limits of interaction, that is, of the participation of persons in the life of society" (5, p. 341). And it may be noted that the geographical limits of intra-group interaction are set by the culture-area generally, and, specifically, in modern times by nation-belonging.

4. Social Interaction and Communication

Social interaction takes place through the medium of communication, a sort of intellectualized stimulus-response relationship, or what Park and Burgess call "intermental stimulus and response" (5, p. 342). Communication is of three types : (1) sensory, (2) emotional, (3) intellectual, the last including the conveying of sentiments and ideas. Sensory communication resulting in perception is strictly personal and private. It may, however, and does often, give rise to the emotions which, though rooted in the biophysical organism, are expressed socially. Communication on the intellectual level results in concepts, which are social, or "collective representations," to use Durkheim's phrase. To quote Park and Burgess again: "Interaction through sensory impressions and emotional expression is restricted to the communication of attitudes and feelings. . . . Concepts . . . are the common symbols wrought out in social experience. They are more or less conventionalized, objective, and intelligible symbols that have been defined in terms of a common experience or, as the logicians say, of a (common) universe of discourse. Every group has its own universe of discourse. In short, to use Durkheim's phrase, concepts are 'collective representations'" (5, pp. 342–43). In other words, social interaction in terms of communication gives rise to attitudes, feelings and concepts.

The tools of communication may be material or non-material—non-material: a facial expression, a gesture, a word, a language; material: a book, a library, the postal service, the telephone, the telegraph, the radio, the TV, the movies, the newspapers, and the various methods of transportation, such as the automobile, the bus, the railway, the ocean liner, the airplane.

In our modern society, the role of mass media of communication is very significant. (1) The newspapers, (2) the movies, (3) the radio-TV—these media of mass communication, reinforced by long-distance telephones, cables and wireless service, are tending to make events, happening far or near, matters of instantaneous knowledge throughout a given nation and throughout the world.

On the stimulus side, communication involves suggestion, inculcation, indoctrination, education, propaganda; on the response side, it involves imitation, reconditioned response or changed behavior.

Elliott and Merrill have pointed out the significant role of communication in all forms of social interaction (4, p. 9.):

Communication is basic to all social interaction and fundamental to all social organization. Indeed, as John Dewey has pointed out, "society not only continues to exist *by* transmission, *by* communication, but it may fairly be said to exist *in* transmission, *in* communication." Only in so far as the members of a group or a society are in substantial communication with one another can we look for organized or effective functioning. Communication must consist of more than the mere formal process of transmitting and accepting verbal and non-verbal symbols if the society is to be adequately organized. Communication in final analysis involves common understanding and common definition of the situation—in short, consensus. Complete unanimity of attitudes and values is seldom reached for any length of time in modern society. Most communication is inevitably incomplete and fragmentary. Symbols can never mean exactly the same thing to all men who use them. Words, phrases, and ideas arouse different trains of thought in different persons. Emotions accompanying the same word differ with different persons. Some degree of communication, however, must continue or the society will cease to exist.

Communication may be either horizontal or vertical. Horizontal communication means the passing on of knowledge and ideas from one group to another more or less of the same generation status—i.e., the idea of self-government communicated by the British public to the Hindese public. Vertical communication involves the passing on of information and knowledge, skills and techniques, from one generation to another in the same group—i.e., parents and teachers educating the young. In sociology, tradition may be viewed as a structuralized form of vertical communication—somewhat analogous to heredity in biology.

5. COMMUNICATION AND CONSENSUS

Not only does society exist in communication but it may also be viewed as being synonymous with consensus. To quote Elliott and Merrill once again (4, pp. 21–23):

Social organization is fundamentally a problem of consensus. Without a general social agreement on basic issues, society cannot be said to exist. As Wirth points out, "There is no society without an ethos, i.e., without shared values, objectives, preferences, and the well-founded anticipation of the members that all the others recognize the rules of the society and will abide by them." When men fail to concur in their purposes, all the machine guns and police which a dictator may amass are impotent to maintain the *status quo*. As De Tocqueville indicated a hundred years ago, "A society can exist only when a great number of men consider a great number of things in the same point of view, when they hold the same opinions upon many subjects, and when the same occurrences suggest the same thoughts and impressions to their minds." In short, a minimum of agreement must exist before collective action is possible. When men begin to lose the fund of common understandings and expectations which make up their consensus, social disorganization may be said to exist.

The concept of consensus may best be understood in the simple terms of its literal derivation—namely, as a process of "feeling together" ("sensing together"—H.T.M.) by the majority of the members of a given society upon the important matters of their common life. This substantial unanimity of opinion is a product of a way of life where all persons are enlisted in the search for a common goal, where men are animated by a common purpose. Consensus is a spontaneous product and cannot be enforced by fiat or force. It is the intangible expression of the inner life of a society which is as difficult as it is important to understand if one is to grasp the essential element of social organization. Without some fundamental unanimity in a society, its physical organization is no more than a hollow shell. Park and Burgess have expressed its crucial importance as follows: "Society is a complex of organized habits, sentiments, and social attitudes—in short, consensus."

The essence of consensus lies neither in the slavish insistence upon formal rules of etiquette nor in the performance of a series of ceremonies grouped about the peripheral elements of group life. Consensus is rather an expression of the common definition of situations that are of vital importance to the society as a whole. Such agreement takes the form of a general agreement upon such matters as the nature, role, and importance of religion in society; the duties of the family group toward its members and the obligations of the members toward the group itself; the nature of the property relationships and the relative importance of these relationships as compared to other values in the society. It is further concerned with the type of educational system in operation and whether the emphasis of that system shall be upon an uncritical preservation of the obsolete elements in the cultural heritage or upon a critical examination of these elements. Consensus applies to the government of the society, the groups which this government serves, and its solicitude for the welfare of the mass of the citizens. Finally, consensus involves a basic agreement with reference to the relationship of the individual to the group. Those societies which have spontaneously developed a high degree of solicitude for the welfare of the group as a whole rather than for the protection of the predatory activities of certain powerful individuals may be said to possess consensus in the fullest sense of the term. When this common point of view does not exist, the society is basically in a state of disorganization, even though the beggars are no longer seen on the streets and the trains all run on time.

The phenomenon of consensus should also be considered from a point of view which we have already suggested—namely, the definition of the social situation. When the definitions of important social situations are essentially similar, when common understandings have grown up about the basic social institutions and relationships, consensus may be said to exist. The values of any society are affirmed and created through the definitions which that society places upon certain important and recurrent situations. Every marriage ceremony in the United States is a reaffirmation of the acceptance of the conception of the monogamous family. Every criminal apprehended and sent to prison is the re-definition of social values with regard to crime. Every department store purchase is an unconscious assent to the social norms related to private property.

The consensus of the group must continually strengthen and reaffirm these and other values if the society is to remain in a state of sound organization. For, the great majority of social acts must have a social definition before they can be adjudged good or bad. Juvenile delinquency, for example, must be constantly defined as such by the group before it can be regarded as truly delinquent conduct. The moral and ethical code of a society is thus in essence a set of regulations and implicit taboos built up by generations of persons who have learned to define the same situation in the same way and have transmitted their definitions to their children. All the manifold forms of group morality, whether immanent in the mores, formally incorporated in the legal statutes, or inscribed in letters of gold in holy books, are basically nothing but "the generally accepted definitions of the situation." By affirming these definitions on every appropriate occasion society maintains its basic consensus.

When all the members of a given society are in virtual agreement on the definitions of certain fundamental situations, that society is harmonious and organized. When there is general disagreement concerning the social implications of particular activities or creeds, the seeds of social disorganization have been sown. The social agreement which produces consensus is highly relative, ranging all the way from the complete social cohesion of the isolated primitive group to the stark conflict of interests within a nation in the throes of revolution. Modern societies fall between these extremes. Consensus is relatively strong in the small rural community and relatively weak in the large metropolitan area. Social disorganization increases where there is no general agreement, and individuals define the important interests of society in purely individualistic terms. Consensus breaks down under the impact of a new and pervasive individualism.

6. Consensus and Cultural Categories

The last statement of Elliott and Merrill may be phrased more generally: Consensus tends to break down under the impact of a new invention, material or non-material. With the invention of the atomic bomb a new consensus must be evolved on a world scale in regard to its use as a weapon of war. With the triumphant rise of the Communist ideology in Europe since 1917 a new consensus must be evolved, again on a world scale, if competing ideologies are to co-exist and resort to war is to be ruled out. In a time of competing values, engendered by an invention, the cultural categories are shaken. In such times as try men's souls, rethinking has to be done. A very interesting illustration is the title of the report of concerned Christian investigators regarding the cultural category of missionary enterprises in the Orient—*Rethinking Missions*, published in the late twenties of this century. Again, the Darwinian hypothesis had shaken to their very foundations some of the most cherished cultural categories of Christendom in the latter half of the nineteenth century.

Consensus really has to do with the upholding of the fundamental categories of a culture. Only a basic invention affecting one or more of the cultural categories disturbs consensus. During the last four hundred years mankind has been in process of arriving at a consensus regarding the series of basic changes in social relationships ushered in by the Commercial and Industrial Revolutions. If tomorrow man should discover how to make life, we would have to rethink all our cultural categories and evolve a new consensus.

To summarize: Social interaction involves compounded stimulus-response relationships and is predicated upon communication. Communication may be either horizontal, from group to group of the same generation status, or vertical, from father to son, from teacher to pupil, from the older generation to the younger. On the stimulus side, communication involves suggestion, inculcation, indoctrination, education, propaganda; on the response side, it involves imitation, reconditioned response or changed behavior. Communication, the significant form of social interaction, defines the limits of society which may be said to exist not only by communication but also, and more significantly, in communication. Finally, consensus, which gives us the most satisfactory dynamic definition of society, is possible only through communication.

REFERENCES

1. V. F. CALVERTON: *The Making of Man.* New York: The Modern Library, 1931.
2. CHANG TUNG-SUN: "A Chinese Philosopher's Theory of Knowledge." Peking: *The Yenching Journal of Social Studies,* Vol. I, No. 2, January, 1939.
3. RUSSELL A. DIXON: *Economic Institutions and Cultural Change.* New York: McGraw-Hill, 1941.
4. MABEL A. ELLIOTT & FRANCIS E. MERRILL: *Social Disorganization,* 2nd edition. New York: Harper & Brothers, 1941. (The third edition, 1950, carries the quoted material, respectively, on pages 9–10 and 17–18.)
5. ROBERT E. PARK & ERNEST W. BURGESS: *Introduction to the Science of Sociology,* 2nd edition. Chicago: University of Chicago Press, 1924 (eighth impression, 1933).

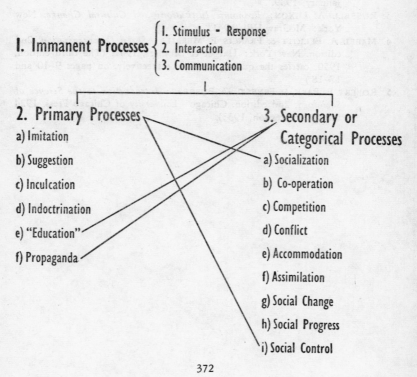

CHAPTER 23

CATEGORIES OF SOCIAL PROCESSES

1. A THREEFOLD CLASSIFICATION OF SOCIAL PROCESSES

WE may classify social processes into at least three groups : (1) immanent processes, (2) primary processes, (3) secondary or categorical processes. The relations of these three categories of social processes may be best seen in the following chart :

CHART 21

CATEGORIES OF SOCIAL PROCESSES

I. Immanent Processes
  1. Stimulus - Response
  2. Interaction
  3. Communication

2. Primary Processes
a) Imitation
b) Suggestion
c) Inculcation
d) Indoctrination
e) "Education"
f) Propaganda

3. Secondary or Categorical Processes
a) Socialization
b) Co-operation
c) Competition
d) Conflict
e) Accommodation
f) Assimilation
g) Social Change
h) Social Progress
i) Social Control

2. THE IMMANENT SOCIAL PROCESSES

The immanent social processes, namely, stimulus-response, interaction and communication, lead to consensus which plays a significant role in holding society together, as pointed out in the preceding chapter.

The stimulus-response relationship is the basic expression of life. In man this expression may be on the biotic, rather symbiotic, level and/or on the psychological, rather psycho-social, level. Hunger as a sensation may be felt on the biotic level, the sight of delicious food may be experienced on the symbiotic and psycho-social levels; but how man should satisfy his hunger is a function of his interaction with the personal and impersonal forces within his culture.

Interaction is definitely a larger process than communication; but in a given situation of communication, it is doubtful whether interaction precedes communication or is preceded by communication or simultaneously accompanies communication. For our purposes, it is unnecessary to attempt a breakdown of the component parts of interaction and communication; suffice it to say that the two are correlated and give rise to the primary social processes on the one hand and to the categorical processes on the other.

We may define interaction as meaningful stimulus-response relationships, while communication may be best defined as stimulus-response relationships entered into for a specific purpose or set of purposes.

3. THE PRIMARY SOCIAL PROCESSES

Imitation and suggestion serve as significant mechanisms of socialization. The French sociologist Gabriel Tarde (1843-1904) and the American sociologist Edward A. Ross (1866-1951) have attempted to account for a large part of the social process in terms of imitation. Faris (3, pp. 73–83) speaks of three types of imitation: (1) immediate, unwitting; (2) gradual, unwitting; (3) conscious, intentional. Folkways, in the first instance, arise from collective imitation of patterns of behavior found to have had survival and enhancement value for the group and hence held in high esteem.

Folkways, mores and institutions, the steel frame of culture, serve as models for the child to imitate. Language is learned in the first instance by way of imitation. Parents' modes of approval and disapproval are imitated by the child. The little girl giving her doll a lecture for misbehavior of the sort for which her mother had given her a lecture is a fine illustration of imitation. Every act of unconscious imitation is a step forward in the process of socialization. Socialization has attained a high degree when the child imitates a model consciously and intentionally.

Suggestion, ranging from inculcation to indoctrination, from hypnotism to persuasion, is a socializing mechanism closely related to imitation. Suggestion is the stimulus side in the situation resulting in the desired or suggested response. The mechanism of suggestion, tied up with an appropriate symbol, a girl in a bathing suit, or a collective representation, *Liberty Bonds*, is utilized by advertisers, newspapers, propagandists, educators, politicians. We are all suggestible, young and old. The youngster is constantly being confronted with a variety of suggestions from his primary group; responding to these suggestions in approved ways, he is building a superstructure of human nature on his original nature.

Though closely related, imitation and suggestion differ in certain specific ways. To quote Park and Burgess (6, p. 346):

The characteristic mark of imitation is the tendency, under the influence of copies socially presented, to build up mechanisms of habits, sentiments, ideals, and patterns of life. The process of suggestion, as differentiated from imitation in social interaction, is to release under the appropriate social stimuli mechanisms already organized, whether instincts, habits, or sentiments. The other differences between imitation and suggestion grow out of this fundamental distinction. In imitation attention is alert, now on the copy and now on the response. In suggestion the attention is either absorbed in, or distracted from, the stimulus. In imitation the individual is self-conscious; the subject in suggestion is unconscious of his behavior. In imitation the activity tends to reproduce the copy; in suggestion the response may be like or unlike the copy.

Inculcation is a process involving efforts to impress upon the mind certain truths or ideas by frequent repetition and/or insistent urging. Parents often inculcate or instill into the child certain modes of behavior, say at the dinner table or in playing with other children.

Indoctrination involves the process of instructing someone in the doctrines, principles, theories, or beliefs of the indoctrinator. The indoctrinator may be an authorized representative of a specific group or of an institution, or a set of cultural compulsives of our society. The value system of society—sportsmanship and dignity of the individual, for instance, in American society—will be passed on to the growing child through example and precept, through suggestion and imitation, and through inculcation. Indoctrination involves an emotional affect in regard to the truth or values learned: to be meaningful, the new truths and values must become emotionally a part of one's experience and way of life.

Dictatorship-ridden totalitarian societies extensively use the mechanism of indoctrination in order to perpetuate the power of the elite at the top. A democratic society rests on the premise that its values are inherently so good that specific efforts at indoctrination are not necessary.

"Education" in the larger sense, that is to say, education as process, as distinguished from education as technology, involves the communication of ideas and facts, conveyed in a manner or tone so as to stimulate and appeal to the rational and intellectual element of man.

4. Propaganda and Its Role

Propaganda, which originally meant propagation of ideas and carried no unfavorable connotation, has come to have a special meaning since World War I. Both the Central Powers and the Allied Powers indulged in disseminating half-truths and in specialized pleading. Propaganda mills were kept humming and busy all through World War II as well by all belligerents. Indeed, totalitarian governments since World War I—the Soviet Government of Russia (the Red Dictatorship), the Fascist Government of Italy (the Black Dictatorship), the Nazi Government of Germany (the Brown Dictatorship)—began to maintain an apparatus of propaganda in peace time as well.

We may define propaganda as the communication of distorted ideas or inadequate facts, or both, conveyed in a manner or tone so as to create in the object of propaganda (the hearer or the reader) an emotional response favorable to the implicit bias of the propagandist.

During World War II, propaganda was fashioned into a powerful weapon of war by all belligerents, in order either to demoralize the "enemy" or to boost the morale of their own people. With the aid of top-notch sociologists, social psychologists and other social scientists, propaganda did indeed emerge as a "fine art." The objectivity of these social scientists engaged in the service of their respective nations is attested by their attempt to classify propaganda into three categories: (1) black propaganda, (2) white propaganda, (3) grey propaganda.

The propagandist appeals to the prejudice of the listener or the reader. The word prejudice, like the word propaganda, originally carried no ill connotation. Literally, prejudice simply means prejudgment. We all have prejudgments or prejudices. For instance, I have a definite prejudice, prejudgment, that every nation is entitled to Swaraj (self-government) or that every human being is an autonomous entity worthy of respect, to be treated as an end and not as a means (to quote Immanuel Kant).

Prejudice, as the term is ordinarily used, however, means prejudgment based on inadequate facts or distorted ideas, involving an emotional attitude. The attitude may be wrong—for instance, that Negroes are inferior to whites in their biological equipment. The prejudice may have no scientific basis, but attitudes and prejudices are as important data of sociology as are wishes and interests.

The term predilection (see supra, CHAPTER 4), used by us in graphically describing the continuum of interpersonal and intergroup relationships, is to be preferred to the term prejudice when unjustified bias is not involved. We all have predilections, which may be defined as predisposing modes of reaction or behavior. Our predilections are the resultant of our previous experiences.

Predilection, prejudice, propaganda, education are all tied in with the enterprise of man's living. Not one of us can escape them. Education can, however, help us to emancipate ourselves from the onslaught of prejudice and propaganda.

5. The Growth of a Press Legend

In times of war, the citizen of every belligerent country is preconditioned, predisposed, and prejudiced against "the enemy." Hence propagandists find it easy to palm off all kinds of half-truths on an unsuspecting population.

After World War I, the National Council for the Prevention of War (Washington, D.C.) published a pamphlet, entitled *The Power of the Press for Peace and War*, which detailed the propaganda device for distorting the facts (1, pp. 749–50, quoted):

1. *The Cologne Zeitung* (Germany):
   "When the fall of Antwerp became known, the church bells were rung (in Germany)."
2. *The Matin* (Paris, France):
   "According to the Cologne *Zeitung*, the clergy of Antwerp were compelled to ring the church bells when the fortress was taken."
3. *The Times* (London, England):
   "According to what *The Matin* has heard from Cologne, the Belgian priests who refused to ring the church bells when Antwerp was taken have been driven away from their places."
4. *The Corriere della Sera* (Milan, Italy):
   "According to what the *Times* has heard from Cologne via Paris, the unfortunate Belgian priests who refused to ring the church bells when Antwerp was taken have been sentenced to hard labor."
5. *The Matin* (Paris, France):
   "According to information to the *Corriere della Sera* from Cologne via London, it is confirmed that the barbaric conquerors of Antwerp punished the unfortunate Belgian priests for their heroic refusal to ring the church bells by hanging them as living clappers to the bells with their heads down."

6. Propaganda Analysis

While totalitarian dictatorship governments began to develop and strengthen their apparatus of propaganda in the wake of World War I, in the democratic society of America there arose a movement which called itself Inquiry or The Inquiry Group—Inquiry into the Christian Way of Life (1923-32). This group, led by such men as Bruno Lasker, A. D. Sheffield and others, began to advocate the technique of cooperative thinking for resolving conflicting ideas and social situations. In 1929, the results of significant researches into children's attitudes toward other races, conducted by The Inquiry, were published in a book entitled *Race Attitudes in Children*, authored by Bruno Lasker (New York: Henry Holt and Company, 1929).

Before long it became apparent that propaganda played a significant part in the stereotypes, or the images we carried in our heads, about individuals, groups, nations, religions, cultures. Hence there arose, quite independently of The Inquiry Group and its work, the Institute for Propaganda Analysis headed by Clyde R. Miller.

The Institute for Propaganda Analysis (1937-41) folded itself up on the eve of America's entrance into World War II. But before it ceased its activities, the Institute made significant contributions to propaganda analysis through its publications. (See especially 5, *passim*.) It pioneered in describing the seven devices successfully used by propagandists:

CHART 22

SEVEN COMMON PROPAGANDA DEVICES[1]
(Illustrations omitted)

---

1. Name Calling
2. Glittering Generalities
3. Transfer
4. Testimonial
5. Plain Folks
6. Card Stacking
7. Band Wagon

---

[1] *The Fine Art of Propaganda*, pp. 23–24. New York: Harcourt, Brace and Company, 1939.

It may be noted that these propaganda devices need not, actually are not, used singly; they are usually employed in combination. The skilled propagandist is apt to utilize two or more of these devices in a single speech or a single paragraph in order to put across his thesis or argument.

7. THE SEVEN PROPAGANDA DEVICES

Name calling involves giving a person, a group, an idea, or an event a bad name, arousing in the listening or reading public an emotional attitude of hostility and rejection. This kind of arguing is what logicians call *argumentum ad hominem*. After calling the Germans Huns, as we did during World War I, or after calling the Russians communists or bolsheviks, as we do today, there is no need for the propagandist to develop elaborate arguments to arouse hostility toward the group concerned. The terms "capitalist," "pluto-democracy," "war-monger," "fascist," and "counter-revolutionary" are enough for Russian propagandists to hurl at America in order to create among Russian masses an emotional attitude of hatred toward America and Americans.

Glittering generality is a handy device for propagandists. With such glib generalities as democracy or the democratic way of life, sanctity of the home and family, equality and justice, the propagandist can concoct his special nostrum and palm it off on an unsuspecting public. The Stockholm Peace Petition, classless society, workers' government—with such glib generalities the communist propagandist indoctrinates communists and fellow travellers and attempts to influence the neutral public.

In the transfer device, the propagandist presents his cause as an integral part of a larger cause by identifying himself and his cause with the collective representation acceptable to the public at large. To safeguard "the people's democracy," communists condemn and persecute all non-conformists as "counter-revolutionaries" or "fascists." They utilize the Red Flag with the hammer and sickle as a collective representation or invoke the names of Marx and Lenin in order to bolster their position.

Testimonial as a device is used extensively for purposes of war as well as peace, for selling cigarettes as well as cereals. The stamp of authority of a celebrity carries great weight with most people.

The plain folks device is used by politicians extensively. Mr. Harry S. Truman ran for the Presidency to succeed himself on the plea that he was just like other folks, with their common virtues and vices. Campaign orators on behalf of Mr. Adlai E. Stevenson, the

Democratic candidate for Presidency in 1952 and again in 1956, tried to capitalize on a hole in his shoe, as a mark of his identification with the plain folks.

Card stacking requires ingenuity and skill. We have shown how skilfully the Allied press of France, Italy and England wove a legend out of whole cloth. People given to a cause sometimes unconsciously—not wilfully—indulge in card stacking. But the most dangerous form of card stacking is to be found in the campaign speeches of politicians in a democracy and in the speeches and writings of ideologists, such as communists.

The band wagon technique relies upon the notion that since everybody is doing it, you may as well do it. Indeed, during the Presidential Conventions of the Republican and Democratic Parties, Betty Furness, appearing on the TV for the Westinghouse Company, actually used to say, "Get on the band wagon!" The band wagon technique, reinforced by the testimonial, may be used effectively to sell consumer goods.

8. PUBLIC OPINION IN A DEMOCRACY, A DICTATORSHIP AND A SLAVOCRACY

A democracy rests upon public opinion. Public opinion is not the sum-total of opinions on a given issue or set of issues *pro* and *con* and the resultant majority either of the *pros* or the *cons*. Public opinion grows out of the interaction of various shades in the positions of *pros* and *cons*, and is usually determined by a combination of the personal predilections of the many and the stated position of the elite or the influential in society.

The so-called public opinion in totalitarian societies is manufactured overnight *pro* or *con*, to suit the convenience or the policy of the elite at the top. The Russian people and the peoples of satellite countries are treated by the Soviet rulers of the Kremlin as a mass to be manipulated at will, not as a public left free to determine its own opinion. Six million communist party members predetermine the opinions and the hates and likes of a mass of almost two hundred million Russians.

On the eve of the War Between the States (1861-65), the slaveholders of the South, in a very modified form, did what the communists are doing every day at present. Out of a total white population of 8,099,760 in the Southern states, in 1860, only 384,000 whites owned all of the slaves, 3,953,580 ; and of these 384,000, only 10,781 owned fifty or more, and, 1,733 owned one hundered and more.

At least 6,000,000 Southern whites were not interested directly in slave ownership. Nevertheless, the fact that the great staple upon which the wealth and prosperity of the South depended was raised largely by slaves under a plantation system gave the institution an importance which the number of slaveholders would not seem to warrant. The slaveholding aristocracy produced able politicians who so molded opinion in the South that when the break came in 1860 the great majority of whites were behind the secession movement. There is no better example in modern history of a handful of the ruling class so shaping public opinion as to bring on a war to preserve an institution which benefited themselves alone. (4, p. 327).

Among other arguments, the threat of economic competition from freed Negroes helped rally the non-slave-holding majority to the side of the slave-holding minority.

9. RELATION BETWEEN PUBLIC OPINION AND DEMOCRACY

Sociologists and social psychologists have been engaged in investigating how public opinion is formed on a given issue, say the presidential candidates in an election year, and poll-takers are refining techniques to inform the citizen of the public pulse.

Public, public opinion, public opinion analysis—these are important aspects of a democratic society; only a democracy permits them to operate and they, in turn, strengthen democracy. Our legislation is enacted by our elected representatives on the basis of " what the public wants." In a democracy, legislation usually lags behind public opinion ; but this is no calamity. The time gap or the lag between the trend of public opinion on a given issue and existing legislation provides our society the opportunity to talk things over, to weigh the advantages and disadvantages, and to arrive at a sound judgment before the demand of the public is crystallized into legislation. (Cf. 2, pp. 19–41).

In totalitarian societies, such as that of the Soviet Union or its satellite countries, as well as in countries whose governments do not rest on a solid middle class, public opinion is technically non-existent. The so-called public opinion in Russia, China, satellite countries, and in non-democratic countries is made to order through the kept press and regimented robots who carry out "public" demonstrations according to the lines prescribed by the governing elite group.

Here is a description of the mechanics of a police state, especially of the way in which public opinion is created in the Soviet Union. That the statement is made in good faith and not distorted for propaganda purposes is indisputable—it was made by a Soviet Russian spokesman in the Moscow *Bolshevik*, Issue No. 4, 1947 (7, p. 111, quoted):

The Soviet State determines the behavior and activity of Soviet citizens in various ways. It educates the Soviet people in a spirit of Communist morality of the system which introduces a series of legal norms regulating the life of the population, imposing interdictions, establishing encouragements, naming of punishment for the violation of these norms. The Soviet State stands guard over these legal norms with all its power. The conduct and activity of the Soviet people is also determined by the force of a public opinion which is created by the activity of numerous public organizations. In creating public opinion, the decisive role is played by the Communist party and the Soviet State, which, through various media, formulates public opinion and educates the workers in a spirit of Socialist awareness.

In countries, which are neither totalitarian nor democratic, the so-called "public opinion" is a cross-section of the opinion of the intelligentsia, including intellectuals and students. Genuine public opinion has unfettered play only in democratic societies.

In the formation of public opinion, both "education" and propaganda play a significant part. As pointed out in CHAPTER 11, the line dividing "education" and propaganda is thin indeed: if we happen to agree with the advocate or proponent of a certain view, we say he is engaged in educating the public; if we disagree with him, we brand him as a propagandist. Regardless of how we view them, proponents of all kinds of views are always directing their "message" at us.

When mass media of communication—the radio, TV, newspapers, movies—and formal agencies of education are used to spread a particular idea or "message," education and propaganda become categorical processes in our society.

REFERENCES

1. JEROME DAVIS: *Contemporary Social Movements.* New York: D. Appleton-Century Co., 1930.
2. A. V. DICEY: *Law and Public Opinion in England,* as adapted in R. E. Park and E. W. Burgess: *Introduction to the Science of Sociology,* 2nd ed., pp. 445–51, Chicago: University of Chicago Press, 1924 (eighth impression, 1933).
3. E. FARIS: *The Nature of Human Nature.* New York: McGraw-Hill Book Co., 1937.
4. H. U. FAULKNER: *American Economic History,* 5th ed. New York: Harper & Brothers, 1943.
5. Institute for Propaganda Analysis: *The Fine Art of Propaganda.* New York: Harcourt, Brace & Co., 1939.
6. ROBERT E. PARK and E. W. BURGESS: *Introduction to the Science of Sociology.* 2nd ed. Chicago: University of Chicago Press, 1924 (eighth impression, 1933).
7. WALTER BEDELL SMITH: *My Three Years in Moscow.* Philadelphia: J. B. Lippincott Co., 1949.

CHAPTER 24

MECHANISMS OF SOCIALIZATION I

THE individual, as pointed out by us in CHAPTER 7, learns through (1) stimulus-response, (2) manipulation, (3) participation, and (4) formal training. Since society is the cultural framework, the great group and the innumerable subgroups become culture-bearers. The group's concern is to see to it that the newborn individual will become a carrier of culture.

1. ASCRIBED AND ACHIEVED STATUS

Immediately upon birth a status is assigned to the individual in the symbiotic family and the larger group. "The mere fact of birth immediately brings the individual within the scope of a whole series of social patterns which relate him to his parents, either real or fancied, his brothers and sisters, and his parents' relatives" (3, p. 122). Besides, there is an age and sex status assigned to the growing child.

What do we exactly mean by status? Status may be defined, after Linton, simply as "a collection of rights and duties" (3, p. 113). Status means the location of the individual within the group—his place in the social network of reciprocal obligations and privileges, duties and rights. The first status received by the child is an ascribed status—ascribed to him biologically. In the course of his experience, the child may achieve a new status or a series of new statuses. Thus it is open to each individual to live not only in the ascribed status but also in the achieved status. Every culture has both types of status and most cultures prize achieved status. Even cultures that prize ascribed status—hereditary hierarchy, for instance—expect appropriate achievements to make good the ascribed status. *Noblesse oblige*!

Culture impels the individual to live up to his ascribed rights and duties and goads him on to achieve new statuses within the limits of cultural categories. In this process the individual develops wishes, interests, and attitudes, which in turn fashion his personality.

2. The Role of Wishes, Interests, and Attitudes in Socialization

"The wish is any purpose or project for a *course of action*, whether it is being merely entertained by the mind or is being actually executed—a distinction which is really of little importance. We shall do well if we consider this to be, as in fact it is, dependent on a *motor attitude* of the physical body, which goes over into overt action and *conduct* when the wish is carried into execution." (6, p. 479, quoted). Thus Edwin B. Holt.

Within the categories of a culture the human being is capable of entertaining or cherishing a variety of wishes, ranging from the desire to have food to the wish to serve humanity, as pointed out by W. I. Thomas. The world of wishes brings into being a correlative world of values. Wishes and values become reciprocal. Values impel the individual to wishes and wishes create values. By definition, "anything capable of being appreciated (wished for) is a 'value.' Food, money, a poem, a political doctrine, a religious creed, a member of the opposite sex, etc., are values." (6, p. 488, quoted).

"The state of mind of the individual toward a value is an 'attitude'" (6, p. 489). In behavioristic terms, attitude may be said to be the neurological organization of the organism, ready and set for action with reference to a given situation. Attitudes are the resultant of previous experiences, physical, emotional, intellectual, etc. Love of money, desire for fame, appreciation of a given poem, reverence for God, hostility toward the outgroup, solidarity with the ingroup, are illustrations of attitudes.

Thomas postulates four wishes: (1) the wish for new experience, (2) the wish for security, (3) the wish for recognition, (4) the wish for response. An individual is characterized by all four wishes, but at a given moment he may be dominated by only one of the four wishes, the other three wishes becoming organized in a subordinate role around the dominant wish.

Anatomically, the wish springs from the motor behavior of the individual organism. On the biotic level, for the feral man, the dominant wish is for self-preservation. On the symbiotic level, for the individual in process of socialization, the dominant wish is for group preservation as well as self-preservation. On the cultural level Thomas's four wishes become meaningful as manifestations of human behavior within the cultural context. Not only that, but culture also defines values, prescribes the bounds within which wishes may be satisfied, and sets forth procedures whereby values and wishes may be attained. While human behavior is rooted in individual anatomy and physiology, the expression of that behavior— including wishes—is culturally conditioned. Hence, in order to understand the process of socialization we must study cultural categories and values. In the attempt to realize his wishes, or the values of culture, the individual gradually acquires familiarity with, if not mastery over, cultural tools and processes—which is to say he is being gradually socialized.

Interests (*see supra,* CHAPTER 13) afford another mechanism for socialization. While wishes, like percepts, may be private, interests, like concepts, are always public. Small's list of six interests—health, wealth, sociability, knowledge, beauty, rightness—is suggestive. Indeed, Small looked upon interests, conceived in the broadest sense, as being at the very core of the life-process: *"The whole life-process, so far as we know it, whether viewed in its individual or social phase, is at last the process of developing, adjusting, and satisfying interests"* (6, p. 456, quoted).

As already noted (CHAPTER 13), the terms interest and group are synonymous. In the realization of an interest, the individual becomes definitely related to a group and achieves a new status— which is the same as to say he is being socialized.

We may define socialization as the process whereby original nature is transformed into human nature and the individual into the person.

Another way to approach the study of socialization is in terms of the culturally defined goals (purposes or values) each member of society should strive for. Hindu philosophers laid down a fourfold goal for every human being: (1) *Dharma,* the performance of one's set of duties; (2) *Artha,* the production of wealth; (3) *Kama,* the satisfaction of the sensuous pleasures or the libido; (4) *Moksha,* the attainment of salvation. *If Artha and Kama are pursued in accordance with Dharma, the end-result will be Moksha*—such is the categorical imperative of Hindu culture. The primary group, serving as a culture-bearer to the new-born infant, acts as a guide in orienting the individual to the goals of life and thus helps in socializing him.

Socialization is acquired through learning which takes place at four levels: (1) stimulus-response relationship, (2) manipulation, (3) social participation, and (4) formal education. At its most elemental level learning arises from the stimulus-response situation. Every response made to the millions of stimuli from within the environment constitutes for the child an occasion for learning. In manipulation the child selects certain items from the environment to respond to. Social participation is a higher level of learning than manipulation because it rests upon a body of experiences already gained and also adds knowledge to the ever-increasing fund of experiences. Formal training or education is the highest form of learning in that it rests upon an ideal setting (environment) in which learning experiences can be concentrated. But throughout, the basic form of learning is the stimulus-response relationship.

Prolonged human infancy provides an excellent setting for the growth of socialization. The family—the group of father, mother, sibs—is there; so is present the newborn infant. The family is the culture-bearer, the child must become the culture-recipient. Through the vast medley of voluntary and involuntary acts, the child has been building up a fund of experiences. In the course of these experiences attitudes are built up. Smile, pleasure, happiness, fondling, love—these form a definite emotional pattern. Crying, displeasure, unhappiness, reproof—these form another emotional pattern. Through trial-and-error experiences, through satisfaction or dissatisfaction with certain emotional patterns, the child subconsciously begins to appreciate the role of praise and blame from the primary group. In the mechanism of praise and blame, of approbation and disapprobation, the primary group has a powerful instrument for socializing even the most unpromising prospect.

3. SEVEN MECHANISMS OF SOCIALIZATION

In addition to (1) the stimulus-response relationship or the elemental learning situation and (2) the praise-blame mechanism, there are at least five other mechanisms available for socialization: (3) imitation, (4) suggestion, (5) sympathy, (6) identification, and (7) social control.

Of these seven mechanisms of socialization, the first four have been already discussed by us. We may, therefore, confine our attention here to the remaining three mechanisms: sympathy, identification, and social control.

Sympathy, the fifth mechanism of socialization, operates in terms of the generation of certain types of feelings in the individual. Sympathy, "the ability to put oneself in another's place and feel as he would feel in the same situation," is, according to Ogburn and Nimkoff, "closely allied with both imitation and suggestion, and in a sense is basic to both," (5, p. 169). Sympathy is directly related to imagination. When the experience of the "other" is imaginatively lived by oneself and an appropriate feeling or emotional response is registered, there comes into operation the mechanism of sympathy. The role of sympathy in socialization and in proper interpersonal relationships has not been fully explored by sociologists. It is the capacity for sympathy that makes a human being truly human. "Sympathy," says an old Hindu saying, "is the root of religion." We are being constantly exhorted to have a sympathetic understanding of the stranger, the underprivileged, the minority group, the delinquent, the pauper, the criminal, the psychopathic. Early in life the child learns to cherish sympathy as a part of its training in socialization.

Identification, the sixth mechanism of socialization, stems directly from sympathy. The child learns the identification pattern early in life. Any uncharitable remark about his father or mother or his brother or sister is immediately considered by the child as an insult to himself; contrariwise, an applause for a member of his family is construed by the child as an occasion for personal gratification. In his early years the child experiences many occasions for identification either through sympathy for persons or empathy for objects. In the play activity, as pointed out earlier (*supra*, CHAPTER 8), occasions for identification are numerous. Each such experience means for the child significant growth of human nature both extensively and intensively. Identification is on the dangerous borderline of dereistic thinking, unrealistic thinking, or the world of phantasy; it is also well within the border of creative thinking, imaginative thinking, or the world of ideas and ideals.

Finally, social control is a most pervasive and potent mechanism of socialization. Social control may be tentatively defined as the influence exerted upon a member of society by social forces. These social forces embrace the presence of groups, tradition, custom, folkways, mores, institutions, ceremonial, myth, religious and political beliefs, dogmas and creeds, collective representations, public opinion, and law. Modifications are made in one's behavior by the very fact of the presence of others—for one thing, one cannot occupy the space occupied by others; second, one must share with others what all want or one must strive with others for the things all want; third, one must abide by certain norms if one expects to enjoy a sense of security.

The impinging of social forces upon the individual results in the transformation of his original nature into human nature and he becomes a fit member of society. He is now ready for social participation the rest of his life.

Let us now sum up the implications of the process of socialization. First, the stimulus-response learning situation may be either active or passive for the learner—usually it is relatively passive for him. He responds to the stimuli and acquires experiences, i.e., learns, in the process. In manipulation the learner is an active agent. Likewise is he active as a learner when he engages in social participation. Formal education, a hot-house method of learning, is good so long as the learner is subjected to the specially created conditions. Over a period of time retention from formal training is meagre, and one may well doubt the wisdom of the money and energy and years devoted to "courses" of study. Manipulation and participation as methods of learning are constantly used by the person in his everyday life, from the presocialized stage through the socialized stage unto death.

Second, it may be noted that the seven mechanisms available for socialization are operative in the life of every person throughout his terrestrial existence.

4. INNER CONFLICTS AND PERSONALITY DISORDERS

Personality formation is a by-product of socialization. In CHAPTER TWO, we suggested three approaches to the understanding of personality: (1) the biological, (2) the psychological, (3) the sociological. Here we may discuss the role of inner conflict in the causation of personality disorders and the relation between culture and personality disorders.

Wishes cherished by a person may be partly harmonious, partly conflicting, his interests likewise may be partly harmonious and partly conflicting, resulting in a conflict of attitudes. Sometimes wishes and interests may be in conflict. Sometimes frustration is experienced from the unattainability of a wish or an interest. These mental and emotional conflicts may interfere with, or partially or wholly set at naught, socialization through which the individual is going or has gone. The malaise engendered by inner conflict is capable of being cured by competent psychoanalysts and psychiatrists. The point to note is that every human being, at least in modern culture, suffers from inner conflicts and frustrations; but the majority of us seem to be able to perform our Dharma most of the time and keep out of the offices of psychoanalysts and psychiatrists as well as out of psychiatric wards in hospitals.

Even so, it is staggering to be reminded by Major General Lewis B. Hershey that during World War II, of the 5,000,000 American citizens rejected for service under the National Selective Service System, 1,000,000 were rejected for mental illness. According to Dr. Thomas Parran, Surgeon-General of the United States Public Health: "(In 1946) eight million persons, more than six per cent of the population, are suffering some form of mental illness"; furthermore, half of all hospital beds in the United States, some 600,000 are occupied by mental patients; finally, 10,000,000 out of the 1946 population of approximately 145,000,000 would require hospitalization for mental illness at some time in their lives. (2, pp. 242–43.) Today the probability of developing a serious mental disorder, regardless of whether the patient be hospitalized or not, is almost one out of ten.

Let us define the terms to be used in this discussion. Insanity, mental disorder, psychosis, psychopathic behavior—all these terms are synonymous: they signify a form of illness stemming from inner conflict, mental and emotional. Furthermore, while insanity means a disorder in the functioning of mental powers, feeble-mindedness means a lack or want in intelligence or mental powers. Similarly, amentia means the lack of mental powers while dementia means a disorder in mental operations. A person suffering from insanity must be viewed as sympathetically as a person suffering from a physical disease, say, infantile paralysis. The insane are not inner enemies of society, like criminals, fifth-columnists, prostitutes. "Persons are (considered) psychopathic when they respond to stimuli in a confused or distorted manner. We compare them with ourselves, that is, with what we expect, and if they deviate widely we class them as abnormal. If the disorders are slight they are called neuroses, or simply nervousness. Those that are more serious, or which incapacitate the individual for life in society, are called psychoses by the physician and insanity by the layman." (5, p. 217.)

Some mental disorders are of an organic or constitutional nature, but most mental disorders are of a functional nature arising from inner conflicts and tensions and having no physical basis. These functional disorders of the mind are created by the conflicting wishes and interests of the individual and by the incompatible values of culture. Rightly does Kingsley Davis observe: "So far as mental disorder is concerned, the significant question is . . . whether the (social) system . . . is unified by a nucleus of common values. When the structure embraces conflicting principles of social organization based on the incompatible values, psychic conflicts inevitably result." (5, p. 224 fn., quoted.)

5. CULTURE AND PERSONALITY MALAISE

Mental disorders and personality malaise arise from two possible sources: (a) inner conflicts within the person, (b) inner conflicts within a culture. Both these types of conflict lead to behavior unrelated to reality. This break with reality constitutes the very stuff of mental and emotional disorders.

The stresses and strains imposed by culture or by certain types of culture upon the original nature of man sometimes seem to be too heavy to bear and lead to mental disorders; under the circumstances, a study of the comparative incidence of insanity in different cultures should give us fruitful clues.

During twelve years of residence in a village of a thousand inhabitants in India I knew of but one person who went berserk. The relative infrequency of insanity in India may be due to two factors: (1) the guarantee of social status, and (2) the cultural imperative of pursuing *Artha* and *Kama* according to *Dharma* to the end that *Moksha* may be attained. The fact that diagnosis of mental sickness is all too inadequate and that there are very few hospitals for the insane in India does not impair the force of this assertion. Most of India lives in villages on the basis of primary group relationship, and a case of insanity cannot be hidden from the primary group.

According to Dr. Frankwood Williams, "the rate of incidence of nervous and mental disease in (Soviet) Russia is falling" (5, p. 235, quoted). At least, that was his judgment as of the year 1934, after several trips to the Soviet Union. Furthermore, Dr. Williams was informed that not a single case of manic-depressive psychosis could be found in any of the hospitals of Moscow for over three months. This is a remarkable phenomenon if true. It may be accounted for by the fact that even though he enjoys no liberty as understood by us, the Soviet citizen does enjoy security. Compared to the feudalistic order of tsarism, the proletariat of the Soviet State does enjoy greater economic security. State paternalism, furthermore, guarantees work, insurance against sickness, provides free medical and other creature-comfort services to all "reliable" Soviet citizens. To what extent the Soviet worker can or does identify himself with the State it is not possible for us of the outgroup to ascertain. Be that as it may, if Dr. Williams' report be true to facts, the conclusion is inescapable, namely, that security—rather, a sense of security—may tend to lessen mental disorders. (*Cf.* 5, pp. 235–36.) And successive five-year plans afford the mechanism for adventure, achievement and high morale.

While primitive cultures have not been studied with a view to ascertaining the incidence of insanity among them, some reports and data are suggestive. Ellsworth Faris found that among the Congo Bantus of the Equatorial Rain Forest insanity was almost non-existent. Not a single member of the staff of four hospitals visited could tell Faris of a single case either of schizophrenia, split personality, or of manic-depressive. The absence of such types of mental illness may be explained by the fact that Bantu society is hierarchical, that there is no sharp competition for status among the Bantus since each person has his rank and place in society assigned to him and he feels secure about it. (5, p. 288.) According to Ogburn and Nimkoff, "it is the general opinion that the graver psychoses were certainly rare among the American Indians. (Ruth) Benedict reports that suicide is not only unknown among the Zuni, but it is incomprehensible to them as well" (5, p. 222).

The study of mental disorders in relation to cultures leads Ogburn and Nimkoff to enunciate a proposition whose implications need to be fully elaborated: "Cultures have their own characteristic (mental) disorders reflecting distinctive cultural influences." (5, p. 223.) I have omitted the "perhaps" at the beginning of the statement, used by the authors as a matter of caution. Each culture embodies cultural categories, compulsives or imperatives, and values. If a participant in the culture fails to make good within the framework of cultural categories, compulsives and values, the result will be mental disorder or derangement. For instance, among modern Americans who prize being in the swim of things, many a senior citizen (over 65 and retired) develops an anxiety neurosis because he is now a back-number, no longer useful, no longer wanted by society.

That cultures have their own characteristic mental disorders may be doublechecked, on the one hand, by a study of the contents and patterns of a culture with a view to discovering possible implicit mental disorders, and, on the other hand, by a study of actual mental disorders in a given society and their possible relation to the contents and patterns of the cultural milieu of that society.

Taking American society, we find that schizophrenia and manic-depressive psychoses are our two chief forms of mental ill-health. Can we relate them to the contents and patterns of our culture? The other approach in our query may be: Are the contents and patterns of our culture, such as they are, related to schizophrenia and manic-depression?

6. JAPANESE CULTURE AND JAPANESE PERSONALITY

Every culture appears to an outsider as a fabric of irreconcilable contradictions. Only to the eye and experience of a sympathetic observer, native or foreign, do the contradictions of culture melt away. For the participant in culture, there are no contradictions, or at most only minor contradictions which can be easily resolved within the framework of basic cultural categories. Let us illustrate this point in the experience of the Japanese people.

Two months after Japan's surrender (August, 1945), Baron Shidehara, the conservative Prime Minister, said: "The Government of the New Japan has a democratic form which respects the will of the people. . . . In our country from olden days the Emperor made his will the will of the people. This is the spirit of Emperor Meiji's Constitution, and the democratic government I am speaking of can be considered truly a manifestation of this spirit." (1, p. 302, quoted).

Is this statement insincere? Do the words mean to the Japanese exactly what they mean to the American? The constitution of 1889, given by the Meiji Emperor to his subjects, taking as it did "every possible precaution to guard against popular interference and the invasion of public opinion," created only a democratic parliamentary structure without the spirit and functions of a democratic government (1, p. 80). In view of this undeniable historical fact, should we brand Baron Shidehara's statement as "inconsistent," as "insincere"?

The answer is not quite so simple as it may appear on the surface. Judged by the ethnocentric norms of American culture, Shidehara's statement is inconsistent, insincere—false! But, then, judged by the ethnocentric norms of Japanese culture, the American belief in the principles of the Declaration of Independence or the Bill of Rights and the American practice of jim-crowism or segregation are inconsistent, insincere—hypocritical!

Shidehara's statement must be evaluated in terms of the cultural categories of Japan, just as the practice of jim-crowism must be evaluated in terms of the cultural categories of America. However inconsistent belief and practice may appear to an outsider, however unrelated or contradictory may seem some elements in the culture of an out-group, every culture is held together by the internal consistence and coherence of its fundamental categories.

Both the sword and the chrysanthemum are a part of the picture (of the Japanese cultural landscape). The Japanese are, to the highest degree, both aggressive and unaggressive, both militaristic and aesthetic, both insolent and polite, rigid and adaptable, submissive and resentful of being pushed around, loyal and treacherous, brave and timid, conservative and hospitable to new ways. They are terribly concerned about what other people will think of their behavior, and they are also overcome by guilt even when other people know nothing of their misstep. Their soldiers are disciplined to the hilt but are also insubordinate. (1, pp. 2–3).

These seemingly contradictory traits of character are welded into a self-consistent configuration and a well-balanced personality by the compulsions and categories of Japanese culture. Hierarchy, "taking one's place," sincerity (i.e., integrity within the hierarchical order), a prescribed ritual for every occasion in life, the "mapping out" of the whole life of man and prescription of appropriate behavior for each life-situation as defined by their culture, belief in the superiority of spirit over matter, rigorous self-discipline as the only aid to the performance of one's allotted tasks, indeed even to the enjoyment of life—these cultural categories have "made Japan a nation of Japanese." (1, *passim*).

The stoicism of the Japanese in war and peace, in joy and sorrow, has impressed all non-Japanese observers. The suicide airplane rides of the *Kamakazis* of World War II are fresh in our minds. The patient forbearance with which the defeated Japanese went about their business to rebuild their country and their national economy is also well known. Unless and until we know him as a member of a primary group, we do not realize that the Japanese citizen can laugh and smile and indulge in humor and banter. To "the generalized other" he presents a stoic front, showing neither joy nor sorrow.

Is this stoicism inborn in the Japanese? Hardly. The personality pattern of the Japanese with the dominant theme of stoicism is fashioned by Japanese culture. During the first two years of his growth, the Japanese child is allowed more freedom than even the American child. But after he passes the age of two, suddenly a whole array of "dos" and "don'ts," of obligations and prohibitions, confront him. If he is to survive and thrive in his culture, the Japanese child must learn to develop a stoic attitude in his personality pattern.

Incidentally, Dr. Benedict's methodological note in the first chapter, "Assignment: Japan," makes a substantial contribution to cultural anthropology. The techniques employed by Benedict may well be employed in the study of American culture or the emerging Soviet-Russian culture. We might, for instance, study American culture in terms of the Statue of Liberty and Jim Crow, or Capitol and Capital. Or, we might study Soviet-Russian society and culture in terms of the slogan of classless society and the fact of rule by the elite, or the workers' government and the workers' serfdom.

7. OUR CULTURE—A HOUSE DIVIDED

Whether a culture is unified by a nucleus of common values and whether its compulsives and values are mutually compatible or not must be judged in terms of the experience of those who are participants in that culture. That there are conflicts and contradictions in our American culture is attested alike by the scholar and the layman in our midst. "The heterogeneous nature of our culture is reflected not only in the great variety of attitudes that are held by different persons, but also in the contradictory and conflicting attitudes of the same individual. Cultural contradictions in society become mental conflicts in the individuals and the source of mental disorders." (5, p. 225).

Even within one's own family there may be incompatible values and loyalties, as pointed out by Margaret Mead (4, pp. 202–03):

. . . the girl's father may be a Presbyterian, an imperialist, a vegetarian, a teetotaler, a believer in the open shop and a high tariff, who believes that woman's place is in the home, that young girls should . . . not smoke, nor go riding with young men in the evening. But her mother's father may be a Low Episcopalian, a believer in high living, a strong advocate of States' Rights and the Monroe Doctrine, who reads Rabelais, likes to go to musical shows and horse races. Her aunt is an agnostic, an ardent advocate of woman's rights, an internationalist who rests all her hopes on Esperanto, is devoted to Bernard Shaw, and spends her spare time in campaigns of anti-vivisection. Her elder brother, whom she admires exceedingly, has just spent two years at Oxford. He is an Anglo-Catholic, an enthusiast concerning all things mediaeval, writes mystical poetry, reads Chesterton, and means to devote his life to seeking for the lost secret of mediaeval stained glass. Her mother's younger brother is an engineer, a strict materialist, who never recovered from reading Haeckel in his youth; he scorns art, believes that science will save the world, scoffs at everything that was said and thought before the nineteenth century, and ruins his health by experiments in the scientific elimination of sleep. Her mother is of a quietistic frame of mind, very much interested in Indian philosophy, a pacifist, a strict non-participator in life, who in spite of her daughter's devotion to her, will not make any move to enlist her enthusiasms. And this may be within the girl's own household. Add to it the groups represented, defended, advocated by her friends, her teachers, and the books she reads by accident, and the list of possible enthusiasms, of suggested allegiances, incompatible with one another, becomes appalling.

Our culture may be said to be a house divided against itself. In the church we exalt altruism, in the market-place we glorify selfishness. We hold forth the ideal of cooperation and actually practice cut-throat competition. We swear by the Declaration of Independence and the Constitution of the U.S.A. and yet practice segregation and jimcrow. We prize the Sermon on the Mount as our most precious religious heritage, and we flout it in practice at every turn. Our science of economics advocates the desirability of a multiplicity of wants; our world of reality is a vast sepulchre of frustrated wants, an abode of limited opportunities.

In addition to some of the inner contradictions just noted, the dominant trends in our culture are: unbridled competition, concentration of power, specialization, urbanization, industrialization, secularization, sophistication, impersonal—indeed, depersonalized, institutionalized—relationships, crowding, fragmentation of personality, glorification of empiricism and pragmatism, insecurity, repudiation of the changeless criteria supplied by High Religion. The list is merely suggestive, not meant to be exhaustive.

How these patterns and configurations of our culture relate themselves to schizophrenia and manic-depressive psychoses is a task for the specialist to investigate. Possible co-relationships may be found.

In conclusion, it may be pointed out that every culture is a house divided against itself, that every cultural framework creates its own satisfactions and frustrations for its participants, bearers (individuals) as well as carriers (groups). The inner contradictions in (every) culture arise from the myriads of possible wishes of individuals—biological, psychological, sociological—and scores of alternative ways of satisfying some or all of the wishes. Hence personality disorder is bound to occur in every culture, in large or small measure. The incidence of personality disorder may be minimized when a given culture is unified and bound together by a nucleus of dominant, mutually compatible, common values.

REFERENCES

1. RUTH BENEDICT: *The Chrysanthemum and the Sword,* Boston: Houghton Mifflin Co., 1946.
2. ARTHUR E. FINK & Associates: *The Field of Social Work,* 3rd ed. New York: Henry Holt & Co., 1955.
3. RALPH LINTON: *The Study of Man,* New York: D. Appleton-Century Co., 1936.
4. MARGARET MEAD: *Coming of Age in Samoa,* appearing in the Trilogy under the title *From the South Seas.* New York: William Morrow & Co., 1939.
5. WILLIAM F. OGBURN & MEYER F. NIMKOFF: *Sociology,* 1st ed. Boston: Houghton Mifflin Co., 1940.
6. R. E. PARK & E. W. BURGESS: *Introduction to the Science of Sociology,* 2nd ed. Chicago: University of Chicago Press, 1924 (eighth impression, 1933).

NOTE: The most significant, and perhaps revolutionary five-year study of the chemical basis of mental disease has been undertaken (1957-1962) by Dr. Linus Pauling, leading physicist of the California Institute of Technology. Should Dr. Pauling's hypothesis be verified, our theories of mental illness and our concepts of socialization will need to be revised. For an introduction to this new theory which would substitute somatopsychic for psychosomatic medicine, see the article " Molecules and Mental Illness " by Gene Marine (*The Nation,* New York, Vol. 184, No. 16, April 20, 1957, pp. 336-38).

CHAPTER 25

MECHANISMS OF SOCIALIZATION II

HAVING described the mechanisms of socialization and personality formation, and the relation between personality and culture, we may now direct our attention to the raw materials from which personality may emerge—namely, the nature of the original nature of man, or the nature of the biophysical and psychosocial traits of the human organism.

Our point of departure is, of course, the classic statement of the late Professor Park: "Man is not born human but to be made human" (11, pp. 79–84). Furthermore, we shall constantly keep in mind our definition of the original nature of man as consisting of: (1) unlearned tendencies and capacity to react to the environment, as manifested in reflex, instinctive and emotive actions; (2) the capacity to organize and systematize the experiences of reactions or responses; (3) the capacity to represent and articulate experiences symbolically (*supra*, especially CHAPTERS 2 and 4).

Discussions of the nature of original nature have become sterile, (1) because of failure to take note of the third ingredient of common-human nature in the above definition, and (2) because of failure to take note of the fact that the individual as an organism has his being in a socio-cultural setting and that his movements and actions are performed in relation to a group or groups within the context of a community.

1. LINTON: THE STRUCTURAL ANATOMY OF HUMAN BEHAVIOR

The late Professor Ralph Linton (1893-1953), the eminent American anthropologist, went farthest in an attempt to account for human behavior strictly in terms of the physiological structure of the human organism. His analysis of the structural anatomy of human behavior is very enlightening (7, pp. 60–68). Here we may reproduce a portion of his discussion (7, pp. 60–64):

Human behavior is vastly different from the behavior of the other mammals, even that of our cousins, the apes. Nevertheless, just as the physical differences between men and apes diminish in importance and cease to be a bar to relationship when they are studied against the background of mammalian variation, the differences in behavior diminish in importance when they are seen in their proper perspective. There is a gap to be sure, and this gap will never be bridged by fossil evidence of the sort which is gradually bringing the structure of men and apes into a continuous evolutionary series. Behavior does not fossilize, and the actual links disappeared when the half-men of the late Pliocene and early Pleistocene became extinct. However, human and animal behavior can be shown to have so much in common that the gap ceases to be of great importance.

The outstanding quality of living as opposed to dead matter is that living matter responds to stimuli in ways which increase its chances of survival. The living being apprehends its environment and acts to adapt itself to it. This irritability of protoplasm, its capacity to receive and transmit stimuli and to react to them purposefully, is the foundation of behavior. It is equally characteristic of the amoeba, that speck of jelly which lies at the root of the animal family tree, and of man, who has perched himself on its highest branch.

In unicellular organisms such as the amoeba, all parts of the individual are sensitive to all sorts of stimuli and the whole individual responds to them. In slightly more complex organisms, where a number of cells have banded together for their mutual advantage, there is a specialization in function. The surface cells receive and transmit stimuli while the interior cells respond to bring about the changes necessary for the survival of the organism. In still more complex organisms, including our own, there is a further specialization in function. All such organisms begin as mere aggregations of cells which become differentiated into a surface layer, highly sensitive to stimuli, and a less sensitive interior. As the individual develops, part of this surface layer remains on the outside and develops into the skin and the various sense organs. Another part is folded in and buried among the less sensitive cells. This becomes the nervous system. The buried part of the original sensitive surface layer specializes in the transmission of stimuli just as the exposed part specializes in their reception.

In animals organized on the radial principle, such as jellyfish and allied forms, the nerves form a continuous net. In those organized along axial lines, which includes all long, bilaterally symmetrical beings from worms to men, there is an axial nervous system. This means that there is a main trunk of nerves running down the center line of the animal with branches leading off from it to the various organs. From our point of view, these organs may be divided into two classes, the receptors, such as eyes, nose, and ears, which are in touch with the outside world and receive stimuli from it, and the effectors, such as the muscles, which act to bring about changes adapting the individual to his immediate surroundings. The function of the nerves is to carry stimuli from the receptors to the effectors much as a telephone line carries messages from one person to another.

The link-up of receptor, conductor, and effector, is known as the *reflex arc* and is the mechanical basis of behavior in all organisms advanced enough to have nervous systems. In those which have axial nervous systems, the structure of the conductor part of this circuit is highly complicated. The nerves which link receptor and effector are composed of a series of specialized cells, *neurons,* whose ends approach but do not actually join each other. The gaps between the neurons are called *synapses* and play a vital part in all the more complicated forms of behavior. Neurons are so organized that they will carry impulses in only one direction. The impulse started by a stimulus impinging on one of the receptors passes along the connecting neuron at the rate of about 400 feet a second until it comes to a synapse, which it jumps, passing on into another neuron, and so on until it reaches the effector. At the synapses there is a resistance of some sort which affects the impulse. It may be slowed down or even blocked at the point. It may also be deflected to any one of several neurons, if their ends lie close enough, or split so that it continues to travel down several of them simultaneously to different effectors. However, the resistance to impulses offered by the synapses diminishes with use. The oftener a synapse has been jumped, the easier it is for the next impulse to jump it. This wearing of paths through the synapses is the neurological basis of learning and habit formation.

In the more complex organisms, such as our own, there is a constant reception of varied and often conflicting stimuli. The impulses arising from these stimuli have to be sorted out and directed to ensure the sort of reaction which will be most profitable to the whole body. The conductors of the various reflex arcs are therefore routed through various *reflex centers*, which serve somewhat the functions of a telephone central. In these centers the ends of many neurons are brought close together so that the incoming impulses can be sorted out, switched from one line to another or distributed. Just how the reflex centers distinguish between impulses, inhibit some, and direct others is still a profound secret, but they do this in frogs and philosophers alike. The mechanics of the reflex arcs and reflex centers are the same in all animals having axial nervous systems.

The main trunk of an axial nervous system (in vertebrates, the spinal cord) is itself a reflex center. All impulses are routed through it on their way from receptor to effector. However, within this trunk there are specialized areas which have superior powers of discrimination. These might be compared to district, as opposed to local, telephone centrals. In axially organized animals one of these superior reflex centers is always located at the forward end of the main nerve trunk, in the head, where it is in close touch with the specialized sense organs also located there. In vertebrates this forward reflex center, the brain, dominates the other reflex centers. To continue the telephone simile, the brain is a sort of super-central which leaves routine business to the district centrals in the spinal cord and elsewhere but which has forwarded to it all calls which are of uncertain significance or which seem to require special action.

The dominance of the brain over the other reflex centers was much less marked in the early vertebrates than in the later ones. In some of the dinosaurs, for example, the brain was actually smaller than the reflex center at the rear end of the body. One of the most important features of vertebrate evolution has been the increase in brain size relative both to the size of the body and to the size of the other reflex centers. Coupled with this there has been a steady increase in complexity of brain structure and in specialization of function within the brain.

In the lower vertebrates the brain functions mainly in the direct reception of stimuli from the sense organs and in making automatic adjustments to these stimuli. At the amphibian level a new division of the brain appears, the *cerebrum*. This specializes in more complex and selective reactions. As we come up the evolutionary scale, the cerebrum increases in size in relation to the other parts of the brain and more and more takes over the function of directing the individual. In primates and especially in man it quite overshadows the rest of the brain and takes care of the organism's activities, with the exception of a few simple necessary ones such as breathing, swallowing, and changing the size of the pupil of the eye.

The cerebrum is made up of an enormous number of neurons set in a bed of connective tissue. There are at least 10,000,000,000 of these in the brain of a normal human being. Each neuron is separated from its neighbors by synapses. The paths of impulses through this maze of neurons and synapses are not organized at birth but are established by the process of path-wearing already described. Every time an impulse passes through the cerebrum on its way from receptor to effector, a large number of neurons and synapses are involved and there is a change of some sort in the cerebral structure. These changes are the structural basis of memory and habit in the individual. The cerebrum is a specialized organ for learning and also for those higher forms of selection and integration of stimuli which we call thought.

The nervous system is the foundation of behavior, and, as far as we can determine by any means now at our disposal, there is nothing distinctive in the human nervous system. In this just as in every other part of their physical structure men fit squarely into the general mammalian patterns. Even the human brain is almost identical with the anthropoid brain. We must grant that the structural and mechanical elements underlying behavior are the same in men and in animals. Let us see whether the uses to which this equipment is put differ in the two cases.

All behavior consists of *reflexes*, combinations of stimulus and reaction made possible by the structural and mechanical features just described. Reflexes are of two types, *unconditioned* and *conditioned*. In *unconditioned reflexes* the path of the impulse from receptor to effector is already established when the individual is hatched or born. The link-up of the elements within the reflex arc is hereditary, like any other part of the individual's physical structure. In *conditioned reflexes* the path of the impulse from receptor to effector is not determined at birth. The link-up of the elements within the reflex arc comes as a result of selection and routing of impulses within the reflex centers coupled with the gradual wearing of paths through the synapses. The unconditioned reflex is the foundation of automatic or instinctive behavior, the conditioned reflex the foundation of learned behavior. All animals with nervous systems have reflexes of both types, but the relation which the reflexes of each type bear to the total behavior of the individual varies tremendously with the kind of animal. For example, insects owe most of their behavior to unconditioned reflexes, while men owe most of theirs to conditioned reflexes.

2. A Sociological Critique of Linton

This learned discussion of the roots of human behavior is on the biophysical or biotic level. Man, however, has always been symbiotic and has had his being on the psychological as well as the biotic level. We may allow, as Linton argues, that the chimpanzee is gifted with "imagination" and "reason"—imagination in the sense of "the ability to picture in the mind situations which are not present," and reason in the sense of "the ability to solve problems without going through a physical process of trial and error" (7, p. 66). But we are justified in doubting Linton's assertion that "the differences in animal and human mentality are purely quantitative" (7, p. 68).

A given chimpanzee may become proficient at the "chimpomat"; another chimpanzee may learn the tricks of the trade by observing and imitating the first one. Even so, it is impossible for the expert chimpanzee to pass on or to communicate to an absent chimpanzee his experience and wisdom. Human beings can and do so communicate by the aid of what we have called the third ingredient of the original nature of man.

It is permissible, even enlightening, to analyze the anatomy of the stomach, the structure of the teeth and the gastric juices and saliva that exude from the eating process; but such an analysis is incompetent to tell us what man shall eat or how he shall eat. What man shall eat is determined by his location, geographical and cultural, and how he shall eat—whether with knife and fork or chop sticks or with fingers—is determined by his culture and by his group.

Sociologists insist that original nature cannot be understood in a vacuum; it must always be thought of as some sort of *being* in process of *becoming* within the cultural context—a potential in process of becoming an actuality in its appropriate environment. Remove the medium—culture—and original nature, a potential, will never become human nature. Feral men bear eloquent testimony to the validity of this assertion.

The capacity to vocalize is part of the original nature of man, but what we shall vocalize and verbalize and how we shall vocalize are determined by our culture and by our group. "Gua," the chimpanzee youngster, could neither vocalize nor verbalize in the Kelloggs' experiment, but their own son, Donald, learned both to vocalize and to verbalize in a manner appropriate to American culture. Donald's neuromuscular system and larynx were adjusted to the potentiality of vocalization; "Gua's" were not. If Donald, like Anna, had been unrelated to groups and culture, his potential capacity to vocalize and verbalize might not have been realized (*Cf. supra*, CHAPTER 6).

In passing, we may pay our respects to the hoary controversy about heredity versus environment, nature versus nurture. The sociologist refuses to recognize this artificial dichotomy. He looks at the total situation—heredity plus environment, which embraces physiographic factors, culture, and group. Geneticists and psychologists to the contrary notwithstanding, the relative contributions of heredity and environment cannot be measured. The classic studies of the Jukes, the Kallikaks and the Edwardses will be dealt with in the next chapter. Suffice it here to say that if a child is born without legs, he will not be able to walk on feet regardless of the insistence of his culture that he walk on organic feet. If he were born without arms, his culture would not be able to sprout organic arms on his body. In the same way, if a child were born with a deficiency in his original endowments, in his common-human nature, the compulsions of his culture could not remedy the defect.

We may grant that there are at birth individual differences in all the three ingredients of original nature—in regard to the quickness or slowness of response, in regard to the capacity for organizing and systematizing the experiences of responses, in regard to the capacity for representing and articulating experiences symbolically. Even so, for the majority of people these individual differences are ironed out by culture; only those at the very bottom—the idiots, the imbeciles and the feebleminded—and those at the very top, the geniuses, may remain somewhat unaffected by the cultural mold.

3. The Role of the Nervous System in Human Behavior

In CHAPTER 13 we discussed the four elements of the original nature of man: (1) the biological, (2) the physical, (3) the psychological, (4) the social, and their relation to the emergence of primary institutions. Let us analyze these constituent elements of human nature, biophysical and psychosocial, to discover what light they have to throw on the process of socialization.

Biologically, the human being is a carrier of the germ-plasm. The germ-plasm is primordial, tied up with the very beginning of life itself. It has persisted through the ages and was present when the species *homo sapiens* had not yet emerged. The germ-plasm may be viewed as consisting of two sets of genes or unit-traits. The two sets of genes, interacting one with the other, give rise to our bodily structure—the body build, the type of hair, the color of eyes, the pigmentation of skin, sex, etc. and, in doing so, make possible the perpetuation of the species as well. The popular phrase, "chip off the old block," contains more truth than poetry.

The body build includes our nervous system and our glandular system. These two systems, one dominantly physical the other dominantly chemical, are correlated to the response mechanism of the human organism. To quote Ogburn and Nimkoff (10, pp. 196–49):

The nervous system is a mechanism capable of receiving and responding to stimuli. It receives impulses or sensations of light, color, sounds, heat, cold, and pain by way of the eyes, ears, and skin. Various internal impulses are also received, particularly from the stomach and from the sex and excretory organs. Hunger may be aroused either by the sight of food or by chemical and motor activities within the stomach. The internal rhythms within man arouse the sex drive even as do external stimuli. It is important to think of man as responding to stimuli from within as well as from the outside environment. The nerves transmit these impulses along fibers to a center in the spine or brain, where the impulses are "switched" to nerves of control emanating to the musculature and glands. Thus responses are achieved such as, for instance, the withdrawal of the hand from pain, the batting of the eye, the placing of food in the mouth, the quickening of the heart beat, or a chemical reaction of the liver.

The glands of internal secretion also have the capacity for stimulating behavior. These glands, the thyroid, pituitary, thymus, adrenal, parathyroid, gonad and pineal, pour chemical substances peculiar to each, called hormones, directly into the blood stream, producing reactions similar to those produced by other stimuli through the nervous system. Thyroxin, the hormone from the thyroid gland, centered near the larynx in the neck, increases the rate of breathing. Adrenalin, the hormone of the adrenals, located near the kidneys, increases the blood sugar from the liver and increases the rapidity of clotting of the blood. One of the hormones of the pituitary gland, located near the center of the head at the base of the brain, stimulates sexual growth and activity. The hormones, whose action is chemical, are associated with the mechanism of the nervous system in the completion of an act.

The nervous system is comparable to a telephone exchange. Messages are carried to a central system—the brain or spinal column—then relayed to their proper destination. In the very simplest behavior, such as the eye wink or the knee jerk, an afferent nerve transmits an impulse from the receptor to a central connection, from which the impulse passes through an efferent nerve fiber to an effector. The unit of this type of action is called the *reflex arc*.

While little of human behavior is so simple as this, it is the basic pattern of response. The reflex action conditioned by afferent and efferent nerves may be reconditioned in a number of possible ways by different intercommunications of afferent-efferent nerves. Pavlov's experiment with the reconditioned response of the dog is a classic example. A dog's mouth normally waters at the sight of food but not at the ringing of a bell. Pavlov set up an experiment in which a bell was rung a number of times simultaneously with the appearance of food. The dog began to associate the ringing of the bell with the appearance of food; and, after a while, saliva would flow from the dog's mouth at the ringing of the bell alone. The exuding of saliva at the sight of food is a natural response; the exuding of saliva at the ringing of the bell is a conditioned response.

The process of learning, for human beings, is essentially a process of conditioning and reconditioning responses. On the base of the organically conditioned responses are built a series of re-conditioned responses in the course of experience. For instance, as an organically conditioned response the first law of life may well be self-preservation; but when the issue of patriotism or a religious ideal is raised, the reconditioned response comes into play and the person is willing, nay glad, to sacrifice his life for the sake of a value, for the good of society.

Soviet Russian scientists, following in the footsteps of Ivan Pavlov (1849-1936), are inclined to rely almost exclusively on conditioned and reconditioned responses as methods of analyzing, understanding, and re-forming human behavior. (*Cf.* the paper read by C. M. Bykov at the American Psychiatric Association's Meetings in San Francisco in 1958.)

4. Drives, Instincts, Emotions, Temperament

The unconditioned response, after rehearsal, becomes the conditioned response. The conditioned response may, in the course of experience, be transmuted into a reconditioned response. This gradual rise in the level from the unconditioned to the conditioned to the re-conditioned response is organically correlated to certain parts of our original nature: (1) drives, (2) instincts, (3) emotions, (4) temperament.

Ogburn and Nimkoff's discussion of drives is very helpful (10, p. 198):

Certain internal stimuli, or *drives*, are an important part of the inherited equipment of the newborn babe. These drives are related largely to the organic needs of the individual, such as those for sleep, exercise, food, water, elimination, and sex activity. A pin stuck into the skin will hurt, without much reference to the internal condition of the body. But the internal stimuli of hunger, let us say, are relatively more important than the external stimuli. These drives provide a kind of dynamic urge, or push, to behavior. When an organic need is unsatisfied, an organic tension is set up which leaves the individual restless and impels him to bestir himself in the effort to satisfy the need. In the case of hunger, for example, the absence of food causes the walls of the stomach to contract, stretching the muscles and producing disagreeable sensations which lead to a state of general restlessness. This restlessness may be interpreted as a diffuse effort to achieve a goal, namely, food. The drives are oriented with reference to goals.

While nature supplies the child with a set of tensions which must somehow be relieved, it remains for nurture to determine the ways in which these tensions will be managed. The craving makes one seek some sort of expression or goal, but it may be conditioned. Thus nature supplies the individual with a hunger drive, but experience determines how, when, and where it will be satisfied. There is great variation in the eating habits and attitudes of different children. One child will accept graciously whatever food is set before him, will eat his meal promptly and with relish. Another will just as regularly refuse what is offered, habitually dawdle, or regret the time that must be given to eating. The differences among children in habits of eating, sleeping and the like suggest the readiness with which the drives may be conditioned. The point is important, for it shows the dominance of the learning process in the formation of human personality.

This discussion of *drives* may as well do for a statement of instincts. An instinct is a complex organization of elementary reflex arcs. There are two possible interpretations of the word instinct or the generalized unlearned tendency to respond with which man is born: (1) an unlearned mechanism to respond to a certain stimulus or a set of stimuli, and (2) an inborn driving-force, an urge to respond to a certain stimulus or a set of stimuli. The exponents of the second definition have no objection to accepting the first as a corollary, but the exponents of the first definition are apt to object to the second as an undue extension of the term instinct. According to the first definition, instinct ceases to be an instinct as popularly conceived—we are not at liberty, for instance, to say, "I instinctively know it" or "I am goaded by my instincts to this action."

The flight of birds is instinctive in the sense that the act represents a complex organization of elementary reflex arcs. The seasonal migrations of certain birds to the North and to the South must also be thought of as instinctive acts. Likewise the nest-building activity of a rat must be laid to an instinct. The bee and the ant colonies operate on the instinct level. Even so, it must be admitted that even among lower animals the generalized unlearned tendency to act may become smothered by an inappropriate medium or by the absence of a pattern. To what extent the presence of a model and the process of learning by imitation and by communication are necessary in the transformation of the generalized unlearned tendency to act into a definite pattern, even among the lower animals, it is difficult to say. According to Z. Y. Kuo's experiments, it was found that of the kittens that saw the mother-cat kill rats, 85 per cent became rat-killers before the age of four months; of the kittens that did not see the mother-cat kill rats, only 45 per cent became rat-killers before the age of four months. It was furthermore demonstrated that "kittens raised with rats as companions killed none of them, nor of any of their kind, and only 16 per cent of other varieties." (10, pp. 34 – 35.)

In man instincts play a very subordinate role. We have attempted to account for all of human behavior in terms of social processes. But we must accept the possible existence of instincts in man, simply because man is part of the animal kingdom. Drives and instincts—call them "prepotent tendencies to react" if you will—provide the substructure upon which is erected the edifice of human behavior.

In addition to drives and instincts, the original nature of man is freighted with emotions and temperament. Emotions represent the *feeling* side of response, while temperament represents the prevailing *mood*. Thus temperament is a matter of emotional response, the underlying or characteristic state of the individual. The temperament characterizing an individual may be one of four basic types or a combination of some of them: (1) choleric or excitable, (2) phlegmatic or dull, (3) sanguine or optimistic, (4) melancholy or sad. The cyclothymic or the manic-depressive alternates between elation and despair, and works by fits and starts.

While temperament is an integral part of original nature, our present knowledge of the mechanisms of inheritance does not permit us to draw any valid conclusions whether it is inborn or acquired prenatally or postnatally. The problem becomes more insoluble by the fact that emotions and temperament tend to be patterned by culture. Not every Japanese is born with a temperament befitting a Stoic but no Japanese could successfully thrive in Japanese society if he did not early in life learn to become stoical in sadness as well as in happiness. (*Cf. supra*, CHAPTER 24).

Again, Ogburn and Nimkoff's discussion of this problem is very helpful (10, p. 202):

While some babies at birth are nervous and others are quiet and calm, it is difficult to know whether these temperamental traits are inherited. In individual cases such differences may be ascribed to circumstances attending the experience of birth; much may depend on whether the birth experience is an easy or trying one for the infant. There is also a little evidence suggesting that some prenatal conditions may be capable of affecting the nervous system of the child. But whether genetic factors are also operative is not clear. The glands are thought to be partly responsible for temperamental differences, and individuals differ in glandular makeup, but "practically nothing is accurately known as to the role of inheritance in transmitting supposedly different glandular types" (according to T. H. Morgan), although of course the glands themselves are inherited. A case might perhaps be made out for such an inheritance if it could be shown that infants of certain races possess temperamental traits different from those of infants of other races. It does appear that South European children tend to be excitable and their time reaction quick, while North European children are more stolid and slower to respond, but unfortunately these differences are not observable in newborn infants. On this account we have no assurance that the behavior noted is not due to culture rather than to biology.

The newly emerging science of ductless or endocrine glands, called endocrinology, may throw light on the relation between these glands and temperament. We know that these glands do influence the emotional potential. "They help to determine whether an individual will, for instance, be vigorous or feeble, energetic or lethargic, in his reactions. Such differences in emotional response are important for personality, but it would be an error to hold, as endocrine-enthusiasts do, that the glands determine the whole personality, including such things as one's opinions, one's habits, and one's skills." (10, p. 203). It is possible to overactivate or underactivate some of these glands, and thereby affect human behavior, by the injection of certain kinds of hormones. In other words, glands respond to outer stimuli as well as to inner stimuli. This renders difficult a determination of the exact inheritable nature of the functioning of glands.

Thus far in our discussion of the biophysical elements of the human organism we have found that the individual at birth is a carrier of the primordial germ-plasm and of the genes determining his body build including the nervous system and the glandular system, drives and instincts, emotions and temperament.

5. THE ROLE OF THE PSYCHOSOCIAL ELEMENTS IN HUMAN BEHAVIOR

Now we may take up a discussion of the psychosocial elements of original nature. The question may well be raised whether the social element is really an indispensable constituent element of original nature. Our thesis in great measure rests upon this assumption. The individual at birth is organically related to the group in exactly the same sense in which his fingers are related to the total organism. We do not sense the similarity because the fingers are joined to the body while the individual is a disparate being. Though separated from others spatially, the individual is organically related to the group within the total time-space frame. In the womb he received nourishment from the mother; at birth he finds himself born to groups—to the family, to the neighborhood, to the community. This is the medium in which he flourishes. It is in this setting that his original nature becomes transformed into human nature and he, the individual, becomes a person. As Cooley aptly phrased it, "Self and society are twin-born, we know one as immediately as we know the other, and the notion of a separate and independent ego is an illusion" (3, p. 5).

Now what kind of psychological equipment does the individual bring into this setting?

While the biophysical equipment of the human organism enables the individual to function with the aid of "unlearned tendencies to respond to the environment, as manifested in reflex, instinctive and emotive actions," the psychological equipment, whatever it may be, enables the individual "to organize and systematize the experiences of reactions or responses" and "to represent and articulate experiences symbolically."

The psychological equipment of man at birth is analyzed by psychologists in terms of intelligence—General Intelligence or the G factor in intelligence—and special aptitudes or capacities, such as those of Rzeszenski who became a chess champion of the world before he was ten years of age or those of Mozart who composed music at the age of five. Musical-mindedness seems to be a unit-trait in the germ-plasm but playing chess is definitely not, though the capacity to image a configuration may well be. Whatever in the G factor or in special aptitudes may be contributed by heredity, sociologists rightly affirm that without cultural approval and without opportunity for training and self-expression the hereditary potential will remain a mere potential. We cannot escape the close link-up between the psychological and the social elements of original nature.

Since there is no generally accepted theory of the psychological equipment of man at birth and of the processes whereby the biotic individual becomes a socialized self, we shall attempt to summarize several theories that have a standing in the field: sociologistic and psychoanalytic.

6. DURKHEIM'S COLLECTIVE REPRESENTATIONS

Durkheim's concept of "collective representations" reinforces the reciprocal interdependence between self and society, as pointed out by us in CHAPTER 12. There we had defined "collective representations," after Park and Burgess, as "the concepts which embody the objectives of group life." There is no conflict between the interpretation of "collective representations" given by Park and Burgess and that given by Gillin and Gillin (4, p. 566) as "a system of ideas, patterns of behavior, attitudes, and values held in common by a group of people, which system is impressed upon individuals by certain sanctions." The chief sanctions whereby the individual appropriates the collective representations and makes them a part of himself are: folkways, mores, institutions, public opinion, laws, social pressures, which are all interwoven into the texture of the social process.

We may identify the mind with the second trait of original nature, namely, the capacity to organize and systematize the experiences of responses. While discussing the emergence of "mind" in the child (*Supra*, CHAPTER 8), we pointed out that the nursery is the birthplace of intelligence, that the playground is the birthplace of ideals; that the child transmutes chaos into cosmos, a "world" of "big booming confusion" into a "world" of unity and order, by differentiating himself from his environment, by differentiating a number of component elements of the environment from one another, by a subtle process of reasoning and ratiocination.

The child has his being within the framework of cultural categories including collective representations and progresses from the biotic to the psychological level through attempts to abide by, and to utilize, the cultural categories of his group. The family, the most elemental primary group, serves to the child as the carrier of culture, indeed, as the embodiment of culture. Later other primary groups and secondary groups as well serve as instrumentalities in making the child an integral part of society, that "immense cooperative concern of mutual services."

7. COOLEY: THE LOOKING-GLASS SELF CONCEPT OF PERSONALITY

We are indebted to Charles H. Cooley (1864-1929) for calling our attention to the crucial role of primary groups in the formation of the self of the newborn and in the formation of the personality of the newborn as well. His "looking-glass self" concept of personality has enriched the literature of sociology. Through symbiotic relationships, through interaction with the group, the individual develops his "self" which is essentially a social self or the looking-glass self. This looking-glass self concept of personality involves three principal elements: (1) the imagination of our appearance to the other, i.e., to a member of the group, or the whole group, (2) the imagination of the other's judgment of that appearance, (3) the response of the individual to the imagined judgment of others in terms of "some sort of self-feeling such as pride or mortification." (2, p. 152).

8. MEAD: THE I AND THE ME

G. H. Mead (1863-1931), the noted American social psychologist, accepts the sociological point of view in his analysis of socialization. It is through interaction with others that the biotic individual develops his self and becomes a member of society. But while Cooley accounted for the emergence of the self in terms of *self-feeling*, Mead would account for it in terms of *self-consciousness*. It seems to me that the two views are complementary rather than contradictory. The role of communication, and of the cultural definition of meaning, in the emergence of mind, in the emergence of the self, has been brilliantly brought out by Mead in the following passage (8, p. 134):

Mind arises in the social process only when that process as a whole enters into, or is present in, the experience of any one of the given individuals involved in that process. When this occurs the individual becomes self-conscious, has a mind; he becomes aware of his relations to the process as a whole and to the other individuals participating in it with him; he becomes aware of that process as modified by the reactions and interactions of individuals—including himself—who are carrying it on. The evolutionary appearance of mind or intelligence takes place when the whole social process of experience and behavior is brought within the experience of any one of the separate individuals implicated therein, and when the individual's adjustment to the process is modified and refined by the awareness or consciousness which he thus has of it. It is by means of reflexiveness—the turning back of the experience of the individual upon himself—that the whole social process is thus brought into the experience of the individuals involved in it; it is by such means, which enable the individual to take the attitude of the other toward himself, that the individual is able consciously to adjust himself to that process and to modify the results of that process in any given social act in terms of his adjustment to it. Reflexiveness, then, is the essential condition within the social process, for the development of mind.

Mead's concept of the "I" and the "Me" essentially embodies the personality makeup of the socialized self: "The 'I' is the response of the organism to the attitudes of others. The 'me' is the organized set of attitudes of others which one himself assumes." (8, p. 175.)

9. FREUD: PSYCHOANALYSIS

Sigmund Freud (1856-1939), the father of psychoanalysis, in his attempt to cure psychogenic illness, was led on to investigate what he called "the anatomy of the mental personality." Freud accepted mind as an operational fact; how it emerged was not his problem. His main concern was to discover how the mind functioned.

Freud postulated three mental processes—rather three mental levels: (1) the unconscious, (2) the preconscious or the foreconscious, or the subconscious, and (3) the conscious. He also postulated three systems of the mind variously referred to as realms, regions or provinces: (1) the id, (2) the ego, (3) the superego.

The experiences an individual goes through are stored away in the mind—in an almost forgotten and buried manner in the unconscious, in a latent manner in the foreconscious (subconscious), in an active state in the conscious. A slip of the tongue, dreams, culturally unapproved acts spring from the subconscious. Names, dates, sources of information, may likewise be tucked away in the sub-conscious, to be used when needed, or in the conscious if we are set to use them immediately.

The id, a chaos, a cauldron of seething excitement, operates on the biotic level, and is concerned solely with pleasure regardless of consequences. The ego receives perceptions and conceptions from contact with the outside world—the world of reality—and passes them on to the id. The superego holds up norms of behavior culturally approved and deemed praiseworthy.

Just as there is constant interaction between the unconscious, the subconscious and the conscious processes, so there is constant inter-action between the three systems of the mind—the id, the ego and the superego. The id, tied up with the biotic level, serves as the storehouse of energy; the ego, confronted with the world of reality, canalizes the id's energies into possible ways; the superego canalizes the ego's activities into desirable, i.e., culturally approved, forms of behavior. While the id is the organ of untamed passions and behaves without restraint, the ego must act with reason and circumspection and the superego with ideals and norms. Under the circumstances, conflict is bound to arise now and then between the three levels as well as between the three systems of the mind. The conflict is re-solved, sometimes successfully sometimes unsuccessfully, by a resort to one or more of the following mechanisms: displacement and transference, repression and sublimation, identification and ration-alization, projection and introjection, dissociation and phantasy.

The relation between the id and the ego and their conflicting interests are brought out by Freud in his comparison of the id with the horse and the ego with its rider. "The function of the ego is that of the rider guiding the horse, which is the id. But like the rider, the ego sometimes is unable to guide the horse as it wishes and perforce must guide the id in the direction it is determined to go, or in a slightly different direction. Freud says that this difference in aims of the id and the ego leads to 'repression-resistances' which merge into the id. It is out of this conflict between the ego and the id that psychosis develops." (4, p. 575).

Finally, Freud postulated two conflicting wishes: the life-wish and the death-wish.

10. Irene and the Country Squire: Two Cases of Inner Conflict

Two cases of mental conflict may be cited, one between the subconscious and the conscious, the other between the ego and the superego:

Irene had nursed her mother through a prolonged illness culminating in death. The circumstances connected with the death were peculiarly painful, and the event produced a profound shock upon the patient's mind. An abnormal mental condition developed, characterized by the frequent appearance of symptoms resembling those exhibited by the ordinary sleepwalker. Irene, perhaps engaged at the moment in sewing or in conversation, would suddenly cease her occupation, and would commence to live over again the scene of her mother's death, carrying out every detail with all the power of an accomplished actress. While this drama was in progress she was perfectly unconscious of the actual events happening in her environment, heard nothing that was said to her, and saw nothing but the imaginary scene in which she was living at the moment. This phenomenon, technically termed a *somnambulism*, would end as suddenly as it had begun, and Irene would return to her former occupation, absolutely unaware of the fact that it had ever been interrupted. After an interval of perhaps several days a second somnambulism, resembling the first in all respects, would appear in the same abrupt manner. If the patient were interrogated during the apparently normal intervals it would be found that she had not only entirely forgotten everything which had happened during the somnambulism, but that the whole system of ideas connected with her mother's death had completely disappeared from her mind. She remembered nothing of the illness or its tragic end; discussed her mother without emotion, and was reproached by her relatives for her callous indifference to the whole subject. This (represents) curious localized loss of memory or *amnesia*. (5, pp. 28–30).

This case was originally described by Professor Janet. The next case was originally described by Jung. We reproduce the story of the country squire as told by Hart (5, pp. 73–74):

A man, walking with a friend in the neighborhood of a country village, suddenly expressed extreme irritation concerning the church bells, which happened to be pealing at the moment. He maintained that their tone was intrinsically unpleasant, their harmony ugly, and the total effect altogether disagreeable. The friend was astonished, for the bells in question were famous for their singular beauty. He endeavored, therefore, to elucidate the real cause underlying his companion's attitude. Skilful questioning elicited the further remark that not only were the bells unpleasant but that the clergyman of the church wrote extremely bad poetry. The causal complex was then apparent, for the man whose ears had been offended by the bells also wrote poetry, and in a recent criticism his work had been compared very unfavorably with that of the clergyman. The rivalry-complex thus engendered had expressed itself indirectly by an un-justifiable denunciation of the innocent church bells. The direct expression would, of course, have been abuse of the clergyman himself or of his works.

It will be observed that, without the subsequent analysis, the behavior of the man would have appeared inexplicable, or at best ascribable to "bad temper," "irritability," or some other not very satisfying reason. Most cases where sudden passion over some trifle is witnessed may be explained along similar lines, and demonstrated to be the effect of some other and quite adequate cause. The apparently incomprehensible reaction is then seen to be the natural resultant of perfectly definite antecedents.

In the two cases just cited, we have described situations fraught with mental conflict for the adult. The child's life may well be said to be a series of conflict situations. It is remarkable that so many children survive the ordeal, become socialized and take their place as respected members of society.

11. The Prince of Wails: A Life of Ambivalence

Here is a charming description of the helpless child on the symbiotic level, "The Prince of Wails," by Marcia Winn, which first appeared in *The Chicago Tribune* (*The Reader's Digest*, September, 1947, p. 131, quoted):

Why is it that every one refers to a baby as a helpless little thing? Give a baby a home of his own, and he is the least helpless object in it. All he needs to do to have his every want filled is to let out one small peep. If help does not come at once, he need only extend this peep into a wail. And by forcing a bellow, he can throw the entire household into a bewildered tailspin from which it may not emerge for days.

He can't walk, he can't talk, he can't feed or bathe himself, and in that he has an unmixed blessing. Unable to walk, he can lie in bed all day and kick his legs—the envy of every adult who sees him. Unable to talk, he need never answer unnecessary questions, become involved in a political argument, or politely tolerate a bore. When oppressed by the last, he can turn his head the other way, yawn, or blandly go to sleep, and have his actions approved by polite society.

He need never worry over what he is going to wear today or what he will eat for lunch. If he doesn't wear a stitch, he is perfectly content, and no one will raise an eyebrow. If he doesn't like his food, he can spit, blow, or bubble it out, no matter who is watching, or he can disdain to eat at all. He can emit, at the end of a meal, a resounding belch, and be applauded for what two years later will be considered most unseemly.

Soon the world at large will criticize the way his hair grows, although now his admirers are enchanted because it grows at all. It will criticize the way he eats, although now all are ecstatic if he gets it down any way. If he turns out to be beautiful, good, rich or successful, part of the world will envy him, and if he turns out to be ugly, mean, poor or a failure, the other part of the world will berate him; but now, for the last time in his life, he is eulogized by poets, chucked under the chin by old ladies, cooed at by Scrooges, and adored by all.

Far from being helpless in this world, he is the only human being who can chin on it. It wasn't idle conversation that prompted a pediatrician to muse, "In the next life I'm going to be a perpetual baby."

12. The Life History of Individuals in Our Culture

In more scientific terminology adapting the material from *Experimental Social Psychology* by Murphy, Murphy and Newcomb (9, pp. 504 ff), Ogburn and Nimkoff describe the life history of individuals in our culture. This description brings out numerous occasions for mental conflict (10, pp. 178–79):

The dynamic character of human interaction is well illustrated by the life history of individuals in our culture. It is illuminating to trace the sequence of processes in the development of the child. The first period in his life is usually one of indulgence. The baby is made the center of attention. Much of the conversation of the family revolves about him and his doings. He is exhibited and his achievement applauded.

Then, quite suddenly, this period of happy co-operation gives way to one of restraint and discipline. When the child is about two years old, his parents undertake to socialize him. Almost overnight they wish him to become an obedient, well-mannered, respectable citizen. The child's usual reaction to such restraint and domination by his parents is conflict of some sort: temper tantrums, defiance, negativism. But soon the child learns that this is an adult's world and he cannot prevail against it.

Thus begins the third period in his life, of reluctant conformity, or accommodation. The child learns how to get along. He discovers that he can get a good deal that he wants if only he does not antagonize his elders. He learns the strategy of putting his best foot forward while "getting away with things." He confides in his superiors, yet has his secrets, too.

So the child's life continues in its ambivalence of catering to adult authority and evading it, until the period of adolescence arrives. Once more there is rebellion against control, as the maturing boy or girl is possessed with a desire for independence and self-realization. In the reaction against parental domination there may develop in the child a violent disdain for values associated with the parents, as, for example, their recreational, occupational, and religious preferences.

As the adolescent tries to put his own ideas into practice, another period of adjustment sets in. Actual responsibility proves quite sobering in its effects. The feeling of superiority to adults diminishes as the young person moves on toward adulthood. Then come marriage and parenthood, and the cycle is repeated.

13. Growing up as a Series of Rebirths

The process of growing up is viewed by a religious writer not as a problem compounded of crises but as a recurring series of rebirths and regeneration. Thus Mr. Harold Blake Walker says (*The Chicago Tribune*, October 16, 1958):

Anyone who thoughtfully considers his own experience is aware that life is a process of repeated rebirth. We keep being born again in the process of growing up. The newly born infant is merely a bundle of unorganized and uncoordinated possibilities. He meets what William James called "the booming, buzzing confusion of the world."

Within a few short weeks, however, the child is born into a world of rattles to be shaken, friendly fingers to be grasped, and smiling faces that inspire response. It is a world of persons and things to be examined with curiosity, a friendly world of love and thoughtfulness.

As time goes on, the child is born into a world of language, wherein sounds like cat, dog, mother, father become identified with persons and things. He is introduced to the miracle of words and sentences that convey ideas. He emerges into a wonderful new world.

In time, the growing youngster meets the world of moral values. At first it is a world of irrational "do's" and "don't's." But in time the "do's" and "don't's" are identified with right and wrong, with something that goes deeper than wants and wishes. The right is an imperative that comes from the mysterious beyond.

Unless growth stops too soon, the child is born into the world of spiritual reality wherein God is meaningful and he knows that "The Lord is my shepherd." Beauty, truth, and goodness come to be the tokens of God's life around him and character takes root. To stop being reborn too soon is to miss the meaning of life itself.

14. INFERIORITY COMPLEX AND PERSONALITY DEVELOPMENT

A variant theory of the psychoanalytic technique, the inferiority complex, elaborated by Alfred Adler (1870-1937), is helpful in an understanding of the process of socialization. As pointed out in CHAPTER 8, the child vis-a-vis the "world"—i.e., his environment including father and mother—realizes his inferiority. This sense or feeling of inferiority must be overcome: subconsciously argues the uninstructed child. In other words, inferiority, the liability of childhood, becomes at once an asset inasmuch as it immediately brings into play its antidote, namely, goal-seeking. The child imposes order upon the universe; the universe in its turn imposes unity of personality upon the child through his goal-seeking activity. The crucial role of the prolongation of human infancy, first discussed by John Fiske (1842-1901), must be fully appreciated if we are to understand the process of socialization. Prolonged human infancy provides just the right setting for the transformation of original nature into human nature, of the individual into the person—in short, for socialization.

15. OTTO RANK: LIFE AS A CONTINUUM OF CRISES

Otto Rank (1884-1939), founder of a variant school of psychoanalysis, looks upon life as a continuum of crises with intermittent equilibrium, precariously achieved. For instance, the child in the mother's womb, after eight months or so, is fully developed and ready to enjoy his life as a parasite upon the mother, when, lo and behold, he is propelled out of the womb! The coming into the outer world, away from the security of the mother's womb, is a most critical experience in the new-born baby's life. Now he must learn to breathe for himself; now he will have to learn to develop his bodily organs for sustaining his bodily framework. This essay at developing motor skills becomes a continuous crisis for days and months—and years. Soon he learns to suckle at the mother's breast (or the milk bottle, in American culture); just when his coordination is perfect and just as he settles down to enjoying and relishing the sucking of the mother's breasts (or the milk bottle), he is compelled to learn to eat solids. . . . When in his boyhood he is ready to enjoy his sheltered position and parasitic dependence upon parents, he is admonished to learn to be independent. When in his teens he tries to be independent, he is scolded that he shows no respect for his parents. And so on and so forth. Otto Rank's theory has great resemblance to Buddha's philosophical postulate of Dukkha (pain) as being at the very heart of *Samsara*, the ongoing universal process.

The Buddha's four noble Truths remarkably anticipated the four steps of modern psychoanalysis and psychiatry in the treatment of human ills. The Buddha's first noble Truth about the fact of suffering is the psychiatrist's first step, namely, that the patient must accept the fact of disequilibrium. Buddha's second noble Truth, the cause of disequilibrium or suffering, namely, desire, is the psychiatrist's attempt to study the etiology of the patient's malady and to discover the causal factors. Buddha's third noble Truth, the realization that the suffering can be overcome, is the psychiatrist's attempt to bring himself into rapport with the patient with a view to giving him confidence that the malady can be overcome. Fourth, the

Buddha's noble eightfold path, as a way of redeeming life, may be likened to the psychiatrist's prescriptions for overcoming inner conflicts and bringing the self into harmony with the outer world. (*Cf. supra*, CHAPTER 21).

Both Freud and Rank have their followers not only among scientific investigators but also among practitioners of social work. The Freudian followers constitute what is known as the Diagnostic school in social work, while Rank's followers are referred to as the Functional school in social work.

Otto Rank postulates the existence of will and looks upon the will as an organizing force in human personality. "In the Freudian view, the postulates of personality structure and organization do not include an organizing force that is equivalent to the functional concept of will." (6, p. 8). Whether the followers of Freud and Rank have unintentionally exaggerated the orientation of their masters or whether the differences are really crucial as between the Diagnostic school and the Functional school, I do not know. But since Social Work schools swear either by the one or the other, it is deemed necessary to reproduce here a discussion of the differences between Freudians and Rankians as seen by a committee of disciples of the two masters (6, pp. 8–9):

Personality organization, according to Freudian tenets, is a composite of differentiated and interacting forces, reacting not only on each other but also to favorable or unfavorable influences in the environment (including people). The relative strength of these forces and the nature of balance they maintain are the result of life experiences of the individual, primarily of his relationships to par- each other but also to favorable or unfavorable influences in the psychic structure, performs various functions, chief of which is that of effecting a balance between inner drives and superego, while, at the same time, reconciling the individual's psychic needs with the demands of reality. The ego is thus oriented to both inner needs and outer influences. Its functions are those of perception, reality testing, judgment, organization, planning, and self-preservation. The strength of the ego is a variable factor, determined largely by the favorable or unfavorable course of the person's psychosocial development. The ego's strength also contracts or expands at points of greater or less inner and outer pressure and is capable of making permanent gains as a result of psychotherapeutically directed treatment. The diagnostic group assumes that an understanding of the personality structure, of the intrapsychic conflicts and their relationship to the current problem of functioning, is basic to furthering change and improvement. It accepts the concept of a norm in psychic functioning; it believes that the nature and extent of the psychosocial disturbance determine the kind and extent of therapeutic endeavor necessary to bring about change.

The functional theory of personality development also postulates the interaction of inner instinctual needs and outer or environmental experience, but in this view such interaction is organized and given direction by the human being's inborn will to individuation and autonomy, which organizes such inner and outer experience to create the ego (in functional casework more frequently called the self). Because of the activity of this will to individuation, the human being, from the beginning of life, is not only acted upon by reality, both inner and outer, but also acts upon it. Thus the ego or self is the result of the creative use of inner and outer experience by means of the will, rather than a product of the interaction of inner and outer forces. Development is seen to take place through relationship to meaningful persons in the environment, first and chief of whom is the mother. In these relationships the individual projects his need upon the other, and while in the earliest stages these needs are largely biological, they are also invested with great psychic significance. The satisfaction of need by the other has the psychic effect of creating a union with this other, of which the organic wholeness of intrauterine experience is the prototype. Because such complete union is not possible in reality, separation inevitably follows, which the will may use constructively, to create an inner wholeness by making the reality limitations its own or, destructively, by refusing to accept the limitations and continuing to strive for completion at that level through the other person.

16. Jung and "Racial Memories"

Carl Gustav Jung (1875-   ) holds that primal *libido*, or *life force*, is composed of both sexual and nonsexual energy. In this he agrees with Freud who postulated a basic mental energy, called the libido, which was equated by the latter with sexual energy, the word sex standing for all pleasure. Jung also agrees with Freud when he accepts an *individual unconscious*, but goes beyond Freud in postulating a *collective unconscious* containing what he calls "racial memories." Within this collective unconscious are locked emotional stereotypes, called *archetypes*, common to all races of mankind—archetypes, such as Mother Earth or earth-mother, the Jovian figure of "the old wise man," etc.

According to Jung, the human mind has three layers: (1) *the conscious*, (2) *the personal unconscious*, and (3) *the collective unconscious*. Having explored yoga and alchemy, fairy tales of the world and tribal rites of the Pueblo Indians, German Romanticism and Zen Buddhism, extrasensory perception (ESP) and the cave dwellings of prehistoric man, as well as 100,000 dreams, Jung, in his "analytical psychology," mixes mysticism with medicine on the theory that psychiatry must take into account all of man's experiences, mystical as well as practical. Against the Freudian view that religion is a form of neurosis and God a projection of the Father image, Jung poses the view that far from being a neurosis, religion is a universally felt human need—embedded in the collective unconscious of man.

If man's personal unconscious be thought of as the repository of one's own experiences, good as well as bad, thrown away by the conscious mind, his collective unconscious is the repository of the archetypes of human experiences from the beginning of man's existence. Supreme among these archetypes, according to Jung, is the transcendent *Self*—the symbol of Oneness found in many religions but best represented by the Hindu concept of *Atman* (Supreme Soul or Self).

The interview plays a significant part in psychoanalyzing a patient. But the technique of interviewing seems to be a no-man's land. Theoretically, the followers of Jung should participate more actively in psychoanalyzing a patient than the followers of Freud. Again, theoretically, the Jungians and Rankians should conduct a "directed interview" in contrast to Freudians who should conduct an "undirected interview." Actually, as Professor Carl R. Rogers stated to the author in a personal communication, "plenty of Freudians . . . conduct very much directed interviews," while "the Rankians . . . tend to hold interviews which involve less direction by the therapist."

Since the interview is part of therapy as well as an instrument of diagnosis, the interview procedures and processes tend to transcend the narrow viewpoints of different schools of psychoanalysis. Then, too, the personality of the interviewer, regardless of the school to which he (or she) belongs, has a great deal to do with whether the interview will be directed or undirected.

17. HINDU PHILOSOPHY: THE PSYCHOLOGICAL EQUIPMENT OF MAN

Finally, we may briefly point out that Hindu philosophy has analyzed the psychological equipment of man in minute details and with the aid of conceptual tools which may or may not be hospitably received by the American sociologist. But the problems raised have a bearing upon our discussion of socialization. I am particularly struck by Freud's comparison of the id and the ego with the horse and the rider; we find the same comparison in Hindu philosophic literature.

Hindu philosophers divide the psychic equipment of man into three categories: (1) Atma (self, soul), (2) Buddhi (intellect, reason, power of discriminating judgment), (3) Manas or Mana (mind, the receptor which transforms percepts into concepts). Buddhi and Manas emerge from the experiencings of the human organism—they view the world through the windows of the sense-organs. Atma is transcendental, an integral part of the Paramatma (Supreme Self or Soul). The Atma as such is indestructible.

In the Kathopanishad, CHAPTER III, verses 3–6 and 9, we find the following statement:

Regard the Atma, the occupant of the chariot, as the master and the body as the chariot. Consider Buddhi as the charioteer—driver—and the mind as the reins. The senses are said to be the horses and sense-objects—cravings, the libido—their pasture-land. The Atma, joined (yoked) to the senses and the Manas, is the enjoyer, so say the wise. He indeed is foolish whose mind is not ever applied; his senses are uncontrollable like the bad horses of the charioteer. He indeed is wise whose mind is always applied; his senses are under control like the good horses of the charioteer. He alone attains the celestial abode of Vishnu (i.e., heaven), whose charioteer is wise and whose mind-reins are under control.

Manu, likewise, states: "The wise man should exert himself to control the senses running wild amid the alluring objects of senses as the good charioteer controls his horses." (*Manu Smriti*, CHAPTER II, verse 88).

Senses are divided by the Hindus into two categories—cognitive (*jnanendriya*) and reactive (*karmendriya*). The five cognitive senses are: (1) the power of hearing, (2) the power of sensing temperature, (3) the power of seeing, (4) the power of tasting, (5) the power of smelling. The five reactive senses are: (1) the power of "voicing" (mouth), (2) the power of touching (hands), (3) the power of locomotion (feet), (4) the power to eject liquids (the male or female sex organ), (5) the power to eject solids (the anus). Hindu philosophers postulated the possibility of the performance of the function of one sense by another substituted in its place—a man without arms training his feet to do a great many of the chores usually performed by the hands. Muscular effort is involved in the functioning of both sets of senses, cognitive and reactive. Such is the physical basis of the ego.

The mind acts as the receptor which transforms percepts into concepts. Cooperating with one or another of these sense-powers, at a given moment the mind selects only certain sensations, and excludes others, from the multiple streams of impacts pouring in upon the individual from all directions of the objective world. The selected impacts are transformed into the various sensation-forms of which we are directly aware. These sensation-forms are the actually " given" of the senses in regard to any particular form of perception. " It is really a movement, a waving to and fro, of the 'seeking' here and there (*eshana*, desire), which is the Manas, Concrete Mentality, when the movement assumes the form of an entity (a 'particle' as the Vaisheshika views it), in much the same way as the ultimate constituents of physical matter are now regarded by science as simultaneously both waves and particles." (1, p. 37).

To describe the interdependence between the mind and the cognitive and reactive senses, Manu went a step farther and in effect suggested that the mind might as well be considered the eleventh sense-organ. Said Manu: "Mind is to be known as the eleventh, belonging by its nature to both (sets of senses); when the mind is conquered (controlled), the two sets of five (senses) become conquered (controlled). (*Manu Smriti*, CHAPTER II, verse 99).

Life, the vital being, is assumed to be endowed with five functions: (1) appropriation (*prana*), (2) rejection (*apena*), (3) assimilation (*samana*), (4) distribution (*vyana*), (5) regeneration (*udana*).

The four first-named functions are obvious. As long as there is Life in the body these are continually going on. To begin with, Life is a selective process. It appropriates, takes into the system, a certain quantity of material which it needs for building up and maintaining the organism in which it operates. It also rejects from the system what is not useful. One of the manifestations of this double activity of Life is seen in the ceaseless process of 'breathing in' and 'breathing out,' which have therefore been taken as the most characteristic feature of life and even regarded as the equivalent of Life (*Prana*). What is selected is further *assimilated* to that form (as, for instance, 'blood') in which it can be built into the system. This activity is compared to that of fire, namely, combustion, so that the result is said to rise up like a 'sevenfold flame.' The fourth function is also apparent in that the assimilated material, such as blood, is distributed all over the body, by means of 'channels' radiating from the heart to every part of the body. (1, pp. 37–38).

The occidentally trained social scientist would understand by the fifth function the perpetuation of the species, and transmission of the germ plasm, the death of the old and the coming into being of the new. But Hindu philosophers understood by it the function which "serves as a link between the Life in the individual and the Life universal, which is *Brahman*" (Supreme Being). (1, p. 38).

To summarize: In the last chapter, we discussed socialization and its mechanisms from the standpoint of society and culture. In the present chapter, we have attempted to present and analyze the individual, the object of socialization, from the behavioristic standpoint (Linton), from the sociological standpoint (Durkheim, Cooley, Mead), from the psychoanalytic standpoint (Freud, Adler, Rank, Jung) and from the standpoint of Hindu philosophy.

Each of these analyses is meaningful and valid depending upon the perspective from which the individual is viewed.

Now we are ready to analyze the processes whereby the individual, at birth a mere bundle of prepotent tendencies to react, becomes a socialized participant in the socio-cultural stream.

18. A SUPPLEMENTARY NOTE ON SOCIALIZATION

It needs to be pointed out that sociologists in general do not sharply define the process of socialization as we have done, though our definition of socialization underlies their thinking when, for instance, they speak of socialization as the process whereby the social and cultural heritage is transmitted from generation to generation, from parents to children, from teachers to pupils, from the elders to the youngsters.

Furthermore, it also needs to be pointed out that the term socialization in economics has an entirely different meaning. When economists, especially Marxist economists, speak of socialization of industry, they mean that the industry is (or is to be) owned and operated socially, i.e., by society as a whole, either through the instrumentality of the State or through the instrumentality of the union of workers engaged in that industry. By and large, socialization in economics means government ownership and operation of industry.

The post offices and their services, the highways and roads, in every country; the public school system and the TVA in the U.S.A., all exemplify socialization in the economic sense. The British Government program of health insurance, embodying the Beveridge Plan, makes available to all British citizens health care at nominal cost in view of the insurance premium being regularly paid by all citizens. It would not be incorrect to call this program "socialized medicine." But the best contemporary example of "socialized medicine" is to be found in the Soviet Union where all doctors are in the employ of the Soviet State and are called upon to render medical service to all citizens without charge; of course, the hidden payment is made for this service as well as for other " free " services in Soviet society by all citizens, in one form or another.

REFERENCES

1. J. C. CHATTERJI: *India's Outlook on Life* (with an Introduction by John Dewey). New York: Kailas Press, 1931.

2. C. H. COOLEY: *Human Nature and the Social Order*. New York: Charles Scribner's Sons, 1902.

3. C. H. COOLEY: *Social Organization*. New York: Charles Scribner's Sons, 1910.

4. J. L. GILLIN & J. P. GILLIN: *An Introduction to Sociology*. New York: Macmillan, 1942.

5. BERNARD HART: *The Psychology of Insanity*. Cambridge: Cambridge University Press, 1929.

6. CORA KASIUS, EDITOR: *A Comparison of Diagnostic and Functional Case-work Concepts*. New York: Family Service Association of America, 1950.

7. RALPH LINTON: *The Study of Man*. New York: D. Appleton-Century Co., 1936.

8. G. H. MEAD: *Mind, Self, and Society*. Chicago: The University of Chicago Press, 1934.

9. G. MURPHY, L. B. MURPHY & T. M. NEWCOMB: *Experimental Social Psychology*. New York: Harper and Brothers, 1937.

10. W. F. OGBURN & M. F. NIMKOFF: *Sociology*, 2nd ed. Boston: Houghton Mifflin Co., 1950.

11. R. E. PARK & E. W. BURGESS: *Introduction to the Science of Sociology*, 2nd ed. Chicago: The University of Chicago Press, 1924 (eighth impression, 1933).

CHAPTER 26

SOCIAL PARTICIPATION: CASE STUDIES

1. A DEFINITION OF SOCIAL PARTICIPATION

SOCIALIZATION is the process whereby original nature is transformed into human nature and the biologic individual is transformed into the sociological entity, the person, i.e., an individual with a status in the group. Social participation refers to the process of the person's taking part in society, "the immense cooperative concern of mutual services." Social participation involves group-relatedness as well as activity on the part of the person in relation to a group or a number of groups. There is no index to measure the degree of socialization; the only way we can judge the presence or the absence, the adequacy or inadequacy, of the socialization of a person is in terms of the efficiency or inefficiency with which he functions in the socio-cultural milieu. But social participation can be measured quantitatively in terms of the frequency of the relation of the person to a given group or a series of groups.

The efficiency of social participation may be determined by the number of groups to which one is related and by the role one plays in different groups. Who is Who, biographies and autobiographies as well as historical documents may furnish us clues to the range of social participation for a given person. Case studies, of course, are most helpful.

Another way to study the range and efficiency of social participation for a given person is to study the number of groups functioning in his community and to analyze his relations to them.

Kolb and Wileden found 351 interest groups in their 1927 study of the sample area of five counties in central and southern Wisconsin (6, p. 332), as shown on page 432.

By tabulating the special interests of a person and the frequency of affiliations with groups and by noting the role of the person in the several groups, we can statistically measure the range and efficiency of social participation. The study of special interest groups

TABLE 25

TYPES OF INTEREST GROUPS IN FIVE WISCONSIN
COUNTIES (1927)[1]

Professional Forms	Number	Per Cent
Total	351	100.0
Parent Teacher Associations	47	13.4
Farmers' Clubs	46	13.1
Community Clubs	43	12.0
4-H Clubs	34	9.7
Homemakers' Clubs	20	5.7
Co-operative Associations	20	5.7
Spray Rings	14	4.0
Breeders' Associations	10	2.8
Horticultural Societies	8	2.3
Cow Testing Associations	7	2.0
Shipping Associations	7	2.0
Milk Producers' Associations	5	1.4
Miscellaneous (63 names)	91	25.9

[1] J. H. Kolb and E. Brunner: *A Study of Rural Society*, 3rd ed., p. 332.

In terms of interests served or functions performed, these groups
or organizations were further studied with the following results :

TABLE 26

INTERESTS SERVED BY THE SPECIAL INTEREST GROUPS
OR ORGANIZATIONS[1]

Interest Classes	Number	Per Cent
All Organizations[2]	351	100.0
Social enjoyment	252	71.8
Better Farming	115	32.8
Help school and teacher	84	24.0
Better business	59	16.8
Young people's interests	59	16.8
Health and social welfare	41	11.7
Home improvement	40	11.4
Public and civic affairs	15	4.3
General community betterment	13	3.7
Unite locals	5	1.4
Mutual improvement	5	1.4
Help church and preacher	5	1.4

[1] Kolb and Brunner: *Op. cit.*, p. 333.

[2] Obviously the sum of the organizations in the various interest classes greatly
exceeds the total number of organizations, because any one organization may fall
into more than one of the classes.

which makes possible an analysis of social participation also enables us to study how active or moribund, efficient or inefficient, a given community is.

Social participation is the climax of socialization. Social participation for Kaspar Hauser or for the wolf-child Kamala would be impossible except in terms of group-relatedness, except in terms of in-group solidarity, except in terms of participation in the cultural stream. Hence we must distinguish between two types of group-relatedness or social participation. The group-relatedness of the newborn child is of a symbiotic type. The nourishment the child received in the mother's womb and the nourishment it receives from the mother soon after birth are strictly on the biotic level. From the biotic, rather symbiotic, level the child—the individual—works up to the psychological level in his relation to the parents and to the parents' groups. On the psychological level the person is in the vortex of the cultural stream and social participation.

2. Differential Social Participation

In our discussion of class and caste, we pointed out the social phenomenon of different groups having differential access to the goods and services available in a community. The same phenomenon from another angle may be spoken of as differential participation in the socio-cultural stream.

In the twentieth century, we have efficient methods of transportation—automobiles, buses, railroads and airplanes. Most Americans have used one or more of these means of transportation to go from one place to another; indeed, in the summer all America seems to be on wheels going in all directions. And yet there are some Americans who seem to have taken literally the injunction of Laotze and Chuantzu and have not stirred out from their community! The social participation of these American citizens in the American cultural stream is limited.

That inadequate or differential social participation is brought about by isolation is demonstrated in the case of the Five Hollows in the Blue Ridge Mountains, about 150 miles from Washington, D.C.: namely, Briarsville, Rigby, Oakton, Needles, and Colvin, each succeeding Hollow community being farther away from the highway and extending progressively more and more into the mountains. The interesting study of *Hollow Folk* (10, *passim*) by Sherman and Henry reveals the effects of isolation, psychological and cultural as well as geographical, upon the inadequate social participation of the Hollow folks in American national life as of the year 1929, when the survey was completed. As summarized by Ogburn and Nimkoff, the five Hollows show differential social participation in American culture (8, pp. 263–64):

Although Colvin Hollow was only eight miles removed from the highway, it was effectively isolated from the outside world. The investigators had to go up hazardous trails on horseback, and then walk the rest of the way. When they finally reached their destination, they came upon a community that had seldom been visited by outsiders in the period of more than 100 years since the first Anglo-Saxons had come up to settle there. Although Herbert Hoover had a camp only ten miles away, the residents of Colvin Hollow had never heard of him. There were no social agencies of any kind in the community. No one could read or write. The English spoken was quaintly Elizabethan. There were scattered families of from five to eleven members living in mud-plastered one-room huts. For food they depended largely on the little maize and cabbage they grew in small patches. The nearest general store and telephone were at Oakton, five miles away, but these were utilized only very rarely. Without multiplying details, it may be said that the rest of Colvin Hollow was in keeping with this picture of a very rudimentary existence.

As one moves down from Colvin Hollow, the communities become increasingly modern. Needles, for example, has some farms. A few of the citizens are literate. There is a combined school and church in the community. Oakton, next down the line, has a general store with a telephone. Rigby has still more social development; and Briarsville, at the foot of the mountain, is a small farm and saw-mill town. It boasts the usual social institutions of our culture: a fine school, church, stores. There are automobiles, radios, and a daily newspaper.

It may be mentioned in passing that the incidence of neuroses seems to have increased progressively from Colvin out toward the highway and the outside world. "The Colvinites were practically without worries" (8, p. 264).

Differential social participation may be caused not only by isolation but also by class status as well as by personality factors. In our discussion of classes (*supra*, CHAPTER 14), we pointed out that the "school tie" was important in English society, and that the inability of sons of poor families to go to public schools, such as Eton, Harrow and others, deprived them of the opportunity to enter public life. Thus they had differential social participation in the national life of Great Britain. In this way class serves as a specialized form of social isolation, so far as social participation is concerned.

Differential participation as a result of personality factors may be demonstrated from practically everybody's experiences and observations. Of two unemployed workmen, one may choose to spend his time in the public library and the other in the park sunning himself. Different emotional involvements lead different individuals to derive different meanings from the same situation. A speech creates different reactions on different persons. Siblings have each a different status and different duties assigned in the home and the school on the basis of their location in the series, and on the basis of their sex. Two individuals go to the art museum, and each is interested in different exhibits and sees different paintings. Instances could be multiplied. The crucial point to note is that because of our differing backgrounds, differing interests and differing emotional involvements, the range of our social participation varies from individual to individual and from group to group.

3. THE JUKESES, THE EDWARDSES, AND THE KALLIKAKS

With this definition of social participation, we may analyze three classic "studies in heredity"—the Jukeses, the Kallikaks and the Edwardses—to discover whether the hypothesis of hereditary endowments is justified, or whether the hypothesis of differential social participation adequately explains the differing situations. (1, 2, 4, 5, 11).

The classic studies of the Jukes by R. L. Dugdale (1841-83), of the Kallikaks by Henry H. Goddard (1866-   ), and of the Edwardses by A. E. Winship (1845-1933), are hailed by their authors as case studies in heredity.

Dugdale gathered data regarding members of the Jukes family

for the years 1800-75 and found that the family had contributed to delinquency, crime, pauperism and disease in the State of New York, and had cost the State $1,308,000 during those seventy-five years. This conclusion regarding the dysgenic aspect of the Jukes family was reinforced by Dr. Estabrook's study of descendants of the same family in 1915.

Depressed by the gloomy account of the Jukes family, published in 1877, Mr. A. E. Winship undertook to offer the world a more cheerful account of another family, the Edwards family. Published in 1900, Winship's account purported to trace the descendants of Jonathan Edwards (1703-59) with a view to depicting the social efficiency of the Edwards family as contrasted with the social inefficiency of the Jukes family.

The Edwards family album contained college graduates, professors, and presidents; clergymen and physicians; officers of the army and the navy; authors, lawyers, judges, senators, congressmen, governors, et al. Indeed, those who advocate the Edwards family as an illustration of hereditary superiority wax eloquent and tell us in unmeasured terms that there is hardly a department of social progress or of public weal which has not felt "the impulse of this healthy and long-lived family" (11, p. 162).

In 1912 Dr. Henry H. Goddard made a study of the "Kallikak" family. Martin Kallikak Sr. was a revolutionary soldier who, during the period of turbulence, "sowed wild oats," his companion in illicit relations having been presumably a feeble-minded girl. The child of this extramarital relationship, born out of wedlock, was Martin Kallikak Jr., who is said to have passed on the hereditary taint of feeble-mindedness to his progeny. Martin Kallikak Sr., in other words, through illicit relations with a presumably feeble-minded girl, became the founder of a line of defectives—480 in all. Of these 480, 143, according to Dr. Goddard, were definitely feeble-minded; 46 normal, and 291 doubtful, borderline cases. The 480 in turn married and procreated a progeny comprising 1,100, of whom 262 were feeble-minded, 197 normal and 581 doubtful.

Removed from the scene of turbulence, Martin Kallikak Sr. later married a respectable girl of good standing; the 496 descendants of this marriage all turned out good.

The Kallikak family [says Dr. Goddard] presents a natural experiment in heredity. A young man of good family (Martin Kallikak Sr.) becomes through two different women the ancestor of two lines of descendants—the one characterized by thoroughly good, respectable, normal citizenship; the other being equally characterized by mental defect in every generation. This defect was brought in from other families through marriage. In the last generation (the study was made in 1912) it was transmitted through the mother, so that we have here all combinations of transmission, which again proves the hereditary character of the defect. (5, p. 116).

4. AN ANALYSIS OF THE THREE FAMILIES

Dugdale, Winship and Goddard alike maintain that the families studied by them illustrate the significance of the hereditary factor in the efficient or inefficient functioning of the members of those families. And yet interspersed in their writings are statements that suggest a preponderant role of the environment, of social participation, in the efficient functioning of some of the cases studied by them.

The case study of the Jukes family is important because it suggests how harlotry, pauperism, syphilis, crime, disease and idleness tend to perpetuate themselves, forming a constellation of socially undesirable traits. But there is no proof that these traits perpetuate themselves necessarily and always through biological heredity rather than through social inheritance, through social contagion in the nursery. (1, *passim*).

The Kallikak family, like the Jukes family, was caught in the vicious circle of social opprobrium. The role of family traditions and standards as well as of neighborhood judgments is apt to account for the degenerate state of the Kallikak family more satisfactorily than the hypothesis of feeble-mindedness. Before we accept feeble-mindedness, undoubtedly a hereditary unit trait, as a causative factor in the Kallikak case study, we must fully analyze the social complex which presumably produced a feeble-minded progeny.

The normal children of the Kallikak family, according to Dr. Goddard, were all "brought up in good families." (5, p. 61). Here are Dr. Goddard's exact words: "One child of two feeble-minded parents who proves to be normal . . . was taken into a good family and brought up carefully . . . (Indeed) it is certainly significant that the only children in these families that were normal, or at least better than the rest, were (those that had been) brought up in good families." (5, p. 61).

Did the good families have an uncanny wisdom which enabled them to pick out "normal" children in preference to the feeble-minded? Two questions may be legitimately raised: (1) Do the scattered instances of "normal" children raised in other families support the theory of early conditioning as a determinant of feeble-minded behavior on the part of children raised in the Kallikak family? (2) Did the wider range and more wholesome type of social participation provided by the "good families" have something to do with other children turning out to be "normal"?

The Kallikak or the Jukes parents would have had no incentive, in the first place, to educate their child to be normal or superior; and, in the second place, had they the incentive they would have been discouraged by neighborhood gossip.

In contrast to the inhospitable surroundings, social as well as physical, in which the Jukeses and the Kallikaks grew up, the Edwards family grew up in socially approved conditions and had the benefit of wide social participation.

John Stuart Mill (1806-73) illustrates the beneficent results of a high type of social participation. As a boy he used to listen to the learned discourses his father James Mill (1773-1836) used to hold in his home with the leading lights of those days. Only on the basis of specialized motivation and social participation can we understand John Stuart Mill's testimony (7, p. 30):

In all these things (quickness of apprehension, accurate and re-tentive memory, active and energetic character), I am rather below than above par; what I could do assuredly could be done by any boy or girl of average capacity and healthy physical constitution.

Let us affirm three propositions: (1) That there are individual differences in native endowment at birth; (2) That feeble-minded-ness as a unit-trait is transmitted biologically; (3) That the influence of hereditary factors, *uninfluenced by the environment, i.e., by social participation*, in determining the whole of the subsequent life of the child cannot be accepted as a valid hypothesis.

To speak of heredity versus environment, of nature versus nurture, is to misstate the problem. The best heredity would be of no avail to the child if, for instance, he were at birth removed from the psycho-social environment of man's cultural setup ; separated from the moulding influences of the environment, he is bound to turn out to be a feral man if he should at all survive ! The study of the Jukes family convinced Dugdale that "heredity (such as that of the Jukes) depends upon the permanence of the environment, and that a change in the environment may produce an entire change in the career which, in the course of greater or less length of time according to varying circumstances, will produce an actual change in the character of the individual." (2, p. 113).

5. SIGNIFICANCE OF TWINS FOR METHODOLOGY

The Austrian monk, Gregor Johann Mendel (1822-1884) worked in his monastery garden, quietly and methodically, from 1857 to 1865, crossing different varieties of peas and studying the differences through several generations. "In 1865 he read an account of his experiments to the society of naturalists in the town of Brno (Brunn), and this was published in the journal of the society in 1866. This journal did not have a wide circulation although it was sent to a number of libraries in several countries. If any scientists read it, they paid no attention to it, for this article, which contained the gist of the modern theory of heredity, lay unnoticed until 1900. Then 16 years after Mendel's death, three other European scientists independently made a similar discovery, unearthed Mendel's forgotten account, and it suddenly became known throughout the world. That was the origin of the science of genetics, which, from that sudden beginning of 1900, has progressed with great speed." (3, p. 42).

Mendel crossed green and yellow peas, tall and short peas, round and wrinkled peas ; from the results observed he formulated the famous principles of unit-traits, recessive and dominant unit-traits, and the Mendelian law of inheritance : Bb × Bb = BB Bb Bb bb. But what Mendel was able to do with peas we are not able to do with human beings, since our cultural category does not permit us to experiment with or upon human beings (except with their free consent).

But an experimental design for the study of heredity and its influence has been made to order for us, so to say, in the existence of twins. Twins are of two kinds, two-egg twins and one-egg twins. The two-egg twins are known as fraternal twins and the one-egg twins are known as identical twins. The fraternal twins are merely a pair of babies who happen to be born at the same time, showing the same hereditary differences as ordinary brothers and sisters. Identical twins, on the other hand, spring from a single fertilized egg which early in its development gets split into two parts and, therefore, passes on the identical hereditary endowment to both.

This nature-made experimental design has been studied by scientists and laymen alike. Professors Dunn and Dobzhansky have summarized the results of scientific researches in an eminently fair manner (3, pp. 27–30):

Physical Traits in Twins

Newman, Freeman, and Holzinger made careful measurements and observations on a variety of physical characters (height, weight, head shape, fingerprints, etc.) in their twins. They also submitted them to a series of psychological tests designed to measure their intelligence, personality, and achievement. A part of their results is summarized in the following table, which gives the average differences between the twins of a pair in various traits:

TABLE 27

AVERAGE DIFFERENCES BETWEEN MEMBERS OF TWIN-PAIRS

	One-Egg Twins Reared Together	One-Egg Twins Reared Apart	Two-Egg Twins Reared Together
Standing height (in centimeters)	1.6	1.8	4.4
Weight (in lbs.)	4.0	9.9	10.0
Head length (in millimeters)	2.6	2.2	6.2
Head width (in millimeters)	2.2	2.8	4.2
Intelligence Quotient (Binet)	5.3	8.2	9.9
Stanford Achievement (in months)	6.4	16.3	11.6

It can be seen that the one-egg twins are, regardless of whether they were reared together or apart, more nearly similar in body height than are the two-egg twins. The average difference in height amounts to 1.6 cm. in the one-egg twins reared together, and to 1.8 cm. when the twins are reared apart. The two-egg twins, although reared together, differed appreciably more—4.4 cm. The same is true for the length and width of the head, the number of finger ridges, and some other traits. In fact, the average difference in head length happens to be even slightly less in the one-egg twins reared apart than in those reared together. But notice that the one-egg twins reared apart differed in weight about as much as the two-egg reared together.

What do these observations mean? Remember that the one-egg twins have similar heredities, regardless of whether they are reared together or apart. Two-egg twins differ in heredity as much as do brothers and sisters born at different times. Therefore, the greater differences found between two-egg as compared with one-egg twins can be safely ascribed to heredity. On the other hand, when the twins reared apart differ on the average more than do twins reared together, it is the environment which is responsible. We can see that different traits are influenced to different extents by heredity and by environment. In physical features, such as eye and hair color, head shape, or height, one-egg twins remained extremely similar even when separated at birth and brought up in different environments. But one-egg twins may become rather different in height. Environment can modify the weight of a person relatively more easily than it can modify his height or his head shape. But it does not follow that heredity has nothing to do with one's weight. Surely, you know persons who find it difficult to "keep their weight down" despite keeping themselves on "reducing" diets, and other persons who cannot gain much weight even on "fattening" foods.

Retention of great similarities amongst separated one-egg twins produced some dramatic situations. A girl of sixteen named Edith was accosted by a young man: "Hello, Fay, how do you happen to be so far from home?" Suspecting an attempt at flirtation, Edith repulsed the young man. But he was a persistent young man who trusted his memory for faces, so in another city he found the real Fay and arranged for her to go and see Edith. Edith met her and was, as she said, "shocked to see myself getting off the train." These girls proved to be one-egg twins separated at birth and adopted by different families.

Mental Traits and Achievement in Twins

There is also the story of identical twin brothers both of whom became, during World War II, generals in the U.S. Air Force, although they had not served in the same military units and had made their careers independently. Can one conclude from this instance that it was the hereditary endowment of these men which was responsible for their similar achievements in the same field of activity? Such a conclusion is quite unwarranted. It is possible that the twin brother of some other general still serves as a sergeant, or that he has become tired of army life altogether.

Newman, Freeman, and Holzinger compared the mental abilities of twins by means of various "intelligence tests." On one of these I.Q. tests (Binet's) the average difference between one-egg twins reared together amounted to 5.3 "points," but when they were reared apart, the difference increased to 8.2 "points." Two-egg twins reared together showed an average difference of 9.9 "points." It follows that *mental ability, though undoubtedly influenced by heredity, is less fixed and more liable to modification by environment than most physical traits.* In different achievement tests, supposedly measuring educational performance, the role of environment proved to be greater still. The Stanford achievement test showed the average difference between one-egg twins reared apart to be even greater than that between two-egg twins reared together. In spelling, the one-egg twins were more alike than the two-egg ones, while in arithmetic environment was much more important. In tests of motor ability and emotional balance, environment assumed the major role, more than half of the differences between twins being due to experience, training, and other environmental factors and less than half to heredity. (*Italics ours.*)

It must also be pointed out that the environments of separated twins studied by Newman, Freeman and Holzinger were not very different. The twins were reared in the same country and generally in a similar class of society and exposed to the same educational system. We do not know how different the twins might have been if one of them were to grow up, say, in a city slum and the other in surroundings of comfort and refinement; or else, if one were to grow up in an American town and the other in a tribe of Asiatic nomads. In fact, where the differences in living conditions were most marked, real differences in personality, in scores on mental tests, and in educational achievement did develop among the twins actually examined, while their physical traits remained closely alike.

6. FUNG KWOK-KEUNG AND PAUL FUNG, JR.

While the wistful thought of Dunn and Dobzhansky regarding one of the twins growing up in an American town and the other in a tribe of Asiatic nomads has not been fully realized, we do have an experimental design illustrating the crucial role of social participation in the lives of two men, an American-Chinese—Fung Kwok-Keung born Joseph Rhinehart—and a Chinese-American, Paul Fung, Jr.

Amram Scheinfeld thus relates the story of these two men (9, pp. 505–07, adapted):

No experiment could be more convincing than the actual stories of two young men now living in New York: one, an American-Chinese; the other, a Chinese-American. Fung Kwok-Keung, born Joseph Rhinehart (of German-American stock), at the age of 2, was adopted by a Chinese man on Long Island and three years later taken to China, where he was reared in a small town (Nam Hoy, near Canton) with the family of his foster father until he was 20. Returning then to New York (in 1938), he was so completely Chinese in all but appearance that he had to be given "Americanization" as well as English lessons to adapt him to his new life. A few years later, after the outbreak of World War II, he was drafted into the American army and sent to Italy. In many ways he was alien to the other American soldiers and tried continuously to be transferred to service in China, but army red tape held him fast in Italy until the war's end. Back again in New York, Rhinehart-Fung at this writing works as a compositor on a Chinese newspaper (an intricate job which few but Chinese could handle), and still speaks English very imperfectly, with a Chinese accent.

Now for a remarkably opposite case, that of a *racially* Chinese but *culturally* American young man: Paul Fung, Jr., another war veteran and now a comic-strip artist. Of second-generation American-born Chinese stock, Paul, like his parents before him, was educated with and lived among White Americans all his life. His thinking, behavior, speech, outlook and sense of humor are completely like that of any other American (and no profession requires this more than does that of an American comic-strip artist!). He has known little of the Chinese language and customs. So it was with the thought of becoming better acquainted with the Chinese people that, after enlistment in the air force at the beginning of World War II and a year of training, he asked for assignment to the American Chinese unit which had just been organized.

But Paul soon found that he was a stranger among the others of Chinese stock. He couldn't understand them properly ; his language and thinking were different ; and—no small matter to a G.I.—there was a food problem, for he preferred American food and couldn't adjust to having Chinese food served him at virtually every meal. Most of the Chinese-American soldiers thought Paul was "putting on an act." Difficulties and conflicts ensued, and he had to seek companionship among White G.I.s from a near-by camp. His predicament was never fully realized by the military authorities, and it was only the misfortune of his father's death, calling him home just as the Chinese unit was about to go overseas, which led to his transfer to a regular unit of the air force. (Subsequently Paul served in the Pacific area for three years, being among the first air-force men to fly over Iwo Jima and Okinawa, and in the atomic-bomb flight over Hiroshima.)

Linking up these two stories, the author (Mr. Amram Scheinfeld) arranged for Joseph Rhinehart (Fung Kwok-Keung) and Paul Fung, Jr., to meet at his studio early in 1950 (as shown in the photograph, *supra* CHAPTER 16). After ten minutes with one another the same thought occurred to both: They were *culturally transposed*. Said Joseph, spontaneously, "He should be like me and I should be like him!" To climax the meeting, a further remarkable fact was brought out. You may have already noted that both men have the same family name, "Fung" (which in Joseph's case is given first, in the traditional Chinese way). So, for a real "believe it or not," it developed that *Paul Fung's grandfather had come from the very same town near Canton where Joseph had been reared and was a relative of Joseph's foster father!*

There may be just as much reason believe that a Negro child, reared among Chinese, would be more Chinese than what we think of as "Negro" in behavior, or that a child of aristocratic European parents, lost and reared among jungle Africans, might grow up with all the traits of a typical cannibal. We might make similar comparisons in the case of an Eskimo child reared by a Hindu, or an Italian child reared by a Swede, or a Turkish child reared by a Boston Cabot.

7. SUMMARY AND CONCLUSIONS

To sum up: Gua could not develop human nature in spite of social participation because she lacked the original nature of man.

Anna and Isabelle in their early years behaved as subnormal children because of "extreme isolation," because of inadequate social participation. (Cf. supra, CHAPTER 6). From his childhood onward, John Stuart Mill experienced rich social participation in terms of listening to learned discussions on politics, economics, history and philosophy his father, James Mill, used to have in his home with his distinguished contemporaries.

The efficiency of the Edwards family may likewise be traced to enriched social participation. While feeble-mindedness could very well have led to inefficiency in the functioning of an individual from the Jukes or the Kallikak family, the hypothesis of social participation must be given some weight. The sociologist accepts the proposition, unqualifiedly, that a child with amentia or lack of mentality could never be normal even with the best environment for social participation. By the same token, it may be asserted that the behavior of borderline or doubtful cases of "feeblemindedness" would depend upon the type of environment and social participation available to the child.

Intensive studies of identical twins have been carried out according to the canons of experimental science. The results show that whereas physical traits remain unaffected when twins are reared apart, even in the case of identical twins social participation plays a major role in the development of motor ability, emotional balance and mental capability.

Finally, the cultural transposition between Paul Fung, Jr., and Fung Kwok-Keung illustrates the crucial role of the superorganic environment and of social participation in the moulding of human personality.

REFERENCES

1. CLARENCE DARROW: "The Edwardses and the Jukeses." The American Mercury, Vol. 6, No. 21, pp. 147–157, October 1925.
2. R. L. DUGDALE: "The Jukes": A Study in Crime, Pauperism, Disease, and Heredity. New York: Putnam's Sons, 3rd ed. rev., 1877.
3. L. C. DUNN & TH. DOBZHANSKY: Heredity, Race and Society, rev. ed. (A Mentor Book, ninth printing, 1956). New York: The American Library of World Literature, 1952.
4. A. H. ESTABROOK: The Jukes in 1915. Washington: The Carnegie Institution of Washington, 1916.
5. H. H. GODDARD: The Kallikak Family. New York: Macmillan, 1912.

6. J. H. KOLB & E. DE S. BRUNNER: *A Study of Rural Society,* 3rd ed. Boston: Houghton Mifflin Co., 1946.

7. JOHN S. MILL: *Autobiography.* New York: Henry Holt & Co., 1874.

8. W. F. OGBURN & M. F. NIMKOFF: *Sociology,* 2nd ed. Boston: Houghton Mifflin Co., 1950.

9. A. SCHEINFELD: *The New You and Heredity.* Philadelphia: J. B. Lippincott Co., 1950.

10. M. SHERMAN & T. R. HENRY: *Hollow Folk.* New York: Thomas Y. Crowell Co., 1933.

11. A. E. WINSHIP: *Jukes-Edwards: A Study in Education and Heredity.* Harrisburg, Pa.: R. L. Myers & Co., 1900.

SPECIAL NOTE NO. 1: Now and then doubts have been cast by some writers upon the authenticity of Dugdale's story of the Jukes family. The latest criticism of this sort is to be found in the article, entitled "The Juke Myth" by Samuel Hopkins Adams in *The Saturday Review of Literature,* April 2, 1955, pp. 13ff. Mr. Adams's criticism of some of Dugdale's methods of investigation is relevant; after all, R. L. Dugdale (1841-1883) lived at a time when sociological methods of investigation and tools of analysis had not been fully devised. That Mr. Dugdale may have sometimes jumped to hasty conclusions on the basis of inadequate data may be admitted, but it is absurd to maintain that no such family as the Jukes (obviously a pseudonym) ever existed.

The student is urged to read Mr. Adams's article in order to discover the many pitfalls confronting the social scientist.

SPECIAL NOTE NO. 2: The case history of most of the so-called child prodigies and geniuses reveals the startling fact that each of them had a specially stimulating and encouraging home environment. We have referred to John Stuart Mill and the special advantages he had as a child. The case histories of James Thomson (1822-1892) and William Thomson, better known as Lord Kelvin (1824-1907), suggest that both of them had been provided by their father with an environment hospitable to intellectual growth. James Thomson made significant contributions to physics and engineering, and Lord Kelvin's many contributions to science are known the world over. Karl Witte (1800-83), who received the Ph.D. degree in mathematics at the age of fourteen from the University of Giessen and the Doctor of Laws degree from Heidelberg University at the age of sixteen, was specially trained by his parents, Pastor and Frau Witte.

The literature of child prodigies needs to be studied and evaluated with scientific tools of analysis.

SPECIAL NOTE NO. 3: The present writer is inclined to the view that the hypothesis of differential association as the cause of crime, set forth by the late Professor Edwin H. Sutherland (1883-1950), becomes more meaningful when presented as the hypothesis of differential participation.

CHAPTER 27

COOPERATION AND OPPOSITION

1. Association and Groupation

THE getting together of a number of individuals in order to achieve an objective involves the process of association. The functional group, too, is referred to by the term association. To avoid confusion between association as the process of getting together and association as the end-result of getting together, that is to say, association as the functional group, some social scientists have suggested that we reserve the term association to connote either the process or the end-result. If the term association stood for a functional group, then we should call the process of getting together by some other term, such as sociation or groupation or groupalization. It is difficult to say whether such a consensus could be secured among sociologists; but the student should note the dual sense in which the term association has been used thus far in sociological literature.

2. Co-Existence of Cooperation and Competition

The reciprocal relation between cooperation and competition among individuals of any given species, especially among members of the human species "congregated and dwelling in any given region," is best set forth by the late Professor Giddings (*supra*, CHAPTERS 5 and 12). In a given region, with specific physiographic characteristics, including food supplies, an "area of characterization" is formed; and human beings dwelling therein tend to "become increasingly alike," and to develop solidarity on the basis of "consciousness of kind."

(In this way, says Giddings) the first two conditions of social life . . . , namely, grouping and substantial resemblance are provided. But since they are alike, individuals of the same variety or race, so brought together in one habitat, necessarily want the same things, and, as often as not, try in like ways to get them, reacting in one

447

manner to any stimulus that incites all of them, or to a common situation. They compete in obtaining things which each is able to get by his own efforts, or (unconsciously or consciously) they combine their efforts to obtain things that no one could get unaided. In either case their interests and activities are not altogether harmonious and easily become antagonistic. Competition tends to engender conflicts inimical to group cohesion; but in aggregations of animals or of human beings, in which individuals generally are substantially similar in behavior and approximately equal in strength, conflicts are self-limiting in a degree. An equilibrium of "live and let live" is arrived at, which makes gregarious life possible for animals and conscious association possible for human beings. (7, pp. 15–16.)

Thus it is evident that wherever there are human beings living together—and live together they must or perish—they become involved simultaneously in two contradictory processes, namely, cooperation and opposition.

3. TYPES OF COOPERATION

Cooperation is manifested in conscious association, in the activity of a functional group; it involves the marshalling of forces to achieve an objective, jointly desired or agreed upon. Slave and master cooperate in a real sense, but their motivations and end-results differ. Cooperation between equals rests upon agreement. It is this form of cooperation, cooperation among free men, that we shall analyze.

Cooperation is achieved either (1) through reinforcement or (2) through division of labor. When four or five men exert themselves to move a boulder or a tree from a highway, their cooperation is in the form of reinforcement. In the Ford factory, on the other hand, hundreds of workers are engaged in working together, each at his assigned task, in order to produce an automobile every few minutes, through division of labor.

The American industrial society of our day rests upon two basic principles: (1) cooperation involving:

(a) specialization of function,
(b) division of labor,

(c) standardized replaceable parts,
(d) credit (involving faith in the bona fides of the other);

and (2) competition involving:

(a) struggle to outproduce and undersell the other,
(b) contractual relations between manufacturer, wholesaler, retailer; between employer and employee,
(c) motivation to make profit by serving the needs of the consumer,
(d) struggle to outshine one's neighbors, "keeping up with the Joneses," conspicuous consumption.

Contract is the essence of modern industrialism, of American capitalism, within the context of the "democratic framework" of our society. In the Middle Ages status governed socio-economic relations. By contrast, in modern capitalistic society we secure cooperation through contract, individual and collective.

The collective bargaining right of our unions demonstrates cooperation at several levels and depths: (a) intense loyalty among workers to the union, (b) the union agent or representative negotiating for all the members of the union, (c) labor and management negotiation—cooperating to settle differences of opinion—in order to achieve cooperation in the productive enterprise of the corporation. After the negotiations are successfully concluded, employers and employees join together, according to the contract, to carry out the terms of the contract in a corporate manner—i.e., in a manner as though the two classes were parts of one body or corpus.

Corporate activity transcends simple cooperative activity in terms of the power released and the gain made. Political activities of a democratic State are of the nature of corporate activity. Indeed, the activities of any Mahajana demonstrate the vigor and dynamic of a corporate body.

One other significant form of cooperation that needs to be analyzed is collaboration. Two authors collaborate, i.e., cooperate as equals, knowingly, for achieving a commonly shared objective. Political collaboration has, however, come to have a special meaning since World War II. A collaborator in politics is a "fall guy," a "stooge" for an overlord, a subordinate toeing the line laid down by his protector and benefactor. In this sense, communists in every country outside of Russia are collaborators of Russian communists. And fellow travellers are collaborators of collaborators.

4. THE GROWTH OF THE COOPERATIVE MOVEMENT

The best illustration of cooperation in the field of economic processes—production, distribution and consumption—is to be found in the cooperative movement. From humble beginnings in 1844 to a worldwide network of cooperatives—that is the story of consumer cooperation. "The objects and plans of this society," wrote the Rochdale Pioneers, "are to form arrangements for the pecuniary benefit and improvement of the social and domestic condition of its members." The humble beginnings of the Rochdale Pioneers with their first grocery store on Toad Lane have been well described by Dr. Harry W. Laidler (3, pp. 3–4, quoted):

It was a Sunday afternoon in November, 1843. The place was Rochdale, England, a growing industrial town hard by capitalism's birthplace, the city of Manchester. The times were dark with misery for the nation's workers. They seemed that afternoon especially dark to Rochdale's flannel weavers, who had just emerged from an unsuccessful strike. Twenty-eight of them were gathered together in the Chartists' Reading Room to discuss what could be done.

Some of the twenty-eight were Chartists who had been fighting with might and main for the political rights of the workers, some were Owenite Socialists whose vision was a cooperative brotherhood. Some were just plain, unphilosophical weavers chained hand and foot by the credit system of the "truck" store and by the wage system—then at its worst.

Many were the remedial schemes proposed. One found favor. It was to start, as soon as capital permitted, a cooperative store of the workers, by the workers, for the workers, which immediately might free its members from dependence on exploiting merchants and from the enslavement of the credit system; which ultimately might lead to the abolition of the wage system, and "so arrange the powers of production, distribution, education and government as to create a self-supporting home colony."

Their dream seemed indeed Utopian. The dreamers were poor. They were unschooled. And who had ever heard of the working class controlling its own industrial affairs? But these dreamers not only had vision, they also had their share of good horse sense and bulldog resolution.

Two pence a week this little band resolved to put aside for the venture. The two pence gradually grew to $140, and with that a dilapidated old store in the back street known as Toad Lane, Rochdale, was hired. The Rochdale Pioneers, as they were called, bought a few packages of flour, sugar, butter and oatmeal with which to supply the store, and finally got up sufficient courage to fling open the doors amid the jeers of surrounding storekeepers and the cat calls of street urchins. Mondays and Saturday nights the store was kept open. Its first week's sale amounted to the munificent sum of $10. One member acted as salesman, one as cashier, another as secretary and the fourth as treasurer. Tenderly the members coaxed along their small establishment. Many a conference was held over its probable demise.

It did not die, however. To the surprise and wrath of merchants and the joy of the few faithful, it actually grew.

The success of the pioneer retail grocery store led to the establishment of other retail stores and to the organization of a wholesale cooperative, in order to supply the retail co-ops. The success of the wholesale co-ops led the consumer cooperative movement into the field of production. Thus producers' co-ops were organized in order to produce goods, such as bicycles, for supply to wholesale and retail co-ops. Today cooperatives are to be found not only in the basic unit, the consumers' grocery store, but also in wholesale trade, in manufacturing establishments, in housing, and in banking and insurance.

In 1942, there were in existence in Great Britain and Ireland " over a thousand cooperative societies of all kinds, operating 12,000 stores, with a membership of nearly 9,000,000 and a retail trade of over a billion and a third. At that time the co-ops in their retail, wholesale, and production sections had a working staff of 330,000. The cooperatives, handling about 13 per cent of the retail trade of the country, were returning over $100,000,000 to their members in net savings." (10, p. 684.)

The cooperative movement, since its beginning in England in December 1844, has made tremendous strides on the continent of Europe, especially in the Scandinavian countries. Sweden's economy may well be said to be a co-op economy, with slight leeway toward state socialism and private capitalism. In 1936, Marquis W. Childs brought to the attention of America and the world the success story of the cooperative movement in Scandinavia through his book, *Sweden: The Middle Way* (5, *passim*).

In the United States, both consumers' and producers' co-ops have been flourishing since World War I. The consumers' co-ops are strongest among American citizens of Scandinavian and Central European background. The producers' co-ops and marketing co-ops on the Pacific Coast are very strong and practically control the supply of "sunkist" oranges, "diamond" walnuts, etc.

The reason for the slow growth of the consumers' cooperative movement in the United States is easy to understand. The American propensity to trade on credit and to have groceries and other articles delivered at home stands in the way of a vigorous growth of the cooperative movement. Then, too, the very narrow margin between cost and sale price in our chain stores does not make the citizen mad enough, or eager enough, to go out and organize a co-op.

The classic stories of the Scandinavian co-op breaking the monopoly of the German bulb industry in Europe and of the Scandinavian-Americans, through their Franklin Cooperative Society (Dairy) in Minneapolis successfully overcoming their competitors, illustrate how team-work and cooperation, grounded in high idealism as well as good business sense, can triumph against seemingly overwhelming odds. (5, pp. 35–42; 6, pp. 581–88).

5. PRINCIPLES OF THE CONSUMERS' COOPERATIVE MOVEMENT

The co-op operates with the same efficiency as does the corporation. Both the co-op and the corporation derive the surplus increment of power from their inherent nature as organic collectivity—they are both Mahajanas and operate as such.

But there are differences, significant differences. The co-op is oriented toward human values while the corporation is oriented toward money values. For instance, while in the business corporation a shareholder's votes are determined by the number of shares he owns, in the co-op each shareholder—regardless of the number of shares purchased—has but one vote.

The seven basic principles of the consumers' co-op may be set forth in the words of Dr. James P. Warbasse, President of the Cooperative League of America from 1916 until 1941 (3, pp. 23–24, quoted):

1. One vote only for each member.
2. Capital to receive interest at not more than the legal or minimum current rate.
3. Surplus savings (or "profit") to be returned as savings returns (or "dividends") in proportion to the patronage of each individual, or to be employed for the general social good of the society.
4. Business to be done for cash or its equivalent.
5. Goods to be sold at current market price—not at cost.
6. Education in the principles and aims of Co-operation, with the view of expansion into larger fields, always to be carried on in connection with the enjoyment of the immediate economic advantages.
7. Federation as soon as possible with the nearest Co-operative societies, with the ultimate purpose of national and world Co-operation.

6. COOPERATIVE COMMUNITIES

Another form of cooperation we may briefly touch upon is manifested in cooperative communities. Some of the early Christians, soon after the Crucifixion of Jesus, sold all their goods and lived in small cooperative communities, owning their worldly goods in common—a sort of primitive communism. Monasteries and nunneries, Buddhist, Hindu, Jain, Christian, exemplify cooperative community living. It was as a member of such a cooperative community—the monastery—that Mendel made his great contribution to science.

Religiously oriented cooperative communities have flourished in every age in most high cultures. Their success has been predicated upon the intensity of the members' loyalty to the religious faith and its principles. Secularly oriented cooperative communities, however idealistically motivated, have had a checkered career and have sooner or later disappeared from the social scene.

Two famous experiments in collective living, attempted in the United States, may be described: New Harmony, Indiana, Colony (1824-27) of Robert Owen (1771-1858), and Brook Farm at West Roxbury, near Boston (1840-46).

Robert Owen, living in the period between the American and French Revolutions and the eve of the Civil War in America, experienced the zest and optimism of the Americans on the one hand and of the French Encyclopedists on the other. He conceived the notion that the highest good of the individual as well as of society could be achieved by abolishing all forms of private property. Convinced that the industrial society of his day had failed to solve the problem of distribution, he advocated the establishment of communities in which both labor and distribution would be equal. "With means thus ample to procure wealth with ease and pleasure to all, none will be so unwise as to have the trouble and care of individual property. To divide property among individuals in unequal proportions or to hoard it for individual purposes will be perceived as useless and injurious as it would be to divide air or light into unequal quantities for different individuals, or that they should hoard them." (10, p. 94, quoted).

In order to put some of his ideas into practice, Owen bought in 1824 for £30,000 the Rappist community at Harmony, Indiana, containing 30,000 acres of land, and renamed it New Harmony. He came to this country, he said, to introduce an entirely "new state of society," a society from which ignorance and selfishness would be banished, a society which "shall gradually unite all interests into one, and remove all causes for contest between individuals" (10, p. 94). In the second year of the experiment, Owen introduced his pet notion of equal compensation to all regardless of effort or productivity. Equality of pay for equal time spent on production was later to be expounded by Karl Marx, hugged to their bosom by socialists and communists, and eventually to be discarded by the communist rulers of Soviet Russia as a result of the fiery ordeal of everyday living. Most of Owen's money exhausted, the New Harmony experiment in cooperative living failed after three years.

Brook Farm is justly famous for the great men and women associated with it. The members of the New England School of Transcendentalism were shining stars in the literary and philosophical firmament of the New World. They were called Transcendentalists because they believed in "an order of truth that transcends the sphere of the external senses"; because they believed in the supremacy or transcendence of mind over matter. The Transcendentalists counted among their members George Ripley, William Ellery Channing, John S. Dwight, Margaret Fuller, Ralph Waldo Emerson, Henry David Thoreau, Nathaniel Hawthorne, and Elizabeth P. Peabody. The interests of the Transcendentalists ranged from literature and philosophy (especially Hindu) to social problems.

It was in quest of a better and more just social order that the Brook Farm experiment in cooperative living was launched in 1840 by George Ripley, Unitarian minister, and his co-workers. Resigning his post as Unitarian minister, Mr. Ripley

chose a 220-acre milk farm at West Roxbury, near Boston, for his proposed experiment. A group of about twenty—including Mr. and Mrs. Ripley, Dwight, Hawthorne, and William Allen—went there to live, and called it "The Brook Farm Institute for Agriculture and Education." Their ideal was a noble one. They desired to substitute "a system of brotherly cooperation for one of selfish competition; to secure for our children, and to those who may be trusted to our care, the benefits of the highest physical, intellectual, and moral education which, in the present state of human knowledge, the resources at our command will permit; to institute an attractive, efficient, and productive system of industry; to prevent the exercise of worldly anxiety by the competent supply of our necessary wants; to diminish the desire for excessive accumulation by making the acquisition of individual property subservient to upright and disinterested uses; to guarantee to each other the means of physical support and of spiritual progress, and thus to impart a greater freedom, simplicity, truthfulness, refinement, and moral dignity to our mode of life."

In pursuance of these aims they maintained a uniform rate of compensation for all labor; a maximum workday of ten hours; free support of children under the age of ten years, of old persons, and of the sick; and free education, medical care, and use of library and bath. They furthermore stipulated that all persons be provided with employment according to their taste and ability.

The community's administration was entrusted to four departments: General Direction, Agriculture, Education, and Finance. In its school an unusually wide range of sciences and arts were taught. While the working hours were many and leisure was scarce, the residents enjoyed an attractive social life. Dances, music, and literary and scientific discussions were provided for the leisure hours, and such visitors as Greeley, Brisbane, the Channings, and Theodore Parker paid frequent calls.

In 1844, following the National Convention of Fourieristic Associations, Brook Farm became a full-fledged Fourieristic experiment, was renamed the "Brook Farm Phalanx," and came to be the very center of Fourieristic activity in the United States. The official organ of the Fourierists, *The Harbinger*, was transferred to the Farm, in editorial charge of Ripley, Dana, and Dwight. Lowell, Whittier, George William Curtis, Parke Godwin, Higginson, Storey, Channing, Greeley, and others contributed to it. And from this center journeyed many a distinguished lecturer to tell the good tidings to other parts of the land.

In 1846 the Farm was beginning to prosper financially, and the residents were living in anticipation of the completion of the unitary phalanx building, the most pretentious of their edifices. But just as the structure was nearing completion, an accidental fire broke out, and the building was burned to the ground. Coming as this misfortune did at a time when the movement was waning in other parts of the country, it proved fatal to the experiment, and in the autumn little of Brook Farm remained but a memory of noble ideals and self-sacrificing devotion. (10, pp. 105-06).

Social life on Brook Farm must have been, as befitted the Transcendentalists, full of sweetness, civility and cooperation; but that it was entirely devoid of clashes and cleavages cannot be affirmed. The obverse process of opposition must find expression even in the midst of a deliberately designed cooperative community.

Ichabod Morton resigned after serving as a trustee for only five months because he felt that sentiment rather than good business judgment governed the practical affairs of the Farm. And Nathaniel Hawthorne, after five months of farm work, asked to be released from the furrows. "Is it a praiseworthy matter that I have spent five golden months in providing food for cows and horses?" he asks in his diary, and answers: "It is not so." Hawthorne was relieved of manual work and given certain executive tasks, but the action, while pleasing to Hawthorne, was displeasing to some of the others, who resented the discrimination. Particularly illuminating is a comment made by one of the students in the school, George Curtis. In writing to his father, he said, having the school in view, "No wise man is long a reformer, for wisdom sees plainly that growth is steady, sure, and neither condemns nor rejects what is or has been. Reform is organized distrust." (12, p. 167).

Russian farm collectives and Kolkhozes or State Farms are forms of cooperative community living, but imposed from on high by the communist dictatorship government. What kinds of emotional stresses and strains are experienced by the members of the farm collectives and the Kolkhozes it is difficult to determine. If the members of these cooperative communities be dominated by a zeal bordering on religious fervor and by an overriding commitment to the communist order of society, emotional stresses and strains should be at a minimum. But whether these conditions are fulfilled we have no way of knowing.

Gandhi's experiments in cooperative community living, two in South Africa and two in India, were all successful, because of the commitment to the ideals and purposes of those experiments on the part of Gandhi and his followers. The story of Phoenix Farm, near Durban (1904); of Tolstoy Farm, near Johannesburg (1910); of Satyagraha Ashram at Sabarmati, near Ahmedabad (1916) and of Sevagram, near Wardha (1936), has been recounted by the author elsewhere (11, pp. 23–29, 31, 59–60).

The Amana Colony in Iowa illustrates how a cooperative community remains a close-knit, communal association so long as religious commitment is strong. When secularism began to replace religious commitment, the Amana Colony tended to give up its cooperative communistic way of life. Gradually the cooperative became a corporation, at first selling stock among members only but later among strangers as well.

It appears that cooperation can flourish unhindered by its reciprocal process, competition, only when there is an overriding commitment. But the humdrum everyday life of our workaday world does not require nor does it call forth deep commitment on the part of any of us. Hence competition is inevitable. Therefore, to an analysis of the process of competition we now turn.

7. OPPOSITION: COMPETITION AND CONFLICT

Cooperation and opposition constitute a continuum of human relations at extreme ends:

CHART 23

COOPERATION-OPPOSITION: A CONTINUUM

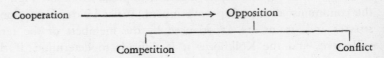

Opposition itself may be subdivided into two categorical processes, competition and conflict.

Competition is more basic in the social process than conflict. Competition is impersonalized struggle among resembling creatures for goods and services which are scarce or limited in quantity. There is no competition for sunshine and air which are unlimited and available to all under identical conditions. But there is competition for five civil service positions among the fifty candidates appearing for the civil service examination, or among the thirty candidates successful in the examination.

Just as cooperation is a continuing process, so is competition, as pointed out by Giddings. Both cooperation and competition arise in the ecological setting and are carried on in the field of social, political, economic, religious, racial, international relations. On the one hand, we have human beings, all basically resembling one another, each with insatiable wants, and on the other hand we have nature which, in spite of its many bounties, is niggardly. Hence people compete for the choice location, for the well-paying job, for status and prestige, etc.

Conflict differs from competition in that while competition, like cooperation, is a general or generalized and continuing process, conflict is a specific event in time. Cooperation and competition can march forward together simultaneously, albeit under different banners; but neither puts an end to the other. Conflict does put an end to cooperation—at least temporarily.

Conflict is opposition or struggle involving (*a*) an emotional attitude of hostility as well as (*b*) violent interference with one's autonomous choice, i.e., violent interference with one's choice or accomplishment of the chosen objective. Conflict may arise between person and person, between person and group, between group and group. War exemplifies conflict *par excellence*.

Conflict is episodic, competition is continuous. Competition is impersonal, conflict becomes personalized. Conflict is a temporary interruption in the reciprocal processes of cooperation and competition.

Rivalry stands midway between competition and conflict:

$$Competition \longrightarrow Rivalry \longrightarrow Conflict$$

Rivalry comes into play when competition becomes personalized without involving emotional hostility.

8. THE CONFLICT SCHOOL OF THOUGHT

The episodic, spectacular nature of conflict has impressed thinkers in every high culture. The Hindu philosophers spoke of Matsya-Nyaya, "the logic of the fish," the larger fish devouring the smaller ones. Thomas Hobbes (1588-1679) premised a presocial state abounding in war of each against all. Charles R. Darwin (1809-82) postulated that new species originated through selection of the fittest in the struggle for existence. Karl Marx (1818-1883) evolved the theory of class struggle which ended "either in a revolutionary reconstitution of society at large or in the common ruin of the contending classes." Ludwig Gumplowicz (1838-1909) reared his system of sociology on the hypothesis of conflict as the central fact in intergroup relations—*der Rassenkampf*.

In our day Marxists and racialists may be best characterized as "social Darwinists," as those who advocate the triumph, respectively, of the "underprivileged" and the "superior" through antagonism and conflict.

9. AVOIDANCE: THE MILDEST FORM OF CONFLICT

Avoidance has been defined as "the purposive restriction of interstimulation" (4, p. 294). Avoidance in any given situation serves one or more of three functions: protection, enhancement, constraint. The hardened criminal is isolated—avoided, put away—for the *protection* of society. Membership in exclusive societies rests upon avoidance of the hoi-poloi and confers special *prestige* and *ego-enhancement* upon the members. Finally, avoidance may result in *constraint*—coercive, punitive, propitiatory. Coercive avoidance takes the form of non-cooperation or boycott, strike or lockout. Punitive avoidance leads to the incarceration of the offender against law. Propitiatory avoidance is replete with totems and taboos.

In our day, the Iron Curtain exemplifies large scale avoidance, hiding from the free world's view military and other preparations going on in Soviet Russia and satellite countries. When the UNTCOK (United Nations Temporary Commission on Korea) was created on November 14, 1947, to organize and supervise elections, South Korea welcomed the UN commission but North Korea enforced avoidance by denying entrance to members of the Commission.

The process of avoidance comes into play in one of four possible ways: (1) staying out, (2) getting out, (3) keeping out, (4) putting out. (4, pp. 294–98).

10. AMALGAMATION, ACCOMMODATION, ASSIMILATION

Amalgamation, like adaptation, is a biological process, while accommodation and assimilation are sociological processes.

Amalgamation involves intermarriage and interbreeding. The various European ethnic groups in the United States, after a generation or two, become amalgamated one with another and with the dominant American group, lose their identity, and pass off as Americans.

Accommodation is a non-violent response or adjustment (a) to a stubborn situation which cannot be changed or (b) to a situation which has changed as a result of violence and hostility, or as a result of new rules and requirements.

"Assimilation," in the words of Park and Burgess, "is a process of interpenetration and fusion in which persons and groups acquire the memories, sentiments, and attitudes of other persons or groups, and, by sharing their experience and history, are incorporated with them in a common cultural life" (13, p. 735).

Endogamy, symbolizing intragroup cooperation, militates against amalgamation with outgroups ; while exogamy, resting upon intergroup cooperation, favors amalgamation. Societies with a caste structure tend to discourage amalgamation, while open class societies, such as the one in the United States, permit amalgamation. Even so, it must be noted that in this country, as between whites and colored, there is tacit, sometimes legal, avoidance so far as intermarriage is concerned.

11. ASSIMILATION, ACCULTURATION, SOCIALIZATION

In what ways does assimilation differ from acculturation and socialization? Socialization involves the new-born child's growing into the culture of his people, mastering its techniques, accepting its values, translating the potential—original nature—into human nature. Assimilation presupposes socialization in another cultural milieu and implies mastery of the techniques and values of the new culture. Finally, acculturation involves transmission of culture traits from one culture to another, through culture contacts or through contacts between bearers of two cultures.

Socialization implies birth in one's culture. Assimilation involves rebirth in a new culture. Acculturation is the objective counterpart of assimilation.

With these terms as our frame of reference, we may inquire concerning the status of the Negro in American society. Is the Negro socialized? Is he assimilated? Has there been acculturation between white and colored? That the Negro has been socialized in the American cultural milieu is an obvious fact. That there has been acculturation between white and colored in regard to music and dance, literature and athletics, is also self-evident.

Then, has the Negro been assimilated in American society and culture? First, the Negro may be said to be assimilated in American society because he has been made like the white man—he speaks the white man's language, he dresses as the white man does, cherishes the same values, enjoys the same sports, etc. In spite of this, it must be pointed out that the Negro is not a full participant in the white man's world and culture.

Second, if we view assimilation in the sense of belonging to the same community or to the same associations, the Negro is assimilated; for he is part of American society and community and plays his role in the on-going process of American culture. Here again, however, certain restrictions militate against full assimilation. Acceptance of the Negro in the American cultural milieu is a fact, but it is partial acceptance.

Third, if we view assimilation from the subjective standpoint of the object of assimilation, the problem of assimilation does not arise in the thinking of the American Negro—or, shall we say, the Negro American? After all, America is as much his country as it is the white man's. In spite of his racial affinity to the Negro in Africa, the American Negro has little in common with the African Negro. In spite of certain avoidances, the American Negro can say he is accepted in the American cultural milieu, he feels at home here, and he identifies himself emotionally with American democracy, not with any alien country, government or ideology. Indeed, the Negro is an American. He does not need to be assimilated.

We must reserve the term assimilation as a description of the process whereby *alien* persons and groups are incorporated into a common cultural life. A member of the out-group may be said to be fully assimilated when he shares the basic definitions of situations which prevail in the in-group, when he has a feeling of belonging, of being accepted, and when he contributes to the realization of collective goals. It should be pointed out, however, that the definition of alien and out-group categories depends upon the social context. The "alien" of yester-year may be accepted, and may function, as a full-fledged member of the in-group today.

Assimilation, thus, becomes a matter of degree. Some members of the in-group may be deviant and operate as marginal men. Some members of the out-group may never fully identify themselves with the in-group and its heritage, and operate as strangers and as marginal men. These marginal men sometimes function inefficiently because of their deviation from the cultural norms ; sometimes they make significant contributions to culture precisely because of their deviation and marginality.

12. THE SPECTRUM AND SUBPROCESSES OF ACCOMMODATION

Just as assimilation is a matter of degree, so is accommodation. Accommodation ranges all the way from acceptance of the situation with a minimum of goodwill to working together (or cooperation) in entire agreement.

Accommodation is either the end-result of adjustment to a stubborn situation which cannot be changed—a totalitarian dictatorship government, for instance—or the end-result of conflict. As the end-result of conflict, accommodation provides mechanisms for cooperation (a) through acceptance of superordination-subordination relations between the parties to the conflict, (b) through mutual give-and-take or compromise, (c) through toleration of the changed conditions and roles of the parties to the conflict. The British refer to politics as the art of compromise.

The subprocesses leading to accommodation are: negotiation, mediation, arbitration. In *negotiation*, the parties to the conflict themselves attempt to get together, to talk over their differences, and to arrive at an accommodation or a *modus vivendi*. In *mediation*, a third party offers his good offices to the two contestants and attempts to arrive at an amicable solution, equitable to both parties. The mediator's services may be appreciated by the contestants, but his judgment is binding upon neither party. In *arbitration*, the parties to the conflict agree to select a third party as an arbitrator and pledge beforehand to abide by the arbitrator's award. The arbitrator may be an individual or a panel mutually agreed upon and selected.

Wars are brought to an end either through surrender on the part of one of the contestants or through negotiation before either party is thoroughly defeated. The United States has formulated the policy of terminating wars through unconditional surrender—of the Confederate Army, of the Central Powers in World War I, of the Axis Powers in World War II. It is conceivable that "peace without victory" on the part of either contestant, in the words of President

Wilson, may provide a better situation for negotiation and long-range accommodation.

In industrial conflicts in the U.S.A., the NLRB (the National Labor Relations Board) set up by the Taft-Hartley Law, provides for making available to employers and employees the services of a government-appointed official as mediator. In the international field, in issues involving differences of opinion or possible conflict situations, the U.S. and Canadian Governments have agreed to resolve their difficulties by arbitration.

Accommodation, in its psychological aspect, may be the result of, or may result in, either conciliation or reconciliation. *Conciliation* involves a psychological reorientation of one or both of the parties to the conflict, giving the benefit of the doubt to the opponent. In *reconciliation*, an effort is made by one or both of the contestants to forget and forgive the past errors of the other party, and to build anew a new set of friendly and cooperative relationships among " new-born" individuals or groups. The Fellowship of Reconciliation in the U.S.A. is an organization dedicated to overcoming society's ills, economic, political, social, racial, international, by the method of reconciliation.

Reconciliation as the end-result of conflict is best illustrated in our day by the warm feelings of friendliness and goodwill between the people of Great Britain and the people of India who had carried on their struggle for freedom from British rule by non-violent methods under Mahatma Gandhi's leadership.

13. Is Accommodation Always an Available Alternative?

That cooperation is better than conflict is attested by the universal experience of mankind. That accommodation is better than continuing conflict will also be granted: for instance, in an industrial strike, a form of conflict, everybody loses—the worker, the employer, the public. Can accommodation, then, be raised to the status of a high principle? In the ordinary affairs of life, yes. But there are situations in which accommodation is unavailable and inadvisable. There are circumstances under which non-cooperation is preferable to cooperation through accommodation. When the values of a society or of a subculture group or of a religious association are threatened, or when the dictates of one's conscience are infringed upon, then accommodation in the sense of compromise is unavailable. An attenuated form of accommodation, live and let-live or toleration, co-existence without goodwill, is a possible solution—or war, hot or cold, violent or non-violent. Incidentally, ethnic and religious minorities would rather be appreciated than tolerated.

Non-violent non-cooperation is preferable to cooperation if cooperation should involve compromise with principle. Compromise or concession on details is necessary in the enterprise of social living, but concession on principles and deeply cherished values would destroy the integrity of the human "soul." Peace is desirable, but not appeasement, because *appeasement* means the buying of peace with sacrifice of principles and values.

14. SOCIAL ORGANIZATION AND PHILOSOPHIC BASE

Different philosophies of life and different types of social organization have evolved on the basis of cooperation or competition or conflict as the dominant principle in the universe, or as the guiding principle in social relations. Ruth Benedict, in her illuminating book, *Patterns of Culture,* describes the competitive society of the Kwakiutl Indians of Northwest Canada, the cooperative and peace-loving society of the Pueblo Indians of New Mexico, the Zunis, and the conflict society of the Dobuans off the southern shore of eastern New Guinea in the Pacific. (2, *passim.*)

In our day, Mahatma Gandhi enunciated his philosophy of life in terms of what he called Soul Force. The philosophy of Soul Force, said Gandhi, rested on cooperation and goodwill, while the philosophy of Brute Force was compounded of violence, conflict and ill-will. The philosophy of Soul Force provided a frame of reference, "an angle of vision," different from that provided by the philosophy of Brute Force.

The hypothesis of Soul Force, according to Mahatma Gandhi, postulates that the universe is hospitable, friendly, loving. In Plato's terminology, the universe may be conceived as the quintessence of the good, the true, the beautiful.

Opposed to the theory of Soul Force, there is the postulate of Brute Force being at the core of the universe. This latter theory holds that the universe is inhospitable, unfriendly, unloving, at best amoral if indeed not immoral. This view is well expressed in the Hindu dialectician's phrase *Matsya-Nyaya*, "the logic of the fish"— "the larger fish devouring the smaller fish."

In Occidental thought this point of view was set forth by Hobbes, Malthus, and Darwin. Hobbes defined the state of nature as "a struggle of each against all." Malthus premised that population tended to outstrip the food supply; thus there ensued the struggle for existence. Darwin studied nature and arrived at the conclusion that there was universal "struggle for existence"; that only "the fittest" survived, giving rise to new species.

Interestingly enough, another student of nature, Peter Kropotkin of Russia, arrived at the conclusion that in nature there was "mutual aid."

Darwin and Kropotkin are both partly right and partly wrong. In nature we have both phenomena: the struggle for existence, and mutual aid. To read in nature exclusively a struggle for existence, or exclusively mutual aid, would be wrong. We must balance the two in terms of the fundamental frame of reference. The experience of nature as well as of man, an integral part of nature, points to an interesting lesson. In the struggle for existence, only that species which had learned cooperation and mutual aid among its members has succeeded, survived, and prospered. Benjamin Kidd (1858-1916) is quite right when he suggests that social progress consists in the capacity for teamwork, in the capacity of the individual member to subordinate himself to the group. Self-preservation, accordingly, becomes group preservation. One finds one's true self when one is willing to lose it for others. (9, *passim*). In this respect the teaching of religion is in harmony with the findings of science. Gandhi maintained that such a conclusion can be arrived at only when man operates within the frame of reference of Soul Force.

Contrariwise, the frame of reference of Brute Force compels different conclusions. Man must be eternally at war with nature and with his fellows. To survive, he must be aggressive and brutal. The more brutal he is, the more likely is he to survive—and to dominate. He must therefore glorify war and create occasions for war. In the war of each against all, there can be no mutual trust, no confidence, no tenderness, in human relations. Man must not only build engines of human destruction; he must himself be an engine of Brute Force.

Hobbes, Malthus, and Darwin, honored social philosophers and scientists as they were, have been responsible to no small extent for the cult of brute force in Western civilization, for "the white man's burden" upon "the lesser breed," for racialism, and for imperialism. In our day, Marxism reinforces the philosophy of violence and brute force. (11, CHAPTER 3).

15. FUNCTIONS OF COOPERATION, COMPETITION, CONFLICT

Functions of Cooperation

We pointed out in CHAPTERS 22 and 23 that the three immanent processes, stimulus-response, interaction and communication, lead to consensus. Consensus holds society together; it precedes cooperation, and cooperation points up and strengthens consensus.

Next, it is obvious that grouping itself, and society as well, would be impossible without cooperation. Finally, cooperation makes possible division of labor and specialization of function. It must be understood that cooperation, based either upon regimentation by the state or upon overprotection say by the mother, would fail fully to develop the powers of some of the cooperators as well as the resources of society.

Functions of Competition

Competition serves five positive functions and three negative functions. First, competition helps determine the status and location of individual members in a system of hierarchy. The process of competition is the same among plants, among subhuman animals, and among human beings. In *The Social Life of Animals*, W. C. Allee describes the pecking order of hens, established in a flock of hens as a result of competition and struggle for status (1, pp. 175 ff.).

Second, "competition tends to stimulate economy, efficiency, and inventiveness," as illustrated by American society. (4, p. 280). Third, competition, rather success in competition, tends to enhance one's ego and to make for a satisfying life. Fourth, competition among

CHART 24

THE PECKING ORDER AMONG HENS

Sketch by Professor John M. Howard, Art Dept., Ark. A. M. & N. College

In his study of dozens of flocks of chickens, Dr. Alphaeus M. Guhl of Kansas State University, Manhattan, Kansas, discovered that " hen society is one of the most rigid in the world," with a hierarchy based on the ability to peck others (or to be pecked by others). The pecking order among hens is established as a result of competition.

individuals of more or less equal strength, as pointed out by Giddings, tends to prevent undue concentration of power in an individual or group of individuals. Fifth, competition among equals rests upon a set of rules, and engenders respect for "the rules of the game." Sportsmanship is the result of fair competition. The concept of sportsmanship is markedly present among the British people as well as the American people. According to the American culture pattern, dating is a sort of competitive game in which neither party to the date should be a loser (8, pp. 109 ff.; see *infra*, CHAPTER 36).

Among the negative functions of competition we may mention the obverse of some of the good outcomes of competition : (1) Competition, which tends to enhance one's ego, may also lead to neurosis through frustration and to violation of the rules, to crime, on the part of those who fail in the struggle for status according to the prescribed rules of competition. (2) Competition, among equals, tends to be self-regulating, with no special advantage to any competitor; but the postulate of equality among competitors is not always tenable. Indeed, uncontrolled competition "among equals" is apt to end up in a monopoly; hence in a democratic society we have legal safeguards to preserve competition. (3) Competition, in some cases, leads to conflict. For instance, competition for markets among nations used to lead to war.

Functions of Conflict

If the primary function of competition be the determination of status, the primary function of conflict may be said to be the distribution or relative concentration of power among the contestants. If cooperation promotes association, conflict definitely promotes dissociation—at least among the warring elements. But this is a simplified way of stating a complex problem.

Conflict does perform some positive functions. First, conflict tends to stiffen the morale and promote the solidarity of the in-group, threatened by an out-group. The crisis tends to bring to the fore competent leaders and to increase the strength, vigor and efficiency of the contestants.

Second, conflict, concluded with victory, leads to the enlargement of the victor group either in terms of power or in terms of incorporation of new territory and population, thus making possible the emergence of a larger in-group. The successful strike means additional power to the employees in terms of better terms and stronger bargaining position in future crises. Victory in war used to lead to the creation of empire in the past. Indeed, some anthropologists, without being Marxist in their orientation, maintain that the State as we know it resulted from a series of conquests. Thus amalgamation and incorporation may be said to be the second positive function of conflict.

Third, conflict may point up more sharply the basic value systems of the antagonists; unessentials that might have been thought to be basic are cast aside, and a redefinition of the situation is undertaken by the contestants. This redefinition may carry within itself possibilities of new types of cooperation and accommodation.

Fourth, alternatives to violent conflict not having been successfully worked out in the past, conflict did serve as a successful mechanism for "breaking the log jam," or for breaking a deadlock. In our generation, several successful non-violent techniques for resolving crises have been worked out. Furthermore, the American insistence on law in preference to war, on the combined wisdom of mankind as reflected through the United Nations rather than on military might, may serve the same function as did conflict in the past—namely, to break a deadlock.

Fifth, conflict does not determine status, as competition does; nevertheless, conflict does change the relative status of contestants and of the non-contestants as well. For instance, after defeating China in 1894-95, Japan began to emerge as a Great Power. And after defeating Russia in 1905, Japan was accorded the status of a Great Power by the Great Powers of those days, and began to be recognized as a leading Asian Power by Asian countries then in the throes of a struggle to overthrow foreign European rule.

Sixth, in view of the destructive nature of armaments at man's disposal, especially the A-bomb and the H-bomb, war in the form of international conflict has lost all its past utility. It may well be that the very destructiveness of modern war may lead to a new consensus regarding abolition of war as an instrument of national policy and to the devising of methods for peaceful changes in the international status quo. (A pioneer discussion of the functions of cooperation, competition and conflict is to be found in the Bossard book—4, CHAPTER 13. I gratefully acknowledge my thanks to my collaborators in that work—Thomas H. Grafton, Marion St. John, and Forrest Keen.)

16. RECAPITULATION

In this chapter, under the general heading of cooperation and opposition, we have dealt with five categorical processes: 1. cooperation, 2. competition, 3. conflict, 4. accommodation, 5. assimilation. The types and subprocesses of accommodation have been distinguished and described because of their interplay in our daily life, both individual and collective. Finally, we have tried to point out the functions of cooperation, competition and conflict.

REFERENCES

1. W. C. ALLEE: *The Social Life of Animals*. New York: W. W. Norton, 1938.

2. RUTH BENEDICT: *Patterns of Culture*. Boston: Houghton Mifflin Co., 1934. Published as a Mentor Book, 1946; eleventh printing, 1953.

3. DANIEL BLOOMFIELD, Ed.: *Modern Industrial Movements*. New York: H. W. Wilson Co., 1920.

4. J. H. S. BOSSARD, Ed.: *Introduction to Sociology*. Harrisburg, Pa.: The Stackpole Co., 1952.

5. MARQUIS W. CHILDS: *Sweden: The Middle Way*. New Haven: Yale University Press, 1936.

6. JEROME DAVIS: *Contemporary Social Movements*. New York: D. Appleton-Century Co., 1930.

7. F. H. GIDDINGS: *Studies in the Theory of Human Society*. New York: Macmillan, 1922.

8. GEOFFREY GORER: *The American People: A Study in National Character*. New York: W. W. Norton, 1948.

9. BENJAMIN KIDD: *Social Evolution*. New York: Macmillan, 1894. (Several later reprints also available.)

10. HARRY W. LAIDLER: *Social-Economic Movements*. New York: Thomas Y. Crowell Co., 1944.

11. H. T. MUZUMDAR: *Mahatma Gandhi: Peaceful Revolutionary*. New York: Charles Scribner's Sons, 1953.

12. WILLIAM F. OGBURN & MEYER F. NIMKOFF: *Sociology*. 2nd ed. Boston: Houghton Mifflin Co., 1950.

13. R. E. PARK & E. W. BURGESS: *Introduction to the Science of Sociology*, 2nd ed. Chicago: University of Chicago Press, 1924. (eighth impression, 1933).

CHAPTER 28

SOCIAL CHANGE

1. STABILITY AND CHANGE

JUST as society is characterized by the simultaneous interplay of the two reciprocal processes of cooperation and competition, so is it characterized by two other reciprocal traits and processes: stability and change. To be permanent, to be effective and dynamic, indeed to exist and to function for long, a society must provide mechanisms both for stability and for change.

The steel frame of culture—i.e., folkways, mores and institutions —makes for stability in the social order in terms of expectation and anticipation, in terms of fulfillment of role expectations, in terms of acceptance of values as well as of individuals and groups. This phase of the study of society we shall deal with in BOOK III. Here we are concerned with the genesis, and operation, and consequences of social change.

Change is the one constant fact in the universe. Day and night; summer, fall, winter, spring; rain and drought; famine and plenty; volcanic eruption and earthquake; submergence of tiny islands under the water or appearance of new tiny islands above sea level; birth, growth, maturation, senescence, death—these are all facts of nature, and they are all facts of change. Some changes in nature are cyclical or form definite patterns of uniformity—day and night, following each other; the seasons following one another in a regular sequence, etc.

Whenever and wherever a pattern of sequence or uniformity in nature is detected, hypotheses are formed to account for such patterns: the rotation of the earth on its axis giving us the sequence of day and night, the revolution of the earth around the sun giving us our seasons in the appointed order, etc. The question has been raised: Are there laws of social change, as there are laws of natural change? Before answering this question, we must answer the question, What is social change?

2. DEFINITION OF SOCIAL CHANGE

Philosophically, change is a continuum of being-becoming. In the process of becoming, being undergoes changes. Collective man's interaction with nature as well as with the superorganic brings about social change of some sort. Food, clothing and shelter are basic material needs of man, but fashions in food, clothing and shelter differ from age to age and from nation to nation. A fad may become structuralized into an institution (a stable social force), which may be constantly played upon and modified by new fads, relevant or irrelevant (social change).

Social change may be defined as a new fashion or mode, either modifying or replacing the old, in the life of a people—or in the operation of a society. Social change includes modifications in social techniques, relationships, behavior patterns, folkways, mores, and institutions, sometimes leading to change in philosophic outlook. If a social change is significant and involves a large segment of the population, usually the entire cultural framework will be eventually changed, or at least modified. In other words, social change and cultural change are inextricably linked together, each affecting the other.

3. THE NEW STATUS OF WOMEN IN AMERICA

Let us illustrate a significant social change in America. The European colonists brought with them to this country their mental as well as household furniture. Part of the mental furniture of Europeans was the notion of woman's inferiority to man. Here in the New World, on the wild frontier, the discovery was made that the "little woman" could use the firearm from behind the stockades as effectively as the "big man." This discovery immediately brought forth a change in the relations between men and women. Later the industrial revolution made woman economically independent of man ; she could get a job for herself. But it was the invention of the typewriter and shorthand that precipitated a most revolutionary change in American society. Since the turn of the century, the gender of the secretary as well as the schoolteacher has been feminine. And at the midpoint of the twentieth century, no occupation or profession was barred to women except actual soldiering and fighting ;

even at that, we do have the WACS, Woman's Auxiliary Corps, attached to army units, WAVES to naval units, SPARS to the Coast Guard, and the WAFS to the Air Force.

The objective conditions in the New World, the frontier amongst them, the industrial revolution, the opening of the public schools, the invention of the typewriter, the Nineteenth Amendment to the Constitution, shortage of man-power during World War II—each of these factors has contributed to the emancipation of woman from a subordinate status and to her enjoyment of equality of status with men.

Profound as this change is, affecting as it does social relationships and attitudes, the impact of this change, in terms of its chain reactions, has been even more profound on American society. The American woman marries for love—not for prestige nor for money —giving rise to our romantic love complex. The American family is by deliberate choice small and atomistic. In the American home the woman reigns supreme—and the American male fights his "Custer's last stand" battle in the basement workshop. The children's training is practically taken over by the mother at home, and by the schoolteacher at school. Under the little woman's prodding, American society has become child-centered, with woman as the boss. Our suburbia illustrate this change most markedly. And economists tell us that American women own a larger amount of the wealth of this country than men and that they spend more money in buying than do men.

This social situation is entirely new—neither the Colonial Period nor the Revolutionary War Period, neither the Civil War Period nor the Reconstruction Period has any similarity to today's conditions. And, of course, it goes without saying that this aspect of American society is duplicated nowhere else in the world. But it may be noted that this culture trait, the new status of woman, having been achieved in the United States, has been travelling around the world making its impact upon European, Asian and African societies.

4. CAUSES AND METHODS OF SOCIAL CHANGE

Social change is brought about by a number of factors: (1) invention, original or borrowed; (2) introduction of a new mode of production; (3) introduction of a new ethnic element in the population; (4) introduction of a new ideological configuration or a new norm or set of norms; (5) rearrangement of elements in the social structure or social organization; (6) charismatic leadership.

In addition to these six causes of social change, we may mention four methods of bringing about social change: (1) the impersonal logic of technology, (2) evolutionary methods, including constitutional procedures, advocated by our Republicans, Democrats and Socialists; (3) brute force methods, advocated by imperialists, fascists and communists; and (4) soul force methods, advocated by Mahatma Gandhi and the historic Peace Churches in Christendom (the Friends or Quakers, Mennonites and Brethren).

5. CONSEQUENCES OF CERTAIN SOCIAL CHANGES

The invention of fire-making enabled the caveman to cook his food and to warm himself by the fire during the cold weather or wintry nights. The invention or borrowing of the bow-and-arrow made possible the hunting type of society. The invention of agriculture changed the entire mode of life of the people: They had to settle down in a permanent settlement, the village, if the fruits of their labor were to be enjoyed. The factory system of production, utilizing power-driven machinery, has changed the nature of whole populations—from rural into urban. These urban concentrations of population have changed the basis of social relationship—from primary group into secondary group relationships.

Social changes brought about by the impersonal logic of technology may be illustrated from the significant role played by (a) the barbed wire, (b) the six-shooter, and (c) the windmill in the opening up of the Frontier of the Great Western Plains area of the United States, between the Mississippi and the Rockies. The barbed wire enabled the frontiersmen to break up the open range into individual farms and ranches well fenced in; the six-shooter enabled the Texas Rangers to give battle to the Indians on horseback, armed with bow and arrows, on better than even terms. The windmill supplied them with subterranean water. (14, *passim*). This vast and rich area could be successfully occupied and developed only in the wake of the three inventions.

6. DEFINITION OF INVENTION

We have been discussing some of the consequences of inventions, but we have not defined the term invention. What, then, is an invention? An invention is a rearrangement of known traits into a new configuration. An invention may be material or non-material. The automobile is a material invention, so is the incandescent electric bulb. But the automobile could not have been invented if there had been no prior knowledge of wheels, axle, chassis, yoke for the ox or horse to pull the carriage, and, above all, the combustion engine. A rearrangement of these known traits into a new configuration gave us the automobile. Analogous reasoning would apply to the invention of the electric bulb, or gramophone, rubber tire, etc., etc.

A non-material invention, whether in the field of social organization or the cultural framework including the value system, is, likewise, a rearrangement of known traits into a new pattern or configuration. The best illustration of such a non-material invention is provided by our city manager form of government, which is simply a rearrangement and introduction of sound business practices into the field of municipal administration.

7. TECHNOLOGICAL CHANGES AND SOCIAL CHANGES

These inventions, whether material or non-material, have led to profound social changes. For instance, the automobile has changed the dating and courting pattern of America; it has also accelerated the mobility of the American people. The electric light makes possible social visits as well as work in the evening. And the city manager plan has given many communities an efficient, businesslike administration, without the graft and corruption and inefficiency that used to be associated with the older forms of municipal government.

In a broad sense, it may be affirmed that the revolutionary changes in our industrial methods of production and in our transportation and communication systems have tended to affect the patterns of population concentration as well as the patterns of social

relationships. Which is another way of saying that these technological changes have brought about profound social changes.

8. THE ROLE OF ETHNIC GROUPS IN SOCIAL CHANGE

Not only do technological changes bring about social changes,
but ideological changes and changes in the population as well as in
the social structure also bring forth significant social changes. For
instance, the presence of the Muslims in large numbers and in a
dominant position (as rulers) in North India for a number of years
has had the effect of weakening certain Hindu social customs and
rituals, especially the caste system; it also led to the adoption of the
Semitic trait of veiling of the woman's face by the Hindus. Indeed,
language, the vehicle of communication and the cornerstone of
culture, was itself modified.

In this country, the Christmas tree as a social ritual was introduced by a German pastor in Cleveland, Ohio, in 1851; just as
Kindergarten was also introduced by the German element in our
population. The whole culture complex of ski resorts which arose in
this country in the thirties was given impetus by Central Europeans,
especially Germans and Austrians, who fled Hitler's persecution. We
could indefinitely multiply instances of social changes introduced in
American society by our ethnic minorities.

9. UTOPIAN THINKING AND SOCIAL CHANGE

Utopian schemes, such as the experiments at New Harmony,
Indiana, and at Brook Farm, were the result of new ideologies and
new norms. Utopian thinking and literature on Utopia are replete
with oblique suggestions for social change and with ready-made
social orders which, presumably, know nothing of the shortcomings
of the existing social order.

Sir Thomas More (1478-1535), living during the Age of Discovery, witnessing the emergence of England from feudalism into a
national state and from a rural economy into a mercantile (money)
economy, indicted the English society of his day through the descriptions of Raphael Hythloday, who described the ideal conditions
obtaining on the island of Utopia. Without risking loss of his head,
More, through his Utopia, performed the services of a critic and a

social reformer. The ideal conditions on Utopia, as described by Hythloday, served as a plea for social change in the English society of his day.

The people of Utopia worked only six hours a day, shared their goods in common, knew the vice neither of riches nor of poverty, lived on streets "commodious and handsome" and in houses "fair and gorgeous" which were never locked or bolted. Utopia believed in universal education and in the greatest happiness of the greatest number of people. (7, *passim*).

This Utopian ideology has led to social changes in England and in other industrially developed countries. In the U.S.A. we already have the eight-hour day (forty-hour week), and labor leaders and social reformers are already talking of a six-hour day or a three-day work week of eight hours per day. The evolving English Poor Laws benefited from More's Utopian ideology.

10. NEGRO-WHITE INTERACTION AND SOCIAL CHANGE

With the abolition of slavery at the end of the Civil War, the whole structure of Southern society was rocked to its very foundation. The slave of yester-year became the freedman and legislator, demanding equal rights with the white man. Backward as he was educationally and economically because of prior denial of opportunity, the Negro freedman was obliged to revert to a subordinate role—not a slave technically, but a serf none the less, a sharecropper. Nobody has scientifically investigated the effect of the Negro *slave's* loose morality upon the moral code of the white man. We do know that the Southern white man's drawl is influenced by the Negro's intonation. Is it conceivable that our national tolerance of premarital and extramarital sex relations may be partly a result of the impact of the Negro *slave's* loose morality upon American society? At least, this is a hypothesis worthy of investigation.

11. THE CHARISMATIC LEADER AND SOCIAL CHANGE

Finally, the charismatic leader brings forth all kinds of social change. The leader is one who has power and authority, recognized by others. These others are the followers who accept the power and authority exercised by the leader. The leader is meaningless without followers, and followers are non-existent without a leader. Thus the total social situation, the unit of sociological investigation, is the leader-followers or the leadership-followership pattern.

Leadership is of three kinds : traditional, bureaucratic and charismatic. The traditional leader gets his authority through the traditional status ascribed to him as a member of a particular group—the feudal lord in relation to his vassals, the Brahmin in India in relation to the non-Brahmin. This traditional leadership, derived from birth, is not rated high in dynamic, secular societies, but is still respected in slowly changing, sacred societies.

The bureaucratic leader gets his authority and power through delegation ; his position of leadership is derived from election as the people's representative, or from appointment in a vast network of bureaucratic organization. The bureaucratic leadership tends to be conservative and tends to maintain the status quo. Thus, the bureaucratic leader is a force for stability in the social order, and the much maligned bureaucratic hierarchy helps keep the ship of State on an even keel.

The charismatic leader, on the other hand, creates his own authority. No individual or organization confers upon him the unique power and authority a charismatic leader exercises. Charismatic leadership arises in an informal setting during a period of crisis. Thus disorganized conditions in a neighborhood may lead to the "birth" of the "leader" of the boys wandering the streets aimlessly. In this crisis situation, the charisma, the halo, of the leader attracts to him footloose boys ; a gang is formed and he "becomes" their leader and "is recognized" as leader. Having created his own authority, the charismatic leader may well develop a formal following obedient to his will—a formal gang, a political party, a religious association, a social reform association, etc. A charismatic leader usually heads a social reform movement or a revolution ; in either case, he symbolizes dissatisfaction with the status quo and acts as a dynamic force for social change.

The difference between the leader and the ordinary man may be stated simply. While the ordinary man tends to conform to outer circumstances, to the environment, the leader—the great leader—

strives to rise above the limitations of outer circumstances and succeeds in compelling the environment to bow before him, before his will. This is especially true of charismatic leadership that has been responsible for significant changes from the days of Moses and Buddha and Jesus to Lenin and Hitler and Gandhi in our day.

12. HITLER AND GANDHI AS CHARISMATIC LEADERS

Let us analyze two sociological phenomena of our times, the charismatic leadership of Hitler in Germany and the charismatic leadership of Gandhi in India. Beyond the fact that both of them were vegetarians and non-smokers, Hitler and Gandhi had little in common. And yet each in his way profoundly affected the destiny of his people and of the world.

Hitler

Adolf Hitler (1889-1945) gathered around himself some of the discontented and unemployed veterans of World War I and began to communicate to them his vision of a Resurgent Germany. The "beer-hall putsch" of November 8-9, 1923, turned out to be a fiasco and its leader was arrested and sentenced to five years' confinement in the fortress of Landsberg. But he was released after serving thirteen months during which he wrote his political testament, *Mein Kampf* (My Battle) which became the Bible of National Socialism (Nazism).

Mein Kampf (6, *passim*) electrified Germany not because it was a literary masterpiece, but because it embodied some of the unspoken, deeply cherished hopes and ambitions of the German people: overthrow of the Versailles *Diktat*, assumption of full sovereignty by Germany, humiliation of Britain and France, regaining of Danzig, the Saar and the Rhineland, the forging of a new German army, abolition of unemployment. To satisfy these ambitions, the German people did not mind accepting the tie-in sale of "Aryan" superiority and Anti-Semitism.

Hitler became Chancellor of Germany on January 28, 1933, by legal and constitutional methods thanks to the strength of his party in the Reichstag, and was soon vested with dictatorial powers by an obedient Reichstag. Thus did the Austrian paper-hanger, corporal of

World War I in the German Army, become the head of the Third Reich.

One by one Hitler began to fulfil his promises. Unemployment was abolished through State-directed activities, an armed force was brought into being in defiance of the Versailles Diktat, soon the Saar and the Rhineland also became parts of the Third Reich.

A believer in the theory of brute force, Hitler had gained power and strength through domestic terrorism and intimidation. It was inevitable that he should strive to attain international power and authority, as well, by an extension of domestic forms of terrorism, intimidation and propaganda. The end-result was the holocaust of World War II. It is interesting to note that while World War I had involved the traditional leadership of Kaiser Wilhelm Hohenzollern and the bureaucratic leadership of his Ministers and army Generals, World War II involved the charismatic leadership of Hitler and two lesser lights, Mussolini and Stalin (as far as charisma was concerned).

Is social change possible through charismatic leadership? Well, let us look at the face of Europe and of the world a little over a decade after the end of the hostilities in 1945! Broken families, displaced persons, stateless persons, refugees, satellite states, slave labor camps in Siberia, on the one hand; freedom and self-government wrested by half the population of the world (Asians) from the reluctant hands of European imperialists! On top of all these consequences, good and bad, we have staring us in the face the unpredictable harm to the human species and to all forms of life through the testing and use of H-bombs, euphemistically referred to as thermonuclear weapons.

Gandhi

By contrast, Mahatma Gandhi (1869-1948) was a believer in the efficacy of soul force, of non-violence and love, as weapons in the struggle to redeem wrong and injustice. Neither the British Government nor any organized body ever conferred upon the humble "weaver and farmer" of Sabarmati Ashram the title of Mahatma (Great Soul). It is a moot point whether this appellation was given to Gandhi first by Mrs. Annie Besant (1847-1933) or by the poet

16

Rabindranath Tagore (1861-1941), Nobel prizewinner. Once the term was applied to Gandhi, people spontaneously took it up and began to refer to Gandhi as our " Mahatma."

There was nothing startling in the boy's background to suggest that he would one day become the charismatic Mahatma of India and of the world. Two incidents in his boyhood days did, however, bespeak the man that was to be : his temporary experiment in meat-eating in defiance of the taboo of Hindu society, and his temporary agnosticism in search of truth despite the all-pervading spirit of religion in his home environment and in Hindu society. (8, pp. 7–11).

In South Africa (1893-1914), confronted by the racial arrogance of the South African Europeans, Dutch as well as English, incapable of insurrection, Gandhi launched his " passive resistance " campaign against the South African Government in behalf of the rights of his compatriots domiciled in that land. In this campaign, Gandhi made a virtue of necessity and reinforced his basic outlook of non-violence by experimenting with the weapons of the spirit, with the weapons of non-violence, variously known as passive resistance, non-violent resistance, non-violent non-cooperation, civil disobedience, Satyagraha, Truth Force, Love Force, Soul Force. (2, 3, 8, 10, *passim*).

Loyalty to *Ahimsa* (non-violence : love), loyalty to *Satya* (Truth), and concern for the well-being of others, especially of the underprivileged, the wronged, the oppressed—these three dominant themes in the life of the Hindu barrister were destined to attract to him the loyalty and devotion of millions of followers in India. It may well be that charisma has little to do with the physical attractiveness of the "leader"; rather that the charisma is derived from the people's spontaneous recognition of certain unassailable and pleasing qualities in the inner makeup of the leader. This hypothesis gains credence from the objective fact, verified a thousand and one times, that the leader stands forth as the embodiment of the hopes of his followers, that the leader speaks the unspoken words of millions who look to him for guidance. At any rate, in death as in life, Gandhi has been adjudged a great charismatic leader because of this threefold quality of his inner self.

13. SATYAGRAHA AS A METHOD OF SOCIAL CHANGE

Satyagraha (holding fast to truth under all circumstances) as a method of bringing about social change may be aptly studied in terms of Gandhi's leadership in India.

Satyagraha and democracy are both revolutionary; they mark a complete break with the past, democracy having overthrown autocracy and *Satyagraha* striving to render useless prevalent methods of violence and warfare. Both democracy and *Satyagraha* are capable of effecting far-reaching changes in society by peaceful, non-violent methods.

We may briefly set forth the premises, modes of operation and consequences of *Satyagraha* as a method of social change.

It is unbecoming to the dignity of man supinely to submit to injustice and wrong. In order to abolish existing injustice and wrong the Satyagrahist studies the system or systems and patterns that make for wrong and injustice. He would try to mend or to end, "to alter or to abolish," the system that is responsible for wrongdoing. In his zest to eliminate the wrong, the Satyagrahist is ever careful not to eliminate the wrongdoer. *Satyagraha* does not aim to cure the rash without cleansing the whole system. If a purge be necessary, let there be a purge—a non-violent purge, to be sure. The Satyagrahist looks behind the flutter of phenomena.

The Satyagrahist gives the benefit of the doubt to his antagonist; he strives generously to understand the other's point of view. He cooperates whenever cooperation involves no compromise with principle, with Truth. He works for conciliation and arbitration. His concern is not only to minimize conflict but also to minimize the occasions for conflict.

Democracy is based upon Soul Force; indeed, the democratic process is *par excellence* the manifestation of Soul Force in action; because democracy, too, strives to minimize conflict and occasions for conflict.

The role of self-invited suffering is most important in the technique of *Satyagraha*. Non-cooperation with the agency of wrongdoing in turn depends upon cooperation among the "revolutionaries." Only self-purification and prosecution of the constructive program make the people fit to offer non-cooperation.

When goodwill and conciliation are unavailing, the Satyagrahist who foreswore violence and warfare has open to him only one course of action, namely, to invite upon his devoted head all the sufferings he can without malice, without ill-will. Sensitivity to suffering is the hallmark of humanity. Hence by inviting suffering upon himself, the Satyagrahist may light up the spark of the divine potential in the wrongdoer.

The process of inviting suffering upon one's self takes two forms : (1) self-purification, internally ; and (2) non-cooperation with the agency of wrongdoing, externally.

Self-purification is meant both for the individual and for society. The Satyagrahist must not hesitate to take upon himself and upon his society, upon his nation, part of the responsibility for existing wrongs. Acts of self-purification call for a reconditioning of the individual and a mending or an ending of internal patterns and systems and institutions that inflict injustice and wrong upon society as a whole or upon certain sections of society. To that end soldiers of non-violence *cooperate* one with another and with other members of society to rid themselves of internal social wrongs.

This is one part of Satyagraha—*the constructive program* based upon self-purification and internal cooperation.

The other part of *Satyagraha* is *non-cooperation* with the agency or system that is responsible for the major wrong or injustice in society.

Concretely speaking, in India *Satyagraha* involved, on the one hand, the fivefold constructive program :

(1) Hindu-Muslim unity,
(2) Abolition of untouchability,
(3) Prohibition of narcotics and liquor,
(4) The greater participation of women in the nation's fight for freedom,
(5) The encouragement of home industries, such as spinning, weaving, and handicrafts of all sorts.

On the other hand, it involved non-cooperation with the British Government and its institutions :

(1) Renunciation of titles,
(2) Non-participation in official functions,
(3) Non-cooperation with government courts and schools, and the setting up of people's courts and national schools,
(4) Non-violent violation of predetermined laws of the government and seeking arrest and imprisonment,
(5) Peaceful picketing of government-licensed opium and liquor shops,
(6) Non-cooperation with the civil and military administration of the country,
(7) Non-payment of taxes.

Gandhi devised the program of non-cooperation not as a substitute for cooperation with the British Raj; he devised it as a substitute for irresponsible, sporadic violence which would have engulfed India as part of the natural cycle of nationalist upsurge. Thus, within the framework of his philosophy of Soul Force, Mahatma Gandhi proved the efficacy of the moral equivalent of war. (8, *passim*).

This technique of *Satyagraha* began to be adopted effectively in the fifties of this century in the United States by certain sections of the Negro minority under the leadership of Rev. Martin Luther King, Jr., and others. This movement for attainment of first class citizenship by Negroes is, likewise, based upon a constructive program—in-group cooperation in various forms and phases—as well as upon non-cooperation with the systems and instrumentalities of segregation. (*Cf. supra* CHAPTERS 16 and 19.)

14. PEACEFUL SOCIAL CHANGE

Not all social changes are, or need to be, brought about by violent or non-violent movements of a dynamic type. Sometimes social changes may be brought about by quiet and peaceful methods.

It is a moot point whether the canning of food was invented because of the American woman's desire to be freed from kitchen drudgery or whether the invention of canning led to her freedom. The hypothesis may not be amiss that in view of America's pragmatic approach and chronic labor shortage, the invention may well have been made to satisfy an acutely felt need. Be that as it may, the operations in the kitchen have been revolutionized since the invention of canning and the can-opener, and the American woman has been freed to work outside the home, to go to club meetings, or to do civic and philanthropic work—or even to espouse causes.

While slavery was abolished in the U.S.A. as a result of war, subsequent changes and improvements in the status of the Negro have been brought about by judicial and legislative procedures. The duel was abolished in America by legislative enactment, but the legislative enactment itself was the result of rising public opinion against dueling as a method of settling personal disputes.

Among the peaceful methods of social change available in a democracy to the "concerned" are: (1) education and propaganda, (2) public opinion, (3) legislation including lobbying, (4) non-violent non-cooperation or civil disobedience, (5) the impersonal logic of technology.

The confusions and conflicts in the international field today are the result of mankind's failure to arrive at a consensus on how to bring about necessary and desired change by peaceful methods. The League of Nations, instituted after World War I, made a valiant attempt to preserve the peace and failed, because it had prescribed no suitable mechanisms for peaceful change in the status quo. The United Nations, organized in the wake of World War II, is groping its way toward creating a consensus regarding peaceful methods of change in the status quo.

15. Social Change, Cultural Lag, and Social Problems

At the beginning of this chapter we pointed out that change is the one constant fact in nature. It is also a constant fact in society. Even so-called static societies do not stand still; we refer to them as static because of the unduly long period of time required even for slight change. Any one of the six causes of change would promptly throw even a so-called static society into a tailspin. But it is true that some societies change very slowly, while other societies change rapidly. These latter types are called dynamic societies. In general, folk societies and sacred societies show a marked tendency toward maintaining the status quo, toward registering little change. National societies and secular societies, on the other hand, are characterized by rapid changes.

Even in these dynamic societies, however, not all parts of culture change at the same rate. In 1900, Philadelphia had an ordinance "limiting the speed of horseless carriages to five miles per hour." The ordinance had validity because the horseless carriages of those days could travel but five miles an hour on smooth level road, and about ten miles an hour downhill. (4, pp. 21–23).

Today's automobiles have enough horsepower to make over a hundred miles per hour. In other words, the speed of the motor car has changed vastly—it has increased twentyfold. But the roads on which it travels have not improved in the same proportion. Some states limit speed to 50, 60, or 70 miles an hour; some simply prescribe "reasonable" speed with the car under the driver's control. Speed laws have attempted to keep pace with the power of modern cars. But the driver, the human factor in the situation, has not changed a whit. His reaction time for sensing danger ahead or stopping the car with a brake is the same today as it was in 1900. Some are temperamentally inclined to be fast drivers and some slow drivers. We see that in the concrete social situation, driving a car on the highways, there may be a dozen or more variables. These variables do not all change at the same rate.

Let us analyze another situation. The pioneers, having braved the high seas in their tiny barks, either settled on the Atlantic seaboard or moved westward. The westward movement of the Pioneers was one of the social and national urgencies of the day. The conquest and habitation of the wild regions on the frontier was imperative for increasing national resources. The logic of the frontiersman was simple: Conquer the wild regions, inhabit them, cultivate them, and thus add to national strength. In the process, trees were cut down, land was cleared and farms were carved out. There came a time of diminishing returns to national strength from this practice. Timber resources began to be wasted without adding much to national prosperity or power. But the practice was continued even when it became harmful to the nation's prosperity and power.

In general it may be said that the two parts of culture, the material and the non-material, change at differing rates. This tendency of the two parts of culture to change at differing rates is technically called cultural lag. If we were to view the material and non-material parts of culture as two horses hitched to a wagon, we would at once see the problem created by one horse pulling forward fast and the other moving slow or not at all.

Usually material culture changes more rapidly than non-material because of the vast number of inventions possible in that field. Non-material culture resists change, and changes very slowly: social organization, patterns of social relationship, and norms strive for continuity and stability. Be that as it may, the uneven rate of change in material and non-material parts of culture constitutes a cultural lag and creates social problems. (9, pp. 200–13).

16. OPPOSITION TO CHANGE

Even though he has attained his present position of eminence in nature by embracing change, man is essentially a conservative creature—i.e., he wants to conserve all the values of the past. When he exchanged his tree habitat for the earth abode, man made one of the profoundest changes in his life. When he graduated from a hunting economy into an agricultural economy, man again made another profound change in his mode of living. But each time he has resisted the new.

Scientific theories, technological inventions, new ways of solving old problems—all of these have been resisted at first and then adopted by the people at large when the new had proved its worth through numerous trials and testings.

In addition to this tendency toward conservatism, man is a creature of habit. When habits are endangered by a new invention or by social change, man rebels.

Third, there is always present a fear of the new. He has already come to terms with all the elements in the status quo; what guarantee is there that the new will not be more painful than the present?

Fourth, tied in with habit and with fear of the new is the simple fact of inertia in social tradition and collective man's intellectual laziness. He would much rather borrow than invent, and he would much rather go along the way he is going than try a new path.

Fifth, ignorance of objective facts, for instance, unawareness of the enormity of slum conditions, may lead well-meaning citizens to oppose change—slum clearance and public housing.

Sixth, failure of the new in the past is considered a valid reason for opposing it in the present and in the future. The failure of the Bull Moose Party in 1912, of La Follette's Progressive Party in the twenties, and of Wallace's Progressive Party in the forties is deemed sufficient reason for opposition to the creation of a new political party in the U.S.A.

Seventh, if the new in a previous trial had proved to be economically expensive or socially disruptive, it would be opposed now and in the future.

Finally, vested interests tend to thwart social change. Those who benefit from the present arrangement, be it economic, political or social, stoutly resist any innovation that may endanger their privileged position.

17. CONTEMPORARY SOCIAL CHANGES

Contemporary social changes in the world are profound and unparalleled, disturbing as well as inspiring. Abolition of the empire system in the wake of World War II, the rise of the totalitarian satellite empire system, the new status of woman the world over, the attainment of swaraj by whole populations of the world inhabiting Asia and Africa, the quest for a higher plane of living, the demand for equality of status on the part of the new-born nations of Asia and Africa, the penetration of the farthest corner of the world by modern technology as well as by modern medicine and hygiene, the trend from a rural-agricultural to an urban-industrial economy— these social changes necessitate new adjustments and accommodations. If mankind should fail to make the proper accommodation, the result would be disturbance, disequilibrium, chaos—and conflict.

Three of the four most significant changes that have come over the world have already been alluded to: (1) universal acceptance of nationalism as a goal for every relatively homogeneous aggregation of people operating either as folk society or as a nationality seeking to free itself from foreign domination; (2) universal acceptance of industrial-capitalist mode of production as a method of improving the people's plane of living; (3) the trend away from rural to urban mode of living (see *supra* CHAPTER 20).

The fourth most significant social change in the contemporary global landscape is the emergence of a hospitable attitude toward change itself. This is indeed a landmark. The Muslims of the world in a sense present the remarkable spectacle of a culture-group that has passed through the cycle of (a) hospitality to change, (b) opposition to change, and now (c) hospitality to change, once again.

Islam, the message of the Prophet Mohammed, itself represented a profound social change—from paganism and idolatry to belief in Allah, the Supreme Creator of the Universe. The early Muslims were avid advocates of social change. Their military arms carved out mighty empires, and their scholars made significant contributions to knowledge during the Dark Ages and the Middle Ages of Europe. Indeed, their services as transmitters of the classical lore of India and of Greece had a great deal to do with the Renaissance and Reformation in Europe.

Then something happened. The Muslims were ousted from all of Europe except the Balkans. Their scholarship began to wither away. Kismet (fatalism, an analogue of the Hindu doctrine of Karma) became the dominant theme of Muslim life and culture. This resulted in cultural stagnation and in opposition to change. The classic example of this may be found in the following answer given by a Muslim in response to a request for information about his community: (11, p. 170):

My Illustrious Friend and Joy of My Liver:

The thing which you ask of me is both difficult and useless. Although I have passed all my days in this place, I have neither counted the houses nor inquired into the number of inhabitants; and as to what one person loads on his mules and the other stows away in the bottom of his ship, this is no business of mine. But above all, as to the previous history of this city, God only knows the amount of dirt and confusion that the infidels may have eaten before the coming of the Sword of Islam. It were unprofitable for us to inquire into it. . . .

Listen, O my son! There is no wisdom equal to the belief in God. He created the world, and shall we liken ourselves unto him in seeking to penetrate into the mysteries of his creation? Shall we say,

Behold this star shineth around that star, and this other star with a tail goeth and cometh in so many years? Let it go; He from whose hand it came will guide and direct it. . . . Thou art learned in the things I care not for, and as for what thou hast seen, I spit upon it. Will much knowledge create thee a double belly, or wilt thou seek paradise with thine eyes?

The meek in spirit,
Imaum Ali Zadi

Compare and contrast this attitude of hostility to change and to scientific investigation on the part of the Muslim world at the beginning of the twentieth century with the dynamism, with the zest for change, which characterized every Muslim nation at the midcentury!

The replacing of the fez with the European-style hat at the dictation of Kemal Ataturk, in the wake of World War I, is but an outward manifestation of the inner revolution in Islamic Turkey. The Turks are today in outlook as modern, as empirical, as scientific, as pragmatic, as the most advanced nations in the world.

The sphinx of Egypt recently awoke from its centuries-long slumber; and President Gamal Abdel Nasser nationalized the Suez Canal in 1956. He and his people are dreaming of building a huge dam at Aswan, of Pan-Arabism, and of spearheading a Renaissance in the Arab world.

The so-called "unchanging East" of yester-year is changing at a dizzy pace. The readers of this textbook are on the threshold of vast changes in Asia and Africa, and their children will see the world from a new perspective.

This hospitality to change is predicated on the premise that collective man can control his destiny, that he is the architect of his own future. The doctrine of social telesis propounded by the great American sociologist Lester F. Ward is today being avidly embraced by Asians and Africans.

18. SOCIAL CHANGE AND SOCIAL PROGRESS

Last, we may distinguish between social change and social progress. Social change is a generic term, an objective term describing one of the categorical processes. It has no value judgment attached to it. To the sociologist, social change as a phenomenon is neither moral nor immoral—it is amoral. This does not rule out the fact that some social changes are beneficial to mankind, and some are injurious. What is implied is that the study of social change involves no value judgment. We may even study changes in the value system without being for or against the change.

The concept of social progress definitely involves and implies value judgments. Social progress connotes improvement, betterment, going up higher from a lower position. The American sociologist Lester F. Ward (1841-1913) was a strong believer in and advocate of social progress. His emphasis upon education as a means of social progress is thoroughly American. His doctrine of teleology or telesis was not just philosophical; he related it to society—social telesis.

It may seem incredulous to the generation studying this book, especially to the American student, but the stark fact is that the concept of progress is relatively new in human history. Progress began to emerge vaguely as a part of the Renaissance in Europe, but it began to manifest itself both as fact and as theory in the New World in the middle of the eighteenth century. St. John de Crevecoeur, the author of *Letters from an American Farmer*, is an exponent of the doctrine of progress. (See *supra*, CHAPTER 19). And after the American Revolution ushered in a new epoch of progress, the French Encyclopedists or the French School of Enlightenment began to preach the doctrine of progress and of human perfectibility.

The central core of the problem of social progress is a balancing between the status quo (in any aspect) with its assets and liabilities and the resultant of change with its assets and liabilities. Should the assets of change outweigh its liabilities and be greater than the assets of the status quo, progress may be said to have taken place. This is a simple formula, but the problem is much more complicated. The very definition of assets and liabilities is culturally conditioned. Then again, what may be an asset, a gain, in one field, say the political field, may be accompanied by tremendous loss in another field—say the economic or the artistic or the religious field.

What, then, is progress? The student must work out his own value system, set up his own norms, and study the social scene (1,

5, 12, 13, *passim*). Whatever else it may be, progress must contain at least the following six ingredients: (1) enhancement of the dignity of man, (2) respect for each human personality, (3) ever-increasing freedom for spiritual quest and for investigation of truth, (4) freedom for creativity and for esthetic enjoyment of the works of nature as well as of man, (5) a social order that promotes the first four values and (6) promotes life, liberty and the pursuit of happiness, with justice and equity to all. A democracy, such as ours, is by definition oriented to "general welfare." Hence the achievement and smooth functioning of a well ordered democracy should be considered one of the indices of social progress.

REFERENCES

1. J. B. BURY: *The Idea of Progress.* New York: Macmillan, 1932.
2. C. M. CASE: *Non-Violent Coercion.* New York: Century, 1923.
3. LOUIS FISCHER: *The Life of Mahatma Gandhi.* New York: Harper, 1950.
4. E. B. GALLAGHER: *Progress in America Which I Have Seen—Since the 1880's.* New York: The Newcomen Society of England, American Branch, 1947.
5. J. O. HERTZLER: *Social Progress.* New York: Century, 1928.
6. ADOLF HITLER: *Mein Kampf.* Available in at least two English translations.
7. SIR THOMAS MORE: *Utopia.* Several editions available.
8. H. T. MUZUMDAR: *Mahatma Gandhi: Peaceful Revolutionary.* New York: Charles Scribner's Sons, 1953.
9. W. F. OGBURN: *Social Change.* New York: B. W. Huebsch (now Viking Press), 1922.
10. VINCENT SHEEAN: *Lead, Kindly Light.* New York: Random House, 1949.
11. W. I. THOMAS: *Source Book for Social Origins.* Boston: Richard G. Badger, 1902.
12. A. J. TODD: *Theories of Social Progress.* New York: Macmillan, 1922.
13. U. G. WEATHERLY: *Social Progress.* Philadelphia: J. B. Lippincott Co., 1926.
14. WALTER P. WEBB: *The Great Plains.* Boston: Ginn & Co., 1931.

CHAPTER 29

SOCIAL CONTROL

1. THE NATURE OF SOCIAL CONTROL

IN CHAPTER 23, we listed social control as the last of the categorical social processes. The assigning of this position to social control in our schema is merely a methodological device; it does not imply the degree or intensity of the utility of social control as a process in society. Indeed, in the schema it was pointed out that whereas it is classified as a secondary or categorical process, social control quite often functions as a primary process.

We may liken social control to atmospheric pressure, ever present and experienced but not consciously felt, noticed by us only when something is missing or goes wrong, such as the breakdown of old controls, or when we consciously and objectively analyze the phenomenon (of either atmospheric pressure or social control).

Social control "is the central fact and the central problem of society." At its elemental level, social control is the process whereby individuals are "inducted" into a given social order, from the time of birth or incorporation, and "induced to cooperate in some sort of permanent corporate existence which we call society." (6, p. 42.)

2. DEFINITIONS OF SOCIAL CONTROL

The term "control" conjures up before the mind's eye a vision of policemen, law courts, prisons, and laws; of force and coercion. While these elements do have a relevance in control, the term social control, as used by sociologists, has a broader meaning. Landis, for instance, defines social control "as a social process by which the individual is made group-responsive, and by which social organization is built and maintained." (3, p. viii.)

Three of the founding fathers of American sociology made significant contributions to an analysis of (a) social control as a process, (b) the consequences of social control, and (c) the methods by which social control is effected: Edward A. Ross (1866-1951), Charles H. Cooley (1864-1929), and William Graham Sumner (1840-1910).

Ross, author of the first book entitled *Social Control*, pioneered in the scientific investigation of this social process (1901; 8, *passim*). The subtitle of his book, "A Study of the Foundations of the Social Order," gives us a clue to the significant role of social control, even though he himself explicitly stated that social control dealt only with social ascendancy—with the purposeful domination over the individual by society. Ross did, however, recognize the fact of unconscious, unintended domination over the individual by society; but he excluded this process from social control as defined by him.

Beginning in 1894, Ross became interested in discovering "the linchpins which hold society together." He set down "thirty-five distinct means by which society controls its members." These were " worked over for six years, and emerged first in twenty articles in the *American Journal of Sociology*, and finally in 1901 in the well-known treatise called *Social Control*. (1, pp. 403–4).

In the 1930's Ross developed the concept of super-social control by which he meant the domination over society by scheming individuals who, through propaganda, lobbying, and/or coercive methods, compel society to do their bidding (7, CHAPTER 40).

In 1902, Cooley formulated a conception of social control that admirably supplemented that of Ross. "Cooley's emphasis is on the effect of group pressure upon the personality of the individual and the necessity for studying a person's life history in order to understand his behavior. In particular, his discussion of 'the looking-glass self' and the social origins of the conscience have been far-reaching in leading others to study the process of socialization and the interaction between the individual and his group." (9, p. 5).

While Ross was concerned with the mechanisms of social control, Cooley was interested in studying the effects of social control, especially in terms of socialization and personality formation. Finally, Sumner investigated what we call social control in terms of the compulsive role of folkways, mores and institutions (9, p. 5):

A third aspect of social control is emphasized by William Graham Sumner. According to this author, social behavior cannot be understood without a study of the folkways, mores, institutions, and value-judgments which underlie the rules of conduct of the group. These socio-cultural forms which organize the responses of individuals are of primary importance in deciding the direction in which social control operates. In other words, the life-values and social organization of the group largely determine whether the agents of social control will encourage or inhibit any specific item of behavior. Sumner's volume, which has been called ' the Old Testament of the sociologists,' treats of social control only incidentally but is of great significance in showing, largely by a profusion of illustrations, how folkways and institutions limit the behavior of individuals—' the mores can make anything right and prevent condemnation of anything.'

In its broadest sense, social control may be defined as the process in which any stimulus determines or modifies the response of any member of a human grouping. Social control has to do with the guiding or directing of human behavior into socially desired or desirable channels, to the end that individual and collective role expectations and fulfillments may promote social continuity and stability.

Sociologists have been inclining more and more toward such a broad definition of social control as given by us in the preceding paragraph. Kimball Young (10, p. 520), for instance, defines

social control as the use of coercion, force, restraint, suggestion, or persuasion of one group over another, or of a group over its members or of persons over others to enforce the prescribed rules of the game. These rules may be set down by the members themselves, as in a professional code of ethics, or they may be those laid down by a larger, more inclusive group for the regulation of another smaller group.

(Parenthetically, it may be noted that Dr. Young omits this definition from the second edition of *Sociology* [11, CHAPTER 29], but implicitly accepts it as a frame of reference in discussing social control.)

Lumley (5, p. 13) speaks of social control "as the practice of putting forth directive stimuli or wish-patterns, their accurate transmission to, and adoption by, others whether voluntarily or involuntarily. In short, it (social control) is effective will-transference."

"Ideally," continues Lumley, "social control would be in the hands and the interests of the inclusive group whatever it is; practically, however, it is in the hands of, and often in the interests of, some few members who have usurped and know how to use it" (5, pp. 13–14).

Finally, Park and Burgess speak of social control emerging only when the control is sanctioned by social forces, such as custom, law, public opinion (6, p. 789):

What we ordinarily mean by social control is the arbitrary intervention of some individual—official, functionary, or leader—in the social process. A policeman arrests a criminal, an attorney sways the jury with his eloquence, the judge passes sentence; these are the familiar formal acts in which social control manifests itself. What makes the control exercised in this way social, in the strict sense of that term, is the fact that these acts are supported by custom, law, and public opinion.

3. Psycho-Social Mechanisms of Social Control

There are two types of psycho-social mechanisms of social control: formal and informal.

Among the informal mechanisms of social control may be mentioned the three immanent processes—stimulus-response, interaction, communication—and four of the six primary processes: imitation, suggestion, inculcation, indoctrination. Gossip and flattery may also be included here. Education and propaganda, whether as primary processes or as secondary processes, play a significant part in social control.

Among the secondary processes, socialization, intimately tied in with all of the primary processes, provides the best mechanism for social control. As for the other secondary processes, cooperation would not be possible without consensus, without a commonly shared definition of the situation, which can only be brought about by social control. Furthermore, "the community and the natural order within the limits of the community . . . are an effect of competition. Social control and the mutual subordination of individual members to the community have their origin in conflict, assume definite organized forms in the process of accommodation, and are consolidated and fixed in assimilation." (6, p. 785). Finally, it is obvious that social control would be exerted in social change through the leadership-followership pattern.

When any of these processes becomes structuralized into an institution, social control becomes formal and institutional. For instance, within cooperation structuralized into the cooperative movement, social control is formalized and exerted by duly appointed functionaries and by formally approved methods. Similarly, conflict structuralized into war as the collective activity of a tribe or a nation carries formal sanctions and formal methods of social control.

With the shift from agrarian to industrial economy, from rural to urban mode of living, from primary group relationships to secondary group relationships, informal mechanisms of control have been steadily giving way before formal mechanisms of social control.

4. FORMAL AGENCIES AND INFORMAL METHODS OF SOCIAL CONTROL

Among the informal methods of social control may be mentioned: praise-and-blame mechanism, socialization, folkways, mores, value-systems, status-systems, and public opinion. Among the formal agencies of social control are the five primary institutions—family, business, church, school, state—and thousands of secondary institutions, each with its formal rituals and sanctions.

That the mass media of communication—press, movies, radio-TV—exert tremendous influence and thereby serve as agencies of social control is evident to all of us. But it is not clear exactly how to classify them. Are they formal or informal agencies of social control? In view of the fact that they are corporate entities and operate as institutions in our society, we may be justified in referring to them as formal agencies of social control. But inasmuch as in a democracy such as ours the public has the right to choose newspapers or radio-TV programs or movies from a wide variety, the strictly formal pattern of social control seems to break down. In a totalitarian, dictatorship-ridden country such as the Soviet Union, on the other hand, all media of mass communication exert formal social control as determined by the higher-ups in the Kremlin. *The Brave New World* of Aldous Huxley with its Director of Hatchery and Conditioning (D. H. C.) illustrates rigid social control available to a totalitarian society (2, *passim*).

The ascendancy-subordination or leadership-followership pattern as well as the set of status-systems in a society exerts both formal and informal types of social control.

Finally, it may be pointed out that social control is achieved (a) through persuasion, coercion, compulsion; (b) through the identification mechanism of esprit de corps and morale or what Durkheim called solidarity; and (c) through collective representations (see *supra* CHAPTER 12).

5. THREE FORMS OF SOCIAL CONTROL

Every society has at its disposal certain "spontaneous forms of social control . . . tradition, custom, folkways, mores, ceremonial, myth, religious and political beliefs, dogmas and creeds, and finally public opinion and law." (6, p. 785). Park and Burgess include law among the spontaneous, or informal, agencies of social control, because in the long run legislation "must have the support of public opinion." (6, p. 786). Even so, it would be better to classify public opinion as an intermediate form of social control and law as an institutional form of social control.

Adapting Park and Burgess' scheme of classification, we may speak of three forms of social control: the elementary, the intermediate, the institutional—(1) elementary forms of social control, such as rapport between individuals in a crowd, or "milling," or a situation predetermined by previously operative forces; (2) intermediate forms of social control, best illustrated by public opinion, and (3) institutional forms of social control, already spoken of by us.

We may reproduce Park and Burgess' discussion of the first two forms of social control (6, pp. 788–96, adapted):

Elementary Forms of Social Control

Control in the crowd, where rapport is once established and every individual is immediately responsive to every other, is the most elementary form of control.

Something like this same direct and spontaneous response of the individual in the crowd to the crowd's dominant mood or impulse may be seen in the herd and the flock, the "animal crowd."

Under the influence of the vague sense of alarm, or merely as an effect of heat and thirst, cattle become restless and begin slowly moving about in circles, "milling." This milling is a sort of collective gesture, an expression of discomfort or of fear. But the very expression of the unrest tends to intensify its expression and so increases the tension in the herd. This continues up to the point where some sudden sound, the firing of a pistol or a flash of lightning, plunges the herd into a wild stampede.

Milling in the herd is a visible image of what goes on in subtler and less obvious ways in human societies. Alarms or discomforts frequently provoke social unrest. The very expression of this unrest tends to magnify it. The situation is a vicious circle. Every attempt to deal with it merely serves to aggravate it. Such a vicious circle we witnessed in our history from 1830 to 1861, when every attempt to deal with slavery served only to bring the inevitable conflict between the states nearer. Finally there transpired what had for twenty years been visibly preparing, and the war broke.

Tolstoi in his great historical romance, *War and Peace*, describes, in a manner which no historian has equaled, the events that led up to the Franco-Russian War of 1812, and particularly the manner in which Napoleon, in spite of his efforts to avoid it, was driven by social forces over which he had no control to declare war on Russia, and so bring about his own downfall.

The condition under which France was forced by Bismarck to declare war on Prussia in 1870, and the circumstances under which Austria declared war on Serbia in 1914 and so brought on the world-war, exhibit the same fatal circle. In both cases, given the situation, the preparations that had been made, the resolutions formed and the agreements entered into, it seems clear that after a certain point had been reached every move was forced.

This is the most fundamental and elementary form of control. It is the control exercised by the mere play of elemental forces. These forces may, to a certain extent, be manipulated, as is true of other natural forces; but within certain limits, human nature being what it is, the issue is fatally determined, just as, given the circumstances and the nature of cattle, a stampede is inevitable. Historical crises are invariably created by processes which, looked at abstractly, are very much like milling in a herd. The vicious circle is the so-called "psychological factor" in financial depressions and panics and is, indeed, a factor in all collective action.

The distinction between control in the crowd and in other forms of society is that the crowd has no tradition. It has no point of reference in its own past to which its members can refer for guidance. It has therefore neither symbols, ceremonies, rites, nor ritual; it imposes no obligations and creates no loyalties.

Ceremonial is one method of reviving in the group a lively sense of the past. It is a method of reinstating the excitements and the sentiments which inspired an earlier collective action. The savage war dance is a dramatic representation of battle and as such serves to rouse and reawaken the warlike spirit. This is one way in which ceremonial becomes a means of control. By reviving the memories of an earlier war, it mobilizes the warriors for a new one.

The dance, which is so characteristic and so universal a feature of the life of primitive man—at once a mode of collective expression and of collective representation—is but a conventionalized form of the circular reaction, which in its most primitive form is represented by the milling of the herd.

Intermediate Forms of Social Control
Public Opinion

We ordinarily think of public opinion as a sort of social weather. At certain times, and under certain circumstances, we observe strong, steady currents of opinion, moving apparently in a definite direction and toward a definite goal. At other times, however, we note flurries and eddies and countercurrents in this movement. Every now and then there are storms, shifts, or dead calms. These sudden shifts in public opinion, when expressed in terms of votes, are referred to by politicians as "landslides."

In all these movements, cross-currents and changes in direction which a closer observation of public opinion reveals, it is always possible to discern, but on a much grander scale, to be sure, that same type of circular reaction which we have found elsewhere, whenever the group was preparing to act. Always in the public, as in the crowd, there will be a circle, sometimes wider, sometimes narrower, within which individuals are mutually responsive to motives and interests of one another, so that out of this interplay of social forces there may emerge at any time a common motive and a common purpose that will dominate the whole.

Within the circle of the mutual influence described, there will be no such complete rapport and no such complete domination of the individual by the group as exists in a herd or a crowd in a state of excitement, but there will be sufficient community of interest to insure a common understanding. A public is, in fact, organized on the basis of a universe of discourse, and within the limits of this universe of discourse, language, statements of fact, news will have, for all practical purposes, the same meanings. It is this circle of mutual influence within which there is a universe of discourse that defines the limits of the public.

A public, like a crowd, is not to be conceived as a formal organization like a parliament or even a public meeting. It is always the widest area over which there is conscious participation and consensus in the formation of public opinion. The public has not only a circumference, but it has a center as well.

When we speak of the tendency or direction of public opinion, we usually mean the trend over a definite period of time.

It is this narrowing of the area over which a definite public opinion may be said to exist that at once creates the possibility and defines the limits of arbitrary control, so far as it is created or determined by the existence of public opinion.

Thus far the public has been described almost wholly in terms that could be applied to a crowd. The public has been frequently described as if it were simply a great crowd, a crowd scattered as widely as news will circulate and still be news. But there is this difference. In the heat and excitement of the crowd, as in the choral dances of primitive people, there is for the moment what may be described as complete fusion of the social forces. Rapport has, for the time being, made the crowd, in a peculiarly intimate way, a social unit.

No such unity exists in the public. The sentiment and tendencies which we call public opinion are never unqualified expressions of emotion. The difference is that public opinion is determined by conflict and discussion, and made up of the opinions of individuals not wholly at one. In any conflict situation, where party spirit is aroused, the spectators, who constitute the public, are bound to take sides. The impulse to take sides is, in fact, in direct proportion to the excitement and party spirit displayed. The result is, however, that both sides of an issue get considered. Certain contentions are rejected because they will not stand criticism. Public opinion formed in this way has the character of a judgment, rather than a mere unmediated expression of emotion, as in the crowd. The public is never ecstatic. It is always more or less rational. It is this fact of conflict, in the form of discussion, that introduces into the control exercised by public opinion the elements of rationality and of fact.

A distinction ought to be made between public opinion and the mores. Custom and the folkways, like habit in the individual, may be regarded as a mere residuum of past practices. When folkways assume the character of mores, they are no longer merely matters of fact and common sense, they are judgments upon matters which were probably once live issues and as such they may be regarded as the products of public opinion.

Ritual, religious or social, is probably the crystallization of forms of behavior which, like the choral dance, are the direct expression of the emotions and the instincts. The mores, on the other hand, in so far as they contain a rational element, are the accumulation, the residuum, not only of past practices, but of judgments such as find expression in public opinion. The mores, as thus conceived, are the judgments of public opinion in regard to issues that have been settled and forgotten.

Public opinion issues from the interaction of individuals. (In the process of public discussion) moral judgments are formed that eventually become the basis of law.

Among the intermediate forms of social control, in addition to public opinion, we should include literature and the fine arts and the media of mass communication.

Institutional Forms of Social Control

Institutional forms of social control are easiest to identify, because each institution has its designated officers, its rules and rituals, its specific provisions for the use of *danda*—for enforcing its rules and regulations.

In complex, secular societies social control exerted by the institution of the state intrudes itself in the other four primary institutions and in the myriads of secondary institutions. The family may have its forms of social control as between husband, wife and children, but the state steps in with imperative declarations of what may and may not be done—i.e., proper treatment of the child.

Professional organizations develop their own code of ethics, but if that code of ethics or the practice of the professional organization should violate the mores of society or the laws, the state would step in.

Social controls exerted by the family, by business, by the school and by the church may be analyzed by the student as a special project: such an analysis should reveal the significant role of social control of the given institution exerted upon the members of the association operating it as well as the equally significant role of social control exerted by the state.

6. THE CENTRAL PROBLEM OF SOCIAL CONTROL

The central problem of social control is the problem of arriving at a nice balance between the rights of the individual citizen and the rights of society, between the obligations of the individual and the obligations of society.

Society may function as community, as a complex of groups (associations), or as state. Community is characterized by common will and commonweal (commonwealth); here the dichotomy between individual and society is at a minimum, and social control becomes collective self-control.

In society as a complex of groups, the rules and regulations of each association are devised for its well-being; but the well-being of a given association, e.g., the trade union, may be—or may be conceived to be—inimical to the well-being of another association, e.g., the N.A.M., the National Association of Manufacturers. To minimize inter-association conflicts, the state sets forth and enforces regulations in terms of "the general welfare."

The relations between state and citizen resolve themselves into problems of freedom and authority. That there can be no freedom without rules, without a frame of reference, is scientifically valid but not generally appreciated. What kind of freedom, for instance, would there be on the highways of this country (the U.S.A.) for any of us if the rule to keep to the right were disregarded by every motorist—or even by a few? Within the compulsion or authority of that rule, we are free to keep to our side of the road and drive peacefully, fully confident that no car would plough into ours head-on from the opposite direction.

While authority and regulation are valuable for social efficiency and harmony, the question arises: how much authority? how much regulation? In a democratic society the state's authority is derived from the free consent of the citizens.

Gandhi defined freedom as the capacity to impose restraints upon oneself. The individual's freedom may well turn out, ultimately, to be a problem of self-discipline. In a democracy, ideally, authority should not go beyond the collective self-discipline of citizens.

7. THE ALL-PERVASIVE NATURE OF SOCIAL CONTROL

Wherever there is group or associated life, social control automatically emerges. Whether it be the medicine man or the tribal chief, king or president, symbols of authority are accepted by the group as regulating their lives. The elementary, intermediate and institutional forms of social control become part of the socio-cultural landscape in every society.

For a comparative analysis of different societies, social control may be utilized as a tool of investigation (a) in terms of its influence upon individual behavior and personality formation as well as (b) in terms of its influence upon social patterns and human groupings.

8. LEADERSHIP AND SOCIAL CONTROL

Recently the study of group dynamics has shed considerable light on the problems of leadership, social control, and group as well as individual achievement. Kurt Lewin (1890-1947), an Austrian social psychologist, and his co-workers at the State University of Iowa set up an experimental design with three types of leadership: (1) authoritarian, (2) laissez-faire, and (3) democratic.

Four boys' clubs, with membership comparable in quality and quantity, were each assigned an adult leader of a different type, alternately: an authoritarian leader, a laissez-faire leader, and a democratic leader (4, pp. 315–30):

Plan For Authoritarian Leadership Role

Practically all policies as regards club activities and procedures should be determined by the leader. The techniques and activity steps should be communicated by the authority, one unit at a time, so that future steps are in the dark to a large degree. The adult should take considerable responsibility for assigning the activity tasks and companions of each group member. The dominator should keep his standards of praise and criticism to himself in evaluating individual and group activities. He should also remain fairly aloof from active group participation except in demonstrating.

Plan For The Democratic Leadership Role

Wherever possible, policies should be a matter of group decision and discussion with active encouragement and assistance by the adult leader. The leader should attempt to see that activity perspective emerges during the discussion period with the general steps to the group goal becoming clarified. Wherever technical advice is needed, the leader should try to suggest two or more alternative procedures from which choice can be made by the group members. Everyone should be free to work with whomever he chooses, and the divisions of responsibility should be left up to the group. The leader should attempt to communicate in an objective, fact-minded way the bases for his praise and criticism of individual and group activities. He should try to be a regular group member in spirit but not do much of the work (so that comparisons of group productivity can be made between the groups).

Plan for Laissez-Faire Leadership Role

In this situation, the adult should play a rather passive role in social participation and leave complete freedom for group or individual decisions in relation to activity and group procedure. The leader should make clear the various materials which are available and be sure it is understood that he will supply information and help when asked. He should do a minimum of taking the initiative in making suggestions. He should make no attempt to evaluate negatively or positively the behavior or productions of the individuals or the group as a group, although he should be friendly rather than " stand-offish" at all times.

This experiment demonstrated how different styles of leadership operate and how each style of leadership brings forth specific results in terms of social interaction. The autocratic leader met with the least favor; the laissez-faire leader was rated "the poorest" leader, and the democratic leader was highly applauded by all the members of the different clubs, first, because each member experienced a sense of security, proper guidance, and self-reliance; second, because each member felt he had a share in the making of policy. Under the laissez-faire leadership, on the other hand, the members began to experience boredom and failed to achieve significant results either individually or collectively. The authoritarian leader sometimes succeeded in getting things done and projects more or less carried out, but the members experienced an acute sense of frustration: they were never in the "know" of things, nor could they anticipate the next move.

The study of role expectations and role fulfillments can be effectively carried on in such small groups susceptible to control and accurate observation.

Group dynamics is an important phase in the creation of social climate of one type or another. Likewise, the sociogram and the sociodrama, evolved by J. L. Moreno, the sociometrist, are important tools in the study of interaction, role playing, and social control.

9. Social Control As Social Progress

Providence, progress, control—such is the progression in man's attempt to understand the universe (including himself) and to adjust himself to it. The dynamic trait of modern culture is the belief in collective man's ability to control nature and to control his destiny. This point of view has been ably set forth by the late Professor Ellsworth Faris (1874-1953) (6, pp. 960–62, quoted):

The idea of progress which has been so influential in modern times is not a very old conception. In its distinctive form it came into existence in the rationalistic period which accompanied the Renaissance. Progress, in this sense, means a theory as to the way in which the whole cosmic process is developing. It is the belief that the world as a whole is growing better through definite stages, and is moving "to one far-off divine event."

The stages preceding this idea may be thought of under several heads. The first may be called "cosmic anarchy," in which we find "primitive people" now living. It is a world of chaos, without meaning, and without purpose. There is no direction in which human life is thought of as developing. Death and misfortune are for the most part due to witchcraft and the evil designs of enemies; good luck and bad luck are the forces which make a rational existence hopeless.

Another stage of thinking is that which was found among the Greeks, the conception of the cosmic process as proceeding in cycles. The golden age of the Greeks lay in the past, the universe was considered to be following a set course, and the whole round of human experience was governed and controlled by an inexorable fate that was totally indifferent to human wishes. The formula which finally arose to meet this situation was "conformity to nature," a submission to the iron laws of the world which it was vain to attempt to change.

This idea was succeeded in medieval Europe by the idea of providence, in which the world was thought of as a theater on which the drama of human redemption was enacted. God has created man free, but man was corrupted by the fall, given an opportunity to be redeemed by the gospel, and the world was soon to know the final triumph and happiness of the saved. Most of the early church fathers expected the end of the world very soon, many of them in their own lifetime. This is distinctly different from the preceding two ideas. All life had meaning to them, for the evil in the world was but God's way to accomplish his good purposes. It was man's duty to submit, but submission was to take the form of faith in an all-wise beneficent and perfect power, who was governing the world and who would make everything for the best.

The idea of progress arose on the ruins of this concept of providence. In the fourteenth century, progress did not mean merely the satisfaction of all human desires either individual or collective. The idea meant far more than that. It was the conviction that the world as a whole was proceeding onward indefinitely to greater and greater perfection. The atmosphere of progress was congenial to the construction of utopias and schemes of perfection which were believed to be in harmony with the nature of the world itself. The atmosphere of progress produced also optimists who were quite sure everything was in the long run to be for the best, and that every temporary evil was sure to be overcome by an ultimate good.

The difficulty in demonstrating the fact of progress has become very real as the problem has been presented to modern minds. It is possible to prove that the world has become more complex. It is hardly possible to prove that it has become better, and quite impossible to prove that it will continue to do so. From the standpoint of the Mohammedan Turks, the last two hundred years of the world's history have not been years of marked progress; from the standpoint of their enemies, the reverse statement is obviously true.

The conception which seems to be superseding the idea of progress in our day is that of control. Each problem, whether personal or social, is thought of as a separate enterprise. Poverty, disease, crime, vice, intemperance, or war, these are definite situations which challenge human effort and human ingenuity. Many problems are unsolved; many failures are recorded. The future is a challenge to creative intelligence and collective heroism. The future is thought of as still to be made. And there is no assurance that progress will take place. On the contrary, there is every reason to believe that progress will not take place unless men are able by their skill and devotion to find solutions for their present problems, and for the newer ones that shall arise.

The modern man finds this idea quite as stimulating to him as the idea of progress was to his ancestor of the Renaissance or the idea of providence to his medieval forebears. For while he does not blindly believe nor feel optimistically certain that things will come about all right, yet he is nerved to square his shoulders, to think, to contrive, and to exert himself to the utmost in his effort to conquer the difficulties ahead, and to control the forces of nature and man. The idea of providence was not merely a generalization on life, it was a force that inspired hope. The idea of progress was likewise not merely a concept, it was also an energizing influence in a time of great intellectual activity. The idea that the forces of nature can be controlled in the service of man, differs from the others, but is also a dynamic potency that seems to be equally well adapted to the twentieth century.

REFERENCES

1. E. S. BOGARDUS: *The Development of Social Thought*, New York: Longmans, Green and Co., 1947.

2. A. HUXLEY: *Brave New World*, New York: Harper and Brothers, 1932, 1946.

3. P. H. LANDIS: *Social Control*. Philadelphia: J. B. Lippincott Co., 1939.

4. R. LIPPITT and R. K. WHITE: "An Experimental Study of Leadership and Group Life" in *Readings in Social Psychology*, ed. by T. M. Newcomb, E. L. Hartley, et al. New York: Henry Holt and Co., 1947.

5. F. E. LUMLEY: *Means of Social Control*. New York: D. Appleton-Century Co., 1925.

6. R. E. PARK and E. W. BURGESS: *Introduction to the Science of Sociology*, 2nd ed. Chicago: University of Chicago Press, 1924 (8th impression, 1933).

7. E. A. ROSS: *Principles of Sociology*, first revision. New York: D. Appleton-Century Co., 1930.

8. E. A. ROSS: *Social Control*. New York: Macmillan, 1901.

9. J. S. ROUCEK, Ed.: *Social Control*. New York (now Princeton, N. J.) D. Van Nostrand Co., 1947.

10. K. YOUNG: *An Introductory Sociology*. New York: American Book Co., 1934.

11. K. YOUNG: *Sociology: A Study of Society and Culture*, 2nd ed. New York: American Book Co., 1949.

CHAPTER 30

GLOBAL PROCESSES—THE EMERGENCE
OF ONE WORLD

1. REVOLUTION IN TRANSPORTATION AND COMMUNICATION

FOR thousands of years collective man has been a captive of limitations imposed upon him by nature. With the accumulation of culture, he began to free himself from bondage to nature. For instance, the earliest form of transportation he had was locomotion—walking as far as his two legs could or would carry him. His communication was confined to the radius of his locomotion. In both transportation and communication, in other words, early man was earth-bound.

Later he began to ply the rivers and traverse on land by ox-cart, by horse-carriage, by reindeer-sled, or by simply riding a horse. Thus he began to enlarge the radius of transportation and communication. But man was still space-bound, and time-bound.

The first steps in transcending the limitations of space and time were taken in the nineteenth century when the telegraph was invented (1832-37) by the American, Samuel F. B. Morse (1791-1872). This invention rested on a knowledge of electromagnetic principles. In 1876 Alexander Graham Bell (1847-1922), also an American, successfully carried on a conversation with his assistant, Thomas A. Watson, over a line which he had erected between Boston and Cambridgeport, Massachusetts. Twenty years later, in 1896, the Italian Guglielmo Marconi (1874-1937) took out his first English patent for wireless telegraphy. The spectacular advances in "wireless" or radio and in TV since World War I have freed man from the limitations of both space and time, so far as communication is concerned.

Since the end of World War II, people in the United States have been used to seeing on the TV screen noted personalities being interviewed in New York, Chicago or Hollywood. So many notables have "faced" the nation or the press that the wonderment has gone

510

out of this revolutionary freedom from the limitations of time and space. But on June 2, 1957, the American nation as well as the world at large suddenly realized the nature of the revolutionary change in communication when Mr. Nikita S. Khrushchev, Secretary of the Communist Party of the U.S.S.R., "faced the nation" over the Columbia Radio-TV network.

Man took the first step toward achieving relative freedom from the limitations of time and space in the field of transportation with the invention of the steam engine (1705) by the Englishman, Thomas Newcomen (1663-1729), and with the improvement of Newcomen's engine (1763-69) by his compatriot, James Watt (1736-1819). The harnessing of steam power to run the wheels of industry as well as to run trains was destined to cut short distances in time and space. And the automobile, an invention of the late nineteenth century, has put all America on wheels—and may soon put the rest of the world on wheels, too.

Man's ability to free himself from the limitations of time and space in the field of transportation is being demonstrated every day by our globe-circling airplanes, regular as well as jet-propelled. The most dramatic demonstration of this fact was brought home to us during World War II when Mr. Wendell L. Willkie (1892-1944) travelled around the world by airplane and wrote his famous book *One World* (1943, 4, *passim*). This book could just as well have been called "The Education of Mr. Wendell L. Willkie," or "The Education of Our Generation."

Today, for the first time in his history on this globe, man is able to establish physical contact with his fellows in the farthest corner in a matter of hours; today, for the first time in history, man is able to communicate with his fellows in the farthest corner of the earth within the twinkling of an eye. Airplane wings, air waves, radio beams, electromagnetic field—these have freed man from the limitations of space and time.

The logical outcome of this revolution in transportation and communication is intensified social interaction on a global scale. News and views travel rapidly from nation to nation and from continent to continent, sometimes resulting in better understanding, sometimes in misunderstanding.

2. On the Threshold of the Interplanetary Stage

The initial launching of two sputniks—one in October and the other in November of 1957—by Soviet Russian scientists and their German collaborators and subsequent launchings of space satellites by American scientists and their German co-workers initiated the space age—the interplanetary stage in man's cultural development.

A high point in this ever-present struggle of man to transcend the limitations of time and space was reached during the Christmas season of 1958 when, beginning with December 19, the four-and-a-half-ton U.S. satellite, the Atlas missile, revolving around the earth in an orbit ranging from 928 miles to 114 miles, began to broadcast from outer space President Dwight D. Eisenhower's Christmas message of "Peace on earth and goodwill toward men everywhere."

The dramatic climax in this process of widening man's conquest of nature came when on the 2nd of January, 1959, the scientists of the Soviet Union shot the interplanetary rocket "Lunik," which soared zooming past the moon at dizzying speed and entered into the sun's orbit on January 7, 1959, to become the first man-made planet revolving around the sun, "an eternal artificial planet of our solar system," and the tenth planet in our solar cosmos.

Not to be outdone by the Soviet Union, the scientists of the United States, two months later, i.e., on March 3, 1959, shortly after the midnight of March 2nd, blasted off their gold-plated space-satellite, Pioneer IV, from Cape Canaveral, Florida. Weighing much less than the Russian "Lunik," the American cone-shaped "artificial planet," the eleventh planet in our solar cosmos, whose gold plate provided an antenna to relay radio instrumentation data back to earth, was packed with instruments to measure radioactivity in space. These data may some day enable man to send down to earth television pictures from outer space as well as to send man aloft into outer space—perhaps to the moon or to Mars. In fact, the American communications satellite TELSTAR began to transmit TV programs instantaneously from the U.S.A. to Europe and *vice versa,* in 1963.

3. The New Ethic in the Making

The world, so formidable to our ancestors, so challenging to Columbus, has today become a small neighborhood. This small neighborhood world, cutting across national, racial, religious and cultural boundaries, is, since World War II, going through the process of developing a new set of norms and a new ethical code appropriate to the changed nature of our world.

We know the conditions under which a small neighborhood may thrive and live in peace. First, there is mutual respect, based upon acceptance of equality, among neighbors. Second, neighbors prosper and live as a cohesive group so long as they observe the twin principles of *Satya* (Truth) and *Ahimsa* (Non-Violence: Love). Third, in order to guarantee stability and long life to the neighborhood, the neighbors must evolve effective ways of bringing about peaceful change.

While the primary group relationships of the small neighborhood cannot be achieved in our small neighborhood world, the principles on which good neighborliness rests must be made effective on a global scale if we are to rid ourselves of the scourge of war.

Peace can be achieved in the world only on the basis of a new consensus. This new consensus must be arrived at on three major issues: (1) nationalism, (2) internationalism, (3) outlawing of war and evolving of peaceful methods for settling disputes among nations.

The paradox of the twentieth century is that it marks the high tide of nationalism and at the same time signals the end of the civilization of nation-states. The countries of Asia and Africa have already achieved their nationalism or will soon achieve it. Nobody with a sense of world-citizenship denies the value of this objective.

Hitler on the one hand and Stalin and his successors on the other demonstrate the trend toward internationalism through the creation of coordinated satellite states. The era of national sovereignty, of national self-competence, was dealt a death blow by the airplane, which flies overhead serenely oblivious of national boundaries, as surely as was feudalism brought to an end by the use of gun powder in warfare.

It is, however, doubtful whether the totalitarian approach, either of the fascists or of the communists, toward developing internationalism through coercion and brute force can yield enduring results. Internationalism can be meaningful only on the basis of the free consent of nations. Mahatma Gandhi, the apostle of a warless world, laid down certain principles which should commend themselves to all members of the small neighborhood world (2, p. 111):

"Internationalism is possible only when nationalism becomes a fact, i.e., when peoples belonging to different countries have organized themselves and are able to act as one man . . . I am patriotic, because I am human and humane. . . . My patriotism includes the good of mankind in general. . . . Isolated independence is not the goal of the world states. It is voluntary interdependence. . . . I see nothing grand or impossible about our expressing our readiness for universal interdependence rather than independence."

Such a consensus on nationalism and internationalism is in the making at the present time.

4. THE ABOLITION OF WAR

All mankind yearns for the abolition of war, for peaceful methods of settling disputes, for the reign of law rather than armed might. But having been prisoners of antecedent conditions which gave birth to the nation-state and which nourish the nation-state, we are unable to find a creative approach toward peace.

We need a new definition of war and peace. Both war and peace need to be viewed as dynamic processes, not as static events that just happen on a particular date or set of dates. We have war whenever and wherever there are present in the relations among men injustice, oppression, tyranny, exploitation, denial of freedom, denial of the worth of human personality, inflicted by one group upon another, whether nationally or internationally. The search for peace, on the other hand, far from consisting in the absence of war, consists in the constant strivings of men for removal of injustice, oppression, tyranny, exploitation, denial of freedom, denial of the worth of human personality; and peace itself consists in the creation of those conditions and instrumentalities, which would, in the words of George Fox (1624-91), founder of Quakerism, lead mankind "out of the occasions of war." (2, p. 111).

This Gandhi point of view on war and peace is reinforced by C. E. M. Joad, the distinguished British philosopher, in his book

Why War? After discussing the irrelevance of methods of violent warfare in our day, Mr. Joad says (1, p. 247):

My case is that war is not something that is inevitable, but is the result of certain man-made circumstances; that man, who made the circumstances in which wars flourish, can abolish them as he abolished the circumstances in which plagues flourish.

The circumstances in which wars flourish are exactly seven: (1) unbridled sovereignty of States, (2) Power Politics, (3) the empire system either of the colonial or the totalitarian satellite variety, (4) denial of freedom to certain nations, (5) racial inequality, (6) absence of even-handed justice to all alike, (7) non-existence of machinery for peaceful change. (3, pp. 213 ff.).

If we were to accept as a base even-handed justice among all nations and erect on that base the edifice of a machinery for peaceful change, we would abolish war from our small neighborhood world.

A two-pronged approach will be needed in order to eliminate war from human affairs: (1) creation of a machinery for peaceful change, and (2) creation of a new consensus regarding the irrelevance of brute force methods in our day, or a sense of dedication to peaceful ways of change. These two approaches must be taken simultaneously; it is not a case of either-or.

If our generation could learn the simple truth that imperialism, totalitarianism, power politics and the war system are all tied together, "the mighty scourge of war" would be on the way out. Should collective man fail to arrive at this truth by critical analysis and sound reasoning, he would be compelled to accept it, under the stress of impersonal forces, by the impersonal logic of technology.

The fear of devastation by the A-bomb and the H-bomb, the fear of radioactive fallout of strontium 90 injuring all or part of the present generation organically, absence of adequate defense against guided missiles and jet-propelled bombers carrying atomic and hydrogen bombs—these technological developments may serve as a deterrent to war and as an accelerant to a new consensus.

Be that as it may, the central problem of our small neighborhood world is the development of a new consensus on war and peace necessitated by the intensified social interaction on a world scale.

REFERENCES

1. C. E. M. JOAD: *Why War?* London: Penguin Special, 1939.
2. H. T. MUZUMDAR: *Mahatma Gandhi: Peaceful Revolutionary.* New York: Charles Scribner's Sons, 1953.
3. H. T. MUZUMDAR: *The United Nations of the World*, 2nd ed. New York: Universal Publishing Co., 1944.
4. W. L. WILLKIE: *One World.* New York: Simon & Schuster, 1943.

BOOK III

CULTURE

(1) The struggle to react, to endure heat and cold and storm, to draw the next breath, to crawl the next yard, to hold out against fatigue and despair, to explore and analyze the situation—this struggle to react with ongoing will and discriminating intelligence became among human beings differentiated, by stages, into religious, esthetic and scientific activities. (2) The struggle for subsistence to repair the waste of reaction—this struggle for subsistence became the economic life. (3) The struggle for adaptation by every organism to the objective conditions of life later broadened into the ethical life. (4) The struggle of resembling creatures—human beings—to adjust themselves (together with their competitions and their adaptations) to one another generated social processes leading either to group solidarity or to group disintegration. While competition would tend to engender conflicts inimical to group cohesion, in aggregations of human beings, substantially similar in behavior and approximately equal in strength, conflicts would be self-limiting in a degree. Thus, with group cohesion achieved on a symbiotic level, human beings were prepared to live on the level of conscious association for mutual services. Thus came into being society and its framework, culture.

CHAPTER 31

CULTURE—AN INTRODUCTORY STATEMENT

WE have defined culture as the sum-total of human achievements, material as well as non-material, capable of transmission sociologically, i.e., by tradition and communication, vertically as well as horizontally. How did culture arise in the first place?

1. THE EMERGENCE OF CULTURE

Culture, in the first instance, arose from the interactions of group-living organisms endowed with original human nature, striving to come to terms with the objective conditions of life—such as heat and cold, altitude and temperature, flora and fauna, hunger and sex urge, etc. The process of coming to terms with the objective conditions of life involved adaptation to nature and accommodation to members of the group. The fourfold struggle for existence, as expounded by Giddings, laid the basis for the birth and growth of culture among human beings.

(1) The struggle to react, to endure heat and cold and storm, to draw the next breath, to crawl the next yard, to hold out against fatigue and despair, to explore and analyze the situation—this struggle to react with ongoing will and discriminating intelligence became among human beings differentiated, by stages, into religious, esthetic and scientific activities. (2) The struggle for subsistence to repair the waste of reaction—this struggle for subsistence became the economic life. (3) The struggle for adaptation by every organism to the objective conditions of life later broadened into the ethical life. (4) The struggle of resembling creatures—human beings—to adjust themselves (together with their competitions and their adaptations) to one another generated social processes leading either to group solidarity or to group disintegration. While competition would tend to engender conflicts inimical to group cohesion, in aggregations of human beings, substantially similar in behavior and approximately equal in strength, conflicts would be self-limiting in a degree. Thus, with group cohesion achieved on a symbiotic level, human beings

were prepared to live on the level of conscious association for mutual services. Thus came into being society and its framework, culture. (3, pp. 14 ff.)

The human organism, characterized by mind, by thinking and reasoning, sought not just to live but to live well. Not life as such but abundant life became—and has remained to this day—man's goal. In the collective quest for the good life, the group developed folkways and mores, religion and law, institutions and techniques, band and hoard, tribe and clan, community and society. The onward progress of humanity has been marked by a transition from ascribed status to achieved status, from status to State.

Before the emergence of the human species on this planet, there was no culture, as the term is used by us. Man seems to have appeared on earth in the third of the great geological periods, the tertiary—a little over 1,000,000 years ago. Between 1,000,000 B.C. and 500,000 B.C. man evolved what is called by anthropologists eolithic culture—i.e., a stage of group living in which people made use of unworked flints, wood clubs, and deliberately worked flints (eoliths). Between 500,000 B.C. and 50,000 B.C. man, collective man, entered the lower paleolithic period of culture when he began to fashion and use flint scrapers, perforators, knives, hand-axes (coups-de-poing); by now he also had hearths and burials. Between 50,000 B.C. and 10,000 B.C., roughly, man built for himself the upper paleolithic culture when he began to sculpture and to engrave on bone and horn, to make awls, chisels and harpoons; to paint polychrome frescoes on cave walls. Between 10,000 B.C. and 7,000 B.C., roughly, man entered the neolithic stage of culture when he began to domesticate animals, practise agriculture, and grind grains into flour with the aid of polished stone implements. About 7,000 B.C., approximately, the use of metal for artifacts was discovered by man and his mode of living began to be revolutionized. The wheel, the wheeled cart, (the chariot of Hindese and Hellenic epics), the spinning whorl, the weaving loom, swords and shields and helmets of bronze and, later, of other metals—these inventions and others in the realm of material culture began to come thick and fast, and, by the very weight of their accumulation, led to further inventions, lateral, collateral, heterolateral. (*Cf.* CHART 25, p. 525.)

When emotive language was reinforced and more or less supplanted by referential language we do not know. Referential language could well have received further reinforcement in communication through symbolic representations—(a) exact pictures, which represented attempts to transfer a three-dimensional object to a two-dimensional surface, (b) pictographs, (c) ideographs, (d) alphabetic writing. According to our present knowledge, alphabetic writing seems to have been invented, in the Fertile Crescent, by the Syrio-Palestinian Semites around 1,500 B.C. or a little earlier (2, pp. 214–17).

The discovery of coal as fuel in China before 1,000 A.D. and its use as a source of energy in England after the commercial revolution (1,500 A.D.); the discovery of oil as fuel in the U.S.A. in the middle of the nineteenth century and its use as a source of power a few decades later; the vague knowledge of electricity, on the part of Benjamin Franklin, at the time of the American Revolution, and the harnessing of electric energy by Edison for light a hundred years later, and its use as a source of power around the beginning of the twentieth century—these are momentous landmarks, from stone implements to electric bulbs, spread over thousands of years, in the upward climb of man from savagery to barbarism, from barbarism to civilization.

If we were to liken the period of man's existence on the planet, 1,000,000 years, to an hour, the Age of Metals would constitute approximately three seconds, and the period of the Christian era would amount to less than a second! Within these three seconds are concentrated the rise and career of the River Valley Civilizations, the rise and career of the historic religions of the world, the rise and fall of Classical and Medieval European civilizations, and the rise of the modern age of nation-states. (Cf. CHART 26.)

An artifact, before it could be made, would necessitate "know-how" on the part of its author or authors. This knowledge, this know-how, might be acquired by the trial-and-error method, by sudden "intuition" or a flash of genius, by patient practising, by experimentation and invention, by tradition and/or communication. The process of making an artifact had to become stylized and ritualized if the technique was to be passed on to others. Thus a given artifact tended to enrich the non-material culture of man in terms of folkways and mores, totems and taboos, that would grow up around it.

Anthropologists have done remarkable work in studying and reconstructing the beginnings of culture. Some of their techniques and concepts as well as some of their conclusions are a great aid to the sociologist; but, as sociologists, we are not concerned with the beginnings of man's life on this planet nor with the beginnings of culture. The twilight zone of human and cultural beginnings is peripheral to us—central to the anthropologists. We are ready to accept whatever light is thrown upon the problems of social and cultural processes and evolution by the investigations of anthropologists. With preliterate and prehistoric cultures we are not concerned except in so far as they shed light upon the understanding of our society; our task begins with the dawn of history—with the rise of River Valley Civilizations.

2. WHY MAN ALONE BUILDS CULTURE

Let us pause for a moment and recapitulate all the attributes we have assigned to man in our discussion thus far, and see what bearing they have upon the evolution of culture. We have taken for granted: (1) man's erect posture, (2) his prehensile thumb, (3) his capacity to vocalize, (4) the relatively larger capacity of his brain, (5) his "original nature" including (a) unlearned tendencies to respond, (b) the capacity to organize and systematize the experiences of responses, (c) the capacity to "represent" and "articulate" the experiences symbolically, (6) his symbiosis or group-relatedness involving the satisfaction of his biological, physical, psychological and social needs; (7) his ability to learn from the stimulus-response relationship, or his greater plasticity, culminating in (a) participation, (b) manipulation, (c) formal education.

These elements in the makeup of man, collective man, provided a background against which arose culture. The rudiments of culture developed by generation A in X territory would serve as foundation-stone to generation B which made its own addition, enlarging the habitation, so to say. Once the building—culture or the cultural framework—was there, each succeeding generation lived, moved

and had its being within the steel frame of culture with its am-
plitude and constriction. To change the metaphor, man, collective
man, the builder of culture, is born in the stream of culture and
must continually swim in it if he is to live as a member of society.
Thus, what we had assumed in our Frame of Reference is
demonstrated: The group in operation evolves and maintains
culture.

The most important aspects of culture, it may be stressed, are not
artifacts but mentifacts, not material traits but non-material traits. In
the non-material phases of culture the most important part is played
by communication. Communication rests upon "language" with its
symbols, spoken and written, with its universe of discourse; with
concepts. The intimate interrelationship between society and culture
may be seen from the central role played by communication in
holding society together through consensus and in the making and
perpetuation of culture through the operation of groups moving
within a universe of discourse.

Besides mentifacts associated with artifacts, besides values and
philosophy of life, which are all integral parts of culture, an important and fundamental part of non-material culture consists in
social organization. The structure, intergroup relationships, and
organization of a society can be studied only by first-hand investigation of the mode of living of the given people. The characteristic
organization, with major and minor emphases, of the five primary
institutions and their multitudinous secondary institutions sets apart
one society from another, just as the characteristic organization of
wishes, attitudes and complexes distinguishes one personality from
another.

We have already pointed out the need for a simultaneous study
of "culture and its categories, society and its culture" (*supra*,
CHAPTER 12). Society, any society, can be best studied and understood in terms of its cultural framework. From one standpoint,
society and culture are coterminous.

Societies are of many kinds: folk societies and national societies,
simple societies and complex societies, sacred societies and secular
societies, rural societies and urban societies. Most of the existing
tribal societies are of the nature of folk society, but some partake of

the nature of national society. However, since all tribal societies are under foreign suzerainty, it is best to speak of existing tribal societies as folk societies.

One society differs and is distinguished from another society by its cultural framework. And the cultural framework is made up of folkways, mores and institutions, including the fundamental categories as well as the implicit values of the culture.

In *Patterns of Culture*, for instance, Ruth Benedict demonstrates how we can best understand the three differing tribes—Kwakiutl, Dobu, Zuni—by an analysis of their "customs"—of their folkways, mores and institutions. Likewise, in an attempt to portray Japan and the Japanese people understandably, the same author utilized anthropological, historical, political and economic as well as sociological data to weave for the reader the Japanese pattern of culture (*The Chrysanthemum and the Sword*).

The sociological thesis is that groups and constituent members of groups flourish only in a cultural milieu. Man is in a real sense culture-bound, just as fish is water-bound.

Stuart Chase has depicted for us how a large number of his behavior patterns are conditioned by the fact of his being "a writer living in a rural town in Connecticut, getting to New York occasionally, and around the country on lecture trips now and then" (1, pp. 293–306).

Anybody can make a list of his activities and behavior patterns in terms of cultural compulsives and imperatives.

In this Book, we shall describe our society in terms of the operation of the five primary institutions.

REFERENCES

1. STUART CHASE: "On Being Culture-Bound," *The Antioch Review*, Fall, 1949, pp. 293–306. Also reproduced in *Contemporary Social Issues* by R. L. Lee, J. A. Burkhart & Van B. Shaw; New York: Crowell, 1955.

2. DAVID DIRINGER: *The Alphabet: A Key to the History of Mankind*, New York: Philosophical Library, 1948.

3. FRANKLIN H. GIDDINGS: *Studies in the Theory of Human Society*, New York: Macmillan, 1922.

CHART 25

THE GROWTH OF CULTURE

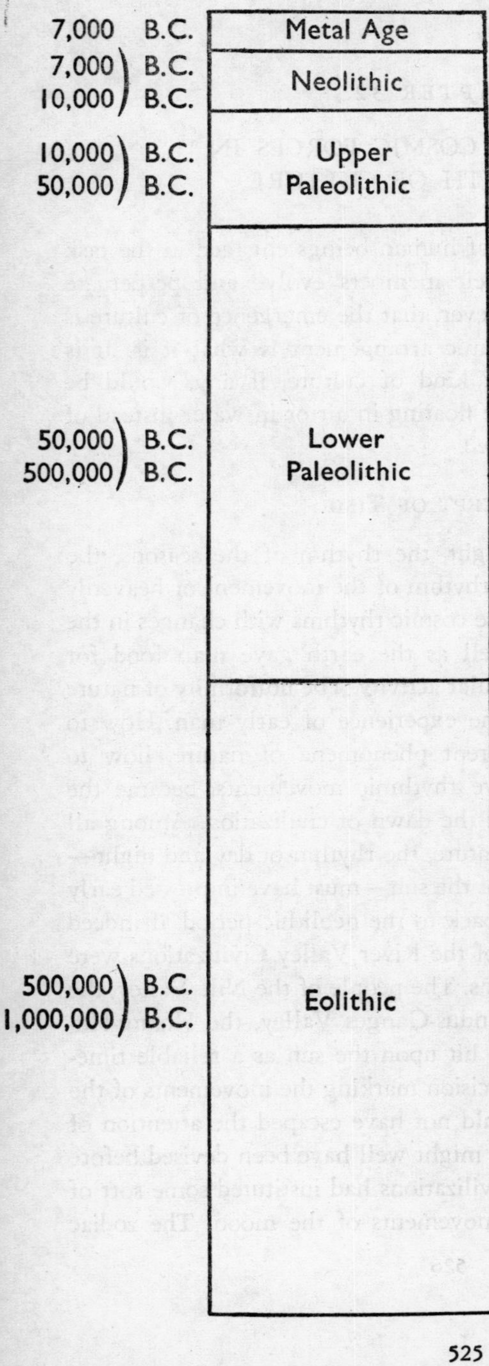

7,000 B.C.
Metal Age
7,000 B.C.
10,000 B.C.
Neolithic
10,000 B.C.
50,000 B.C.
Upper Paleolithic
50,000 B.C.
500,000 B.C.
Lower Paleolithic
500,000 B.C.
1,000,000 B.C.
Eolithic

CHART 26

THE SHORT DURATION OF THE POST-STONE AGE

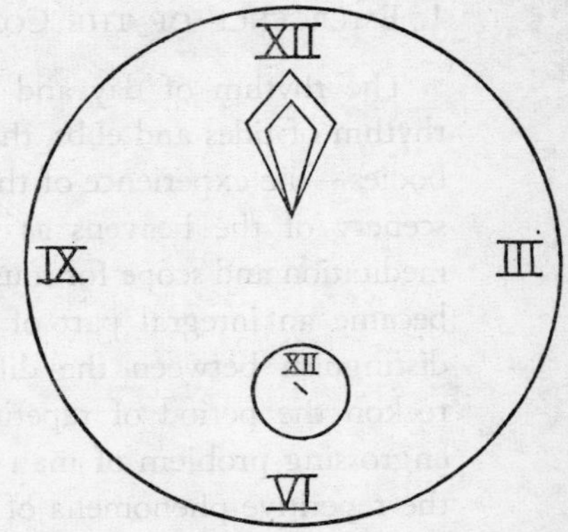

XII
III
VI
IX
XII

The Age of Metals Equals Three Seconds of a Million-Year Hour

CHAPTER 32

THE ROLE OF COSMIC FORCES IN
THE GROWTH OF CULTURE

WE have said that groups of human beings engaged in the task of satisfying the needs of their members evolve and perpetuate culture. It may be added, however, that the emergence of culture is possible only because the cosmic arrangement is what it is. It is fascinating to speculate what kind of culture, if any, would be evolved if collective man were floating in air or in water instead of walking on earth, on *terra firma*.

1. EMERGENCE OF THE CONCEPT OF TIME

The rhythm of day and night, the rhythm of the seasons, the rhythm of tides and ebbs, the rhythm of the movement of heavenly bodies—the experience of these cosmic rhythms with changes in the scenery of the heavens as well as the earth gave man food for meditation and scope for muscular activity. The uniformity of nature became an integral part of the experience of early man. How to distinguish between the different phenomena of nature, how to reckon the period of repetitive rhythmic movements, became the engrossing problem of man at the dawn of civilization. Among all the repetitive phenomena of nature, the rhythm of day and night— i.e., the rising and the setting of the sun—must have impressed early man most. Sun-worship goes back to the neolithic period, if indeed not farther back. The people of the River Valley Civilizations were engaged in studying the heavens. The people of the Nile Valley, the Euphrates-Tigris Valley, the Indus-Ganges Valley, the Hoang-Ho-Yangtse-Kiang Valley had all hit upon the sun as a reliable time-keeper. The regularity and precision marking the movements of the earth's satellite, the moon, could not have escaped the attention of early man. The lunar calendar might well have been devised before the solar calendar. All high civilizations had instituted some sort of rites in connection with the movements of the moon. The zodiac

526

was known to all high civilizations, though it is difficult to prove whether the knowledge was arrived at by each River Valley group independently or was borrowed from one source.

The concept of time was derived from the movement of heavenly bodies. The concept of reckoning—numbers—was derived from the rhythms of nature. Modern man speaks of three types of time— astronomical, geological, and chronological. The last is an arbitrary man-made measuring device: The beginning of a reigning dynasty, the appearance of a Prophet or an Incarnation of God, the discovery of metal, the fission of the uranium atom—any of these events might serve as the starting-point of chronological time.

Chronological time, however, required the postulation of an un-varying, stable unit, if meaningful computations were to be made. One total unit embracing all the seasons could be rhythmically experienced by all human beings. Within that unit certain constant relations between the sun and the earth were observed to constitute a complete cycle. Thus arose the large chronological unit—a year. In the attempt to correlate the earth-sun cycle, what we call the earth's revolution around the sun, and the earth cycle of day and night—what we call the rotation of the earth on its axis—proper subdivisional units of the year were worked out. None of the great thinkers of the River Valley Civilizations has left us a record of the exact methods whereby they successfully achieved the notion of time and subdivided the chronological year into 365¼ days, each day into 24 hours, each hour into 60 minutes, each minute into 60 seconds (and each second into 60 Matras among the Hindus).

2. Conditions Favoring the Emergence of Culture

Without the life-giving, light-giving energy (heat) of the sun, no organic form of being could exist. But the sun, of itself, could bring into being neither life nor culture. The particular shape of the earth with its enveloping atmosphere is responsible for the existence of man and culture.

Five significant constituent elements of the earth—of course, in cooperation with the rest of the cosmos—are responsible for the emergence of man and his culture: (1) the globular shape of the earth, (2) land forms, (3) water bodies, (4) soil and minerals, (5) climate. These five constituent elements of earth are responsible for plants and animals, for men and their culture.

The diagram by Huntington (2, p. 4), showing the elements of human geography, vividly brings out the correlation of the five elements of the earth to the rise and persistence of culture (see p. 529).

The globular nature of the earth and the tilting of the earth's axis are responsible for the present land and water masses and for the tides and the seasons. To quote the late Professor Huntington (2, p. 27):

The earth is an oblate spheroid, that is, a sphere flattened at the poles and bulging at the equator, so that the diameter from pole to pole is about 7,900 miles, or nearly 27 miles less than at the equator. If the solid part of the earth were a perfect sphere, the effect would be the same as if there were a gentle slope downward all the way from the poles to the equator. Hence an ocean of great depth would completely surround the earth in low latitudes, and there would be no land there. Each pole would be surrounded by an enormous circular continent where the winter would be very dry and almost incredibly windy and cold. In summer strong winds would blow inward from the equatorial ocean, and the low belt along the coast would be extremely rainy as well as warm. The bitterly cold and violent winds of winter, however, would make even this belt almost uninhabitable according to our ideas. Plants, animals, and men, if they existed at all, would have to be different from those with which we are familiar. It is useless to pursue the subject further; this is enough to show how completely all life is adapted to a globe with a definite shape, size, and set of motions.

Furthermore, the fact that "the earth's axis is inclined to the plane of the earth's orbit instead of being vertical" has had profound effects upon life on the planet, in that the tilting of the axis is responsible for the rhythm of the seasons. To quote Huntington once again (2, p. 38):

The earth's yearly revolution around the sun makes a difference to mankind mainly because the axis on which the earth rotates is inclined to the plane of the earth's orbit, and thus causes seasons. The inclination of the earth's axis causes the sun to remain above the

CHART 27

THE ELEMENTS OF HUMAN GEOGRAPHY

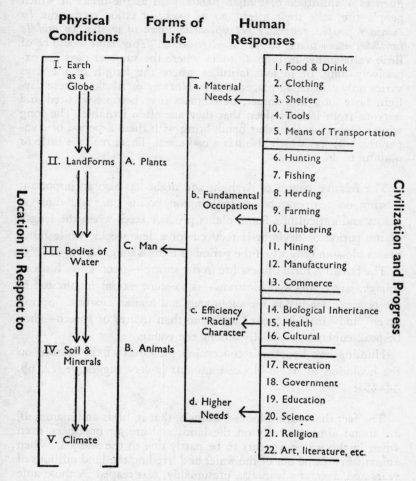

Physical Conditions — **Forms of Life** — **Human Responses**

Location in Respect to

Civilization and Progress

I. Earth as a Globe

II. LandForms

III. Bodies of Water

IV. Soil & Minerals

V. Climate

A. Plants

C. Man

B. Animals

a. Material Needs
1. Food & Drink
2. Clothing
3. Shelter
4. Tools
5. Means of Transportation

b. Fundamental Occupations
6. Hunting
7. Fishing
8. Herding
9. Farming
10. Lumbering
11. Mining
12. Manufacturing
13. Commerce

c. Efficiency "Racial" Character
14. Biological Inheritance
15. Health
16. Cultural

d. Higher Needs
17. Recreation
18. Government
19. Education
20. Science
21. Religion
22. Art, literature, etc.

NOTE: "The arrows indicate the chief ways in which the physical conditions influence one another. Climate, for example, is influenced by the earth's sperical shape, by the form of the land, and by bodies of water such as oceans. It in turn influences the form of the earth's surface, the quality of the soil, and the nature of mineral deposits. It also influences bodies of water, but this relationship and certain others are omitted to avoid crowding."

horizon far longer in some places and at certain seasons than at others. Hence *daylight and night vary greatly in length*. This influences a multitude of human habits, such as the hours at which people rise, take their meals, go to work, or enjoy recreation. *In summer people generally get up earlier than in winter. In middle latitudes many places adopt " daylight time."* This habit would be of little value either in high altitudes where the summer days are excessively long, or in low latitudes where the length of the days varies only a little. In places such as Norway or Alaska, where daylight lasts long in summer, newcomers may become so tired and nervous from lack of sleep that they are often irritable. The long winter nights, on the other hand, bring with them a period of comparative idleness which also has a bad effect. There really is little or nothing to do.

The relative length of daylight and night has also an important bearing on temperature, as Huntington points out, and thus on plants and agriculture. Some plants produce seeds when the length of the period of daylight is reduced for a few weeks, while other plants blossom only when the period of light is long. (2, pp. 38–39).

The bursting forth of new life in the spring—green grass, luscious foliage, gay colors and blossoms—is to some extent manifested in the renewed vitality in the subhuman and human creation. "Spring fever" and "mal de coeur" are more than figures of speech—they bespeak euphoria, especially among the young.

Huntington's hypothesis concerning the effect of the seasons on the evolution of warm-blooded animals is very suggestive. (2, pp. 44–45):

The fact that warm-blooded animals, that is, birds and mammals, are found almost wholly on the lands and are air breathers, even when in the water, appears to be partly due to the seasons. When animals first came out of the water and lived on the land millions of years ago, a great advantage, presumably, was reaped by those able to warm themselves a little and thus continue their activities in cold weather. Warm blood involves a higher rate of activity than cold blood. It thus puts a great premium on intelligence and on the development of the higher qualities such as parental care and love for offspring. The cold-blooded animals practically never care for their eggs or young. They do not need to. Among warm-blooded animals, however, if there are cold seasons, the eggs must be kept warm and the young must be protected from bad weather. This was apparently one of the primary reasons why the parents took an interest in their young. Little by little the swing of the seasons selected for preservation the types of animals that had these new and higher instincts. This gave a peculiarly good chance for natural selection to preserve those whose brains were most highly developed. Thus along with the parental instinct the development of intelligence was fostered by the seasons.

All this meant that the young animals became more and more dependent upon the mothers. Hence when types that placed the young in pouches were developed in addition to those that merely laid eggs, they had an advantage in the struggle for existence because the young could be protected not only from enemies but from the inclement weather as well. The last step was the evolution of true mammals whose helpless young are born alive. Their evolution, so far as we can tell, took place chiefly in the great continental interiors where the contrasts of the seasons are greatest, and where the rigors of winter are among the most powerful factors in eliminating many types and preserving those whose intelligence is relatively high.

The physiological reactions of man to the seasons are important. Everybody talks about the weather but nobody does anything about it—this statement of Mark Twain's has been true of the major segment of man's existence upon the planet. Only yesterday, so to say, as cultural history goes, man learned to temper the inclemencies of weather by installing heating apparatus in homes and offices and operating them in the winter. Air-conditioning in the summer will soon be inexpensive enough to be enjoyed by everyone in America. Huntington's discussion of the effects of the seasons on man's physiology are of interest to the sociologist. (2, pp. 45-46):

Among men the influence of the seasons is no less than among plants and animals. One of the best-known effects is variation in health from season to season. *In climates such as those of the northern United States and western Europe the death rate is systematically lowest at the end of summer and highest late in the winter.* Certain diseases, however, such as digestive troubles, show an opposite variation, being most numerous and most likely to be fatal in summer. Births also vary in number according to the seasons. In the most densely populated parts of the United States they are most numerous in the early spring and again in the late summer. In western Europe there is a strong and widespread tendency toward a maximum in the early spring. In other climates both deaths and births show a different adjustment to the seasons according to the temperature. Everywhere, however, human beings respond to the seasons in essentially the same way as plants and animals except that man has learned how to overcome many effects of the weather, but by no means all.

Finally, the tilting of the earth's axis and the resultant seasons have not only instilled in man the need for foresight but have also made man, singly and collectively, a capitalist and the builder of culture. By the term capitalist is meant of course one who uses capital—i.e., production goods, such as machinery or raw materials— for further production. The farmer who saves some corn or wheat for seed during the next sowing season is operating as a capitalist. This saving implies, subjectively, foresight and, objectively, the sway of folkways, mores, and rituals. This is what Huntington has to say on the role of the seasons in civilizing mankind. (2, pp. 46–47):

Without the seasons mankind might never have become civilized. When early man began to rely on his mind instead of on physical strength, one of his first important ideas was to store up food for seasons of scarcity. So far as he lived by hunting this was relatively unimportant, but if he gathered nuts it was important, and as soon as he relied mainly on farming he could not live unless he stored up food in summer to last him through the winter. In regions with strong seasonal changes this was far more necessary than in warm regions with no real winter or dry season. Moreover, the strong contrast between the seasons stimulates him not only to store up food, but also to make new inventions. In every stage of life those people are most successful who plan intelligently for the future which lies months or even years ahead of them. The inclination of the earth's axis and the resultant seasons have been among the chief incentives to this kind of foresight.

3. TECHNOLOGY, AN ATTEMPT TO EMANCIPATE MAN FROM NATURAL FORCES

To emancipate himself from the tyranny of the forces of nature, man has resorted to various devices: (a) magical incantations, (b) invoking of divine aid, (c) the philosophical attitude of harmony with nature, (d) the empirical search for conquest of nature by scientific procedures and by the application of science to production.

These devices became part and parcel of man's ever-growing culture. The application of science to the problems of production has resulted in the culture complex called technology. And technology is broadbased upon the roundabout method of production—or upon the device of capitalism. In a classic description, Böhm-Bawerk vividly portrays the processes of roundabout or indirect methods of production in contrast to direct production and immediate consumption (1, pp. 66–68, quoted):

A peasant requires drinking water. The spring is some distance from his house. There are various ways in which he may supply his daily wants. First, he may go to the spring each time he is thirsty, and drink out of his hollowed hand. This is the most direct way; satisfaction follows immediately on exertion. But it is an inconvenient way, for our peasant has to take his way to the well as often as he is thirsty. And it is an insufficient way, for he can never collect and store any great quantity such as he requires for various other purposes. Second, he may take a log of wood, hollow it out into a kind of pail, and carry his day's supply from the spring to his cottage. The advantage is obvious, but it necessitates a roundabout way of considerable length. The man must spend, perhaps, a day in cutting out the pail; before doing so he must have felled a tree in the forest; to do this, again, he must have made an axe, and so on. But there is still a third way; instead of felling one tree he fells a number of trees, splits and hollows them, lays them end for end, and so constructs a runnel or rhone which brings a full head of water to his cottage. Here, obviously, between the expenditure of the labor and the obtaining of the water we have a very roundabout way, but, then, the result is ever so much greater. Our peasant need no longer take his weary way from house to well with the heavy pail on his shoulder, and yet he has a constant and full supply of the freshest water at his very door.

Another example: I require stone for building a house. There is a rich vein of excellent sandstone in a neighboring hill. How is it to be got out? First, I may work the loose stones back and forward with my bare fingers, and break off what can be broken off. This is the most direct, but also the least productive way. Second, I may take a piece of iron, make a hammer and chisel out of it, and use them on the hard stone—a roundabout way, which, of course, leads to a very much better result than the former. Third method—

Having a hammer and chisel, I use them to drill a hole in the rock; next I turn my attention to procuring charcoal, sulphur, and nitre, and mixing them in a powder; then I pour the powder into the hole, and the explosion that follows splits the stone into convenient pieces—still more of a roundabout way, but one, which, as experience shows, is as much superior to the second way in result as the second was to the first.

Yet another example. I am short-sighted, and wish to have a pair of spectacles. For this I require ground and polished glasses, and a steel framework. But all that nature offers toward that end is silicious earth and iron ore. How am I to transform these into spectacles? Work as I may, it is as impossible for me to make spectacles directly out of silicious earth as it would be to make the steel frames out of iron ore. Here, there is no immediate or direct method of production. There is nothing for it but to take the roundabout way, and, indeed, a very roundabout way. I must take silicious earth and fuel, and build furnaces for smelting the glass from the silicious earth; the glass thus obtained has to be carefully purified, worked, and cooled by a series of processes; finally, the glass thus prepared —again by means of ingenious instruments carefully constructed beforehand—is ground and polished into the lens fit for short-sighted eyes. Similarly, I must smelt the ore in the blast furnace, change the raw iron into steel, and make the frame therefrom— processes which cannot be carried through without a long series of tools and buildings that, on their part again, require great amounts of previous labor. Thus, by an exceedingly roundabout way, the end is attained.

The lesson to be drawn from all these examples alike is obvious. It is—that a greater result is obtained by producing goods in round-about ways than by producing them directly. Where a good can be produced in either way, we have the fact that, by the indirect way, a greater product can be got with equal labor, or the same product with less labor. But, beyond this, the superiority of the indirect way manifests itself in being the only way in which certain goods can be obtained; if I might say so, it is so much better that it is often the only way!

4. THE NATURE OF THE MACHINE

The roundabout method of production required the use of tools, of machines. A machine is an embodiment of energy and force, energy being defined, after Lewis Elhuff, as "ability or capacity to move an object," and force as that part of the energy that is used at any one time. Machines are labor-saving devices as well as energy-multiplying devices. A big rock I cannot move with my bare hands. With the aid of a lever I can move it. The lever saved me labor, personal exertion, and multiplied my energy and force. "Give me a lever large enough and I shall move the world!" said the Greek philosopher Archimedes.

How the machine operates is best stated by Lewis Elhuff (3, p. 46, quoted):

A machine is a device used to transform or transfer energy, and to apply force for doing useful work. Illustration of how a machine can transform energy: when coal is burned in the firebox of a boiler, the heat of the coil makes steam of the water, and the steam in running the engine develops mechanical energy, which can be made to develop electricity or electrical energy by turning a dynamo. The electrical energy can be changed back to mechanical energy and drive street cars along the tracks. All kinds of steam and gas engines and electrical machines are devices for transforming energy as well as for transferring it, while the simple machines are either devices for transferring energy or devices to which force can be applied and useful work [may] result.

The simple machines, according to Elhuff (3, p. 46), are six in number: "The (a) lever, (b) inclined plane, (c) wedge, (d) screw, (e) pulley, and (f) wheel and axle. Of these the lever and inclined plane are basic types. The pulley, and the wheel and axle are modified forms of the lever, while the wedge and screw are modified inclined planes. All complex machines are only combinations of two or more simple machines. . . ." When and where these inventions were first made we do not know, but we do know that all high civilizations, excepting the pre-Columbian American Indian cultures, utilized all these simple machines.

These simple machines launched man on his astounding career of invention and capitalism.

REFERENCES

1. PAUL F. GEMMILL: *Fundamentals of Economics*, fourth ed. New York: Harper & Brothers, 1943.
2. ELLSWORTH HUNTINGTON: *Principles of Human Geography*, fifth ed. New York: John Wiley & Sons Inc., 1946.
3. THAMES ROSS WILLIAMSON: *Readings in Economics*. New York: D. C. Heath & Co., 1923.

CHART 28
THE SIX SIMPLE MACHINES

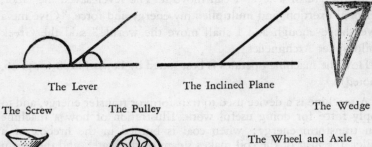

The Lever   The Inclined Plane

The Screw   The Pulley   The Wedge

The Wheel and Axle

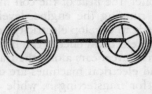

CHAPTER 33

ANALYSIS OF CULTURE

BROADLY interpreted, folkways and mores and institutions, whether concerned with material or non-material phases of man's activities, may be said to constitute the total content of culture. The five primary institutions and scores of derivative or secondary institutions carry on their existence within ordered social relations because of the folkways, mores and institutional procedures that have become attached to them. This generalized statement on the content of culture, however, does not help us in comparing different cultures. Hence anthropologists and sociologists have been in search of universal culture patterns with concrete details for use in comparative studies.

1. WISSLER: THE UNIVERSAL CULTURE PATTERN

Clark Wissler (5, p. 74) suggests that nine basic culture traits, by interaction among themselves, give rise to the universal culture pattern composed of:

1. Speech and Language
2. Material traits
    (a) Food habits
    (b) Shelter
    (c) Transportation
    (d) Dress
    (e) Utensils, tools, etc.
    (f) Weapons
    (g) Occupations and industries
3. Art
4. Mythology and Scientific Knowledge
5. Religious Practices
6. Family and Social Systems
7. Property
8. Government
9. War

537

Kimball Young, (6, p. 39) suggests as universal patterns of culture the following thirteen items:

1. Patterns of communication: gestures and language.
2. Methods and objects for providing for man's physical welfare:
   a. Food-getting   c. Shelter
   b. Personal care   d. Tools, instruments, and machines
3. Means or techniques of travel and transportation of goods and services.
4. Exchange of goods and services: barter, trade, commerce, occupations.
5. Forms of property: real and personal.
6. The sex and family patterns:
   a. Marriage and divorce
   b. Forms of kinship relation
   c. Guardianship
   d. Inheritance
7. Societal controls and institutions of government:
   a. Mores
   b. Public opinion
   c. Organized state: laws and political officers
   d. War: institutional form of conflict of tribes, societies, or states.
8. Artistic expression: architecture, painting, sculpture, music, literature, dancing.
9. Recreational and leisure-time interests and activities.
10. Religious and magical ideas and practices.
11. Science (in civilization chiefly).
12. Mythology and philosophy.
13. Cultural structuring of basic interactional processes, such as competition, conflict, co-operation, differentiation, stratification, accommodation, and assimilation.

2. ANALYSIS OF CULTURE

Culture may best be analyzed, so far as the beginning student is concerned, in terms of the following five conceptual tools: (1) Culture Trait, (2) Culture Complex, (3) Culture Pattern, (4) Cultural Category, (5) Ethos. Sutherland and Woodward's table showing the level of cultural integration in regard to the first three of the five items listed by us is very helpful. (4, p. 35):

TABLE 28

UNITS USED IN DESCRIBING THE CULTURE OF A PEOPLE

Units	Level of Cultural Integration	Illustrative Examples		
		The Kwakiutl Indians	The Crow Indians	The United States Today
The Culture Pattern	Brief Characterization of the Dominant Themes in the Culture as a Whole	Sedentary but nonagricultural people. Great emphasis on individual prestige based on property distribution and nobility titles	Nomadic hunters, living in small bands. Emphasis on individual exploits and on the power of visions	A machine culture. Emphasis on competition and the profit motive, on democracy and humanitarianism. A highly mobile and generally "urbanized" population
The Culture Complex	Clusters of Functionally Associated Traits	Potlatch complex. Salmon-fishing complex	Tobacco complex, Guardian-spirit religion, Buffalo complex	School Complex, Touring Complex, Sports Complex, Political party election Complex
The Culture Trait	Individual Folkways and Institutions	Totem poles, plank houses, cannibal dance society, media of exchange, shamans	Tipi dwelling, sweat lodge, "counting coup," tobacco society, sun dance	Textbooks, automobiles, baseball, voting machines, honeymoons, banquets, policeman, tuxedos

A culture trait is the smallest or ultimate unit into which culture may be resolved: e.g., the baseball. A cluster of culture traits, functionally related and interdependent, forms the culture complex: e.g., the baseball complex. Several related culture complexes, making a configuration, give us the culture pattern: e.g., emphasis on competition within a cooperative framework. The cultural category is the imperative of value-judgment derivable from the culture patterns. However, once the cultural categories are recognized as valid, they regulate the culture patterns, culture complexes, and culture traits. Ethos signifies the characteristic organization of culture traits, complexes and patterns of a total society—in contrast to groupings within society—in such a way as to accentuate the role of cultural categories within that society. William Graham Sumner, one of the American pioneers in social science, defined ethos as the *totality of characteristic traits by which a group (i.e. a society) is individualized and differentiated from others.* (3, pp. 36–37).

Ethos differentiates one society from another: Sparta and Athens, India and the United States of America, China and the U.S.S.R. The German word, *Weltanschauung,* is an appropriate synonym for ethos.

3. STEREOTYPES ABOUT DIFFERENT CULTURES

Some popular jokes about members of different nations contain profound commonsense insight into the ethos of different societies. Thus, for instance, in an essay competition on the elephant, in the good old days before World War II, the Englishman wrote on "The Elephant and the British Empire"; the Frenchman on "The Love Life of the Elephant"; and the Pole on "The Elephant and the Polish Question," while the German wrote on "An Introduction to the Study of the Elephant" in two volumes.

Here is another popular attempt at peering into the ethos of different societies: Three college students—a Japanese, a Hindu and an American—once visited the Niagara Falls. The Japanese boy was bewitched by the sheer beauty of the grand spectacle, while the Hindu boy began to philosophize to himself about the Supreme Being manifest in this phenomenon of nature. The silent communion of the two Orientals with the Niagara Falls, each in his own fashion, was sharply interrupted as the American boy asked: "Boys, how much horsepower is there in *them* Falls?"

Yet another interesting attempt at characterizing the ethos of different peoples is to be found in the witty statement of a Frenchman quoted by Shiridharani (2, pp. 245–46):

One German:	A scientist
Two Germans:	Conspiracy
Three Germans:	War
One Chinese:	Company
Two Chinese:	A crowd
Three Chinese:	Humanity
One American:	The almighty dollar
Two Americans:	A corporation
Three Americans:	Heaven on earth
One Englishman:	An idiot
Two Englishmen:	Two idiots
Three Englishmen:	The greatest power in the world
One Hindese:	A philosopher
Two Hindese:	Argument
Three Hindese:	Confusion

4. U.S.A., India, U.S.S.R.—A Comparison

Here is a tentative list of comparative cultural categories obtaining today in the U.S.A., India and the U.S.S.R.:

TABLE 29

CULTURAL CATEGORIES IN U.S.A., INDIA, U.S.S.R.

The U.S.A. Today	India Today	The U.S.S.R. Today
1. Conquest of and Mastery over Nature	Harmony with Nature	Conquest of and Mastery over Nature
2. Rights of the Individual	Duties of the Individual toward the group	Statism—Subordination of the Individual to the State

The U.S.A. Today	India Today	The U.S.S.R. Today
3. Scientific Outlook	Philosophic Outlook	Scientific Outlook within a pre-accepted political framework: Pseudo-scientific
4. Pragmatism	Idealism or Transcendentalism	Pragmatism and Transcendentalism
5. Dominance of the Machine	Dominance of Handicrafts—striving toward a Machine Technology	Furious Striving toward a Machine Technology
6. Mad Rush—Self-imposed or Culturally conditioned: " Eventually, why not now?"	Leisureliness	Ruthless Planning and Rush, with slipshod results
7. Constitutionalism	Personalism	Dictatorship: The Führer Principle

Herewith we may also tentatively list some elements in the ethos of the three societies:

TABLE 30
ETHOS: U.S.A., INDIA, U.S.S.R.

The U.S.A. Today	India Today	The U.S.S.R. Today
1. Democratic Procedures	Oligarchic Procedures— Tending toward Democratization	Violence as the means of Social Change—Permanent Revolution
2. Bigger and Better— Accent on the Future	Conservation of the Past —Tending toward Bigness	Abrupt Break with the Past —Worship of Bigness
3. Dominance of Secularization — Subordination of Dharma	Dominance of Dharma— Subordination of Secularization	Dominance of Secularization and ersatz Dharma
4. Ambivalence toward Means and Ends	Ends do not justify Means	Ends do justify Means
5. Competition	Cooperation—voluntary	Cooperation — Imposed from above

5. Reasons for Differences in Ethos

What is responsible for differences in the ethos of different peoples and societies? The ethos of a people is the resultant of the cumulative experiences of the people enmeshed in the network of social relationships. These experiences include, *inter alia*: (1) the topography and geography of the region with its flora and fauna, (2) the climate of the region, (3) the nature of the cycle of the seasons, (4) abundance or scarcity of the bounties of nature necessary for man's upkeep, (5) the state of industrial arts, (6) contact with other groups, either peaceful or warlike—or isolation from other groups, (7) strategic location on the highroad of commerce, (8) the possibility of cultural borrowings from others, (9) the memory of the people, congealed into tradition, in respect to their historic antecedents, regardless of their factual or mythical basis.

If the original nature of man be common-human, as we have said, it is reasonable to expect that man in Asia, Europe, Africa or the Americas, confronted by identical stimuli, might conceivably respond in an identical fashion. The same solution may be independently found in more places than one. Anthropologists and sociologists accept the possibility of parallel or independent invention of the same culture trait in different places, or in different ages, by different peoples. But more often than not, a culture trait is apt to be borrowed by one group from another and integrated within its own cultural framework. According to this theory, an invention having been once made is diffused, spread, to other parts of the world and borrowed by other peoples. It is conceivable that the lunar calendar and the zodiac might have been independently invented by the peoples of the River Valley Civilizations. On the other hand, we know it to be a fact that the so-called Arabic numerals, today used by the whole civilized world, were invented but once— by the Hindus of India. This Hindu invention was borrowed and refined by the Arabs and introduced by them to Europe. The Europeans, during their career of expansionism in the wake of the Commercial Revolution (circa 1500 on), took the Hindu-Arabic numerals all over the world including India and Arabia.

Regardless of whether they were independently invented or borrowed, new culture traits would become an integral part of the culture pattern and would thus have a bearing on the ethos. The people's memory—or conception—of their historic antecedents is a more forceful determinant of the ethos than the validity of their historic construct.

6. ETHOS CAN CHANGE

The ethos of a people may change and undergo profound transformation under the impact of new experiences. Karl Marx' thesis that the method of production is the sole determinant of the ethos of a people is too narrow and particularistic. As a part of the new experiences, changes in the method of production may and do affect the ethos. But there are other factors equally compulsive, or even more compulsive, that affect the ethos. Under the impact of technology, i.e., a change in the method of production, one people ceases to be warlike and another blossoms forth into a military nation.

Two classic examples from the contemporary world may be cited. The Scandinavians, the aggressive Vikings of the ninth century, the terror of Europe during the early phase of the Reformation, have been for the last two hundred years model examples of peace, non-aggression and the "middle way." In sharp juxtaposition to the Scandinavians, we have the Japanese with a history of peace and non-aggression unmatched in the annals of any country in the world including the traditionally peaceable China and India.

During the first eleven centuries of her recorded history she (Japan) was engaged in only one war abroad. Indeed this sole conflict ended in 1598, and from that time until 1853, when Japan opened her doors to intercourse with the world outside, the building of all ocean-going boats was forbidden by imperial decree to make certain that Japan would preserve her policy of isolationism. The ceremoniousness, the light-heartedness, the aesthetic appreciation of the Japanese were traits that passed current as their essential qualities. Since 1853 they have fought five times overseas and are (were—H.T.M.) well on their way to becoming one of the most aggressively warlike nations of the world. (1, p. 14).

Forced by the black ships of Commodore Perry to open her gates to contact with the Occident, Japan looked about herself and discovered that all her neighbors, who had subordinated military virtues to civic duties and whose industrial arts did not rest on a scientific and technological base, had fallen prey to the might of the Occident with its black ships and guns. Promptly the Japanese decided methodically to borrow all they could from the Occident with a view to strengthening themselves. The power complex of Occidental ethos made inroads upon the Japanese culture pattern, with the result that Japan became an excellent Asian version of the Occident's glorification of brute force. Since her surrender in World War II, August 15, 1945, Japan is trying to learn and adopt democratic procedures and to eschew violence and aggressiveness. In Japan, stunned by military defeat, Mahatma Gandhi, the successful votary of non-violence and Satyagraha, began to be held up as the highest exemplar of heroism. And the new constitution of Japan definitely renounced resort to war for any reason whatsoever. However, I am afraid that the emergence in Japan of the new—rather old—ethos of peace and non-aggression may be retarded, perhaps frustrated, by the uncertainties of the postwar divided world.

The point to note is that the ethos of a people can change under appropriate conditions. When the ethos is in process of change, the cultural categories are in a flux. During such a period of flux, the even working of social forces is interrupted. The masses are at the mercy of saviors and wreckers, charlatans and madmen, leaders and misleaders. Men with a philosophic calm, men with an either-or point of view, men wedded to reason and divorced from emotion, are pushed aside in such a period of social disorganization and cultural rearrangement. Men with vision and simple emotional appeal come to the fore and direct social forces into channels deemed to be beneficial to the group.

Sometimes, over a period of time, without benefit of leadership, profound changes may creep into the ethos through impersonal interaction between a new culture pattern and an old one. The gradual substitution of chair for crosslegged squatting on the floor in India will in time create a new temper, a new outlook, among the people.

In order to understand a given society fully, we must know the ethos of the people constituting that society and the cultural categories characterizing the society.

18

7. CULTURAL LAG

Two final points regarding the cultural framework, already alluded to (CHAPTER 28), need to be re-emphasized at this stage of our discussion. (1) Culture, i.e., the social heritage, is constantly undergoing change, thanks to additions of new culture traits or modifications of existing culture traits. But some cultures change faster than others. Western culture, for instance, since the onset of the industrial revolution, has been changing much faster than pre-industrial Western culture or Asian cultures in the recent past did. However, since the emergence of the ideology of nationalism in the Orient, Asian cultures, engulfed simultaneously in the throes of nationalism and industrialism, are tending to change at a faster rate than previously.

(2) In addition to the differing tempo of change as between cultures, it must be noted that the different parts of each culture change at uneven rates. Thus, the material aspects of the culture of a people tend to change faster than the non-material aspects, including folkways, mores, institutions, values, social organization, philosophy of life, etc. It is easier to adopt and/or adapt new mechanical tools in order to increase efficiency than to adopt or adapt new social inventions. This uneven or differential rate of change between the different parts of culture constitutes cultural lag, and usually gives rise to social problems.

In the next chapter we shall attempt to study the meeting of East and West, of Orient and Occident, the rise of modern civilization, and the emergence of the small neighborhood world; and in the chapter after that, we shall attempt to study the cultural categories characterizing American society, as a prelude to a study of the primary institutions of our society.

REFERENCES

1. RUTH BENEDICT: *Race: Science and Politics.* New York: The Viking Press, 1945.
2. K. SHRIDHARANI: *My India, My America.* New York: Duell, Sloan & Pearce, 1941.

3. W. G. SUMNER: *Folkways*. Boston: Ginn & Co., 1906.
4. R. L. SUTHERLAND & J. L. WOODWARD: *Introductory Sociology*, 3rd ed. Philadelphia: J. B. Lippincott Co., 1948.
5. CLARK WISSLER: *Man and Culture*. New York: Thomas Y. Crowell Co., 1923.
6. KIMBALL YOUNG: *Sociology*: *A Study of Society and Culture*. New York: American Book Co., 1942.

CHAPTER 34

EAST AND WEST: A STUDY IN CULTURE
CONTACTS

1. EAST AND WEST MEET

"EAST is East and West is West and never the twain shall meet,"
so wrote the bard of British imperialism, Rudyard Kipling. With a
play upon the words, during World War II, a Soviet Russian jour-
nalist tersely wrote: "East and West shall meet—in Berlin." Well,
East and West are conventional points of the compass, dependent
upon one's location and orientation. East, as generally understood,
embracing Asia and Egypt, has constantly met West, as generally
understood, embracing Europe and the Americas.

Man, East and West, has had through the centuries two things
in common, original human nature and physical nature. Original
human nature has been a constant in the sense of the unlearned
capacity for response; but the intensity and swiftness of responses
vary with different individuals, the variations being caused by heredity as well as by environment. Physical nature, likewise, has been a
constant, East and West, in the experience of man; but here, too,
differences in climate and in the contours of the earth have been as
varied as the particular parts of the world we happen to be studying
—not to mention the transformation wrought into the self-same
natural phenomenon by advances in man's knowledge and culture.
The physical fact of the Niagara Falls, for instance, has not changed
much from the early colonial days to the present day; but to the
contemporary man this physical fact is a source of power, something
unknown to the colonists.

Thus despite the common sharing of original human nature and
of physical nature, man in the East built up different modes of
reactions and created different culture patterns from those of man in
the West. But men, East and West, have, all through the historic
period at least, known of each other and learned from each other.

548

And the process is still going on—East and West are today engaged in learning from each other and in building a common world civilization.

2. MAN IS OF THE EARTH, EARTHY

The earth is man's habitat. More than that, in a real sense man is the child of Mother Earth. The heavens above—the sun, the moon, the stars—interacting upon this terrestrial planet, producing climatic and seasonal changes, conditioning the very existence of life, are part of man's environment. The atmosphere surrounding the earth, the land masses and the bodies of water, mountains and rivers, forests and deserts, rainfall and drought, lightning and thunder, flora and fauna, as well as other human beings have constituted part of the natural scenery upon which man has gazed from the time he could register experience.

Willynilly man has had to respond to the universe of which he has been a part. In the process of response, experience was accumulated. By the trial and error method, he learned to differentiate between "good" and "bad" responses, between survival-value responses and life-destroying responses, between growth-value responses and mere survival-value responses. In a large sense, man's responses to the universe are creative acts, acts of creation, rather than acts of invention. Man's specific attempts to adjust himself to the earth and to the fullness thereof call forth inventions and lead to the upbuilding of culture.

Man's adjustment to the earth can be and has been studied objectively. To quote an eminent geographer (4, pp. 1–2):

Man is a product of the earth's surface. This means not merely that he is a child of the earth, dust of her dust; but that the earth has mothered him, fed him, set him tasks, directed his thoughts, confronted him with difficulties that have strengthened his body and sharpened his wits, given him his problems of navigation or irrigation, and at the same time whispered hints for their solution. . . . Man can no more be scientifically studied apart from the ground which he tills, or the lands over which he travels, or the seas over which he trades, than polar bear or desert cactus can be understood apart from its habitat. Man's relations to his environment are infinitely more numerous and complex than those of the most highly organized plant or animal.

3. THE RISE OF RIVER VALLEY CIVILIZATIONS

Civilization began "chiefly in four river valleys (or pairs of river valleys): the valley of the Nile (Egypt), of the Tigris and Euphrates (Mesopotamia), the Indus and Ganges (India) and the Hwang-ho (China); and in one island in an island sea, Crete. In each of the first four areas geographical conditions for civilization are to a greater or less extent realized. In each, the rivers provided a constantly fertilized soil; in each, mountains, sea, or desert afforded natural protection; each was a naturally defined unit, with the river serving as an easy means of internal communication." (1, p. 21).

Growth-value responses to the river are predicated upon inventions enabling man properly to utilize the waters of the river and the surrounding areas. In the early days of man's upward march from savagery to barbarism, from barbarism to civilization, the river served as a most potent factor in social and political unification.

It was, of course, an easy means of communication between the dwellers on each side of its banks throughout its entire basin. To this day, 'the Chinese call such roads as exist in China "*dry* ways"— the natural sequence to the idea that *the* way is a wet way, a river.' The river is, therefore, very obviously a bond of union between great numbers of men. And it is a bond in another sense, since it sets them all certain common problems and gives them all certain common interests. *Rivers unite.* And they do this, of course, most fully and effectively where the advance of civilization has not as yet produced other and even more efficient means of unification. (1, p. 26).

"This unifying and stimulating national task of utilizing and controlling the water," rightly observes Miss Semple, "was the same task which in various forms promoted the early civilization of the Hwang-ho and the Yang-tse basins, India, Mesopotamia, Persia, Peru, Mexico." (4, p. 329).

4. THE MEDITERRANEAN, THE HIGHWAY OF RIVER VALLEY CIVILIZATIONS

Of the early river valley civilizations, only India and China have maintained an unbroken continuity to this day. Others passed the torch of civilization on to the lands and peoples around the Mediterranean—the Middle sea, the Sea in the midst of land—and themselves disappeared from the pages of history. The Mediterranean served as the one and only significant highway of commerce and culture between the river valley civilizations. Both material and non-material gifts of Egypt, Mesopotamia and Palestine were introduced to Europe by way of the Mediterranean. The glory of Greece and the power of Rome were dependent upon gifts from the East. Stories of explosives and the printing press, invented by the Chinese, were brought to the Mediterranean world by Marco Polo in the thirteenth century, not to mention noodles Italianized into spaghetti and macaroni. The Hindu numeral system including the zero, the decimal system of notation and algebra, invented by the Hindus and refined by the Arabs, were introduced to Europe in the Middle Ages by the Arabs via the Mediterranean. Not only did the Arabs act as middlemen in the carrying of commerce and culture between India and Europe, but they also stimulated the Renaissance, the New Learning, in Europe by making available to Europeans the treasures of classical Greek learning.

The Crusades had been an occasion for the rude barbarians of Europe to learn good manners and chivalry from the Arabs. (5, pp. 172–73). The conquest of Spain by the Arabs was a signal for the implanting of Oriental culture on the soil of Europe. The Orientalization of Europe was never fully achieved, but the Saracen Arabs left an abiding impress upon the intellectual life of Europe. Some of the greatest historiographers of the Middle Ages were Arabic: it is, for instance, impossible to estimate fully the influence exerted by Ibn Khaldun (1332-1406) upon European scholarship. Furthermore, to quote the late Mr. Alfred W. Martin (1862-1933), leader of the Ethical Culture Society of New York (2, p. 230):

During those centuries of ecclesiastical despotism when the Christian Church suppressed all intellectual activities save those that were theological, causing the talent that reproduces to supplant the genius that creates, Mohammedans did all in their power to encourage and stimulate research in every branch of human inquiry. No medieval Pope or bishop ever sent thanks to a thinker for scientific discovery, but the sheik, Ul-Islam, sent congratulations and the benedictions of Allah to Al-Hassan for his discovery of a fundamental law in optics.

The Muslim contribution to the material culture of Europe is equally significant. "Today we decorate our walls and floors with fabrics that Mohammedans taught us (Occidentals) to weave. We regale our senses with perfumes they taught us to make; we teach our children the algebra and higher mathematics they taught the fathers." (2, pp. 230–31).

The Orientalization of Europe was prevented by a number of factors. For one thing, the new learning and the point of view of the Arabs acted as a tonic to the somnolent Europe steeped in theological bickerings; the dynamic thus released led to the rejuvenation of Europe and the downfall of Arab power on the continent. Second, the experimental attitude, the formalized attempt to unlock the secrets of nature, the dominant wish to control nature by applying the results of scientific explorations to the methods of production— this new temper just then arising in Europe gave the Europeans an advantage over the rest of the world. Third, the commerce and culture of the Mediterranean lands were carried up the Rhine to the Germanic tribes in the Middle Ages. Adventurous German merchants banded themselves together into the Hanseatic League and converted the Baltic Sea and the German (North) Sea into inland seas—highways of commerce and culture. Fourth, the opening up of this northern Mediterranean—the Baltic and the North Sea— stimulated the growth of commerce and culture, leading, specifically, to the development of the economic philosophy of Mercantilism in England and elsewhere on the continent of Europe. Fifth, Mercantilism, thriving upon competition and conflict with out-groups, led to the development of political nationalism in the European world by the end of the Middle Ages.

5. THE ATLANTIC, THE NEW MIDDLE SEA

The center of civilization shifted from the Mediterranean to the North, from the North to the West. The epoch-making voyage of Columbus, undertaken to find a direct searoute to the fabulously wealthy India, made the Mediterranean a mere pond and made of the Atlantic the new Middle Sea. Northwest Europe and the eastern seaboard of the New Hemisphere became the sending and receiving points in the traffic of commerce and culture. Indeed, Yankee clipper ships, on their own power, began to ply the high seas on their journey to India and China. While the Colonies were engaged in their War of Independence, the British were engaged in laying the foundation of their vast empire in India.

The conquest of India by Britain, equipped with deadlier instruments of human destruction, resulted in an intensified culture contact between India and Europe. The discovery of Sanskrit literature by European scholars marks an important milestone in the intellectual regeneration of the world during the last two hundred years. Not to mention the daily bath and personal hygiene (the morning ablutions) which the English learned from the Hindus, the English also acquired certain artifacts and skills from India. To quote F. Baltazar Solvyns (3, pp. 250–51, quoted):

In ancient times the Indians excelled in the art of constructing vessels, and the present Hindus can in this respect still offer models to Europe—so much so that the English, attentive to everything which relates to naval architecture, have borrowed from the Hindus many improvements which they have adapted with success to their own shipping. The Indian vessels unite elegance and utility, and are models of patience and fine workmanship.

The discovery of Sanskrit and Vedic literature by the Europeans in the eighteenth century and their acquaintance with Panini (circa 700 B.C.), the greatest grammarian known to mankind, laid the foundations for the study of comparative linguistics, of philology. The literary skill of Kalidas (200 B.C.?–600 B.C.?) thrilled the great Goethe who, in paying tribute to Kalidas' famous play Sakuntala, rapturously exclaimed:

Wouldst thou the life's young blossoms and the fruits of its decline,
And all by which the soul is pleased, enraptured, feasted, fed—
Wouldst thou the earth and heaven itself in one sweet name combine?
I name thee, O Sakuntala, and all at once is said.

The flowering of New England, the New England School of Transcendentalism, was made possible by the interaction of the newly discovered lore and learning of the Hindus with the newly rising dynamic culture of the United States of America. Ralph Waldo Emerson's debt to Hindu lore can never be overstated. And one of the greatest geniuses of that School, Henry David Thoreau, once whimsically remarked: "One wise saying of the Hindus is worth the whole state of Massachusetts." Incidentally, Thoreau, the author of the Essay on Civil Disobedience, gave Gandhi, through Gandhi to India, the weapon of non-violent resistance, the technique of civil disobedience, of non-violent revolution. *The circle is thus fully made around the globe.* During the period of intensified culture contacts between East and West, the art forms of China and Japan as well as those of India have significantly influenced the Euro-American world.

But it has not been a one-way traffic. The East has been learning a great many new things from the Western world. To cite but one or two illustrations. Japan, opened to the commerce of the West in the middle of the last century, decided to borrow and adopt all the patterns of the West that had relevance to the philosophy of might and power. Universal education, public health and hygiene, industrialism, militarism, party politics, parliamentarism, centralism— these patterns of the West Japan grafted onto her ancestral culture and emerged as a Great Power after defeating China in 1895 and Russia in 1905. The whole of the East has been engaged during the last hundred years in developing political nationalism as a defense mechanism against the aggressions and violence of the West. A prolonged period of intimate contact with the British has created in the Hindese heart and mind deep respect for the political philosophy of civil rights and civil liberties, of parliamentary procedures and constitutional methods, of freedom and democracy. The pattern of the public school system, invented by the State of Prussia, adopted by the United States on a national scale over a hundred years ago, is looked upon very respectfully by the Eastern world; in India, at least, that pattern will be made an integral part of national life now that the nation has become free from British control. The scientific attitude, so thoroughly characteristic of the West in the recent past, has been already accepted by the intellectual elite of the East and will become the focal point for a new culture complex in the East as soon as education is diffused among the masses.

6. THE PACIFIC, THE LATEST MIDDLE SEA

This process of worldwide acculturation has been significantly aided by newer inventions in the realm of communication and transportation. The use of metal in shipbuilding, the international postal system, the telegraph and the cable, and most recently the radio and the airplane have compressed this vast world of yesteryear into a small neighborhood world. With the conquest of the Philippines by the United States of America at the turn of the century, the Atlantic made way for the Pacific as the new Middle Sea. The waters of the Pacific are lapping the coasts of those very regions whence the river valley civilizations began to traverse outward and beyond. *Another circle has been completed.*

For the past half century the Atlantic has been a mere pond and the Pacific the real Mediterranean. But this position of the Pacific is not likely to endure for long. The European phase of World War II (1939-45) has brought into prominence a much neglected body of water as the real Mediterranean of the present and of the future— the Arctic Ocean, which once separated but now unites the land masses of the New World, Europe and Asia.

7. MAN CLIMBS UPWARD BY INVENTIONS

The history of mankind may be divided into several epochs on different bases of classification. In terms of transportation: locomotion on foot, riding on the back of domesticated animals, horse-drawn chariots, horseless carriages; river navigation, inland sea navigation, ocean navigation; air navigation. In terms of materials used for the making of tools: stone age, copper age, bronze age, iron age, iron-and-coal age, electricity (water-power) age, atomic age. In terms of warfare: mild intertribal warfare with bow and arrow; warfare in which the missile's range may be increased by the warrior riding on a horse or in a chariot or a boat; warfare in which the missile's range is increased by propulsion, i.e., by the use of gunpowder; warfare in which the missile's range is increased both by propulsion and by the warrior's swift movement, such as use of modern artillery tanks, naval vessels and airplanes. In still different terms of warfare: war as the business of the chief and his warriors; war as the business of robber barons and their feudal vassals; war as the business of monarchs, their military chieftains and mercenary troops; war as the business of the whole people, initiated by the Revolutionary War in the New World, reinforced by Napoleon and the post-Napoleonic monarchs of Europe in terms of universal conscription, consummated into totalitarian war by Hitler and his antagonists in World War II. In terms of economic evolution, from food-gathering to food-producing: hunting and fishing, the pastoral stage involving domestication of animals and nomadism, the settled agricultural stage, the agricultural and manufacturing stage, finally the modern economy of agriculture and manufacturing and world trade.

From another standpoint, the history of civilized peoples may be conveniently divided into two eras, the pre-technological era (roughly ending with the end of the Middle Ages in Europe) and the technological era (roughly beginning with the Renaissance), as suggested by Quincy Wright. (6, p. 168). In the pre-technological era, societies and civilizations, though they were never in complete isolation from one another, had nevertheless distinctive features of their own and developed in accordance with their individual genius. In the present technological era, culture contacts having been accelerated and multiplied, the old values of different societies and civilizations are in process of modification through interaction, and new values are emerging.

8. MODERN CULTURE PATTERNS IN THE MAKING

The transition from the pre-technological era to the modern period in Europe, illustrative of what is happening the world over, really a story of modern culture patterns in the making, has been admirably set forth by Professor Wright (6, pp. 168–69):

Among the significant developments of the century from 1450 to 1550 were the effective use of explosives, of clocks, and of printing;

the discoveries of America and of new routes to the East; the rise of vernacular literature, the rediscovery of ancient literatures, and the renascence of art; the fall of the Eastern empire, the reformation of western Christianity, and the rise of strong national dynasties in England, France, and Spain; and the acceptance by the European leaders of the ideas of critical scholarship, of science, of territorial sovereignty, and of business accounting. Western civilization came into contact with ten living and dead civilizations as well as with many primitive cultures. Institutions and methods, values and ideas, were compared and exchanged by the rising elites. The geocentric, anthropocentric, religiocentric, hierarchical order, established by revelation and tradition in Western Christendom and in most of the other civilizations, confining the human mind and spirit to a static economy and immutable truths, became infected by fevers of inquisitiveness and skepticism which would eventually prove fatal. In the West pioneers were by 1550 looking out upon vast unknown realms of nature, art, and opportunity, confusing and bewildering, but perhaps capable of being ordered by human energy, especially if that energy could be directed by new methods of observation, experiment, analysis, and representation, and could utilize new techniques of expression, communication, persuasion, and control.

These changes were so momentous that the civilization of Europe in the seventeenth century was wholly different from that in the fifteenth. Some of the institutions of medieval Christendom, it is true, survived. Some survive even in the twentieth century, but their spirit is as feeble as was the spirit of classical institutions in the sixth century. A new civilization, inspiring new states, new churches, new corporations, and new universities, had turned its back on the European Middle Ages and was advancing to occupy the hitherto uncivilized lands of America, the Pacific, and Africa and to penetrate and gradually to supersede the ancient civilizations of Mexico and Peru; Russia, Turkey, and the Arab countries; India, China, and Japan.

Survivals of the patterns suitable to pre-technological cultures are to be found among all peoples, races and nations. Those culture patterns that are harmlessly recessive may yet be perpetuated; those culture patterns that are, on the other hand, aggressively antagonistic to the spirit of the modern age will be cast aside—with forethought and wisdom by some groups, and after violent cataclysms by others. Today we are called upon to forget the ethnocentric norms and viewpoints of the river valley civilizations, of the Mediterranean civilization, of the Atlantic civilization, of the Pacific civilization;

today we are called upon to look to the Arctic civilization of tomorrow which shall bind the whole world into one common cultural fellowship.

9. THE ETHICAL IMPERATIVE OF THE GREAT SOCIETY

The small neighborhood world has entailed upon the Great Society the ethics of primary group relationships: Ahimsa or non-violence and love, Satya or truth, accommodation and reconciliation; live and let live and help live, mutual understanding and appreciation.

In terms of the imperative of the ethics of our small neighborhood world, our generation must explore afresh the religious heritage of mankind with a view to discovering the specific contributions different religions have made and may yet make to the doctrine and practice of Ahimsa and good neighborliness. The motto of this journey of exploration may well be: "A good thought by whomsoever initiated, a good word by whomsoever spoken, a good deed by whomsoever done—they all belong to me, they are a part of my heritage. No good is alien to me; I shall appreciate, appropriate and participate in all the spiritual streams and values of mankind, ancient and modern, colored and non-colored. Aye, I dare to dream to be the co-doer of the good a thousand years hence!"

REFERENCES

1. J. F. HORRABIN: *An Outline of Political Geography*, New York: Alfred Knopf, 1942.
2. ALFRED W. MARTIN: *Great Religious Teachers of the East*, New York: Macmillan, 1911.
3. RADHAKUMUD MOOKERJI: *A History of Indian Shipping*, London: Longmans, Green and Co., 1912.
4. ELLEN C. SEMPLE: *Influences of Geographic Environment*, New York: Henry Holt & Co., 1911.
5. HENDRIK WILLEM VAN LOON: *The Story of Mankind*, New York: Boni & Liveright, 1921.
6. QUINCY WRIGHT: *A Study of War*, Vols. I & II, Chicago: The University of Chicago Press, 1942.

NOTE: S. RADHAKRISHNAN'S *East and West—Some Reflections*, delivered as the Beatty Memorial Lectures in Canada in 1955, and published in America by Harper & Brothers in 1956, deserves the serious attention of sociologists as well as philosophers.

CHAPTER 35

THE AMERICAN SOCIAL HERITAGE*

THE processes and factors that have given rise to the modern American mind, to the American character, to American culture, may be traced as far back as the rise of the River Valley civilizations, if one wishes to indulge in stimulating intellectual exercise. Not wishing to essay such a task, we shall content ourselves with the role of the Colonial background in the making of the twentieth century America.

1. THE NEW AMERICAN SOCIAL SYSTEM

The American social system has been a distinctly new innovation in the history of modern times. Commentators on the American scene have noted this fact from the earliest times. Nine special features differentiate the new American social system from previous social systems the world over:

First, permissiveness in child rearing;

Second, a high premium placed upon achieved status rather than upon ascribed status;

Third, freedom and equality as the warp and woof of the social fabric;

Fourth, reliance on voluntary associations to achieve the desired objectives on the basis of a contract, formal or informal;

Fifth, the easy informality of the frontier, resting now upon rugged individualism and self-reliance and now upon team work, reinforcing the basic belief in freedom and equality, and thus giving rise to the American creed whose first article is freedom, democracy and equality and whose second article is education;

Sixth, abundant living for all, not just for the privileged few, on the basis of hard work and mass production and on the busi-

* In a slightly abbreviated form, this Chapter has appeared as the concluding chapter in *Introduction to Sociology*, edited by JAMES H. S. BOSSARD and OTHERS (Harrisburg: The Stackpole Co., 1952).

ness principle of a small margin of profit per unit with a large turnover of goods.

Seventh, separation of Church and State;

Eighth, the federal structure of government, with checks and balances;

Ninth, religion and education to be kept apart and yet commingled one with the other.

First, from the days of George Washington to the present, American parents have been in the habit of permitting their children wide latitude and extraordinary freedom. The youngster is treated as a person with rights and privileges. Children are not only to be seen but also to be heard—indeed, they are to be listened to with greater interest and more ecstatic devotion than the adults! This attitude of respecting the child's personality is derived from the gospel of freedom and democracy; in turn, such treatment instills into the growing youngster a strong sense of loyalty to freedom and democracy. Carried to extreme lengths, this permissiveness in child-rearing leads to ego-centrism, to self-centeredness—and to juvenile delinquency when the youngster feels frustrated.

Second, in the New World generally and in the United States of America specifically, the new man called American is judged not by his pedigree nor by his title but by his brains and brawns. Writing during the Revolutionary period (1776-83), Hector St. John de Crevecoeur stated that once the immigrant arrived on this new continent, "a modern society offers itself to his (the newcomer's) contemplation, different from what he had hitherto seen. It is not composed, as in Europe, of great lords who possess everything and of a herd of people who have nothing. Here are no aristocratical families, no (royal) courts, no kings, no bishops, no ecclesiastical dominion, no invisible power giving to a few a very visible one. . . . The rich and the poor are not so far removed from each other as they are in Europe. . . . We have no princes, for whom we toil, starve and bleed: We are the most perfect society existing in the world." (3, pp. 49, 50).

De Crevecoeur goes on to describe the new man, called American, in equally ecstatic terms: "*He* is an American who, leaving behind him all his ancient prejudices and manners, receives new ones from the new mode of life he has embraced, the new government he obeys, and the new rank (of citizen) he holds. He becomes an American by being received in the broad lap of our great *Alma Mater*. Here individuals of all nations are melted into a new race of men, whose labors and posterity will one day cause great changes in the world." (3, pp. 54–55).

Embarassingly enthusiastic over America, over American society as it was then emerging, and over America's role in world affairs, de Crevecoeur hit upon the central point of the new American social system, namely, that here a man is to be judged not by his pedigree but by the degree of his accomplishment, that achieved status is more important in the new society of America than ascribed status. (Compare *supra* CHAPTER 19 for de Crevecoeur's analysis of the transformation of the European into the American citizen.)

Third, the American social system rested on the proposition that all men are created equal and are endowed by their Creator with the inalienable right to life, liberty and the pursuit of happiness. This was a revolutionary doctrine enunciated in a fledgeling society into which had crept the monstrous wrong of slavery. That beset by slavery as they were, the Founding Fathers could enunciate the doctrine of freedom and equality for all testifies to their vision of "the most perfect society" of which de Crevecoeur had spoken. Precisely because freedom and equality are part of their ethos, the American people have been constantly engaged in regaining equal rights for certain minority groups who had been victims of historical forces beyond the control of the Founding Fathers—to wit: American Indians and Negroes.

Fourth, the efficient use of voluntary association as a mechanism to achieve desired objectives may be said to be an invention of the American people. A voluntary association rests upon contract willingly entered into among those who form and/or perpetuate an association. The role of the theory of social contract in the making of the American nation as well as in the making of the American character has been fully appreciated neither by the "children" of the Founding Fathers nor by other nations. Even though the theory of social contract arose in Europe (Plato down) and in India (Buddha), the stamp of social contract is indelibly impressed on America's face:

(1) The Mayflower Compact;

(2) The American Declaration of Independence (affirming the right of the people "to alter or to abolish" a tyrannical form of government and "to institute new government" by contract among themselves);

(3) The U.S. Constitution ("We the People of the United States, in order to form a more perfect union, . . . do ordain and establish this Constitution for the United States of America" by a social contract among ourselves);

(4) Individual and Collective Bargaining in Industrial Relations;

(5) Widespread use of the system of payment by checks rather than by cash, implying trust in one's fellow man;

(6) Universal acceptance of the social mechanism of voluntary association as a useful tool in getting things done, regardless of the nature of the objective, religious or recreational, economic or educational, societal or familial, etc.

What part the virgin soil of the New World, the fear of the American Indians as an outgroup, or the bold and optimistic outlook of the frontiersmen played in the invention and cultivation of this new social instrument, namely, voluntary association as a mechanism for achieving objectives, it is difficult to say. Suffice it to note that competent foreign observers, notably de Tocqueville in the 1830's and Bryce in the early part of the twentieth century, were struck by the frequent use made by Americans of the mechanism of voluntary association for the achievement of desired objectives, in sharp contrast to governmental paternalism prevalent elsewhere in the world. To quote de Tocqueville (5, Vol. I, p. 216; Vol. II, p. 128. *Cf.* 2, Vol. II, p. 281):

In no country in the world has the principle of association been more successfully used, or applied to a greater multitude of objects, than in America. . . . Americans of all ages, all conditions, and all dispositions, constantly form associations. They have not only commercial and manufacturing companies, in which all take part, but associations of a thousand other kinds—religious, moral, serious, futile, general and restricted, enormous and diminutive. The Americans make associations to give entertainments, to found seminaries,

THE AMERICAN SOCIAL HERITAGE

to build inns, to construct churches, to diffuse books, to send missionaries to the antipodes; they found in this manner hospitals, prisons, and schools. If it be proposed to inculcate some truth, or to foster some feeling, by the encouragement of a great example, they form a society. Wherever, at the head of some new undertaking, you see the government of France, or a man of rank in England, in the United States you will be sure to find an association.

Fifth, the crucial role of the frontier in the making of the American mind is now an accepted fact among historians and observers of the American scene. Frederick J. Turner, contemporaneously with the theoretical vanishing of the frontier (1890), set the fashion of analyzing the role of the frontier in the making of America by reading his paper at the World's Fair in Chicago, 1893, on "The Significance of the Frontier in American History." (6, *passim*). What lay beyond the Atlantic was a frontier to the European on-lookers in the days of Columbus. Since the settlement of the Atlantic coast areas by these "frontiersmen," by these "pioneers," the thrill of pioneering, of expanding out to the Alleghanies, to the Mississippi, to the Rockies, to the Pacific, possessed the hearts and minds of men settled on the eastern seaboard. The American character has been moulded by these pioneering ventures.

Sixth, the American's economic activities are characterized by a number of startlingly new and highly efficient ingredients:

(1) that hard labor is necessary for abundant production;
(2) that no type of labor is degrading if it is honest;
(3) that "competition is the life blood of trade";
(4) that the customer is always right;
(5) that every citizen is a potential customer for the manufacturers' wares, from automobiles and refrigerators to pens and pencils;
(6) that all consumption goods should be mass-produced in order to satisfy the demands of all customers;
(7) that new customers can be created by mass advertising;
(8) that business success and accumulation of wealth depends upon a large turnover of goods with a small margin of profit per unit;
(9) that a worker is entitled to "fair wages for a fair day's work";

(10) that exploitation of labor, through under-payment, is contrary to the democratic philosophy;

(11) that government should not enter into competition with business unless "the general welfare" requires, as in the case of the postal service and the TVA;

(12) that labor and management should be free to enter into individual and collective bargaining and contract without government interference, except when the national interest is threatened;

(13) that a high standard of living is the birthright of every American citizen—of every citizen of other nations as well.

Aided by high-powered tools, the American worker produces three to four times more than the European worker, and perhaps ten times more than does the worker in Asia (excepting Japan). The thirteen ingredients of American economic activity, if adopted by the rest of the world, are calculated to bring about worldwide prosperity and abundant life for all nations. The thirteenth ingredient in our list above has been responsible for American prosperity and for unprecedented American aid to other nations either for rebuilding their war-shattered economies or for developing a strong industrial superstructure on their agricultural economic base.

The seventh and eighth features of the new American social system, namely, separation of Church and State and the federal structure of government with built-in checks and balances, have made America what it is—a land where each one is free to worship God in his own way, and where each citizen enjoys the rights of a sovereign citizen with loyalty to the place of his residence, the city, the state and the Nation.

The ninth feature of the new American social system is the dominant role of religion and education in the life of the people. Religion manifests itself as social gospel, without detriment to the gospel of salvation. And while religion and public education are to be kept strictly apart, the theme of American culture is the unity of religion and education, like a sword with two edges: Religion, for the American, means starting with God and working down to man, while education means starting with man and working up to God.

2. Ten American Traits

Just as there are dominant and recessive biological traits in an organism, so there are dominant and recessive cultural traits in every society. What follows herewith is the presentation in brief form of ten dominant American traits.

The *first* and outstanding trait of the American people is the spirit of pioneering. Pioneers and daredevils, braving the furies of the high seas in their tiny barks, discovered the New World. The spirit of pioneering and daredeviltry are among the original traits of the American people. Not only was the discovery of the New World the result of pioneering and daredevil exploits but colonization also required the cultivation and exhibition of the same spirit.

The experimental attitude, the tentative view of the universe, the pragmatic approach—these are the logical outcomes of pioneering conditions of living. The American never was, and never is, frightened by the lack of a consistent philosophy of life. Enough for him to solve the problems of the moment by the roughest and readiest methods at hand. Pragmatism is as natural to American culture as is the Woolworth Building or the assembly line. Furthermore, the insistence upon solution of a given problem by the roughest and readiest methods, without regard to the whole situation, is in thorough harmony with scientific procedure. Thus, the pragmatist and the scientist made possible the invention of the atom bomb; the idealist would have asked himself a number of relevant questions regarding the utility of the atom bomb in the cosmic scheme of things before he undertook to perfect it.

Pioneering conditions of living necessitated in the New World of the 17th and 18th centuries equality of the sexes, each taking its share of the burden of making life more enjoyable. The New World thus repeated the experiences of the pioneer Aryas who had colonized and settled in India centuries before the beginning of the Christian era.

The *second* important trait of the American people may be traced to the Pilgrim Fathers and the Puritans. The Pilgrim Fathers were a God-fearing people, cut loose from old-world traditions of theological bickerings and animated by the pioneering, experimental spirit of the New World. To be sure, staunch religious communities in America, especially the Puritan, persecuted those of other faiths in the early days, thus setting at naught their own plea for religious freedom in Europe. There is no denying, however, that both Protestants and Catholics were deeply religious and remarkably free from the chicanery practised by their fellow communicants in Europe.

The *third* important ingredient of American character has been derived from the castaways of Europe—from paupers, criminals and convicts who used to be dumped on the shores of the New World by European governments. A number of these castaways made good in the New World, thereby pointing to the moral that many human derelicts are made by society, not by God nor by nature. But some of these derelicts could not rise above the early conditioning of their lives in Europe and became the physical and spiritual progenitors of the lawless elements in America. Nor did the mores of pioneering society militate positively against experiments in lawlessness.

Fourth, America stands for nothing if not for the will to freedom. Stout hearts and unlimited expanses of land gave men and women a thrill of freedom to which it is America's privilege to bear witness. "No taxation without representation" was a political slogan pointing to the more abiding spiritual aspiration for freedom. Long before the Revolutionary War, the New World had successfully asserted the principle of freedom of the press; Benjamin Franklin and Peter Zenger, not so well known to the outside world, may be said to be the patron saints of the American press. The political revolution was but an aspect of the larger spiritual transformation which the New World undertook to bring into the lives of its own citizens and of the other peoples. Yes, let freedom ring! "Proclaim liberty throughout all the land, to all the inhabitants thereof." It may be truly asserted that Americans love freedom more dearly than all other values combined. *Freedom is the American's first love.* Love of freedom is rooted in and reinforces patriotism.

Fifth, pioneering is opposed to established ways of doing things, opposed to stability in the social order, opposed to the concept of the organic nature of the social process. It is, on the other hand, hospitable to new and ever-changing ways of doing things, hospitable to a quick succession of changes in the social order, hospitable to the concept of the contractual basis of society and of the political order. The Social Contract theory, though propounded in Europe, found firm lodgment in this country precisely because pioneering conditions favored such a view of the social process. To the pioneer, society is an artifact and government a contract.

Jean Jacques Rousseau and John Locke, expounders of the Social Contract theory in Europe, are the patron saints of the American Revolution. The American Declaration of Independence speaks of "the laws of nature and of nature's God;" among the "natural rights" it mentions "life, liberty and the pursuit of happiness." Furthermore, it enunciates the right of the people to "alter or to abolish" a government repugnant to man's conscience and destructive of "natural rights." Finally, the Declaration affirms the right of the people, contractually, "to institute new government." And the Preamble to the Constitution breathes the spirit of Social Contract: "We the people of the United States in order to form a more perfect union . . . do ordain and establish this constitution for the United States of America" by contract among ourselves.

Sixth, in his role as the frontiersman of America the European pioneer developed and fostered the virtues of individual initiative and self-reliance. The pioneer, the typical frontiersman, according to Meiklejohn, is "strong, shrewd, resourceful, zestful, mirthful, untiring, ingenious, resolute, and ambitious." (4, p. 146). The pioneer brooks no interference. He prefers individual initiative—civic enterprise if necessary—to governmental paternalism. Self-reliance is a characteristic of the pioneer, of the frontiersman. The frontiersman hugs to his bosom the motto: "God helps him who helps himself." The aim of philanthropy and of social service should be to help one to help himself—such is the American attitude. The Americans keenly admire the spirit of frontier independence, of self-reliance, of going on one's own, of working one's way through college. In the American cultural milieu the achieved status is prized more than the ascribed status.

Seventh, the post-Revolutionary stream of immigration to the newly (contractually) established United States of America was composed, to a large extent, of resourceful men and women who had either found no scope for their talents in war-torn Europe or had been disinherited or denied freedom and justice by their governments. This stream of immigrants was definitely dominated by the zeal to make this world over so that their sad lot might not befall others. The fusing of this immigrant element with the evolving American type resulted in stamping upon American character a "Messianic" hope and a "Messianic" role. America, it holds, shall serve as a beacon-light to harassed mankind. America shall be the torch-bearer of democracy to the world at large. America "the land of the free and the home of the brave"—America, "God's own country"; America, the promise of abundant life to humankind!

Eighth, the pioneer was always happy when he discovered something new, when he went a few steps ahead. His joy knew no bounds when he "got there" first. This joy had its thrills, but the frontiersman was practical enough to lay claim to the land and mineral resources he was the first one to survey. In this fashion the frontiersman combined the thrill of adventure with material abundance of life. Frontier conditions and pioneering alone explain why the magic word "progress" and the equally compulsive word "new" to this day create in the American a sense of adoration and worship.

Ninth, progress, new achievements, and scientific discoveries are rendered possible only by education, devoutly believes the American. Hence, *education, his second love,* has become to the American a panacea for all the ills of the world, a thing with which to conjure. Education, reasons the American, not only cures the ills of the world, but is also essential for the preservation of freedom, his first love, and democracy. Ignorant as he is of the many problems involved in the formulation of a philosophy of education, the average American prizes education above everything else but liberty. This naive deference to education on the part of the American is a thrilling phenomenon for an Oriental American to observe.

Tenth, if concern for child life be considered one of the significant tests of civilization, as it might well be, then the American people are the most civilized in the world. American civilization is child-centered. The woman is "the boss" of the American household but the reigning monarch of the house is in reality the child. The Old World saying, "The child is to be seen but not heard," is magnificently disregarded in the New World.

Pioneering and daredeviltry, the experimental attitude and pragmatism, competition and the goals of success, i.e., advancement to a higher level, equality of the sexes and God-fearing puritanism, reconditioning of human derelicts and the provision of ample scope for unregenerate law-breakers, love of liberty and the "Messianic" role, the worship of progress and dedication to education, the dominance of the child and the emancipation of woman—these values through reciprocal interrelationship and interaction during the last four centuries have led to the making of the American character as we know it today. One may assert, without fear of contradiction, that each of these traits today flourishes in the American cultural milieu without let or hindrance. It is difficult, however, to state the nature of the emergent "character" resulting from the fusion of such diverse traits.

3. THREE AMERICAN BEHAVIOR PATTERNS

We may make a tentative attempt to see what type of behavior or culture pattern results when some of the traits of the American, just discussed, are crossed one with another. Three such patterns are presented.

Lawlessness

Pioneering and daredeviltry, the experimental attitude and pragmatism, provision of ample scope for unregenerate law-breakers, ingroup-outgroup hostility, and the social contract theory—these traits do not militate against lawlessness; indeed, they reinforce lawlessness in a very marked fashion by supplying material and moral justification.

One may recall the spicy statement of the late Theodore Roosevelt: "Show me a man who never broke a law, and I'll show you a fool!" The advice would hardly seem necessary so far as the *genre* American is concerned. The average American's favorite pastime is to "beat"—to circumvent—the law, whether it be in regard to crossing the street against the light or in regard to sumptuary legislation. This trait of "beating" the law, in contradistinction to "breaking" the law, permeates every aspect of American civilization. The idea of "getting by," to be found now and then in education as well as in other fields, is a phase of the larger problem of lawlessness.

It may be safely affirmed that lawlessness in the United States of America was born of the original sin of social contract and that it was reinforced by an exaggerated emphasis put upon the contractual basis of social relationships by a pioneer society. By substituting for social contract an organic view of society and of the cultural process, we may eliminate the historic American culture pattern of lawlessness. On the other hand, we may note in passing that the social contract theory is responsible for the American emphasis upon the dignity of the individual as well as for the democratic rights and liberties of American citizens.

Zest for Living

Pioneering, the spirit of adventure, and ample scope for the exercise of initiative developed in the American a zest for living—for doing things, for proceeding at a fast pace. The rough and ready pioneer's zest for living expressed itself in the aspirations for opening up the frontier, for building up the country, for developing industries, and for making money. It is true that the American applies himself to the task of making money more avidly than anybody else. But it is a misconception to say, as transient tourists, especially from Europe, maintain, that the American's chief preoccupation in life is "the chase after the dollar." As a matter of fact, no people on earth are more indifferent to wealth than the Americans. The American can build up a billion-dollar fortune magnificently and give away the whole of it, or nine-tenths of it, still more magnificently. Of no other people in the history of mankind can such a proposition be affirmed.

Commenting upon the American scene of 1892, Henry Adams has this to say (1, p. 328):

They (the American people) had lost the sense of worship; for the idea that they worshipped money seemed a delusion. Worship of money was an old-world trait, a healthy appetite akin to worship of the gods or to the worship of power in any concrete shape; but the American wasted money more recklessly than any extravagant court aristocracy; he had no sense of relative values, and knew not what to do with his money when he got it, except (to) use it to make more money or to throw it away . . . The American mind had less respect for money than the European or Asiatic mind, and bore its loss more easily; but it had been deflected by its pursuit till it could run in no other direction. It shunned, distrusted, disliked, the dangerous attraction of ideals, and stood alone in history for its ignorance of the past.

To paraphrase the last statement of Henry Adams in positive terms: The only objective that could attract the American with the force and compulsiveness of an ideal was, and is, the zest for living in the present.

I Will

The uninterrupted successes of the pioneers have created the legend that the American can do anything he lays his hand to—that the only self-respecting thing for the American to do in the face of difficulties is to maintain and exhibit the "I will" spirit, which has been so aptly appropriated by the City of Chicago as the motto for its escutcheon. This trait of American character has been best expressed in the oft-quoted lines of the Poet Henley:

It matters not how strait the gate,
How charged with punishment the scroll;
I am the master of my fate,
I am the captain of my soul.

In refreshing contrast to the older peoples of the world, the American throws caution to the wind; the existence of three thousand miles of unfortified border between Canada and the United States is a tribute to the sanity of the New World, to American statesmanship.

The existence of this unfortified border between Canada and the United States since 1815 is made possible by the basic orientation of American foreign policy derived from the Founding Fathers, from the famous Northwest Ordinance of July 13, 1787. This Northwest Ordinance (July 13, 1787) laid down two fundamental *political* principles: (1) exclusion of slavery from the "Northwest Territory," and (2) inclusion of the Territory—rather of Territorial units —as equal members of the emerging American Nation-State on a par with the original Thirteen States, as soon as the Territorial units fulfilled certain conditions including population strength.

The first principle implemented the promise of the Declaration of Independence, namely, that "all men are created equal," and re-asserted the central value of American culture regarding the dignity of man. The second principle threw overboard the old-world prac-tice of subjecting and exploiting territories for the benefit of the "mother" country. These two basic principles of American pioneer-ism and of the American "I WILL" spirit should stand the Ameri-can people in good stead, now that they have been willynilly thrust into the position of world leadership.

The American's vocabulary is free from the taint of *nitchevo, manana, kismet, karma,* and *fatalism.* His vivacity and open-hearted hospitality, his sportsmanship and utter lack of distrust, above all, his buoyant optimism and contagious enthusiasm—these virtues the older peoples of the world would do well to appreciate, and to appropriate if possible.

The American's glorification of the common man has no parallel in the recorded history of mankind. Contradictory traits harmon-iously blend in the American character—individualism and team-work, aggressive salesmanship and the Rotary motto of service, nationalism and concern for the well-being of other nations.

4. Certain Liabilities in American Orientation

For all of these positive constituents of the American mind, cer-tain liabilities must be set down. Progress is conceived primarily in terms of secular evolution, with the result that "bigger" is auto-matically identified with "better." Worship of size has its own nemesis, for quantity and quality are not necessarily synonymous. The American's open-hearted hospitality has made this country a stamping-ground for all kinds of propagandists, cranks, soothsayers, utopianists, messiahs, health-vendors, food-dealers, "psychologists," charlatans, both domestic and imported. The activities of such quacks are comparatively innocuous; but, while patronizing lec-

THE AMERICAN SOCIAL HERITAGE 573

turers from abroad are a nuisance, subversive fifth columnists, boring from within, with impunity, are a definite menace to the American way of life.

The easy informality between teacher and pupil is a striking feature of the American scene, but it is an open question whether the teacher arouses in the pupil a sense of wonderment, a sense of something transcendental to which he may aspire. The American's geographical frontier has vanished; he is today engaged in exploring the technological frontier. The price which he is paying for this pioneer exploration is the breakdown of his family. The spiritual frontier seems to be receding farther and farther into the background. Certain culture patterns have become structuralized; more are in process of becoming structuralized. It remains to be seen whether the American spirit of "I will" and the American conception of education as a solution of all ills can break through the shell of structuralized culture patterns, or whether the impersonal logic of technology will triumph over man's will. This, it may be noted, is a world problem, not specifically an American problem.

5. THE IMPACT OF THE NEW DEAL UPON THE AMERICAN ETHOS

The ten American traits and the three American behavior patterns have been traced by us to the Colonial background of America. They are all expressions of "rugged individualism" and flourished without let or hindrance until the onset of the Great Depression of the thirties of this century.

In the early thirties, between 10 and 15 per cent of the total population of this country—i.e., between 25 and 30 per cent of the employable population—was unemployed and thrown on the relief rolls of private and public agencies. Apple-selling—individual self-help and initiative—mitigated the horrors of unemployment for some.

Cooperative projects for mutual self-help in some communities helped a few of the unemployed. But these activities of self-help and mutual aid were like a drop in the ocean of misery created by unprecedented unemployment.

Some states created State Emergency Relief Agencies, and the Federal Emergency Relief Agencies (FERA) were set up under the New Deal (1933-onward) of President Franklin D. Roosevelt. In 1935 the Federal Government passed the Social Security Act.

The self-reliance and the rugged individualism of the American citizen were dealt a body blow by the New Deal philosophy which glorified security rather than pioneering adventure, and substituted government handouts for self-help and teamwork. That the unemployment situation was drastic is accepted by all students, at least in retrospect; that it required drastic measures is also obvious.

Unemployment in our complex society is caused more often by forces beyond the worker's control than by his laziness, shiftlessness or unwillingness to work. And the dimension of unemployment is nationwide. Hence the responsibility of the Federal Government for this national ill may be granted—indeed, must be recognized. The emergence of a sense of social responsibility is a positive gain.

But the sociologist is also under obligation to point out that during the last generation the moral fiber of the American citizen has been weakening. He who considered it humiliating to accept private or public "charity" today longingly looks with outstretched hands to the state capital and to Washington for a "free" handout. A politician's reputation today rests upon the size of the pork barrel he can bring to his constituents. The old-fashioned virtues of self-reliance and thrift are thrown away as rubbish. And in place of the old-fashioned values of pioneering and risk-taking, the New Deal philosophy has substituted the new-fashioned "values" of "security" and government handouts.

A process of universal pauperization has been set in motion during the last generation by the New Deal and the Fair Deal and its offshoots: On the one hand, the American people, who are being psychologically pauperized through extortionate taxes, are happy to stretch forth their hand for government handouts in a million different forms; and, on the other hand, the people of the world are being pauperized through dependence upon American governmental handouts.

Whether this modification of American character under the impact of the New Deal philosophy is destined to be permanent or transitory remains to be seen. Whether the change in American ethos—i.e., longing for security rather than liberty—will lead to the emergence of a dominant or recessive culture trait in American culture, it is difficult to assess at this time. But the student of the American scene must realize that, for good or for ill, the old foundations of American character have been rudely shaken.

6. MAN IN THE MACHINE AGE

Science and technology have brought forth two new culture traits —rather culture complexes—in America: industrialization and urbanization. Both are held in high esteem. Notice the vogue of referring to industrially underdeveloped countries as "backward" countries. Urbanity and a civilized mode of living are often considered synonymous terms. That industrialism and urbanization have contributed certain positive values there is no denying. But the negative by-products of these two dominant traits in American culture cannot be overlooked if we are to develop a healthy social order and balanced personalities.

Industrialism has been brought about by the application of the results of science to the processes of production. The philosophy of present workability, pragmatism, not telesis, has ever been the guiding spirit in the evolution of industrialism to date. Vast manufacturing plants necessitated the concentration of large numbers of people in the areas round about them. Where urban centers already existed, industrialism enlarged them to the size of a metropolis, even a megalopolis.

Associated with industrialism and urbanization is the phenomenon of "crowding." Linked with them, likewise, is "social insecurity." In the pre-industrial era, the craftsman was his own boss; he had a steady source of income made doubly secure by rules governing apprenticeship and by requirements for membership in the guild. In the industrial age, the tools of production belong not to the craftsmen, nor to the laborers, but to the "capitalists" who possess the right to hire and fire their workers at will. To offset such arbitrary hiring and firing, the workers have been "organized" into unions. A sort of tug-of-war is going on between the owners of the tools of production and those who operate them—between employers and employees, between "capitalists" and "laborers." One is interested in giving as little recompense as possible, the other in getting as much as possible. The result is the "job psychology," "impersonal relationships" between two groups whose cooperation is essential for the production of goods, within the framework of the present system. This pattern of "impersonal relationships" is carried over from the realm of the production of goods to that of the rendering of services. In other words, we get both goods and services "impersonally."

As a configuration, the industrial-urban complex has both positive and negative patterns—positive: the capacity for mass production for the satisfaction of the wants of all the people, the raising of the plane and standard of living of whole populations, the elimination of poverty, the availability of opportunities to large numbers of people for the development of inner resources through access to great works of art and literature, of science and religion; negative: crowding, social insecurity, tendency to organize conflict groups (labor and capital), impersonal relationships, depersonalization of services.

Retreat from the industrial-urban complex is neither possible nor advisable. The machine is here to stay. The urbanization of our population, both geographically and psychologically, is an accomplished fact. Attempts are under way, in American culture, for the taming of the machine, so that man shall be its master, not its slave. The capitalist economy has, for the first time in human history, solved the problem of production. The niggardliness of nature has been overcome. No man need suffer from want. We have at our disposal techniques and tools for indefinite expansion in production so that man may live abundantly. Add to this the advances in life-saving and health-promoting fields of human activity, namely, medicine, surgery, sanitation, public health, and we get a measure of the abundant life available to all the people.

7. ENHANCED STATUS OF THE INDIVIDUAL

It is within such a cultural milieu that the modern American lives and moves and has his being. Our democratic framework rests upon the firm foundation of equality; at the polling booth, the vote of the President of the United States of America or the vote of a Wall Street tycoon is no better and no worse than the vote of John Doe—each counts as just one vote. Our democratic philosophy is predicated upon the dignity of the individual and the worth of human personality. The ministrations of religion in America have been developing in us a sensitized conscience and making us conscious of and responsive to the sufferings of outgroups as well as to the sufferings of some members of our ingroup. In spite of the phenomena of crowding and mass-mindedness, the logic of American culture always refers us back to the individual human equation.

As products of American culture, we undertake an obligation to make good the basic principles of the American way of life, and to enrich it. This is a goal worthy of all true men and women. In a sense, however, we are today more than American citizens; we are truly citizens of the world. Science and technology have knit this world of ours into a neighborhood. Modern methods of transportation and communication have brought to us knowledge and experience of the noblest achievements of mankind the world over, of past generations as well as of the present generation in every land.

Specifically, we are heirs to the noble American social heritage; in a general sense, however, we are heirs to the great social heritage of all mankind. "God hath made of one blood all the nations of the world to dwell on the face of this earth"—this is not only good religious teaching, it is also an excellent description of the universal cultural reality of our day, transcending the boundaries of race and country. This basic principle of High Religion exalts the worth of the individual as a participant in the world's cultural stream, ennobles nations, and lays the foundation for peace and harmony among nations.

The new, enhanced status of the individual, at least in American culture, is bound to affect history in the making.

REFERENCES

1. HENRY ADAMS: *The Education of Henry Adams*. New York: The Modern Library, 1931.
2. JAMES BRYCE: *The American Commonwealth*, Vols. I & II. New York: Macmillan, 1911.

19

3. J. HECTOR ST. JOHN DE CREVECOEUR: *Letters from an American Farmer*, reprinted from the Original Edition (1782), with an Introduction by Ludwig Lewisohn. New York: Albert & Charles Boni, 1925.
4. A. MEIKELJOHN: *What Does America Mean?* New York: W. W. Norton & Co., 1935.
5. A. DE TOCQUERVILLE: *Democracy in America*, Vols. I & II. Cambridge: Sever & Francis, 1862.
6. F. J. TURNER: *The Frontier in American History*. New York: Henry Holt & Co., 1921.

A SPECIAL NOTE *on Potter's Hypothesis of Economic Abundance in the Making of the American Character*: In a penetrating analysis of the American character, David M. Potter has set forth the thesis that not the frontier as such, but economic abundance, is the primary factor in the moulding of the American character. (Potter: *People of Plenty: Economic Abundance and the American Character, passim*; Chicago: Univ. of Chicago Press, 1954.) Insofar as the frontier provided economic abundance, Turner's thesis is identical with Potter's. But Potter's main contribution is that economic abundance, including the frontier, must be considered the crucial factor in the making of the American mind and personality from the Colonial days to the present.

Potter quoted approvingly T. W. Adorno's thesis that whereas personality development takes place within the setting of the family, the family as an institution is profoundly influenced by economic and social factors—a sociological truism. " Broad changes in social conditions and institutions will have a direct bearing upon the kinds of personalities that develop within a society." (Adorno: *The Authoritarian Personality*, pp. 5–6; New York: Harper & Brothers, 1950.)

The newborn child in the American cultural milieu is confronted by a series of stimuli, physical, psychological, social, quite different from those confronting newborn children elsewhere. The difference is to be traced, maintains Mr. Potter, to the presence of economic abundance in American society and culture.

Bottle-feeding, separate room for the child, heated house, comfortable lighter clothing, younger parents, permissive toilet training, co-active democratic family pattern, the nursery school for play with the child's peers, the romantic love complex for adolescents and adults, American democracy and the democratic way of life, wide latitude to the child for indulging his fancies, exemption for the child and the adolescent from economic responsibility—these concrete realities of the contemporary American scene, " hastening social maturity and prolonging economic immaturity," are related by Potter to the existence of economic abundance in American society and culture. (See especially CHAPTER IX.)

CHAPTER 36

THE FAMILY ORDER

1. The Role of Institutions

In the operation of the institutional system of each society, folkways, mores and institutions all play a significant part. Let us reproduce what was said earlier (*supra*, CHAPTER 12):

The folkways outline the general frame of reference of a culture; the mores embody value-judgments within the framework of the folkways; the institutions create elaborate structural patterns for the promotion of the functions of the culture. The non-acceptance of folkways marks out one as an outlandish person, as a marginal man. The non-acceptance of mores marks out one as a stranger, as a rebel, as a fit object for ostracism, for persecution, for extermination. The institutions provide techniques including *Danda* for imposing conformity to the folkways and mores upon all members of the group.

The family order, the economic order, the dharmic order, the socio-state order have their roots, as already pointed out, in the original nature of man. These four orders are to be found, either in a simple or complex form, in every society, primitive as well as civilized. The elaborations of the five primary institutions—family, business, religion, education, state—have varied with different people, but the core of their functions has remained. For instance, mating, procreation, upbringing of children, emotional satisfactions of wishes within the context of primary group relationships—these core functions of the family are to be found in every society. Different societies, however, have devised different mechanisms and instrumentalities for the accomplishment of these objectives through the creation of secondary institutions. Marriage as an institution, for instance, has been evolved and elaborated in order to promote smoothly and harmoniously the satisfaction of the sex urge and the functioning of the family. Sometimes, however, elaborate institutional patterns tend to restrict and circumscribe the drives of original nature—a price man must pay for his group-membership.

Similarly, the core function of physical sustenance, associated with the economic order, is to be found in all societies, simple as well as complex, among food-gatherers no less than among food-producers. The core functions of the dharmic order, namely, (a) induction of the new (newly-born as well as newly adopted) members of society into the stream of culture, making them co-sharers of the legacy of the forefathers, (b) helping all members of society to develop rounded personalities and (c) to be at home in the universe—these core functions of the dharmic order are performed in every culture through the instrumentality of the medicineman and the initiation ceremony (simple societies) as well as the priest and the teacher (complex societies). Finally, the core functions of the socio-state order, namely, *danda* (literally, the right to punish; broadly interpreted, sovereignty), distribution of goods and services, competence for the resolution of conflicts among "members," competence to safeguard, against outgroups, the group interest, whether the group be family, clan, tribe or nation—these core functions of the socio-state order are universally performed in every society and culture, primitive as well as advanced.

2. FAMILY AS ASSOCIATION AND AS INSTITUTION

The family may be studied both as an association and as an institution. Among all social groups, the family as an association occupies a unique place. The family is a primary group in a very special sense.

Within the family circle the newborn child undergoes the processes of socialization; here he becomes transformed from an individual into a person. Not only does the family bestow status upon the newborn; but it is within the context of family interaction that the original nature of the child becomes transformed into human nature. Sympathy, love, co-operation, sacrifice for others and all other primary virtues and ideals are acquired and absorbed by the child as a result of his association with other members of the family. As pointed out by us in CHAPTER 8, the nursery in the family is indeed the birthplace of the child's intelligence as well as of the primary ideals that hold society together.

As Park and Burgess state it, "The biological interdependence and cooperation among the members of the family, intimacies of the closest and most enduring contacts have no parallel among other human groups." The family, both as association and as institution, is the primary field for "the interplay of the attractions, tensions, and accommodations of personalities" (14, p. 216). Because of its crucial role, the family has been described by Ernest W. Burgess as "a system of interacting personalities."

As an institution, the family stands for a network of relationships and functions collectively assigned and accepted by society. The family should be studied in this twofold aspect of association and institution.

3. ARISTOTLE: ORIGIN AND FUNCTIONING OF THE FAMILY

The interest of the human species in perpetuation of itself, in sustenance and growth of its members, gives rise to the family grouping, to the Family Order, and to the family as one of the five primary institutions of society.

Aristotle's classic discussion of the origin and functioning of the family may be reproduced in order to throw light upon this institution to be found in every society in one form or another (*Politics* I, 1: 2–5):

In the first place, there must be a union of those who cannot exist without each other; for example, of male and female, that the race may continue; and this is a union which is formed, not of deliberate purpose, but because in common with animals and plants, mankind have a natural desire to leave behind them an image of themselves. And there must be a union of natural ruler and subject, that both may be preserved. For he who can foresee with his mind is by nature intended to be lord and master, and he who can work with his body is a subject and by nature a slave ... Out of these two relationships between man and woman, master and slave, the family first arises.

Setting aside Aristotle's defense of slavery, we may note that he encompasses within the family husband, wife (children to be born later), and household help.

Even though it is primarily intended to serve the purposes of procreation and care of the young, the family, according to Aristotle,

attempts to attend to the other "affairs of life" as well (*Ethics,*
BK. VIII, 12):

> Between husband and wife friendship is thought to exist by
> nature; for man is by nature a being inclined to live in pairs rather
> than in societies, inasmuch as a family is prior in point of time and
> more necessary than a State, and procreation is more common to
> him, together with animals. To other animals, therefore, community
> proceeds thus far only; but human beings associate not for the sake
> of procreation (alone) but for the (other) affairs of life (as well).

How the family naturally leads to the evolution of the State, in
Aristotelian thinking, will be dealt with in CHAPTER 40.

4. FAMILY AND MARRIAGE

Family and marriage are so intimately tied together that some
social philosophers have gone so far as to suggest primacy for marriage as an institution and to deduce the family from marriage. Of
course, such a construction is entirely wrong from a theoretical
standpoint. The family order on the biological level is foreordained
by nature. From this order emerges the family as a primary institution—the union of male and female and the birth of children.

In order that equity and justice may prevail in the establishment
of union between male and female and in order that proper care
may be provided the progeny of such union, every society has
evolved rules and procedures competent to solve the problems involved. Marriage, as an institutionalized ritual, is one of the mechanisms devised by society to ensure its own stability as well as the
well-being of the family. We may, therefore, define marriage as a
socially sanctioned union of male and female, or as a secondary
institution devised by society to sanction the union and mating of
male and female, for purposes of (a) establishing a household, (b)
entering into sex relations, (c) procreating, and (d) providing care
for the offspring.

5. CLASSIFICATIONS OF FAMILY

The family may be classified on a number of bases: (1) on the
basis of type of marriage relationship, (2) on the basis of authority

and descent, (3) on the basis of residence, (4) on the basis of ingroup or outgroup affiliation, (5) on the basis of blood relationship, (6) on the basis of organization.

In terms of marriage, there are three possible combinations: (1) one man, one woman (monogamy); (2) one husband, plural wives (polygyny); (3) one wife, plural husbands (polyandry). This may be illustrated diagrammatically as follows:

CHART 29

TYPES OF MARRIAGE

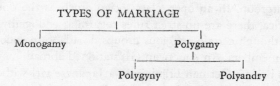

Theoretically, there is possible what some anthropologists have called "group marriage": several men and several women conjoined together. Whether group marriage is today practised by any tribe is doubtful. But we do have something new emerging among certain groups in America, namely, "successive monogamy": one man, one woman *at a time*; with great laxity in divorce, life becomes a series of monogamies—a fashion first set by Henry VIII (1491-1547) of England, and now popularized by the Hollywood set. Some have called this practice "serial monogamy."

The family may be monogamous, polygynous or polyandrous, according to the customs of a people. Most societies prescribe monogamy, but some societies, while exalting monogamy, may yet permit polygyny (as among the Muslims). There are a few societies which permit polyandry—notably Tibetan society and the tribal Toda society in the Nilgiri Hills of India.

On the basis of authority and descent, families are either patriarchal or matriarchal, either patrilineal or matrilineal. And in terms of residence, a family, according to the custom of the tribe or society, may be either patrilocal or matrilocal.

With us the family is patrilocal and patrilineal. The father of the family, the *pater familias*, has been the headman in Hindu, Chinese, Hebrew, Greek, Roman and modern Euro-American cultures: the wife goes to the husband's abode and the children take the father's name. But in some cultures, the husband goes to the wife's abode and the children take the mother's name. It may be noted, however, that in matrilineal and matrilocal societies, the mother's brother rather than her husband has authority over the children.

On the basis of ingroup or outgroup affiliation, we have the two concepts and practices of endogamy and exogamy. Endogamy sanctions marriage only among members of the ingroup, while exogamy sanctions marriage of members of an ingroup only with members of an outgroup. In an open class society, such as the one we have in America, there are no strict rules regarding endogamy or exogamy, even though certain religious groups do advocate endogamy among their members. An American GI, stationed abroad, may readily take as his bride a German Fräulein or a Japanese girl without creating a cultural crisis in American society. But our society does have legalized endogamy in some states and implicit endogamy in other states as between whites and colored. Thirty states in the U.S.A. prohibit intermarriage between whites and colored. And it would appear that our implicit religious endogamy is observed more rigorously than our so-called class endogamy.

So far as blood relationships are concerned, a family may be organized either on a conjugal (non-blood-relationship) basis or on a consanguine (blood-relationship) basis.

In societies organized upon the *conjugal basis* we can picture the authentic functional family as consisting of a nucleus of spouses and their offspring surrounded by a fringe of relatives. In those organized on the *consanguine basis* we can picture the authentic family as a nucleus of blood relatives surrounded by a fringe of spouses. . . . Under the first system the blood relatives of the spouses are of only incidental importance to the functioning of the family unit. Under the second, the spouses are of only incidental importance. (13, p. 159).

Even though the consanguine type of family is more stable and a more efficient agency for the transfer of property and privilege, the majority of mankind have chosen the conjugal basis for the family (13, pp. 159–61).

Finally, in terms of organization, Carle C. Zimmerman (15, pp. 39ff), refining the concepts of Frederic Le Play (1806-82) suggests three possible types of family: the trustee type, the domestic type, and the atomistic type. (Also cf. *Life*, July 26, 1948).

The trustee type of family, prevalent in Europe during the Middle Ages, has some resemblance to the joint family or the extended family or the large family of India and China. In the trustee type of family as in the joint family system of India, the role and behavior of each member are determined by the family in terms of the welfare of the whole. The individual member has no rights except those that the family may extend to him.

In the domestic type of family, the patriarchal form prevails, but the patriarch's powers are less extensive than those of the trustee family; here public law begins to assume ascendancy over the private law of the patriarch.

In the atomistic family, the individual is esteemed to be supreme; family bonds and obligations and rights are construed as sources for the individual's own growth and enhancement; he holds himself accountable to the State for his role-playing and behavior. In the atomistic type of family, marriage is looked upon strictly as a private matter between two individuals, and as a contractual relationship subject to periodic review by either party. The American family, especially in the urban setting, has come to resemble more and more the atomistic type of family.

6. THE MODERN AMERICAN FAMILY

The ideal American family pattern is: Patrilocal, Patrilineal, Co-active-Democratic, Monogamous, free from restrictions as to Endogamy and Exogamy. The actual American family does in large measure correspond to this ideal construct. The co-active-democratic pattern of the American family has emerged since World War I under the impact of (a) woman's economic independence and (b) woman suffrage since 1920.

Our industrial setup has made it easy for woman to earn an income, to enter the professions, to carve out a career. The economic independence of woman is one of the most important factors affecting the size and the functioning and the role of the family in our culture today. In the old days woman had to look forward to matrimony for her economic well-being; now she can rely on her own self for her maintenance if she chooses. Thus in our day when boy meets girl, it is not necessarily in terms of marriage and family. And when they do marry, it is not because they must but because they want to marry each other. We call it romantic love.

7. THE DATING PATTERN

The dating culture trait on American college campuses, and even in high schools, is a recent innovation. Courting in the horse-and-buggy days down through the Civil War and up to the closing of the frontier (1890) used to be done under the supervision of chaperons. At the end of World War I, the chaperon began to be conspicuous by her absence. The automobile enabled young people to drive out together, away from the gaze of parents and chaperons. Coeducation, in full swing especially in the Midwest, hastened the departure of the chaperon except at all-college dances.

Geoffrey Gorer, the English social anthropologist, has given us an interesting analysis of the anatomy of the dating pattern (7, pp. 109ff; also *Life*, Aug. 18, 1947):

Dating is a highly patterned activity or group of activities, comparable in some ways to a formal dance, in others to a very complicated competitive game. . . . In a successful date there should not be a loser; both parties should feel their self-esteem, their assurance, enhanced. Because . . . it (dating) employs the form—but not the content of love-making—it has been the cause of innumerable and serious misunderstandings whenever young Americans have come in contact with foreigners of the opposite sex. . . . Dating is normally ended by betrothal, which is the almost inevitable sequel of a boy's concentration on one girl. . . . Marriage is meant to be founded on romance, on love, without any other considerations being involved.

8. THE ROMANTIC LOVE COMPLEX

Since romance plays such a significant part in American marriage and family, it may be helpful to analyze the American ideology of romantic love.

In American culture, the value most prized in relation to marriage, family, or any situation, is the cult of personality and personal happiness. In the marriage of two persons, no one else is theoretically involved. With the sanction of the State, the two embark upon matrimony, to make or mar their future. And the two of them embark upon matrimony as the climax to romantic love.

The theory of romantic love is simple: two persons of the opposite sex become attached to each other by virtue of the attraction each one has for the other, by virtue of "purely personal qualities." These personal qualities or bases of attraction may refer to: looks, the color of the eyes, the color of the hair, the size and shape of the body, etc. The qualities may again refer to temperament or mental abilities and skills, or to sociological factors such as socio-economic status.

The person is identified with any one of these purely personal qualities that may appeal to the party of the second part. There is no guarantee that good looks and mental abilities or high status and well organized personality will necessarily be conjoined one with the other traits.

Thus, in the pursuit of romantic love, any one factor that exerts attraction is generalized by the other party to stand for the whole man or woman. This process of idealization, which in this case is a break with reality, is an important base of romanticism. Add to this idealization the thrill of anticipation, the poignancy of uncertainty, the exercise of skill, and the challenge of competition—and you have the culture complex of romantic love in the American cultural milieu.

The five ingredients of romantic love mentioned by Kingsley Davis (5, pp. 587–92)—idealization, anticipation, uncertainty, skills, and competition—are all integral parts of American culture. That is why this new pattern or configuration of romantic love is avidly accepted and practised by the American.

The luxury of romantic love demands a twofold price from the American people: (1) Eugenic considerations are almost entirely absent in mate selection except as they happen to be realized accidentally; (2) the cult of personality and personal happiness among us results in the highest divorce rate in the world.

There is a valid answer to each of these two criticisms of romantic love: (1) As for eugenic considerations, the typical American attitude is that environment, not heredity, is crucial in the life of a person—so why should we let eugenic considerations cut out the thrills of romantic love? (2) As for our high divorce rate, far from being a symptom of social pathology, it is integrally interwoven with other traits into the dynamic fabric of American culture.

9. MATCHMAKING IN THE ORIENT

In contrast to romantic love as the basis of marriage and family, the Oriental world has practised matchmaking by the elders—for what seem to them valid reasons. In the Orient, when two individuals of the opposite sex are united in wedlock, in a real sense the family of the bridegroom and the family of the bride are joined together. The marriage of the two persons is thus tied up with the honor and good name of their respective families. Under such conditions, the elders of the two families would exercise great care in the selection of mates for their sons and daughters.

Matchmaking by the elders in the Orient has had at once a good result and a bad result. The bad consequence of the Oriental practice is that courtship and romance are phenomena relegated to fiction-writing, not to be experienced by the prospective bride and groom. The positive consequence of matchmaking is twofold: (1) The elders take into account eugenic considerations as well as family status and breeding before they accept a suitable mate for their son or daughter; and (2) the ideology of the union of two families has meant the practical absence of divorce, or very low incidence of divorce where it does occur.

To achieve these two positive results in enriched marriage and happy family life, the Oriental world has been willing to sacrifice romantic love in courtship and to consider the price not too high. However, it may be pointed out that intensified culture contacts between America and the Orient, especially through literature and the movies, reinforced by expanding industrialization and urbanization and secularization, are tending to weaken the hold of the matchmaking pattern among young people throughout the awakening Orient.

10. The Romantic Theme in the Movies

An exploration of the American ideology of romantic love as reflected in the movies is highly rewarding.

The movies, along with the press and the radio and TV, are appropriately classified among the media of mass communication. A medium of mass communication, to be effective, must appeal to the masses, to the man in the street. It must utilize those themes and values that strike a responsive chord in the heart of all to whom it is addressed. While there are specialized publics interested in special topics, a medium of mass communication must attempt to take hold of those themes and values that would appeal to all, regardless of the specialized interests of different individuals and groups.

The newspaper attempts to tell the happenings of the day in terms of human interest stories and thus catch the interest of its readers. The radio including television, likewise, attempts to address its audience in terms of human interest stories with a minimum of controversial issues except as commentators are given freedom to slant the news according to their preconceived notions and philosophy of life. The movies attempt to cater to all of us—from the children to adolescents to adults and old persons, to the lonely as well as to those who enjoy domestic felicity. This the movies attempt to do in terms of entertainment, at a profit.

To appeal to everybody in society, the entertainment must utilize themes and values which are dominant in the culture, integral to the culture, known to everyone, prized by everyone even if they should be attained only by a few. *Romantic love is a theme that fills the bill.* Everybody, including old bachelors and spinsters, is interested in the love story. The great epics of India and Greece derive their abiding quality from the intricate stories of love and death. Classics, likewise, depend upon such themes for their appeal to mankind from generation to generation.

The movies as vehicles of entertainment in a sense mirror the unspoken as well as spoken thoughts, feelings and emotions of our people. BOY MEETS GIRL—this theme can be worked over in a million different variations. Add to it the triangle, and the tension and excitement increase. The romantic theme appeals to us, first, because we are culturally conditioned to it and, second, because it is a fiction, an idealization, compared to the humdrum activities of daily living.

American movies, as pointed out by Martha Wolfenstein and Nathan Leites (5, pp. 559–66), attempt to combine sacred and profane love in a single relationship, with reference to one's object of love. And therein lies a major psychological conflict.

Freud has pointed out that the difficulty of choosing between a good and a bad girl constitutes one of the major problems in the love life of western man. The difficulty is that of fusing two impulses in relation to the same woman. On the one hand, there are sexual impulses which a man may feel to be bad and which he may therefore find it hard to associate with a woman whom he considers fine and admirable. The image, and the actuality, of the "bad" woman arise to satisfy sexual impulses which men feel to be degrading. On the other hand, there are affectionate impulses which are evoked by women who resemble the man's mother or sister, that is to say, "good" women. A good girl is the sort that a man should marry, but she has the disadvantage of not being sexually stimulating. (5, p. 560).

This psychological conflict may be resolved in one of several ways: (1) satisfy one of these impulses at the expense of the other; (2) satisfy them both, but with different women; (3) combine the two impulses in a single relationship.

The solution favored by Hollywood is a combination of sex and affection in a single relationship. "The image of what we may call a ' good-bad' girl has been created" (5, p. 561). The girl must be— or must be conceived to be—good enough for one to take as spouse, but just bad enough or naughty enough to stimulate desirableness of an adventurous sort.

The French films mirror French culture by separating good women from bad women. Good women have their place and role, but bad women are depicted as the more alluring. The Frenchman has his wife for carrying on the work of the world and his mistress for the romantic escapades. The bad girl in British movies ends up by dying.

In American films the good-bad combination is presented to satisfy the requirements of respectability as well as allurement. She is really not bad but appears to be bad—that point disposed of, hero and heroine marry and live happily ever after.

This treatment of romantic love in American movies is tied up with American culture and with the American temper. The Americans are the most optimistic people in the world. They do not believe in resignation to any kind of deprivation. The American male must have the girl with the right bodily proportions, with grace and charm, with virtue and a wee-bit naughtiness, with intellectual attainments and emotional stability—all this and Heaven too!

Romantic love leads to marriage on the hypothesis that all these traits would be found in one's partner. The American girl has her own idea of the ideal husband. She wants not just one man but three combined in one—good-looking and dashing, the husband must be (1) a handyman, (2) a lover, and (3) a good money-maker.

Given these ideals and these conditions, the American high divorce rate is entirely normal. If the marriage did not satisfy the ideal image of one party or both parties, it is dissolved—and the quest is begun anew for another partner who shall satisfy the demands of idealization.

11. FUNCTIONS OF THE FAMILY

The crucial role of the family in culture arises from the two-fold fact that (1) it is the most unimpeachable mechanism for ascribing status to new as well as old members of society, and (2) it is a serviceable device for the accumulation and transfer of property and privilege. Indeed, the family is basic and unique among all social institutions, because it performs biological, economic, psychological and sociological functions. "Considered biologically, the family is made up of a number of organisms, having certain reproductive relations with each other. Considered economically, the family is made up of persons who produce and consume goods and services, in part cooperatively. Considered psychologically, the family is made up of interacting personalities." (8, p. 5; with a change in the order of sentences—H.T.M.). Considered sociologically, the family is the seat of authority with quasi-sovereignty—at once an institution and an association of persons for the fulfillment of the functions assigned to it by culture.

Historically and traditionally, the family in every culture has been —better, had been—called upon to perform the following eight functions: (1) reproductive, (2) affectional, (3) economic, (4) protective, (5) recreational, (6) religious, (7) educational, (8) socializing (of the newborn).

In an agricultural economy under rural conditions, the family's eight functions were all made to order. On the farm the entire family worked together and satisfied their economic wants. Since there were no commercialized recreation centers, the family had to provide recreation for all its members—youngsters, adolescents, adults. Taking care of one another, i.e., protecting one another, especially the youngsters, was part of the functions of the family. Religious instruction as well as training in the three R's had to be provided within the family circle. Since marriage was a necessity to women, reproduction rarely took place out of wedlock. And through interactions and interstimulations within the bosom of the family the newborn child went through the process of socialization. Finally, the family admirably served as a mechanism for the satisfaction of the need for affection by human beings. That lack of affection is responsible, in greater or lesser degree, for personality disorders and social malaise in our day is recognized by psychologists, sociologists and social workers.

Our industrial-urban culture has effected vast changes in our mode of making a livelihood, in our mode of recreation, in our mode of receiving and imparting education and religious instruction, in our relations one to another within the very bosom of the family. The assumption of the omnipresent State is that the parents are not among the most competent protectors and educators of their children—that, therefore, the State must enact legislation prescribing penalties for parental transgression of the rights of children. The State, likewise, requires the establishment of schools for the education of the young. The church is being regarded more and more as the only agency competent to impart religious training and inculcate religious values. No consumption goods are made by the members of the family occupying an apartment in a city—they must buy their meat and bread as well as their clothes and soap and hundreds of other consumption goods which used to be produced on the farm by the family. Now the apartment-dwelling family buys all its consumption goods in the market by paying money which is earned as salary or wages either by the husband or the wife, or by both. As for recreation, our thriving commercial establishments have taken over the job of providing recreation for young and old. And even in the sacrosanct field of socialization of the newborn, the nursery school, the kindergarten, the grade school, the Sunday school, and the playground, all supervised by outside persons, are making inroads upon the family's role. Finally, the secularization of our outlook has been responsible for extramarital reproduction.

These changes are the inevitable result of industrialism and urbanism. Passing judgment upon them, whether they are good or bad, is not very helpful without an analysis of the nature of changes and their possible effect on personal and social well-being. We notice that the family is deprived of most of its functions—economic, recreational, protective, religious, educational, partly or wholly— with socialization partly threatened and reproduction slightly encroached upon.

The one function the family has not yet been called upon to share with other institutions or agencies in society is the affectional role. Can the family be built on the sole foundation of affection? That is the question American society is trying to answer.

Here is the way Professor Hill puts it: "Once the one and only major institution among the preliterates, the family now shares the stage with four other major institutions: the State, the church, education, and industry (economica, in our terminology—H.T.M.). . . . We prefer to think of the loss of functions in this way: Much of the weight and responsibility is now off the shoulders of the family, leaving that institution free to improve its effectiveness in the segments of those functions which are left." (3, p. 627). Professor Ogburn phrases the answer thus: The modern family may not be producing "thread and cloth and soap and medicine and food," but if it does produce happiness it may be doing not a bad thing after all (5, p. 573, quoted).

12. PRESENT TRENDS AND FUTURE PROSPECTS

We may note some of the changes that have taken place in American society with reference to the family.

First: Age of Marriage. In the Colonial period practically everybody married, and that at an early age. Western migrations in the period of national consolidation brought about wide discrepancies in the sex ratio in boom towns and on the frontier, many unattached men experiencing the thrill of pioneering footloose. But in the settled parts of the Eastern seaboard the old pattern prevailed until after the Civil War. Then the suffragette movement, the ability of women to earn their own livelihood, invasion of the teaching and secretarial professions by women—these and other factors after the closing of the frontier (1890) led some women to refrain from marriage and many women to marry late. This trend began to be reversed during World War II. Young people began to marry at an earlier age than previously. The present trend promises to remain operative in the near future, what with early dating in high schools and steady dating in colleges.

Our young ex-servicemen, going to college on the GI Bill of Rights, have demonstrated that marriage is no handicap to college education. We may look forward to many married couples attending our colleges and universities. In fact, some colleges and universities have actually been providing "dormitories" or "barracks" or special dwelling-units for married students on the campus.

The coactive nature of our family is bringing about a profound change: Many an erstwhile struggling student of law, medicine or engineering is today being "put through" school by the wife.

Second: Size of the Family. In the Colonial period large families were the general rule. The size of the family began to shrink under the simultaneous impact of (a) immigration, (b) westward migrations, (c) industrialism (See CHAPTER 19). Since World War II, America has been enjoying a bumper crop of babies—a reversal of the previous trend. Also, since World War II a dysgenic factor in the birth rate is being corrected: while previously college-trained couples used to be either childless or with one child at the most, today the college-educated youth are in line with the rest of the population in the number of children in their family.

Third: Incidence of Divorce. Between 1890 and 1950, our population increased roughly two and a half times, while divorces increased twelve times.

The annual number of divorces in the United States increased from about 33,000 in 1890 to a high of over 600,000 in 1946. In 1950 divorces numbered around 385,000. In 1950 the population was less than two and a half times greater than in 1890, but the number of divorces was almost twelve times greater. The marriage rate was 9.0 per 1,000 population in 1890; 10.3 in 1910; 10.1 in 1929; 7.9 in 1932; 12.1 in 1940; 16.4 in 1946; and 11.1 in 1950. The divorce rate for the same years was 0.5 per 1,000 population in 1890; 0.9 in 1910; 1.7 in 1929; 1.3 in 1932; 2.0 in 1940; 4.3 in 1946; and 2.6 in 1950. (6, pp. 330–31).

Comparing the incidence of divorce with the incidence of marriage, we get the following figures: "In 1870 there was just one divorce for every 32.1 marriages; in 1900 the rate was 1 to 12.7. Just before World War II the ratio was 1 to 6. In 1946 a sharp postwar rise in the divorce rate brought the ratio to one for every 3.8 marriages. In 1951 the rate was one for every 4.2 marriages." (4, p. 245). In other words, at the middle of the twentieth century, one out of four marriages ended in divorce.

During World War II (1941-45), with eleven million men and women in uniform, the family as an institution received rude shocks. Marriageable as well as married men were away in training camps and on battle fronts. Lured by the uniform, some girls entered into hasty marriages, spent thrill-packed honeymoons of 24 hours, saw their men go off to war, and stayed home wondering what to do next. Romance had its day, but the family as an institution received a jolt, first, because some of the men did not return; second, because war experiences changed their personalities; third, because the stay-at-homes found new romantic adventures. These conditions leading to instability were reinforced by a "scientific" study of *Sexual Behavior in the Human Male* (1948) and *Sexual Behavior in the Human Female* (1953) by Kinsey and others. The effect of the Kinsey Reports has been to condone, if not to promote, premarital sex relations among young people.

These situations—our high divorce rate and the sex behavior of youth prior to marriage—have led some sociologists to conclude that the family is "in trouble," that we are on the eve of the breakdown of the family, that our high divorce rate is a symptom of social disorganization; while others maintain that the new conditions including our high divorce rate are symptomatic of the transition we are going through from the old scale of values to a new one. Professor Koenig calls upon society to "institute reforms designed to facilitate the transition from old to new values" (11, pp. 148–49).

Fourth: Prospects. We may expect our religious leaders, social scientists, social workers, judges and others to make intensive efforts properly to diagnose the contemporary nature and status of the family. Next, we may look forward to our churches, colleges, universities and other organizations developing Adult Education Institutes and Clinics for those who are married or are to be married. Finally, without denying the right of divorce, the leaders of our society may undertake to infuse anew into our culture a sense of the responsibilities attached to the romance and adventure of matrimony.

Glorification of the child, equality and exaltation of the woman, the concept and fact of coactive democratic membership in the family—these new traits, born of experience in the New World, promise to abide with us, and may conceivably strengthen the American family and enrich American culture.

REFERENCES

1. ARISTOTLE: *Ethics* (Jowett's translation).
2. ARISTOTLE: *Politics* (Jowett's translation).
3. HOWARD BECKER & REUBEN HILL: *Marriage and the Family*. Boston: D. C. Heath & Co., 1942.
4. JOHN BIESANZ & MAVIS BIESANZ: *Modern Society*. New York: Prentice-Hall, 1954.
5. KINGSLEY DAVIS & Others: *Modern American Society*. New York: Rinehart & Co., 1949.
6. LUKE EBERSOLE: *American Society*. New York: McGraw-Hill Book Co., 1955.
7. GEOFFREY GORER: *The American People, A Study in National Character*. New York: W. W. Norton Co., 1948.
8. HORNELL HART & ELLA B. HART: *Personality and the Family*. Boston: D. C. Heath & Co., 1941.
9. ALFRED KINSEY & ASSOCIATES: *Sexual Behavior in the Human Female*. Philadelphia: Saunders, 1953.
10. ALFRED KINSEY & ASSOCIATES: *Sexual Behavior in the Human Male*. Philadelphia: Saunders, 1948.
11. SAMUEL KOENIG: *Man and Society*. New York: Barnes & Noble, Inc., 1957.

12. *Life* (New York), July 26, 1948.
13. RALPH LINTON: *The Study of Man.* New York: D. Appleton-Century Co., 1936.
14. ROBERT E. PARK & E. W. BURGESS: *Introduction to the Science of Sociology*, 2nd Ed. Chicago: University of Chicago Press, 1924 (8th impression, 1933).
15. CARLE C. ZIMMERMAN & LUCIUS F. CERVANTES: *Marriage and the Family: A Text for Moderns.* Chicago: Henry Regnery Co., 1956.

CHAPTER 37

THE ECONOMIC ORDER

1. ECONOMY AND WASTE DEFINED

THE need for physical sustenance—for food, clothing and shelter —gives rise to the economic order. The term economy implies the management or husbanding of resources at man's disposal with a view to securing the utmost results for the satisfaction of human wants. The proper husbanding and utilization of resources is essential because, in spite of its bountifulness in many ways, nature is niggardly and man's wants are insatiable. Without sunlight, air and water, provided by nature freely, life could not endure. In order to survive and procreate, however, organic beings need, in addition, food—and in the case of man, covering for the body and shelter from the inclemencies of weather. Now, nature did and does still supply roots and herbs, nuts and fruits—but not in quantities sufficient to satisfy the appetite of all men the year round.

When man fails to make the most of his resources in terms of either personal or social well-being, or when he is getting less than the theoretically possible output, or when he is receiving less satisfaction either intensively or extensively, either personally or socially, under the given circumstances, he is said to be indulging in waste.

2. FROM FOOD GATHERING TO AGRICULTURE

In the earliest economic order, namely, food-gathering or direct appropriation of food, population tended to be sparse over vast regions. Folkways and mores developed with appropriate totems and taboos as to which type of food might be gathered and eaten in what season. Under the food-gathering economy, man was a helpless plaything at the mercy of nature. Too much rainfall or too little rainfall, unseasonable weather or violent storm, shifting of a river-bed or the outbreak of pestilence—these and other "acts of God" determined whether man would be well fed or poorly fed, indeed whether man would survive and procreate his kind.

Faced by the niggardliness of nature, man was compelled to become a food-producer. Even in the food-gathering stage, he was in a sense a producer. The exertion involved in picking up roots and berries, nuts and fruits, did constitute an act of production; but in the next stage man went beyond the rudimentary form of production. He deliberately set out to exert himself for getting, for "producing," more food for himself either by cooperating with nature or by warring against nature. He began to hunt and to fish, to domesticate animals and to cultivate the soil.

Agriculture constituted one of the most revolutionary changes in man's culture. When he lived by hunting or fishing or by herding sheep or cattle, man moved from place to place with the seasons; but with the development of agriculture he was tied to the soil. Now he and other members of his tribe had to live out the whole cycle of seasons—the entire year—in one place if the products of agriculture were to be enjoyed. This meant the growth of community life which provided a suitable background for the interplay of social processes and for the growth of culture.

The earliest form of agriculture is called by anthropologists "hoe culture" or "dibble culture," in which, usually, the women made a hole in the ground with the aid of a stick or a dibble and sowed the seed—corn, for instance. When the plough was invented, agriculture came of age. Agriculture was man's chief source for securing needed goods and services for over 6,000 years. Only recently, about 200 years ago, was industrialism developed as a new method for the production of goods and services. During the long period when agriculture was dominant, religious rites and festivities were developed in connection with agricultural pursuits by all advanced peoples—the Hindus, the Greeks, the Romans, to name only three. Some of the religious rites have lingered on to this day among many peoples even though precise knowledge of nature and its laws might have rendered them outmoded and even superstitious.

3. ECONOMIC PROCESSES

Before describing the evolution of American economy, we may briefly set forth the theoretical framework of economy. The smallest unit in economy is a utility or a use-value. A good (commodity) or service having use-value to human beings is a utility and becomes an economic good or service when it is also scarce (automobiles, for instance, in contrast to air which is a free good). There are four types of utility: (1) form utility, (2) place utility, (3) time utility, (4) ownership utility. The creation of any of these four utilities constitutes production. Popularly, production is thought of as the trans-*forming* of raw materials into finished products—iron ore into steel, steel into automobiles, flour into bread. This is a narrow conception of production, the creation of form utility: economists refer to it as physical production.

There are three main economic processes: (1) production, just defined by us; (2) distribution, which involves allocation of a share of the product to the agents or factors of production, and (3) consumption, using or using up the product—the ultimate goal of production.

Unless man is living in a food-gathering stage, there must be production before consumption can take place. Production is the secret of an abundant economy, of abundant living. The more goods and services are produced, the larger the amount of goods and services there is to go around among the population. Production is limited in an economy of direct consumption, as pointed out by Böhm-Bawerk (*supra*, CHAPTER 32). In an economy of roundabout production, production is multiplied. The economy of roundabout production presupposes specialization and division of labor and a well articulated medium for the exchange of goods and services.

The shoemaker, a master craftsman, let us say, makes only shoes, but he must feed, clothe and shelter himself and his family. He is able to obtain food, clothing and shelter by exchanging the product of his handiwork. The shoemaker may supply shoes to the farmer and his family, to the tailor and his family, to the carpenter and his family, and in exchange receive food, clothing and shelter, respectively.

Such a process of barter is theoretically feasible but is actually very clumsy and unworkable. Just the right number of pairs of shoes and the right quantity of grain or grains would have to be matched if no injustice were to be done to either producer. Hence mankind early found it expedient to devise a standard of value by which all goods and services could be evaluated on a uniform basis. Not only was a standard of value necessary but a medium of exchange was also indispensable if exchange was to be carried on to everyone's satisfaction. Thus evolved the concept of *money*, which is another name for *a standard of value which also serves as a medium of exchange*. Before a standard of value could serve as a medium of exchange, it had to have the quality of being desired and accepted by all persons in a given society.

4. EVOLUTION OF MONEY

In the history of economic evolution, many articles have served as money: shells, beads, wampum; rice, tea, tobacco; hides and skins; sheep and cattle; metals both base and precious.

The so-called precious metals, silver and gold, were finally accepted by advanced societies as money, (1) because they were universally desired, (2) because they were scarce, (3) because they neither deteriorated nor lost their substance, (4) because they could be subdivided into small, uniform units. Gold and silver served as money among all civilized peoples long before the beginning of the Christian era. Of the two metals, gold was the more prized because of its greater scarcity and because of its greater durability.

This concept of money was an accepted culture pattern when America was discovered. Indeed, the lure of money—of gold—played not an insignificant part in the discovery and settlement of the New World, and in European expansion all over the world in the wake of the Commercial and Industrial Revolutions (*circa* 1500 A.D. and 1750 A.D., respectively).

The beginnings of American economy were already money-oriented, though in the early days of colonization the Indian and the European engaged in barter transactions for the exchange of goods and services. Thus, thinking in terms of pounds, shillings and pence, and, later, in terms of dollars and cents is part of the heritage of the American people from their European background. The American habit of evaluating economy—economic goods—in terms of dollars and cents, rather than units of use-value or degrees of satisfaction, is understandable. To us the dollar means so much purchasing power, whether in food, clothing or shelter, or any luxury item. Money is the nexus that ties production to consumption. We produce goods and services and get paid in money, in dollars and cents; with money we buy the things we need. Without this intermediation of money as a distributing agent, both production and consumption would suffer. The dominant role of money has led some economists to characterize our economy as a money economy, the economy of the cash-nexus. The characterization has a certain validity, but underlying the cash-nexus or the money economy are the fundamental economic processes of production, distribution and consumption. We do not live by the dollar but the dollar helps us get what we want in order to live. (*Cf.* Henry Adams, *supra*, CHAPTER 35).

5. ECONOMIC EVOLUTION

In CHAPTER 14 (TABLE 4), we have indicated the economic stages through which collective man has passed. The economic processes of food-producers may be diagrammatically represented as follows:

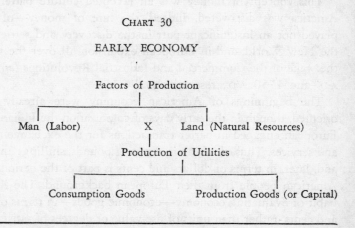

CHART 30

EARLY ECONOMY

Factors of Production

Man (Labor)   X   Land (Natural Resources)

Production of Utilities

Consumption Goods   Production Goods (or Capital)

CHART 31

SLIGHTLY ADVANCED ECONOMY (ADAM SMITH, 1776)

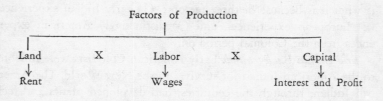

CHART 32

MODERN ECONOMY

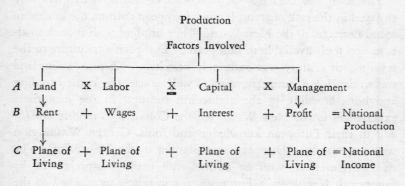

Note: The symbol X stands for interaction.

In Chart 32, *A* represents cooperating agents or factors of production, *B* the process of distribution, and *C* the process of consumption. These three economic processes are to be found in every complex society, be it capitalist or socialist, or communist. The bookkeeping in a communist economy may be different, but the three processes do obtain there.

Within this framework we are ready to study the evolution and distinctive patterns of American economy.

6. AMERICAN AGRICULTURE

Modern American agriculture, the most productive in the world, is what it is because of three factors: (1) early Indian experiences, (2) European experiences, and (3) distinctively American experiences from the Colonial period on.

The Indian Background. Early American Colonists were indebted to the American Indian for survival in the New World. The American Indian, through the centuries, had developed plants and techniques suitable for full utilization of New World land. American Colonists borrowed from the Indians techniques for the raising of corn and tobacco, staple agricultural products of the Indian, as well as other vegetables, such as pumpkin, squash, yam, potatoes, etc. Incidentally, potatoes were considered inedible by the early settlers.

The European Background. American Colonists, willynilly, were engaged in the task of transplanting European culture, the European social heritage, to the New World. They brought with them knowledge and tools available to Europeans. "European agriculture of the seventeenth century was extremely primitive" (2, p. 57). England was to develop scientific farming as well as scientific cattle-breeding and horse-breeding in the eighteenth century. In the meantime, experiences in the New World led the Colonists to modify and/or add to their European knowledge and tools. George Washington was not exactly a European transplanted to the New World—he was an American with an outlook not easily comprehended by Europeans. Napoleon, a European, for instance, succumbed to the temptation of an imperial crown, but not George Washington. In experimenting with the new environment, Colonists on the Atlantic seaboard discovered that "most of the common grains, vegetables, and fruits of northwestern Europe were suitable to American soil and climate, as were the various farm animals" (2, p. 58).

The American Background. The existence of a vast frontier began to influence American culture as a whole and American agriculture in particular, for better as well as for worse, from the beginning of colonization. Only with the closing of the frontier in 1890 did the experience of American agriculture begin to be appraised in the proper perspective.

The frontiersman considered himself above the law, if not actually an outlaw. The frontiersmen contributed not a little to the winning of the Revolutionary War; they precipitated the War of 1812; they influenced Jefferson's thinking and policy about the Louisiana Purchase; they brought the Lone Star State, the Southwest and the Oregon Territory into the Union.

The frontier was responsible for the perpetuation of old-fashioned and criminally wasteful methods of agriculture. To get rich quickly, colonists in the South grew tobacco on most available land, which soon became impoverished, especially as knowledge of fertilizers and of scientific farming was lacking. The "soil butchers" moved on westward and repeated the same act of vandalism against Mother Earth. Forests were cut down and timber squandered without thought of the morrow. A little later, when use of subsoil minerals became known, the process of wasteful production was repeated.

After the invention of the cotton gin by Eli Whitney in 1793, cotton became king in the South. Cash crops—tobacco and cotton— impoverished Southern soil, though they brought temporary prosperity to the big plantation-owners. Cotton culture fastened slavery on the South until the violent war between the states put an end to it—legally.

The Middle West—the old Northwest—became the granary of the new nation and of the world. The opening of the Erie Canal (1825) and construction of railroads (after 1830) stimulated agricultural activities in the American granary by transporting agricultural products to the populous East and to Europe. The gold rush of the (eighteen) forty-niners opened California to settlement. The Westward moving frontier from the East and the eastward moving frontier from the West finally closed the gap when the Union Pacific and the Central Pacific Railroads met at Ogden, Utah, in 1869. The fever of the gold rush having died down, the East and the West having been tied together by bands of steel, California became the orchard of America, its annual citrus crops now yielding more than all the gold mined in that state.

Over a period of three hundred years—from 1620 when the Pilgrims landed to 1920 when America became the leading power in the world—American economy, without a plan, without premeditation on the part of anyone or any one group, became integrated as a self-sufficing unit on the basis of specialization and division of labor:

Thus, but several generations ago, the frontier country was occupied by trappers and hunters; behind them lay great stretches of country devoted almost entirely to grazing; further east, agriculture predominated; east of the Mississippi, commercial activity appeared on a large scale; manufacturing was concentrated heavily in the North Central states and New England; and financial control and the largest industrial units centered along the Atlantic seaboard. (1, p. 47).

Today, the integration, interdependence and self-sufficing nature of American economy present the following pattern: the Northeastern states as manufacturing, with Wall Street, New York, as the money market; the Middle West as the granary; the South as the area of cash crops; the Mountain States as the ranching and cattle country; California as the fruit orchard and home of truck gardening; the Pacific Northwest as the lumber country. The pioneering spirit, the existence of the frontier, dominance of the profit motive, allegiance to the principle of competition as the inner core of economy—these factors, interacting upon one another, have made American economy and American economic institutions what they are today.

7. AMERICAN AGRICULTURAL ECONOMY

The central problem of American economy, whether in agriculture or industry, whether in transportation or commerce, has been a shortage of labor. Hence the quest for labor-saving devices and inventions. The development of labor-saving machinery, an outgrowth of the factory system and the industrial revolution (to be dealt with later), was " slow in the quarter century after the Revolution, but gathered speed in the years from 1810 to 1840 and thereafter proceeded with lightning-like speed " (2, p. 219).

Scientific farming, scientific cattle-breeding and horse-breeding, like the industrial revolution, had their beginnings in tight little

England in the eighteenth century. Arthur Young, Jethro Tull, Viscount Townshend and Robert Bakewell were among the leaders in scientific farming in England. Their work was known in the Colonies, but thanks to the existence of the frontier, the Colonists paid scant attention to scientific farming and went their merry way "butchering" the soil. Complaining of the "exhaustion" of the soil by the cultivation of tobacco, the far-sighted Father of this country "turned from tobacco raising to an intensive cultivation of other products" (2, pp. 222–23). Thomas Jefferson, likewise, was an agricultural experimenter.

By the time of the Civil War, knowledge of superior breeds and breeding of cattle and horses, knowledge of the new inventions, and of the improved methods of tillage began to be disseminated in America by five means: (1) agricultural societies, (2) agricultural fairs, (3) farm periodicals and literature, (4) agricultural schools, and (5) government aid. (2, p. 223).

The feat accomplished by the pioneers had never before been achieved anywhere in history by any people. Within two hundred and fifty years they not only conquered a vast wilderness but they also made America the richest and the most prosperous country in the world. In the process, undoubtedly, natural resources were wasted a great deal. In spite of George Washington's warning, the American people began to be conscious of waste not until a century later—just about the time the frontier began to disappear. In 1893, at the World's Fair in Chicago, Professor Frederick J. Turner read his memorable paper on "The Frontier in American History."

Theodore Roosevelt was the first President actively to espouse the cause of conservation of all natural resources, especially of agricultural resources and rural man-power. The Rural Life Commission, established by him in 1900, was the starting-point for the study of rural society in America and for the development of Rural Sociology. President Franklin D. Roosevelt, with the aid of a cooperative Congress, went much farther in the enunciation and execution of conservation policies. The Tennessee Valley Authority (T.V.A.) stands as a monument to F.D.R.'s conservation measures. The U.S. Department of Agriculture, the county agents, Schools of Agriculture, and private citizens have all been recently doing yeomen's service in the direction of conserving America's agricultural resources and promoting scientific farming. The conservation of non-farm natural resources is also one of the crying needs of America today. Government regulation is helping achieve this objective to some extent.

The role of agriculture in American economy in the post-Civil War period has been aptly described by Dr. Faulkner (2, pp. 382–83):

Since the 1860's the American farmer has not lacked aid from either the state or the national government. This is attributable to three reasons. In the first place, the fundamental importance of agriculture has always been recognized. Although the estimated annual value of agricultural products averaged (1919-29) only about 11 billion dollars and that of manufactured products 60 billion dollars, more than half of the important manufacturing industries—for example, slaughtering and meat packing, milling, the production of cotton and woolen cloth, boots and shoes, and many others—are dependent upon agriculture. Farm products are also an important, in some sections the most important, item of railroad freight. Agriculture still remains the foundation of much of our economic life.

In the second place, during most of our history the farmer has exerted a potent influence on the legislative branch of the government. As late as 1880, 49 per cent of the gainfully employed population was engaged in agriculture; although this had fallen off in 1910 to 32.5, and in 1930 to 21.4 per cent, the fact that the industrial population is largely centralized has given the farmer special weight in the upper house, where southern and western Senators are naturally very susceptible to the demands of agriculture. The so-called "agricultural bloc" in the House has been quick to coalesce when the farmers' interests are at stake.

In the third place, the policy of laissez faire, so strong during the first decades of the Industrial Revolution, has been gradually breaking down, and nowhere had this change of attitude been more apparent than in the relation of government to agriculture. This has been due not alone to the political strength of the farmer, but to the realization of the farmer's handicaps in dealing with other economic groups, and of his consequent special need of protection. Consequently, government aid has taken three forms: first, research and education; second, protection by legislation against other groups; and third, help in reclamation and irrigation.

The founding of Agricultural and Mechanical Colleges throughout the nation as a result of the Morrill Act of 1862; various tariff acts to discourage competition of foreign products of farms and factories and mines in the American market; guarantee of parity price for farm commodities by federal support of prices of farm commodities in order to assure the farmer equitable distribution of the national income; soil bank projects—these and other direct and indirect aids given to the American farmer reflect the political strength of the farm bloc, cutting across party lines.

The paradox of American agriculture is that in the midst of plenty a few American citizens have to experience poverty. Our granaries are bursting with grain, we have vast amounts of dairy products and cotton stored away—and yet the prices we must pay for food, clothing and shelter are exorbitantly high. Furthermore, while we have the highest standard and plane of living in the world, with vast surpluses to share, there are millions and millions of people in the underdeveloped countries of Asia and Africa who are perennially in the grip of famine and starvation—and yet, we cannot dispose of our surplus among the needy of the world because of a possible (or imagined) loss of income to the farmers and businessmen of those countries. We cannot eat our surplus, and we cannot dispose of it without being accused of "dumping" by some of our friends who also have surplus—among them Canada and Australia —and without being accused of depressing the prices of agricultural commodities grown abroad.

No satisfactory answer has been found to this dilemma, but in our small neighborhood world a rational answer to the problem, acceptable to all parties, should go a long way toward banishing famine, starvation and poverty from the earth.

8. RISE OF INDUSTRIALISM

The Background of the Industrial Revolution. The year 1776 marks an important point of departure in the history of culture: it not only ushered in political democracy through the Declaration of Independence; it also witnessed the publication of *An Inquiry into the Wealth of Nations* (6, *passim*) by Adam Smith which effectively

20

protested against State interference with economic activities. While George Washington, Thomas Jefferson, Benjamin Franklin, and others were dealing a death blow to the doctrine of political autocracy, Adam Smith, following in the footsteps of the Physiocrats, was knocking the props from under the system of Mercantilism and State-regulation of economic activities.

Adam Smith postulated that every individual was motivated in his economic activity by self-interest, by the desire to get the most returns for the least effort. "The individual man, in seeking his own profit, will necessarily seek to produce and sell that which has most value for the community, and so 'he is in this, as in many other cases,' as Adam Smith puts it, 'led by an invisible hand to promote an end (the public good, the consumer's well-being) which was no part of his intention' " (5, p. 504). Self-interest of the businessman, of the entrepreneur, could have unhindered play only if government let business alone and if competition were free and unfettered. Adam Smith, prophet of industrial economy, enunciated four principles under whose operation capitalism has evolved: (1) the doctrine of self-interest, (2) laissez faire or the let alone policy, (3) the theory of competition, (4) the profit motive.

The roots of the industrial revolution go much farther back than the year 1776, but Adam Smith's monumental work laid the foundation for the theoretical framework of industrialism and capitalism. *The Wealth of Nations* signalizes the beginning of a new epoch in man's economic activities.

Man is a tool-making and tool-using animal. A tool that is used for production of goods and services is technically part of capital. In this sense, primitive man who used the bow and arrow, spear or ax, was technically a capitalist. But the wide use of capital in productive processes came about after the eighteenth century — first in England, second in the U.S.A., and, later, in European countries and, still later, i.e., in the latter part of the nineteenth century in Asia. Except for South Africa, the whole continent of Africa may be said, at this writing, to be in the pre-industrial stage.

The antecedents of industrialism are not difficult to trace. As pointed out in CHAPTER 34, the centers of civilization shifted from the four River Valleys to the Mediterranean, from the Mediterranean up the Rhine to the North Sea, from the North Sea to the Atlantic, from the Atlantic to the Pacific.

The beginnings of the Atlantic era (1492) ushered in the Commerical Revolution. West Europeans began to trade—i.e., exchange goods and services—with the New World and with Asia on a scale never before known in human history. A little earlier, the merchants of Genoa, Venice and Florence in Italy, in their trade with the Orient, had devised and developed the methods and instruments of modern banking. The Hanseatic League merchants elaborated upon the Italian practices and developed prototypes of modern merchandising methods. (4, pp. 177–78). Thus, at the dawn of the Atlantic era, the role of banking institutions including money—gold in this case—and credit was grasped more or less adequately by West Europeans and American Colonists. Land, which had been a prized possession through the ages, began to be subordinated to gold and to capital goods by the Commercial and Industrial Revolutions.

Merchant princes, "robber barons," autocratic monarchs, feudal lords, church dignitaries—all became conscious of the value of money, of gold. The nation-state that began to arise toward the end of the fifteenth century on the ashes of feudalism adopted the mercantilist theory which stated that a nation was rich and prosperous in terms of the amount of gold it possessed. The acquisition of gold became the alpha and omega of economic activity, regardless of whether it was agricultural, manufacturing, or trading. Now, gold could be had in one or all of three ways: (1) by mining, (2) by trade, (3) by robbery. Western Europe had no gold underground; hence the Atlantic nations of Europe were reduced to acquiring gold by fair means (trade) or foul (conquest of the American Indians and Asians, or piracy on the high seas). The whole of the sixteenth century was devoted to the hoarding of gold by West Europeans under the aegis of their national state.

In the seventeenth century merchant princes began to supplement trade with a new economic activity as a source of income. This new economic activity was the introduction of the "putting-out" system, also known as "household" or "domestic" economy. The new system was in harmony with changing times and concepts. Its essence was simple. The merchant princes, with a portion of their gold, would buy raw materials and "put out" those raw materials in the homes of those artisans and craftsmen who would transform the raw materials into finished products. To illustrate: Our merchant prince buys a bale of cotton: he "puts out" that bale of cotton in the homes of a dozen craftsmen who would separate the seeds from the cotton. Next, he would put out the "ginned" cotton to those who would transform it into thread. Next, he would put out the thread with the weaver who would *manu*facture cloth for him. The finished product—cloth—our merchant prince would sell in the open market at a price far above the total cost of the original cotton and the total payments made to the different domestic workers. Thus was the merchant prince transformed into the merchant capitalist. Whereas in the self-sufficing agricultural economy all the functions —ginning, spinning and weaving—would be performed in the farmer's home, now under the new putting-out economy there came into being four special types of economic workers: (1) the capitalist, (2) the ginner, (3) the spinner, (4) the weaver. Broadly speaking, there came into being two distinct classes: the capitalist and the worker. (*Cf.* Discussion of Karl Marx' Communist Manifesto, *supra*, CHAPTER 14).

The putting-out economy brought about two sharply differentiated classes and introduced the principle of division of labor as well as specialization of labor. While specialization and division of labor tended to increase production and the capitalist's profit, it soon became apparent that the putting-out system was not so well articulated as it could be. Sometimes, for reasons unforeseen and uncontrollable, one or a whole group of specialized workers—ginners, spinners or weavers—might fail to deliver the goods at the appointed time. This would entail unproductive or idle capital and a delay in reaping profits by the capitalist. To obviate such a contingency, the factory system was invented.

The difference between the domestic economy and the factory economy was crucial: formerly, work was taken to the worker, now the worker went to the place where there was work, namely, the factory. The factory system involved the assumption of extra responsibilities by the capitalist: in addition to the raw materials, he had now to provide the worker with tools and with a place to work in—

a building set aside for *manu*facturing. In one factory only ginners might work, in a second only spinners and in a third only weavers, all under the supervision of superintendents or foremen responsible to the capitalist; or the different processes might be carried on simultaneously in different parts of the same building or factory. The foreman was empowered to replace a sick or incompetent worker with another.

The invention of the factory system has revolutionized modern economy. Indeed, neither industrialism nor capitalism could have advanced very far without the factory system, which is ideally suited for articulation of all phases of production in a given industry. Once articulation of productive activities was achieved through the establishment of the factory, the next problem was that of increasing productivity. Inasmuch as specialization of labor had already extracted maximum productivity from the worker, any further increase in productivity had to be extracted from capital—from better tools, from powered tools, from better raw materials. The attention of capitalists as well as of workers was now directed toward the improvement of tools, toward endowing tools with power, so that they could increase productivity. Power, applicable to tools, is of two kinds: mechanical and motor.

The application of both these types of power has resulted in the industrial revolution. To illustrate: In a spinning factory there are a hundred spinning wheels and a hundred operatives. If a belt could connect two spinning wheels, fifty workers would be able to operate the hundred spinning wheels. This is the application of mechanical power. If horse-power, water-power, steam-power or electric power were substituted for human power in the turning of the wheels, still fewer workers would be needed to operate the original hundred spinning wheels. The application of mechanical and motor power to the tools of production has resulted in multiplying the productive power of tools and, therefore, the productivity of workers.

These patterns of industrialism were first evolved in England. With the advantage of a strong national State consolidated under the Tudor Dictatorship, with the flow of goods and gold from India, with the inexhaustible reservoir of raw materials in the American Colonies, with an undisputed rule of the seas after the defeat of the Spanish Armada (1588), with a thriving commerce and a prosperous economy under Mercantilism, England was ideally suited to pioneer in industrialization. England's early experiment in industrialism served as a foundation for industrialism in the U.S.A., and elsewhere in the world. Wherever industrialism was adopted, the scientific outlook became a new culture trait.

9. AMERICAN INDUSTRIAL ECONOMY

Pre-Civil War: *Infant Industries.* The world which had witnessed the American Revolution and the French Revolution was going through the birthpangs of a new order of society on a global scale. Slow as they were, the newer methods of transportation and communication of the day were effectively bridging distances in time and space. The political edict of the British government of the day, outlawing dissemination abroad of the new knowledge and techniques of industrialism was impotent in the face of culture contacts, especially when there was cultural readiness and receptivity on the part of the new-born American nation.

In spite of successive legislation, between 1765 and 1789, by the British Parliament prohibiting (*a*) emigration of operatives trained in textile, iron and steel, and coal-mining industries, and (*b*) export of textile machinery, plans or models, British know-how was diffused in the new nation. Evading the British laws, Samuel Slater, an English textile expert, came to the United States as an immigrant and erected the first textile factory in America at Pawtucket, Rhode Island, in 1790. Similarly, two brothers, John and Arthur Scholfield of Yorkshire immigrated to the United States in 1792 and aided in the establishment of woolen factories in Massachusetts and Connecticut.

Soon inventions, basic as well as collateral-technological, began to come thick and fast. As against an average of 77 inventions annually reported by the U.S. Patent Office between 1790 and 1811, in 1830 there were 544; and as against 6,480 patents in the decade 1840-50, there were 28,000 patents issued in 1850-60. In the twentieth century, the *annual* inventions between 1901 and 1950 have averaged 40,224. Of course, not all patented inventions are basic; but all inventions, if acted upon by society, do make an impact of some sort upon the cultural heritage.

If Adam Smith be considered the prophet of industrialism, then Eli Whitney may well be called the patron saint of industrialism. Not only was he the inventor of the cotton gin in 1793, but he also made possible the modern assembly line method of production by applying the principle of standardized, interchangeable parts during the War of 1812—the logic of identity, on which the whole fabric of industrialism rests. Henry Ford, in the twentieth century, put America—and the world—on wheels by using the assembly line method of production in the manufacture of automobiles. And some of Edison's inventions have revolutionized our every day mode of living.

In addition to inventors, American industrialism has been indebted from the very beginning to the vision and initiative of American captains of industry. Among the pre-Civil War captains of industry may be mentioned: Francis Cabot Lowell, Nathan Appleton, Abbott Lawrence, Edmund Dwight, William Gregg (of South Carolina), and Patrick T. Jackson.

Patrick Tracy Jackson (1780-1847) may be taken as an example of the sort of entrepreneurs who created American industrialism (2, p. 257):

Apprenticed to a Newburyport merchant at the age of fifteen, he became a sea captain in his early twenties, retired from the sea at 28 to engage in the exporting and importing business, and with the curtailment of his shipping interest by the War of 1812 found an outlet for his energy in the manufacture of cotton. Joining his brother-in-law, Francis C. Lowell, he aided in the establishment of the famous Waltham factory and managed it in its early years. When the local power resources were exhausted, Jackson and his associates moved to the Merrimac and erected mills around which grew the city of Lowell, the "Manchester of America." Jackson turned a ready ear to the reports of steam railroads and was chiefly responsible for the first one in New England. Sailor, merchant, manufacturer, railroad builder—his life epitomizes the economic history of New England during the first half of the nineteenth century.

Experiments in water transportation by Rumsay, Fitch and Fulton (1807); the invention of the sewing machine by Elias Howe (1846); the smelting of iron ore with anthracite coal by John Stevens and the independent or parallel discovery and invention of the Bessemer process by William Kelly, the invention of the telegraph by S.F.B. Morse (1837)—the pioneer work of these men, reinforced by those who operated in the field of textile and transportation and food-processing industries, was destined to make the infant industries of America into giant industries, giant corporations.

American Industrialism Comes of Age. The post-Civil War period has been characterized by the coming of age of industrialism in America and by the growth of American political power abroad. By the time of the Civil War, the present boundaries of continental United States had been well defined and the whole subcontinent had been Americanized. French-speaking and Spanish-speaking peoples, resembling cultural islands, not to mention the many American Indian tribes, had all been incorporated within the American polity. Alaska was purchased from Czarist Russia in 1867 for $7,200,000. Hawaii was formally annexed to the U.S.A. in 1898 during the Spanish-American War which also gave America a foot-hold in the Caribbean and in the Pacific. The Monroe Doctrine of 1823, supplemented or rather reinterpreted by Theodore Roosevelt's Corollary of 1904—the right of the U.S.A. to intervene in the internal affairs of the countries of the Western Hemisphere in cases of mismanagement—and the "dollar diplomacy" of the early part of the twentieth century gave America economic hegemony over the Western Hemisphere.

At the turn of the century American political power and growing American commerce were responsible for saving the economic, territorial and political integrity of China through the enunciation of the "open door" policy in China by Secretary of State John Hay. The Open Door Policy in China may in a sense be said to be an extension, in the international field, of America's domestic policies and instruments embodied in the ICC (Interstate Commerce Commission) and the FTC (Federal Trade Commission).

World War I changed America from a debtor into a creditor nation and shifted the world money market from Lombard Street,

London, to Wall Street, New York. World War II transformed America into the arsenal of democracy and ended with the emergence of the United States as the strongest power in the world.

This vast power, unknown previously in human history, is broad-based upon the resourcefulness of the American people, upon freedom and democracy, upon a well-articulated technology, upon capitalism (to be discussed later).

The post-Civil War era, so far as American economy is concerned, is the story of the emergence of Big Business first, Big Labor second, Big Government third, Big Agriculture fourth.

The canals and canal barges of the pre-Civil War period facilitated commerce but added no significant folklore to American culture. The adventurous forty-niners, on the other hand, live in song and legend. The railroads that crisscross the country have contributed the immortal ballad of Casey Jones. Big Business has enriched American legacy by the Horatio Alger type of story and achievement. Big Labor has been bankrupt so far as folklore is concerned unless one were to think of enshrining the raucous eyebrows of John L. Lewis. Big Government has functioned smoothly without depriving people of their liberties but with a deal of padding, with "feather-bedding" in labor terminology.

Money and Banking. Within this framework modern American capitalism arose. Spectacular developments in money and banking, in transportation and communication—culminating in world-girdling banking; transportation by rail, road, sea and air; communication through telephones, telegraphs, cables and radio and TV—throw considerable light on the working of capitalism. The American Telephone and Telegraph Company's financial empire all over the Western Hemisphere, in Europe and Asia and Africa is in dollars and cents worth many times some of the largest colonial empires of the past.

Money and banking are integral institutions of capitalist economy; they are also integral institutions in the "communist" economy of Soviet Russia as well as of socialist and semi-socialist nations.

The first mint was established in 1652 in Massachusetts Colony whose government was also the first in the New World (1690) to issue paper money in the form of bills of credit in order to raise revenue in anticipation of taxes. The issue, at first limited to £7,000, was later increased to £40,000; this credit money depreciated in value in comparison with coin money until it was made convertible into silver in 1693. The Constitution of the newly formed United States of America gave Congress the exclusive right to coin money and to regulate its value, with the subsidiary right to emit bills of credit. The dollar bills, until the advent of the New Deal (1933 on), were in substance warehouse receipts for gold; one could take a ten-dollar bill to a bank or to the U.S. Treasury and get in exchange a gold eagle worth ten dollars. Or, one could take gold to the U.S. Mint and have it converted into gold coins of desired denominations.

The dollar, the unit of money accounting in the U.S.A., has become a part of the institutionalized procedures of the business world both at home and abroad. Dollars could be lent abroad or used to buy goods or services abroad; they would then be used by the dollar-receiving nation in payment for goods and/or services bought from us. Until the beginning of World War I, the English pound was dominant in international trade and finance; in the interwar period it continued to lose its hegemony in world trade, and in the era following World War II the American dollar has reigned supreme as the most desired unit of money. The value of any unit of money—dollar, pound or ruble—in the markets of the world ultimately rests upon (1) peoples' confidence in the stability of the government sponsoring it, (2) the productivity of the people using it, and (3) the annual production of the nation or the national income. Judged by these criteria, the primacy of the American dollar is assured for the foreseeable future.

10. EVILS OF INFANT CAPITALISM

Capitalism, in its nascent stage, has had evils of exploitation associated with it, in some countries and at some periods more ruthless, elsewhere and at other periods less ruthless. Here are two typical illustrations of the exploitation of women and children in the early stages of industrialism in England and the U.S.A. (3, p. 18, quoted):

My two sons (one ten, the other thirteen) work at Milne's factory at Lenton (England). They go at half past five in the morning; don't stop at breakfast or tea time. They stop at dinner half an hour. Come home at a quarter before ten. They used to work until ten, sometimes eleven, sometimes twelve. They earn between them 6s. 2d. (less than a dollar in American money, 1958) per week. One of them, the eldest, worked at Wilson's for two years at 2s. 3d. (less than half a dollar, 1958) per week. He left because the over-looker beat him and loosened a tooth for him. I complained, and they turned him away for it. They have been gone to work sixteen hours now; they will be very tired when they come home at half past nine. I have a deal of trouble to get 'em up in the morning. I have been obliged to beat 'em with a strap in their shirts, pinch 'em, in order to get them well awake. (*Testimony of a father of two working boys, given to the factory commissioners, appointed by the British Parliament, in* 1833.)

Contemporaneous New England displayed slightly more civilized conditions, but not good enough to brag about. For instance, the Hope Factory of Rhode Island, in 1831,

. . . . rang its first bell ten minutes before sunrise. Five minutes after sunrise the gates were locked against tardy comers, not to open again until eight at night. (A committee of laborers claimed that the employer stretched this horrible "day" by twenty or twenty-five minutes more, by always keeping the factory clock slow.) The only respites from toil during the fifteen or sixteen hours were twenty-five minutes for breakfast and a like period for "dinner"—both meals being cold lunches brought by the operatives. And more than half the operatives were children. This was not an exceptional instance; it was typical.*

Evils of nascent industrialism elsewhere have been equally ruthless, even more ruthless in Czarist Russia and in Oriental countries which had been until recently under European imperialist control. The evils of infant industrialism as witnessed by him in three continents—England (1888-91), South Africa (1893-1914), India (1915 on)—turned Mahatma Gandhi (1869-1948) into a "foe" of industrialism and into an advocate of simple agrarian mode of living.

* In those days, women and children were preferred to men as operatives in textile mills because they could be hired at much lower wages; operatives had to attend to the simplest tasks, the machine doing the most complicated jobs.— H.T.M.

It was this sort of thing that aroused the ire of Christian socialists in England as well as of Karl Marx and Friedrich Engels and other reformers and revolutionaries.

11. PEOPLE'S CAPITALISM IN AMERICA

Thanks to (a) the glorification of the common man in our culture, (b) government legislation and intervention in bahlf of labor, (c) rise of unionism and Big Labor, American capitalism has no resemblance whatsoever to the gruesome pictures just depicted. Yet doctrinaires in Europe and Asia, whenever they think of America as the bastion of capitalism as well as of democracy, conjure up before their mind's eye the horrendous picture of an exploiting capitalism. This imaginary picture conditions the attitude of intellectuals abroad toward America.

The truth of the matter is that under the people's capitalism in America, the laborer has more rights and privileges and enjoys a higher plane of living than the worker in any other society under any other economic system. St. John de Crevecoeur's description of two hundred years ago regarding the new dignity of man in American culture is true to this day. (*supra*, CHAPTER 19.)

To remove the emotional cobweb of misunderstanding about capitalism, either for or against, we may endeavor objectively to describe the nature of capitalism. In the broadest sense, capitalism may be defined as the economic system making the widest use of capital in the process of production. In the technical sense, capitalism may be defined as the economic system of production in which capital goods are owned privately by individuals or corporations.

At least, ten traits of capitalism may be identified: (1) wide use of capital, (2) money and credit system, (3) right of private property in production goods or capital as well as in consumption goods, (4) freedom of enterprise, or private initiative, or the system of laissez faire, (5) competition, (6) profit motive, (7) freedom of contract: (a) individual and (b) group, (8) law of supply and demand as a regulator of price, (9) rise of corporations, and (10) an expanding market with an ever expanding economy.

American capitalism, far from being a system of wage slavery as falsely believed by intellectuals abroad, is a system which grants and safeguards the laborer's right to enter into a contract, of his own volition, on terms satisfactory to him, either for himself singly or for himself and his co-workers joined together in a union. The process of collective bargaining between employers and employees in the U.S.A. is indeed the process of arriving at a group contract. Since the end of the Civil War, American society has tolerated no "involuntary servitude" except for criminals and for those few (conscientious objectors) whom the State has adjudged to be in defiance of some of the basic laws of the land. And even in our prisons, the goal of the new penology is to rehabilitate the erstwhile wrongdoer by entrusting him with the responsibilities of freedom.

The coffee break in American business houses has practically become a folkway on a par with the Englishman's afternoon tea. Curiously enough, the same intellectuals of Europe and Asia who criticize scientific management and efficiency methods in production, widely used in America, wax ecstatic over Stakhanovism in the Soviet Union, which seems to be a combination of efficiency methods and the stretchout system!

12. Traits of Communist Economy

Let us see which of the ten traits of American capitalism are present or absent in the "communist" economy of the Soviet Union. (1) Wide use of capital is present in Soviet economy. (2) Money and the credit system also obtain. (3) Right of private property in consumption goods is assured, but right of private property in production goods is denied except in those rare cases where there are but three or four employees. (4) Freedom of enterprise is entirely missing. The State does the planning and the ordering and the execution of all industrial activities as well as plants. (5) Competition is absent because of State regulation. (6) The profit motive is absent simply because the private citizen has no initiative in organizing industrial enterprises. Soviet citizens may and do invest money with the Soviet government on an interest basis—a thoroughly capitalistic device. In a large sense, the profit motive is not entirely absent—the State could run some of its corporations at a loss all of the time, or all of its corporations at a loss some of the time, but never all of its corporations at a loss all of the time. (7) As for freedom of contract, individual and group, there seem to be enormous restrictions. Voluntary associations in our sense are not tolerated. So-called voluntary associations, such as trade unions, are but adjuncts of the State machinery in a communist society. (8) The law of supply and demand as a regulator of price does not obtain in the Soviet system, because the State sets production quotas on all goods and sets official prices; in the black market, however, the law of supply and demand does set the price. (9) Corporations, giant corporations, are to be found doing business in the Soviet Union, but these corporations are, like our TVA, government-sponsored corporations, not private corporations as we know them in the U.S.A. (10) Ever since the launching of the communist experiment in the Soviet Union, its rulers have been dedicated to the task of expanding their economy through successive five-year plans. While their domestic market seems to have expanded in some measure compared to Czarist days, the expansion of the market suffers from lack of consumers' goods as well as from inadequate purchasing power. It would be intriguing to speculate what kinds of changes might be wrought in Soviet economy and polity if and when the twin conditions of American capitalism, adequate purchasing power and abundance of consumers' goods, were realized.

13. Problems of Industrialism and Capitalism

One. Industrialism-Capitalism has solved, for the first time in human history, the problem of production. Today we are in a position to produce enough to satisfy the needs of all human beings. But in the field of distribution, there are serious shortcomings. Interestingly enough, the communists of Russia, instead of following the Marxian notion of equal pay for equal time of work, have been successfully using the capitalist device of incentive pay for higher category of work as well as for more efficient production. Perhaps American economy does need to be more consumption-centered than production-centered.

Two. Vast aggregations of population crowded into urban centers by industrialism are a fairly new phenomenon in the experience of man. We do not know as yet whether man flourishes best in a rural setting, in a medium city, or in a large metropolis.

Three. Whether there are serious ill effects of monotonous work at the assembly line on human personality, we do not know. This is a problem not for capitalist economy alone but for all forms of economy.

Four. The separation of the powers of ownership and the process of management in our giant corporations, as pointed out in Chapter 14, is a very recent phenomenon in the development of capitalism. Its implications have not yet been fully analyzed by economists, sociologists or social philosophers. If a worker in the Ford factory, who owns stock in the Ford Company, goes on a strike, is he striking against the impersonal entity, the corporation, or against himself? The communist theory is that since the factories theoretically belong to the people, to the workers, the worker has no right to strike against himself. Is it conceivable that thanks to labor's partnership with capital through widely diffused ownership of stock, capitalist economy is indirectly approaching the theoretical base of communism?

Five. The Guaranteed Annual Wage (GAW) is no doubt a highly desired and desirable objective; it has already arrived in some industries, and promises to be widespread throughout the business world. Will this have the consequence of freezing the worker in the same business establishment?

Six. Would the pension plan in industry, likewise, have the tendency to demand freezing of the worker's work with the same establishment? If this should be one of the unforeseen consequences of recent demands by labor, how profound will be the change in the American pattern of pioneering and freedom of movement?

Seven. Can political democracy indefinitely postpone industrial democracy? Will industrial democracy be productive of efficiency and of satisfaction, individual and social?

Eight. With our high-powered tools, the American worker produces three or four times more than his European counterpart and perhaps five to seven times as much as his Asian counterpart (excluding the Japanese). This has resulted in higher wages and shorter hours. The forty-hour week is standard with us, and in some industries they have a thirty-five-hour week. The trend has been toward shortening hours and increasing the payroll. The question is: Have we developed in our working population—some seventy million of our fellow citizens—the inner resources to enjoy the time freed from work? This question will have to be answered in terms of the logic of American culture and in terms of the ministrations of our educational and religious institutions.

REFERENCES

1. RICHARD T. ELY: *Outline of Economics*, 6th ed., New York: Macmillan. 1937.
2. HAROLD U. FAULKNER: *American Economic History*, 5th ed., New York: Harper & Brothers, 1943.
3. BRUCE W. KNIGHT: *Economic Principles in Practice*, New York: Farrar & Rinehart, 1939
4. JOHN W. MCCONNELL: *Basic Teachings of the Great Economists*, New York: The New Home Library, 1943.
5. ROBERT E. PARK & E. W. BURGESS: *Introduction to the Science of Sociology*, 2nd ed., Chicago: University of Chicago Press, 1924 (8th impression, 1933).
6. ADAM SMITH: *An Inquiry into the Wealth of Nations*, (1776). Any standard edition or an abbreviated edition should serve as an excellent introduction to Adam Smith's economic theories.

CHAPTER 38

THE DHARMIC ORDER—RELIGION

1. FUNCTIONS OF THE DHARMIC ORDER

THE core functions of the dharmic order are three: (1) to induct new members of society into the stream of culture, making them co-sharers of the legacy of the forefathers; (2) to help all members of society to develop rounded, well-adjusted personalities capable of functioning smoothly in the particular milieu, and (3) to help them all to be at home in the universe.

These core functions of the dharmic order are discharged in highly evolved societies by the various institutions of religion on the one hand and by the several institutions of education on the other; but in simple societies religion and education were not differentiated.

2. ATTRIBUTES OF HIGH RELIGION

High religion—exemplified by the three Semitic religions, Judaism, Christianity, Islam (i.e. Surrender or Submission to the Will of Allah or God); by the three Aryan religions, Hinduism, Buddhism, Zoroastrianism; and by the three Chinese-Japanese religions, Confucianism, Taoism and Shinto—is characterized by at least five attributes: (1) Belief in the existence of a Higher Power or Higher Powers; (2) Belief in the relation of man to the Higher Power or Powers; (3) Belief in the competence of the Higher Power or Powers to "control," i.e., to direct and redirect, the flow of natural events; (4) Belief in salvation; (5) Belief in a code of conduct, sanctioned by the Higher Power or Powers, and, therefore, capable of guiding man in his journey through this world and the next.

This does not mean that the religions of the world have the same or identical beliefs; it does mean, however, that all highly developed religious systems worthy of the name have a set of beliefs in each of the five categories. These sets of beliefs may agree in some respects and disagree in others as among religions, but the sets of beliefs in each religion are usually mutually consistent and make up an integrated whole.

For instance, the Hindu concept of salvation is very different from the Christian concept. Accepting as basic the theory of evolution, the Hindu believes that man has arrived at his present stage through a number of incarnations and that his ultimate destiny is release from the cycle of births and deaths (Moksha) and final submergence or absorption into the Infinite Spirit. This blessed state, to the Hindu, involves complete loss of his individuality and attainment of his true destiny by merging with the Infinite—as a drop of ocean water becomes immortal by being reunited with the ocean. This notion of loss of individuality is unbearable to the followers of Semitic religions, especially to Christians and Muslims. To them salvation means the immortality of their individual selves through eons of time in the presence of God, or in paradise. The important point to grasp is that both Hinduism and Christianity have a set of beliefs in regard to salvation.

3. ORIGIN OF RELIGION

Armed with his five senses of perception—sight, hearing, touch, taste and smell—and with the unidentifiable sixth sense of conception, man was foreordained to experience and elaborate religion or Dharma, "that which holds together" the universe, society, and himself. Religious ideas are bound to arise from the following four situations in which man found himself, and still finds himself, enmeshed: (1) Observation of crises, such as births, deaths, thunder, etc.; (2) observation of the regularity of nature, the rhythmic repetitions of day and night and of the seasons, as well as a pattern of sequence in the movement of heavenly bodies; (3) the compelling need of the human mind to find order and logic in the universe and to account for phenomena; (4) the tendency of the human mind to impose order upon the universe in terms of the world of observable facts and in terms of the world of fantasy or the world of logical constructs, which is to say, in terms of the world of "reality" and in terms of the world of "ideality."

For instance, before Arya Bhatta of India (born 476 A.D.) and Copernicus (1473-1543), a thousand years later, developed the heliocentric theory of the universe, mankind had gone about its business quite successfully with the help of the logical constructs: (1) that the earth was flat and (2) that the sun revolved around the earth, causing day and night. Subsequent logical constructs and empirical data, such as Columbus' voyage to the New World (1492) and the circumnavigation of the world by Magellan (1480?-1521) and Drake (1540?-96), proved that the earth was a sphere and that it revolved around the sun. Before the facts of the earth's sphericity and its revolution around the sun were discovered, mankind needed to account for certain phenomena; and this it did in terms of the world of fantasy or the world of logical constructs.

Religion, philosophy and science all attempt to account for phenomena, to explain the meaning of events in the universe, each within its own frame of reference.

Awe-inspiring phenomena needed to be explained. The "reality" of dream had to be explained. Birth and death had to be explained. Who am I? Whence did I come? Whither am I bound? These eternal questions, systematically first posed by Hindu philosophers, have confronted collective man from the beginning of his emergence on this planet, rather from the beginning of the dawn of his conceptual powers.

Auguste Comte speaks of three modes of thinking: (1) mythological ("theological"), (2) philosophical ("metaphysical"), (3) scientific ("positive"). Religion had its origin in the mythological mode of thinking and reasoning. We are not using the word myth in any derogatory sense. When, for instance, lawyers speak of a corporation as a person that can sue and be sued at law, they are referring to a legal fiction, a myth. A myth is simply an ideal construct devised to answer a specific question or a set of questions. The myth remains a serviceable fiction until it is either validated or invalidated by further observations and empirical data.

Myth-making led to the emergence of two ways of looking at the phenomena of the universe: (1) the animistic theory, and (2) the animatistic theory. According to the animistic theory, it is believed that primitive man looked upon natural phenomena as presided over by spirits or deities—for instance, Agni, as the god of fire among the ancient Hindus. To come to terms with natural phenomena, one must enjoy proper relationships with the gods of those phenomena. Hence the emergence of rituals for propitiation, to ward off evil consequences and to court the favor of the gods.

According to the animatistic theory, it is believed that primitive man posited an impersonal power, called *mana*, a word employed by Melanesians to signify the special power possessed by a person, animal, vegetable or inanimate object. According to the American anthropologist Robert H. Lowie, the Polynesians look upon *mana* as a kind of "electrical fluid that could charge persons and things and be diverted from one to another" (6, p. 303). Incidentally, the word *mana* is a pure Sanskrit word meaning mind.

Far from being antagonistic, animism and animatism overlap each other in some beliefs, rituals, and constructs. Both animism and animatism tended to develop ghost-worship, and later the worship of many gods, and still later the worship of the One God. Both of these systems attempted to answer the supreme questions confronting primitive man: How can I, how can we, ward off possible evil consequences? And how can I, how can we, reap good consequences?

In answer to these questions magic, a ritualistic mode of behavior and practice, was developed. Magic postulated cause-effect relationships between phenomena and sought to "control," to direct and redirect, the natural sequence of events by certain rites and rituals, practices and incantations. Sympathetic magic, for instance, going on the theory that like begets like, would advocate mutilation of the image of one's enemy. In course of time, magical practices and rituals, broadbased as they were upon the process of idealization, led to the emergence of religious practices and rituals and to the belief in personified superhuman powers.

What sorts of beliefs preceded animism and animatism and magic we have no way of knowing. Some anthropologists have formulated fear as the origin of religion. Fear may well have played a part. But so may also adoration of the sun and other natural phenomena have played a part in the emergence of religion. The Hindus speak of compassion for the suffering of others as being at the root of religion.

We may roughly speak of three layers of thought in the growth of religion as we know it today: (1) pre-animistic, (2) animistic, (3) religious. The River Valley civilizations had already elaborated religion in our sense of the word.

4. A SOCIOLOGICAL ANALYSIS OF RELIGION

With the development of speech and concepts, both products of man's collective life, there emerged early in the experience of man two important ritualistic systems of thought and action: totem and taboo. Totem served as a mechanism for the identification of the group and also as a source of strength, while taboo regulated human behavior through interdictions and prohibitions. The close connection between totem and taboo may be observed in our word sacred, which comes from the Latin *sacer*, meaning both something to be dreaded and something to be worshipped. A clan that has the deer as its totem would refrain from killing the deer, but once a year or on some special occasion, the deer clan must kill and feast on the deer, because it is sacred.

Freud has attempted to explain the symbolism in the Christian communion service—the body and blood of Christ—in terms of totem and taboo, (5, *passim*). Of course, an explanation of this sort does not mean that the ritual loses its potency to regenerate human beings. Precisely because it is a collective representation and because as a collective representation it has a plus value added on to it, the communion service retains and will continue to retain its power to transform human lives—at least for those who accept the collective representation.

Emile Durkheim (1858-1917) in his classic book *The Elementary Forms of the Religious Life* (1912; English translation 1915, 4, *passim*) maintains that collective ritualistic activities, such as rites and ceremonies, were the elementary forms of religion, not belief in gods or supernatural beings. With the accumulation of collective representations, rather in the process of accumulating collective representations, primitive man was led on to distinguish between the profane (secular) and the sacred, between flesh and spirit, between body and soul.

Sociology does not deny the role of inspiration and revelation in the formulation and development of religion, but it puts upon those terms an interpretation at variance with that of theology. While theology, for instance, looks upon the Ten Commandments as derived from on high, as revealed by God, Sociology contends that the Ten Commandments are derived from below, from the experiences of the people. Moses, the charismatic leader in this case, towered above his people in his capability of seeing clearly and coordinating into a system the experiences that had a value for the survival and welfare of the group. The prophet is one who prophesies or foretells; another word for the prophet is Seer. Moses as Seer clearly saw which behavior patterns tended to promote the well-being of the group and he simply systematized them into the Ten Commandments.

Interacting among themselves, totems, taboos, magic, and collective representations gave rise to all the institutions of religion known to us. In primitive religion the medicineman combined secular and spiritual authority; he could heal the sick and lay down the law for all members of the clan or the tribe to obey. The *rites de passage*, initiation ceremonies in connection with puberty, became institutionalized. Incantations and ceremonies for "controlling" adverse natural forces (drought, for instance) became formalized and institutionalized. These and other institutional procedures served as a mechanism for transmitting the lore of the forefathers to incoming generations as well as for maintaining the stability of the social order.

Our baptism and confirmation ceremonies, wedding ceremonies, funeral services, Sunday morning church services, indeed our very churches and temples and synagogues have all become part of religious institutions.

Springing from the bosom of society, religion has also attempted to formulate a code of conduct serviceable to society. Thus high religion has always made ethics an integral part of religion. It is obvious that morals and ethics, derived from the mores, are integrally related to man's experience as a participant in the socio-cultural milieu. High religion has attempted to systematize those canons of behavior and response that have the highest value for safeguarding the integrity of man as well as society. These canons of behavior, then, become ethical norms and are backed up by the sanction of religion.

Accepted ways of doing things, in terms of everyday experiences as well as in terms of norms of behavior, tend to become structuralized into institutions. Now the paradox of man's membership in society is that he cannot live without institutions, and yet he feels himself at times circumscribed and fettered by institutions. An institution arises in the first place as an instrumentality to subserve a given end. Soon the end becomes subordinated to the maintenance of the institution. This, then, is the supreme dilemma of the human race, especially in the field of religious experience, namely, that man unknown to institutions is less than human and man dominated by institutions is also less than human. Yet, man constantly strives, as he must, by means of institutions, to realize his worth as a citizen, his dignity as a child of God.

Eternal vigilance is the price of freedom from the tyranny of institutionalism. From time to time, "in every cycle of time," as the Bhagavad Gita has it, man must re-evaluate whether a given institution is functioning as an instrumentality or whether it has arrogated to itself the role of the end. In the sphere of religion as in other spheres of human activity and relationship, prophets, seers and charismatic leaders are needed from time to time to proclaim that "the Sabbath is made for man, not man for the Sabbath."

Finally, religion manifests itself in the lives of people. Some cultures have made religion segmental to life, others have made it central to life. According to the Hindus, for instance, religion embraces the totality of life; it is a way of life. Religion, as manifested and observed in the religious life, is more than creed and dogma, more than institution and ritual: it is, said Mahatma Gandhi (1869-1948), a heart grasp—it cannot be taught, it can only be caught.

5. FOUR PHASES IN THE GROWTH OF A RELIGIOUS MOVEMENT

A religious movement conforms to the basic processes characterizing every social movement—moving from dissatisfaction with the status quo to the creation of a social movement, culminating in an ecclesia.

Every religion—or religious movement—starts out, as does every social movement, with a humble beginning—with a concerned individual or with a group of concerned individuals, and if it has inner vitality, it will end up as the most significant institution in society.

First, a particular mode of response—shall we say worship?—is found to be meaningful and satisfactory by an individual or a set of individuals. If a section of the population is attracted to this mode of response, we are on the threshold of a cult. A cult may be said to be a temporary collective fad, organized around a dominant leader or around a dominant idea—usually leader and idea are combined. It is not necessary to join a cult; one may become the follower of a cult by merely accepting and following its practices.

Second, if the cult generates a dynamic power and persists as part of the social process for a time, it may become a sect. The sect is a conflict group—the sect must try to maintain its integrity, its difference from the rest of the world, and it must fight to maintain its existence in a hostile world. Thus, both by inward motivation and by outward resistance, the votaries of a sect are compelled to constitute themselves into a conflict group.

Third, when the sect persists over a period of time and loses some of its combative tendencies, when it begins to be accepted as a normal part of the social process and attains respectability, it is transformed into a denomination. Functionally, the denomination is an accommodation group, while the sect is a conflict group and the cult is a fad group.

A denomination, in the process of attaining respectability, also begins to become congealed structurally, that is to say, it tends to become an ecclesia, an ecclesiastical organization affecting the whole of society. The ecclesia may be said to be a power group.

Here, then, are the four stages through which every religion, and every religious movement, passes and must pass: cult, sect, denomination, ecclesia. (I am indebted to Professor Howard Becker for these conceptual tools, though my interpretation is slightly different from his.) (See 3, CHAPTERS 20 and 21).

6. CASE STUDY OF CHRISTIANITY

Let us illustrate this theoretical framework by reference to the rise of Christianity as an integral institutional part of the Western world.

First, Jesus of Nazareth found a certain mode of response—in terms of worship and conduct in life—meaningful to himself. Those around him became attracted to him and to his teachings—the Twelve Apostles and nameless individuals. Even so, it must be noted that in the lifetime of Jesus only a small segment of the population, attracted to him and to his teachings, constituted his following. This was the stage of the cult.

Next, the cult persisted and began to be propagated by the original Apostles as well as by the new converts such as Paul. Now we had the makings of a sect whose members gloried in their withdrawal from the world and who were compelled to live in catacombs. The Christian sect was harried and hounded by the Roman Empire with whose religion it came into conflict.

Third, Constantine became converted to Christianity at the beginning of the fourth century, and Christian sectaries became respectable—in fact, too respectable. They became an established religious denomination in the Roman Empire—and began to persecute non-conformists!

Fourth and finally, an ecclesiastical organization affecting the whole of society began to be fashioned with rules, rituals, creeds and hierarchy as part of the persistence and practice of the teaching of Jesus.

7. SOME EXAMPLES OF CULTS AND SECTS

It is possible to make a similar analysis of the rise of any one of the Protestant denominations within the Christian Church—in terms of cult, sect, denomination, ecclesia.

The Father Divine Peace Mission movement—"Peace is wonderful"—is in our day a sect. This sect may logically be conceived to be a lineal descendant of the Negro slave's collective activity to seek release from his sad lot by composing and singing spirituals which in double-talk used to express his people's longing for freedom. It would be interesting to investigate to what extent the Father Divine Movement is a subconscious revolt of the Negro against his inferior status in American society. Steeped in religious rituals, it has brought a new, regenerated life and happiness to many a colored and white follower of Father Divine.

The Jehovah's Witnesses sect, as pointed out by Marcus Bach (*The Christian Century*, Feb. 13, 1957), is today in the process of becoming, and being accepted as, a denomination. At one time Christian Science was a sect—it is now a denomination in America. Similarly, the Mormons have passed through the stage of cult and sect to that of denomination and have a well-knit ecclesiastic order.

In this country the followers of Hindu centers, where Hindu religion and philosophy are taught by Swamis, constitute a cult—neither a sect nor a denomination.

It may be pointed out that the rise or persistence of a new sect is a normal part of the social process, much like the rise and functioning of a new class—or a new cause. A democratic society permits and encourages all kinds of voluntary grouping to the end that all the citizens may satisfy all their varied interests. When some of these interests come into conflict with one another, the State in a democratic society lays down directives, procedures, and "rules of the game" in order to safeguard the well-being of concerned interest groups as well as of the public at large.

8. COOPERATION, CRYING NEED OF OUR ONE WORLD

Mahatma Gandhi used to say that the followers of different religions should unite in fighting the common enemy of us all, namely, materialism and secularism. Religion alone is competent to perform the ministry of healing and reconciliation among human beings. But religions are fettered by creeds (or religious beliefs) and tend to imprison God within a definition appropriate to each creed. Hence we have had conflicts of creeds which are then viewed as religious conflicts.

In the name of religion, the common denominator of all mankind, many heinous crimes have been committed. Not so long ago

Protestants and Catholics burned each other at the stake. The devout Muslim ruler had been wont to present three alternatives to the non-believer: (1) accept Islam, (2) pay a poll tax, the jizziya, or (3) fight. Emperor Marcus Aurelius was a great exponent of Stoicism and a devout Stoic, yet he took special delight in persecuting Christians.

An investigation of the social psychology of religious conflict and persecution reveals two important facts: (1) that the new convert to a creed is more fanatical than the one born in the faith; (2) that single-hearted devotion and loyalty to one's creed *as the only universally valid creed* inevitably leads to intolerance, conflict, and persecution. The sensible rule for an individual or a group, in the field of religious belief, would seem to be: "My faith satisfies me completely, and I shall give my allegiance to it unto death. I hope others have arrived at the same conviction with regard to their faith. I respect their faith and expect them to respect mine. At all times I stand ready to share my faith and convictions with others, but not at the price of engendering ill-will."

To be sure, each religion has its distinctive and unique features; and each religion is, *to its followers*, the best. But if religions continue to strive against one another on the plane of violence in thought, word or deed, we may all be engulfed by the demon of materialism and secularism.

The logic of our one world, of our small neighborhood world, requires that we cooperate one with another without sacrificing our inner convictions, beliefs, and principles.

Agencies for the strengthening of religious resources and for the harmonizing of divisive religious groupings have been in operation in this country for some time. The National Conference of Christians and Jews, founded in 1928, with headquarters in New York City, has been consistently and successfully engaged in bringing about better understanding and cooperation among Catholics, Protestants and Jews. The Federal Council of Churches in America, organized in 1908, served as coordinator for the activities and viewpoints of 25 Protestant denominations in America. Its work is now taken over and strengthened by the National Council of Churches, organized in 1950.

The drive toward the Catholic (Universal) Church and the drive toward the Ecumenical Church among the Protestants are movements designed to promote cooperation among Christians throughout the world. Is it conceivable that these worldwide movements of cooperation among Christians are stepping-stones to cooperation with the non-Christian world? At any rate, the logic of our One World demands cooperation among the votaries of all high religions on the basis of equality and mutual respect.

9. COMMUNISM—AN IDEOLOGY OR A RELIGION?

In view of the compulsive role of religion in human affairs and in view of the compulsive role of the communist ideology in the lives of Soviet people, the question may legitimately be raised whether communism serves the purposes of religion in Soviet society and culture.

Religious beliefs are values in our culture because they are accepted and shared by practically all members of society; segmental beliefs in process of becoming universal in a culture form a part of ideology. Since the communist theories are accepted not by the whole of Soviet society, as it would appear to us at this distance, communism should be properly referred to as an ideology with norms and prescriptions for human behavior. It should be remembered that an ideology, to its believers, is as compulsive as is religion to its votaries. Indeed, in the early stages of its career, an ideology generates more dynamic and power among its followers than does an accepted system of values such as religion. The accepted values of religion are taken for granted, they are "old stuff"; while the newly emerging values of an ideology capture the imagination and loyalty of the people. This is the only valid explanation for the success of recurring Protestant movements within Christendom as well as for the success of the communist ideology in our day.

The communist ideology is today as dynamic a factor in the lives of its followers as was the Christian ideology in the early days of Christianity in the lives of Christ's followers. Indeed, the ideal communist and the ideal Christian are in some respects blood brothers. The devotion of present-day communists to their cause can be matched only by the devotion of early Christians to their cause. Sensitivity to the suffering of the exploited and the persecuted is compulsive and similar in both cases. Some of the articles in the constitution of the Third International can well be imagined to have been lifted bodily from the practices of the early Christians.

Some scholars have gone so far as to institute an analogy between Christianity and communism. Like Christianity with its Bible, Communism has its *Das Kapital*. What Jesus was to Christianity, Karl Marx has been to Communism. The role of St. Paul in communism is played by Lenin. In other words, Communism, like Christianity, has its Book, its Founder, its Prophets. And the emotional response to the book, the founder and the prophets is identical in both cases. To quote Marcus Bach (1, pp. 10–11):

Communism's form is strikingly like that of a religion. It appeals to the same kind of dedication to a selfless cause. For more than forty years since the 1917 Revolution, Communism has had to provide a satisfactory substitute for what we think of as man's spiritual drive.

Communism's god is the State. Its holy books are the writings of Karl Marx. Its temples are the institutions of learning. Its holy city is the Kremlin. Its most famous shrine is the tomb of Lenin. . . .

It has its sacred trinity: Marx, Engels, and Lenin. Its creed is Dialectical Materialism which says, "It is not the consciousness of men that determines their existence, but, on the contrary, their social existence determines their consciousness." Its code is the pronouncement of Lenin: "The new spiritual leader must be the proletariat." Its gospel insists that the production of life's necessities and the exchange of products is the fundamental law of existence. The major problem with which it is concerned is not sin and salvation, but the conflict between the "exploiting class" and the "exploited masses."

The fundamental difference between the two is that while Christianity glories in God, communism exults in atheism. Soviet Russia today affords an interesting laboratory for the study of the implications of a godless society—whether a culture inhospitable to a belief in Higher Powers can develop integrity and rectitude among the primary virtues, or whether religion will ultimately triumph over atheism.

10. THE GOLDEN RULE UNIVERSAL IN ALL RELIGIONS

The golden rule, in one form or another, is to be found in all religions. The universality of this ethical norm, developed independently by the Seers of the world, attests to the validity of the religious experience. Here are the different ways in which the golden rule has been expressed by historic religions (7, p. vi):

TABLE 31
THE GOLDEN RULE IN DIFFERENT RELIGIONS

HINDUISM: The true rule is to do by the things of others as you do by your own.

ZOROASTRIANISM: Do as you would be done by.

BUDDHISM: One should seek for others the happiness one desires for one's self.

CONFUCIANISM: What you would not wish done to yourself do not to others.

TAOISM: Recompense injury with kindness.

JUDAISM: Whatever you do not wish your neighbor to do to you, do not unto him.

CHRISTIANITY: All things whatsoever ye would that men should do to you, do ye even so to them.

ISLAM: Let none of you treat a brother in a way he himself would dislike to be treated.

BAHAI CAUSE: If you look toward mercy, regard not that which benefits yourselves, but hold to that which will benefit mankind. If you look toward justice, choose for others that which you choose for yourselves.

REFERENCES

1. MARCUS BACH: "Can Russia Challenge Our Faith?" *Better Homes and Gardens* (Des Moines, Iowa), April, 1958.
2. MARCUS BACH: "The Startling Witnesses." *The Christian Century* (Chicago), Vol. LXXIV, No. 7; Feb. 13, 1957.
3. HOWARD BECKER: *Man in Society*. Mimeographed book in two volumes. Madison: Univ. of Wisconsin, Dept. of Sociology, 1947.
4. EMILE DURKHEIM: *The Elementary Forms of the Religious Life*. New York: Macmillan, 1915.

5. SIGMUND FREUD: *Totem and Taboo.* Originally published in 1913. Several American and English Translations are available.
6. R. H. LOWIE: *An Introduction to Cultural Anthropology,* 2nd ed. New York: Rinehart & Co., 1940 (7th printing, 1947).
7. M. A. SOHRAB, Ed.: *The Bible of Mankind.* New York: The Caravan of East and West (132 East 65th St.) 1939.

NOTE: *God and the Soviets* by MARCUS BACH (New York: Crowell, 1958), not available to the present author when this chapter was being prepared, is an excellent report on Soviet Russia as a "laboratory for the study of the implications of a godless society."

CHAPTER 39

THE DHARMIC ORDER—EDUCATION

THE American's first great love, as I have pointed out elsewhere, is freedom; his second great love is education (*supra*, CHAPTER 35).

Every stimulus-response relationship is an occasion for learning—for education. A great deal of our learning and education takes place informally.

1. SEPARATION OF RELIGION AND EDUCATION

In unsophisticated societies, the functions of teaching and of religious ministration—indeed, of tribal administration, as well—were incorporated in the headman or the medicineman and in the folkways, mores and institutions. Among preliterate societies, the institutions of totem, taboo and initiation ceremonies—*rites de passage*—served as mechanisms for transmitting the lore of the past and for inducting new members into the cultural stream. Because of the sacred nature of society and because of the lack of sophistication, among preliterate peoples education and religion merged into the single dharmic order.

With advances in secularization and with increase in sophistication, as in post-Homeric Greek society and post-Buddhist Hindu society, education began to emerge as a special aspect of the dharmic order, distinct from the religious aspect. Even so, education and religion remained more or less tied together until the birth of the United States of America whose constitution (1789) specifically laid down "separation of church and State." This meant that public education, that is to say, tax-supported schools, could not be tied to any institutional form of religion.

2. THE ROLE OF GREAT TEACHERS

As pointed out earlier (*supra*, CHAPTERS 7 & 24), on the basis of (1) the stimulus-response relationship, man learns by three other specific methods: (2) manipulation, (3) social participation, and (4) formal training or education.

The role of charismatic leaders, of great men, in promoting education, in founding schools, has not been fully appreciated. From one standpoint,

> all great men are founders of schools, either in the sense of having a following, i.e., a body of persons banded together formally or informally around the great man's teaching, or in the sense of establishing a center of learning. Buddha and Jesus, Confucius and Laotze were founders of schools in the first sense. Socrates with his "school" in the market-place of Athens, Plato with his Academy, Aristotle with his peripatetic "school" were all founders of schools in both senses of the term. In recent times Pestalozzi and Froebel and Montessori, Gandhi and Tagore have been founders of schools in both senses. (3, p. 75).

3. THE CRUCIAL ROLE OF THE PROTESTANT REFORMATION

A survey of world history reveals that formal education, ever since its emergence as an institution in society, was the monopoly of the elite. Whether in Hindu society or Hebrew society or Chinese society, whether in Greek society or Roman society, the instrumentalities of formal education could be availed of only by members of the upper class.

This educational monopoly of the elite was broken, without any premeditation on his part, by Martin Luther (1483-1546), leader of the Protestant Reformation in Christendom. Luther's enunciation of the twin doctrines that man could establish personal relationships with God without the intermediation of priest or Pope and that every Christian had the right to read the Bible for himself and by himself led straight to the doctrine of universal education. One could not read the Bible without knowing how to read and write; hence the imperative need for everyone to have a schooling.

It took two hundred years for the implicit goal of Luther's teaching, namely, universal education, to be realized. In 1763 Prussia issued a decree making education for children from the age of five compulsory. And in the New World, while as early as 1642 Massachusetts had enacted a law requiring parents to educate their children and while the Northwest Ordinance of 1787 encouraged education, it was not until the 1840's that the culture trait of the public school, free and compulsory, began to become an accepted part of American culture.

4. THE PUBLIC SCHOOL, A GLOBAL CULTURE PATTERN IN THE MAKING

Prussia and America may legitimately divide honors for contributing the culture trait of the public school system to the modern world. The so-called public schools of England—Eton, Harrow, Winchester—are in reality private schools. England did not have a universal compulsory school attendance law until 1876, and France passed a similar law in 1882; while Japan, emerging from feudalism with the Meiji Restoration (1869), passed the first public school law in 1872. India passed a similar law soon after attaining freedom in 1947, but lack of facilities as well as of trained personnel has impeded realization of the goal thus far; the government of the Republic of India expects to overcome these handicaps in the not distant future.

The specific American contribution to a well-articulated educational system is being borrowed today, in part or in whole, by the newly freed nations of Asia and Africa: (1) grade school, eight years; (2) high school, four years; (3) undergraduate college, four years; (4) graduate schools of universities for specialized training in law, medicine, engineering, journalism, social work, etc.; (5) research laboratories maintained by universities, government agencies, and by industry.

5. AMERICAN HIGHER EDUCATION

The dominant concern of American society has been "service to God and Commonwealth." Among the very first activities of the Pilgrim Fathers were (a) establishment of churches to minister to their spiritual needs, and (b) founding of Harvard College (1636) in order to prepare educated citizens who would serve God and Commonwealth. In order to achieve this objective of preparing citizens for service to God and to Commonwealth, Harvard College (1636) and Yale College (1701) took over bodily the curricula of mediaeval European universities; they even borrowed the academic regalia and rituals of mediaeval European universities. Other colleges and universities, as they arose in this country, followed in the footsteps of Harvard and Yale.

The following requirements for entrance to Harvard and Yale prior to the Revolution should make interesting reading for the modern American student who knows little Greek and less Latin, and even not much of his own mother tongue (2, p. 14 quoted):

When any Scholar is able to understand Tully, or such classical Latin Author *extempore,* and make and speak true Latin in Verse and Prose, *suo ut aiunt Marte;* And decline perfectly the Paradigms of *Nouns* and *Verbs* in the *Greek* tongue: Let him then and not before be capable of admission into the College (Harvard). (Spellings modernized—H.T.M.).

The requirements for admission to Yale College, as laid down a hundred years later (in 1745), reveal no significant deviation from the Harvard standards of 1643, as cited above:

That none may expect to be admitted into this college unless upon examination of the President and Tutors, he shall be found able Extempore to Read, Construe and Parce Tully, Virgil and the Greek Testament; and to write True Latin in Prose and to understand the Rules of prosodia, and Common Arithmetic, and shall bring Sufficient Testimony of his Blameless and inoffensive Life.

The specifically American contributions to higher education began to be made after the establishment of Land-Grant colleges and universities. The Agricultural and Mechanical colleges of the various states, in the post-Civil War period, emphasized vocational training as part of higher education. And since the end of World War I (1914-18), America has been a leader in the general education movement, designed to inform the student about his cultural legacy and its specific values.

6. A Sociological Analysis of Education

The question has been raised, and quite legitimately: How can we train our children to make the most of their abilities and to attain full intellectual powers? The root meaning of the word education in Latin is "to draw out" the latent powers of the child.

First. John Locke's notion of the human mind as being a *tabula rasa* (a clean slate), on which sense-impressions from the outside world are registered, is no longer held to be valid. Learning is a creative experience. In the process of responding to stimuli, natural as well as socio-cultural, the human being acts in a creative manner. Education, in other words, is a creative act for the learner.

Second. Education is rooted in social experience and flows back into social experience more enriched and vitalized.

Third. Of the four fundamental ways of learning—stimulus-response, manipulation, social participation and formal education—the first three serve, continuously through life, as mechanisms for learning as well as for reinforcing previous learning.

Fourth. Formal education is a socially devised technique, a highly elaborated procedure, for creating (artificial or ideal) situations in which the pupil may learn. We go through formal education only a short period of our life—for some of us in the United States, it means eight years of grade school; for some, four more years of high school; and for a few of us, four more years of college. Thus we have the 8 : 4 : 4 ratio in our formal education.

Practically all children of grade school age are in school, excepting perhaps a few non-white children in some of our Southern states. And four out of five children of high school age are enrolled in our high schools (79.4 per cent in 1950). Thus, an overwhelming majority of American youngsters spend twelve years of their lives in grade school and high school, public or private, devoting the most plastic and impressionable period of their lives to formal education.

The enrollment in our colleges and universities has been increasing by leaps and bounds since the closing of the frontier in 1890. From an enrollment of 237,592 in our publicly and privately controlled colleges and universities in 1900, the number has steadily increased at every decennial count: 355,215 in 1910; 597,880 in

1920; 1,100,737 in 1930; 1,494,203 in 1940; 2,659,021 in 1950
(4, p. 122).

TABLE 32

ENROLLMENT IN AMERICAN COLLEGES AND UNIVERSITIES,
BOTH PRIVATELY AND PUBLICLY SUPPORTED,
IN CERTAIN YEARS

Year	No. of Students
1900	237,592
1910	355,215
1920	597,880
1930	1,100,737
1940	1,494,203
1950	2,659,021
1956	3,450,000

Fifth. American society has succeeded in implementing the gospel of democracy by devising methods and techniques and evolving institutions for educating "all the children" of school-going age, coming as they do from diverse racial, religious, cultural and family backgrounds. The neatly devised time ratio of 8 : 4 : 4 is a serviceable tool at the disposal of administrators and teachers in fulfilling the task of "democratizing" education. But in the process, American education has become a prisoner of its own well devised scheme and a victim of the tyranny of the time ratio. Except in some special schools for the handicapped and except in some private schools, all children are "treated" alike, regardless of their competence and background. For some time now, the need for special opportunities and training for the superior student has been keenly felt in academic circles.

Sixth. The American belief in education as a means of solving all the ills of mankind is a refreshingly new experience in human history. Thomas Jefferson wanted to be known, among other things, as the Founder of the University of Virginia (1819). The figures for expenditure on education bear out the American's high regard for education.

On public schools, elementary and secondary, for which reliable figures are available, the American people spent: $214,965,000 in 1900; $426,250,000 in 1910; $1,036,151,000 in 1920; $2,316,790,000 in 1930; $2,344,049,000 in 1940; and $5,837,-643,000 in 1950; and $9,092,449,000 in 1954. And on higher education, both publicly and privately supported, America spent: $216,366,000 in 1920; $632,249,000 in 1930; $605,755,000 in 1940; $2,123,275,000 in 1950; and $2,802,100,000 in 1954. The grand total of expenditures on education at all levels from the kindergarten to the university, privately as well as publicly supported, in 1954, was: $13,248,628,000. (4, p. 122).

The cost of new public educational building construction has also jumped by leaps and bounds in the same years: $190,000,000 in 1920; $364,000,000 in 1930; $156,000,000 in 1940 (World War II); $1,133,000,000 in 1950; and $2,548,000,000 in 1956. (4, p. 752). The estimated worth of all capital outlay in educational buildings, equipment, etc. for both public and private institutions at all levels, in 1957-58, was in the neighborhood of $4,300,000,000 according to a reply from the Research Division of the Department of H.E.W. (Health, Education and Welfare). TABLES 33, 34, 35, vividly illustrate the rise in expenditure on education in this country.

TABLE 33

EXPENDITURE ON PUBLIC SCHOOLS IN CERTAIN YEARS

Year	Amount in Dollars
1900	214,965,000
1910	426,250,000
1920	1,036,151,000
1930	2,316,790,000
1940	2,344,049,000
1950	5,837,643,000
1954	9,092,449,000

TABLE 34

EXPENDITURE ON HIGHER EDUCATION INCLUDING PUBLICLY
AND PRIVATELY SUPPORTED INSTITUTIONS
IN CERTAIN YEARS

Year	Amount in Dollars
1920	216,366,000
1930	632,249,000
1940	605,755,000
1950	2,123,275,000
1954	2,802,100,000

TABLE 35

EXPENDITURE ON NEW PUBLIC EDUCATIONAL BUILDING
CONSTRUCTION IN CERTAIN YEARS

Year	Amount in Dollars
1920	190,000,000
1930	364,000,000
1940	156,000,000
1950	1,133,000,000
1956	2,548,000,000
1957	4,300,000,000

Of the total number of government employees, 7,685,000, at all levels—federal, state, local—in 1956, 2,286,000 or 29.7 per cent were employed in educational work (4, p. 418). Of the total number of persons, 5,275,000 employed by state and local governments in 1956, 43 per cent or 2,283,000 were working in the field of education (4, p. 420). And while the number of federal employees in education was 10,555 in 1954, the total number of faculty personnel in all institutions of higher learning in the same year was 265,911 (4, pp. 369, 123).

Education in the United States is in the category of a twenty billion dollar enterprise annually (News release, Jan. 8, 1958, by the Dept. of H.E.W., Office of Education—Research and Statistical Services Branch). By the school year 1963-64, the cost of public elementary and secondary schools alone began to approach the amount of 20 billion dollars a year.

Percentagewise, we spend in the neighborhood of five per cent of our national income on education, while the Soviet Government spends 17 per cent of its national income on education (1). Even though the percentage of the national income spent on education in the Soviet Union is three times higher than in America, in dollars and cents the American expenditure on education just about equals the amout spent by the Soviet Union—because the American national income is a great deal over three times Soviet Russia's.

"The battle of the bulge" in American education is graphically revealed by the latest figures for enrollment. For the school year 1963-64, according to the Associated Press, the most reliable estimate is an enrollment of 75 million young Americans in educational institutions at all levels—75 million young people enrolled out of a total population of 190,000,000 (1963). This means that almost 40 per cent of all Americans are engaged in some sort of educational endeavor. Here are the estimated figures for students at all levels:

TABLE 36

ESTIMATED NUMBER OF AMERICAN STUDENTS ENGAGED IN EDUCATIONAL STUDY AT ALL LEVELS (1963-64)

Kindergarten	2,300,000
Elementary School	30,600,000
High School	11,500,000
Higher Education	4,500,000
Adult Education Institutions	17,000,000
Independent Study	9,000,000
Total	74,900,000

Seventh. Something seems to have gone wrong with the noble purposes of the "progressive education" movement fathered by John Dewey (1859-1952) and his disciples in the wake of World War I. Disregarding the value of intellectual discipline in learning sponsors of progressive education threw overboard the three R's— reading, writing and 'rithmetic. The result has been devastating in the lives of some of the youngsters who were led to believe that there was no price to be paid in hard work and in other forms for any objectives or goals in life. Such beliefs bred irresponsibility, intellectual laziness, spoon-feeding in college class rooms, and loss of thrill of the adventure of learning.

Progressive education begins with where the child is, not with where the child ought to be. Lack of goals and objectives leads to disorganized personality. Education may well start with the dictum: A man should be judged not by what he is but by what he aspires to be.

Be it said in defense of progressive educators that their objective was to stimulate intellectual curiosity, to intensify the learning process, and to develop a socially adjusted personality as well as good citizenship. But whether their techniques are competent to achieve these laudable objectives is another matter.

One contribution of progressive education promises to abide with us, and that is John Dewey's dictum that education is the living of life, not a preparation for life. Even here, however, a modification is necessary: Education is both the living of life (in the network of social relationships in the classroom and outside) *and* a preparation for life. Preparation for life involves (a) capacity to earn a livelihood, (b) capacity to enrich one's life through enjoyment of the cultural heritage and of one's own inner resources, (c) capacity to function efficiently and constructively as a member of society, as a citizen of the State.

Eighth. Education involves or should involve (a) mastery of the tools of learning, such as reading, writing, arithmetic, and (b) mastery of our relations to our inner self, to our neighbors, to the universe, to God. These aspects of man's living are always present. And the logic of the dharmic order compels him to practise these relations daily. Gandhi's doctrine of noble character as the end-product of education (3, CHAPTER VI) is in thorough harmony with the sociological analysis of education.

7. CHALLENGES TO EDUCATION

The only things learned in education that our conscious self does not forget are the things we continually practise every day. The results of an interesting experiment conducted by several colleges and universities pose a challenge to education: A simple test in American history, administered to recent high school graduates and to college graduates of five or ten years' standing, invariably disclosed a better showing by the high school graduates than by college graduates.

Two questions arise from these experiments: (1) Why did we waste the college student's time by asking him to take American history if he was not going to remember its contents the rest of his life? (2) Is it possible that the way we teach history or other liberal arts subjects is not the right way?

Thus the *first* challenge to formal education is: How shall our curriculum be built? What shall it contain? How shall it be executed?

The *second* challenge to formal education is in regard to its limited objective: In the attempt to develop intellectual powers, education addresses itself primarily to the conscious self of man. Now, man's total self is like an iceberg, as pointed out by Johann Friedrich Herbart (1776-1841) long ago and as emphasized by Freud in our day: over 11/12 submerged and only 1/12 visible. In a sense, our formal education tries to deal with the 1/12, ignoring the 11/12 of our total self. To be meaningful, education should attempt to develop body, mind and heart. To quote Gandhi (3, pp. 84–85):

I hold that true education of the intellect can only come through a proper exercise of the bodily organs, e.g., hands, feet, ears, nose, etc. In other words, an intelligent use of the bodily organs in a child provides the best and quickest way of developing his intellect. But unless the development of the mind and body goes hand-in-hand with a corresponding awakening of the soul, the former alone would prove to be a poor lopsided affair. By spiritual training I mean education of the heart. A proper and all-round development of the mind, therefore, can take place only when it proceeds *pari passu* with the education of the physical and spiritual faculties of the child. They constitute an indivisible whole. According to this theory, therefore, it would be a gross fallacy to suppose that they can be developed piecemeal or independently of one another.

Allied to the problem posed by Gandhi is the *third* problem discovered by Professor Ralph Harlow's sociology class at Smith College: A questionnaire submitted to students at Smith College and to students at other colleges (in the thirties) revealed that whatever attitudes the student had regarding war, peace, religion, and labor had been arrived at as a result of extracurricular activities, not as a result of classroom experiences.

These revelations do not permit us to dodge certain central issues confronting formal education: (1) To what extent shall formal education follow the lead of the social education movement, which attempts to inculcate values through indoctrination and even propaganda? (2) Is formal education confined to classroom work alone, or does it also embrace informal, indirect methods of learning, such as extracurricular or cocurricular activities on the campus? (3) If the purpose of education be to train the whole man, can we accomplish it by bypassing the realm of values? (4) Have educators in totalitarian societies, such as communist Russia, discovered a formula for blending properly the education of body, mind, and heart?

The *fourth* challenge to formal education is posed by the tyranny of the 8 : 4 : 4 ratio. Not only is it a handicap to the superior student but it also effectively frustrates one of the fundamental purposes of education, namely, to impart to the pupil an appreciative acquaintance with the universe. For instance, certain subjects are never brought to the attention of the child in the elementary school on the plea that they are beyond the comprehension of the young learner. These "tabooed" or "reserved" subjects are meant to be pursued, some at the secondary level, others only at the college level. What happens to the child who does not go through college? Does he develop a proper understanding of the universe? Is he trained to function effectively as a citizen?

The *fifth* challenge is in regard to vocational education. The problem of vocational education has been squarely faced and solved with fair success by American educational institutions. Vocational education is justified on two grounds: (1) We remember longest the things we do daily, and excel in the doing of those things for which we have had practice; (2) vocational education admirably fits the student to take his place as a respectable, self-reliant, resourceful citizen in the community. But even in this field, a pertinent question needs to be raised: Shall education concern itself with turning out expert craftsmen, or shall it address itself to the task of turning out men and women of noble character who are also expert craftsmen, each excelling in his or her craft?

The *sixth* and last challenge to formal education is in relation to its role in the social process. By its very nature, formal education is called upon to perform simultaneously two functions, somewhat contradictory: (1) It must propagate the values inherent in the culture; (2) it must train people to explore and introduce new values. Conserving past values and reconstructing society—these two tendencies cannot very well go hand-in-hand; and yet no social order can long remain free from cataclysmic change unless it has these two functions of education well integrated.

It is in terms of this dual problem of conserving values and introducing social change that there arise conflicts between the teacher and the community, between the administrator and the teacher.

In totalitarian societies, formal education may not address itself to the problem of exploring the need for change in the content of its ideology or in the structure of its society. The framework of democratic society, on the other hand, permits the citizen-educator both to conserve old values and to introduce new changes, without disruption of the social order and without loss of status (or life) to the citizen-educator.

By the logic of the dharmic order, the educator in every culture plays the triple role of prophet, innovator, conserver.

8. EDUCATION IN SOVIET SOCIETY

In more ways than one the Soviet Union provides a laboratory for the study of an integrated cultural framework emerging under the impact of a new ideology. Enjoying the first flush of triumph and enthusiasm, Soviet leaders tried to make a complete break with the past, with capitalist ideology, with bourgeois ideas and practices. All the basic institutions of society were modified to conform to the communist ideology. Rules for marriage and divorce, structuralized into institutions under the Czarist regime, were abolished: A man and a woman simply could go to the marriage bureau and register themselves as husband and wife. Likewise, no impediments were put in the way of divorce: either party went to the bureau and registered his or her separation from the spouse. And children were to be taken care of by the State as in Plato's *Republic*. Experience, however, led Soviet leaders to see the wisdom of age-old regulations for marriage and divorce, esteemed by capitalist society; and today in the Soviet Union, divorce is more difficult to obtain than in some of the states in the United States. Likewise, the inner autonomy, if not the sanctity, of the family has been restored in the Soviet Union.

Similarly, in the field of education the Soviet Union has gone through several modifications and, today, has a rigorous curriculum for the grade school, the high school, and the university more in conformity with the strict standards of Czarist academicians and of American and European capitalist academicians of the pre-progressive education era.

In the twenties Professor Herbert A. Miller, the American sociologist, was visiting the new-born Soviet Union. The then Minister of Education, Lunacharsky, and other leaders of the Soviet Union plied Professor Miller with questions about the basic theories and practices of American education. Answering their queries as best he could, Professor Miller told them that for definitive answers to American educational theory and practice they should approach Professor John Dewey. Professor Dewey visited the Soviet Union in 1928 and sold to Soviet leaders the dominant ideas of pragmatism, of scientific approach, and of progressive education.

For a decade or so, the Soviet Union tried out the Dewey pedagogy on a national scale. Experience proved to them the validity of some of Dewey's ideas and the invalidity of others. Retaining in their reorganized educational system those aspects of Dewey pedagogy that had relevance to the strengthening and advancing of Soviet citizens, the Soviet Union reworked its curriculum and recast its theory in terms of the generation of power for Soviet society: cutting out the frills of progressive education, insistence upon intellectual discipline, emphasis upon science and mathematics as well as upon communist ideology, instituting of a system of rewards and punishments—a highly capitalistic device and bourgeois notion, which we are in process of forgetting and the Soviet Union is utilizing most effectively in the strengthening of its cultural base.

The attitude of Soviet children toward school and school work is very serious because Soviet culture inculcates that success in life depends on success in school. The Soviet educational pattern is different from our 8 : 4 : 4 ratio.

Seven years of grade school or elementary schooling and three years of secondary schooling, roughly, correspond to our twelve-year elementary and secondary education, with this difference that more is expected of and achieved by Soviet pupils in those ten years than is achieved by our high school graduates. For instance, the graduate of a Russian *grade school* would have "a good knowledge of the Russian language, one foreign language, mathematics and sciences." (5). So far as their knowledge of the world of human beings is concerned, it must be confessed that their view is definitely distorted by "social education."

Farm children have available to them schooling up to the 7th grade, and sometimes up to the 10th grade. Some of the prospective factory workers attend primary school for the first four years only and then enter special trade schools, while others may take in 7 or 10 years of regular schooling before going to work in factories.

Technicums, or special secondary schools for the training of technicians, may be entered after the seventh year of general schooling. The technicums have a three- to four-year course, and there are 4,000 of them in the Soviet Union with an enrollment of 2,000,000. "Currently some 600,000 students are admitted to them each year." (5).

Heavy emphasis upon science and mathematics is evident from the work-load of the Russian senior in high school (10th grade). He "*is spending one third of his classroom time on science and another quarter of his time on math, mechanical drawing, and applied technology. This means that a graduate from secondary school who wishes to become a technician, engineer or scientist has already a good start toward such a career.*" (5).

Only the very best students from among secondary school graduates are admitted to higher educational institutions; hence their number is limited. Thus, for instance, out of 1,100,000 high school seniors in 1954-55, only 286,000 students were admitted to institutions of higher learning in 1955-56. "The total of students enrolled in institutions of higher education—institutes and universities—runs about 2,000,000," of whom 30 to 40 per cent are "correspondence students" employed in full-time jobs. (5). This compares satisfactorily with our enrollment in American colleges and universities of 2,659,021 in 1950, not so favorably with our enrollment of 3,450,000 in 1956-57.

"Higher education in the Soviet Union takes from four to six years for a diploma. In the sciences, however, even after such a course, the student often continues in graduate work—mostly research—for another three to four years to receive the title of Candidate of Sciences—equivalent to an American Ph.D. Completion of such a graduate course fits a student to become a teacher in higher education or a research scientist. These professions are at the top of the Soviet pay scale." (5). According to Dr. Samuel B. Gould, formerly President of Antioch College and now Chancellor of the University of California at Santa Barbara, "The average annual salary for a college professor in the United States is $5,400; his Russian counterpart earns $35,000 annually and more." (1).

It may be pointed out that in Russian higher education there is nothing to correspond to our notions of general education and liberal arts education. What we seek to achieve within the framework of general education and liberal arts education, Soviet society seeks to achieve through indoctrination in the communist ideology and through interpretations of art and literature as well as political and international events in conformity with the tenets of communism.

Why and how the Russian schools are successful in turning out scientists, technicians and engineers has been well answered by Mr. Thomas P. Witney (5), Associated Press Foreign News Analyst (to whom, among others, I am indebted for some of the information on Soviet education detailed in this chapter):

The basic reasons that Russian schools are good in training future engineers, scientists, technicians and workers are that the teachers are excellent and devoted to their work and that the pupils are serious about learning.

Russian teachers put no stock in the ideas of progressive education which are so popular in American teachers' colleges. They base their work on a strict system of rewards for students who do well and punishments for those who fail.

They grade all students in all subjects on a nationwide 5-4-3-2-1 basis in which 5 represents top accomplishments and 2 or 1 failure. Grades determine the progress of a child in school and are important criteria for selection of those to go on to higher education.

There are no elective subjects. All pupils take the same universal curriculum which emphasizes fundamentals.

The teacher is expected to be friendly but authoritative, and his or her position is not to be questioned by either pupils or parents. Pupils wear uniforms and follow certain strict rules in personal appearance and classroom behavior.

Homework assignments are given regularly and must be done. Examinations are given periodically on a nationwide basis to test both pupils and teachers.

Standards of passing and failure are held to be absolute. Teachers are judged by authorities on the basis of the smallness of percentage of failures in their classes.

Extracurricular activities are encouraged—but not permitted to interfere with studies.

Political indoctrination in patriotism and loyalty to the Soviet system occupies an important place in Soviet education. This takes place both in classes, particularly in the history course, and outside classes in the Pioneers (Communist children's organization) and the Komsomol (the Young Communist League).

The place which science occupies in the Soviet schools is worth particular note. A Russian student who graduates from the 10th grade has already acquired a thorough knowledge of physics, chemistry and biology and has learned rudiments of astronomy and psychology. In addition, he has had a full grounding in mathematics, and has received instruction in mechanical drawing and a good deal of practical technology.

Finally, Soviet society is now engaged in establishing boarding schools, somewhat after the fashion of academies established in this country after the Revolution. In 1956 Communist Party Secretary Nikita S. Khrushchev directed the establishment of a new boarding school in Moscow. The plan is to enroll one million Russian school children in these boarding schools by 1960. "They are intended to teach and indoctrinate an elite of specially educated young people, free of family influence and ties, who will dedicatedly serve the Soviet Communist Party." (5). Shades of Plato!

As for higher education, "most Soviet students in institutes and universities receive scholarships paying their tuition and some of their living expenses, but in return for this they must, when they graduate, accept assignments wherever the Soviet government chooses to send them" (5). That there are no privately controlled schools at any level in the Soviet Union goes without saying.

9. SOVIET SCHOOL REORGANIZATION LAW OF 1958

In order "to strengthen the ties of school with life," the USSR Supreme Soviet adopted a new education law on December 24, 1958. "The major intent of the new law is to combine education with socially productive labor, to help hasten the process of eliminating the separation between mental and manual labor which was so characteristic of the old society." (*USSR*, No. 5 (32), p. 38). The new education law lays out the pattern for a combination of study and work. "From the very first grade, children are to be prepared psychologically to make their future contribution as socially productive workers. They will be taught to do work commensurate with their age level. They will have work lessons at school workshops and on school experimental plots. As they grow older, these lessons will be increasingly supplemented with practical work in factory shops or collective farms." (*Ibid.* p. 39). The educational excellence of Soviet schools is not to be sacrificed in the new emphasis on relating study to work, for "the law stresses the care that must be taken in assuring that the schools function at the very highest possible level" (p. 40).

To quote the author of "The New School Law: Education for Socially Productive Labor," once more (pp. 39-43):

The present universal compulsory seven-year school is to be extended another year, as the first rung in the (new) system of education. Its guiding principle is to prepare the boy or girl for future productive work. It will combine a general and polytechnical education, give the science fundamentals, the basic humanities, and inculcate a respect and readiness for work.

The second rung in the educational ladder for the graduate of the eight-year school will be one of these three, depending upon the desire and inclination of the student. He may (a) take a job and continue his study after work at an evening or correspondence secondary general-education school; he may (b) continue his study to complete the full program of secondary schooling at what is called a general-educational labor polytechnical school; or he may (c) enter a specialized secondary educational establishment called a *tekhnikum* (technicum). . . .

The changeover is to begin with the 1959-60 school year and is to be completed within three to five years . . . More boarding schools are to be established. By 1965 it is expected that they will have as many as 2.5 million children as students, 14 times the number currently enrolled. These will be organized both as eight-year schools and as secondary general-vocational schools.

(As for vocational training), in the eighteen years since the national system of vocational schools was founded, they have trained 10,250,000 young workers. . . . The (new) law provides for a uniform system of vocational training. Urban and rural vocational schools will be opened to provide training for young people who will take up employment in production upon the completion of the eight-year school. The urban schools are to give one- to three-year courses; the rural schools one- to two-year courses.

The new schools will be training skilled workers for more than 800 trades. There will be schools training workers for the metal industries, others for mining, power, chemicals, textile, construction, railroads, motor transport, and so on. . . .

(As for higher education), the principle embodied in the law— the meshing of schooling with productive labor—is carried through to the college level. The country's schools of higher education have been training 260,000 to 290,000 specialists annually and will before long be training 300,000 to 350,000.

Heretofore these graduates have had little training in practical work. The very predominant emphasis on book learning to the virtual exclusion of productive labor has been reflected in the curriculum. . . .

The function of the Soviet school as expressed in the new law is to ensure a creative approach to learning, a love for labor, and the ability to work independently. These fundamental aims, carried through from the earliest days of schooling through the college level, will make for the roundly educated worker, equipped to handle the many and diversified problems of building a communist society.

The need for the school reorganization has been dictated by life itself.

The school reorganization of 1958 in the Soviet Union is bound to be highly successful. It has honorable precedents. In 1937 Mahatma Gandhi enunciated the Wardha Scheme of Education, also known as the Basic Education Scheme. In order to make education self-supporting in a poor country like India, Gandhi advocated a seven-year schooling program imparting "general education, plus a vocation used as a vehicle for drawing out the minds of boys and girls in all departments of knowledge." "For the all-round development of boys and girls all training should so far as possible be given through a profit-yielding vocation," the State to guarantee "employment in the vocations learnt" and to "buy the pupils' manufactures at prices fixed by the State" itself. (3, pp. 89–90).

The basic assumptions of Soviet school reorganization are not unknown to American education. Indeed, one might say that the Soviets have borrowed the entire idea from American education, with slight modifications to suit their requirements. "Working one's way through school"—high school or college—was an idea invented in America. Under the impact of the New Deal and the badgering of unionism, the practice of working one's way through school in America has recently suffered a setback to some extent. Only the obtuse-minded would deny the educational value of earning while learning. Previous generations of Americans, when they entered college, had already developed maturity and self-reliance as a result of earning while learning; while today's generation of American students alas! need counseling and spoon-feeding when they enter college! While we are in process of discarding our own unique educational invention, the Soviet Russians are in process of reorganizing their school system by borrowing our invention, to the end that the future Soviet citizen may have the enriching experience of working his way through school.

In substance, the Soviet school reorganization law of December, 1958, aims at helping students to work their way through school via a planned vocation. I prefer the unplanned vocation of American education; but the Soviet leaders have devised a scheme in harmony with their ideology and thoroughly in accord with the highest pedagogical principles.

10. PRESENT TRENDS AND FUTURE PROSPECTS

The successful launching of two Sputniks in October and November of 1957 by Soviet scientists and their German collaborators has had a tremendous impact on American society in general and on American education in particular. We may look forward to a reevaluation of some of the basic theories and practices in American education.

First. Revitalization of American education may take the form of (*a*) cutting out the frills of progressive education, (*b*) infusing a new sense of dedication to the high calling of teaching among prospective teachers, (*c*) enhancement of the status of the teacher, not necessarily in terms of higher salary though that may partly help, (*d*) promotion of basic research by universities, government agencies and by industry, (*e*) expecting more of our students at all levels of schooling, (*f*) re-introducing the system of rewards and punishments at all educational levels.

Second. We may look forward to a greater infusion of general education in vocational training.

Third. Special opportunities and institutional procedures are apt to be developed on a large scale for the training of bright students.

Fourth. Adult Education programs, formal as well as informal, through correspondence and evening classes, are likely to be multiplied and enriched. The public platform as a tool of promoting adult education has been in the doldrums since World War II, but is apt to be revitalized in some form or other in the future. Radio and TV, especially the closed circuit TV programs of an educational nature, are already doing good work in the field and may increase their effectiveness in the future.

Fifth. Education, the American's second love, may be re-evaluated in terms of a worship not just of education as such but in terms of a high premium on scholarship. "Eggheads" are not people to be scoffed at, but to be highly respected. When our culture begins to put as high a premium on scholarship and superior academic achievement as on athletics, we may witness the dawn of a new educational era in American society.

Sixth. We are on the threshold of a new era which demands an intensive analysis of the primary and secondary functions of education. American schools are today being criticized by some for doing too little in the way of secondary functions and by others for doing too much. Is the primary aim of education to train the whole man or to develop his intellectual powers? Is the primary aim of education to accomplish social adjustment or to develop the intellect, or to develop a rounded personality, or yet to develop a balanced *Weltanschauung* (world-view)?

Today American public schools have taken over most of the functions of the family, including custodial care. Should this trend toward assumption of secondary functions be reinforced or curbed?

These are some of the fascinating problems young Americans will have to answer in their role as citizens, regardless of whether they enter the teaching profession or any other profession.

REFERENCES

1. SAMUEL B. GOULD: "A Turning Point in Education." *Association of American Colleges Bulletin*, Vol. XLIV, No. 2 ; May, 1958, pp. 325–38.
2. E. D. GRIZELL: *Origins and Development of the High School in New England Before* 1865. New York: Macmillan, 1923.
3. HARIDAS T. MUZUMDAR: *Mahatma Gandhi*: *Peaceful Revolutionary*. New York: Charles Scribner's Sons, 1953.
4. *Statistical Abstract of the United States*, 1957. Washington: U. S. Govt. Printing Office, 1957.
5. THOMAS P. WHITNEY: " Reds Take Their Schools Seriously." *Denver Post*, Dec. 8, 1957.

NOTE: *USSR*, the illustrated monthly, published by the Soviet Embassy in Washington, D.C., has been carrying articles on Soviet education in most of the issues of 1958 as well as of 1959. It is regrettable that the issue, quoted in the Chapter, carries no mention of the month of publication. I received it early in May, 1959, if my memory serves me aright. It contains pictures celebrating May Day festivities in the Soviet Union ; these pictures obviously must have been taken on May Day in some previous year.

This practice of Soviet leaders not to identify precisely and unequivocally anything, even the month of publication of a given issue of *USSR*, is in keeping with their ever-present tendency to hide from world-public (even Soviet public) gaze anything and everything that may perchance lead to objective discussion and criticism. This secretiveness, this defense mechanism, on the part of Soviet leaders, is in my judgment entirely unnecessary. If they are still in doubt, let me assure them that in the fields of education, technology, and certain aspects of " public relations," they have " arrived," and are in some respects doing better than we are.—H.T.M.

CHAPTER 40

THE SOCIO-STATE ORDER

SOCIETY is characterized by two "organic" features: order and stability on the one hand and change on the other. In the last chapter, it was pointed out that no social order could escape cataclysmic change if it did not provide mechanisms for conserving the values of the past as well as for introducing new changes.

In order to understand the nature of the socio-state order, it is necessary, now, for us to gather up all the terms we have thus far used to describe society and to point out their specific connotations. In this book we have not used any term, any conceptual tool, without defining it. At the journey's end in our quest for an understanding of society, a final and enriched meaning of those conceptual tools may be set forth.

1. SOCIETY AND SOCIETAL ORGANIZATION

The term society, as used by sociologists, is indeed a complex of groups as well as a complex of institutions (*supra*, CHAPTER 3); but it needs to be pointed out that the term society as a conceptual tool is an abstraction, a logical construct. The essence and central features of this abstraction, society, are to be found wherever human beings are living together. But society can neither be seen nor studied, except by way of a logical construct. What we actually see and study is a society or a set of societies: English society, American society, Chinese society, Japanese society, Hindu society, etc.

Each society may be studied in terms of what the sociologists call Social Organization, which encompasses associational activities as well as institutional procedures. Anthropologists have pioneered in describing the Social Organization of certain tribes. The classic study, *Patterns of Culture* (3), by Ruth Benedict, for instance, attempts to give an insight into the way of living of three interesting tribes—the Kwakiutl, the Dobu, the Zuni—by describing their associational activities and institutional procedures.

The term social organization is, however, ambiguous. It has two meanings. On the one hand, it refers to society in its concrete manifestation, as just pointed out; and, on the other hand, it refers to institutional groups or associations in societies, such as fraternities and sororities on college campuses, to civic clubs, chambers of commerce, etc. Hence we should avoid using the word social organization as encompassing the totality of a society; instead, we should use the word societal organization, and retain the term social organization for a formal group in society. With this difficulty in terminology out of the way, we may proceed to define societal organization. The following two definitions are in substance identical but view societal organization from different perspectives:

(1) Societal organization is the well integrated *relationship* between institutions and groups articulated in such a way as to achieve optimum *social control* and to enable various groups and individual members of society to satisfy their needs and interests.

(2) Societal organization is a network of *relationships* conditioning the mode of behavior of each member of the population and prescribing ways and means for the *participation* of each member in the wide range of activities possible and permissible within a given cultural framework.

Within this frame of reference, it is evident that Soviet society—societal organization—differs in marked ways from American society or societal organization. Societal organization may be studied in terms of (*a*) structure and (*b*) functions. The structure is embodied in the folkways, mores and institutions; and functions comprise the various activities of associations.

Each society, each societal organization, is an integrated, well-knit whole, except in periods of crisis and transition. " The various parts of the social structure do successfully interlock. The family structure, the economic organization, the class system, education, religion, and politics—these are different aspects of the same total phenomenon, and they reinforce one another." (4, p. 704).

2. CLARIFICATION OF OTHER CONCEPTUAL TOOLS

(1) Group is the fundamental datum of sociology and grouping is one of the fundamental social processes. The term group stands for

any aggregation of individuals, with reciprocal interstimulation among the members, brought together by an interest.

(2) An association is a functional or purposive group.

(3) A functional group is a group which functions (i.e., operates) as a unit and which has a function (i.e., a purpose) in the social order and which, therefore, by the fact of its operation and purposiveness enables its members to realize their interests. A functional group being synonymous with an association, this definition of a functional group gives a fuller description of an association.

(4) The State is an association of all citizens within a given area into a political body; i.e., in terms of power relations; that is, the State is the entire group, the whole people, functioning politically within a given area. Of course, the State is also an institution, that is to say, a collective mode of behavior that has outlasted a generation and is kept in operation by rituals, symbols, and self-renewing associations, officers and citizens. From the institutional standpoint, the State is the embodiment of Danda.

(5) Community comprises the entire group sympathetically entering into a common life within a given area, regardless of the extent of area or State boundaries.

(6) The nation, characterized by strong ingroup loyalty, is a militant organization—militant, potentially or actually—of a community delimited by the State. "Indeed, not only did the Nation-State arise from competition and conflict; it also thrived on competition and conflict, and it has been armed to the teeth for ever-present competitions and conflicts" (6, pp. 116–17). While the civilization of the Nation-State is in process of disruption, the emerging nations of the Orient are substituting militant political nationalism for their cultural nationalism.

(7) Society is a complex of groups in reciprocal relationships, interacting upon one another within the cultural context, enabling human organisms to carry on their life-activities and helping each person to fulfill his special wishes and accomplish his special interests in association with his fellows.

(8) The distinctions between community (*Gemeinschaft*) and society (*Gesellschaft*) need to be brought out sharply.

In the *Gemeinschaft* the group has a life of its own, superior to that of its temporary members. The group is an end in itself. In the *Gesellschaft* the group is merely a means to an end. In the *Gemeinschaft* we have faith, customs, natural solidarity, common ownership of property, and a common will. In the *Gesellschaft* we have doctrine, public opinion, fashion, contractual solidarity, private property, and individual will. (7, p. 280).

Community and community spirit are, in other words, distinguished from society and its contractual solidarity by the fact that members of the community emphasize their common will and commonweal—parks, for instance, in the domain of material culture, and mores in the domain of non-material culture—whereas members of society emphasize their rights, rely on laws, and operate on the basis of contract and formal legalism.

(9) The correlation between institution and association may be re-emphasized. Institutions are prescribed ways of doing things, and associations act in terms of those prescriptions.

(10) Finally, we may point out that whereas problems of intragroup relations involving interpersonal relations fall within the purview of ethics, problems of intergroup relations involving relationships between groups are of the nature of politics—that is to say, they underline pressures and rival quests for power.

3. ANALYSIS OF THE SOCIO-STATE ORDER

The social element in the original nature of man gives rise to a million and one groupings in society as well as to the socio-state order, with the State at the apex.

The ever-present operational characteristics of a group are: (1) Mental and emotional interstimulation of its members, (2) give and take among members, (3) constraint over "unlimited" freedom of action for some or all of its members, (4) attainment and enjoyment of status by its members within the group and vis-a-vis other groups. Thus, for ensuring order and stability, the problem of social control, of coercion, of Danda, is central to the functioning of any group.

As the supreme embodiment of Danda, the State enjoys sovereignty. Indeed sovereignty is an essential attribute of State: We cannot conceive of a State without sovereignty. Sovereignty means unchallenged power to regulate the behavior of members of the ingroup. Sovereignty implies unlimited freedom—the state of being a law unto itself, being held accountable to no one.

The two attributes of the State, Danda and sovereignty, are possessed by each group, in some form or another, attenuated or wide-ranging. Social organizations, such as churches, trade unions, associations of employers, etc. exercise power of constraint over their members and, in a measure, over members of outgroups as well; they define the status of their members and regulate both intragroup and intergroup relationships.

A respectable line of social and political philosophers—among them: Jean Bodin (1530-96), Johannes Althusius (1557-1638), Otto von Gierke (1844-1921), F. W. Maitland (1850-1906) and Miss Mary P. Follett (1868-1933)—have analyzed society and state as a complex of groups, each group having a "personality," real, according to some; fictitious, according to others. Be that as it may, in some ways each group acts as a little State or shares the powers of the State. And the State, at least in a democratic society, does not violate their "personality."

Sociological analysis of the socio-state order, thus, reveals the nature of the State to be pluralistic. The pluralistic concept of the State, in substance, says that State sovereignty is compounded of the powers of a series of groups within society, "all having some of the qualities of public law and most of them showing clear signs of a life of their own, inherent and not derived from the concession of the State, (which) could recognize and guarantee . . . the life of these associations—the family, the club, the union, the college, the church; but it no more created life than it created the individual, though it orders his birth to be registered," as pointed out by J. N. Figgis (1866-1919), the English exponent of the pluralistic concept of the State, (5, p. 320, quoted). (In this quotation, I have taken the liberty to substitute the term 'associations' for the term 'societies.'—H.T.M.) In other words, the State, expressing itself as political authority, is to be viewed as an association, not as an overlordship.

Thus, from the functional standpoint, the State is one of the associations in society; though all-inclusive, yet one among many. And from the structural standpoint, the State is one of the five primary institutions of society.

The State has been endowed with personality by some political philosophers, with mystical powers by others, with real existence by most. Actually, the State, like society, is an abstraction, a logical construct, a very serviceable conceptual tool. The State can be studied objectively in terms of its manifestation in government, a specific government in power, which serves as the delegated agent of the State.

There are a number of theories about the origin and functioning of the State, chief among which are: (1) The Natural-Organic Theory of the Origin of the State, (2) Divine Origin of the State, (3) Social Contract Theory, (4) Conflict Theory, and (5) the Organismic Theory.

4. Aristotle: The Natural Theory of the State

Aristotle is one of the earliest and best exponents of the natural-organic theory of the State. It must be remembered, however, that to the Greeks the *polis* (the City-State) meant the community, the socio-state, not just a political State. Having asserted that the family was natural (*supra*, CHAPTER 36), Aristotle goes on to make the point that the State, too, was a natural development, derivable from the social nature of men (*Politics*, I, 2 : 5–9):

The family is the association established by nature for the supply of man's everyday wants . . . but when several families are united and the association aims at something more than the supply of daily needs, then comes into existence the village; and the most natural form of the village appears to be that of a colony from the family composed of the children and grandchildren. . . . When several villages are united in a single community, perfect and large enough to be nearly or quite self-sufficing, the State comes into existence for the sake of a good life. And therefore if the early forms of society are natural, so is the State; for it is the end of them, and the completed nature is the end. For what each thing is when fully developed we call its nature, whether we are speaking of a man, a horse, or a family. . . . Hence it is evident that the State is a creation of nature, and that man is by nature a political animal. And he, who by nature and not by mere accident is without a State, is either above humanity or below it; he is the

'Tribeless, lawless, hearthless one'

whom Homer denounces—the outcast who is a lover of war; he may be compared to a bird which flies alone.

Here the natural-organic growth of the State is attributed to the social nature of man. The organismic theory of State thought of the State, the body politic, as a person with various organs performing in society tasks analogous to those performed by bodily organs in the body. The organismic school is thoroughly discredited, but its central concepts, interdependence of parts and the integrated wholeness of the State, have reinforced the original contributions of the natural-organic school.

5. THE DIVINE ORIGIN OF THE STATE

The Divine Origin Theory maintains that the State was divinely instituted among men. This theory was enunciated among peoples of diverse racial and religious backgrounds. It may still be held by some people, but sociological analysis proves its invalidity.

Wherever and whenever the Divine Origin of the State theory was in the ascendant, its exponents developed a corollary, namely, the Divine Right of Kings. In England, this theory of the divine right of kings was sedulously promoted by the Tudor dictatorship, from Henry VII to Elizabeth I, and even by the early Stuarts.

6. SOCIAL CONTRACT THEORY

The basic concepts of the Social Contract theory were set forth by Buddha in the sixth century B.C., and by Plato in the fourth century B.C. Chief among its celebrated modern exponents are Hobbes, Locke and Rousseau (6, pp. 122–26).

Hobbes, Locke and Rousseau. The theory of Social Contract premised a pre-social state of man, "the state of nature," which was conceived to be either utter lawlessness, "a war of each against all," or idyllic blissfulness, freedom for all and goodwill of each toward all. The former point of view was espoused and admirably expounded by Thomas Hobbes (1588-1679), the latter by John Locke (1632-1704) and Jean Jacques Rousseau (1712-78).

The theory of the original sin of man led straightway to Hobbes's "state of nature," redemption from which was possible for man only through the grace of the all-powerful, autocratic, regulative Leviathan, the despotic State. The theory of the divinity of man, on the other hand, led to the Rousseauesque type of "state of nature," a picture of idyllic blissfulness, from which man fell because of the corruptions of human nature engendered, among other factors, by the emergence of private property. The State, broadbased upon democracy, according to Locke and Rousseau, was essential to help man overcome the corruptions of human nature.

Elements of the Social Contract Theory. The elements of the Social Contract theory are: (1) That there was a pre-social state of man, "the state of nature." (2) That men in "the state of nature" had to enter into a contract or a compact one with another in order to regulate the wicked propensities of their nature, both original and acquired. (3) That, once the compact was entered into, "the state of nature" ceased to exist and man became, in Aristotelian phraseology, a "political animal," either as a "member" or as a "citizen" of the State.

A Critique of the Social Contract Theory. That man could ever live in a so-called pre-social state is denied by Sociology. The very birth of man, it is apparent both a priori and a posteriori, is dependent upon at least two human beings, the parents. Man is neither born in a vacuum nor can he thrive in isolation. The existence of parents, man and woman, presupposes the existence and awareness of their parents and relatives. The family, in the biological sense, is an integral part of man's being. Indeed, from the very origin of the human species, man has found himself surrounded by fellow men; which is to say, man has always been born in society, never in a presocial state. A group of families, endogamous among themselves, would represent a clan, a small society. Exogamous clans would lead to the formation of a tribe, a large society. Some anthropologists, with justification, describe the modern nation as a tribe.

In other words, there could possibly be no period of time in human history when man at birth did not have membership in at least the family. Indeed, we are justified in saying that at all periods of time man at birth has had membership in the family and in the clan, if not in the tribe as well.

Sociology further leads us to believe and Anthropology corroborates that rules and regulations, rituals and taboos, evolved through the trial and error method and through the experience of preceding generations, have been part and parcel of every cohesive group. The rules and regulations of primitive society, along with the machinery for their enforcement and for punishment of transgressors, correspond to the laws and regulations of the modern State. In other words, in every society, be it the most primitive or the most advanced, there is present the State, if by State is meant a regulative machinery in society with power to coerce obedience to its "laws."

Contributions of the Social Contract School. The Social Contract school was wrong on both of its major counts: Man was never born in a pre-social state nor did he have the liberty to enter into a compact to "create" the State. Even so, the Social Contract theorists were responsible for the "institution" of government, for the "creation" of a new State, in the New World on a contractual basis among the Thirteen Colonies. Rousseau's spirit is present in the American Declaration of Independence; his teachings and the teachings of Montesquieu (1689-1755) and Locke set the pattern for the democratic State of the United States of America: the general will; popular sovereignty; sovereignty, indivisible, infallible, inalienable, universal; checks and balances (Montesquieu); contractual relations among citizens.

Furthermore, under the impulse of the speculations of the Social Contract school, the State machinery began to be looked upon as the outgrowth of human experience, not something too mystical or too divine to be comprehended by mere mortals. The Social Contract theory once and for all enunciated the doctrine that the State was, and is, one of the institutions of human society, capable of investigation, observation and improvement—or abolition, according to Karl Marx as well as the exponents of anarchism.

7. Conflict Theory

With the new concept that the State was a man-made institution
and with the new tools of analysis, provided by the Social Contract
theorists, the way was prepared for an intensive and fruitful analysis
of the origin of the State and its functioning in the socio-cultural
milieu.

The conflict theory of the origin of the State has had venerable
exponents: Heraclitus, sixth century B.C., in Greece; Polybius
(second century B.C.), Lucretius (96?-55 B.C.), and Horace (65-8
B.C.) in Rome; Ibn Khaldun, the Arabic scholar of the thirteenth
century in Spain; Niccolo Machiavelli (1469-1527); Bodin and
others.

Among the modern exponents of the conflict theory are Karl
Marx (1818-83), Ludwig Gumplowicz (1838-1909), Gustav Ratz-
enhofer (1842-1904), Franz Oppenheimer (1864-1943), and Achille
Loria (1857-1943) (2, *passim*).

The conflict theory of the origin of the State is subscribed to by
a number of sociologists as well as anthropologists. Its essence is
that the State arose from conflict between two clans or tribes, as a
regulatory mechanism. In order to enjoy the fruits of the conquest—
loot and subjection of the outgroup—the conquering group would
set forth certain directives and procedures, rules and norms, to the
end that the new social order would not be disturbed.

Karl Marx, the socialists and the communists have a variant
theory, namely, that the State arose not out of intergroup conflict
but out of intragroup conflict between the oppressor and the
oppressed.

That the element of conflict may well have played a part in the
development of the State there is no need to deny—especially in its
elaboration. But it is well to remember that cooperation is as basic a
social process as are competition and conflict. What we call the
State could very well have existed and operated among a peaceful
tribe, knowing neither intragroup nor intergroup conflict.

A cooperative, peaceful tribal society would have evolved mechanisms for conserving old values, for introducing new values, and,
most important, for assigning status to its members. If a status

society does not exhibit the paraphernalia of the modern State, it nevertheless does have all the mechanisms of the State in a rudimentary form. The transition from Status to State may well be attended by conflict, either intragroup or intergroup, the latter more likely than the former. And the process of sanctifying property rights and the new status of the conqueror would be synonymous with the process of the emergence of the State.

8. A Sociological Analysis of the State

The modern nation-state arose, as pointed out in Chapters 16 and 17, out of competition and conflict, and it has so far thriven on conflict. That the modern State is intimately tied to the institution of war must be properly grasped. This means that before war can be abolished, certain modifications would need to be made in the institution of the State.

Historically the State has performed at least five functions:

1. It has served as a mechanism and symbol for generating the collective power of the citizens in a thoroughly respectable and approved manner.

2. It has functioned as a law unto itself, accountable only to itself and to nobody else, not even to its citizens. "Reasons of State"— this argument is all-sufficing.

3. It has served as a mechanism for the distribution of goods and services.

4. It has served as a mechanism for the resolution of conflict among its "members."

5. It has served as an instrument for the safeguarding of the "national interest" in a world of competitive and conflicting as well as cooperative "national interests."

The State as the Embodiment of Danda. The State is sometimes defined as a political association of the citizens. This is a definition in a circle. But the meaning is not far to seek. In its functional aspect, the State is an equilibrium of pulls, pressures, politics, (i.e., undue influences), lobbies, competitions and conflicts. The equilibrium is normally maintained through the peaceful processes of adjudication. But above and below and interwoven with the process of adjudication is Danda, the power to punish. Indeed, the State may as well be

22

defined, from one standpoint, as an embodiment of Danda, i.e., of brute force.

Rarely does the State resort to Danda in its dealings with ingroup members. The judicial machinery providing punishment of the guilty, unto death where necessary, takes care of stresses and strains and tensions that are bound to arise in organized relations among human beings.

The New World States Minimize Danda. In its dealings with other entities like unto itself, the State relies upon Danda, upon brute force, as the first recourse and also as the last recourse, because no judicial machinery acceptable to States with conflicting interests or points of view has yet been evolved, either on a world scale or even on a Regional scale. The best approach to a judicial machinery encompassing two or more States is to be found in the New World —in the U.S.-Canadian Treaty of Arbitration and Conciliation, and in the Pan-American Union, renamed the Organization of American States (OAS).

All States in the world excepting those in the New World are wedded to the proposition that might makes right; that God is on the side of the big battalions (a cynical English saying, this!); that diplomacy is an arm of the war department; that, persuasion failing, the "mailed fist" must come into operation. This glorification of brute force is characteristic not alone of Totalitarian States; it is true of all States.

Nature of Sovereignty. It is only on the basis of worship of brute force that we can understand the nature of sovereignty so jealously regarded by all States. Is not one of the ingredients of sovereignty the right to make war and peace at will? And is not another ingredient the right to maintain armaments at will, limited only by the State's capacity or by its estimate of the need? Whenever we have had bilateral or multilateral agreements for maintenance of armaments not above the prescribed level, the States concerned have experienced partial renunciation of sovereignty. But please note how the Outlawry of War Treaty—the Kellogg-Briand Pact of 1926—was whittled down with reservations by the Great Powers of Europe and Asia, until the outlawry part of the Treaty was fully outlawed!

Throughout history the State has acted as an embodiment of brute force, but it is only recently that we have been able to investigate the nature of society and its institutions including the institution of the State, the institution of property, and the institution of war. For this insight into the institutions and processes of society we are indebted, first, to the School of Social Contract theorists and, second, to the rise of Sociology.

"A Sociological View of Sovereignty," propounded by Professor John R. Commons (1862-1945), should be acceptable to sociologists. Comparing certain attributes of private property with those of sovereignty, Commons said (2, pp. 131–32, quoted):

Private property is but another name for that coercive relation existing between human beings through which the proprietor commands the services of others. This is also sovereignty.

Commons made an original contribution when he broke down sovereignty into its three ingredients—coercion, order, and (moral) right. Commons' theory of sovereignty may be summarized in his own words (2, p. 133, quoted):

Society precedes the state just as it precedes the family, the church, the corporation, the political party. It unites all of these as a tree unites its branches.

The state is the coercive institution of society. It is not an ideal entity superimposed on society, but is an accumulated series of compromises between social classes, each seeking to secure for itself control over the coercive elements which exist implicitly in society with the institution of private property. Sovereignty is built up gradually by a transfer of coercive power from private property to social organization (societal organization—H.T.M.).

We have three constituents of sovereignty—coercion, order and right. Coercion originates as private property. The struggle for existence causes this to survive in the form of monopoly and centralization. Order emerges as a constituent of sovereignty in place of caprice only when sovereignty has extended over wide areas and when subordinate classes have earned the veto power in determining the sovereign will. Right takes its place as the moral aim of sovereignty when freedom has displaced material and competitive necessity.

A democratic State would minimize coercion and maximize order and right.

Finally, it must be emphasized that the State is one of the institutions of society, like the family, business, education and religion. Just as a human organism functions through the operation of various organs, so society functions through the operation of its institutions. Among institutions, the State occupies a place of pre-eminent authority as the all-encompassing agent of formal social control, and serves as a coordinating and integrating agent in society.

9. TYPES OF STATE

Aristotle conceived the State to pass from one stage to another because of certain defects in each—kingship, constitutional government with the king at the head, aristocracy, oligarchy, tyranny, democracy. A democracy may break up because of (a) disregard for common law, (b) sedition, (c) maldistribution of wealth among the citizens, and (d) the tendency of citizens in a democracy to believe that because they are equal in one respect (in respect of law), therefore they are equal in all respects. (*Politics* v).

Modern nation-states exhibit all the forms of State described by Aristotle. In addition, there is one base of classification of States, not thought of by Aristotle, namely, totalitarian States and democratic States. The Soviet State today is totalitarian, as were the Nazi State in Germany and the Fascist State in Italy. The Soviet State may also be conceivably described as being either an aristocracy or an oligarchy.

Paradoxical as it may seem, a totalitarian State professes to serve the total good of all citizens. It is the logical culmination of a Welfare State—a beehive in which every bee is content to do its allotted part.

In the modern world, we find flourishing (a) absolute monarchy (Arabia, for one), (b) constitutional monarchy (Great Britain), (c) republican form of government (the United States), (d) totalitarian form of government (the Soviet Union). Sometimes oligarchies and aristocracies may masquerade under one of the four forms of government.

10. THE AMERICAN STATE

The American State emerged from conflict with Britain. It was born of contract among the Colonists-Americans, whose Declaration of Independence and Constitution breathe the spirit of the Social Contract theory as well as the spirit of Natural Law and embody the results of compromise and pragmatic approach. For instance, while Washington and Jefferson manumitted (freed) their slaves, the problem of abolishing slavery was omitted from the Declaration of Independence. Second, the principles embodied in the Bill of Rights, as the first ten amendments to the Constitution are called, were fully known to and cherished by the framers of the Constitution; but those principles were not organically included in the original constitution. The reason for the omission was threefold: (1) fear that the projected federal government might become a leviathan, destructive of the rights of the people and the states; (2) uncertainty, in the realm of theory, whether the basic freedoms should be guaranteed by each of the thirteen states or by their creature, the federal government; (3) desire on the part of exponents of differing schools of thought to evolve an instrument, the Constitution, as a symbol of their new status as a nation-state.

The successful working of federal government over such a vast territory has been one of the enduring achievements of the American people. The Constitution as the basic law of the land has been interpreted and reinterpreted, and modified to suit changing times, in accordance with the legal and constitutional methods and mechanisms provided by the Constitution itself. While others may find it unworkable, the American system of checks and balances—as between the Executive, Legislative and Judicial branches of government—is best suited to the American temper.

The greatest contribution of the American State has been the successful implementation of the famous Northwest Ordinance of July 13, 1787. That Ordinance laid down two political principles: (1) exclusion of slavery from the "Northwest Territory," (2) inclusion of the Territory or territorial units in the Northwest as equal members of the American Nation-State on a par with the original Thirteen States. This second principle threw overboard the old-world practice of subjecting and exploiting territories for the benefit of the "mother" country.

Thanks to the Northwest Ordinance, America is made up of 50 free and equal states, enjoying the sovereignty of commonwealths.

Because of the democratic beliefs of the American people, the form of government evolved had to be Republican. To assure each state the collective power of all states, the principle of federalism was introduced into the government structure. To make sure that the federal government would not be a tyrannical leviathan, "residual powers" were vested in the states and citizens.

The American State is pluralistic in more senses than one: while the President and the Secretary of State hold office in the Federal Government, they deal with other States as representatives of the American people, of the fifty states in the Union. The American State is composed of (a) the Federal Government, (b) State Governments, (c) County and Local Governments.

While Karl Marx's notion of "the withering away of the State" is sociologically invalid and practically unattainable, the concept, "withering away of the state," has been partially realized in the United States of America. Inasmuch as the State is the supreme embodiment of brute force, the withering away of the State would involve the process of divesting the State of the powers and functions that pertain to it as an agency of brute force, that is to say, of the powers and functions of maintaining armaments and of making war and peace at will. This is precisely what happened to each of the Thirteen States when they gave up the most significant of their sovereign rights and powers in favor of the United States of America —they literally experienced "the withering away of the State." The Soviet State, the spiritual child of Karl Marx, has not, on the other hand, after forty years, taken even the first step in the direction of "the withering away of the State." If and when the Soviet State is ready to renounce part of its sovereignty, mankind may experience a world composed of nations with limited sovereignty on the model of the 50 states in the Union—the United Nations of the World.

As for *trends and prospects*, statistics could be marshalled to prove that the federal government has grown big since the days of the founding fathers in every field: in the number of its employees, in income and expenditure, in the size of the national debt, in the number of functions it performs. In the early days, the American State was pragmatic enough to believe in the doctrine of laissez faire and violate it when the circumstances demanded it. Thus among the first laws passed by the First Congress was legislation regarding tariff—protection to infant industries, surely not a let-alone policy. The pendulum later swung in the direction of an interventionist philosophy: The government has an obligation to promote the good life of the citizen. "The general welfare" clause of the Constitution began to be interpreted and reinterpreted to suit changed conditions and the temper of the times. Nostalgically believing as he still does that "That government is best which governs least" (Thoreau), the modern American has resigned himself to government intrusion into his life—and even glories in the philosophy that his government is dedicated to the welfare of the people.

The Welfare State is here to stay. The only problem that remains in the realm of public discussion is: (a) how to achieve the welfare of all citizens, (b) how many more unspecified "residual" powers the federal government should be permitted to appropriate. The American frontiersman, the American pioneer, would shudder to see the all-pervasive role of the American State in the lives of modern citizens.

REFERENCES

1. ARISTOTLE: *Politics* (Jowett's translation).
2. H. E. BARNES: *Sociology and Political Theory*, New York: Knopf, 1924.
3. RUTH BENEDICT: *Patterns of Culture*, New York: The New American Library (Mentor), 14th printing, 1957.
4. KINGSLEY DAVIS et al: *Modern American Society*, New York: Rinehart & Co., 1949.
5. H. W. LAIDLER: *Social-Economic Movements*, New York: Thomas Y. Crowell Co., 1947 (4th printing).
6. H. T. MUZUMDAR: *The United Nations of the World*, 2nd ed., New York: Universal Publishing Co., 1944.
7. C. C. ZIMMERMAN & M. E. FRAMPTON: *Family and Society: A Study of the Sociology of Reconstruction*, New York (now, Princeton, N.J.): D. Van Nostrand Co., 1935.

CHAPTER 41

GLOBAL CULTURAL CATEGORIES

THE twentieth century has been referred to by some as the American Century. If the element of chauvinism be removed from it, the statement describes an objective reality. American movies, radio, TV, refrigerators, cars and globe-girdling airplanes have penetrated the farthest corner of the world, including the countries behind the so-called iron curtain. But this is the American Century in a far different and higher sense. The logic of the One World is inevitably leading mankind to re-enunciate the basic principles of the American Declaration of Independence in terms of a worldwide Declaration of Interdependence. Herewith an attempt is made to formulate such a worldwide declaration (1, pp. 42–44):

1. WORLDWIDE DECLARATION OF INTERDEPENDENCE

When in the course of human events, it becomes necessary for several nations to dissolve the forms of independence, self-competence and sovereignty of States and to create a federal union of interdependent nations, each coequal with the others in status regardless of size of territory, population, natural resources or industrialization, a statement of the causes leading to the change is in order.

We hold these truths to be self-evident: That all men are created equal in the sight of God and ought to be treated as equal in law; that, in the political process, the vote of a citizen, however well placed or richly endowed or highly gifted, counts for no more and no less than the vote of another citizen less fortunate; that, in the economic process, all citizens are entitled to an equitable opportunity for employment and for the enjoyment of the fruits of their labor; that in the cultural process, all citizens and all nations should have unhampered freedom to enjoy the values cherished by preceding generations and to enrich those values by new creative contributions.

That man is endowed by his Creator with certain inalienable rights—that among these are life, liberty and the pursuit of happiness. The attainment of these ends is facilitated by the enjoyment of civil rights by the people of a country. Experience has proved the wisdom of the American Bill of Rights. Entrance into the New World of Tomorrow may be fittingly made through the Plymouth Rock of the American Bill of Rights.

That to secure and maintain these rights is one of the main functions of governments.

That governments, to be acceptable of all men, must derive their powers from the consent of the governed.

That government of the people, by the people, for the people, is most conducive to peace, both internal and external.

That the advances of science and technology have well-nigh annihilated distances in time and space and made the whole world kin—at least physically and materially, if not spiritually. Willynilly, thanks to technology, the world of man has become a small neighborhood. How to develop good neighborliness toward every race and every nation is the challenge of our times.

That the problem of race relations is at bottom a problem of disabusing the minds of members of certain nations, races and religions, who suffer from the curse of the "chosen race" dogma, from racial pride, and from a superiority complex.

That the doctrine of sovereignty is in need of prompt modification; that symbolic nations like Luxembourg or the State of Monaco have outlived their usefulness as separate entities and need to be consolidated with neighbor nations; that even nations such as Denmark, Netherlands, Belgium and others, to speak of the European nations alone for the moment, stand in need of renouncing unlimited sovereignty and becoming members of the European Region.

That unlimited sovereignty of a Nation-State, involving the right to make war and peace at will and the right to maintain armaments, has periodically plunged mankind into war; and, therefore, in the interest of the present generation and of generations to come, the doctrine of Nation-State sovereignty must be modified to conform to the actual status of the forty-eight (now 50) states in the United States of America. The states in the American Union maintain no independent armies of their own nor do they have the right to make war or peace. These aspects of sovereignty are transferred to the United States. In like manner the Nation-States of the world of today must renounce their rights to maintain armaments and to make war and peace in favor of the United Nations of the World of Tomorrow. (This Declaration of Interdependence was penned by the present writer in 1942.)

2. "LIFE, LIBERTY AND THE PURSUIT OF HAPPINESS"

The cultural category of life, liberty and the pursuit of happiness, which the Founding Fathers made an integral part of American culture, promises to become the cultural category of the whole world. Everywhere, Man is interested in living his *life* peacefully, in *liberty* and freedom, and engaging in those activities and pursuits that would bring him *happiness*. The sanctity of life, the value of liberty, freedom to pursue happiness within the cultural framework of one's nation—these values are denied by none. A positive affirmation of these values would electrify the world.

3. LIBERTY AND SECURITY

That every man should have the right and the opportunity to work and to earn his bread is a cultural category made fashionable by the newly emerging culture of the Soviet Union. When the class of exploiter and the class of exploited disappear, then will emerge the true society, as Franz Oppenheimer phrased it. The Soviet Constitution commendably declares, "He who does not work shall not eat." Here the term work means productive labor—it may be work either by hand or by brain.

Complete security would rob man of liberty; unlimited liberty would rob man of security. Hence our One World is engaged in finding a formula for a balance between liberty and security.

4. THE OPEN BOOK OF SCIENCE AND TECHNOLOGY

The scientific outlook was nurtured and today thrives on free, unhindered access to the discoveries and theories among the scientists of the world, who in a sense constitute a brotherhood of Brahmins. The imperative of science is: *Share with others and learn from others.*

This imperative of science recently received a rude jolt, first, at the hands of the United States government and, later, at the hands of the Soviet government. Immersed in the world Armageddon, World War II, the U.S. Government decided to make use of atomic power first for war purposes and later for peaceful purposes. A hush-hush program of research was carried on and led to the development of the first atomic bomb by the U.S.A. The Germans had been on the trail, but had been frustrated when their research laboratories and plants were blasted by British bombers. The Russians, hard pressed though they were by the exigencies of War, nevertheless kept a wary eye on atomic developments in the U.S.A. with the aid of their sleuths. In this they followed in the venerable footsteps of American pioneers who, soon after the Revolution, successfully evaded British laws and brought in men and ideas competent to initiate industrialism in America. (*Cf.* CHAPTER 37).

At the end of World War II, the Russians, too, addressed themselves to the task of developing the A-bomb and the H-bomb. Today, victimized by the psychosis of the cold war, both Russia and America are trying to keep from each other the scientific knowledge gained by each. But regardless of the present posture of affairs, it is safe to say that the imperative of science shall become an accepted worldwide category in our One World in the not distant future. The wholehearted cooperation between Soviet Russian scientists and American scientists, indeed among the scientists of the whole world, during the IGY (International Geophysical Year, 1956-58), in the Antarctic is a happy augury.

5. THE PUBLIC SCHOOL, A NEW WORLDWIDE CATEGORY

The public school system, as pointed out in CHAPTER 39, is in the process of becoming a highly valued global culture pattern. In all national societies, democratic or totalitarian, the public school system is deemed to be an integral part of national life, though it must be pointed out that the adoption and actualization of this new culture pattern is in various stages of realization in the newly freed nations of Asia and Africa, because of (a) lack of funds, (b) lack of physical facilities, (c) lack of trained personnel.

6. ECONOMIC INTERDEPENDENCE

In spite of the fever of Autarchy on the eve of World War II and during the present cold war period, the reality of the economic interdependence of the world shall be accepted by all nations. Adam Smith's dream of each nation or region specializing in the production of those goods and services it is best suited to produce may yet be realized. Indeed, without its realization, the stability of our One World will always be in danger.

7. INSTRUMENTALITIES FOR EFFECTING CHANGE

Instead of war, which in the past served as an instrumentality for effecting change, the world of tomorrow will devise peaceful methods of change, *machinery for peaceful change.* The League of Nations, even in its death, left mankind some valuable lessons. In the forum of the United Nations, new lessons are being learned whereby the demon of war may be scotched and unjust and inequitable conditions in the status quo may be changed by peaceful methods.

A world organization, whether it be the present United Nations Organization or a modified one with all nations as members, promises to be one of the cultural categories of the world of tomorrow.

Federalism on the United States model is not likely to emerge in the near future; but substantial limitation on each nation's sovereignty, through mutual agreement, is one of the distinct possibilities. This limitation of sovereignty is the only way war can be banished from our world.

8. AHIMSA AND SATYA

Finally, the twin principles around which Mahatma Gandhi (1869-1948) had organized his life are admirably fitted for our small neighborhood world—Ahimsa (non-violence : love) and Satya (truth). Even those who may ideologically choose not to believe in God cannot fail to see the power of these two principles in binding together our small neighborhood world.

Indeed, with these two principles as cultural categories, mankind can get along well with a poor constitution or with no constitution for a world organization.

These two cultural categories are capable of binding and keeping the One World together indefinitely.

REFERENCES

H. T. MUZUMDAR: *The United Nations of the World,* (1st ed., 1942), 2nd ed. New York: Universal Publishing Co., 1944.

APPENDIX

THE SOCIOLOGY OF KNOWLEDGE*

OCCIDENTALS, Chinese, Hindus—we are all guilty of ethnocentrism. But if the civilization of nation-states is collapsing and the One World is emerging before us, the social scientists of the whole world take on an added responsibility to interpret aright different cultural traditions and to help evolve a few categories of thought acceptable to all peoples. Occidental scholars and laymen write books on peace from their biased standpoints and are amazed when other peoples do not wholeheartedly welcome their diagnosis or their prescriptions. That the Occidental is today in possession of power need not be denied, but whether power is to be considered a criterion for the determination of right and wrong may well be questioned.

Occidental sociologists have ably studied the behavior of man within the cultural context of the Occident and have arrived at valid conclusions. They are wrong, however, in considering the validity of their conclusions as being applicable to people in other cultures as well.

Contemporaneously there are four great cultural traditions, each with a special set of categories of its own—the Hindu, the Muslim, the Chinese, the Occidental. (Some would add a fifth—the communist cultural framework, now in process of emergence.) Each has attempted to look at the universe and at the problems of human behavior within the framework of its own culture-correlated categories.

A Chinese philosopher has raised problems of transcending importance for Occidental philosophers and sociologists. In his article "A Chinese Philosopher's Theory of Knowledge" (*The Yenching Journal of Social Studies,* Vol. I, No. 2, January 1939) Professor Chang Tung-sun discusses the sociology of knowledge in a most illuminating way. Here an attempt is made briefly to summarize and set forth Professor Chang's theory of knowledge.

"The Western theory of knowledge," sagely comments Professor Chang, "has taken knowledge as the *universal* knowledge of mankind.

---

* Paper presented at the Annual Meeting of the Midwest Sociological Society held in Kansas City, Missouri, April 12-14, 1956, and published in *The Midwest Sociologist,* Vol. XIX, No. 1, December, 1956, pp. 12–17, under the title, "A Chinese Philosopher's Theory of Knowledge."

As a matter of fact, however, it is only one kind of knowledge, other kinds being present in other cultures."

The sociology of knowledge received great impetus, at least in the Western world, from Marxism. But inasmuch as the Marxist sociology of knowledge is characterized by class interests and antagonisms, it "cannot be properly called a sociological theory of knowledge but rather a class interpretation of knowledge. It is evident that the influence of social relations upon thought will not be adequately accounted for merely in terms of economic interests."

Kant addressed himself to an investigation of "the fundamental conditions of knowledge," without reference to the content of knowledge. "Kant himself thought that he was treating the universal categories employed in the thinking process of all mankind, while as a matter of fact he has treated the forms of thought characteristic only of Western culture." This is not to deny the possibility of "universal categories applying to human thought in general" nor to affirm that "only ethnically and culturally determined forms of thought are possible."

Spengler is eminently right in "attributing the genesis and differences of the categories of thought to cultural differences. A given culture must have a given set of categories. This does not mean that a given culture is derived from a given set of categories, or that a given set of categories gives birth to a given culture. It means that the establishment of culture and categories is one and the same thing. The formation of a given culture lies in the use of a given set of categories, but the relation between them is not in terms of cause and effect. They are two aspects of the same entity."

Professor Chang's four propositions are:

1. A theory of knowledge and cultural history must be treated simultaneously;
2. Not only does concrete social thought have its social background but logical forms and theoretical categories also have their cultural determinants;
3. The difference between Western and Eastern thought can be explained from this point of view;
4. From this we may understand that Western philosophy is nothing but a particular form of knowledge characteristic of and for the use of Western culture.

Knowledge is derived from two sources; perceptions and conceptions. While perceptual knowledge is in a sense private, conceptual knowledge is always public (social, collective). Perceptions must be experienced by each person—mayhap, differentially. The experience of perception can be transmitted to others only by emotive behavior or by description. Conceptions can be communicated through language, obviously a social product. Even so, "It may be noted that perceptual knowledge cannot be outside the conceptual, nor can conceptual knowledge be separated from the perceptual. As a matter of fact, any conceptual knowledge contains perceptual elements and *vice versa*. The difference between the two is always for the mere convenience of discussion. They do not exist separately."

"In so far as the conceptual guides the perceptual, the importance of the former surpasses that of the latter. This point is often neglected by the empiricists, but from the standpoint of cultural history it is desirable to have it emphasized."

"Conceptual knowledge is also interpretative in nature. By interpretation we understand the manipulation of concepts and the employment of categories. For instance, the apprehension of a flower is a perception, but it is an interpretation to say that flowers are derived from leaves, or that the formation of the flower is for the purpose of reproduction. In an interpretation of this kind, at least, the following concepts are being used: any event must have its antecedent; each change must have its cause; and, the final result in a concept of evolution is so much the more derived from interpretation. Therefore, interpretative knowledge, because it contains concepts and results in concepts, is conceptual knowledge. The manipulation of concepts is for the purpose of interpreting perceived facts. Thus, it is evident that conceptual knowledge is interpretative knowledge, and interpretative knowledge is theoretical knowledge."

Pareto has classified theoretical knowledge into two kinds: the experimental and the non-experimental, either of which may be buttressed by the logical and non-logical methods. Pareto's use of the logical and non-logical categories is subject to criticism in that a logic, a real logic, inheres in every culture, regardless of whether or not it conforms to the tenets of formal logic as developed in the West. But he "has made a real point in saying that approval and disapproval of non-experimental knowledge depends upon sentiments, and thereby (he) speaks of the 'logic of sentiment.'"

Carnap, an exponent of the newly arisen Vienna school, has made a valid distinction between the problems of facts and the problems of logic. "The former are those arising from facts while the latter are problems of words symbolizing things, and of the judgments which are made about things. This distinction may be of use by bringing before us the fact that much of our knowledge is not directly related to things, but merely to views about things. This kind of knowledge has a great place in human life. In our discussion we are dealing with this kind of knowledge which in concrete cases is comprised of political thought, social thought, philosophical thought and moral points of view, as well as the theoretical part of religious beliefs. Scientific knowledge, apart from its experimental elements, belongs here also in the form of interpretative theory."

Experimental knowledge is derived from perception; even so, it is worth noting that "experimental knowledge is guided by conceptual knowledge. Whitehead is very clear on this point. According to him, science is a synthesis of two kinds of knowledge, one direct observation, the other interpretation. Thus he speaks of an 'observational order' and of a 'conceptual order.' The former is explained as well as supplemented by the latter. Points of view among scholars may differ as to the priority of the two, but since the emergence of higher animal forms both of them have co-existed. New observations may modify original concepts while new concepts may lead to new points of observation. . . . It is easy to see that experimental knowledge can modify conceptual knowledge, while it is not so obvious to many people that conceptual knowledge may be underlying and guiding the perceptual knowledge."

The social nature of conceptual and theoretical knowledge is discussed by Professor Chang in the following terms: "All experimental knowledge is derived from the senses, and thus is individual and private, in other words, non-social. Consequently, perceptual knowledge can hardly be social knowledge. Yet no knowledge can do away with its social content, the emergence and existence of which occurs only in the field of interpretative knowledge. S. Alexander has pointed out that the problem of valuation has a social nature and that without presupposing society we cannot speak of value. It is needless to say that valuation is possible only in the field of interpretative knowledge. So far as perceptual knowledge is concerned, by the nature of the fact that it is private and individual, there is no problem of objective valuation. The importance of perceptual knowledge is self-evident, while non-experimental knowledge is apparently unimportant because its importance is not so evident, though nevertheless real."

"The reason for the social nature of theoretical knowledge," says Professor Chang, "is not far to seek; it is that it is thinking expressed in terms of language, which in scientific terminology is called 'linguistic thinking.' It is needless to say that language is a social product . . . Although language and thought cannot be identified, they cannot be separated . . . Should we consider the two points together, namely, that thought develops with language and that language is a form of social behavior, it will be clear that apart from the experimental elements all knowledge is social."

"With the cognizance of the determination of thought by social conditions, there develops the sociology of knowledge." That is to say, the theory of knowledge becomes grounded in the social reality—groups and culture, i.e., immediate forces and remote forces. "The immediate forces determine the trend of our thought, while the remote cultural heritage determines the forms in which thought is made possible. All these forces help to determine interpretative knowledge. With different interpretations come different cultures. And, being born into different cultures, people learn to interpret differently. Thus we may use culture to explain categories, and categories to explain mental differences, e.g., those between the West and the East."

Language, a social product and the vehicle of thought including theoretical knowledge, has been classified by Ogden and Richards into "emotive language" and "referential language." "The first is used to arouse, with necessary gestures and appropriate sounds, the corresponding gestures or mental attitudes in the person to whom they are addressed. The latter is used to refer to things and ideas about things, largely in terms of organized symbols or articulate language. According to Darwin, the animal expressions in the form of singing and roaring may be taken as the precursors of human language. Thus emotive language is nearer to elemental expressions and more concerned with mental attitudes, while referential language, being nearer to abstract thinking, is more concerned with grammatical constructions than mere changes in sounds."

"With grammar and sentence-structure comes logic, and in this connection we have to deal for a moment with the nature of logic. Western logicians take it for granted that the object of logic is rules of human reasoning. This assumption, however, is not quite justified. Take Aristotelian logic, for example, which is evidently based on Greek grammar. The differences between Latin, French, English and German grammatical forms do not result in any difference between Aristotelian logic and their respective rules of reasoning, because they belong to the same Indo-European linguistic family. Should this logic be applied to Chinese thought, it will prove inappropriate. This fact shows that Aristotelian logic is based on the structure of the Western system of language. Therefore, we should not follow Western logicians in taking for granted that their logic is the universal rule of human reasoning."

"In so far as the object of logic lies in the rules of reasoning implied in language, the expression of reasoning must be implicitly influenced by language-structure, and different languages will have more or less different forms of logic. Hence the difference between Chinese logic and Aristotelian logic . . . The traditional type of subject-predicate proposition is absent in Chinese logic. According to the usage of Western logic, in such a sentence as 'A relates to B' the form is not a subject-predicate proposition but a relational proposition. Another sentence like 'A *is* related to B' is in the form in question, because there is the distinction between the subject and predicate. For both forms, however, there is in literary Chinese only one, *chia lien yi* . . . . Although we may say colloquially *chia shih lien yi* . . . . the function of the *shih* is that of the so-called 'empty words' . . . . which are used only for emphasis or intonation, without any grammatical function. Both of these Chinese propositions mean the same thing, without grammatical distinction except that the latter is more emphatic. Neither is a subject-predicate proposition. *Lien* relates the two terms *chia* and *yi* but it is not a copula."

Aristotelian logic is based on the Greek sentence-structure, characterized by the subject-predicate form. "Should we alter the sentence structure, the validity of the traditional Aristotelian logic may be questioned."

It is of the essence of Professor Chang's thesis that logic, a method of arriving at knowledge, and, indeed, all knowledge, are culturally conditioned, dependent as they are on language, a social product. The differences in language-structures give rise to different types of philosophical problems.

Aristotelian logic, conditioned by the sentence-structure of Indo-European languages, has given rise to the Occidental problems of philosophy. The subject-predicate sentence of the Greek language required the use of the verb "to be" and its many forms. Inasmuch as "be" is synonymous with "exist" in Indo-European languages, "it is" is translated to mean "it exists." "Because the verb 'to be' has the meaning of existence, the 'law of identity' is inherent in Western logic; without it there can be no logical inference. Western logic, therefore, may be called 'identity-logic'."

The subject-predicate proposition, coupled with identity-logic, leads Western thinkers to the postulation of substance. Underlying the subject is postulated a substratum in thought. The substratum leads to the postulation of substance. The investigation of the nature of substance becomes the central problem of Western philosophy. "For example, when we say, 'this is yellow and hard' yellowness and hardness are the so-called 'attributes' which are attributed to something, the something in this case being 'this.' The 'something' in general is the substratum. With a substratum emerges the idea of 'substance' . . . . This is the reason why in the history of Western philosophy no matter how different the arguments may be, pro and con, about the idea of substance, it is the idea of substance which itself constitutes the central problem."

"Because the idea of substance is related to the idea of causality, most of the sciences are still determined by the concept of causality. . . . We may maintain that there are three fundamental categories in Western thought: substance, causality and atoms. Religion has a foundation in substance. With causality science is developed, and from atoms materialism is derived. Behind these three categories there is another to string them together, namely, that of identity. The French philosopher Meyerson has done a service in pointing out that all scientific theories and quests are concerned with identity. It may be easily seen that with identity there must be substance; with substance there must be causality; and the atom is between the two. Thus Western thought is essentially based on these four categories. Without understanding the importance and priority of these categories, we cannot thoroughly understand Western culture and thought."

"Chinese culture," asserts Professor Chang, "has no relation whatsoever to the above-mentioned categories." Furthermore, Western thought, based on the law of identity, must develop the law of contradiction. of mutual exclusiveness—A and not-A. "But Chinese thought puts no emphasis on exclusiveness, rather it emphasizes the relational quality between above and below, good and evil, something and nothing." Indeed, the Chinese explain above in terms of below as a relational phenomenon, good in terms of bad, yin in terms of yang. Yin is inconceivable to the Chinese mind without its correlate yang. Furthermore, in definitions the Chinese rely on analogies and are not concerned with the requirements of formal logic, Western style, which must set forth the genus and the specific differentia of the subject defined. These considerations lead Professor Chang to suggest that "correlation-logic, non-exclusive classification, (and) analogical definition" are characteristic of Chinese culture.

Finally, the Occidental puts the question: "What is it?" while the Chinese, confronted by the same situation, asks: "How should one react to it?" Western thought is characterized by the what-priority, Chinese by the how-priority. "Neglect of 'what' accounts for the neglect or absence of epistemology in China." The dominance of how man must react to a situation has led Chinese philosophers to concern themselves with human affairs—how man must react to nature, how man must react to fellow man. Chinese thought is supremely concerned with politics and social relationships and the logic of correlation is a more serviceable tool in this field than the logic of identity. "In social phenomena anything may be considered in terms of correlations, such as male and female, husband and wife, father and son, the ruling and the ruled, the civil and military, and so forth. It is but a short step from this realm to that of cosmology. For example, we say, 'with Heaven being superior and the Earth inferior the universe is fixed.'"

In contrast to the traditional Occidental logic of identity, the Chinese logic of correlation is derived from the concept of correlates (and opposites)—*yin* and *yang*, good and evil, thesis and antithesis. In this respect, Chinese logic has certain elements in common with the Hegelian and Marxist dialectic. "Marxism has done away with the law of identity, and has advocated the law of opposition in thinking, being essentially a philosophy concerned with political and social affairs. But its difference from Chinese thought lies in the fact that while Marxism puts emphasis on opposition and thus class struggle, Chinese thought puts emphasis on the result or adjustment of such an opposition. When Mencius said, 'Mental laborers rule while manual laborers are ruled,' the emphasis is in the division of labor, and mutual aid as conceived by him is thus made possible. In contradistinction to the Chinese logic of correlation, the Marxian type of logic may be called the 'logic of opposition.'"

Professor Chang's discussion of theories of knowledge has laid sociologists under a heavy debt. His may be said to be a pioneer effort in the formulation of the sociological theory of knowledge, or the sociology of knowledge. The subject (perceiving agent)-object (external world) relationships have been analyzed by him in terms of (a) "structure" (the outer world—object), and (b) "sensa," (c) "constructions," and (d) "interpretations" (subject—the perceiving and reacting agent). Here is this great Chinese philosopher's theory of knowledge in his own words:

"It seems to me that human knowledge may be considered in four groups, each penetrating into and dependent upon the others. The first is the external 'structure,' which accounts for immediate sensation. The external world being merely 'structure,' we can only know its 'mathematical properties,' to borrow a term from Bertrand Russell. As to its qualitative nature, we know nothing. But it must be pointed out that these mathematical properties are not static and rigid, but flexible and changeable. The second group is the 'sensa,' to use the terminology of neo-realism. Our sensation is a curious thing. Although externally aroused, it is different from the external world in nature. There may be said to be correspondence and not identity between the two. Sensation by its nature is something independent. The third group consists of 'constructions.' The ordinarily perceived tables, chairs, houses, friends and what not, are 'constructions.' These constructions are often taken naively as independent self-existent things. But as a matter of fact, these things are constructed through the perceptions of the observer. The fourth group is what we have already discussed as 'interpretation.' These four groups are interdependent. Comparatively speaking, the first two are more closely related to the external world and, therefore, more objective, while the last two are more closely related to the inner world and, therefore, more subjective. The process from the last two to the first two may be called the process of 'attachment' while the reverse may be called that of 'detachment.' Theoretical knowledge is a process of detachment. After detachment theoretical knowledge still invisibly underlies positivistic knowledge. The problem of validity occurs only after the process of detachment. Because of the fact that there may be different interpretations, the problem arises as to which is right and which is wrong, or which is reasonable and which is not. (As a matter of fact, from the cultural point of view there is only difference, and no correctness or incorrectness.) And this is characteristic of theoretical knowledge to which philosophy, social thought, political theories and religious beliefs all belong."

Professor Chang's theory of knowledge, properly grounded in sociology, is a wholesome corrective to traditional philosophy and psychology. Traditionally both philosophy and psychology, it is now evident, have gone astray in conceiving of the subject-object relationship in terms of the individual perceiver, while as a matter of fact the subject ought to be viewed as what I have called "collective man," i.e., man related to other men in groups within a cultural context. The sociology of knowledge, still in its infancy, is destined to make fruitful contributions to our understanding of human behavior.

REFERENCES

1. CHANG TUNG-SUN: "A Chinese Philosopher's Theory of Knowledge." Peking: *The Yenching Journal of Social Studies*, Vol. I, No. 2, Jan., 1939.

INDEXES

NAME INDEX

Abhedananda, Swami, 230.
Adams, Henry, 570–71, 577, 602.
Adams, Samuel Hopkins, 446.
Addams, Jane, 177.
Adler, Alfred, 84, 128, 421–22, 428.
Adorno, T. W., 578.
Akhilananda, Swami, 66.
Alexander, S., 688.
Alger, Horatio, 617.
Allee, W. C., 467, 471.
Allen, William, 455.
Allport, F. H., 60, 66, 72–75, 78, 84.
Althusius, J., 287, 667.
Appleton, Nathan, 615.
Archimedes, 535.
Aristotle, 42, 111, 113, 133, 137, 280–81, 283, 297, 344, 581–82 ; 596, 641 ; 668–69, 676, 679, 689–90.
Arya Bhatta, 37, 627.
Asoka, 297.
Ataturk, Kemal, 491.

Bach, Marcus, 634, 637–39.
Bacon, Francis, 297.
Bagehot, Walter, 161–62, 168, 173, 284.
Bakewell, Robert, 607.
Bales, Robert F., 288.
Baltimore, Lord, 292.
Barker, Ernest, 230.
Barnes, H. E., 187, 288, 679.
Beard, Charles A. and Mary, R., 317.
Becker, Howard, 289, 596, 632, 638.
Bell, Alexander Graham, 510.
Benedict, Ruth, 230, 238–43, 252–54, 257, 263, 393, 396, 398, 465, 471, 546, 663, 679.
Benham, F. and Boddy, F. M., 203–04, 213.
Bentley, A. F., 169, 187, 286.
Berkeley, George, 224.
Berle, A. A. and Means, G. C., 203, 213.

Bergson, Henri, 108.
Bernard, L. L., 80, 84.
Bernhardi, Friedrich von, 67.
Besant, Mrs. Annie, 481.
Beveridge, Lord William, 429.
Biesantz, John and Mavis, 596.
Bismarck, Otto von, 500.
Block, Harlan Henry, 316.
Bloomfield, Daniel, 471.
Bluecher, G. L. von, 264.
Blumer, H., 142–143, 148.
Boas, Franz, 244.
Bodin, Jean, 287, 667, 672.
Bogardus, Emory S., 289, 509.
Böhm-Bawerk, E., 533–34, 600.
Bossard, J. H. S., 470–71.
Bowers, R. V., xi.
Bradley, John Henry, 316.
Briand, Aristide, 674.
Brisbane, Albert, 456.
Bristol, L. M., 288.
Brunner, E. de S., 432, 446.
Bryce, James, 562, 577.
Buckle, H. T., 50.
Buddha, 37, 39, 65, 67, 282, 297, 355–56, 422–23, 480, 561, 641, 669.
Bunche, Ralph, 262.
Burgess, E. W., see Park and Burgess.
Bury, J. B., 493.
Bykov, C. M., 407.

Calverton, V. F., 371.
Carmichael, Leonard, 128.
Carnap, Rudolf, 687.
Carr-Saunders, A. M., 324, 352.
Cartwright, D., 288.
Carver, George Washington, 189, 262.
Case, C. M., 493.
Cervantes, Lucius F., 597.
Chang Tung-sun, 15, 21, 365, 371, 685-93.
Channing, William Ellery, 455–56.

697

GENERAL SUBJECT INDEX

23

261, 376, 428, 446–47, 540, 596, 685.

Social security, 300, 312, 392, 574 (Act), 682.

Social Solidarity, see Solidarity.

Social system, 559–64 (American).

Social Work, Social Worker, ix, 11, 95, 99, 222, 359–60, 423–24, 425–26 (interview), 434 (agencies), 567, 592, 596, 642.

Societal organization, 46, 664 (defined); 675.

Society, 33, 44–45 (defined), 51, 68–69, 72, 77, 79–80, 82, 92–93, 108; 110 (Cooley's definition); 110–11 (definition by Park and Burgess); 112–14 (in relation to educative process); 124 (primary ideals of); 133–35 (democratic contrasted to totalitarian); 135–37 (compared to community); 129–58 (made up of types and categories of groups); 159–68 (held together by sociological mechanisms); 169–87 (functions through associations and institutions); 188–213 (class groupings); 215–30 (caste groupings); 231–63 (interracial relations); 264–78 (functioning through nations and nation-states); 279–88 (theories about); 290–96 (evolved by American pioneers); 296–317 (created by the American nation); 318–52 (in the throes of evolving interdependent world; 357–65 (in terms of interaction); 365–67 (in terms of communication); 367–71 (as consensus); 372–83 (held together by immanent and primary social processes); 384–430 (as setting for socialization and personality formation); 431–45 (as background for social participation); 447–70 (as setting for operation of secondary social processes: cooperation and opposition); 472–93 (in relation to social change); 494–509 (upheld by social control); 510–15 (emergence of world society); 519–24 (relation to culture); 537–46 (synonymous with cultural framework); 556–58 (emergence of the Great Society through culture-contacts); 559–78 (American); 579–96 (and family); 598–624 (and economical); 625–38 (and religion); 640–61 (and education); 663–79 (and the State); 680–84 (and emerging global cultural categories).

Sociology, 3–21 (theoretical framework); 23 (scope); 33ff. (definition); 46–52, 57, 83 (analysis); 52–54 (experimental design); 24–26 (results of sociological inquiry); 29–31 (sociological approach to personality); 31–32 (universality of the socio-cultural process); 97–106 (Sociological thesis re. human nature); 107–15, 640–62 (thesis re. education).

Socio-state order, The, 9, 176–79, 579–80 (core functions); 663–79.

Solidarity, 76–77, 136, 159, 161, 163, 165–68, 211, 221, 251, 259, 264, 266, 268–69, 277, 279, 284, 286, 336–37, 369, 385, 433, 447–48, 469, 499, 513, 666, 671.

Soul Force, Philosophy of, 465–66, 475, 481–83, 485.

South (U.S.A.), 189, 192, 197, 256–57, 297, 299–300, 306, 308–09, 380–81, 478, 605–06, 608, 644.

Southern Christian Leadership Conference, 310.

Sovereign, Sovereignty, 265, 270, 273–76, 480, 513, 515, 557, 564, 591, 666–67, 671, 674–76 (analysis of), 678, 680–81, 684.

Soviet Russia, Russian, viii, 135, 141, 190, 208–09, 211, 229–30, 251, 261, 265, 271–76, 297, 303–04, 326–27, 329–30, 344, 375, 379–82, 392, 396, 407, 429, 450, 454, 457, 460, 466, 470, 498, 500, 511–12, 540, 541–42 (cultural catego-